HISTORY OF
THE SECOND WORLD WAR

UNITED KINGDOM CIVIL SERIES

Edited by Sir Keith Hancock

WAR PRODUCTION SERIES
Directed by M. M. Postan

STUDIES OF OVERSEAS SUPPLY

BY

H. DUNCAN HALL

AND

C. C. WRIGLEY

with a Chapter by

J. D. SCOTT

LONDON: 1956

HER MAJESTY'S STATIONERY OFFICE

AND

LONGMANS, GREEN AND CO

First published 1956

Crown Copyright Reserved

HER MAJESTY'S STATIONERY OFFICE

London: York House, Kingsway, W.C.2 & 423 Oxford Street, W.1
Edinburgh: 13a Castle Street   Cardiff: 109 St. Mary Street
Manchester: 39 King Street   Bristol: Tower Lane
Birmingham: 2 Edmund Street   Belfast: 80 Chichester Street

LONGMANS, GREEN AND CO LTD
6 and 7 Clifford Street, London, W.1
Boston House, Strand Street, Cape Town
531 Little Collins Street, Melbourne

LONGMANS, GREEN AND CO INC
55 Fifth Avenue, New York, 3

LONGMANS, GREEN AND CO
20 Cranfield Road, Toronto, 16

ORIENT LONGMANS, LTD
Calcutta, Bombay, Madras
Delhi, Vijayawada, Dacca

Price £1 17s. 6d. net

Printed in Great Britain under the authority of H.M. Stationery Office by
The Chiswick Press, New Southgate, N.11

CONTENTS

v

APPENDICES

DIAGRAMS

LIST OF TABLES

PREFACE

STUDIES of Overseas Supply, as the title indicates, is a series of studies of different aspects of the subject rather than a narrative of events. It complements an earlier book in this series – *North American Supply* by H. Duncan Hall – which gives an account of the principal events forming the background of most of these studies.

Overseas Supply, in the meaning given to it in this book, is largely an aspect of British War Production; thus such matters as food, petroleum and maritime transport are excluded from its scope. The book forms part of the sub-series on the history of War Production edited by Professor M. M. Postan, who has indicated the scope of the series in the preface to his *British War Production*.

The conditions governing the writing of books in the British Civil Histories series are indicated in the preface to Professor W. K. Hancock's *British War Economy*. Here it should be noted that the practice in British official histories requires that as a general rule British officials shall be mentioned by their offices rather than by their names.

The studies in this book are devoted to an analysis of some of the major problems and topics to which only a reference could be made in the wide sweep of *North American Supply*. The scope of the second book both as to subjects and geography is wider than the first, since its chapters include aspects like the Combined Boards, British supply organisation overseas, scientific collaboration, and munitions supply from the Eastern Hemisphere. The first four chapters are devoted to major problems of munitions supply from North America, beginning with a general survey of the kinds and quantities of munitions procured in both Canada and the United States. These chapters were contributed by Mr C. C. Wrigley. The chapters on the Combined Boards, the Combined Raw Materials Board and British War Organisation were written by Mr H. Duncan Hall. Mr Wrigley contributed also the chapter on the Eastern Hemisphere. Each of the authors is responsible for the writing of, and the judgements made in, his own chapters. But the collaboration of the authors has covered the book as a whole and has not been confined to the contribution of individual chapters.

The chapter on Scientific Collaboration was written by Mr J. D. Scott, joint author, in this series, of *The Administration of War Production*. His chapter concentrates on three major examples in the

large and immensely varied field covered by its title. In scientific
and technical matters, far more than for munitions, collaboration
was a two-way traffic across the Atlantic. The three examples dwelt
on in the chaper – Radar, the Jet Engine, and the Atomic Bomb –
show sufficiently the magnitude of the British contribution in the
scientific field.

That the space given to a chapter is no measure of the relative
importance of its subject is illustrated by the single chapter on the
Eastern Hemisphere as against the many devoted to North America
in this book and its predecessor. It is true that supply from North
America was far greater in bulk and involved more complex problems. But supply from the Eastern Hemisphere was of immense
importance, if only because of the factors of time and place; for part
of the supply from this area came in very early at a time when a few
guns or a few hundred thousand rounds of small arms ammunition could outweigh in value thousands of guns and millions of
cartridges received from British factories or from North America a
year or two later. Moreover supply on the spot for campaigns in the
Pacific and South Asia involved an invaluable economy in shipping.

The nature of the materials used in writing the book and some of
the problems involved in their use are indicated in the preface to
North American Supply. The Studies are based on British official records
in London, Washington, Ottawa and New Delhi. As in the case of
North American Supply use has been made where necessary, and with
the consent of the American and Canadian Governments, of Combined Documents.

The writers had full access to all these records and the right to use
them freely. But the book, like its predecessor, is not a combined
history, since it can give the combined picture of the matters with
which it deals only as that picture emerges from a study of the
British records, eked out by occasional references to the very few
official or semi-official sources that have been published in other
countries.

Free use has been made of the historical narratives prepared by
officers of the British Missions in Washington, whose names are
mentioned in the preface to *North American Supply*. Amongst those
whose narratives have been used in this book the authors wish
to acknowledge their indebtedness to: Mr Douglas Campbell,
Mr H. O. Hooper, Mr K. H. Huggins, Mr C. B. Wilson, Mr V.
Bates, Mr H. Tetlow and Mr H. Munro. Chapter IX owes much
to a draft by Miss E. Baker.

H. Duncan Hall
C. C. Wrigley

ABBREVIATIONS

A.A.	Anti-Aircraft
A.R.C.	Aeronautical Research Council
A.S.P.	Army Supply Programme
A.T.	Anti-Tank
B.A.C.	British Air Commission
B.C.S.O.	British Central Scientific Office (later British Commonwealth Scientific Office)
B.E.W.	Board of Economic Warfare
B.P.C.	British Purchasing Commission
B.R.M.M.	British Raw Materials Mission
B.S.C.	British Supply Council
C.F.B.	Combined Food Board
C.M.A.B.	Combined Munitions Assignments Board
C.P.O.	Central Provision Office
C.P.R.B.	Combined Production and Resources Board
C.R.M.B.	Combined Raw Materials Board
D.S.R.	Director of Scientific Research
D.S.I.R.	Department of Scientific and Industrial Research
F.E.A.	Foreign Economic Administration
H.E.	High Explosive
J.A.C.	Joint Aircraft Committee
M.A.C.	Munitions Assignments Committee
M.A.P.	Ministry of Aircraft Production
M.W.T.	Ministry of War Transport
N.A.C.A.	National Advisory Committee for Aeronautics
N.D.R.C.	National Defence Research Committee
O.P.M.	Office of Production Management
O.L.L.A.	Office of Lend-Lease Administration
O.S.R.D.	Office of Scientific Research and Development
R.A.E.	Royal Aircraft Establishment
R.A.F.	Royal Air Force
R.C.A.F.	Royal Canadian Air Force
R.F.C.	Reconstruction Finance Corporation
S.A.C.	Scientific Advisory Committee
S.P.A.B.	Supply Priorities and Allocations Board
T.R.E.	Telecommunication Research Establishment
U.N.R.R.A.	United Nations Relief and Rehabilitation Administration
U.S.A.A.F.	United States Army Air Force
W.P.B.	War Production Board
W.S.A.	War Shipping Administration

CHAPTER I

NORTH AMERICAN MUNITIONS –
KIND AND QUANTITY

(i)

A Note on Scale and Proportion

THE DRAWING by the Island on supply from the seven seas is the theme of this book. The journeys which the book makes into different fields of war supply, administration and geography, can cover only part of the vast subject of Overseas Supply. Yet the journeys are extensive and varied enough to raise in the reader's mind important questions of perspective and scale. The problem of comparative war effort is a highly complex subject which cannot be dealt with in a preface to a chapter.[1] Only a hint can be given as to the kind of scale of comparison which the reader should bear in mind. What Britain received from Overseas has to be measured against the scale of what the United Kingdom herself contributed. Her contributions on the political and military side – as the Island that set an insuperable barrier in the way of Hitler by winning the Battle of Britain, that while carrying alone the weight of the defence of the free world preserved the Middle East and the Suez Canal from the Axis powers, and that formed the base and contributed a large part of the power for the liberation of Western Europe and North Africa – all belong to other parts of the British Official war histories. The contributions to allied victory made by British war production by Britain's economy and by her finance, are dealt with in other volumes of the Civil Series.

The volume on *North American Supply* refers to some of the British contributions on the economic side that outweighed in the scales even the great Lend-Lease and Mutual Aid contributions made by the North American continent to the Island. These contributions from North America helped to maintain the productive capacity of the centre – economic as well as military – of the British Commonwealth of Nations. How great the United Kingdom's contribution was in the matter of munitions is shown by a single figure. Over the whole period of the war the United Kingdom supplied 69.5 per cent. of

[1] See brief discussions in *History of the Second World War, United Kingdom Civil Series*, H. Duncan Hall, *North American Supply*, Chapter X, section (iii) and Chapter XI, section (vi).

I

the munitions available to the entire Commonwealth – including the United Kingdom itself. The other 30.5 per cent. came from the following sources: Canada 7.9 per cent.; the rest of the Common-wealth 1.6 per cent.; the United States 17.3 per cent. by Lend-Lease and 3.7 per cent. purchased by the United Kingdom for cash. In the critical early period of the war the United Kingdom's contribution was higher still; in the first fifteen months the United Kingdom supplied no less than 90.7 per cent. of the munitions of the Commonwealth.[1]

This, crude though it may be, is the most important clue to scale and proportion. Several others can be mentioned here. If Lend-Lease aid to the United Kingdom was colossal, so was British recip-rocal aid to the United States. The conclusions reached in *North American Supply* were (1) that both the United States and the United Kingdom contributed about 4¾ per cent. of their national income to mutual aid, (2) that the United States contributed about 11 per cent. of their war expenditure as Lend-Lease to the British Commonwealth as compared with nearly 9 per cent. of war expenditure contri-buted by the United Kingdom as reciprocal aid to the United States.[2] If the United States went heavily into debt to finance Lend-Lease, so also did the United Kingdom to finance reciprocal aid and the war overseas. But with this great economic difference: that the American debt was internal whilst a great part of the British debt was owed abroad. Thus at the end of 1944 Britain's *overseas* debts totalled $10,000 million.[3] Moreover, Britain's contribution was made out of a smaller labour force and with a greater percentage of its total labour force in the Armed Forces than was the case in the United States.[4] Such comparisons belong to the later stages of the war when time for survival and victory had already been won. It may be that in a total view of the war British cash expenditure in the United States and British capital investment in American munitions plants may be judged to have been of greater historical importance than the much vaster sums of the period after Pearl Harbour. For British orders for American machine tools, aircraft and tankers, and British capital expenditure in equipping American munition factories, were the largest single factor in the more than doubling of the American munitions output before Pearl Harbour.

(ii)

The Content of British Needs

For the greater part of the war British requirements from the United States were not related to any fully coherent plan. It is possible to

---

[1] See Table in *North American Supply, op. cit.*, p. 428.
[2] ibid., pp. 432–3, 481–2.   [3] ibid., p. 444–6.
[4] Percentage of total labour force in the Armed Forces on the eve of V.J. Day: United Kingdom 24 per cent., United States of America 18 per cent., ibid., p. 473.

conceive of an ideal system in which the British would have sat down at the outset of the war to consider the following problem: 'It is certain that from our own resources alone we cannot equip forces on the scale needed for victory. Now what shall we make for ourselves and what shall we ask the Americans to make for us?' If it had been possible for the economist's principle of division of labour to be applied in real earnest to the war efforts of the two countries, it would have been at once apparent that there were many sectors of production from which, theoretically, the United Kingdom could profitably retire altogether, in order that it might reduce its dependence on the United States in other sectors where it was better fitted to sustain itself. Thus, from a purely production point of view, the British Army's tanks might have been made in the United States, with a great saving of resources (but in that case might there not have been a twofold loss – of the developments represented by the Cromwell group and the elements of design contributed by the British to the Sherman tank?). Alternatively, the decision might have been to raise only such forces as *could* be equipped from British production, the United States being looked to for troops rather than munitions. In any future emergency one or other of these principles may have to be adopted – not necessarily in the rigid form in which they are here stated. But such clear-cut planning, difficult enough in any case, was of course out of the question in the special circumstances of the Second World War, in which the United States slipped by slow stages from a remote though friendly neutrality to active belligerency. The British Government had to assume at the outset that it must rely substantially on its own resources, first because it could not pay for more than a small quantity of warlike stores and secondly because America was not in a position, either politically or practically, to provide more. After Dunkirk, self-sufficiency was abandoned under the sheer pressure of necessity, but only piece by piece. The prospect of American supplies was still so uncertain that Britain had still to make as much as possible of nearly everything for herself, even though she had also to seek some quantity of a great many things from the United States.

British demands upon American industry thus grew up haphazardly, the results of a host of individual emergency decisions at many different levels rather than of a rational division of labour. Very broadly speaking, four main categories of requirements may be distinguished. First, there were certain classes of equipment for which the strategic demand was so nearly unlimited as to require both an all-out effort in the United Kingdom and a very large reinforcement from overseas as well. Among the most prominent were aircraft of all types, but particularly heavy bombers, on which British hopes of victory were pinned; merchant ships and their escorts, without which

defeat was certain; small arms ammunition; and in the later phases of
the war, landing craft, the indispensable prerequisite of almost every
offensive. The other three categories which are referred to below,
comprised, (2) types produced mainly in the United States, (3) stores
which Britain could make but not in the time limit set by military
plans, (4) supplies for which there was an increasing dependence on
the United States because of the acute shortage of manpower in the
United Kingdom in the later stages of the war.

The production of aircraft, as Professor Postan has shown, dominated the whole of British rearmament planning, and throughout the
war enjoyed a highly favourable position.[1] Yet the supply from
British factories never came anywhere near sating the hunger of the
Air Staff and of the military planners as a whole; and aircraft therefore occupied the foremost place also in overseas supply. The first
substantial munitions contracts placed in the United States (in 1938)
were for 450 military planes; the Air Ministry alone was free, or
relatively free, from the crippling restrictions imposed on dollar
expenditure in the first nine months of the war; and purchases of
aircraft and associated stores accounted for over 60 per cent. of all
the cash commitments incurred by the British Government up to
March 1941 in respect of warlike stores. In the Lend-Lease era the
relative position of aircraft in British supply from the United States
showed a steady decline. In the first Lend-Lease appropriation the
sum earmarked for aeronautical supplies was still 45 per cent. of the
total provision for munitions; but in the final analysis such supplies
represented just under a third of all the munitions furnished under
Lend-Lease throughout the war, and just over a fifth of all supplies.
Absolutely, however, Britain became, if anything, rather more
dependent upon American supplies of aircraft. The British Government was forced to recognise in 1941 that the Air Staff's requirements
went far beyond the utmost capacity of the United Kingdom, and
the fulfilment even of the modified programme then adopted had to
be repeatedly deferred. It was therefore only by means of a vast
reinforcement from the United States that the desired impact on the
enemy could possibly be achieved. The potential reinforcement from
this source was almost unlimited. Though the number of military
aircraft produced in the United States before 1940, in relation to the
output of other Great Powers, including several with much less real
claim to greatness, was extremely small, an efficient and flourishing
aviation industry had grown up to serve the needs of transcontinental
travel; and the early British orders had done much to divert this
industry into military channels and to stimulate expansion. In
reserve, moreover, there lay the immense and prolific automobile

---

[1] See *History of the Second World War, United Kingdom Civil Series* M. M. Postan, *British War Production*, Chapter II.

industry, which was in large measure converted, hesitantly in 1941 and whole-heartedly in 1942, to the production of aircraft. The output of America's military aircraft rose spectacularly from 3,770 in the latter part of 1940 to 51,122 in the first six months of 1944, in which period it exceeded that of British planes by more than 3½ to one. Between September 1939 and June 1945, Great Britain produced 123,819 planes; the United States in a shorter period of five years from July 1940 produced 284,295.

British expectations, however, were never fully realised. This was because America's contribution to the war in the air increasingly took the form of American squadrons complete with crews rather than of individual machines. From the military point of view this was more or less irrelevant. The impact on the enemy was probably delayed a little but the rubble of German cities testified that it was achieved in the long run. In all some 13 per cent. of all the planes (15 per cent. of the Service aircraft) produced in the United States were transferred to the British Commonwealth, which received from this source during the war 36,182 American machines – 20 per cent. of its total supply, or 24 per cent. if trainers are excluded from the count.

In no other sector of war production was British dependence on the United States as great as in the construction of merchant ships. This was, of course, the one branch of production in which from the very outset – indeed, in the pre-war preparations – British planners anticipated a large contribution from a much-expanded shipbuilding industry in America. The experience of the First World War showed how great were America's potentialities for mass production of merchant ships. At the same time the British plans and prospects of naval construction together with the inevitable repair work did not appear to leave room for a very large programme of cargo ships. One million tons annually, or a little more, was the figure which in the early war plans appeared to measure the full potential of British merchant shipbuilding in war-time.

In the event, these expectations were more than borne out. In the course of the war Britain proved even less able to cover her full needs for merchant ships out of her own production than the planners may have anticipated. The need for merchant vessels was as great as it had ever been expected to be, and at certain times (especially when the Battle of the Atlantic was at its height) it was even greater; at the same time the domestic output could not be much expanded. The actual tonnage of merchant vessels built in Britain at times overtopped the million mark, and the total output of cargo shipping throughout the war was about 8.3 million tons. This was, of course, very much less than was needed, yet a great increase beyond this point was out of the question. The shipbuilding industry in general was not as indefinitely expandable as the American. Though at least in theory the supplies of slips and berths should have been sufficient for a higher output, the supplies of labour and machinery were not. British shipyards had irrevocably lost during the depression a large proportion of skilled craftsmen on whom they depended; the technical equipment (at least until 1943) was often backward and obsolescent. The electric welding and prefabrication teams which were to prove to be the key to American success were not adopted on a large scale in Britain until the closing stages of the war, partly because there was never time for the necessary conversion of shipyard plant and lay-out. Above all, the pressure of other demands on the shipbuilding industry was very great and growing. The programmes of naval construction imposed a high and ever-growing load; and, in addition, British industry had to cope with a vast amount of repair work.

Fortunately, the expectations of American achievement and of American aid in this field were far outstripped by the actual performance of American industry. America had startled the world in 1918 by building some five million deadweight tons of merchant shipping – about as much as was built in the entire world in 1913, or for that matter in 1938, and when the British Government in December 1940 implored the Americans to make an all-out effort in shipbuilding, it was thinking of an output of this order of magnitude. But in the event the achievement of America's shipbuilders in the First World War was as nothing to their achievement in the Second. In 1942 they produced eight million, in 1943 nearly nineteen million deadweight tons, the latter figure being more than two-thirds of the entire tonnage on the British register at the outbreak of war. Altogether American shipyards turned out 50 million deadweight tons of shipping.

The figures have more significance than any account of the actual supply of ships from the United States. Ships were not in general transferred to the British outright like guns or planes, but were merely placed at the disposal of the Ministry of War Transport for particular voyages. How much cargo capacity the British gained in this way is a matter for the shipping historians to whom we thankfully leave the unravelling of this complex theme.[1] Besides this help from American shipping resources, however, there were certain more definite British acquisitions. In the first eighteen months of war the Ministry of Shipping was very active in the world market for second-hand ships, and from the United States alone it acquired 111 vessels of just under a million deadweight tons. By the autumn of 1940 this source of supply was nearly exhausted, and British needs being more desperate than ever, the Government at last decided to adventure what were practically its last remaining dollars on the construction of sixty

---

[1] See *History of the Second World War, United Kingdom Civil Series*, C. B. A. Behrens, *Merchant Shipping and the Demands of War*.

tramp steamers, totalling some 600,000 tons[1]. These ships coming forward as they did between October 1941 and November 1942, at the height of the Battle of the Atlantic, were in themselves contributions to victory whose real value it is almost impossible to compute; and the construction of the new yards in which they were built was the first major step in the war-time expansion of American shipbuilding capacity. Finally, in the summer of 1943, the War Shipping Administration altered its normal policy to the extent of undertaking to hand over to Britain, in the course of the next year, 200 ships on bare-boat charter. The main reason for this step was the difficulty of finding American crews; whereas British shipping losses had created a pool of unemployed seamen.

Closely associated with merchant vessels were the warships which protected them. But Britain herself carried the main burden of naval construction and her dependence on American-built warships was rather small. Ninety-nine American-built escort vessels (78 'destroyer escorts' and 21 frigates)[2] passed under the control of the Royal Navy during the war, against 303 sloops, corvettes and frigates and 220 destroyers built in British yards. And this comparison overrates the real value of American aid, for the majority of the 99 came into service after the worst of the danger had passed. After its initial rebuff at the very beginning of the war[3] the Admiralty did not again raise the question of securing from America warships of any size until June 1941 when, with shipping losses mounting alarmingly, it put forward a request for 100 vessels of the corvette or frigate type. The requirement was finally incorporated in the Navy Department's programme immediately after Pearl Harbour, but progress, compared with America's achievements in other fields, was very slow. The United States Navy was preoccupied with the restoration of its battle-fleet supremacy, which had been so rudely overthrown, and was slow to realise that the protection of sea communication against underwater attack was a no less pressing need. Not until the end of 1942 were convoy escorts given their proper place at the head of the Navy's priority schedules. The first destroyer escort was completed in February 1943, and by the end of June, when a remarkable fall in shipping losses had already signalled victory in the Atlantic struggle, only eight had been delivered to the Royal Navy. Such are the vicissitudes of war production planning that the large number of escorts still under construction on both sides of the Atlantic, whose completion only a few months earlier would have been the most welcome of all possible events, were now not actually superfluous,

---

[1] See *North American Supply, op. cit.*, Chapter VI.

[2] Not counting the 50 over-age destroyers, which were used mainly for convoy escort.

[3] See *North American Supply, op. cit.*, Chapter IV.

but certainly far less valuable than many other vessels that could have been built with the same resources.

A valuable naval contribution from the United States was the auxiliary (or escort) aircraft carrier. A problem which greatly perplexed the naval authorities was the provision of air cover for convoys in that central part of the Atlantic which was beyond the range of aircraft based on either shore. Ordinary aircraft carriers were clearly not the answer, for they took from two to five years to build, according to size. The Admiralty therefore hit on the idea of fitting flight decks to certain large vessels of merchant type in the course of construction. The first of these, *H.M.S. Audacity*, during a short life in 1941, proved beyond doubt the value of this experiment. But the number of suitable ships being built in Britain was small, and most of these had to be retained for trading. The Admiralty therefore turned to the United States in the spring of 1941 with a request for six auxiliary carriers. In the event, while only three more ships of this type were completed in Britain, American shipyards delivered no less than 84, of which 38 flew the White Ensign.

Then there was the landing ship tank, or transport ferry. This was an ocean-going vessel much larger than ordinary land-ing craft. It was absolutely vital for amphibious operations and there was hardly any room for it in British yards. Thus up to the end of 1943 the British built only three, apart from a few ex-perimental vessels, and received 115 from the United States. This dependence then came to an end, for the Admiralty, despairing of getting American aid for its Far Eastern operations, had to tear up its merchant shipbuilding programme and fill several yards with landing ships.

It was, however, in landing craft proper that the main American contribution to combined naval requirements came. It is perhaps doubtful whether these should be placed in the same category as the supplies we have been considering. For although a great effort was made to build landing craft in the United Kingdom, it was an effort that had perforce to be contained within narrow limits. When it became evident in 1941 that a return to the continent of Europe was impossible without an armada of very special vessels, the British shipbuilding industry was already fully extended, and no relief could be afforded in other directions. Therefore, except for a brief period immediately before Operation 'Overlord', landing craft were built in Britain only outside the regular industry, by the employment of structural engineers in various derelict yards. The result of such an expedient could not be spectacular, and it was understood from the beginning that the main burden of providing the equipment for amphibious operations would have to be carried by the United States, which produced no less than 64,000 vessels of 2.7 million tons against Britain's 4,133 vessels of 752,000 war load displacement tons. Here again overseas supply is really a minor feature in the total picture. The vessels transferred under Lend-Lease were 391 major and 2,004 minor landing craft – about 90,000 tons in all. The needs of the Royal Navy in the earlier operations, such as the North African landings in 1942, were largely met by actual transfer, but the great majority of the craft used in the later stages of the war either remained under American operational control or were loaned to the British for specific duties.

An inconspicuous but absolutely basic requirement which formed an important part of overseas supply was small arms ammunition. In the pre-war plans the expenditure of small arms ammunition in war-time was underestimated and undue reliance was placed on stocks; and consequently no orders were available on which the necessary productive capacity could be built up or maintained. The arrangements made during the rearmament period for the production of this store in Britain were therefore less than usually adequate. One reason was the multiplicity of types required. Thus in types .303-inch and .5-inch alone, more than a dozen different kinds were asked for by the Services. To meet the demand two steps were taken: first, new factories were set up in the United Kingdom, and second, home supplies were supplemented by placing orders for supplies from overseas. At first Canada was the preferred source, not only for the usual reasons but because Canadian ammunition was markedly superior in quality to the American product at the time. Nevertheless the United States came into the picture very early, and became more and more prominent as the demand outstripped the limits of Canadian capacity. At the beginning of 1941 the position was as follows. Total requirements of .303 cartridges were estimated at 450 million rounds a month, against which 300 million rounds were expected from United Kingdom sources, 40 million from a factory 'east of Suez', 80 million from Canada and 75 million from the United States. The requirement was probably inflated; certainly it was never met. British production of small arms ammunition of all calibres reached 260 million rounds per month in 1943, but a large proportion of this consisted of calibres other than .303-inch. The output of the latter did not exceed 170 million rounds in any month; Canada's maximum production for her own as well as United Kingdom needs, was 90 million, and the highest monthly rate obtained from the United States was 50 million. .303-inch ammunition, however, was only a fraction of the American contribution which included also large quantities of .30-inch, .50-inch, .45-inch and 9-mm. (Sten gun) calibres. United States production of small arms ammunition exceeded that of the United Kingdom by an exceptionally wide margin – at one time it was seven times as great –

and Britain received an exceptional proportion, 16 per cent., of the total production.

Tanks were an even more striking example of British dependence on American supplies, even though, in theory and in accordance with earlier plans, the bulk of British needs should, and could, have been covered from domestic production. In the end, however, more tanks were procured from the United States than were built in Britain and at one time (certainly between the end of 1941 and the end of 1943) the demand for American tanks was almost as unlimited as that for American aircraft. The actual figures of output and supplies from overseas up to 30th June 1944, were as follows: United Kingdom production, 24,800, or 46 per cent. of the total supplies available for British and Commonwealth forces; from Canadian production – 3,600, or 7 per cent. of the total; from the United States – 25,600, or 47 per cent. of the total.[1] Supplies from the United States included nearly 8,000 light tanks of less value than the great majority of British machines; but even if attention is confined to the medium and heavy classes, the American contribution is still more than two-fifths, that of the United Kingdom still less than half of the total. Moreover, in 1943 and 1944, the United Kingdom was receiving nearly twice as many tanks from the United States as it was building for itself.

In no other main sector of war production was so great a proportion of the output of the United States devoted to meeting the needs of its foreign customers.

> In this field, probably more than anywhere else [Mr Stettinius wrote in October 1943] we have been the arsenal of our allies. Over fourteen thousand tanks had gone abroad under Lend-Lease by the middle of 1943, and many more were on the docks or rolling out of the factories. This means to-day about thirty-eight out of every hundred tanks produced in the United States – a higher percentage for Lend-Lease probably than of any other military item we produce.[2]

Many of these were going to the Soviet Union. None the less, over the whole period from July 1940 to the end of the war Britain received about thirty per cent. of all the American tanks produced.

The reason for this state of affairs is not far to seek. Owing to delays and disappointments in the development of new tanks, the supply of battle-worthy British tanks fell further short of British needs than the supply of almost any other category of munitions. Although it was sheer quantitative shortage that forced the British Army to rely so largely on America for its supplies of tanks, the

---

[1] See M. M. Postan, *British War Production, op. cit.,* Table 36, p. 247.

[2] Edward R. Stettinius, Jr., *Lend-Lease, Weapon for Victory* (The Macmillan Company, New York and London, 1944), p. 356, Pocket Book edition.

British deficiency was not, strictly speaking, one of insufficient out-put. By the end of 1942, and possibly even earlier, United Kingdom output could have met the bulk of the Army's needs if every tank had really counted. But it was unhappily clear that a large pro-portion of the machines produced were not yet fit for use in battle against the German tanks. At the same time, American tank design progressed somewhat more rapidly and smoothly, and, as a result, American tanks of adequate quality were available in considerable numbers at crucial points of the war while high quality British tanks were not yet to be had. At its first serious attempt in 1940, the United States Ordnance Corps produced a machine which possessed at least one important operational quality – first-class mechanical reliability. When, at the next stage, British operational experience was married to this basic design, the result was the General Grant which, although still somewhat inadequate, proved quite useful at its first introduction in North Africa in May and June 1942. At their third attempt, again with British advice and help, the Americans produced the Sherman which was highly successful in North Africa in 1942–3 and with which General Patton drove from Normandy to the banks of the Elbe. Finally, British designers brought forth, in the Cromwell, a tank which matched the Sherman in armament and reliability and was in other respects somewhat superior. But while the Sherman was in full production by February 1942, the Cromwell did not reach this stage until the very end of the year. When, in 1943, the development of enemy armour had made it necessary to develop a tank capable of mounting a still more efficient armament, the British produced the Comet tank which made its appearance in the last quarter of 1944. But the Americans by arming the Shermans with their 76-mm. high velocity gun had found at least a partial answer many months earlier.[1]

It is, therefore, not surprising that British demands for American tanks were so large as to appear at one time to be limitless. Indeed, it could be argued that it would have been in British interests to have asked for still more tanks and to have done it earlier. With the large proportion of the British machines produced before 1943 fit only for training or for other subsidiary roles, it might perhaps have suited Britain better to curtail the current output and to take more Shermans from the United States. In fact this was the solution of the tank problem which at one time in 1943 American military opinion appeared to favour. But just how far this process should have been carried was a controversial question to which we shall return.[2]

The fact that large orders for these classes of equipment were

---

[1] The British had achieved the same result by fitting the new 17-pdr. gun into the Sherman Tank. See below, p. 13.

[2] See p. 18.

placed in the United States did not mean, except in the case of landing craft, any corresponding relaxation of effort in the United Kingdom. If aircraft dominated the story of overseas supply, they also had supreme priority in all British production plans. It is true that the vast American output of merchant shipping enabled the British to concentrate on warship construction, but if no warships had been built in Britain at all, the output of merchant vessels might have been doubled – perhaps trebled; it would still have been short of British needs. The requirements notified to the United States thus represented not so much a division of labour as the overspill of a demand too great for one nation to satisfy.

There was, however, a second category of munitions whose production was definitely delegated, wholly or in very large part, to the United States. There were certain particular types of American equipment for which the British had no satisfactory equivalent. There were others for which the demand first arose during the war, when production could not be started up in Britain without undue disturbance to other things. An early example of the former was the Thompson sub-machine gun. The Army was not slow to recognise the value of a weapon more lethal than the revolver, cheaper and more portable than the lightest of orthodox automatic weapons, and for over a year the 'tommy-gun' held the field, though it was later rivalled by the development in Britain of the still cheaper Sten. Another example was the American car, '5-cwt. four-wheeled drive', more familiarly known as the jeep, for which the British Army's appetite was never sated, though it received over 86,000 vehicles. Nor did the British find any real equivalent to the American amphibious vehicles, the landing vehicle, tracked, and the wheeled D.U.K.W. Then there were the very heavy vehicles, the 20-ton and 40-ton tank transporters and the 10-ton load carriers. These became indispensable in 1941 for the Middle East campaign,[1] but the British, having diverted most of the makers of heavy lorries to tank production, could make very few (and the Canadians, who were the main overseas suppliers of other types of vehicle, could not make any). The 4,793 tank transporters and the 13,541 10-tonners which the British Army received from the United States thus represented 79 and 76 per cent. respectively of its total supplies.

Self-propelled artillery, one of the most important tactical developments of the war, was another American speciality. The need to give field and anti-tank guns greater mobility became obvious in the Desert campaigns and the expedient of mounting them on powered platforms with some armour protection was not difficult to conceive. But although a few marriages between artillery pieces and

---

[1] ' Tanks without transporters', wrote Lord Beaverbrook at the time, 'are like chickens without their tails.'

lorry or tank chassis were improvised as early as 1941, the British Army authorities were not convinced that the self-propelled gun had more than a limited usefulness. General Staff requirements did not take definite shape until the summer of 1942. By this time the Americans, who were able to tackle the problem in a less extempore fashion, had evolved several models, in three of which – a 57-mm. anti-tank gun on a half-track chassis, a 105-mm. howitzer on a Grant tank chassis and a 3-inch gun on a Sherman – the British Tank Mission of March 1942 had shown a keen interest. The first was not a very great success, but the other two did yeoman service in both armies, the Grant howitzer as early as Alamein. The British were therefore content to leave this field mainly to the Americans. At the end of 1942 self-propelled artillery was listed among the stores for which dependence on American supplies was almost absolute. This was something of an exaggeration, for the British continued to experiment on a small scale, and one hybrid weapon, a British 17-pounder gun mounted on imported Sherman chassis, won high repute. Owing to the compound nature of the equipment, the statistics of the subject are complex. It appears, however, that some 46 per cent. of the Commonwealth supplies of self-propelled artillery using tank chassis came from the United States, two-thirds of the remainder consisted of a Canadian weapon, a Ram tank chassis carrying a 25-pounder field gun.

Within the general field of aircraft supply also, there were certain sectors in which American aid was so prominent as to represent a real division of labour. Over the whole war 38 per cent., and in 1943 over 50 per cent., of the Fleet Air Arm's aircraft came from the United States. In transport planes the Americans held a virtual monopoly, providing 98 per cent. of Britain's supplies. The need for such aircraft did not become apparent till about the end of 1941, when lines of communication lengthened to the ends of the earth, and the United States, with a large civil aviation industry still in being, was the obvious source of supply.

The third category of requirements consisted of stores which Britain was perfectly well able to make, and in adequate quantities, but not within the time-limit set by military plans. These were mainly equipment for the ground forces. In general (tanks apart) the Army did not depend for its main weapons on American supplies to the same extent as the other Services. One of the reasons (by 1942 it had become the main reason) why more Army equipment was not procured from the United States was the failure of the two countries to agree on common designs. The American-designed aircraft could and did perform very well in British squadrons. American-designed tanks at one time provided the main equipment of British armoured units. But when it came to other weapons, Britain could not receive a large contribution from the United States as long as American production for its own Forces was devoted to weapons of different design and calibre from those with which the British Army was being equipped. Travelling British Military Missions in 1940 tried to persuade the American military authorities of the superiority of the British 25-pounder and the 3.7-inch anti-aircraft gun to the corresponding American weapons. In this they failed, and, as a result of the failure, it became as impossible for the British Army to re-equip itself anew with American weapons as it was to expect the Americans to set aside a large proportion of their war industry for the manufacture of weapons which they themselves were not going to use.

In this, and in other respects, the problem was also one of timing. Doubtless, had the possibility of ordering large quantities of American guns and shells been there in 1939 and 1940, long before the British Army had acquired large quantities of home-made equipment, the failure to persuade the Americans to adopt British designs might not have mattered very much. At least, in theory, it would then have been possible for the advocates of greater division of labour between the two countries to persist and to succeed in their hopes that the British Army might be equipped with American guns and shells. But by 1941, and still more by 1942, the re-equipment of the British Army had already gone too far for this possibility to have been seriously considered.

By then it was also too late for other reasons as well. Generally speaking, the planning of Army supplies differs from that of supplies for the other Services in that it is much more nearly finite. The number of aircraft and warships required by one belligerent depends to an important extent on the number possessed by the enemy, and as the latter continually increases so also must the former. This is true also of some ground equipment, notably of tanks. But whilst the ultimate limits of manpower affect all the Services, they affect most of all the Army. For in general the size of an army is inexorably governed, not by the size of the opposing forces, but by the limits of available manpower. And although more and more equipment can be lavished on an army of a given size, this process has, if not a saturation point, at least an area of sharply diminishing marginal utility.[1] Theoretically, once the initial equipment of the previously determined number of divisions has been provided, production should drop to the maintenance level.[2] Originally, this stage was

---

[1] In practice the line between Army supplies and supplies for other Services is less sharply defined at a number of points than the statement implies, e.g., in the matter of ammunition and other types of requirements.

[2] In practice the production of vital equipment and the maintenance stage overlapped to a very great extent.

supposed to be reached in Britain by the end of 1941, the Army taking the field in its full strength in the following spring.

This date was, of course, highly unrealistic. The Army could not have been equipped by that date without very large assistance from the United States: larger than it had actually asked for, and larger than that which American industry, at that time, could have supplied. But as the terminal dates were being postponed and the horizon of Army planning receded, the proportion of the total demand which could be met from British sources steadily increased, and the need for American supplies, real or potential, declined. Writing in March 1942, a high official of the Ministry of Supply summed up the position as follows:

Long before the United States reaches its peak of production we shall have all the weapons that British manpower can use. If, for example, the United States could, by some miracle, produce colossal numbers of anti-aircraft guns by next June, we would gladly take many thousands. But if we make the calculation up to December of this year our deficiency will be appreciably smaller. By June 1943 it will be measured in hundreds or will have disappeared, while by the end of 1943 we shall have guns to spare.

In short, what we want from America is help now and very little next year.

The same official repeated this theme a year later. 'In 1941', he wrote, 'the worth of American supplies was measured in rubies; in 1942 it was silver; in 1943 it is copper, and in 1944 they will be a drug on the market.' There was an element of rhetoric in these remarks, which indeed their author qualified by the gloss that copper in 1943 was a very precious metal. Nor, for that matter, were drugs altogether valueless in 1944. For there were a number of factors working in a contrary direction, to enhance the value of American supplies even of ground munitions. As its minimum needs were met the Army's standards naturally became higher. Ammunition scales, for example, which were drastically cut down in 1941 and again at the beginning of 1943, were revised upwards in some cases early in 1944. Then, as tactics changed, there emerged requirements for wholly new types of weapons such as self-propelled artillery; and weapons which had seemed adequate in the early days had now to be replaced by something better of the same general class. Cruiser tanks were the most obvious example, but there were others. The Boys anti-tank rifle was succeeded by the P.I.A.T. and by various rocket-firing devices, and the 20-mm. Polsten was intended mainly as a substitute for the .303-inch machine gun for close anti-aircraft defence of field units. The latter requirement led to an urgent call for large-scale assistance from Canada and the United States. Even more important, however, was the fact that the claims of the supporting arms and services also became more extravagant. Towards the end of 1942 there was a remarkable increase in the demand for signal equipment, engineer stores and transport. Thus while the above-quoted analysis of the trend of demand for American anti-aircraft guns was correct enough, it could not be applied without qualification to Army equipment as a whole; and although it was broadly true that the completion of the British Army's 'capital' equipment, always excluding tanks, was in sight by the end of 1942, both the requirement and the supply of American ground equipment reached their peak in 1943 and fell off only slowly in the following year.

One reason for this was the emergence of the fourth and the more general factor making for dependence on American supplies, the acute shortage of manpower in the United Kingdom in the last two and a half years of the war. It is more accurate to speak of a fourth factor than of a fourth category, because it is difficult to point to any particular class of supplies which was procured from the United States for this reason alone. Indeed, the whole analysis by categories of requirements would be very misleading if taken as a rigid scheme. And, of course, all American supplies, whatever the main reason for their being sought, helped to relieve the strain on British manpower. But in the later stages of the war the general overloading of the British economy, and the excess demand for labour in particular, came into the foreground and influenced British planners to request from the United States many supplies which, taken individually, could have been produced in the United Kingdom, and to increase the quantity of orders which they would in any case have had to divert overseas. The shifting to America of a large part of the total load, rather than Britain's inability to meet particular needs of her armed forces, became the dominant theme. In the planning of 'Stage II', the final campaign against Japan after the defeat of Germany, it was almost the sole theme. Though there were still a few specific requirements (landing ships, naval aircraft, naval anti-aircraft guns) which the British would have found it difficult to meet, in general they were perfectly capable of producing for themselves all the munitions they needed for that phase of the war – but not if they were to make a start on reconstruction at the same time.[1]

Manpower, though a very important factor in British plans and eventually the main cause of Britain's growing dependence on the United States, was not a very effective argument to use on the other side of the Atlantic. By 1943 the labour problem had succeeded the scarcity of raw materials as the main anxiety of American as well as of British planners; and although it was easy to demonstrate that the situation in the United Kingdom was far worse, it was only at the

---

[1] On Stage II see *North American Supply, op. cit.*, Chapter XI.

highest level that the demonstration really went home. Therefore the British missions in the United States preferred to present requirements on their individual merits rather than to embark on wider economic discussions. The history of Stage II clearly showed the insecurity of agreements based on the equities of reconversion and the proportionate sharing of loads; such few supplies as the United States furnished to Britain in the brief interval between victory in Europe and the capitulation of Japan were almost all of types for which the actual operational need was clearly proved; the main agreement passed rapidly into limbo.

In general, overseas supply was a supplement rather than a complement to munitions production in the United Kingdom. The items most prominent in American supply were also those to which the British gave the highest priority at home. The exceptions listed in our second category were exceptions of relatively minor importance in the whole scheme of war production. And even here the division of labour became not more but less clearly marked as time went on; towards the end of the war the British began to make landing ships, transport aircraft and more heavy vehicles for themselves. When the pressure for army equipment was heavy, it was heavy on both sides of the Atlantic, and when the production of ordnance was allowed to slacken in the United Kingdom, so also were the demands made upon the United States. The need for more signal equipment, mechanical transport and engineer stores in 1943 was met partly by increased production at home, partly by increased supplies from America. The output of gun ammunition after a temporary reduction was stepped up in 1944 both in the United Kingdom and overseas (in this instance, in Canada).

As a result, the actual distribution of munitions production between the two countries was often far from the theoretical ideal. The concentration of the R.A.F. on fighter production (at the expense for the time being of bombers) was a strategical necessity to the defence of the United Kingdom, but the production of heavy bombers could not be neglected since they could not be obtained from the United States. The British aircraft factories went on to produce the Lancasters and Halifaxes that later in the war were to carry a far greater load of bombs than the American day bombers. In the early days of the war British orders for aircraft from the United States had to be concentrated on usable types that could be obtained from them in the shortest possible time and this meant that most of the early contracts negotiated with American firms were for light bombers and fighters; before the advent of Lend-Lease only the French had placed production orders for heavy bombers, and their orders were very small. Thus although the first Lend-Lease programme went some way to correct the balance, only a small proportion of the capacity set up in the United States for British use was devoted to heavy bombers.

This illustration is not perhaps particularly apt, for the demand was such that American supplies would probably have had to be multiplied several times to have had any appreciable effect on British planning. Indeed the huge bomber programme of 1941 assumed the receipt of considerably more American planes than were actually delivered. But there were many instances where the British could have been spared much effort if only American production could have developed even a few months earlier, or if only they could have been sure of receiving a definite allocation therefrom. By 1943, for example, the United States were in a position to furnish many more bombs than they actually were doing. But in 1941 it would have been risky to rely on this, so that expensive development of British production had had to be undertaken as a measure of insurance.

Yet it was not solely the lateness and the uncertainty of American supplies that restricted the opportunity for a radical division of labour between the munitions industries of Britain and of the United States during the Second World War. Beyond a certain point the path of rationalisation was inherently very difficult to follow. For example, it was agreed in principle in 1942 that, to save shipping, the needs of the Forces based on the United Kingdom, including so far as possible those of the vast American forces that were to be assembled there, should be met from British production, whilst British forces in the Middle and Far East should be equipped mainly from North America. Very considerable adjustments of this kind were actually put into effect, but the Americans could not bring themselves to adopt weapons of British type, so that American-type field guns continued to move across the Atlantic to Britain while outward-bound convoys carried 25-pounders from the United Kingdom to North Africa and India.

The history of tank supply also illustrates the limitations of combined planning. By the spring of 1943, American tank production had reached a point at which the surplus remaining after United States and Russian needs had been met could comfortably cover almost the whole British Army requirement, and that with machines markedly better than the majority of those which were emerging from United Kingdom plants. Even the much smaller British output was made possible only by continuing supplies of American components and machine tools; and at the same time the British were asking the Americans to increase their deliveries of locomotives and other heavy engineering equipment which the Americans could not easily supply and which the British could make for themselves if certain plants were released from tank production. On every ground therefore, the

War Department argued, it was desirable that the British should virtually cease to build tanks and should take what they needed out of the American surplus. Now the British Government had already gone some way in this direction and was prepared to go further, but to go out of the tank business altogether was another matter. There were persistent fears of assignment difficulties and there was the prevailing (though not unanimous) view that in the Cromwell tanks just coming into production the British would have machines superior to anything the Americans could offer. But over and beyond these arguments was a consideration of high national policy; to put it bluntly, a country whose army was wholly dependent on a foreign source of supply for so important a part of its equipment could not easily maintain the status of a fully independent Great Power. Therefore, although the United Kingdom did curtail its domestic tank programme and accept larger numbers of Shermans in lieu, the cuts in home production were only partial, the increases in imports not more than marginal. In default of a stronger British demand, the Americans allowed their tank production to fall in 1944 to a fraction of what it had been in 1943. Thus when in the latter part of 1944 the United States Armoured Corps found that it had underrated its needs, the American surplus disappeared and allocations to Britain were suspended. Some British authorities now congratulated themselves on having maintained an independent source of supply; but it has to be remembered that if the British in 1943 had asked for more tanks, more would have been available in 1944.

(iii)

Supply from the United States

THE PRELUDE, TO DECEMBER 1941

Of the twenty-one billion dollars' worth of munitions which accrued to the British Commonwealth from United States production during the Second World War, less than one-tenth became available before the end of 1941. Moreover, whereas over the whole war the United States furnished the Commonwealth with 21 per cent. of the dollar value of its munitions supplies, in this first phase the percentage was only 10½. In one sense, indeed, the whole period of American neutrality can be seen in retrospect to have been a mere prelude to the main body of the work, its real significance lying not in the actual supplies received from cash and Lend-Lease but in the preparation of the ground, the political as well as the industrial ground, for the great harvests of the future. In this period two distinct themes were in evidence. The British Government's primary object was to secure from America the largest possible amount of first-aid, by negotiating for the release of munitions from existing stocks and from current production and by placing orders for such kinds and quantities of war material as could be furnished during the immediate struggle for survival. But besides this there was a second and remoter objective: to create – or rather to assist and encourage the United States Government to create – a munitions industry on the scale that would be needed if ultimate victory, positive and conclusive victory, were to be something more than a romantic vision. This emphasis on this second aim was more apparent in some departments than in others. But the aim was kept very much in mind by a number of leading officials in London and by Mr Arthur Purvis[1] in the United States. The Ministry of Aircraft Production tacitly endorsed it by setting its seal on programmes of supply which would clearly tax the utmost resources of the American aircraft industry and which, equally clearly, could not be implemented in full until well into 1942. The other supply departments, however, though recognising that the full realisation of the American war potential was a British interest, were of necessity more deeply concerned with fairly early gains and tended to look askance at long-term schemes which might interfere with these. According to 1940 plans, as we have seen, the Army was to be fully equipped, trained and ready for action by the spring of 1942. The Ministry of Supply, therefore, limited most of its North American orders to the relatively small quantities of equipment which American factories could provide by the end of 1941. This did not apply to stores such as explosives for which there would be a continuing need after the basic equipment of the forces had been completed; and in all cases the knowledge that the orders given would create permanently available production capacity was an important factor in the Ministry's calculations. But orders were never given without the prospect of deliveries in 1941. In the naval sphere, it was not until near the end of the period that the United States was asked to build warships of any size.

But although the Government as a whole did not in 1940 unequivocally adopt as a primary objective the general mobilisation of American industry for purposes of long-term supply, the measures which it took contributed largely and progressively to that end, and not only in the matter of aircraft production. In September of that year reliance on purchases of second-hand American merchant shipping was abandoned, and the decision was taken to order new ships, notwithstanding the long interval that would have to elapse

---

[1] For the part played by Mr Arthur B. Purvis, first Director-General of the British Purchasing Commission and first Chairman of the British Supply Council, in the early history of United States supply, see *North American Supply, op. cit.*, Chapters III to VIII.

before they could be produced. Only the most wishful of thinkers could really have supposed that the large orders for American tanks and rifles sanctioned about the same time by the Ministry of Supply would be executed in full during 1941. The undertaking given by the United States Government in November 1940, that it would furnish the British with the complete equipment of ten Army divisions was in reality a step forward in American rearmament, and was accepted as such in London, far more than it was a direct contribution to immediate British supply problems. Already the horizon was receding, and the first Lend-Lease programme of February 1941 formally extended it, for ordnance as well as for aircraft, to the middle of 1942. Well before Pearl Harbour it was realised on both sides of the Atlantic that the main production effort and the main American contribution to British supply, so far from approaching their terminus, were only just beginning. With that realisation, which was made explicit in the 'Victory Programme' of October 1941,[1] the preliminary phase of first-aid and of half-hearted approaches to the problem of supply was over. In endorsing this programme, albeit only in principle, the Americans had set their hands to the plough, and although there was still needed the disaster of 7th December to make them drive it fast and furiously, the main work had begun. But since the large-scale projects for the mobilisation of American munitions production on Britain's behalf, except those relating to aircraft and explosives, had not taken shape until the latter part of 1940, and since they were proceeded with under conditions which, for most of 1941, were very far from those of 'total defence', it was not to be expected that many of them should have yielded substantial results before Pearl Harbour.

A very large part of United States munitions supply in 1940 and even in 1941 was thus of the nature of first-aid, taking the form, not of a continuous flow of deliveries from new production, but of occasional bulk reinforcements prompted by the challenge of special emergencies. The first and greatest of the emergencies, which arose when the British Army was almost denuded of its modern equipment at Dunkirk, brought forth the most spectacular response, the shipment of three-quarters of a million rifles, eighty thousand machine guns and nearly nine hundred field artillery equipments, along with much other war material, in the summer of 1940. This great operation, which has been described at some length in *North American Supply*[2] helped to tide the British through the supreme hazards of the months that followed the fall of France. But when 1941 opened the emergency was scarcely less acute. The British Government knew

---

[1] See *North American Supply, op. cit.*, Chapter VIII.
[2] Ibid., Chapter V. The rifles and other supplies were not from new production but from old reserve stocks dating back mainly to the First World War.

C

that it stood on the eve of a great struggle in the Atlantic, as crucial and as uncertain in its outcome as the air battle of the previous summer. The decision for 1941, the Prime Minister had written in December, 'lies on the seas'. Shipping losses had fallen somewhat during the winter, but a new assault by much stronger U-boat forces was imminent; convoy escorts, though reinforced by the American 'four-stackers' and by the first-fruits of the Admiralty's Emergency Programme, were still desperately scarce; new merchant ships were coming forward very slowly; and confusion reigned in the congested and heavily bombed western harbours, where already 1½ million gross tons of damaged cargo shipping lay immobilised. Equally grave was the situation in the Eastern Mediterranean. The new Balkan front was menaced by German armies massing in Hungary and Bulgaria, and its collapse would expose the whole British position in the Middle East. At the same time, the defences of the United Kingdom itself were still dangerously thin; and the threat of invasion, though it had receded a little, could not yet be ignored.

The United States Government was eager to do all that it could to help. In January 1941, the War Department told the British Military Mission not to hesitate to ask for further releases out of stock; and meanwhile, Mr Harry L. Hopkins had gone to London at the President's bidding, partly to find out at first hand what the British wanted most and why. The answers were plain enough: aircraft (especially flying-boats and heavy bombers) and aero engines; ships (merchant vessels, escorts, motor torpedo-boats) and naval anti-aircraft guns; rifles, small arms ammunition and anti-tank guns.

The extent to which the United States Government could meet these requests, however, was narrowly circumscribed by the inadequacy of current production and of its existing stocks of war material. Ever since the crisis of May 1940, persistent attempts had been made to secure the release of American combat aircraft in advance of British contract deliveries, but with very little success. Even if the United States air forces had been entirely deprived of efficient aircraft, the clouds of planes which in its extremity the Government of the French Republic had sought to conjure up could not possibly have materialised. As it was, the comb-out of stocks in June 1940, had yielded some three hundred planes, but these were obsolete machines which could not have been accepted for combat purposes in any but the direst emergency. Later in the year, however, certain releases were effected which, though numerically small, were of considerable operational value. The Air Ministry was especially eager to acquire heavy bombers, for long-distance communication flights as well as for attacks on Berlin; and six Liberators and twenty Flying Fortresses, among the very first to be completed, were released from American contract delivery in the autumn of 1940. The other most urgent requirements were flying-boats. Very early in the war the Ministry had realised the great services that American Catalinas might render on anti-submarine patrol in the North Atlantic and in seeking out raiders in the wide spaces of the Indian Ocean. In September 1940 the United States Navy, which also badly needed Catalinas for its Pacific vigil, agreed to share alternate deliveries with the Royal Air Force, to which as a result ten were handed over before the end of the year. These were valuable reinforcements, for it was not until late in 1941 that deliveries began to be made against British production contracts for heavy bombers or flying-boats.[1]

When Lend-Lease came into effect the prospects for much larger releases of aircraft seemed bright. In March 1941, an agreement negotiated by Air Commodore J. C. Slessor (as he then was) promised the British not only the entire output of the capacity which their own contracts had brought into being and of the new capacity which was now to be financed from Lend-Lease funds, but also 'the allocation of a continuing output from the United States capacity, existing or approved, in such numbers as the military situation might require and the circumstances permit'. An attempt to translate this nebulous formula into quantitative terms produced a figure of 5,817 aircraft to be diverted from United States Government contracts up to June 1942. But this promise, if it was a promise (the United States Government never recognised the agreement as binding), was not fulfilled. There was no practical limit to the number which the military situation required, but the number which circumstances permitted was for the time being negligible. Thirty Martlet and ten Tomahawk fighters, destined originally for the Balkan allies, found their way to British forces in the Mediterranean theatre, and that, with a few transport planes, was the entire allocation for 1941. (The 'circumstances' were chiefly the sharpening hunger of the American Air Force and the emergence of a powerful third claimant in the Soviet Union.)

One great reinforcement the Royal Navy had received from the United States in 1940 were the famous fifty 'over-age' destroyers. Once these had been transferred the United States Navy had very little that it could spare. After long negotiations, which had begun in June 1940, the transfer of 28 motor torpedo-boats was eventually authorised in the Presidential directive of 11th March 1941, which declared Great Britain eligible for 'defence aid'. Shortly afterwards ten armed cutters, the property of the United States Coastguard Services, were handed over for Service or convoy escorts – a small but useful stopgap contribution to an enormous and growing need.

---

[1] It was one of these first Catalinas that in May 1941 tracked the *Bismarck* to her doom. Flying Fortresses took part in a raid on Wilhelmshaven about the same time. This however was little more than a demonstration, in their original form neither the Fortress nor the Liberator was really fitted for attacks on well-defended targets.

Also included in the directive of 11th March were five 5-inch, 150 4-inch and 300 3-inch naval guns, which the Admiralty had been seeking for several months past, chiefly in order to complete the defensive armament of merchant ships. The main American contribution to the battle of ocean supply lines in 1941, however, was not to be found in the actual transfer of ships or equipment but in the cargo space which they placed at the disposal of the British and in the opening of repair yards to damaged British warships and merchant vessels.

Some valuable assistance was still to be had from the United States Army's stocks of war material which the Army was the more ready to deplete as the prospect of early replacement from new production became brighter. One of the first results of Hopkins' mission to London, together with the advocacy of Purvis and his military colleagues in Washington, was the release of a further quarter of a million .30-inch rifles, which helped to arm the Home Guard and other static units and so freed .303-inch weapons for the Field Army. Steps were also taken as soon as Lend-Lease allowed, to stiffen the Balkan and Libyan fronts with all possible war material. Greece, declared eligible for aid on the same day as Great Britain, Yugoslavia, during the brief period in which she was at war as an organised state, and Turkey, to whose reinforcement the British gave at this time a high priority, all received immediate allocations of field guns, scout cars and other equipment. These were probably too little and certainly too late; not much had been shipped and nothing had reached its destination when the German Army swept through the Monastir Gap and on to the Piraeus. But, together with similar allocations of obsolescent equipment made directly to the British, they did something to strengthen the hands of the defenders of Egypt.

Much more was needed, however, for after the loss of Greece and Crete and the arrival of the Afrika Corps in Cyrenaica, the situation in the Middle East was hazardous in the extreme. At Hopkins' suggestion there came to Washington in May a special emissary from Cairo, Brigadier J. M. Whiteley, bearing with him a list of the stores which would have to be supplied in the next three months if Suez were to be saved, and which could not be provided from the United Kingdom. This novel and unorthodox procedure was designed to dramatise the situation and to convince the Americans both that the stated requirements were urgent and that, if they were met, Egypt could and would be held. (Current opinion in Washington was nearly as sceptical of this as it had been of the survival of Britain in the previous summer.) The 'Whiteley list' was a long one, covering practically the whole range of military equipment from tanks, artillery and 10-ton trucks down to barbed wire and typewriter ribbon. The main emphasis, however, was on engineer stores such as road-making and water-supply equipment, and on the supplies needed for the creation of a vast military base in a non-industrial country – iron and steel in various forms, machine tools, welding sets, air compressors and workshop equipment generally. Much of this was civilian-type equipment which could be acquired easily enough by immediate purchase. For artillery, further inroads were made into War Department stocks: and the great majority of the stores for which General Wavell had asked were on their way to Suez before the summer ended.

The first clashes with the Afrika Corps had shown that the worst weakness in the British position was lack of armour, and it was therefore on the supply of tanks that interest was mainly focused. Allocations from stocks and from current production could not help very much here, for until June 1941, only one firm was producing tanks, and these were light machines hardly strong enough to take a successful part in intensive armoured warfare. Nevertheless the 'General Stuart', as this tank was called, could and did give valuable service in the Desert campaigns. It was fast and reliable and won the good opinion of its users. Hopes of acquiring a battalion's worth in time for General Wavell's offensive of December 1940 did not materialise, but from February 1941 onwards Stuarts were shipped in steadily increasing numbers; which reached 772 before the end of the year.

For all practical purposes, however, the British could acquire modern types of major war equipment such as aircraft, medium tanks, artillery and ammunition only from new production initiated by their own contracts or by Lend-Lease contracts let on their behalf. Up to the end of 1941 the latter played an almost negligible part. By the time of Pearl Harbour nearly thirteen billion dollars had been appropriated by Congress for defence aid and over nine billion had been allocated to the procurement agencies. But the value of the aid actually received by the British – goods transferred and services rendered – was only just over one billion dollars ($1,000 million), and no more than a fifth of this consisted of munitions supplies. Of this $200 millions' worth most was accounted for by transfers of existing material of the kind just described, and very little, naturally enough, was the fruit of contracts placed since the Act had been passed.

Receipts of new equipment before Pearl Harbour thus depended very largely on the size and progress of British cash contracts. These began to yield a substantial harvest in many fields before the period was over: indeed deliveries from these contracts reached their peak in the autumn of 1941. In the supply of small arms weapons and ammunition there was a particularly notable contribution. Deliveries of new rifles on British account did not begin to come forward until the last days of 1941, but the United States were already the main source of pistols and, so far, almost the sole source of sub-machine guns. Here the British were not breaking wholly fresh ground: Smith and Wesson and Colt pistols and Thompson sub-machine guns were established products, and output was expanded readily and swiftly in response to the British demand, and the demand was great. In this way personal weapons of that type had been provided from the United States for over 350,000 British officers and men before Pearl Harbour. The total supply of rifles of American manufacture, including the rifles released from stock, was not far short of the total number supplied from United Kingdom sources between the outbreak of war and the end of 1941. The British also received from the United States in the same period some 1,300 million rounds of small arms ammunition – not very many fewer than were produced in their own factories.

The supply of artillery and of artillery ammunition was altogether different. Here there were no ready sources of supply and British purchases did little to develop any. Apart from one small stopgap order after Dunkirk for 37-mm. anti-tank guns (which after long delays in manufacture proved to be useless), the only new guns which it was thought might possibly be obtained from America before the end of 1941 were 20-mm. Oerlikon guns.[1] These were regarded as the most promising weapon for the defence of ships against low-flying aircraft. Swiss deliveries being interrupted in 1940, it became necessary to find alternative sources of supply. Production was started up in the United Kingdom, but a supplement from America was obviously desirable, and an officer of the Royal Navy was sent out in the autumn of 1940 to establish production there also. Having failed to interest any American firm in the project he took over a factory in Rhode Island and himself organised a system of sub-contracting which resulted in the delivery of the first gun within seven months. Eventually a massive output was secured from this and from other plants set up by the United States Navy, which evinced a keen interest in the Oerlikon from the start: and the British, who made some sixty thousand Oerlikons for themselves, received a further 14,660 from the United States. But only 217 were made available in 1941.

American supplies of gun ammunition represented little more than five per cent. of British production up to the end of 1941. The only important contributions so far were medium and heavy howitzer shells, which had been contracted for as early as the spring of 1940, armour-piercing shot for tank and anti-tank guns, and 75-mm. shells

---

[1] Orders for loose barrels and predictors for anti-aircraft guns were placed with American firms before the war, and supply began almost at the beginning of the war (in the case of predictors even before the war).

ordered for the use of the field guns released from stock at the time of Dunkirk.

No supplies were more eagerly awaited from America than medium tanks, on which, more than on any other single factor, it seemed that the issue of the North African war would turn. Before its dollars ran out the British Purchasing Commission had succeeded in placing orders with four American engineering firms for a total of 2,085 tanks, to which were added Lend-Lease orders for 2,100. In addition, it was understood that 1,271 would be allotted to Britain out of the deliveries accruing from earlier War Department contracts, so that in theory the British could look forward to something over five thousand medium tanks by mid-summer 1942, the terminal date for the first programme of Lend-Lease supply. But in the spring of 1941 it already seemed unlikely that these expectations would actually be met. Though the great firm of Chrysler had been set to making tanks there was not yet any general mobilisation of the automobile industry. A British suggestion that General Motors should be brought in as well was not followed up, and the production of civilian cars and trucks continued without serious restriction until the autumn of 1941. Moreover, since American munitions production was geared not to British but to American needs, among which tanks were by no means the most urgent, the tank-building firms were finding it impossible, in face of competing demands from Navy Department and Army Air Corps contractors, to get early delivery of the machine tools they needed. Thus on 23rd March 1941, the British Purchasing Commission had to report that total deliveries to the middle of 1942 were now expected to be only 3,335 medium tanks, of which the British were provisionally allotted 2,116. More serious still was the fact that although production was to start in May 1941, it would not get into its full stride until the following year: in the whole of 1941 no more than 335 medium tanks were likely to be completed.

To the British Government, faced with a gap of eight thousand tanks between military requirements and estimated home production up to the spring of 1942, this situation was disappointing and disquieting in the extreme. In June the Prime Minister decided that the moment had come for one of his sparingly used personal interventions on supply matters. In cables to the President and Hopkins he asked for the utmost effort to increase supplies in the next six or nine months. Specifically, he asked for two thousand medium tanks in 1941.

The impact of these communications was immediate. The President at once issued a strong directive calling for a great drive to accelerate tank production. He decreed that the ultimate planned rate of output should be raised from five hundred to a thousand medium tanks a month – this rate to be attained by May 1942; also that the six hundred or so machine tools required by the tank contractors should be made available forthwith, so that a total output of some 1,700 medium tanks in the remainder of 1941 now seemed possible. The vigorous hoist thus given to tank production was one of the big events in American mobilisation for war, the measures now taken paving the way for the tremendous expansion of output after Pearl Harbour. For the time being, however, progress was inevitably rather slow and halting. The contractors were entirely without recent experience in this type of work, and the first tanks were full of minor faults. The supply of engines, of transmissions and above all of guns and mountings lagged badly behind, so that the assembly plants, living from hand to mouth, could not develop the smooth rhythm of quantity production. Nevertheless, 1,342 medium tanks were completed during the last seven months of 1941 – many more than had seemed possible in the spring, though fewer than had been hoped for in July. But of these only 269 were built to British order, and, partly because of competing Russian demands only 85 were actually allotted from War Department contracts. American supplies of tanks thus contributed little, after all, to British fighting strength in 1941, for of the 354 delivered, only 229 had actually been shipped by the end of the year, and very few had reached their destination. In the campaigns of that year, and for a while longer, British-built Valentines, Matildas and Crusaders had to bear nearly the whole burden of the Desert war.

The supply of aircraft was perhaps an even more urgent need. Local air supremacy was vital to the defence of Britain and Egypt. Aircraft were among the most efficient hunters of U-boats and protectors of convoys. And, until the Red Army was drawn into the struggle, the bomber plane was the only conceivable counterpoise to German land power. Fortunately, in this field more than in almost any other, United States assistance made itself appreciably felt even in the first two years of the war. Lend-Lease had little to do with this. Within three weeks of the passing of the Act the President allocated funds for the 'immediate purchase' of 5,600 aircraft on British behalf, and by September 1941, Lend-Lease requisitions had been accepted for over 11,000. But immediate purchase in this context could not mean immediate delivery; the production facilities had to be created first. In fact, the British received only 189 planes on Lend-Lease terms during 1941. The decisive factor was the British purchasing of aircraft, which started earlier and was carried on more vigorously than the purchasing of any other store. Throughout the rearmament period and the early years of the war inferiority in the air was the British Government's greatest single anxiety, and despite the utmost effort at home it was forced to rely more and more upon American aid. Seven hundred and fifty aircraft were ordered from American manufacturers before the outbreak of war, and 1,320 more, costing $100 million, within its first six months. Already the assistance of the United States had been invoked in every section of the aircraft supply programme except that of heavy bombers, and already a large area of the existing aviation industry had been invaded by British purchasers. So far, however, procurement from the United States was not regarded as more than an interim measure, to tide the Royal Air Force over the period in which British production was being expanded. But the horizon of air supremacy was still receding, and in the spring of 1940 it became clear to the Allied Governments that a far greater venture would have to be undertaken. All previous measures were eclipsed by the 600-million-dollar scheme approved by the Supreme War Council on 29th March, whereby the Allies were to place orders for 4,700 American planes, all of combat types.[1]

This Anglo-French project, the French share of which, together with the unfulfilled balance of earlier French orders, was inherited by the British shortly afterwards, represented a major effort to harness the industry of the United States to the service of the Allies and a major departure from the ruling British policy of self-sufficiency. It looked far ahead, for deliveries were to run from October 1940, to September 1941, and continuation orders for supply in 1942 were not ruled out. Indeed, the number of aircraft ordered was much less significant than the fact that to fulfil their new commitments the manufacturers would have to increase their rate of output by seven hundred planes a month; and thanks to the helpful attitude of the United States Government these would consist of the most modern and efficient types yet developed (Tomahawk, Kittyhawk, Lightning and Airacobra fighters, Boston, Baltimore and Hudson light bombers, Bermuda dive bombers and a few four-engined Liberators). Taking the previous orders into account, the United States aircraft industry, which in the whole of 1939 had produced only 1,800 military planes, would have to provide a thousand a month for export by the summer of 1941, quite apart from meeting the growing, though still much smaller, demands of its own Government. Nearly all the principal airframe and aero-engine firms were to be drawn into the Allied orbit and a hundred thousand more Americans set to work for the Allied cause. According to the plans now framed, the United States would ultimately provide well over a quarter of Britain's total supplies of aircraft.

The foundations of aircraft supply from the United States were thus laid very early. Though much vaster schemes, involving the expansion of total American production to six thousand planes a

---

[1] See *North American Supply, op. cit.,* Chapter IV.

month, were discussed after the fall of France, and though by the spring of 1941, when direct purchasing by the British Air Commission ceased, the number of planes ordered on British account had risen to 11,359, the actual production capacity earmarked for British use was not much augmented during the latter part of 1940. Provision was made through Lend-Lease for the supply of additional types of aircraft, notably medium and heavy bombers, transport planes and naval aircraft, but this did not much affect the numbers supplied, in total. At no time during the war did the British receive more than the thousand planes a month which was the theoretical output capacity of the plants contracted for before the fall of France.

Throughout 1940 and 1941 they received very considerably less. The Anglo-French scheme was not implemented in full according to the original timetable. Many of the new types concerned did not come into production until the summer of 1941; and in the twelve months ending on 30th September 1941, during which 4,700 planes were scheduled for delivery under the scheme, the contracts placed after March 1940 actually yielded only 1,859. Nevertheless, thanks to the earlier contracts and in a lesser degree to the special releases described above, the Royal Air Force was already receiving a very considerable reinforcement from the United States even in this early period, as the following figures show:

	U.K. Production	*U.S. Supplies*
1939	7,940	701
1940	15,049	2,006
1941	20,094	5,194
	43,083	7,901

The increment was thus, on paper, already a substantial one; by the summer of 1941 American supplies of aircraft bore to British production very nearly the proportion that they were to bear for the rest of the war. The actual contribution to British fighting in this period, however, was not as great as the figures suggest. Owing to the time-lag between delivery at the factory and absorption into British squadrons, the actual receipts in 1940, according to British records, were 1,040 aircraft; and in June 1941, the Royal Air Force still acknowledged the receipt of only 2,764 American planes, of which little more than a third were then included in its front-line strength. Many of the remainder, especially among those bequeathed by the French, were obsolete machines hardly fit for combat in current conditions: 200 Mohawk fighters, for example, had to be relegated to the training schools. In spite of the preference in the expenditure of dollars which the Air Ministry and the Ministry of Aircraft Production had enjoyed throughout, American supply was not a big factor in the development of British air strength during the first two years of war. In 1941, hardly less than in 1940, the great majority of the aircraft which guarded the English and Egyptian skies and which carried the war to the cities of Germany were made by British hands.

THE FIRST YEAR OF AMERICAN BELLIGERENCE

At the end of 1941 a fundamental change took place in the relations between the American arsenal and its foreign customers, in that the arsenal now became itself a belligerent with clamant operational needs of its own to satisfy. The danger, inherent in this change, of a catastrophic interruption in the flow of warlike stores from the United States to Britain was averted, however, by the munitions assignment organisation and by the statesmanship which inspired its creation and its operation;[1] and was in any case more than offset by the powerful stimulus to American production which was afforded by actual participation in the war – the one factor which had been absent in 1941. Thus the value of munitions supplies furnished to Britain in 1942 was more than double that of the previous year's receipts – about $3,360 million against $1,515 million: and although United Kingdom and Dominion production was also very much on the increase the proportion of total Commonwealth supplies that was procured from the United States rose from 11½ to 17 per cent. This year, in fact, may be regarded as the first in which American munitions supply was a really important factor in the growth o Britain's war-making power as a whole. The long labour of clearing and ploughing was over; sowing was now in progress everywhere and in many fields a sizeable harvest was already being reaped.

Nearly the whole of the war material supplied now came from new production initiated by British cash contracts, the early Lend-Lease contracts or United States rearmament orders. Nevertheless, supply still retained much of its first-aid character. Ammunition was allotted to British forces, not in accordance with any previously agreed programme, but because British guns would otherwise have very soon ceased to fire. The British front was broken at Gazala in June, and 300 Sherman tanks were taken off the assembly line, by special arrangement, in order to stem the flowing tide. It was not until near the end of the year that the planners of supply could pause to draw breath, to stop doling out supplies against particular emergencies in this or that battle-front and frame coherent programmes for the building up of the offensive strength of the United Nations as a whole.

The rate of growth in 1942 was least noticeable in the supply of aircraft. This was partly because production was already more

---

[1] See below, Chapters IV and V, and *North American Supply, op. cit.,* Chapter IX.

advanced in this field than in most others, so that war mobilisation had proportionately less effect on total output, and partly because the British, through their own numerous contracts and early Lend-Lease requisitions, had already acquired a claim over a definite sector of American aircraft production capacity. They were still allowed to receive the bulk of the output from this sector, but expectation of additional receipts from the new capacity now coming into operation were, in the main, disappointed; it was almost exclusively the American air forces that benefited from the expansion of the aircraft industry after about the middle of 1941. Thus deliveries to the British rose only from 5,194 aircraft in 1941 to 6,847 in 1942. The most grievous disappointment was the supply of heavy bombers, on which great hopes had been pinned. Receipts in 1942 amounted to only 176 planes against 135 in 1941, although total American production of these types had multiplied more than eight times. In this field American supplies were less than ten per cent. of British production in 1942.

For the Royal Navy, American supplies did not bulk very large even in 1942. In that year it received steadily increasing supplies of guns and ammunition (though assignments were never as large as the Admiralty thought that its needs warranted), together with a few torpedoes, mines and shells; also a very important supply of engines for landing craft and other small vessels. Apart from landing craft, of which the British were allotted sufficient to make the North African landings feasible, very few American warships were as yet available for Britain's use; the most important were four auxiliary or escort aircraft carriers (out of six requisitioned early in 1941 and a final total of thirty). The completion of escort vessels, which were not given what the British considered adequate priority in the American production set-up until the end of 1942, did not begin until the following year. Indeed, when heavy sinkings began to take place off the American coast, the British had to allow the United States Navy to take delivery of ten corvettes which had been built in Canada to United Kingdom order. In this year of rapidly mounting shipping losses there was only one really bright ray of light in the gloom of the struggle on the seas, and that was the extraordinary American merchant shipbuilding achievement. Contrary to all the indications in the early part of the year, United States shipyards attained and slightly exceeded their objective of eight million deadweight tons – nearly eight times as many as were completed in 1941. From this success Britain gained comparatively slight direct benefits; the Americans felt themselves to be in too great need of ships to spare many for British use. There were, however, the sixty cargo steamers, each of 10,000 tons deadweight, which the British had ordered in December 1940, and which were actually transferred to the British flag. All these were delivered between October 1941 and November 1942 – a remarkably prompt performance considering that two brand-new shipyards had to be laid out before construction could begin. This acquisition alone was equal to a third of the United Kingdom output in 1942, which was the peak year in British merchant shipbuilding.

It was the Army which benefited most among the British Services from the impetus given to American munitions production by Pearl Harbour. The value of ground munitions delivered to the British in 1941 was $430 million, in 1942 $1,530 million. Small arms weapons and ammunition retained a prominent place in the list of supplies furnished. Over 2,500 million rounds of ammunition were provided from the United States in 1942, rather more than were produced in Britain herself. The majority of these were for use in the machine guns mounted in American-built tanks and planes, but there were also valuable supplies of ammunition for rifles and sub-machine guns of British tanks and planes. There were also over 400,000 rifles (all of which were new and most of which were of .303-inch calibre), matched by an almost equivalent number of revolvers and sub-machine guns. Owing to the rapidly rising output of rifle and Sten guns in Britain, however, supplies of personal weapons lost the peculiar and paramount importance which had been theirs in 1940 and 1941. But now for the first time substantial numbers of new American artillery equipments began to be acquired by the British Army. This was chiefly due to the coming into production in March 1942, of two very important weapons, originally British but now common to both armies – the Bofors light anti-aircraft gun[1] and the 6-pounder (57-mm.) anti-tank gun. No Bofors were allotted to the British until July, but in the second half of 1942 Britain received 2,334 guns or 30 per cent. of total production. On the other hand, up to September the entire output of 6-pounders was assigned to Britain, and 2,511 guns out of 3,877 produced in the whole year.

United States deliveries also became a major element in the British Army's supplies of mechanical transport in 1942, although in numbers, as distinct from the peculiar value of special American types such as the tank transporter and the jeep, Canada was still a much more important source. But by now the catalogue of American supplies was almost endless. Indeed, variety is quite as much a feature of the story as increase in total quantity. At first British demands upon the United States were more or less confined to the major types of specifically armament stores. But from 1941 onwards both requirements and supply came to include a vast miscellany of other kinds of military equipment – signal apparatus and that wide variety of

---

[1] The Bofors was designed in Sweden but was now a standard weapon of the British Army.

material which is classed as engineer stores and includes pumps and generators, road-making and earth-moving equipment, workshop tools, assault boats, bridges, cranes, steel loading mat for improvised airfields and caterpillar tractors. In this field the Army's wants were constantly multiplying as the war progressed and the absorption of general manufacturing industry into armaments production made it less and less easy for its wants to be satisfied from home sources. The year 1942 saw a great increase in American exports of such stores, though the full development still lay in the future.[1]

Perhaps the most important development of all, however, was the fruition of the plans laid for tank supply. The output of medium tanks in the United States, though well short of the 'goal' announced by the President immediately after Pearl Harbour, increased at a prodigious rate, from 1,348 in the last six months of 1941 to 4,170 in the first half of 1942 and 8,763 in the second half, by which time it was already more than double the output of the United Kingdom. During the year the British received from United States production 4,389 medium tanks, or about a third of their supplies from all sources. Over half of these, moreover, were of the latest and best model, the Sherman, whose advent had an incalculable influence on the course of events in North Africa.

THE PERIOD OF PLENTY, JANUARY 1943 TO JUNE 1944

A number of factors combined to make the autumn of 1942 the end of one phase and the beginning of another in the story of supply from the United States. The great military successes of October and November, together with the virtual abandonment of plans for a major land offensive in 1943, dissolved the atmosphere of emergency and gave the planners a clear run of about fifteen months in which to arrange the build-up of the forces needed for the final onslaught. At the same time the production plans of the United States, hitherto little more than an assemblage of competing aspirations, were reduced into something more like an orderly programme, related (though not as closely as the British would have liked) to genuine military needs on the one hand and to industrial realities on the other. In consequence the raw material crisis, largely a matter of excessive demand rather than of real shortage, was overcome, and with the great plant construction programmes of 1941 and 1942 now more or less completed, the country's mass-production industries were enabled to display without hindrance the full measure of their fertility for war. In 1943, 54,000 combat aircraft were produced as against 25,000 in 1942, and 21,000 medium gun tanks against 13,000.

---

[1] Deliveries of engineer stores rose from $6 million in 1941 to $35 million in 1942 and $153 million in 1943.

The tonnage of naval ships and craft completed rose from 0.86 to 2.58 million displacement tons, that of merchant ships from 8.2 to 19.3 million deadweight tons. These, together with the creation of two new giant industries, synthetic rubber and aviation fuel, were the highlights of achievement, but the whole volume of industrial production increased by about twenty per cent. and the output of munitions by 76 per cent. Moreover, the development of a realistic American programme made possible what the exigencies of British planning, in particular the need for very precise distribution of manpower, now made more than ever desirable – the preparation of fairly accurate long-term forecasts of the supplies which Britain would receive from the United States. It was now less important that munitions should be distributed according to the operational needs of the moment, more important that the planners in each country should know in advance what they could expect to get. The closing weeks of 1942 thus saw the formulation of a number of agreements which sketched in broad outline both the production and distribution of munitions in 1943.[1] And these were far more nearly fulfilled than any previous agreements of similar type.

The agreement signed by representatives of the United States Army Air Corps, the United States Navy's Bureau of Aircraft, the Royal Air Force and the Fleet Air Arm reflected a notable change of American policy in regard to aircraft supply. The principle that American aircraft must be manned by American crews if at all possible was modified by the superior principle of maximum impact on the enemy. The American Air Forces in the main overseas theatres, the South-West Pacific, the Mediterranean and the United Kingdom, were to be built up *pari passu* with the Royal Air Force, and only when these were fully equipped was the metropolitan air force of the United States to be expanded. From this declaration of policy there emerged a provisional allocation of 6,150 combat planes to the British in the year 1943, plus 1,800 fighters in aid of their commitment to the Russians. This allocation was warmly welcomed by the Chief of the Air Staff, for it meant that the most important attrition requirements of the Royal Air Force would be fully covered, with a net gain of at least 287 Liberators for anti-submarine patrol. In addition there was to be the most valuable increment of 600 Dakota transport planes; though little more than half the stated need, these would be the first substantial contribution that the Americans had yet made to the solution of the acute British air transport problem. Moreover, nearly all the promised planes were modern types of high quality. Actual allocations came within reasonable distance of the forecast. The British received the full quota of fighters for transfer to the Soviet Union and 5,359 combat aircraft for their own use. The

---

[1] See Chapter IV, section (iii), and *North American Supply, op. cit.*, Chapters IX and X.

supply of heavy and medium bombers exceeded expectation, and the short-fall was concentrated mainly on the now less important dive-bomber and flying-boat categories. (The execution of the British contracts for Bermuda dive-bombers had been so long delayed that the number on order was drastically reduced, the machine having become obsolescent. Production of the Coronado flying-boat, intended successor to the Catalina, did not develop according to plan.) Only 474 Dakotas were assigned in place of the 600 promised, but the British received 289 other smaller transports.

The formulation of the 1943 programme of ground munitions supply will be described in Chapter IV below, where it will be noted that deliveries to the British amounted to 86 per cent. of the provision made for them. This represented a further remarkable increase in the absolute value of the British Army's receipts from the United States – from $1,530 million in 1942 to $2,610 million in 1943. This latter figure was estimated to represent in turn between a quarter and a third of its supplies from all sources. In the supply of most land weapons this was easily the peak year. Over 10,000 medium tanks – twice as many as in any other calendar year – were allotted to the British in 1943, not to mention some 2,000 light tanks, 3,000 armoured cars and nearly 5,000 machine-gun carriers. The bulk of the tanks were delivered in the first half of the year, in which period the United States contributed no less than 61 per cent. of all British supplies. Other notable supplies included 90,000 vehicles and over half a million rifles; with revolvers and sub-machine guns added, the United States provided in this one year personal weapons for only a few less than a million British troops.

On the naval side the main feature of the year was the fruition of the escort vessel programme. In 1943 the British Navy received from the United States shipyards 26 auxiliary aircraft carriers and 72 destroyer escorts and frigates, whose advent helped to bring about the decisive defeat of the German attack on the ocean communications of the United Nations. In addition there were numerous mine-sweepers, smaller anti-submarine vessels, tugs and landing craft; and the total supply of naval ships and craft from the United States was of the order of 800,000 displacement tons, which may be compared with the 500,000 tons built in United Kingdom yards. And this although in theory Britain was devoting her main effort to naval construction and America to merchant ships. The great bulk of American warship supply was concentrated in this one year. Earlier very few ships of the type required by the Royal Navy had been completed in the United States. Afterwards escort vessels were no longer needed, and as we shall see, the vessels which took their place at the head of British needs were not forthcoming in any number.

It can be asserted as broadly true that in 1943 the United Kingdom was for the first time receiving from the United States all the supplies that it really needed. There were exceptions, of course. There was the major universal shortage of landing ships and craft, which was to have a profound effect on the course of operations in the following year and which impelled the British Government to embark on a feverish programme of construction at home in the last few months before Operation Overlord. There were minor exceptions such as heavy vehicles, some types of small arms ammunition, and many varieties of engineer and signal stores, though it is at least arguable that in some of these cases British requirements were inflated beyond the level of real need. In general, however, it was a year of plenty. The total value of munitions supplies received by the British Commonwealth from the United States was $6,670 million, nearly twice as much as in 1942 and 27 per cent. of the Commonwealth's total supplies.

Munitions supply in 1944 began to be actively considered in London and Washington in the spring of 1943, very soon after that year's programmes had been settled. At this time the planners were still looking through a glass darkly; there was much that was uncertain about the shape and size of the demand and the trend of production. The Battle of the Atlantic was still in the balance; the timing of the main offensive in Europe had not yet been finally settled, nor could the intensity and duration of German resistance be accurately forecast; the needs of the liberated territories could only be guessed at; and it was by no means clear how far Britain would be able to sustain her own production in face of a continuing loss of industrial manpower to the Services, nor to what extent the American authorities would have to yield to pressure for more domestic consumer goods.

The main outlines were none the less tolerably clear. By the end of 1943 the 'capital' equipment of the British Army would at last be substantially complete, and a few months later the United States Army would reach the same position. Generally speaking, the demand would then fall to the maintenance level. Many obsolescent weapons would still need replacement, and there would still be a large unsatisfied requirement of vehicles, engineer stores and signal stores. But on balance it seemed safe to assume that ground forces would make a considerably smaller claim upon the combined resources in 1944 than in the current year.

On the other hand, the strategy of the combination allowed no respite for aircraft production until undisputed air supremacy had been attained. Output was not scheduled to reach its peak before the middle of 1944, and although it might then fall off numerically there would be a countervailing emphasis on higher quality. It seemed unlikely, therefore, that there would be much freeing of resources from this sector of production on either side of the Atlantic.

D

It appeared also that shipbuilding would have to be continued in 1944 at a rate certainly not less than that attained in 1943. Losses at sea in March 1943 were the highest of the war, the U-boat packs were still increasing in strength, vast armies and shipments of food and raw materials to the United Kingdom had yet to be moved across the ocean. At the same time there would clearly have to be some increase in the supply of many types of civilian stores which had a direct relation to the war effort and whose production had been too sharply curtailed – agricultural machinery, to make possible a very necessary increase in food production, with a reduced labour force; locomotives and wagons, to help in the restoration of Europe's battered transport system; clothing and drugs for relief work; mining machinery, to arrest the decline in British coal output, and equipment for public utilities which had everywhere gone too long without normal maintenance.

Thus the British view was that the United Nations would have little opportunity in 1944, at least until the year was well advanced, to relax from the tremendous exertions of 1943 on the production front. While there was likely to be a reasonable plenty of munitions in general, supplies would still fall far short of the ideal in several vital sectors. The combined objective for the year should therefore be to concentrate all available resources on the production of ships, aircraft, new weapons and 'material for the maintenance of essential services', particularly transportation equipment.

This view was not altogether shared by the American authorities. The mighty surge of United States production in 1943 and the Allied victories in the field, limited though they were, produced a more and more widespread belief among the American people that the main job was done and that they could begin to look forward to peace and plenty. In some degree this optimism began to permeate the offices of the production planners, where before the end of the year the fear of surpluses, of 'munitions graveyards' to which the guardians of the public purse in the legislature might justly take exception, had largely replaced the earlier fear of shortage. Strenuous and successful efforts were made by the War Department in 1943 to hold *down* the production of tanks, artillery, small arms, bombs, aircraft armament and army clothing. Nor were these cuts altogether offset by increases in other fields. Aircraft production, indeed, continued to rise during the first few months of 1944, but at a much slower rate than hitherto; and by that time both merchant and naval shipbuilding were on the decline. Originally, it had been planned to spend 85 billion dollars on war production during 1944, but by December 1943 the figure had fallen to 71 billion. This was slightly less than the rate of expenditure then current, although with the completion of most war plants and the elimination of most raw material difficulties, a largely increased output was obviously possible. Thus the War Production Board, early in 1944, was in a position to take the first tentative steps in the direction of reconversion. There was, indeed, already some anxiety about the pockets of unemployment which were the result of cutbacks in the munitions programme.

These trends presented the British with a danger and an opportunity. The danger was that once production was allowed to slacken and American thoughts turned towards peace it would be more and more difficult to get British requirements accepted for manufacture. Moreover, as time went on there would be fewer and fewer completed stores to go round, so that there would be a recurrence of assignment troubles whenever the American Services found that they had underrated their own needs. On the other hand, since stated American requirements were on the wane and there was a wide margin between the potential and the planned output of the American munitions industries, it was clearly easier for the British to obtain assistance from the United States, provided that they stepped in quickly and secured provision for their needs in time to arrest the threatened decline in total output.

At first it did not appear, however, that assistance would be wanted on any great scale. A Ministry of Production memorandum written in May 1943 commented: 'The call on the United States for war supplies is falling as has been foreseen'. Ministry of Supply requirements presented a month later, for inclusion in the 1944 Army Supply Programme, amounted only to about eighty per cent. of the provision made for 1943. Now this, on the face of it, was odd; for the United Kingdom's difficulties were not markedly diminishing. The problem of manpower in particular was more acute than ever. The easing of the general shipping situation about the middle of 1943 brought no relief to British shipbuilders, who had to cope with a host of fresh demands for landing craft, fleet auxiliaries and special-purpose merchant vessels. The Ministry of Aircraft Production was clamouring for yet more workers and the Ministry of Supply, faced with an additional cut of 80,000 in its labour force, was hard put to it to find ways of pruning its domestic programmes further than they had already been pruned in the previous winter. With the last inches of slack in process of being pulled in, the United Kingdom was seeking to sustain its substantial production and at the same time increase the personnel of its armed forces. It was argued that these facts posed an insoluble problem, and that a further squeeze of the civilian sector, including production, had to be accepted, the 'huge and resilient' capacity of the United States being relied on to fill the resulting breach. The current trend, in fact, should be reversed, and wherever the case was doubtful, the decision should be to seek supplies from the United States rather than from domestic producers.

The difficulty was, however, that the type of munitions which Britain most needed and could least readily supply from her own resources were in the main those of which production was still lagging behind the demand in the United States. An obvious example was landing craft. Not only was there no prospect of relief for the United Kingdom in this quarter but the British Government had to embark, in the last few months before Operation Overlord, on a feverish programme of additional construction involving the uneconomic use of a number of yards normally devoted to merchant shipbuilding. Again, during the animated debate on the British aircraft programme which took place in the early summer of 1943, it was suggested that the Ministry of Aircraft Production's demands for manpower could be made less exorbitant if it would rely more upon American supplies. But the Ministry discounted this possibility. It pointed out that the total United States programme had lately been reduced by 13,000 planes and that, since the Army Air Corps was sure to have provided crews for the number originally scheduled, the chances of an increased allocation to Britain were remote. Clearly there could be no question of any further shifting of the burden of aircraft production on to American shoulders.

Nor were the prospects much brighter on the Army side. When the Army Supply Programme for 1944 was printed in August 1943, it was found that fully a quarter of the stated British requirements of ground munitions, relatively modest though they were, had been left unsatisfied. This was due to the persistence of certain black spots in the American production scene. Among these were still signal apparatus, British requirements of which received 79 per cent. satisfaction in the programme, and certain types of engineer stores (68 per cent. satisfaction). Easily the worst shortage, however, was that of vehicles. The British were trying hard to secure in 1944 some part of what had been denied them in 1943, but with very little success. Pressure on the War Department and the War Production Board led to a general review of truck manufacturing capacity in August 1943, as the result of which there was some increase in total production schedules and in the international aid allotment; but the gain to Britain, some 8,000 additional vehicles, was described by the British representative as 'a mere bagatelle in comparison with the shortfall'. The War Department could still undertake to provide less than a third of the stated British requirement.

On the other hand it was significant that the United States programme contained provision for practically the full British requirement of armoured fighting vehicles and ordnance. Here were fields in which production was stable or contracting; and British representatives in Washington argued that the best way of securing a relief for British manpower problems was to seek from the United States, not difficult items such as heavy lorries or teleprinters, but rather the 'easy' items, even though these might be easy for the United Kingdom also. That is, the British should ask for more tanks, rifles, small arms ammunition, bombs, 6-pounder shot and so on, cutting back the corresponding production in the United Kingdom even more sharply than had been planned and using the resources thus set free to make the stores which the United States could *not* supply.

But adjustment of this sort was not as simple as might appear. There might be a good deal of surplus capacity in the United States, but public opinion, more and more clearly, required that it should be restored to the production of consumer goods for the American market and not used for increasing the supply of Lend-Lease munitions, especially if there was any suspicion that such aid would enable the British to switch some of their own resources to civilian use. This attitude was reflected in a War Department letter of 1st April 1944, which caused much stir in British circles. Explaining the rejection of certain requisitions for engineer stores, the letter pointed out that British production of the equipment in question was by itself sufficient for British military needs, but that part of that production was being used for civilian purposes; in effect therefore the requisitions were for civilian goods, and procurement must be initiated through the Foreign Economic Administration – the War Department would have none of it. The letter was written by a subordinate, and discussions at a higher level revealed a more moderate attitude. The episode none the less underlined the difficulty which the British had from about the beginning of 1944 onwards in securing supplies which, taken in isolation, they were well able to provide for themselves.

Nor was the suggested adjustment at all easy for the British. It entailed transport of labour and capacity from one form of production to another that was exceedingly difficult to arrange. Some steps were taken in this direction: a new Ministry of Aircraft Production schedule of requirements brought to Washington in July 1943 contained greatly increased quantities of bombs, armament and auxiliary items. But the authorities responsible for Army supply were loath to add to their demands on the United States for 'easy items'. Apart from the limited readjustment of the combined tank programme described above, revolvers were almost the only ordnance items for which an increased demand was sanctioned in the summer of 1943. In general, despite the difficulties, it is hard to resist the conclusion of a Ministry of Production official that the scope for increased military supplies from the United States in 1944 was not quite as narrow as the supply departments appeared to believe, and that the fear of a breakdown in assignments, which was one of the main deterrents, was a 'relic of 1942 thinking'.

Be that as it may, in the ground munitions sector the tide of supply was clearly passing the flood early in 1944 as the preparations for the European offensive entered their final phase. When the Army Supply Programme came up for review at the turn of the year the War Department found it possible to concede the British a rather larger proportion of their 1944 requirements than hitherto. Even so, the provision was 40 per cent. below the provision made for 1943 and 30 per cent. below the value of stores actually delivered in that year. Up to midsummer the programme was honoured at least as fully as in 1943, about 45 per cent. of the whole year's provision being duly assigned in the first six months. But many of the stores which had been most prominent hitherto showed a sharp decline. Supplies of rifles and small arms ammunition were petering out, and deliveries of Bofors and 6-pounder anti-tank guns had ceased altogether. Deliveries of tanks were still substantial, but not quite on the scale of the previous year. Increases in some other categories, such as heavy artillery, signal equipment, heavy trucks and jeeps, did not wholly offset these losses.

It was otherwise, however, with aircraft supply, which reached its peak in the first six months of 1944, assignments exceeding those of the previous half year by 13 per cent. in mere numbers and by considerably more in structure weight and value. Assignments of heavy bombers in particular rose from 284 to 478, and of transport planes from 483 to 798. Such was the predominance of aircraft in the general scheme of American supply that, in spite of the falling off of most other supplies from the beginning of the year and the rapid decline of assignments in nearly all fields which set in during its latter part, the total value of munitions delivered to the British Commonwealth in 1944 was appreciably greater, both relatively and absolutely, than in 1943. Deliveries were valued at approximately $7,090 million, which represented nearly 29 per cent. of the Commonwealth's total receipts.

THE FINAL PHASE

Some diminution in the flow of supplies after the mounting of Operation Overlord was natural and expected, inasmuch as the main task of equipment had been completed and the end of the most arduous part of the war was in sight. But the reduction of American aid went in some ways beyond what was appropriate to the new military situation. It has to be recognised that the volume of American-made munitions hitherto received by the British had been determined by the special conditions prevailing in the early part of the war, when Britain was a belligerent and the United States, at most, an arsenal. Even after Pearl Harbour the British were for another two years or so more deeply engaged in combat than the Americans and so maintained a valid claim to a large share of American arms; in any case their plans had been laid on the assumption of large-scale material assistance, and to have disappointed these hopes would have been to disorganise the combined effort. Now, however, a new situation had arisen, in which a more natural relationship between the two countries asserted itself. American armies were taking the larger share even of the land fighting in Europe, and the role which was to be allotted to Britain in the Pacific war, though as yet obscure, was certainly to be a subsidiary one. It was therefore no longer part of the natural order of things that the United States should supply Britain with munitions of war. Rather it was to be expected that each country should put into the field such forces as it could equip and maintain, and the British would have to show cause for exceptions to this general rule. This is an extreme statement of the position. The comradeship of war did not permit of a ruthless application of this logic; nor, as a matter of practical expediency, could the innumerable ties which, as a result of the history of the past two years, linked the British forces to American production, be severed now without loss to both parties. Nevertheless, during the last year of war, international aid in munitions came to be regarded by the Americans less and less as a matter of accepted routine, more and more as an exception, an incubus or an anachronism.

In the latter part of 1944 attention was divided between two distinct aspects of the situation – the maintenance of the supplies required for the current campaign in Europe, and the preparations for the ensuing offensive against Japan. Over the former, a minor crisis had arisen. German resistance was more prolonged and the wastage of equipment heavier than the American authorities had budgeted for, and even before the Ardennes battle the units in the field were in real danger of running short of some vital stores. As a result reconversion plans were shelved and steps taken to raise the level of munitions output, which had been allowed to fall too far earlier in the year. But this could have little immediate effect, and the first American reaction was to curtail assignments to Britain. Often there was good justification for this, inasmuch as British forces had in many cases stronger reserves. But the result was that despite the good start made in the early part of the year, only 76 per cent. of the provision made for British ground munitions in the 1944 programme was liquidated by deliveries. In the last quarter the British received no more than one-tenth of the year's provision. The value of Army supplies received in 1944, $1,660 million, was less than two-thirds of the previous year's income. The shortfall was due almost entirely to a breakdown in the supply of tanks and of gun ammunition, the latter largely a corollary of the former. During the first half of 1944 the total American output of medium tanks had been cut back to less than half the peak figure reached early in the previous year, and in consequence, when American field commanders called urgently for reinforcements in the autumn, the only course open to the War Department was to curtail British allocations very sharply. In November, indeed, deliveries were completely suspended, and over the year as a whole the British received less than two-thirds of the promised numbers. Especially disappointing was the assignment of only 1,300 (out of a scheduled 4,000) of the latest and most efficient type of Sherman mounting a 76-mm. high-velocity gun.

The changing character of Anglo-American supply relations was naturally more clearly apparent in the negotiations over supplies for the Japanese war, which was bound to be a predominantly American affair. Difficulties emerged first and were most acute on the naval side. The United States Navy's attitude to British participation was markedly cool, and its reluctance to provide supplies for the purpose was very clear. At the beginning of 1944 the British were informed that American production of landing ships and craft had been arranged so as to provide for balanced American amphibious forces, and that there would be none to spare for Britain. At first the Navy appeared to accept this position, on the assumption that it would be able to borrow craft from the Americans for specific operations. But by February it was clear that this would not do. The British needed 120 tank landing ships on stations in the Far East by 1st May 1945; 80 were to be built in the United Kingdom and in Canada, but only 47 were expected to be ready in time. After further investigation it was established there would be an absolutely minimum deficiency of 34 tank landing ships in the spring of 1945. It was found also that the United States could fill the gap merely by keeping production at the peak rate instead of allowing it to fall after June 1944, as planned. This, however, the Americans declined to do. There was a similar disappointment over the great fleet of auxiliaries – depot ships, repair ships, victualling ships, etc. – required by the Royal Navy if it was to operate in strength at a great distance from its home dockyards. The American naval authorities concurred at Cairo in the strategic and tactical arguments in support of the Fleet Train, but when discussions were opened on the supply of American ships the Navy Department could offer only five repair ships. These were to be deducted from the 200 merchantmen which the Maritime Commission had agreed to turn over to Britain on bare-boat charter, and in point of fact only two were delivered. Taken together, these setbacks meant already a grave reduction in forces which Britain could effectively deploy in the Far East war.

The later history of Stage II supplies, the negotiations, highly successful in appearance, conducted in the autumn of 1944 by Mr J. M. Keynes and Sir Robert Sinclair, and the disillusionment that followed, have been described at length in the final chapter of *North American Supply*. The story was essentially one of international politics and finance. It was concerned less with operational need and the physical possibilities of supply than with the scope of British participation in the Pacific campaign, the propriety of using Lend-Lease for purposes which had more to do with the post-war balance of power in Europe and the Middle East than with the prosecution of the present war, or the extent of America's moral obligation to help in the restoration of the shattered British economy. Here we need only sketch briefly the concluding phase of the decline in munitions from the wartime peak to the zero of peace. The decline was extremely rapid. The value of munitions received by the British Commonwealth from the United States in the first six months of 1945, $2,065 million, was less than three-fifths of the 1944 average. And although the British Government had originally hoped to secure the same general proportion of its total supplies from overseas during the Japanese war as it was receiving in 1943-4, the proportion of Commonwealth munitions contributed by the United States actually declined from 29 per cent. in 1944 to 22 per cent. in the first half of 1945. Moreover, the great bulk of these supplies were delivered in the first three or four months, while war was raging in Europe.

Table 1. Deliveries of certain major war stores by the United States to the British Commonwealth

	1944	1945		
	2nd qtr.	1st qtr.	2nd qtr.	3rd qtr.
Service aircraft . . .	2,578	1,362	1,117	222
Tanks	3,129	242	200	—
Universal Carriers . .	2,625	604	—	—
Small arms ammunition (million rounds) . .	259	48	49	—
Vehicles	13,476	12,002	3,990	—
Wireless sets (Army only) .	6,056	1,516	2,005	300

Table 1 shows, for some of the major items, the quantities delivered in the first three quarters of 1945 and, for comparison, in the second quarter of 1944, before the real decline began. Supplies in January–March 1945 were largely related to Stage I: the second quarter of 1945 covers the transition from one Stage to another; and the third, so far as it falls within the war period, was wholly Stage II. After the close of the German war the British received from the United States practically nothing except special types of equipment which they could not provide for themselves. Almost all the aircraft supplied in the third quarter, and most of those supplied in the second were naval fighters and torpedo bombers, that is, types which were of particular importance in the Pacific war and in which the United Kingdom was notably deficient. The last vehicles were mainly amphibians, the last tanks, light machines to which there was no British equivalent. Almost the only American small arms assigned to Britain in 1945 were carbines – another American monopoly. Attempts to use American munitions supply in Stage II as a means of providing general relief to the sorely burdened British economy were an almost total failure. It was indeed fortunate for Britain that the Japanese war ended when it did, so that Stage II planning proved to have been little more than an academic exercise.

(iv)

Munitions Supply from Canada

THE SIZE AND CHARACTER OF CANADIAN SUPPLIES

The Dominion of Canada had no difficulty in claiming fourth place among the United Nations as a producer of warlike stores; and the 9,000 million dollars' worth which it produced between September 1939 and June 1945 represented almost 8 per cent. of the British Commonwealth's supplies from all sources – no mean achievement for a population of thirteen millions whose industrial development was largely of recent date and whose facilities for armaments production at the outbreak of war were virtually non-existent. Not all this production was of direct benefit to the United Kingdom or of direct relevance to the story of 'overseas supply'; Canada not only had large Forces of her own to arm, but was an important source of supply for other nations of the Commonwealth and also for China. (Her assistance to the Soviet Union, which in armoured fighting vehicles was considerable, helped to implement the British Government's protocol commitments and so counted as supply to the United Kingdom.) The proportion of total Canadian production which was transferred to the United Kingdom is not accurately ascertainable in every case, but the general picture can be inferred from the fact that the latter received 60 per cent. of the tanks, 67 per cent. of the artillery, 70 per cent. of the rifles and 53 per cent. of the combat aircraft made in Canada during the war.

Within the obvious quantitative limitations Canada was in many ways a much more attractive source of supply than the United States. This was, of course, especially true in the period before Pearl Harbour and still more so before the passing of the Lend-Lease Act, when political and financial considerations weighed most heavily. As a belligerent, Canada could be expected to devote her full energies to the execution of any munitions programmes that she undertook, and whether or not the products actually passed under the control of the United Kingdom they would certainly be put to some use directly connected with the war in which Britain was engaged. Again, although the Canadian dollar was not noticeably softer than its American cousin, the monetary barrier was less formidable in 1940 because the Canadian Government was willing to accumulate sterling. This was not always the position. The British never actually went short of supplies for financial reasons, but it was not until the spring of 1943 that the Canadians put war supply on to a solid non-monetary basis comparable with Lend-Lease.[1] Thus there were seasons, notably at the beginning of 1941 and again at the end of 1942 – the Mutual Aid project being then in an inchoate condition – when the British Treasury had to insist on greater caution in the ordering of Canadian than of American munitions.

The United States could theoretically have made a much earlier start than Canada on the supply of munitions to Britain, but as a matter of practical politics this was not so. Canada was going uninhibitedly ahead with physical preparations at a time when domestic rearmament and aid to Britain were alike bogged down in the United States by a mass of political, administrative and economic difficulties. As a result Canadian output in 1941 was more than a third of its ultimate peak, while the United States output had hardly begun to show its strength. In 1942 the Americans were still barely half way to their goal, though the Canadians had almost reached theirs. Deliveries of some of the most important weapons made for British use in both countries, such as the .303-inch rifle and the Bofors gun, were first effected in Canada; and even with tanks the Canadians were only a few weeks behind. Thus, allowing for the inherent difference of scale, Canada was able to make a relatively larger contribution than the United States to the equipment of the British Army at the critical period of its growth.

In addition, the British Government enjoyed a far larger measure of influence over the content of Canadian munitions programmes than it could hope to exercise in the United States. This statement should not be misunderstood. After the dissolution of the British Supply Board at Ottawa, the Canadian Department of Munitions and Supply wielded a wholly sovereign control over war production in Canada. It acted largely as agent for United Kingdom supply departments, but it was an entirely free agent, accepting or rejecting British supply orders, placing contracts, and manipulating priorities at its own discretion.

The influence which the British Government exerted was, as it

---

[1] See *North American Supply*, *op. cit.*, Chapter VII, Canada.

were, not political but economic, being simply that of the largest customer. Since munitions production was initiated in Canada mainly for the United Kingdom 'market', United Kingdom needs inevitably determined to a large extent what kind of armament should be produced, how much and when. It is true that the Hyde Park Agreement signed by President Roosevelt and Mr Mackenzie King in April 1941, opened up alternative markets, in that it enabled Lend-Lease contracts to be placed in Canada.[1] Although the production thus set up was primarily for the benefit of the United Kingdom, from the American point of view it constituted 'the U.S. programme in Canada', and the United States Government was, of course, able to dispose of the products as it chose.[2] By the end of the year London was feeling some concern at the re-orientation of Canadian production, at American instance, away from the United Kingdom and towards China, which in the latter part of 1941 was taking 10 per cent. of the total Canadian output. Moreover there was an obvious temptation for the Canadians to allow the execution of British orders to take second place to that of Lend-Lease contracts which brought in badly needed United States dollars. This, however, was not more than a minor disturbing factor. Generally speaking, the United Kingdom had far less competition to fear in Canada than in the United States, and could count on its supply programmes being accepted and implemented promptly.

Most important of all, Canada had in general no objection to producing equipment of British type. There were exceptions: the standard Canadian tank, the Ram cruiser, was a close relative of the Grant and the Sherman, and certain American aircraft types (Catalinas, Helldivers, Cornells) were introduced into the Canadian programme. But these were not regarded as adverse to United Kingdom interests, and in the sphere of ordnance, where the standardisation of British designs was most important, it was virtually complete. The 25-pounder field gun, the 3.7-inch A.A. gun, the 2-pounder anti-tank equipment, the Boys anti-tank rifle, the Bren gun, the 20-mm. Polsten – all these were weapons rejected by the United States but adopted and readily supplied by the Canadians. Thus Canadian production was often of much greater value to Britain than an equivalent quantity of supply from the United States.

On the other hand Canadian war production had serious limitations, qualitative as well as quantitative. Though there was no type of war equipment, except large warships, which the Canadians could not make, there were some, and those the most highly prized, which they could not make easily or in large quantities. The industry

---

[1] See *North American Supply, op. cit.*, Chapter VII.

[2] This refers to the period before the setting up of the assignment machinery. Thereafter Canadian Lend-Lease production was placed in the Washington 'pool', and bid for by the British representatives in the same way as the products of American industry.

of the Dominion was dominated to an undue extent by automobile production. True, a mass-production vehicle industry is an inestimable asset, but a wider spread of general engineering would have provided a more solid basis for war production. Moreover, the whole of this industry and a large part of the others had been created by American firms. Some of these American-owned plants merely assembled imported components; few were fully self-sufficient production units. The dependent character of Canada's industrial development was betrayed at many points. Thus there was concern both in Ottawa and in London at the meagre Canadian contribution to research in the aeronautical field. The reason was obvious: neither aircraft designers nor the scientists behind them could feel much urge to original work while production was concentrated on planes of British or American origin. More serious was the complete dependence of the builders of automobiles, and therefore of the builders of tanks and aircraft, upon United States supplies of many of the more elaborate components, especially power plants. This dependence was modified during the war by the development of domestic capacity for the manufacture of, for example, aircraft propellers and suspension units for tanks. But no engines were built in Canada either for tanks or for aircraft. As a result, these forms of production occupied a relatively small place in the Canadian war effort; for there was clearly little advantage to Britain in encouraging the creation of a really large capacity which would have had to be fed with supplies of the most crucial limiting components from the United States. Canadian production of Service aircraft was at its peak only one-fortieth, and Canadian production of tank chassis one-twentieth of the output achieved in the United States.

The munition-making capacities of Canada were thus even less complementary to United Kingdom production than were those of the United States, since the Dominion was unable to furnish really significant quantities of the two kinds of armament which Britain needed most. A table drawn up early in 1944 to show the magnitude of overseas supply, in terms of equivalent United Kingdom manpower and its distribution between the three Services, illustrates the composition of Canadian aid. The Ministry of Aircraft Production absorbed 43 per cent. of all United Kingdom output and 35 per cent. of all United States supplies, but barely 12 per cent. of Canadian supplies. Canada was providing 14 per cent. of the Royal Navy's supplies and 15 per cent. of the British Army's, but only 3 per cent. of the total receipts of the Royal Air Force. An earlier comparison would have shown a still greater contrast, since it was only in 1944 that aircraft production in Canada was fully developed. The story of the development has been told in *North American Supply*,[1] and only

---

[1] *Op. cit.*, Chapter II.

the outline need be repeated here. The main feature of the Canadian aircraft programme was undoubtedly the production of planes for the great air-crew training scheme which was initiated in the Dominion at the outbreak of war. Some 22 per cent. of the Commonwealth's trainers were built in Canada, though only 4 per cent. of its Service aircraft. Among the latter were 1,451 Hurricane fighters, all but 400 of which were built on United Kingdom account. Production of this famous aircraft, planned in 1938, started early in 1940 and was at its peak in 1941-2, thus making contribution to Britain's air defences in the crucial phase. The other project initiated in 1938– manufacture of the Hampden medium bomber – was less fruitful, for this machine was obsolescent by 1941 when production got going in Canada; only 160 were completed, and it does not appear that any of these went into action. It had been intended from the outset that Canadian manufacturers, having cut their teeth on Hampdens, should proceed to one of the new four-engined bombers as soon as the development of these was finished. Fulfilment of this project, however, was much delayed, chiefly because of the prolonged uncertainty as to which model was the best. The choice finally fell on the Lancaster, but too late for Canada to make as valuable a contribution as she might have made. In the circumstances the completion of 395 of these large and elaborate machines was a creditable achievement, but half this total was built in 1945, when the period of really pressing need was over. From 1942 onwards the growing experience and capacity of her aircraft industry and the slackening demand for trainers, enabled Canada to undertake the manufacture of three other important combat models. One was the Mosquito fighter-bomber, of which 961 were built to British order in the last two years of war. In the same period the Canadians completed 1,068 American carrier-borne bomber planes of the Helldiver type. Most interesting and important of the newcomers, however, was the Catalina flying-boat. Although production did not start till 1943, Canada actually produced more flying-boats (770) than were either built in Britain or procured from the United States during the whole war.

The great bulk of the war material supplied by Canada to Britain – over 60 per cent., by labour-value, at the beginning of 1944, and probably rather more at most stages of the war – consisted of supplies for the Army. The type of land armament which the British most needed, tanks, accounted for only a small part of this. Only about 5 per cent. of all the United Kingdom's tanks came from Canada. These included 1,420 Valentines, almost all of which actually went, not to Britain, but direct to Russia, and 2,000 machines which were not strictly tanks but self-propelled artillery – 25-pounder field guns mounted on a Ram tank chassis. For the rest the Canadian contribution to British Army supplies was three-fold. Generally, the Canadian Government arranged to produce a moderate surplus, over and above the needs of its own Forces, of most ordnance weapons and their ammunition; and this surplus served first as an insurance margin and later as a small but useful supplement to United Kingdom output. Thus Canada supplied the British Army with, *inter alia*, 13 per cent. of its rifles, 22 per cent. of its 2-inch mortars, 21 per cent. of its 2-pounder and 8 per cent. of its 6-pounder anti-tank gun equipments and 13 per cent. of its anti-aircraft guns, both heavy and light.

In some few cases, however, the surplus was distinctly larger and constituted a definite Canadian speciality. Such, notably, was the Bren light machine-gun. This was the only weapon for which a Canadian firm received a contract before the outbreak of war, apart from a small order for 25-pounder equipments referred to below. The original 1938 order for 12,000 guns was multiplied many times in the next four years, and by the end of 1940, Canadian Brens figured not merely as a useful additional windfall or as an element of insurance, but as a major factor in British supply plans. In the end Canada provided nearly a third of all the British Army's supplies of this weapon. Still more remarkable was the output of anti-tank rifles – over 40 per cent. of the total; it was not Canada's fault that the development of enemy armour outstripped this weapon's penetrative powers, so that production had to be prematurely wound up. Another very valuable Canadian achievement was in the production of small arms ammunition. There was a small nucleus capacity for this store in existence at the outbreak of war, and expansion during the next two years was very rapid. In the whole war Canadian arsenals manufactured over four thousand million rounds, against ten thousand million produced in the United Kingdom.

The Canadian output of vehicles, however, stands in a class by itself as a major factor not merely in British but in global war supply. The prolific automobile industry of the Dominion, unlike its counterparts in Britain and the United States, was left almost undisturbed by the insistent demand for tanks and aircraft, and was thus able to achieve a prodigious output of military trucks which in the end proved hardly less valuable than either tanks or aircraft. Here, indeed, more than anywhere else, may be found the specific Canadian contribution to the victory of the United Nations. Nearly 600,000 unarmoured vehicles of various types were delivered from Canadian factories during the war. This was over 70 per cent. of the United Kingdom output and more than twice as many as were supplied from the United States – indeed the entire American output was only four times as large. It is true that Canada could not help much with the special types that were in greatest demand; she built no trucks of more than 4-tons load, nor any amphibians or jeeps. But in the production of the standard 3-ton and 15-cwt. trucks she rivalled the United Kingdom and was not altogether eclipsed even by her giant neighbour.

This fecundity extended also to the production of the minor types of armoured fighting vehicle – armoured cars, scout cars, and especially the light tracked vehicle devised originally for carrying Bren guns over exposed ground but later adapted to many other uses. The United Kingdom drew more than a fifth of its carrier supplies from Canada.

Shipbuilding, however, was perhaps the most remarkable feature of the Canadian, as it was also of the American, industrial war effort. Starting from very small beginnings, the Canadians established by 1943 an output of merchant shipping only fractionally less than that of the United Kingdom. Nor was this achieved at the expense of warship construction, to which roughly half Canada's shipyard capacity was devoted throughout the war. Only a small part of this production, however, accrued to the United Kingdom. Only two ocean-going cargo ships were actually transferred to the United Kingdom register, though the bulk of the output was chartered for longer or shorter periods to the British Ministry of War Transport. Transfers of warships were more numerous, though here too the majority of the vessels remained under the Canadian ensign. The Royal Navy acquired from this source 25 corvettes and frigates and 62 fleet minesweepers as well as a large number of small craft. Canadian escort vessel construction was far more valuable than the figures suggest, because it began two and a half years earlier than in the United States. Ten corvettes were actually completed to British order in the winter of 1940–1. After that, production was for a long time devoted to the Royal Canadian Navy, assignments to Britain re-commencing in 1943. In the last phase of the war Canada came to the rescue when American aid failed; she undertook a huge construction programme of 35 tank landing ships and 21 maintenance ships for the Fleet Train, though owing to the unexpected dénouement of the Pacific campaign only 12 of the former and 6 of the latter had been completed when the war ended.

THE PRELIMINARY PHASE, 1936–40

The chronological development of Canadian supply followed a somewhat different pattern from that of United States aid. Here neither the Lend-Lease Act nor Pearl Harbour were major landmarks. The preliminary phase of fragmentary progress and of political and financial frustration begins earlier than in the United States, since it may be said to start with the first approaches by

Canadian manufacturers in 1936. It also comes to an end sooner. In June 1940 there was a complete revolution in the attitude both of the Canadian and United Kingdom Governments towards munitions production in the Dominions. Thereafter progress was rapid and continuous, limited only by the country's physical resources. The autumn of 1942 marks the end of the build-up, and the beginning of a period of adjustment similar to that carried out in United Kingdom production and in supply from the United States. From then on the problem is not so much the further expansion of total munitions output but rather the full exploitation of the capacity built up during the past two years, in order to meet the rather different needs now emerging.

The reasons for the slow start made in the development of Canadian munitions supply have been described in *North American Supply*. Briefly, they were, before the war, the doubts of the Dominion Government and the general lack of funds at the disposal of the supply departments in London, particularly the War Office, for either production or 'educational' orders (in fact the total orders available were insufficient to build up capacity in the United Kingdom let alone put orders into other Commonwealth countries). A second reason after the outbreak of war, was the shortage of dollars and the belief that Canadian production, at any rate of the more elaborate forms of munitions, could not be got going in time to be of real value. As a result, throughout this period a situation existed which in the light of later events seems wholly paradoxical. Canadians, that is to say, Canadian manufacturers in time of peace and the Canadian Government later on, were continually urging London to make fuller use of the Dominion's industrial resources. But the United Kingdom Government in this early period was constrained to adopt, in the main, an attitude of reserve and caution, such orders as it did give often having the character of concessions. (The reserve was partly due to the fact that the formidable day to day problems of expanding production in the United Kingdom left those concerned with little time to think about any early development of production in the unknown conditions of Canada.) Thus the First Canadian Division arrived in England soon after the outbreak of war with very little equipment of its own, and had to be supplied out of United Kingdom production. Instead of deploring this, the Government welcomed the windfall of dollars which thus accrued to it. A Canadian offer to replace the equipment in kind met with but a cool reception at the War Office for, in the words of representatives of the Canadian War Supply Board, 'the crux of the whole situation is financial . . . when we buy from (the British) such supplies as manufactured articles which are made in volume in the United Kingdom they do not want those supplies replaced

E

in kind, but would prefer money in order to purchase supplies which were more urgently needed such as foodstuffs, raw materials, etc.'

The story of the Bren gun carrier is also instructive. As early as March 1939, the War Office suggested unofficially to the Department of National Defence at Ottawa that Canada should build some of these vehicles for Britain. The proposal was taken up with alacrity; for the Canadians were already thinking of making a few carriers for their own army, and a supplementary British order would make production economic. In June the War Office gave an undertaking that 100 carriers would be ordered on British account if a reasonable price could be secured. Contract negotiations then began and technical preparations were put in hand. But when in December the Ministry of Supply sought authority for the necessary expenditure of some half a million dollars, the Treasury demurred, arguing first that the proposal was 'not based on any lack of capacity at home', and secondly that the outbreak of war, the vast expenditure of dollars on the air training scheme and the existence of a Canadian expeditionary force nullified the previous undertaking; any carriers made in Canada should be made at Canadian expense and supplied to the Canadian contingent. The matter was taken up again in March 1940, when a Canadian mission visiting London pressed for the reinstatement of the original order and its extension if possible to 200 vehicles. At first the mission made little headway, for the Ministry of Supply had no requirement for carriers from overseas; indeed the United Kingdom production programme had just been cut back. However, after a warning from the Dominions Office that cancellation would be most unfortunate politically, it was agreed that the original plan should be proceeded with. But so far from eagerly seeking Canadian assistance the United Kingdom was reluctantly accepting equipment which it did not appear to need and could not easily afford. Yet within a year the British Army was to require all the Canadian-built carriers that it could get, and in the event Canada was to provide the United Kingdom not with 100 or 200, but with nearly 24,000 carriers, besides 10,000 which she built for her own use.

Equally unhappy was the early history of Canadian tank supply. One of the projects under consideration at the outbreak of war was the manufacture of 300 Valentine tanks on British account. In March 1940, however, the Ministry of Supply concluded, on the report of a visiting expert, that Canadian firms were not really competent to build tanks. The Canadians vigorously asserted that they were. But admittedly they would have to import engines and some other components, and admittedly deliveries could not be looked for until the spring of 1941. This robbed the project of most of its value in the eyes of the Ministry, and it remained in abeyance until June 1940.[1]

Too much should not be made of these case-histories. There may have been no apparent requirement for carriers, and Canada's ability to build tanks quickly and economically may have been in doubt. But there were other munitions stores which Canada could unquestionably supply and which London was most anxious that she should supply; and in some cases the need was so evident that Treasury objections were successfully overborne. This was notably true of gun ammunition. At the beginning of the war the Ministry of Supply authorised the erection at British expense of nine new shell plants, in addition to those already being operated by the National Steel Car Company of Hamilton, Ontario, which had received its first War Office contract back in 1936. The total output was planned to reach about 33,000 rounds a week. But in January 1940, having found a grave deficit in prospect, the Ministry decided that capacity for a further 80,000 rounds a week should be established in Canada. Even so the output which Canada was being asked to supply was only a small fraction either of United Kingdom production or of the deficit. Thus for the biggest single item, 25-pounder H.E. shell, the total requirement was 491,000 rounds a week, the deficit 251,000 and the proposed supply from Canada 30,000. By the time of Dunkirk arrangements had been made or were being made for a total monthly output of some 600,000 shells. Since production was at no time during the war more than about three times that amount, it may be said that in this field a valuable beginning had been made during the preliminary phase. Also before Dunkirk a British requirement of 400 million rounds of small arms ammunition had been notified to Canada, and preparations were in hand for a monthly output of 35 million rounds – about a tenth of the supply needed from all sources.

Arrangements for weapon production were so far much less well advanced. The project for the manufacture of Bren guns at the rate of 200 a month by John Inglis Co of Hamilton had passed through the squalls (mostly political) which accompanied its inception, and the first gun was completed in March 1940. Marine Industries Limited, of Sorel in Quebec Province, were making good progress towards the implementation of the contract for 100 25-pounder field guns which they had accepted just before the outbreak of war, though, as we shall see, they were soon to run into rough water. No other complete weapons were ordered from Canadian firms before Dunkirk, but a supply of loose barrels for anti-aircraft guns had been

---

[1] The problem was complicated by the uncertainties of British tank policy. In the spring of 1940 the Valentine was out of favour, and a new, heavier model was being developed. The idea was thus that instead of attempting complete Valentines, the Canadians should make parts of this new model as soon as it was ready for production.

arranged; and although this difficult type of production was wholly new to Canada, deliveries were in sight by the middle of 1940. A scheme for the manufacture of 2-pounder anti-tank gun carriages, on the other hand, had been disorganised by a change in the design.

Canada assumed responsibility for the larger part of the great North American explosives and propellants programme which the Ministry of Supply worked out early in 1940. The Canadian chemical industry was well developed, and already had some experience in the manufacture of explosives. By the end of May, preparations were well advanced for the construction of four great new plants designed to produce between them an annual 15,000 tons of cordite, 12,000 tons of nitro-cellulose cannon powder and 24,000 tons of T.N.T. In addition, Canada provided seven factories for the filling of the empty ammunition made both here and in the United States. The rapid construction of these plants, which contained capacity for a million rounds a month and cost approximately £10 million, was a very notable achievement; they were quite outside the range of previous Canadian experience.

By contrast with the provision made for the supply of ground munitions, the aircraft production planned before Dunkirk came much closer to the limits imposed by the physical resources of Canadian industry, at least so far as combat types were concerned. Hurricanes, as well as a number of local models, were already in production, and deliveries of Hampden bombers were to start before the end of the year. And it was a fact of supreme importance that corvettes were already under construction in Canadian shipyards, for the Royal Canadian Navy as well as for Britain.

THE BUILD-UP OF PRODUCTION, 1940–2

In most fields, however, the progress made up to the middle of 1940 was insignificant in comparison with the ultimate achievement. In two respects the summer of 1940 was the turning-point in the story of Canadian war production, after which there was no further hesitation or looking back. In the first place, the Ministry of Supply decided that Canada should be given definite orders for the utmost quantity of every type of weapon and ammunition which she could be expected to supply before the end of 1941. These supplies were originally conceived of as providing a margin of insurance against the failure of United Kingdom production. But the insurance proved a valuable stimulus to Canadian firms and the capacity thus created buttressed United Kingdom production. Moreover, Canada was no longer content to receive and execute United Kingdom orders, but set to work also to provide on her own account the bulk of the equipment of her own Forces, thus relieving the United Kingdom of what would soon have been a heavy burden.

In its original form the Canadian section of the North American 'insurance programme' as formulated by the Ministry of Supply in July 1940, was still fairly modest in scope. It called for a great increase in ammunition production, but for no more than 600 complete guns, and those only 2-pounders. But after discussions between Mr A. B. Purvis and Mr C. D. Howe, Minister of Munitions and Supply, the Canadians not only undertook a larger share of the ammunition orders, but began to consider making complete anti-aircraft guns, both heavy and light, as well as anti-tank rifles and the carriages of medium artillery equipments. By the autumn it was clear that British-type weapons, with few exceptions, could not be procured from the United States and that only Canada could fill the breach. This meant, amongst other things, a great expansion of the Bren gun and 25-pounder plants. Meanwhile the small British order for tanks, finally authorised in June, had been greatly augmented by Canadian orders; arrangements had been concluded for the manufacture of Universal carriers, also on the initiative of the Canadian Government; the production of military lorries had been started on a grand scale; and work had started on a rifle factory, the greater part of whose output was to be available to Britain.

The latter part of 1940 saw important developments also in the story of Canadian aircraft production and shipbuilding. In the former the great need was for trainers, without which the Commonwealth scheme must have collapsed or remained on an insignificant scale. Canada now undertook to build large numbers of this class of aircraft, including 1,000 twin-engined Ansons. At the same time, however, the British order for Hampden bombers was raised from 80 to 160, and the order for Hurricanes from 80 to 600. For the shipyards the great event of this period was the beginning of cargo ship construction. In the matter of warships the Canadians were doing on their own account almost all that was required, the Admiralty adding only 12 minesweepers and 12 motor torpedo-boats to the 10 corvettes which it already had on order in Canada. But the British Merchant Shipbuilding Mission which came to the United States in October 1940 supplemented its activities there by placing orders for 18 (shortly afterwards increased to 24) ocean-going vessels with Canadian shipbuilders.

Table 2 (incomplete) shows in summary form the immense advance made during the latter part of 1940 in the mobilisation of the Canadian war potential.

The task represented by these figures was one which was bound to tax the utmost resources of Canadian industry, even if some elasticity was to be allowed in the original time-limit of December 1941. Artillery, machine guns, warships, tanks were wholly outside the experience of Canadian manufacturers. No ocean-going merchantmen had been built in Canada for many years, and the production of modern military aircraft was barely out of the experimental stage. In the previous war Canada had made little more than ammunition

Table 2. Canada: Munitions Orders Placed or Under Negotiation, 1940

Item	Unit	To 30th April 1940 On U.K. account	To 31st December 1940		
			On U.K. account	On Canadian account	Total
Combat aircraft .	number	450	1,075	315	1,390
Other aircraft . .	,,	—	—	2,759	2,759
Warships . . .	,,	10	22	108	130
Merchant ships . .	,,	—	18	—	18
Tanks . . .	,,	—	300	1,645	1,945
Universal carriers .	,,	—	1,000	1,279	2,279
Vehicles . . .	,,	—	72,434	23,414	95,848
Artillery equipments and naval guns .	,,	—	3,450	1,690	5,140
Machine guns . .	,,	5,000	42,600	20,250	62,850
Rifles . . .	,,	—	100,000	50,000	150,000
Gun and mortar ammunition . .	thousand rounds	4,755	12,940	3,362	16,302
Small arms ammunition	million rounds per annum	400			1,500
Aircraft bombs . .	thousand lbs.	—	50	9	59
Explosives and propellants . . .	tons per annum	56,000			73,600

for the allied armies, and that only with much difficulty. This is not a history of Canadian war production, and it would be inappropriate to describe here the methods by which government and industry tackled the formidable programme which they undertook in the summer of 1940. We need only note that, in marked contrast to the contemporary situation in the United States, the next two years were occupied in Canada by single-minded effort and steady though undramatic progress towards a remarkable achievement.

Deliveries of munitions in 1940 were of course very small, amounting to only two and a half per cent. of total Commonwealth supplies. The more important items were 130 combat and 716 other aircraft, 14 corvettes, 1,267 Bren guns, 198 loose gun barrels, some 25,000 vehicles, a little over two million shells, 113 million rounds of small arms ammunition and about 8,000 tons of explosives and propellants. But the authorities were confident that before the end of the following year Canada would be turning out aircraft, ships, tanks and ordnance in substantial quantities; nor were they being unduly sanguine, although full fruition had to wait until 1942.

Shipbuilding and aircraft production may be passed over briefly, the former because in this period it played only a minor part in

United Kingdom supply, the latter because it has been described in some detail in *North American Supply*. Eight of the ten corvettes ordered by the Admiralty at the beginning of 1940 were duly completed in the autumn of that year, before the St Lawrence froze; the other two were removed to Halifax for fitting out and were handed over early in the following year. The twelve 'Bangor' minesweepers ordered in November 1940, were all completed in the spring of 1942, as were the twelve torpedo-boats. Otherwise the Canadian warships built in 1941–2 were all retained by the Royal Canadian Navy or, in a few cases, assigned to the United States. It is hardly necessary to add that, although technically Canadian output did not much augment the strength of the Royal Navy, ships plus men were a more valuable contribution to the common effort in the Atlantic than ships alone. The extent and timing of the contribution may be gauged from the fact that in the last six months of 1941 alone Canadian yards delivered 20 corvettes and 28 minesweepers. Cargo ship construction, initiated nearly a year later than warship building, did not begin to show results until the very end of 1941, but in the following year 81 tramp ships, each of 10,000 tons deadweight capacity, were completed; Canadian output, in fact, was already nearly half that of the United Kingdom.

The achievement in aircraft production during these years was less spectacular, though progress was steady, output rising from 130 service planes and 713 trainers in the whole of 1940, to 650 of the former and 1,465 of the latter in the first six months of 1942.

The main interest of the period, however, lies in the development of the production of Army equipment, which was to be Canada's predominant interest. Of the new weapons undertaken by the Canadians in the summer of 1940, nearly all – 2-pounder anti-tank guns, Bofors, trench mortars, rifles and Browning aircraft guns – came into production in the latter part of 1941, more or less according to plan. Anti-tank rifles and naval guns were a little later, and the first 3.7-inch anti-aircraft gun, the heaviest of the artillery weapons to be produced in Canada, was not delivered until May 1942. The reason was that negotiations with the United States War Department dragged on throughout the winter of 1940–1 before the Americans finally decided that they would not make this gun themselves and the British that they would not take American 90-mm. guns in lieu. Thus it was not until June 1941, that arrangements were concluded for the production of the 3.7-inch gun in Canada (with Lend-Lease money). Tank production made a remarkably early start. By the end of 1941 Canadian firms had assembled 73 Valentine tanks to British orders and 27 of their own Ram cruisers. The former were particularly opportune, in that they helped to meet the Red Army's most urgent need. By the beginning of April 1942,

30 Valentines were already in Russia and 140 more were on their way. Carrier production was in full swing well before this. Indeed, the first carriers came forward before the end of 1940, and nearly three thousand had been completed by the time of Pearl Harbour.

Meanwhile there had been rapid expansion in the output of those types of munitions whose production had been undertaken before the fall of France. Supplies of filled gun ammunition, indeed, did not become important until 1942. Less than a million rounds were produced up to the end of 1941, but nearly ten million in the next six months. Long before this, however, Canada had been providing considerable quantities of empty shell components for assembly in the United Kingdom; Canadian cartridge cases, in particular, were of the utmost value, these having been one of the worst 'bottlenecks' in British production. The Canadian output of small arms ammunition was also very considerable in 1941, viz., some 350 million rounds of .303-inch calibre, which may be compared with the 1,080 million produced in the United Kingdom in the same year. Enormous strides were being made meanwhile with Bren gun production. By the spring of 1941 the planned capacity of the Inglis plant had been raised from the original 200 to 3,500 guns a month, and this rate of output was duly attained by the middle of 1942; it was to be more than doubled during the following year. The other pre-war project, however, had a more chequered history. When a contract for 25-pounders was awarded to Marine Industries Limited just before the outbreak of war, it had been arranged that, since neither the management nor the local labour force had relevant experience, the firm would engage French technicians from the famous armaments firm of Schneider-Creusot. This it did, but the Frenchmen went home in the summer of 1940, leaving the whole project in a precarious position, which caused the Canadian and British Governments much anxiety. This was the only prospective source of 25-pounders in all North America, and it was desired to increase the capacity of the plant from eight to twenty-four and then to seventy-five equipments a month. The Department of Munitions and Supply accordingly stepped in, providing both money and a general manager and setting up a control committee which consisted of the Chairman of the firm, a member of the Department and a former Woolwich man who had been serving with the defunct British Supply Board. The outlook none the less remained bleak, and it was therefore decided towards the end of 1940 to enlist the aid of the great Chrysler Corporation. With the immense managerial and sub-contract resources of this firm at its disposal, the project now went ahead smoothly and quickly. The first gun was ceremonially presented to the Minister of National Defence on 1st July 1941; the full rate of seventy-five equipments a month was reached by the middle of 1942; and little over a year later the plant was turning out over a hundred 25-pounders and thirty 4-inch naval guns a month, as well as components for these and other weapons.

It was natural that the first call on Canadian munitions production should be the equipping of Canadian troops. Nor was this unwelcome to the British Government, except in so far as the priority was extended to home defence units. To an appreciable extent, however, it was thus extended; and this fact, coupled with the inexorable consequence of the failure to start full-scale preparation at the beginning of the war or sooner, meant that in most cases the British Army had to wait until well into 1942 before it received large-scale assistance from Canadian production. There were exceptions: the first batch of Canadian Brens was tested in England (with excellent results) in February 1941; Canadian-built carriers began to arrive before the end of that year; and ammunition supplies were appreciable even in 1940. Up to the end of 1942, that is to say, to the end of the British Army's expansion period, the position with regard to a few key items of equipment was as shown in Table 3.

Table 3. Canadian and United Kingdom Production of Certain War Stores

1940–2

	Canadian Supplies			United Kingdom production
	Total for the Commonwealth	For home defence	For the United Kingdom	
Tanks	2,143	1,157	986	6,466
Universal carriers . . .	11,710	3,505	8,205	24,037
25-pounder guns . . .	929	420	509	9,041
6-pounder A.T. guns . . .	841	207	633	9,244
40-mm. A.A. guns . . .	1,516	323	1,193	9,363
3.7-inch A.A. guns . . .	451	174	277	5,394
Rifles	200,502	90,960	109,542	772,440
Bren guns	52,950	13,781	39,169	140,075

The figures are sufficient to show that Canada played a significant if not a very conspicuous part in the creation of the British Army's 'capital' equipment. Moreover, the table does not include Canada's outstanding contribution, mechanical transport, for which the division between home defence and overseas use is not ascertainable for the whole of this period, though it is clear that the great majority were exported. Production of military vehicles rose from 25,000 in 1940 to 190,000 in 1942; and the mobility displayed by the Imperial forces in Africa was due in very large measure to the fertility of the Canadian automobile industry and its rapid adaptation to the needs of war.

CONSOLIDATION, ADJUSTMENT AND DECLINE, 1942-5

By the summer of 1942 the phase of expansion was virtually complete in Canadian as in United Kingdom war production. The established munitions plants had either reached or were in sight of reaching their maximum rate of output, and there was little margin left in the economy for fresh developments. Labour supply for war industry, though not absolutely as tight as in the United Kingdom, could not be much further augmented by the methods of recruitment and distribution at the disposal of the Canadian Government. The question now was: 'What next?' The Canadians would undoubtedly have wished to continue production of existing types of munitions indefinitely at the peak rates of output which they were now achieving. But this was not as simple as might appear. Owing to the British manpower shortage the need for overseas supplies in general was still acute, and the Ministry of Production laid down as a general principle that the transfer of any part of the burden of production from the United Kingdom to Canada should be regarded by the supply departments as an achievement. In September 1942, the Minister of Production asked the War Cabinet to approve the thesis that existing capacity in Canada should be kept fully employed and further orders placed there wherever possible.

As often happens, however, a policy which appeared eminently sensible in the abstract was found full of difficulties when its implementation was considered in detail. It has already been explained that Canadian munitions production was weighted very heavily in favour of Army supplies. This was particularly true of that sector of production which was maintained by direct United Kingdom orders: of about $1,500 millions' worth of warlike stores ordered on behalf of British Government departments for delivery between September 1942 and December 1943, nearly $1,300 million consisted of Ministry of Supply stores. Now the demand for such stores was already beginning to decline as the equipment of the Army with weapons and ammunition approached saturation point; and this tendency was accentuated by the great review of manpower held in London in the autumn of 1942, the main consequence of which was a severe cut in War Office scales of equipment. Thus what Canada could most readily supply was what the United Kingdom now needed least. The more closely Canadian production was analysed the more clearly did this fact emerge. To a very large extent it consisted of those standard Army weapons and ammunition which had been very scarce in 1941 and early 1942, but were now or soon would be in ample supply. There were many exceptions, of course. There was no sign of any slackening in the demand for armoured fighting vehicles or of rifles or of Bren guns, and the demand for mechanical transport was immense and still growing. But Canadian production of field guns, of anti-tank guns and of medium artillery carriages, undertaken in the first instance as a measure of insurance, was already strictly superfluous to War Office requirements. For the time being anti-aircraft guns were still needed in large numbers, but the demand was likely to fall off, even to cease completely, before the end of 1943. The great reduction of British ammunition scales worked out early in 1943 entailed some consequential reduction in Canadian output rates, even though its main object was to relieve the burden on the United Kingdom. The general conclusion was that while the full output of existing capacity could be maintained throughout 1943 there was little prospect of fresh orders or of continuation orders beyond that date for many of the stores in current production.

The Ministry of Supply had always foreseen the danger that a too enthusiastic build-up of Canadian munitions production would result in the creation of plants whose output would be superfluous by the time they were in full production. Its general attitude in 1940 had been: 'We want all the munitions you can send us in 1941, but we are *not* interested in the creation of capacity which will not be effective until 1942'. On this ground, for example, it had dissuaded the Canadians from setting up a second 25-pounder plant. As things turned out, nearly all Canadian output was exceedingly welcome in 1942, and much of it was still valuable in the early part of 1943. Nevertheless the production of the types of munitions established in 1940 obviously could not, with advantage, be continued indefinitely. The problem of timing, in fact, which so greatly complicated the planning of overseas supply in general, was particularly acute in the case of Canada. Up to a certain date munitions were required from Canada in almost unlimited quantities. After a certain date they were often not required at all. Thus many plants could only be allowed a very short run at the maximum rate of output. For example, a factory was built at Hamilton to employ 5,000 workers and produce 300 Bofors guns a month. This rate it was not expected to attain until May 1943, but by September its orders would have been completed. Similarly, the production of anti-tank rifles started in March 1942, reached its peak rate of 6,000 a month at the beginning of 1943 and was closed down in June of that year. Clearly such abrupt cessation of production which had been built up largely to meet United Kingdom requirements, and the consequent dismissal of labour, could have very unfortunate political repercussions, and it was recognised in London that this was an additional reason for maintaining production in Canada whenever it was at all reasonable to do so. Nevertheless the Canadians had to face, and did face, the fact that the demand for most types of munitions was not unlimited and that, where it was not, rates of production would have to be fixed accordingly in agreement with the Ministry of Supply. Matters of this kind were settled by helpful discussions between high officials of the Ministry and of the Canadian Department of Munitions and Supply.

The obvious solution to the problem was that Canada should switch her production from the stores that were superfluous to those that were still in great demand. This was less easy for Canada, however, than for most other countries. More than most, Canadian manufacturers were comfortable only when given a long, straight run on an established type of equipment. They were much less competent to deal with new weapons which called for tool-room methods in the early stages and constant changes in the detail of production. The period of adjustment enforced on all the munitions-making countries in mid-war was thus one of very great difficulty for Canada. That the difficulties were largely overcome is sufficiently proved by the fact that her total output of munitions was higher in 1943 than in 1942 and fell off only very slightly in 1944; furthermore that her percentage contribution to Commonwealth supplies increased steadily throughout this period.

The adjustment was carried out in a number of ways. One was a marked increase in the relative importance of aircraft production, which accounted for less than 12 per cent. of the total value of Canadian output in 1942, but for 16 per cent. in 1944. This in turn entailed drastic changes within the aircraft industry. In 1942 the United Kingdom orders for Hampdens and Hurricanes, both by now obsolescent, were running out, and the need for trainers was beginning to decline. Their place was taken, as we have seen, by some of the most currently valuable types of aircraft – Catalinas, Lancasters, Mosquitos and Helldivers. The output of the shipyards increased by over 50 per cent. as between 1942 and 1943. Merchant ship construction alone rose from 810,000 to 1,430,000 deadweight tons. It was half a million tons less in 1944, but largely because of the impact of the landing ship and Fleet Train conversion programme.

There were also great changes in the composition of the ground munitions programme. Nineteen forty-three saw the virtual elimination of Canadian artillery production, a steep decline in the output of most types of ammunition and the end of the Valentine tank programme. These losses were offset, partly by the maintenance or expansion of the demand for other types of ordnance, partly by the introduction of new or relatively new forms of production. The output of carriers was kept at a steady rate of 700–900 a month from mid-1942 right up to the spring of 1945. Production of Bren guns did not reach its peak until the summer of 1943, that of rifles until the beginning of the following year, and both were fairly well sustained through 1944, the slackening British demand for Brens being partly counterbalanced by the needs of the Chinese armies. The output of tank chassis also remained almost stable in total, the Ram model being converted from an orthodox cruiser tank to a self-propelled artillery equipment.

Several novel weapons were adopted by Canada in the latter part of the war, notably the 9-mm. automatic pistol and the 20-mm. Polsten anti-aircraft weapon. Over 7,000 of the latter were completed in Canada during 1944, more than half as many as in the United Kingdom. The output of 9-mm. and 20-mm. ammunition in this period more than offset the decline in .303-inch ammunition. More important, perhaps, Canada was able to render notable assistance in meeting the clamant need for signal apparatus and clothing and to a lesser extent engineer and transportation stores. The percentage of total munitions production occupied by the 'signals and instruments' group doubled between 1942 and 1944; in the latter year Canada provided the Commonwealth with more army wireless sets than the United States, more charging sets than the United Kingdom. In the category of engineer stores, Canadian supplies in the period 1943–5 included 1,300 reconnaissance boats and 240 mobile cranes. The Canadians also came to the rescue of the Indian railway system, whose sad plight is mentioned in Chapter IX below, supplying nearly 400 broad-gauge locomotives.

A final example of the adaptability of Canadian war production may be taken from the story of gun ammunition. At the beginning of 1944 the War Office persuaded the War Cabinet that it could profitably use much larger supplies of field and medium artillery shell than it was currently receiving, and Canada's help was sought in this matter. By this time, as a result of the cuts imposed a year earlier, production of 4.5-inch shell had ceased altogether and the output of 25-pounder shell had fallen from the peak rate of 400,000 to about 30,000 rounds a month. Labour had dispersed and plant had been diverted to other uses. Nevertheless the Canadian Government responded nobly and with less recrimination than might have been expected. By the summer, production of 4.5-inch shell had been re-started and that of 25-pounder shell restored to its original level.

CHAPTER II

PROBLEMS OF
CASH PROCUREMENT IN THE
UNITED STATES

(i)

Introduction

THE MOST striking aspect of the procurement of warlike stores by Great Britain from the United States during the Second World War was the way in which its whole scope and nature changed as the war proceeded. It began with a few scattered purchases from commercial suppliers in a neutral country – transactions of a type perfectly familiar, and exceptional only in that they were confronted with more formidable legal obstacles than were customary. It became an essay in co-operation between nations that not only had no parallel but did not even remotely resemble anything in previous history, and which left a deep mark upon the thinking of the peoples which took part in it. At the outset American supplies were a tiny marginal element in the calculations of British planners. Before the war was half over they had become one of the dominant factors, determining the scale of the whole British war effort and the standard of life of the British people. In 1939 and the first few months of 1940 there were long and anxious discussions over the expenditure of say, a hundred thousand dollars. By 1941 negotiations were in terms of hundreds of millions of dollars, and in the later years of the war a hundred million dollars could be represented as a decimal fraction. The organisation which handled this business shows the same furious rate of growth. In February 1940, the whole staff of the 'British Supply Board in Canada and the United States', set up in Ottawa in September 1939 under Colonel J. H. M. Greenly, numbered 33 persons, excluding clerical assistants, typists, draughtsmen, etc.; and its branch office in New York, the British Purchasing Commission, by which it was destined to be overshadowed, was as yet slightly smaller. The Ministry of Supply was represented in the North American continent by seven persons, the Air Ministry by three, and the Admiralty by two. Within a couple of years each of the several supply missions in the United States constituted a major branch of its parent Ministry, and the total personnel was numbered in thousands. Before July 1940, there were only two sets of telegraphic correspondence on supply matters – one between departments in London and the Supply Board at Ottawa, the other between Mr Arthur Purvis, head of the Anglo-French Purchasing Board in New York and his opposite number in London, M. Jean Monnet. The former cables were mingled with the regular traffic between the Dominions Office and its High Commissioner. The latter constituted a special series, of which there were in all less than four hundred in seven months. Later there were more than a dozen special series of telegrams (or cables) dealing with supply some of which ran into tens of thousands in the course of a year. There was a sort of domesticity about the whole atmosphere in the early days. The reports home of the Controller General in Ottawa were mainly in the form of letters to the Permanent Secretary of the Ministry of Supply in which discussions of policy mingled with the interchange of personal friendship. Similar letters were of course written in later stages of the war as well, but their authors were then no more than cogs, or, to be more complimentary, fly-wheels, in a machine much bigger than themselves; and the letters have the air of conversation conducted amid the roar and rattle of a giant factory. At the beginning, individuals counted for very much. In 1940 the personality of Arthur Purvis dominated the whole scene in a way which was not possible for any man later on. Even before his death in August 1941, his influence, though still very great, was ceasing to be of such unique importance. The ramifications of supply had become so wide that no one outside the inmost circle of government could play a commanding part.

It was not merely the size of the operation that changed as time went on, but also its character and method. At first, as we have said, procurement was a commercial activity. The agents of the British Government had in each case to locate a manufacturer able and willing to supply the stores they had been instructed to procure. Having found one, they had to negotiate terms of payment and schedules of delivery. When the contract had been signed, they had to watch over the progress of production, inspect the finished articles and arrange for their shipment. The Government of the United States took a natural interest in the proceedings from the outset – an interest dictated on the one hand by its desire that the Allies should win the war and on the other by its concern lest its own rearmament should suffer. It advised on the selection of one firm and vetoed another. It issued priority instructions which affected the progress of British contracts. It gave or withheld export licences. From June 1940 onwards it was increasingly concerned to arrange 'complementary' programmes of production which would allow for the satisfaction of both British and American needs. In one or two cases it went so far as to place a joint contract with the British, financing in the first instance the firm's entire capital outlay. But with these exceptions procurement during the first eighteen months of war remained in all its aspects, legal, financial and manufacturing, a transaction between the British Government on the one side and individual American producers on the other. Even when supplies came out of stocks which were the property of the United States Government a private firm had to be formally inserted as an intermediary, the sole exception being the political deal which resulted in the transfer of the famous fifty destroyers.

All this was changed by a few strokes of President Roosevelt's pen on 11th March 1941, when the Lend-Lease Act became law. Lend-Lease, as *North American Supply* has shown, was far more than an arrangement whereby the United States Government financed British war supplies. Procurement itself was taken over by the agencies of that Government, and thus became in form and manner what it had increasingly become in substance during the latter part of 1940, a political, inter-governmental affair. Its extent was controlled, firstly, by the funds which Congress could be induced to assign for the purpose, secondly, by the general volume of American defence production, and thirdly, by the proportion of that production which the United States Services were prepared to forgo.

The relations between the two countries remained, however, essentially those of supplier and user; until the second great change took place, with equal abruptness, on 7th December 1941. Thereafter the question of procurement for Great Britain in and by the United States was merged in the wider questions of the proper apportionment of production and of productive resources between the nations which constituted the grand alliance. Munitions, shipping, raw materials and in a more nebulous sense production capacity in general were 'deemed to be in a common pool'. Lend-Lease as such faded into the background (to emerge ominously at the end of 1944 when victory was in sight and the bonds of the alliance loosened). Its place was taken by munitions assignment and the combined planning of production.

It is obvious, therefore, that there was little uniformity in the history of procurement. Underlying the whole, indeed, there was the grand theme of the continuous development of the Anglo-American combination, which can be traced, as it is traced, in *North American Supply*, from the discussions between Lord Riverdale and members of the United States Administration in the summer of 1939 to the completion of the formal and manifest structure of the Combined Boards in 1942. But on the surface of things, in the procedures and mechanisms of supply which are the main subject of this chapter and several that follow it, the changes were more apparent than the unity. The problems of cash procurement, small in scale for the most part and essentially commercial in character, though coloured by the constant need to enlist the help and avert the opposition of the American Government, differed fundamentally from the problems of procurement by the novel instrument of Lend-Lease; and these again from the problems of the period in which supply to the British from the United States was a subsidiary element in the planning of the whole United Nations war effort. Each phase therefore needs to be considered separately.

(ii)

The Concentration of Procurement Through Official Channels

THE GENERAL ISSUE

The first problem which confronted the British Government when it began to contemplate fairly extensive purchasing of war supplies in the United States was how such purchases should be conducted. By the summer of 1939 it was generally agreed that some form of central organisation was essential. Lord Riverdale confirmed in August the need for a British Purchasing Commission, and one was duly established in New York early in November, as soon as the amendment of the Neutrality Act had made such a step politic.[1] But the exact scope of its activities was at first obscure. It was certainly not conceived as a monopoly on the model of the Soviet trading corporation, 'Amtorg', although that body figured as a precedent in Lord Riverdale's report. The purchase of munitions in the narrowest sense – planes, guns, ammunition, explosives – would clearly be its responsibility. Equally clearly it would have little to do with such commodities as tobacco and cotton which had no direct connection with the war effort and were handled by complex commercial organisations of long standing. Between these extremes, however, there was a wide area of uncertainty in which were to be found machine tools, miscellaneous ancillary equipment such as chain cable, and materials such as steel and aluminium which were being bought in various stages of fabrication for incorporation in British-made munitions.

In this area a considerable degree of confusion prevailed during the early months of the war. Some orders were placed through the

---

[1] See *North American Supply, op. cit.*, Chapter III.

F

Commission, others through private trade channels. A flagrant example was chain cable for harbour defence, for which the torpedoing of the *Royal Oak* in Scapa Flow produced a sudden large demand. At the beginning of January it came to the attention of Purvis that a British firm with an Admiralty contract had a representative in the United States negotiating for chain cable, although the British Purchasing Commission had also been asked to procure similar material. Thus in effect, as Purvis pointed out, 'the British Government was endeavouring to obtain competitive quotations with ourselves'. He urged that 'these other purchasing channels should withdraw from the market, or we should, if money is not to be wasted. As you know, this is only one of many similar situations which is involving us in increasing criticism in this country, of wasteful buying methods'. Although the Admiralty a fortnight later agreed that 'practically all' its future orders would be placed through the Purchasing Commission ('the exception being where contractors have regular trade suppliers for special goods'), the situation was still not cleared up in March, when enquiries as well as large orders for chain cable, regarded by the Admiralty as of great urgency, were converging on a tight North American market from four directions: from the United Kingdom Government, the Canadian War Supplies Board, the Australian Government, and from private traders. The inevitable result was a rise in prices.[1] Taking the field of procurement as a whole, such incidents were not very frequent, though there were similar competing demands for ball bearings, fire hose and some other supplies. French purchases were a further complication, however. The French had greater control over their private traders than the British, since the head of their Purchasing Mission was given sole authority to arrange for payment for orders whether government or private. Kraft pulp, for example, was bought by the French through their Mission, but by the British through the London agents of American firms. Competition between the Allies and interruption of Scandinavian supplies brought matters to a head in May 1940, when kraft prices were reported by the Anglo-French Board to be rising at an alarming rate. London agreed that Anglo-French purchases should be made through one channel, but doubted whether the British and French Mission had the necessary technical knowledge.

Private trade thus continued on the British side in the United States long after it was dispensed with for French purchasing. It continued despite the experience of the First World War and the advice of Purvis. In 1915 J. P. Morgan & Co had urged that it was in the interest of the British Government to eliminate private buying of such things as raw materials and machine tools which the

---

[1] The upshot was that the representative of the British firm mentioned above was attached to the Commission as a purchasing agent for Admiralty stores.

Government itself needed in large quantities. This was not done for machine tools until 1918. The history of the Ministry of Munitions noted that for British purchases generally concentration of buying in the Ministry was 'achieved with difficulty owing to the reluctance of Government departments and private buyers to give up their usual channels of supply'.

But it seemed that history had to be repeated and its lesson learnt again. The question of co-ordination over the whole field of Allied requirements, which arose over machine tools in November and at a special Embassy meeting called in December to discuss 'centralisation of dollar purchasing', stands out as the chief single preoccupation of Purvis from December 1939 to May 1940, receiving more personal attention from him than any other matter save perhaps strategic materials. He saw from the outset that, as he put it to Monnet, there must be 'concentration of all French and British buying through the respective missions'. His reasons were twofold. One was economy and efficiency in procurement, the exploitation of the Commission's potential monopolistic advantages. 'The practice of negotiating in France and England or through independent buyers here destroys our background with the suppliers here'. The other was that the United States Government so desired it. As indicated in *North American Supply*, the Administration, though well disposed towards Allied procurement, was concerned about the effect which it might have upon its own present and future rearmament, both through the actual absorption of plant capacity and through the general inflation of prices which it was bound to cause if not carefully controlled. The Allied Missions had therefore been required to submit to the President's Liaison Committee a weekly statement of the purchases which they were making or intending to make. In January 1940, it was requested that these statements should cover *all* purchases – not only those made through the mission, but those like aluminium, steel, textiles and oil, which were made outside it – and should be given at the 'enquiry' stage. Purvis therefore wrote to London asking that, where buying was carried on outside the missions, the buyers should either be attached to the missions or remain in close contact with them. He must know, he said, the relation of a requisition to the total requirements for that material.

The departmental consultations in London on these representations took some time to complete; but Monnet warned him in a private letter on 2nd February that whilst the two Governments could go a long way it did not seem possible for them entirely to meet the wishes of the United States Administration in regard to private purchases. Their objections have already been suggested. Briefly, they were that for the purchase of most supplies other than munitions proper there existed long-standing commercial connections, any hasty disturbance of which would be likely to be highly damaging, at least in the short run, whatever the theoretic advantages of centralised buying. In its reply on 7th February the Anglo-French Co-ordinating Committee pointed out that the two Governments had already given to Secretary Morgenthau, head of the American Treasury (through the British Embassy), estimates of total British and French purchases to be made in the first year of war. These together were put at some £200 million; the figure included all purchases, i.e., both 'government purchases of controlled stores and private purchases of uncontrolled stores'. But the giving of detailed estimates of all purchases for imports other than munitions was quite another matter. The two Governments agreed that government purchases, as they were concluded, should be notified to Purvis (through the Ottawa and French Missions), and also, as far as possible, private purchases of commodities like cotton and steel which were bought in large quantities and subject to some degree of control. But for other private purchases it would be impossible to do more than furnish information shown in trade returns. Nor could advance information on specific orders be given at the enquiry stage. The United States market for most of the commodities concerned was extremely sensitive, the Committee pointed out, and the interested departments were concerned lest any leakage of information on their intentions might lead to a considerable rise in prices.

To this Purvis replied that this inability to satisfy the American demand for data at the enquiry stage was causing the Anglo-French Purchasing Board much anxiety. It would not help relations if the Administration had to get from its own traders information about British negotiations with them. He urged also that things like machine tools, duraluminium shapes and metal strip should be classed with munitions. For materials belonging to the more sensitive markets, which were not strictly munitions, like cotton, oil, copper and ingot steel, it might be enough if purchases were made in such a way as to avoid unnecessary advances in price.

MACHINE TOOLS

Two of the items here mentioned – machine tools and steel – represented specially important and difficult aspects of the general problem, and must be singled out for special treatment. Already by November 1939, fears were being expressed on both sides of the Atlantic about the possible results of 'unco-ordinated buying of machine tools', which occupied a dominant position in the British Government's pre-Dunkirk overseas procurement plans. The matter was under discussion in that month by the British Supply Board in Ottawa and by the Exchange Requirements Committee in London, whose chairman urged co-ordination of the enormous purchases being made in the United States; otherwise competing orders might raise prices and lengthen delivery dates.

It was decided that the Anglo-French Co-ordinating Committee should examine the matter. But this was little use without some change in the policy of purchasing through private trade channels. The Ministry of Supply, however, warned the British missions in Ottawa and New York that centralisation of purchases in North America under government control would disturb supply by eliminating British machine tool importers, many of whom had made advance arrangements with American tool makers. The issue continued to be discussed throughout December in a series of personal and secret messages between Greenly and Purvis on the one hand and high officers of the Air Ministry and the Ministry of Supply on the other. It was recognised in London that the huge British requirements of machine tools ($225 million worth were needed, according to the estimate of one high official, for the British aircraft programme alone), together with a substantial French demand, could be satisfied only by the diversion to the Allies for a period of eighteen months of a very high proportion of the total United States output. (Here Purvis commented on the margin of his copy of the telegram: 'Can be done only with United States Administration's permission'.) It was realised that in these circumstances a rise in prices was inevitable and indeed 'a necessary condition of diversion of United States output from its normal channels'. (Here in the margin Purvis doubted whether, if the process took place with the Administration's permission, any price rise would be necessary except to the extent of capital assistance for the building of new factories.) The Ministry of Supply, the London message pointed out, would resort to some direct government purchases for its machine tool needs, but only to a limited extent. The demand of the Air Ministry, on the other hand, came from private firms, though these firms were in large measure financed from public funds. Owing to the highly specialised nature of the machines needed they could only be ordered by the firm which designed and produced the aircraft. (Here Purvis wrote: 'Technically yes, commercially no'.) Already, London went on, a substantial part of the Air Ministry's contractors' orders had been successfully placed through these private channels. The result so far had been to lengthen the period of delivery rather than to increase prices. (The real point, Purvis noted here, was whether they would be *allowed in the end to ship* the tools they had ordered.) The fear of the Air Ministry was that 'inadequately prepared action . . . might disorganise and delay the equipment of the new factories', on the timing of which the air programme depended. (Here Purvis noted that it was the 'present unco-ordinated action which is creating danger of disorganisation'.)

The upshot was that, while Greenly and Purvis were given full discretion in taking the United States Administration into their confidence on the whole problem of machine tools, they were warned that existing trade channels should not be unnecessarily disturbed. An expert might be sent as adviser to the Mission, but he would not purchase. Representatives of firms sent to buy in the United States would be asked, however, to report to the British Purchasing Commission immediately on their arrival in New York, and would be regarded as temporarily attached to the Commission, which would thus be able to exercise some supervision over the contractual aspects and terms of purchase of machine tools. Monthly global totals of expected dollar releases would be given by London. This promised some advance; but it still fell short of the centralisation of payments in the Commission, which Purvis had made up his mind was necessary if the British Government was to secure its full requirements of machine tools at reasonable prices.

In this view he was confirmed by finding that British firms had been accepting demands for down payments of 100 per cent. for special tools, whereas 25 per cent. would have been a reasonable figure. (The Australian Government, faced with a similar request, decided that it would be best for Australia to place her orders through the British Purchasing Commission.) At the beginning of January he learned that a single British firm, the Bristol Aeroplane Company, had placed machine tools orders totalling some £6 million since November without consulting the Commission. This necessitated an amendment to the weekly statement of purchases prepared for Morgenthau. In reporting this incident to Ottawa Purvis wrote that the unco-ordinated methods of buying adopted by the Allies ... were convincing the Administration that machine tools were the bottleneck of rearmament'. He went on to predict a possible breakdown in some of the deliveries of tools 'which have been and are being bought through so many channels'. As a result the purchases of this particular firm were channelled through the Commission; but other importers continued to place their orders direct with the manufacturers.

The crisis Purvis had foreseen came at the end of January. At this time the Allies were negotiating on a big scheme for the supply of aircraft,[1] which would create a heavy demand by American aero engine makers for the very machines which the British were seeking to buy for export. For ten days it even looked as if the supply of machine tools to Britain might be interrupted. In the event Morgenthau was able to straighten matters out with the machine tool makers, and British orders were made secure for the time being. But the incident had served to intensify the desire of the Administration for the centralisation of all future British, French and Canadian

---

[1] See *North American Supply, op. cit.*, Chapter IV.

orders and enquiries through the Allied missions, in order that. adequate consideration might be given to 'the combined necessities' and a system of priorities established for Allied and American defence needs. On 31st January, at a joint Allied-American meeting in the Treasury, attended by representatives of the machine tool and aero engine makers, Morgenthau had asked that the entire programme of machine tool requirements, both domestic and foreign, should be presented to him a week later. No new orders, he added, could be placed 'until a joint Allied programme had been established'.

The industry itself took the same line. On 31st January, both in conversation with Purvis and at the Treasury the manufacturers confirmed their desire for co-ordinated buying and a 'combined' programme.

Machine tool makers here [Purvis had written to Greenly on 31st January] feel that unco-ordinated buying through numerous channels, small and large, is resulting in failure to get priority of output for the tools which are most important for the production of war supplies and much of the energies of the industry are being dissipated in the making of relatively unimportant tools.

Purvis accordingly asked for data on all machine tool orders in the United States, including those which might be the consequence of aircraft programmes still under consideration, for priority ratings and dates of delivery. The language which he used showed that even at this early date there was a clear concept of 'combined necessities' and of the importance of avoiding the high prices and belated deliveries which were 'inherent in the unco-ordinated method of purchasing'.[1] As a later message made clear, he wanted the Commission itself to negotiate the placing of orders, to settle prices and to make the payments. Only then would it be possible to satisfy the demand of the Administration for 'synchronisation' at the enquiry stage.

None of the Ministries concerned was prepared to go quite so far. The complete centralisation of buying, the Ministry of Supply explained early in March, was limited by two factors. First, the organisation of importers in the United Kingdom was essential, not only for the initial equipping of factories, but also for the subsequent servicing of machine tools. Secondly, the volume of orders and the related correspondence was probably much greater than the British Purchasing Commission could handle for some time to come. The Ministries were, however, willing that the importer should send a copy of his order to the Commission, which would make the final payment and be given wide discretionary powers of intervention.[2]

---

[1] See *North American Supply*, *op. cit.*, Chapter IV, Section (ii).

[2] The arrangement was to include all orders directly or indirectly on Government account. Machine tools privately imported – mainly for non-war purposes – would be excluded; but these were a small part of the whole, probably less than five per cent.

This was a further advance, but the Commission was still not wholly satisfied; and in April the head of its Machine Tool Division was sent to London to try to secure a final agreement on this matter, still unsettled after months of cabling. The whole question, including the placing of orders through the Commission, the use of importers for pre-sale and post-sale servicing and the commission fees of agents, was discussed in detail with the different Ministries and with the importers. The discussions revealed considerable differences of opinion between the Ministries, the Air Ministry being especially reluctant to curtail the functions of the importers. But a tentative agreement was reached, subject to confirmation after discussion between the Ministries and the machine tool importers' panel, that future machine tool orders in the United States and Canada for war needs should be presented by importers to the British Purchasing Commission and placed by it with the manufacturer. Existing orders were excluded from the agreement.

Difficulties both in London and Ottawa held up final action on this matter. In North America the main difficulty was the overlapping jurisdiction of the British Supply Board in Ottawa and the Purchasing Commission in New York. The Board, although in practice it had nothing to do with the purchase of machine tools, was still formally responsible for making the arrangements which the Commission had to carry out; and to safeguard its nominal control the procedure had to be far more complex than was otherwise necessary. This difficulty vanished in June with the decision to suppress the Board.[1] But meanwhile those who were not held up by procedures – the other Allied Missions and American manufacturers – were buying rapidly as the tempo of the war accelerated; and in May there developed a new threat to the fulfilment of British orders which was not wholly lifted until the late autumn.

This gave Purvis the opportunity to secure at last the essential minimum of co-operation and concentration. On the 24th May he asked for, and got immediately, a final decision that machine tool orders should be placed through the British Purchasing Commission. Next day all British importers were urgently instructed to cable their principals in the United States requesting them to give the Commission at once a complete list, with delivery dates, of all the machine tools on order. And on 29th May a circular letter from the head of the Machine Tool Division informed 150 American machine tool makers that the Commission had taken over the responsibilities of purchase.

STEEL

The co-ordination of steel purchases ran a very similar course. At first they were made entirely through private channels; and up to

---

[1] *North American Supply*, op. cit., Chapter II.

mid-February, when the issue came to a head, had never been mentioned in the weekly statements supplied to the President's Liaison Committee. Like machine tool purchases, however, they were of sufficient volume to cause the United States Administration particular concern. Even in the first five months of war they totalled $35 million, and they were to rise very sharply after the German invasion of Norway and Western Europe, making steel by far the heaviest single charge on shipping across the Atlantic in the second half of 1940.[1]

On 6th March Purvis reported to London that Morgenthau had asked for 'immediate information' on purchases which the Allies expected to make in the next two or three months. At the Anglo-French Co-ordinating Committee in London on 21st March, the representative of the Ministry of Supply took the view that it would be highly dangerous to give such advance notice. A week later there was an unfortunate slip over certain large French orders. Secretary Morgenthau told Purvis that he had learned from private sources that orders for 30,000 tons of steel had been placed in the United States from London on account of the French Government. Neither Purvis nor his French colleague Bloch-Lainé, head of the French Purchasing Mission, knew of these orders or of others then being placed through London. The Secretary asked Purvis to express his 'very great regret that he was not provided with the information for which he had made a special request to the Allied governments'. Evidently the procedure London had announced in February (of notifying through its Mission large private purchases of steel) was not working.[2] 'As you know', Purvis added, 'Mr Morgenthau has been exerting himself to the utmost to accomplish practical results of value to the Allies in connection with the various requests we have made to him and occurrences of this nature seriously weaken our position'. Morgenthau had emphasised his 'very definite view' that it was only by making purchases through the two missions that 'synchronisation' between the Allies and the United States could be secured. London's reply on 13th April expressed regret to Morgenthau for the failure, which was due to a misunderstanding, to notify the purchasing missions regarding the French orders. The necessary information on the steel programmes, it reported, had now been furnished. But neither government, it was pointed out, was at present buying steel through the missions. On the British side, indeed, purchases of steel, as of other raw and semi-finished materials, were made on private account.

---

[1] British steel imports from the United States before the war fluctuated widely. About 200,000 tons were imported in 1938, and only 52,000 tons in the first eight months of 1939. Orders were placed for over five million gross tons of iron and steel (including scrap) between 1st September 1939 and 31st July 1940, by which time over two million tons had been delivered.

[2] See p. 72.

The reply by Purvis (17th April) raised the question of financing these private steel purchases. They were apparently being made on 100 per cent. irrevocable letters of credit. This would undermine the successful efforts of the Anglo-French Board towards 'breaking down such arduous exactions'. (Light alloys, machine tools and other commodities were involved as well as steel.) 'If the result of purchasing independently of the Mission involves suppliers receiving preferential payment terms it seems obvious that we shall be forced into a position whereby cash payments or irrevocable letters of credit will have to apply to the bulk of our purchases.'[1] Moreover, purchases of steel by the Mission would be a useful lever in its difficult negotiations over shells and toluol, which were also supplied by the steel manufacturers.

The Ministry still considered, however, that commercial steel should be bought by the British Iron and Steel Federation, because of its technical experience and contracts with the principals of the United States steel companies as well as their agents in London. But it announced that both data on purchases concluded and advance programmes of new orders would be communicated regularly to Purvis by the Ministry of Supply and the Ministère de l'Armament. Moreover, the Iron and Steel Controller would write frequent personal letters to Purvis giving him full information on developments in the United Kingdom. The first of these letters explained that the industry paid for its own imports of steel. The view of the Steel Control was that 'a change from the system of purchasing through commercial channels to a system of purchasing through the Anglo-French Mission in New York, with the governmental background which this so obviously creates, must gravely imperil the maintenance of the advantage of securing competitive prices'. For commercial steels the American market was likely to remain a buyer's market. Allied orders were only a fraction of the American steel output; and their needs could be met easily by the United States and Bethlehem Steel Corporations. For alloy steel, however, the situation was radically different. Allied and American demands might well over-tax the capacity of the industry unless handled and co-ordinated with the greatest care. Hence it had been agreed in London and Paris that a 'joint forward programme' was necessary, that orders should be placed to cover needs up to September, pending investigation of the supply position by a technical mission.

In the view of the Anglo-French Purchasing Board, as reported by Purvis on 6th May, this was still not enough. Meanwhile the situation was being affected both by the grave turn taken by the fighting in

---

[1] On 23rd May Purvis again protested against the continued use of irrevocable letters of credit for steel orders, which was 'stultifying Anglo-French Board policy, damaging Allied credit'.

France and by heavy Allied ordering of steel. At the beginning of May the French Ministère de l'Armament advised the French Mission in New York of its intention to place immediate orders for the delivery of several hundred thousand tons of steel a month. The Mission expected that the monthly figure would be at least 500,000 tons. French Government purchases, Purvis noted, were being prejudiced because the French had no means of knowing the price agreed in London for private British purchases. The American steel executives took the view that the Allied requirements could be met better if co-ordination of purchases took place in the United States rather than abroad. It was suggested that the Iron and Steel Federation could send a representative to the United States to operate under the aegis of the Board. He would have the advantage, which the Board already enjoyed, of association with the executive heads of the steel companies, with benefits to prices and deliveries. At present decisions were being largely based on contacts with London agents alone. 'There is much goodwill here', Purvis added, 'upon which we cannot capitalise when dealing at long range'. A further point was that purchasing through agents meant paying commissions which added to the dollar cost of steel. Many producers of steel and copper products had said that they would welcome direct contacts with Allied representatives and had indicated that better prices and perhaps better deliveries would result.[1]

On 11th May Purvis reported that Morgenthau definitely disapproved of the British policy. A few days later it was learnt that the American Ambassador in Paris had 'strongly emphasised Mr Morgenthau's wish that this problem be immediately settled in the sense of the request of the United States Administration', i.e., that all British and French steel purchases in the United States be 'channelled through Mr Purvis in direct agreement with the Administration'.

The Ministry of Supply's decision to bow to the wishes of the American Government was communicated to Purvis on 15th May. It agreed to make all steel purchases in future through the Anglo-French Purchasing Board in New York. For this purpose an Anglo-French technical mission was to leave immediately to study the situation and to make arrangements. It would leave behind it 'British and French experts who will be appointed members of the British and French Missions respectively'.

The Mission, composed of three British and five French members, arrived in New York at the beginning of June. The British members remained on as officers of the British Iron and Steel Federation, in

---

[1] On 22nd May the Board issued a release saying it was the 'established policy' of the two Purchasing Missions to conduct negotiations only with principals and not with intermediaries.

whose name steel contracts continued to be made. Purvis in fact secured only a general supervision over the purchase of steel. This situation was ended after the Lend-Lease Act on the peremptory orders of Lord Beaverbrook. The steel group then became one of the regular 'supply directorates' of the British Purchasing Commission, where it remained until, in January 1942, it was transferred to the new British Raw Materials Mission.

By the time of Dunkirk, then, the scope of centralised official purchasing was fairly well defined. It covered beyond question all munitions of war, including components thereof and ancillary equipment. It included also machine tools and, in the limited sense described, steel. Purchases of copper were entrusted to it in May 1940, at the instance of the Ministry of Economic Warfare.[1]

(iii)

The Conditions of Supply

THE STATE OF THE MARKET

Although prices might be high and terms of payment onerous, the actual procurement of most raw materials, whether through the Purchasing Commission, through the various Ministry of Supply Controls or through ordinary channels, presented little difficulty in this early stage of the war. Preparations for American rearmament began to cause some stringency in the latter part of 1940, more especially in semi-finished products such as drop forgings, bearings and brass strip, but also in zinc, alloy steel and many chemicals.[2] But by and large supplies were still ample; and, despite grave difficulties in shipping, British imports of raw materials from the United States were larger in 1940 than in any year before or since.

Munitions, however, were a very different matter. Owing to her preoccupation with the problem of dollar finance and her under-estimate of her real military needs, the quantities of warlike stores proper which Britain sought to purchase before Dunkirk were very small. Apart from the Allied aircraft programme of March 1940, they were insignificant in relation to the war potential of the United States which, measured by the crude but significant index of steel production, was at least two and a half times as great as that of either Germany or of Britain and France put together. The country's heavy industries, capable as time was to show of fabulous achievement in

---

[1] The Commission dealt reluctantly and for a short time only, with petroleum, because of its inheritance of certain contracts from the French in June 1940.
[2] *History of the Second World War, United Kingdom Civil Series*, J. Hurstfield, *The Control of Raw Materials*, p. 268.

armaments production, lay open to the Allied purchasers, from November 1939, without any formal restrictions save those of 'cash and carry'. Lord Riverdale, on his exploratory visit in August 1939, had found that the Administration, so far from placing obstacles in their path, was eager to encourage and assist them; and Purvis' first contacts with Morgenthau and the President confirmed and strengthened that impression.[1] Economically, conditions were equally propitious. When war broke out in Europe, the American economy was still struggling towards recovery from the great depression of the thirties, and in particular from the grave setback of 1938. The volume of industrial production was still below that achieved a decade earlier; nine million men were unemployed; and the general level of activity can be gauged from the fact that more than a quarter of the country's steel-making capacity was out of use. Expectations of big war orders generated a minor boom in the autumn of 1939; by November the steel industry was working at over 90 per cent. of its capacity. But by April the percentage had fallen back to 61. Clearly, therefore, there was a very considerable amount of slack to be pulled in before any serious strains were felt; and it was legitimate to assume that, quite apart from political sympathy for the Allied cause, orders for munitions would be warmly welcomed by American industry.

PURCHASING POLICIES AND PROCEDURES

Yet the results achieved in the first nine months of the war fell short even of the limits dictated by the British Government's financial policy. For example, in November 1939, the Exchange Requirements Committee gave the Ministry of Supply authority to spend up to $48 million on army equipment and components thereof in the United States during the first year of war. The total value of such contracts actually placed up to the end of April 1940, was only about $26 million, much of which would not be disbursed until well into the second year. One reason was that British 'requirements' from the United States were not only very small but also far from firm. They were for the most part contingent on the securing of satisfactory conditions of price and delivery, and also very often on a hypothetical loss of output at home due to enemy bombardment. Certain striking exceptions there were, even before Dunkirk. One was the Allied programme for the supply of explosives which was communicated to New York on 10th January 1940. In conjunction with its French counterpart the Ministry of Supply had surveyed the entire problem of Allied requirements throughout the period of a three-year war, calculated the output which could be achieved in France and Britain without disrupting other programmes, and worked out definite proposals for the supply of the whole deficit from

---

[1] See *North American Supply, op. cit.*, Chapter III.

the only possible external source, North America. The proposals involved the planning of an annual output of 70,000 tons of high explosive and propellant powder, the erection of the necessary factories in Canada and the United States, and the provision of a considerable sum in capital expenditure. The scheme was conceived as a whole and was pressed forward with vigour and determination. For the supply of explosives was so fundamental to the Allied war effort that it could not be allowed to fail. Even more important was the great Allied air programme formulated in January 1940, and set in motion at the beginning of April. This provided for the manufacture in the United States of 4,800 combat planes in a twelve-month period, at an estimated cost of more than six hundred million dollars.[1]

But apart from these, and a few small purchases of equipment peculiar to the United States, such as the Thompson sub-machine gun and the Sperry A.A. predictor, the requirements notified to the Purchasing Commission were rarely firm orders. More often they were merely enquiries about supplies which the Government might wish to purchase, if they could be had cheaply and quickly, if British production were interrupted. As soon as the Commission was established the Ministry of Supply cabled a list of possible requirements to an estimated value of $23 million. This list covered only relatively simple items – shells, small arms ammunition and spare gun barrels. But from time to time more ambitious ideas made a tentative appearance. In February 1940, the Director-General of Munitions Production asked unofficially if there was 'any hope of medium and heavy guns in the United States of America'. Nothing came of this, and very little of the November 'programme', much of London's interest in which evaporated as the weeks passed and no bombs fell on British factories; several enquiries were cancelled on the ground of 'no requirement'.

It followed from the provisional and uncertain nature of British requirements, and from the acute anxiety about dollar finance, that the freedom of action, both of the Purchasing Commission and of its parent body at Ottawa, was very closely circumscribed in the first phase of cash procurement. The initial instructions given to Sir James Rae, administrative head of the Mission in Ottawa, laid down that he was to place contracts only to cover specific requirements notified by the Ministry of Supply. Fixed prices were to be obtained, unless variation clauses were demanded, in which case the right to verify costs was to be insisted on. A break clause was to be inserted in all contracts covering more than six months production. Advance payments were not to be made without a banker's guarantee or progress payments without inspection of the product. Finally, the

---

[1] *North American Supply, op. cit.*, Chapter IV.

Mission was not allowed, without prior reference to London, to agree to capital assistance or to orders on which deliveries would not begin within six months. Many of these restrictions were not unreasonable in theory, but as the Supply Board soon pointed out, they made it almost impossible to do business in the conditions prevailing in the United States. Some modifications were conceded in respect of cost-plus contracts, advance payments, and in particular of the crippling six-months limitation. But the Board was still required to refer back to London on arrangements regarding capital assistance, abnormal depreciation, seller's options in respect of further orders, and royalty payments. It had also to certify that the payments agreed to in each contract were fair and reasonable.

Mounting impatience was displayed by the Purchasing Commission at the shackles thus imposed upon it, and especially at the lack of definite authority to go ahead with specific purchases. 'Once requirements were settled', Purvis wrote in December 1939, 'full authority to place orders should be vested in the Missions. A system of general enquiries and of reporting quotations seldom produces the best prices and deliveries'. It was obvious that manufacturers who had wasted time and money on the preparation of estimates which led to nothing were not going to be eager to repeat the performance when London really wanted supplies. Again, *à propos* of the explosives scheme he commented: 'The picture provided by a comprehensive programme of this nature, with some degree of authority to act, is most encouraging as it provides us with an opportunity of buying which is almost entirely missing in the case of spasmodic enquiries unrelated to such a programme'.

After Dunkirk the Commission, released from its dependence on the British Supply Board in Ottawa, had in general a much freer hand. The requirements notified from London were not only much larger in volume, but much more definite in character and more frequently assembled into comprehensive programmes. The aircraft purchase scheme was extended in time and expanded in scale. The Army 'insurance' programme of July 1940, and the 'deficiency' list brought to Washington in September by Sir Walter Layton, embraced practically the whole inventory of major ground weapons and ammunition.[1] In December a limited discretion was given to the Commission in advancing capital assistance to firms and in making payments which exceeded by a small amount the upper limit specified by the home department. But by this time the procurement of munitions had run into the difficulties (described in *North American Supply*), which were associated with the growth of American rearmament and the approaching exhaustion of British funds.

---

[1] *North American Supply, op. cit.*, Chapter VI.

CAPITAL ASSISTANCE FOR AMERICAN INDUSTRY

Even when the demand was firm, progress in the early days was fragmentary and slow. Despite what has been said about the favourable conditions existing in the United States at the beginning of the war, the difficulties of establishing munitions production in a foreign country by commercial methods were extreme. American manufacturers were often not over keen to do business with the Allied Governments. Those who had done so in 1914–8 had subsequently been pilloried as 'merchants of death', and the echoes of the Nye Committee's investigation of the arms industry were still reverberating in the background. Over and above this fear of a moral stigma there were the grave commercial risks inherent in the acceptance of contracts from belligerent states. The Winchester Repeating Arms Company, for example, had been forced into receivership after the First World War, when it had made rifles for the Allies. Thus it proved impossible to interest any of the big automobile corporations (Ford, Chrysler, General Motors) in the manufacture of certain components for British tanks (though in this case there were other firms that were willing to contract). In spite of pressure from its own Government the Ford Motor Co declined in mid-1940 to make aero engines for the British. Some months were needed to overcome the disinclination of Messrs. Du Pont de Nemours to go into the explosives business on behalf of the Allies.

Even when they could be brought to negotiation at all, firms commonly stipulated very arduous terms. Take, for instance, the requirement of 100 million rounds of .303-inch ammunition, which was confirmed by the Ministry of Supply in March 1940. The Government arsenals which met the needs of the American Army and Navy (except for certain special calibres) were not available to the Allies. Outside these there were only two possible sources of supply, the Remington Arms Co of Bridgeport, Connecticut, and the Winchester Repeating Arms Co of New Haven in the same State. Both were approached in March with a view to an order of 50 million rounds, and both stipulated terms which then seemed prohibitive. Remington wanted $2 million to pay for the reconditioning of plant, a price of forty dollars for a thousand rounds (which in France and the United Kingdom then cost the equivalent of about eighteen dollars), and a minimum order of 300 million rounds. Winchester had no existing capacity for rifle ammunition, and even on its own terms, which included payment of the entire cost of new plant and 100 per cent. down payment with the order, was reluctant to contract. Hence it was not until June, when circumstances were very different, that any orders for small arms ammunition (apart from one or two small contracts for sub-machine gun and revolver cartridges) were placed in the United States. So also with gun barrels. During the winter of

1939–40 negotiations were carried on with the great Bethlehem Steel Corporation over a possible contract for 500 4-inch naval gun barrels. The firm asked for a million dollars in capital assistance alone – a sum clearly out of all proportion to the size of the production order. No more was heard of this matter until much later in the year.

This question of capital assistance was fundamental. The Ministry of Supply had recognised from the beginning that little could be expected from Canada in the way of munitions without the outlay of British money on the construction of new plant, and had earmarked £1 million for this purpose out of the £9 million which it was prepared to spend there in the first year of war. But no corresponding provision had been made at this early stage for capital expenditure in the United States.[1] It seems to have been widely believed that 'a considerable war potential would in fact exist in the United States and be ready for immediate use'. That impression was very rapidly dispelled. We have indeed suggested that the 'war potential' of the United States was enormous. But that was to use a rather elastic term in a very wide and perhaps illegitimate sense, indicating merely the plant, labour and industrial organisation that could in time be made to serve the purposes of war. The resources readily available for munitions production were quite another matter. There was, of course, an aviation industry in being, so that the procurement of aircraft, being a question of expansion rather than of new creation, was easier than that of most other war material. There was also a small nucleus capacity for the manufacture of certain types of small arms used by the guardians, or the enemies, of law and order; and other warlike stores that closely resembled civilian products – army lorries, for example – could have been secured easily enough if they had been required. But for tanks, guns, rifles, shells and other purely military products there was virtually no capacity in being outside the arsenals of the United States Government. Nor were private firms willing to speculate on setting up plant to meet a highly specialised and at best temporary demand. Thus to get any purely military supplies, or large quantities of any supplies, it was necessary that the British Government should take the initiative, and bear the financial burden, of creating new manufacturing facilities. This the Government could not lightly undertake. It meant, in the first place, waiting – and in most cases it was still believed that once the difficult period of transition from peace to war was over British factories would be able to do all that was required. It meant also an additional drain on British dollar assets. Nor, obviously, was it worth while unless a large and continuous volume of production was required. Only in a few instances before Dunkirk was this condition satisfied. In many others

---

[1] On capital expenditure in the United States in 1940–1, see *North American Supply, op. cit.*, pp. 102–104, 287–289, 290–291, etc.

G

the vicious circle remained unbroken: no supplies could be got without new plant; new plant implied a big order; but a big order was out of the question, either because demand was lacking or because the Treasury demurred at the expense.

Apart from aircraft[1] the most important of the early steps taken by the Allies to finance American production arose from the 'joint comprehensive programme' for explosives which they had drawn up in January. The Anglo-French Purchasing Board was asked not merely to place orders but to act at once to induce the Du Pont, Hercules and Atlas Companies, as well as Canadian firms, to expand in order to increase their output of propellants and explosives.[2] Much discussion ensued as to the form which the necessary capital assistance was to take. An initial difficulty was that the manufacturers had to pay a 20 per cent. income tax on capital sums spent on the expansion of plant.[3] The first French contracts in 1939 had included large sums for factory expansion, provided in the form of higher unit costs. These were fixed high enough to pay both for the actual expansion and for the tax charged thereon, and must, Purvis noted, have involved tens of millions of dollars. In December 1939, the Secretary of the Treasury had advised Purvis to settle the matter first with the Treasury before any aircraft and explosives contracts were made which involved capital outlay. A formula had been worked out to cover production on American defence orders which might serve as a precedent for the Allies and save them large sums. The manufacturer was to apply for a 'Treasury ruling' to enable him to treat the sums as secured loans bearing interest. The formula was not acceptable to most firms, and further discussions with the Treasury produced no solution. Purvis, in a letter to the Ambassador on 9th February 1940, noted the 'anomalous position that in addition to being cut off from any normal credit facilities, usually regarded as vital to permit buyer and seller to come together, income tax should have to be levied upon cash outlays we are asked to put up towards the capital cost of expanded facilities, and perhaps, indeed, tax upon that tax'. It made still less sense when the Allies were creating at their own expense 'additional plant facilities of great national strategic value to the United States under existing world conditions'. The British Purchasing Commission was therefore taking legal advice to see whether there was not some means whereby the expansion facilities could not

---

[1] On aircraft see *North American Supply, op. cit.*, Chapter IV, Section (iv).

[2] On explosives in Canada see above, p. 56.

[3] A number of States, e.g., California and New York, also levied sales taxes of one or more per cent. on purchases within their territories. Since the tax was included in the price of the product, the British Purchasing Commission could not claim immunity as the agency of a foreign government. The matter first assumed importance in connection with aircraft produced in California. The British Purchasing Commission's lawyers had the foresight to insert in the contracts a provision that delivery should be made outside the State; and after much legal argument the Attorney-General of California finally ruled in July 1941 that tax was not due.

be 'fenced off from other plant belonging to the supplier'. This might be possible with a new plant, but he saw little hope of a way out being found in the case of an expansion of an existing plant.

This income tax point held up some of the very urgent explosives contracts for a considerable time. The Atlas Company, indeed, accepted the Treasury formula, and in January signed a contract for the supply of T.N.T. to the British and French Governments, from which it was to receive a total of $1,327,000 capital assistance (the British share being $667,000). But the formula was rejected by the Hercules Powder Company, and after negotiations lasting from December 1939, to 3rd April 1940, the British Government had to undertake to pay income tax of about $435,000 as part of capital assistance totalling $2,175,000.

Though at first 'definitely disinclined' to accept 'powder business', as Purvis put it, Messrs. Du Pont de Nemours agreed in a contract for the manufacture of 300 tons of smokeless cannon powder, to be delivered by September 1940. This small order on existing plant raised no questions of capital assistance, nor did it go far to meet the long-term needs of the Allies. On 25th April, however, Bloch-Lainé reported that Du Pont had offered to build a plant for the production of 15,000 tons or, if desired, 30,000 tons of powder a year for the Allied Governments. Next month, at the height of the Dunkirk crisis, London gave its approval to the construction of a plant with an annual output capacity of 24,000 tons of powder; and terms were then arranged with the firm.

Du Pont's proposals contained a novel feature; the Allied Governments, having put up the necessary capital, were to retain ownership of the plant. Accordingly, on 31st May 1940, the 'Tennessee Powder Company' was incorporated in the State of Tennessee with a share capital of $100,000 which was held by nominees of the British and French Purchasing Commissions. (A fortnight later the French nominee transferred his right to the British as part of the general assignment of French contracts.) On 10th June this Company signed a contract with Du Pont engaging them to construct the new plant at Memphis for a fee of $1,000,000. The plant, erected at the expense of the Tennessee Powder Company, was to remain its property. It was to be operated by Du Pont with full discretion as to details of production and maintenance, but subject to Tennessee's direction on production policy. Tennessee paid for the actual cost of the powder produced, plus an operating fee of 6c per lb. for the first 48 million lb. and 3.5c per lb. for any additional quantity. Du Pont were given an option to purchase the plant at cost (less depreciation at 10 per cent. per annum) at any time within ten years of the termination of the contract. Construction was begun about 25th July 1940, and the first deliveries of powder came forward in the following January, two months ahead of schedule. In the meantime similar arrangements had been made with Hercules, which agreed in the summer of 1940 to build and operate additional powder plants financed and owned by a second British-owned 'shadow' company, the 'New Jersey Powder Company'.

The Tennessee powder plant marked the beginning of an important change of policy in dealing with the problem of capital assistance. The new policy, of which a contract for heavy shells actually provided the first example in point of time,[1] was to retain title to the new plants created by British capital.

It was of special importance for aircraft. Several of the early British aircraft contracts contained what in effect were large amounts of capital assistance disguised under the description of 'expediting charges' in which provision for income tax was included. But the rapidly increasing expenditures in the spring of 1940, and especially the Allied air programme of $600 million, made it still more imperative to save dollars wherever they could be saved. On 5th and 8th April Purvis signed letters of intention with the Curtiss Wright and General Motors (Allison Division) Corporation for the production of aircraft engines. The new policy of plant ownership was worked out during the course of the negotiations leading up to these letters, and was embodied in the formal contracts when they were finally signed. Advance payments of a million dollars were made in April to each company by way of capital assistance.

The Curtiss Wright contract (finally signed on 31st August 1940) provided for the supply of 3,174 Wright Cyclone engines at a total cost of $51½ million. This included expediting charges amounting to $7 million; in addition capital assistance of over $13 million was to be advanced to the firm for the purchase by them, as agent for the British Government, of land, buildings, machinery and equipment, all of which were to be leased to the manufacturer for the performance of the contract. The final contract with General Motors, dated 25th May 1940, provided for an undetermined number of various types of Allison engines, to be supplied at fixed unit prices per engine. The British Government was to lend the manufacturer the estimated amounts required for land, improvements and additions to buildings, and for tools, dies and so forth, all of which remained the property of the manufacturer. The loans were to be repaid over the life of the contract in proportion to the deliveries made. But in addition, the British Government was to advance the cost of new machinery and equipment which the manufacturer would purchase as its agent. The machinery and equipment were to remain the property of the British

---

[1] The contract signed on 24th April, was with the American Car and Foundry Co for 200,000 9.2-inch howitzer H.E. shells. It provided that in addition to the cost of the shells, which was $7,568,000, the British Government should advance $1,096,000 for plant and machinery which should remain its property.

Government, but to be leased to the manufacturer at a rental based on the number of engines delivered.

FINANCIAL AID FROM THE UNITED STATES GOVERNMENT

The new policy was adopted by the French Commission during the remaining weeks of its operation, and became the established practice until the time when the United States Administration itself took over the burden of creating capacity for war production. When that time came, the facilities owned by the British Government in the United States provided a valuable means by which its depleted dollar reserves could be replenished by sale to the American Government and to manufacturers. Purvis had raised the point about the United States Government taking over such facilities in connexion with the original proposal for the Tennessee Powder Plant. In a memorandum dated 27th April 1940, for Secretary Morgenthau, he pointed out that the projected powder plant was of a purely military nature and of obvious strategic value to the United States. Would the United States purchase it ultimately on an agreed basis? The reply in the affirmative could only come after the Lend-Lease Act. On 19th March 1941, an agreement to purchase was signed. The plant was sold on 23rd May to the Defence Plant Corporation (a subsidiary of the Government-owned Reconstruction Finance Corporation) for the actual cost of construction, which was $25 million. Similar arrangements were concluded at various stages of the war for the sale to the United States Government, of the New Jersey powder plants, of certain machine gun and tank factories, and of the two new shipyards laid out early in 1941 at Portland, Maine and Richmond, Oregon, for the construction of merchant ships on British account.

But many months before Lend-Lease the provision of capital for American munitions plants had become an acute and urgent problem. After Dunkirk British munitions programmes in the United States, and with them the sums required for capital expenditure, were enormously expanded. In August 1940, it was estimated that $1,000 million dollars would be required for the capital cost alone of the new aircraft programme, and a further $80 million for aircraft armament and for Admiralty and Ministry of Supply requirements, which were then very incompletely formulated. A calculation of 17th December 1940 showed that for pending munitions contracts requiring payments before September 1941, capital assistance would have to be given to the order of $1,218 million.

Expenditure of this order of magnitude was quite beyond the capacity of the British Government, which was actually able to find no more than about $200 million for capital assistance between September 1939, and March 1941. This was the most crucial point of the whole financial problem. Payments on account of deliveries could mostly be deferred until a time when, it was confidently hoped, the United States Government would be in a position to relieve the British of their financial burdens. But capital advances had to be made at once. It was therefore vital, if any substantial progress were to be made with munitions production on British account in the period before the Presidential election of November 1940, and in the ensuing months while Lend-Lease was germinating, that some means should be found of supplementing, if not replacing, the advances which the British Government was then able to make.

Proposals put forward by Secretary Morgenthau in June 1940, and repeated in more explicit terms in August, seemed to offer a solution. He suggested, according to Purvis' report, that wherever possible the United States procurement agencies and the British missions should co-operate in the creation of munitions plants, placing 'complementary' orders for the same product with the same firm. In such cases the Administration would be prepared to advance the whole cost of factory construction and equipment, the British paying their share later on in the form of payments for units of deliveries. The advantages were obvious: the elimination of income tax payments, the limitation of profits (under the Vinson Trammel Act) to 12 per cent., and above all, the postponement of dollar expenditure. In one important case, that of tank engines, this expedient was put into effect; the United States Army certified that the creation of capacity for the production of 20 engines a day, which was the combined British and American requirement, was essential to the security of the United States, and that the Administration should pay the producer for the fixed assets. In mid-September the British placed an order with the Continental Motors Co for 3,500 engines, and the United States War Department followed suit with an order for 2,000.

Unfortunately, however, the wide extension of this system proved very difficult. It could be applied only to munitions required equally by the British and American forces, that is to say, to standardised equipment, which, as will be seen shortly, was only a part of the whole. It could be applied, also, only where the American requirement was in volume a very substantial part of the whole. The expedient broke down over the manufacture of Rolls-Royce Merlin engines by the Packard Co, since the American share was to be only 3,000 out of 9,000 engines. The Reconstruction Finance Corporation, the government agency from whose funds the capital was to be provided, found that it could not finance schemes unless the American share of the produce was to be at least 50 per cent. – a condition likely to be satisfied in few contracts. At the best, the expedient was liable to cause delay. Negotiations over capital assistance for a machine gun contract – a vital element of both the tank and the aircraft programmes – dragged on through the autumn without positive result, until the Purchasing Commission decided that it could wait no longer and must place an order in the ordinary way. The R.F.C., like most organs of the United States Government, was a semi-autonomous body with a mind and will of its own, and an accountability to Congress for the handling of its funds; and its influential chief had to be won over separately to the idea. It was not until January 1941, that it definitely agreed to set aside $880 million for the construction of facilities required partly by the British, but certified by the Chiefs of Staff to be essential to American defence. By that time Lend-Lease was already over the horizon, and the lesser expedient was merged into the greater. Meanwhile the placing of munitions contracts by the British had slowed almost to a standstill. Although cash procurement could not in any case have continued for very much longer, the inability to furnish capital assistance to contractors was the rock on which it actually foundered.

(iv)

The Standardisation of Arms

THE PROBLEM

Before the war, of course, the design and development of military equipment proceeded quite independently in the United States and in Britain, so that at the outset the weapons in use or being prepared for use by the armed forces of the two countries were in very few, if any instances, identical. Thus one of the greatest problems confronting the British Government when it sought munitions from the United States was whether it should try to have equipment of British type made there, or should accept equipment similar to that used by the American forces. The problem had no direct connection with the system of procurement, and was still a live issue long after Lend-Lease had come into effect. But it first emerged, and was on the whole most prominent, during the era of cash contracts and may conveniently be considered here.

At first there did not appear to be much question but that the latter course would be adopted for aircraft; all the pre-Dunkirk aircraft orders had been for machines of types designed by American manufacturers. The bulk of other American munitions appeared, however, at this time to be unsuited to British requirements, and the Army authorities refused to accept any American weapons except the Thompson sub-machine gun. When the long-term planning of army munitions purchases began in June 1940, the Ministry of Supply was emphatic that if substantial deliveries were to be obtained within a reasonable period, the acceptance of American patterns of equipment already in production in the United States would have to be considered. One of Monnet's first actions after the principle of starting large-scale production in the United States had been sanctioned had been to ask Purvis for information on American designs of tanks and of anti-tank and anti-aircraft guns but, for the time being, the Ministry of Supply went on planning production on the assumption that British war industry would have to bear the main burden of military requirements.[1]

The ingrained prejudices of the Service departments in favour of their own tried types of equipment were not ill-founded, even apart from the obvious difficulties which a mixing of types would cause, especially in the Army. Thus as early as 18th June Purvis was asked to investigate the possibility of producing the British 25-pounder field gun in the United States instead of the Franco-American 75-mm. type, and a later telegram on 11th July set forth at length the advantages of the former gun. On 26th June he was instructed to press the claims of two British tank models, the Matilda and the Crusader. It was of the essence of the Army Insurance programme of 5th July (that is, the scheme whereby capacity was to be set up in the United States for the production of a more or less fixed percentage of the total British requirement of each of the major ground weapons with its ammunition, so as to cover the probable loss of output in Britain due to air-raids) that specific British types should be provided. So later with aircraft. On 26th July Lord Beaverbrook presided over a meeting in London to discuss what was referred to as the promise of 3,000 additional aircraft a month, which he understood would become 'effective in the comparatively near future' with deliveries reaching 'a steady flow' by mid-1941. Apart from this initial misconception the meeting proceeded on the basis of an assumption which was to prove untenable – that British types of aircraft might be produced under the scheme in the United States. According to the instructions given to the British Air Commission on 31st July, American types of dive bombers, light bombers, reconnaissance machines and trainers (such as were already on order) were acceptable; but the single-engined fighters were to be Spitfires or Typhoons, the twin-engined fighters, Beaufighters (powered by American Wright engines), and the heavy bombers, Stirlings.

The British authorities had two main reasons for taking this line. One was their very natural belief that the American equipment

---

[1] See *North American Supply*, *op. cit.*, pp. 173-177.

available was in fact much inferior to their own.[1] Discussions on the new aircraft programme in London were influenced by the strong conviction that high quality was more important than numbers,[2] and that British types of fighters and heavy bombers already in existence and under development were definitely superior to any known American types likely to be obtainable within the time set. As regards two-engine fighters the Air Minister expressed the general view in a letter to Lord Beaverbrook on 30th July: 'There is really no choice – it must be the Beaufighter'. The position was much the same as regards short-range fighters; either the Spitfire III or the Typhoon was held to be better than any known American type. Of the new British heavy bombers only the Stirling had yet flown satisfactorily, and it was regarded as the clear choice for production in the United States, especially as arrangements for its production in Canada were well advanced. Technical reports showed that the American B.24 (the Liberator), as then designed, was inferior to the Stirling in range, bomb-load, internal lay-out, defence armament and tyre pressure.

Reports from the British experts on the spot confirmed, in the main, the opinions held in London. Their view was shown clearly in a 'Note for Mr Morgenthau' amongst Purvis' papers. Written across the note are the words . . . 'This is dynamite . . . not given to H.M.' It pointed out that, whilst orders had been placed for several pursuit types, the contracts had had to provide for the incorporation of a number of changes dictated by British battle experience; since all such changes added weight they were limited by the high wing-loading of the American aircraft; and they had added considerably to the cost of the contracts. Many of the numerous experimental projects, it was reported later, looked good on paper, but they had not been tried out under service conditions or related closely enough to war experience. 'One is faced', London was told, 'with a lack of knowledge of the essential details of armament, combined with advanced technical development in theory and very wavering opinions as to air staff requirements'. 'Armamentally, they are passing through the same phase as we did eight years ago'.

The Army authorities were equally reluctant to adopt unproved American weapons whose design was not based, as was that of the latest British types, on direct experience in the field. Each of the two American types of tank in production or under development in the

---

[1] On the technical aspects of the controversies here described the authors have no sort of competence to pronounce. They can only record what was thought and said, but it was at least clear that the 75 mm. gun was out of date as compared with the 25-pounder and the Americans themselves showed their recognition of this later by introducing the 105 mm.

[2] The Air Ministry's Director of Production pointed out in a minute of 29th July: 'Numbers in themselves can achieve nothing if the equipment is inferior, since this inferiority will destroy the morale of our pilots'.

summer of 1940 (the medium M.2 and the light M.2A4) was held to be far too lightly armoured to be of any real use in conditions such as the British Army had recently experienced; Purvis was told that he must on no account let the Americans think they might be adopted for British contracts. The 75-mm. field gun was ballistically inferior to the British 25-pounder, and had the crippling disadvantage of a complex recoil mechanism which was difficult to make and impossible to repair in the field. The War Office was also anxious to see its own proved and excellent anti-aircraft guns adopted as the model for production in America. As to the merits of the internationally famous Bofors it seemed that there could be little argument, whilst the 3.7-inch gun, though not as quick-firing as its American equivalent, had a much higher ceiling.

The second objection to the use of American-type weapons was that in nearly every case they would be supplementary to, not a substitute for, weapons made in Britain, and that such mixture of types presented grave practical difficulties. The Ministry of Aircraft Production had stressed the need to avoid as far as possible an increase in the number of types used by the R.A.F., since this would complicate operations, add fresh problems in the matter of provisioning and spares, and increase the difficulty of training pilots and mechanics. With aircraft, however, and also with tanks and ground weapons whose role was mainly static, such as anti-aircraft guns, the mingling of various types was a nuisance but not a real stumbling-block. But when it came to the basic weapons of a mobile infantry division, such as rifles, anti-tank guns and field artillery, the difficulty of securing accessories and replacement parts, and above all the need for separate stocks of ammunition, with all the complications and risks that these implied, were held to be an absolute bar to the acceptance of foreign types, however efficient. The problem had cropped up in June when the British and French were trying to arrive at a common programme of orders in the United States. The Prime Minister had then ruled that the British should join with the French in ordering 75-mm. field guns, curtly silencing any contrary argument. 'There are objections to having two types in one army but we are not in a position to indulge them'. This, however, was in the hectic atmosphere of the fall of France, when any kind of armament seemed better than none. For the long-term equipment of the Army the War Office soon reverted to the position that British types of most guns and small arms were essential.

On the other side, the American authorities, firmly opposed to the allocation of productive capacity for competing types, insisted on the standardisation of the weapons produced for export and for use in their own Forces. One reason for this was the desire to exploit to the full the mass-production techniques which were the key to the marvellous productivity of American industry. The decisive reason, however, was that the production of purely British types would not contribute, as they desired that British orders should contribute, to the security of the United States. The French contracts taken over by Britain were a case in point. A great many of these, being for equipment used only in the French forces, were of little value to the British, who had been compelled either to accept unsuitable material or to start afresh with orders of their own. The Americans were resolved not to be put in the same position if Britain went the way of France, and insisted that any plants set up to produce munitions for the British should be capable of being turned over, without re-tooling, to work for the American forces. In fact, over the whole field of munitions production, the American decision to standardise was more or less a *fait accompli* before discussions were begun.

Almost equally certain was it that the decision would be to standardise upon American types. The United States Services were by no means disposed to admit that their designs were inferior to those evolved by the British. In many respects, indeed, the facts were not quite as London thought. The information there available as to American equipment was at first very scanty, and when further investigations were made the difference of quality was found to be appreciably narrower. The field gun which the United States Army was about to adopt was not the 75-mm., but an entirely new model, the 105-mm. gun/howitzer, whose inferiority to the 25-pounder was by no means so clear. The medium tank was not the M.2 but the M.3, which made an immediately favourable impression on the British Tank Mission sent out at the end of July. On the air side, investigations showed that the latest American types were rather better in armament and performance than had been realised in London. Moreover, if firms were to change over to British types production could not be in full swing before the middle of 1942; and the American experts were convinced that by that time they would have in production follow-up models, then on the development list, which would be superior to known British types, both in speed and armament – a long-range fighter faster than the Beaufighter, and a single-engine fighter with six .50-inch machine guns against the Spitfires' eight .303-inch guns.

The American authorities were also, in the summer of 1940, in a very great hurry. In mid-July, when Mr J. G. Weir arrived from England to open discussions on the Army problems, he found that American opinion had already hardened against the adoption of British types and even against further consideration of the question. It was made clear that the War Department had 'already decided in the most unequivocal manner' to proceed with its own type of field gun. As for tanks, it had been deeply impressed with the British and French error of holding up quantity production for interminable discussions on the ideal design. The main object in its view was to secure rapid delivery of 'reasonably effective' equipments; and it was accordingly going ahead at once with its own medium tank. On the air side, the case for standardisation on British types had already been prejudiced by the adoption of American models for the Anglo-French programme of the spring.

It is conceivable, none the less, that with prompt and decisive action the British Government might have induced the Americans to adopt British designs, at least of ground weapons, in which field their own progress was rather less far advanced than in that of aircraft design. But for this two things were necessary: expert technical salesmanship and the ability to demonstrate specimen British equipments on the spot. Neither of these was forthcoming early enough or on a sufficient scale. The British Purchasing Commission lacked men versed in manufacturing technique and it lacked military experts. Its only technicians were a small number of Army officers inherited from the defunct British Supply Board; their duties related mainly to inspection, and they hardly had the standing which would have enabled them to argue with the Chiefs of the United States Army. In one sector this gap was quickly and admirably filled. At the end of July there arrived in the United States a special British Tank Mission. Its leader was Mr Michael Dewar, an industrialist with a wide range of manufacturing interests who had had experience in the organisation of munitions production in the First World War. With him came Brigadier D. H. Pratt who, as Commander of the 1st Army Tank Brigade in Flanders, was as well fitted as any man living to represent the user's point of view, and Mr L. E. Carr, who had helped to design the Matilda tank. As we shall see, this Mission, though it failed to gain its original objective, met with a great measure of success in reconciling British and American needs. The Tank Mission was followed in August by a military mission with wider terms of reference, but one whose composition was singularly ill-adapted to its task. Its leader, Major-General Pakenham-Walsh, was an engineer officer, and neither he nor his assistants had special knowledge of the weapons whose merits they were supposed to expound. It was not until December, with the arrival of the so-called '200 Mission', the nucleus of the later British Army Staff, that British technical and user experts began to be systematically assembled in Washington to aid in supply negotiations.

The absence of specimen British equipments was a handicap to British negotiators over the whole field of these discussions on standard-isation. Officials of the British Air Commission were never able to demonstrate British types of aircraft. There was desultory discussion until early in 1941 of the possibility of sending over a Stirling and a

Typhoon, but none was available. The Tank Mission had no Crusader tank to show to the Americans. A static model of the Bofors was available in Canada in August 1940, but without the fire-control gear which was one of its essential merits. The despatch of specimen 4.5-inch medium guns and 6-pounder anti-tank guns, weapons in which the Americans had shown a definite interest, was repeatedly delayed. Very often the absence of specimens was unavoidable, for the simple reason that the models in question had not yet gone into production in the United Kingdom. But whatever the reason might be, it was in each case fatal to the success of the negotiations, for the Americans could hardly be expected to adopt for their own use weapons which they had not even seen. When British equipments were in fact demonstrated, conversion of American Service equipment frequently followed. The 2-pounder anti-tank gun, indeed, when tried out in August against the American 37-mm. gun, disappointingly failed to establish a definite supremacy. The Bofors, on the other hand, when it finally came on view in December, at once proved itself and was adopted as the United States Army's standard light anti-aircraft gun. The 20-mm. Oerlikon, which was to save many British and American ships from the on-slaught of low-flying aircraft, found favour with the American Navy in November. The timely arrival of a Matilda tank towards the end of August 1940, though it did not lead to the adoption of British types, clinched the argument in favour of the incorporation in all American-built medium tanks of the power-traverse turret which the British held to be operationally vital.

But in the summer of 1940 the hard facts were that the decision as to the standardisation on British designs lay with the Americans and that in the main the decision was adverse. The British had there-fore to decide whether, notwithstanding all the objections to such a course, they should agree to place orders for American types or whether they should persist in the attempt to secure a separate niche, within the general framework of American munitions pro-duction, for the manufacture of at least some weapons of purely British type. Against the latter policy there were two arguments so obvious and decisive that to invoke them seemed almost superfluous. One was that it would mean foregoing the chance of American capital assistance for British orders. On 24th August there was an important meeting between British and United States representatives, the theme of which was 'the adoption of common types so as to create one productive capacity'. Here was renewed Morgenthau's offer to con-sider financing the manufacture for British orders so long as the United States were satisfied that the type of weapon manufactured for England was the same as the United States Army and Navy had adopted. If the United Kingdom pressed its own types, it did so at the risk of having to pay the whole capital cost as well as purchase the output and with no prospect of later American assistance. The other argument was the Administration's control over priorities and shipments. British supply representatives in America united in underlining the folly of trying to start separate British programmes which would be bound to take second place to production for the United States Services. For example, the better-known aircraft firms would be unlikely to accept British orders in preference to American. It might, therefore, be necessary to fall back on untried and inexperienced firms. This would hardly be practicable unless the United Kingdom could provide fully equipped production teams, as well as much larger capital assistance. Moreover the United States Government was always in a position to bar British access to American firms, which it did temporarily in August 1940 pending a settlement of the question of types. Purvis summed up the whole position as he saw it in a very important cable of 24th August. 'We believe that it is only if (as in the last resort will be inevitable) we agree promptly with the Americans on common types of weapons, so achieving complementary programmes, that we can hope to take advantage of the plan . . . whereby the American Administration finances our capital expenditure . . . or obtain United States consent to . . . priorities on deliveries.' The point about priorities was that the Administration would allow 'British' plants to be built and equipped more quickly than its own if, but only if, the material produced thereby could be diverted in case of need to its own use; also that it might sometimes release to the British material produced under its own contracts if it knew that there would be identical material coming along later on British contracts, from which it could be recouped.

THE PROBLEM RESOLVED – TANKS, AIRCRAFT, ORDNANCE

No systematic solution was ever worked out to this problem. The deadlock was broken down gradually and empirically, item by item, the general result being a compromise, though a compromise heavily weighted towards the adoption of American designs as the common standard.

Decision came first on the question of tanks. Here a solution was made easier by the supreme urgency of the British need, which made it impossible for them either to forgo or to delay the supply of American tanks, and also by the manifest fact that the latest American design was at least as good as anything the British had in prospect. The armour of the M.3, of which Brigadier Pratt saw a mock-up at the beginning of August, was considered quite adequate for a cruiser tank. Its speed and range were similar to those of the rival British model, Crusader. It was to carry in the hull a 75-mm. gun firing a 15-lb. shell, as well as a 37-mm. gun in the turret, whereas the

Crusader would have only a 2-pounder. The authorities in London, however, were not at first convinced that as an engineering job M.3 was anything more than experimental, while they felt that, lacking the three-man, power-operated turret, it did not compete with British tanks in fighting capacity. But in Pratt's view its engineering was not in any way experimental (in fact, it was the mechanical soundness of all American tanks that proved their greatest asset); and the Americans were willing to consider re-design of the fighting compartment. Pratt, Dewar, and Purvis strongly urged acceptance, which would carry with it the full co-operation of the United States Government, including the granting of priority to British orders. Preliminary negotiations were started with the leaders of American engineering industry, who were called into council at a most import-ant meeting presided over by Mr Knudsen of the Defence Advisory Commission on 6th August; and it was hoped that capacity could be created for the full British requirement of twenty tanks a day, deliveries starting within eight months.

The British Government, however, was not yet ready for decision. It insisted that no action should be taken until the arrival of Major-General Pakenham-Walsh, who had been instructed, like Dewar and Pratt, to press the case for British weapons. Yet there was nothing the new mission could do to alter the situation. It contained no one with special knowledge of the design, manufacture or military use of tanks. It could therefore only accept the technical advice of the men already on the spot as to the merits of M.3, while it was obliged to recognise as final the American refusal, already reported to London, to consider British designs. On 18th August London was warned that the sands were running out. Some American orders for medium tanks had already been placed. British orders must be given within a few days, or the Americans would go ahead alone; and the orders must be for M.3, with such modifications as could be secured. In London, Sir Arthur Salter added his voice in favour of concession: 'If we do not at once accept the basic design of M.3, and cable our acceptance in the next few days, we shall probably lose, and, I am tempted to add, deserve to lose our chance of getting any substantial tank production in America, and in addition prejudice our negotia-tions for all other forms of supplies'. The remaining hesitations of the War Office were now quickly overcome, and on 22nd August the British Purchasing Commission was authorised to place orders for 1,500 (shortly afterwards raised to 3,000) cruiser tanks of American design, subject to an alteration of the fighting compartment on the lines which the Tank Mission had suggested.

The settlement thus arrived at, which led immediately to the con-clusion of contracts between the Purchasing Commission and four American firms for a total of 2,085 tanks (lack of funds preventing more), and ultimately to a position in which the United States was able to furnish more than half the Commonwealth's total supply of tanks, was certainly not the least momentous event of that eventful month, August 1940. The gains accruing to both parties were immense. The American authorities, whose own requirements were as yet relatively small, were enabled to plan their production programme on a basis three times broader than would otherwise have been possible, in the full knowledge that whatever happened the whole of the new capacity would be of value to them. They could do what they wanted to do, i.e., help Britain, and at the same time satisfy their critics that adequate provision was being made for the security of the United States. Britain, for her part, was now able to count on a large delivery in the not too distant future of tanks at least as good as any which had yet been designed at home.

The course of negotiations over aircraft types followed a broadly similar though more gradual course. Here also the British Government, having done its best to secure the adoption of British types, yielded with good grace to the inevitable, lest production be delayed. American planes were already being built for the British on a considerable scale, and it was obvious, as the Ministry agreed in August, that follow-on orders for the same capacity must be for similar types. It did, however, hope for a while, as we have seen, that in the new and larger programme being worked out in the summer of 1940 some room would be found for British types, at least for Stirlings (or Halifaxes) and Typhoons. But at the beginning of October it was agreed, though reluctantly, to accept part of the heavy bomber requirement in the form of Liberators. The end of any serious attempt to secure standardisation of British types was shown by the remark made by Lord Beaverbrook on 20th October (in a transatlantic telephone talk with Morris Wilson) that his knowledge led him to believe that success was unlikely, 'for I know that the Americans will never depart from their own models'. He was not mistaken. British hopes died hard – Typhoons made a somewhat forlorn appearance in a list of requirements presented to the Americans as late as February 1941. In the Second World War no aircraft of British design was built in the United States.[1]

It was in the sphere of Army ordnance that the controversies over British and American types were most acute and most protracted. Here the case against a mixture of different types in service was strongest, and here too the argument for yielding to the wishes of the Americans was least potent, since the demand was in few instances as pressing as the demand for aircraft or tanks. For the most part production of guns, small arms and ammunition in America was

---

[1] During the First World War the DH4 – a British design – was built in large numbers in the United States as a standard day bomber.

required only by way of insurance, and it was emphasised that the provision, late in 1941, of alien types of weapon would not really meet the insurance need at all. For some items, indeed, notably rifles and tank and anti-tank guns, the need for American supplies seemed exceedingly urgent: but these were just the weapons for which it was most important to have British types. The War Office was, it is true, eager to lay hands on as many American-calibre rifles as could be made available, for issue to the Home Guard and other static units, but for the main Field Army, rifles of British design were essential. A suggestion that further releases of .30-inch rifles might count against the requirement of .303s was firmly rejected.

Practically no progress was made on these ordnance problems during the summer. Their solution was one of the main tasks of Sir Walter Layton, the special emissary of the British Government who arrived in Washington at the end of September.[1] After a thorough exposition of British supply needs he asked that, notwithstanding the admitted advantages of standardisation, 'the rule barring the placing of planes or weapons which are not standard in the American Army should be relaxed where the ordering of alternative types is needed to make good specific deficiencies in the British programme, to provide insurance against a severe loss of British output as the result of enemy action, or to increase fighting efficiency at the earliest possible date'.

In the circumstances this was the crucial point of his mission. As regards planes, there was little hope, as we have seen, of a favourable response. In the matter of ground weapons the answer came, after an interval of uncertainty, towards the end of October. It was in the nature of a compromise. First came the proposal, described in *North American Supply*, that the United States should make available to Britain American-type equipment for ten complete divisions. This was designed to meet the argument about the confusion of types, since the divisions would constitute a fully self-contained force, wholly American in its supplies. In addition, the British were to be allowed to place orders for a strictly limited range of British-type weapons, viz., 2,000 2-pounder tank guns, 2,250 2-pounder guns for installation on British-built tanks and a million .303-inch rifles. In the event, various further objections were raised to the manufacture of 2-pounders, and the .303-inch rifle was the only important complete weapon peculiar to the British Army that was manufactured in the United States.

After October 1940, the 'battle of the types' faded out of the foreground of the picture. As a result of the compromise then adopted the high feeling which the controversy had engendered began to die

---

[1] See *North American Supply*, *op. cit.*, Chapter VI.

down. Henceforward the British avoided raising the issue of general principle, and, as was forecast by Sir Walter Layton, a situation was gradually created in which individual weapons could be judged on their merits at the technical level. Before the end of the year, as already mentioned, the Bofors and the Oerlikon anti-aircraft guns had been adopted by the United States Services. These were followed later on by the 6-pounder (57-mm.) anti-tank gun and the 4.5-inch medium gun, though none of the latter were actually supplied to the British.

The significance of the ten-division programme was always primarily political. The British had little use for most of the weapons planned under this programme. The idea of raising special divisions with British or Allied manpower was abandoned early in 1941; and the production to which the programme gave rise was gradually merged into the general tide of American rearmament. On the other hand, there were certain American weapons which the British Army was glad to use. It had been quick to see the value of the Thompson sub-machine gun, for which there was no British equivalent until the appearance of the Sten gun in 1941. A small number of 'tommy guns' was ordered from the Auto Ordnance Corporation in February 1940. It was repeated and expanded many times, and the total number of guns supplied ran into several hundreds of thousands. In June 1940, the War Office agreed to a stopgap order for 37-mm. anti-tank guns in default of 2-pounders. But in the main, wherever common types or ordnance could not be established, the British either did without supplies from overseas or turned to Canada instead. British-type weapons for which Canada was the sole North American source of supply included the 25-pounder field gun, the 3.7-inch heavy A.A. gun, the 2-pounder anti-tank gun, the Bren light machine gun and the Boys anti-tank rifle.

BRITISH INFLUENCE ON AMERICAN DESIGN

Very limited success thus attended the effort to get British models standardised as equipment common to the Forces of both countries. But this was not the whole of the story, for at a great many points British experience and British needs had profound influence on the development of American weapons. The influence was continuous throughout the war, but it was naturally greatest in the early stages when the Americans, having no battle experience of their own to draw on and few designs finally evolved, were most ready to listen to foreign advice.

Here again tanks provided the first conspicuous example. M.3, when the British first saw it, was already a first-class piece of engineering, but to make it a fully battle-worthy tank certain changes were essential, and these were made. At a meeting on 28th August on the

Aberdeen proving ground, the British succeeded in convincing United States Ordnance Department officers and the Commander of the Armoured Corps that the British power-operated traverse should be incorporated in the design. A jubilant message from Dewar next day reported that 'almost all our requirements in respect of the fighting chamber have been met'. Thus in a very real sense M.3 was an Anglo-American achievement, American in its basic structure but owing much of its fighting quality to British experience in the field.

Collaboration did not end at this point. After much discussion the Americans agreed in December to adopt the British spudded track, better suited than their own for operation over muddy or snow-covered terrain. Another British suggestion, however, led to a departure from the principle of standardisation. In October 1940, Mr L. E. Carr produced revised drawings of a new type of turret with a bulge at the rear in which the British No. 19 wireless set could be accommodated. This was not acceptable to the Americans, but, since the change did not affect the basic identity of the tanks for manu-facturing purposes, they agreed that it might be adopted for the vehicles built under British contract. Thus there emerged, after all, separate American and British versions of the M.3 tank, the one known as the General Lee and the other as the General Grant.

Neither the Lee nor the Grant, though each was good enough for 1941, could be accepted as the ultimate in cruiser tank design. As soon as the design of M.3 had been settled and long before any had been built, work began on the preparation of its successor. For a while, however, in the winter of 1940–1, the scene shifts to Montreal. The Canadian authorities were anxious to build cruiser tanks: and, as their manufacturers were dependent on the United States for many components, it was clearly desirable that they should in this instance follow the American rather than the British lead. The British Tank Mission in the United States seized this opportunity to evolve a tank using the basic components of M.3 but with its defects removed. The result was the Canadian Ram cruiser. This machine was based on the General Grant, but the 75-mm. gun was eliminated from the hull and the turret made capable of mounting the new British six-pounder in place of the original 37-mm. gun. It was to be built also with a single casting for the upper part of the hull in place of the usual rolled plates – a development which followed on the successful manufacture of turret castings for British-built tanks in American foundries. United States Ordnance officers visited Montreal in January 1941, and were suitably impressed. When the design of the new American medium tank, the M.4 or Sherman, made its appearance in May it was found to follow the Canadian prototype very closely. Thus the British parents of the Ram have some claim to be numbered among the grandparents of the Sherman, which was to contribute so much to the Allied victories in Africa and Europe.

The position of aircraft was in one respect somewhat dissimilar. In the United States, military aircraft were frequently designed by private firms and offered by them to the War or Navy Department. Most of the American aircraft which were supplied to Britain had in fact been thus designed and offered. Therefore in buying the standard product of an American aircraft firm the British might or might not be acquiring machines identical with those used by the American air forces. There was in fact a class of planes which, though not 'British' in the sense of being of the same type as planes built in the United Kingdom, were not 'common' either, though they might become so. Such was the Lockheed Hudson light bomber and general reconnaissance machine, for which the first orders had been placed as far back as 1938. Such also was the Mustang fighter. This was the nearest approach to a 'British' aircraft to be built in the United States. It was the outcome of collaboration early in 1940 between British experts and the North American Aviation Company, whose technical resources, incidentally, were largely the result of earlier British orders for Harvard trainers. Although its airframe bore every mark of a good and highly promising design, the early versions of the aircraft fell somewhat short of expectation and found no favour with the United States Army Air Corps. But after going through a number of successive modifications, and above all a marriage with the Rolls-Royce Merlin engine, it established itself as one of the best fighters in service, and was eventually adopted by the Americans for their own use as well as for export under Lend-Lease. In the later years of the war it shared with the Thunderbolt the position of standard American single-engined fighter. It was to be built in Australia also and to survive as an operational type well into the jet era.

Even where the aircraft bought by the British were basically the same as those supplied to the American air forces, the early British contracts often stipulated modifications in detail which produced a markedly different type. When the standardisation issue became acute in the summer of 1940 the British authorities were anxious that such 'British improvements' should continue to be made; that, if they could not get their own types built in America, at least they should receive 'United States aircraft of British adaptation'. The Ministry of Aircraft Production expressed the hope that the American Government would take full advantage of British experience, especially in regard to armament, armour, power turrets and self-sealing tanks. In the British view one very serious drawback of American types was that American turret development was in a rudimentary stage. It was suggested that British power turrets might be produced in the

United States under licence and installed, with suitable modifications, in American types. There were also other divergences, including a fundamental cleavage of opinion as to the method of stowing bombs. The technical difficulties involved in standardisation were in fact so many and so serious that they could not be resolved by either side giving way on the question of principle without a great deal of investigation and the pooling of the conclusions of research and production teams from both countries. This process began in the summer of 1940 and was to result not in the adoption of British types but in important changes in the design and equipment of American aircraft.

Meanwhile the value of British types was being amply demonstrated in the Battle of Britain, the results of which made a profound impression on the American public as well as on American experts. In the midst of the Battle of Britain a British technical mission, led by Sir Henry Tizard, brought to the United States and demonstrated before American experts the scientific and technical achievements – especially in the field of radar and armament – by which the victory in the air was being won.[1]

This double demonstration clinched the already strong argument for collaboration between the United Kingdom and the United States at the stage of design and development. The result on the air side was the Joint Aircraft Committee, the earliest and one of the most important of the formal organs of Anglo-American co-operation.[2] The Committee, which held its first meeting on 20th September 1949, was concerned with standardisation as well as with the planning of production schedules. One of its first actions was to secure agreement on a standard specification for the Curtiss P.40 fighter. Hitherto there had been two versions of this aircraft in production, British and American. The differences between them were numerous and were hampering production. The freezing for six months of an agreed design resulted in an increase of output in which both countries shared. A conspicuous example of increased readiness to introduce British improvements was the B.24 or Liberator. Production of the existing model was slowed down in October, following the visit of a joint Anglo-American party to the factory; and a new version was promised for May 1941, with better armour, armament and self-sealing tanks.[3]

On the naval side, again, the problem of the adoption of British designs or British improvements took a somewhat different form. It did not arise on any significant scale until after the end of the cash purchase period, for, apart from a few small craft, it was only in June 1941, that the Admiralty definitely decided to seek warships

---

[1] See *North American Supply, op. cit.,* Chapter VI, Section (iii).
[2] See *North American Supply, op. cit.,* Chapter VI, and below, Chapter V.
[3] On the jet engine see below, Chapter VIII.

from the United States. The point here was that the Americans had no real equivalent for the vessels of which the British stood in especial need. Absorbed by the prospect of major fleet actions in the Pacific, the United States Navy had given relatively little thought to the defence of trade against submarine and mine which was the main preoccupation of the Royal Navy. There was thus no obstacle to their supplying British types of warship, or adaptations thereof, once they had been convinced of the need. They took over from a successful British experiment the idea of producing large numbers of small auxiliary aircraft carriers by building a flight deck on cargo vessels in course of construction. American shipyards built versions of the little British motor minesweeper (in United States Navy nomenclature the B.Y.M.S. or British Yacht Minesweeper), the larger Algerine class of minesweeper (B.A.M.S.), the Vosper motor torpedo-boat and the 72-foot Fairmile motor launch. It is to be noted, however, that at least one of those best qualified to judge considered that the construction of British-type warships in the United States was not on the whole a success, and in particular that the Fairmile project was a great mistake. The transformation of the original design to suit American specifications and production methods resulted in what was in effect a different and inferior vessel. It was better, therefore, that the Americans should undertake the design from the beginning.

This was done in the case of escort vessels, of which the British asked for 100 in 1941. The United States Navy had at the time nothing between a fleet destroyer proper and a small patrol craft. To meet its own as well as British needs it evolved a 285-foot vessel known as a destroyer escort. The design was influenced by that of existing British vessels, and the British Admiralty Delegation put forward its operational requirements, collaborating closely in the early stages on such matters as the layout of bridges and armament, depth charges and towing gear. The vessel, however, was from beginning to end an American project. The Maritime Commission, on the other hand, when it was called in to help with the escort programme in 1942, adapted a British frigate design for construction in mercantile yards.

The design of landing craft was a matter of special interest. Here both countries, in 1941 and the early part of 1942, were feeling their way towards the solution of wholly novel problems. They were solved in co-operation. The Landing Ship Tank, that indispensable element in all the great amphibious operations of the later part of the war, was developed by the Navy Department from a suggestion put forward by the British Admiralty Supply Representative for an 'Atlantic Tank Landing Carrier'. Similarly the Landing Craft Infantry (Large) was the result of a request for giant raiding craft emanating from the Combined Operations Executive in London.

Liaison continued throughout the process of development, the British naval officer most concerned being given a desk in the Design Section of the Navy Department's Bureau of Ships. 'On the building side', it has been written, 'the landing craft programme is probably the most outstanding example of joint effort and the pooling of ideas in solving a major problem on which the whole conduct of the war depended, and on which previous experience was practically nil'.

How greatly United States preparedness for war was helped and stimulated by the earlier necessity of supplying Britain with munitions, has been emphasised in other parts of this study and in *North American Supply*. It was not least in the field of design that this stimulus was felt. Though few British weapons were actually taken over, at all the most important points, tanks, aircraft, warships and many more besides, the British had something of value to contribute from their fund of experience, technical and military, towards the evolution of satisfactory American equipment *before* the test of battle came.

(v)

The Submergence of Cash Procurement

It has already been suggested that up to the time of Dunkirk British purchases of munitions in the United States were on a very small scale. Apart from aircraft, indeed, they were almost insignificant. Actual disbursements by the British Purchasing Commission in the twenty weeks ending on 14th May, amounted to about $59 million only. Expenditure in any one week of this period never rose above $8 million. In the fifth week it was $6 million, but only in the last week did it exceed $7 million. That payments rose from $21 million in April to $186 million in July, continuing at about that level until January 1941, is eloquent testimony to the revolutionary extension of procurement operations that was occasioned by the military disasters of May and June.

These disbursements, however, included only payments for actual deliveries of warlike stores, capital advances and the varying 'down payments' required by the suppliers. A more complete picture of cash procurement is afforded by the estimated total value of the contracts let, as shown in Table 4.

Thus when Lend-Lease came into effect the British Government had ordered munitions valued at rather more than $2,500 million, together with some $200 million worth of machine tools. This was by no means the whole of its purchasing. The total value of orders placed by or through the British Purchasing Commission was estimated in April 1941, at $3,154 million, the balance consisting mainly of iron and steel but including also non-ferrous metals, electrical equipment and small quantities of textiles, tobacco, petroleum and other products. These are omitted from Table 4

Table 4. United Kingdom cash contracts placed in the United States to 30th April 1941

$ million

1	To 30th April 1940	To 31st October 1940	To 30th April 1941	Ex-French Contracts (Included in cols. 3 and 4)
	2	3	4	5
Ships and Marine Equipment	14.8	25.6	163.1	—
Airframes . . .	173.4	721.8	849.3	211.8
Aero engines . . .	22.7	480.5	608.7	196.7
Aircraft Accessories .	1.0	59.3	116.4	29.2
Tanks	2.5	99.5	131.0	—
Motor Vehicles . .	—	41.7	51.9	21.9
Ordnance Equipment .	7.4	114.5	232.7	21.4
Ammunition . . .	9.9	124.8	221.1	2.9
Explosives . . .	9.0	39.9	39.9	3.1
Machine Tools . .	42.4	127.6	209.9	74.2
Total Products . .	283.1	1,835.2	2,624.0	561.2
Capital . . .	8.4	154.8	197.6	2.2
	291.5	1,990.0	2,821.6	563.4

because changes in the method of procurement make it difficult to obtain a true comparison between different periods, and because even the final total for raw materials, and still more for petroleum, etc., would be incomplete, many purchases having been effected through other channels. The figures shown, on the other hand, do not represent the value of munitions actually received from the United States on cash terms since a considerable part of the material produced under British contracts, as well as of the production facilities set up with British money, was later transferred to the United States Government.

Three thousand million dollars is an imposing figure, especially when compared with the meagre results achieved in the first ten months of the war. It was considerably more than the total value of the United States Government's defence expenditure in 1940. None the less, to those who saw in the all-out mobilisation of American industry the only hope of ultimate victory, the contractual provision for munitions supply still seemed miserably inadequate. It fell far short of Britain's true needs, and far short also of what America could provide. The national income of the United States was reckoned at some $80,000 million. Contracts totalling little more than $3,000 million, deliveries from which would be spread over much more than a single year, were thus but a drop in the ocean of the American potential. They represented, moreover, only a fraction of the stated requirements of the British Government, though these were themselves, in the opinion of many, still far too modest. Early in November 'proposed programmes', chiefly for aircraft, were valued at a further \$3,755 million. By the turn of the year, with the addition of the ten-division programme and other commitments, it was estimated that British requirements of munitions for delivery over a period of two years totalled between \$8,000 million and \$9,000 million.

The gulf between the supplies required and the supplies for which provision had been made was evident in every sector. It will be seen from the table that orders for aircraft and associated stores, though they had not retained the absolutely commanding position which was theirs before Dunkirk, still accounted for well over half the total of procurement. None the less, the contracts actually let provided for less than half the desired supply. The British air supply programmes as formulated in the summer of 1940, called for the delivery of the following quantities between July 1940 and June 1942: first, 8,200 planes representing the undelivered balance of existing contracts, plus 1,500 for which orders were then pending, plus 4,200 by way of continuation orders for the capacity set up under the Anglo-French project of March 1940, which was originally to terminate in October 1941; secondly, 12,000 planes which were to be the first instalment of a great new expansion scheme. In all approximately 26,000 aircraft. But the number actually contracted for by the United Kingdom was only 11,359. It included, moreover, very few of the heavy bombers which were Britain's greatest need, the composition of the orders being as follows:

Heavy Bombers	185
Medium Bombers	695
Light Bombers	4,468
Fighters	4,009
Flying Boats	109
Naval Aircraft	181
Transports	9
Trainers	1,694
Miscellaneous	9
	11,359

In addition the Canadian Government had ordered 50 flying-boats and 770 trainers and the Australian Government 18 flying-boats, making a grand total of 12,197 aircraft. More significant, however, than the numbers on order was the extent of the manufacturing capacity set up to meet British needs. The British Government repeatedly emphasised during the financial impasse of the winter preceding the enactment of Lend-Lease that the creation of fresh facilities was far more important than the provision of follow-on orders for those already in existence. In this they had not been successful. By the time of the fall of France arrangements had been made for the eventual supply to the Allies of aircraft at the rate of a thousand a month. In subsequent discussions with the United States Government the idea had been conceived of setting up new plant which should yield a further three thousand planes a month. But no positive steps could be taken to put this scheme into effect until Lend-Lease was law, so that in this case cash procurement had taken the British only a quarter of the way towards the ultimate goal.

By contrast, merchant ship requirements, in one sense of the word 'requirements', had been provided for in full. Sixty cargo tramp ships, totalling some 400,000 gross register tons (or 600,000 dead-weight tons) had been asked for, and sixty ships had been duly ordered. This, however, was only a fraction of the true need. The Prime Minister wrote in December: 'To ensure final victory, not less than three million tons of additional merchant shipbuilding capacity will be required'. In the event the United States produced five million gross tons in 1942 and 13 million tons in 1943; and even so the Allies came very close to defeat in the battle of the ocean supply lines.

By March 1941, 2,085 tanks were on order in the United States on British account. Here again it is difficult to compare contracts with requirements, because of the varying bases on which the latter could be computed. The requirement notified by the Ministry of Supply was 3,000 cruiser tanks, but this was really a calculation of what might be produced in the fairly near future rather than a statement of the ideal requirement, which was undoubtedly far higher. An earlier message had spoken of a need for 5,000 (2,000 infantry tanks as well as 3,000 cruisers). And the comparison, elicited by Purvis in December 1940, between military needs and probable production in the United Kingdom and Canada, revealed a deficit of 9,150 tanks, including 2,150 for the ten-division scheme, which would have to be met, ideally, from the United States by mid-1942.

The situation of ordnance, ammunition and other Army requirements was even more complex and uncertain, owing to the multiplicity of programmes and schedules that were put forward on the British side during 1940. It was often far from clear whether these were cumulative demands or successive approaches to the same problem. Some of the 'deficiency' requirements presented by Sir Walter Layton in October were restatements of items in the earlier but largely inoperative 'insurance' programme of July 1940; others

were additions thereto. The ten-division programme was to some
extent a substitute for earlier programmes, but to precisely what
extent was a matter for dispute and doubt. In any attempt to assess
the sum total of British requirements in this sector there is thus a
risk of duplication and over-statement. Some points, however, are
tolerably clear. The requirement of rifles, for example, was 1 million,
plus 205,000 for the ten-division scheme. Against this, arrangements
were made during the winter of 1940–1 for the production of 833,000
rifles, but although letters of intention had been signed the financing
of the contracts had to wait for Lend-Lease. The minimum requirement of land anti-aircraft guns was 3,400; none was on order in
March 1941. Indeed, although the insurance programme alone had
called for the supply of 3,000 army artillery equipments of various
types, a solitary contract for 500 small anti-tank guns was all the
Purchasing Commission had to show for its efforts.

On the other hand provision had been made for the annual production in the United States of 45,000 tons of propellant powder and
nearly 20,000 tons of T.N.T. An experimental order for 750 sub-
machine guns had been built up by stages to a total of over 100,000,
deliveries from which were to prove invaluable during the acute rifle
shortage of 1941 and before the British Sten gun came into quantity
production. More than a thousand million rounds of small arms
ammunition and some six million shells of various natures were on
order. Admiralty representatives had arranged for the supply *inter
alia*, of 118 motor torpedo boats, 50 primitive landing craft, and a
much larger number of engines for installation in similar craft built
in the United Kingdom; also – a most important beginning – of
2,000 Oerlikon guns. The Ministry of Supply was making steadily
increasing use of American semi-manufactured components to clear
'bottlenecks' in United Kingdom production – brass strip for
ammunition; ball and roller bearings; engines, transmissions,
suspension units and armour castings for tanks; gun barrels and
recuperators in various stages of completion; drop forgings for motor
vehicles. Eleven thousand complete vehicles formed one of the most
valuable portions of the inheritance from the French. To these had
been added on British initiative small but significant contracts for
10-ton lorries, tank transporters and other special types. For the
standard load-carrying types, however, Canada was already marked
out as the principal source of supply.

The 'failure' of cash procurement is thus a relative rather than an
absolutely valid description. It is true that when British dollar assets
had been exhausted provision had been made for a small part only
of total British needs. But, whilst many of the more ambitious
schemes of supply remained in suspense and the volume of munitions
so far ordered was discouragingly small the foundations of British

war supply had none the less been laid when the era of Lend-Lease began. The nature of the supplies was already fairly clearly defined. In British plans the United States had now been allotted a highly important role in the provision of aircraft, tanks, merchant shipping, personal weapons (rifles, sub-machine guns and revolvers), Oerlikon guns, small arms ammunition, explosives and heavy vehicles. With all these a beginning had been made. Firms had been chosen and contracts let, and in most cases, if quantity production was hardly yet in sight, buildings were rising, plant being assembled and technical preparations put in hand.

Moreover, cash procurement can be said to have failed only because it had been asked to do more than could legitimately be expected of it. So long as the function of United States supply was merely to fill gaps in Britain's war equipment, the purchasing mission working on commercial lines was a reasonably appropriate instrument. But since the fall of France the position had been that Germany and her allies could be defeated only by the entire strength of the British Commonwealth *plus* a very large part of the latent strength of the United States. Thus what the United Kingdom desired in effect was little less than the mobilisation of the American war potential. Some at least of the procurement programmes formulated in the latter part of 1940 in consultation with the Administration went far beyond British needs in the narrow sense. The American ten-division scheme, theoretically a supplement to British supplies, had in reality much more to do with the equipping of the American Army. It is highly doubtful whether the Royal Air Force would have known what to do with a monthly increment of 3,000 American aircraft, if it had ever received so many. In point of fact United States deliveries of aircraft never at any time during the war exceeded the 1,000 a month for which provision had been made under the earlier contracts, so that in a sense cash procurement had here succeeded in its object, although from 1942 onwards most of the deliveries had to be paid for out of Lend-Lease funds. A large part of the proposed 3,000 did indeed appear later on in British theatres of war, but with American crews.

Now the mobilisation of the munitions industries of a foreign country by means of ordinary commercial contracts was an intrinsically impossible task. It was not solely a question of finance. True, the exhaustion of British dollar resources was the proximate cause of the breakdown of cash procurement. But even if funds had been inexhaustible the system could not have continued very much longer, if its larger objectives were to be attained. The practical difficulties were too great. For one thing, at every stage in the process of supply, from the making of the first enquiries to the shipment of the finished goods, British purchasers had to win the consent of the United States

Administration. Failure in this at any point might nullify their whole efforts. They would approach a firm only to find that it had been earmarked for a War Department contract. They would bring negotiations to the point of finality with a firm outside the War Department's orbit (and so probably second-rate), and the project would be vetoed on the ground that the area in question was already overloaded with defence contracts and short of suitable labour. A contract would be placed, and the supplier would be unable to secure plant or material because other firms with United States rearmament orders received priority. Machine tools would be delivered for export to Britain and the Administration would claim them for some other purpose.

Moreover, the negotiations of contracts was only a part, and not the most important part, of the organisation of munitions supply on a grand scale. It was also necessary to see that the contracts were executed efficiently and in good time. Many of the contractors were wholly inexperienced in munitions work, and in some cases the choice of firms, restricted as it was by the competition of United States rearmament, was not very happy. Notable examples were contracts for 9.2-inch howitzer shell and for the 75-mm. guns required for General Grant tanks. The British Purchasing Commission was much stronger on the commercial than on the production side. It was staffed at the outset largely by American business men. Some of the Purchasing Agents had engineering and other technical qualifications; and the Commission was loaned the services of a few British production experts, and could enlist the help of the military Inspection Department. But in general the available expert knowledge of manufacturing processes and of the planning of production was quite insufficient for a proper watch to be kept over the fulfilment of contracts.

'Progressing' was not merely a technical matter. It involved such questions as the acquisition of machine tools, lengthening of the hours of work, introduction of double and treble shifts. It was far from easy for foreign missions to intervene in such matters, though on occasion they did intervene, and not without success. But still larger issues were involved. By the end of 1940 British procurement plans were of such magnitude that when put into effect they would affect the whole economic life of the United States. Entire industries, such as the aviation and machine tool industries, had to be reorganised and expanded. Others, in particular the great automobile firms, had to be diverted in considerable measure out of their normal courses. The supply of the raw materials vital to munitions production, such as alloy steel, aluminium and copper, had to be safeguarded and their use controlled. Labour had to be trained for novel tasks. There was a risk of demand inflation stemming from the sudden prosperity of American heavy industries. These, of course, were problems quite outside the compass of purchasing missions, however large and efficient. Their solution required, as the solution of similar problems was requiring in the United Kingdom, the whole energies of a major part of the administration of the State, with all its apparatus of persuasion and enforcement. The United States Administration was beginning to grapple with these difficulties. But, so long as a great part of the procurement which gave rise to them was carried on independently and outside its immediate control, its task was unduly complicated. Hence the demand which the Administration had pressed since the beginning of British purchasing, for close liaison and for early and complete disclosure of contracts negotiated and planned. But liaison and information were not enough. A vast amount of time and effort could obviously be saved and much confusion averted if the Administration were itself to take over the whole business of procurement on behalf of the British and their Allies, and treat it as an integral part of its own defence programme.

Other considerations pointed the same way. It was wasteful, for example, to have separate inspection and proof facilities, at least, so far as stores of 'common' type were concerned. United States Departments could arrange for the transport of material from factory to port much more easily than could the British mission. Moreover, the wider the range of supplies under a single control, the more flexible could be the arrangements. If one contractor failed, the more urgent needs could be met from the deliveries of another who was ahead of schedule. Now there were during the cash purchase period, some releases to the British of material produced under United States Government contracts, replaced later from British contracts; but these were always the result of delicate and often protracted negotiations at the highest level. In the summer of 1941 both 'British' and 'American' contractors were ready to start assembling tanks, but both were held up, the one by a shortfall of transmissions and armament, the other for lack of armour plate. Arrangements to make good British deficiencies from 'American' sources and vice versa required considerable discussion, a joint committee and the appointment by Presidential decree of a special 'co-ordinator'. If both groups of contracts had been the responsibility of the United States Ordnance Department from the start, the necessary adjustments would have been a matter of simple routine.

It is noteworthy that some weeks before the idea of Lend-Lease as a quasi-financial measure had germinated, the essential features of its procurement aspect were already a part of the thinking of United States Government officials. At a meeting in the Pentagon on 4th November 1940, the British representatives were told that the War

Department wanted to give practical and positive assistance to the British munitions programme. Hitherto the best that could be hoped for had been acquiescence – 'no objection'. Now, it was suggested, many important Government facilities, such as production control, inspection, proof transport and distribution, would be placed at the disposal of the British. As far as the orders required for the implementation of the ten-division programme were concerned, once London had settled types and quantities, the British Purchasing Commission would have nothing to do except sign the formal contracts. The War Department would select the firms, arrange for the creation of new facilities where they were needed, and supervise production. The orders would be handled as part of the Department's own programme; and, a very important point, it was agreed that deliveries to the British might not necessarily come from the contracts which they had themselves signed. Administratively, it was a very short step from the system here outlined to the eventual structure of Lend-Lease procurement, though its extension to programmes in which the United States authorities had a less direct interest than they had in the ten-division scheme, and in particular to the procurement of 'non-common' stores, came rather less naturally.

CHAPTER III

LEND-LEASE PROCUREMENT

(i)

The Lend-Lease Machinery

INSTITUTIONS AND PRINCIPLES

O N 11TH MARCH 1941, President Roosevelt signed an 'Act to Promote the Defence of the United States', whereby he was empowered by the Congress 'to sell, transfer title to, exchange, lease, lend or otherwise dispose of ... any defence article' to 'the government of any country whose defence (he) deems vital to the defence of the United States'.[1] These words implied, amongst other things, a revolutionary change in the methods of British procurement. In this respect, indeed, the passing of the Lend-Lease Act was a more decisive event than Pearl Harbour. As a result of America's entry into the war, munitions assignment and combined planning were superimposed upon the procurement process; but the process itself continued, not indeed unchanged, but with a recognisable identity, from March 1941 until August 1945, and can therefore be treated as a single theme.

Lend-Lease being a phenomenon without precedent in the history of international relations, its advent naturally gave rise to many problems and perplexities, which neither the first bold outline sketched by the President nor even the terms of the Act itself wholly resolved. What kinds of supply would it cover? Under what terms and conditions would they be furnished, and how repaid? How were the recipient countries to be prevented from abusing the privileges accorded them, without the introduction of rigidities which would go far to defeat the Act's purpose? But apart from these questions of high policy, which have been discussed in *North American Supply*,[2] Lend-Lease posed formidable administrative problems – far more formidable than any one had realised before the Act was passed. There was no blueprint to the machinery of this novel system. Its construction, modification, testing and 'running in' occupied the

---

[1] The text of the Lend-Lease Act is appended to *North American Supply, op. cit.*
[2] Ibid., Chapter VIII. See also, *History of the Second World War, United Kingdom Civil Series*, W. K. Hancock and M. M. Gowing, *British War Economy*, Chapter IX.

whole of the remainder of 1941, and were not even then altogether completed.

The basic idea was essentially simple. The British missions would stand aside from the actual business of procurement. They would say what supplies were needed, and the regular purchasing agencies of the United States Government would do the rest, choosing sources of supply, negotiating and signing contracts, supervising their fulfilment, paying for the finished goods and handing them over for shipment. These agencies were five in number. There were the War and Navy Departments, which, like the British Admiralty but unlike the War Office or the Air Ministry, had retained the functions of procurement, and which were to supply all the main military and naval Lend-Lease stores. In addition, the Navy Department, as the largest user, controlled purchases of petroleum, and the War Department's Ordnance Corps handled the procurement of machine tools. Merchant shipping was the responsibility of the Maritime Commission.[1] The Department of Agriculture was to procure food and tobacco, and also cotton and certain other raw materials, such as rosin and turpentine, which were classed as 'naval stores'. Finally there was the Procurement Division of the Treasury, a general purchasing agency which for Lend-Lease purposes handled metals and minerals, timber and most other raw materials, as well as civilian and some minor military manufactured products.

Lend-Lease, however, was far more than a matter of simple procurement. It was intimately connected with foreign policy and with military strategy; it profoundly affected the economic life of the country, and it was a very delicate issue in domestic politics. It could not therefore be left entirely to the several supply agencies to handle as they thought fit. Moreover, the Act made the President himself directly responsible for its administration. It was to him, and not to the procurement agencies, that the funds which were the life-blood of Lend-Lease were appropriated. He, and not the departmental chiefs, had to report to the Congress on their disposal. It was therefore judged necessary to set over against the executive departments some special organisation under the direct control of the President to keep watch on the development of Lend-Lease as a whole, administer the funds and secure a uniform interpretation of the provisions of the Act. Several proposals were canvassed, mostly variants on the theme of a 'Cabinet Supply Policy Committee' consisting of the Secretaries of War, the Navy and the Treasury.[2] Such schemes, however, were doomed to failure. It cannot be too often emphasised that the United States neither possessed at the start nor

---

[1] From 1942 onwards, the War Shipping Administration.
[2] U.S. Bureau of the Budget, *The United States at War* (Washington: War Records Section, Bureau of the Budget), Chapter III.

succeeded in developing during the course of the Second World War a system of cabinet control remotely resembling that which has been established for over two centuries in Britain. A 'Cabinet Supply Policy Committee' was perhaps foreign to the American system of government. It was certainly foreign to the ideas of President Roosevelt, who preferred to keep the final responsibility in his own hands, appointing special aides and executives as new problems arose. So it was for rearmament and all the aspects of the war effort, and so also for Lend-Lease. In this case there were special reasons at work. Lend-Lease was his own creation, and in its working he took a keen personal interest, over and above that which was demanded by his statutory responsibilities. A very marked degree of direct presidential supervision was thus a feature of the first phase of Lend-Lease administration. Though some sort of delegation was clearly necessary, it was significantly to Mr Harry L. Hopkins, now the President's closest associate, that the delegation was made.

Hopkins, just back from his first visit to England and full of the enthusiasm for the British cause which that visit had helped to kindle, set about his new task with energy and determination, as his biography has amply shown. He worked at first in an informal way, with a small staff drawn mainly from that of the President's Liaison Committee, which was now dissolved. But before many weeks had passed it became evident that the work was more complex and exacting than anyone had imagined; and at the beginning of May his office was given a formal constitution as the 'Division of Defence Aid Reports',[1] and an executive officer, Major-General James H. Burns, was appointed to organise its routine and handle matters of detail. The name suggests that the collection of data for the three-monthly reports to Congress was what the President chiefly had in mind. But in point of fact the functions of the division were much wider than this. As soon became apparent, they were much larger than, as then organised, it could efficiently handle, and in August 1941, there came a further change. Hopkins now withdrew, and the division was placed under the direction of Mr Edward R. Stettinius, Jr., who thus entered on the international career which was to have its climax at San Francisco in 1945. On 28th October it was again reconstituted as the Office of Lend-Lease Administration (O.L.L.A.). These changes were undoubtedly beneficial. The new organisation had greater authority and a higher status than the old – from 'division' to 'office' was a long step up the Washington hierarchy. It was also a gain to have the administration in the hands of one less trammelled with other cares than Hopkins had been, while the advantage of being able to enlist the aid of so influential and

---

[1] A division, that is, of the Office of Emergency Management, the insubstantial matrix from which most of the war-time agencies derived their constitutional origin.

sympathetic a statesman was not lost, since Hopkins retained the right to be consulted on matters of high policy.

The Office of Lend-Lease Administration continued in being and under the same direction for nearly two years. During that period, however, there had been a proliferation of other agencies concerned with the economic aspects of American foreign policy. The Board (later Office) of Economic Warfare had always had a separate existence. An Office of Foreign Relief and Rehabilitation Organisation had been set up to consider the problems later handled by the United Nations Relief and Rehabilitation Administration (U.N.R.R.A.). There was the Foreign Purchasing Department of the Commodity Credit Corporation. The State Department, almost wholly excluded from the administration of Lend-Lease, had set up its own Office of Foreign Economic Co-ordination. It seemed good to the Administration, therefore, that all these bodies should be tied together with O.L.L.A. in a single organisation, more especially as the connexion of Lend-Lease with post-war foreign policy was becoming steadily clearer. This was accomplished in September 1943, by the establishment of the Foreign Economic Administration (F.E.A.) under Mr Leo T. Crowley, Mr Stettinius having taken up the post of Under-Secretary of State.

The main functions of the successive bodies which administered Lend-Lease were: to see that the funds provided by Congress were not overdrawn and that they were duly replenished from time to time; to decide whether individual supplies requested by the British or other foreign claimants were or were not eligible for Lend-Lease treatment; and to serve as the recipient countries' advocate before the authorities which controlled the sources of war supplies. Of the fiscal problems we shall have occasion to speak later. The question of eligibility was at first fairly simple. The Act itself had defined the phrase 'defence article' in terms so wide as hardly to constitute a definition at all;[1] and O.L.L.A. showed itself concerned to interpret its authority in the most generous manner possible. Not merely war material in the more obvious senses but anything which could be shown to be necessary to the war effort of the British Commonwealth or to the maintenance of a reasonable standard of life for its peoples, was judged eligible for supply on Lend-Lease terms. Raw materials,[2] petroleum, and food were included and so were tobacco, and beer for the troops in the Middle East, and electric light bulbs, and tractors for farmers in the United Kingdom and the Dominions, and type-writers and so on indefinitely. Freight charges and the costs of storage in the United States were rather more contentious, but these questions

---

[1] Section 2 listed various things, such as ships and munitions, that were to be so regarded and concluded with the words '. . . or any other article for defence'.

[2] Including Cuban molasses, and hemp and timber from the Philippines, and the refining in the United States of copper ores from the Congo.

too were eventually settled in a manner very favourable to Britain. In the first two years of Lend-Lease exception was taken only to requirements which appeared to have but a very tenuous connexion with the war. Such, for example, were requests for the supply of civilian goods to Britain's colonies far removed from theatres of operations. Over these a large question-mark hung for a long period. Constructional steel for Malaya (before the Japanese attack) seemed to O.L.L.A. much less clearly essential than constructional steel for the United Kingdom. Early in 1942 part of a requisition for oil to be supplied to Nigeria was definitely rejected; but it was not until the spring of 1943 that the general principle was settled. O.L.L.A. then ruled that products for direct military use in such territories were eligible, whilst raw materials for incorporation in military products, together with equipment for the production of strategic raw materials, would be considered on their merits. But goods for civilian uses not directly connected with the war effort would be excluded from Lend-Lease. This was a blow to the British Government; it desired for reasons both strategic and political to keep the population of the colonies contented and efficient; it could not afford dollars for purchase in the United States, and it was unable to maintain its own normal exports. But the action was hardly unreasonable from the American point of view.

The only other class of supplies whose eligibility was doubtful was capital equipment of a permanent nature, particularly when postwar advantage to Britain was combined with a possible detriment to American interests. Thus the British Supply Council strongly advised London not to proceed with a request for plant and material needed for the expansion of the Abadan oil refinery.[1] Similarly, O.L.L.A. would not extend the benefits of Lend-Lease to the steel plate required by the gold mines of the Rand, although both Pretoria and London insisted that the production of gold was an essential war-time activity in that it helped the sterling countries to pay for supplies outside the United States. But there was always difficulty in making clear in Washington the nature of the Sterling Area. Since she was a large producer of gold and was not living as austerely as some other members of the Commonwealth, South Africa's claims on Lend-Lease were always more difficult to uphold; and at the beginning of 1943 the American authorities ruled that South Africa must pay for all civilian supplies.

About this time there was a noticeable change in the general

---

[1] There seems to have been a tendency in London to take Lend-Lease a little too much for granted, for the North American Supply Committee had to ask Departments for a more rigorous scrutiny of requests at source, in order to prevent those which might be politically damaging from going forward. It has to be remembered that behind all particular cases lay the all important long-term problems of the balance of payments between the sterling and the dollar areas. See *North American Supply, op. cit.*, Chapters VII and XI.

climate of Lend-Lease administration. The cause was political. It
was closely related to the problem of securing a renewal of the Lend-
Lease Act and a fresh Lend-Lease appropriation from a Congress
whose composition had not been improved, from the Administration's point of view, by the mid-term elections. The only important
actual change, however, for the time being was the exclusion of
tobacco, other than that supplied to the armed forces. Despite
O.L.L.A's anxieties the Act extending Lend-Lease for a further year
was duly passed by the House of Representatives in May 1943, with
only four irreconcilables against it, and by the Senate without a
dissentient vote. None the less, the situation continued to deteriorate,
a more and more restrictive view being taken of eligibility as time
went on. The unpopularity of Lend-Lease was growing, as the
American consumer began to feel the pinch of war more sharply and
the American trader began to worry about his post-war markets.
And at the same time the Administration could point to a rise in
British gold and dollar balances. Actually the reserves then stood at
about $1,000 million. Against them were outstanding liabilities of
$7,000 million. Moreover, the reserves belonged to the whole of the
Sterling Area; but the liabilities were Britain's debts. In October
1943, the Foreign Economic Administration announced that after
15th November Lend-Lease requisitions would no longer be accepted
for five classes of supplies: 'projects of a permanent nature', machine
tools, portable electric and pneumatic tools, industrial equipment
generally, and machinery or materials used in the production or
refining of petroleum. The special mention of this last obnoxious
item betrayed the political motive, which F.E.A., indeed, made no
attempt to hide but rather paraded as its justification. London took
strong exception to the manner of the proposal, which was presented
as a decision, British concurrence not being sought. But it did not take
their substance tragically. It was on the whole in the British interest
to revert to cash purchase of machine tools, and the other items did
not constitute a very heavy charge. The total cost was at first reckoned
at only $50–100 million in a full year, though later estimates ranged
as high as $400 million – about one-tenth of all non-military supplies.
Nor were there many further additions to the list of supplies which
were to be excluded on principle. But, if the main outlines of Lend-
Lease eligibility held firm between November 1943, and the final
collapse which has been described at the end of *North American Supply*,
there was a steady whittling away of individual items. Whereas in
the first two years or so of operation the development of case-law
had in the main broadened the concept of Lend-Lease, now it
worked wholly in the reverse direction. F.E.A. began to scrutinise
requests for aid more closely, questioning not merely the strict
eligibility of supplies, but also their necessity. The British Missions

thus found that they had to furnish ever fuller and more cogent justifications of their claims, if they were to stand a chance of success.

Even in the days when eligibility was rarely called in question, the administrators of Lend-Lease had always insisted on being provided with full evidence of the British case for assistance. In May 1941, the British Purchasing Commission warned London that cabled 'demands' would have to be accompanied not merely by practical details such as the precise specifications and estimated value of the stores required but also by a statement of the main purpose for which they were intended. This was not at first a very onerous task, as a statement in general terms sufficed. There was, however, the complication that O.L.L.A. insisted on all supplies being labelled either 'direct military' or 'essential civilian'. In practice the distinction was often difficult or impossible to make. The British could not guarantee in advance, for example, that such and such drugs would be administered only to soldiers, nor was it desirable that they should attempt to do so; it would hardly be argued that the Prime Minister's recovery from pneumonia was less vital to the British war effort than that of Pte. Atkins, T. Indeed, O.L.L.A. frankly admitted that they could not suggest how the distinction was to be made, and left it to the British to decide; all they wanted was 'a record to quote'. Mr Stettinius emphasised – all the evidence, from his own book downwards, supports him – that the demand for justification and documentation of British requirements did not arise out of any desire on the part of O.L.L.A. to be finicky or obstructive, but from the fact that in 1941 and again towards the end of the war, Congress and the public were acutely sensitive to any misuse of Lend-Lease funds. Any suspicion that O.L.L.A. was being too free and easy with the British would, he urged, gravely damage both it and them, since it would make the replenishment of the funds more difficult. Moreover, O.L.L.A. had to defend British requirements not only to Congress but also to those who actually made the supplies available and who, being themselves rival claimants upon a limited volume of production, had a strong interest in keeping British supplies to the minimum. The advocate, in fact, had to be briefed if he was to do his job.

Sensitivity to public criticism of possible misuse of Lend-Lease funds also produced rulings which caused the British Government a great deal of trouble in the first year or two of Lend-Lease. One was the insistence of O.L.L.A. that the British Government should not seem to make money out of Lend-Lease supplies by 'selling' them to the public. This took the form of a rule that such goods should not pass out of Government ownership or at least out of strict Government control, at any stage before they reached the final consumer. The second, which was a variant of the first, related to raw materials supplied under Lend-Lease. Obviously in the case of raw materials used in the production of goods for the use of consumers in the United Kingdom, the ordinary channels of distribution had to be used. The real complication arose in connection with the raw material content of goods exported from the United Kingdom. The Administration was particularly sensitive to any charge that raw materials supplied under Lend-Lease were aiding British exports with the implication of unfairness to American exporters.[1] The raising of these problems resulted in a wider expansion in the United Kingdom of Government procurement and detailed control than would otherwise have been necessary to avoid wasteful use of materials. This represented a diversion of administrative time and energy which could be ill afforded at the height of the war.

The pressure of American public opinion on the Administration was heaviest in the last two years of the war because civilian supplies, from beef to lorry tyres and from shoe leather to coal-mining machinery, had become generally scarce in the United States, and because, while military supplies were relatively plentiful, there was a strong demand for the reconversion of munitions plants. It was impossible that the American consumer should not reflect that rationing would have been unnecessary but for the vast shipments of free food to Britain, and that if the British were not still demanding guns he could soon be buying refrigerators again.[2] It was hard to convince him that the British were not taking advantage of American munitions supplies to begin building up their civilian economy and their export trade ahead of time. Elements hostile to Britain exploited the situation to the full. Certain politicians and sections of the Press went to great pains to ferret out every British action which could possibly be interpreted as a misuse of Lend-Lease supplies. Such attacks could only be countered if the Administration were in a position to explain in circumstantial detail the reasons for every request which it granted. The documentation of British requirements thus increased to such an extent that it became a very heavy burden both upon the British missions in Washington and on the Ministries in London.

These none the less co-operated, not without grumbling, as best they could. On certain points, however, they took a firm stand against activities of O.L.L.A. which seemed to them to exceed its proper functions. Thus in the period when shipping was extremely

---

[1] On these matters see pp. 247-8 of this volume and *North American Supply, op. cit.*, pp. 295-296, 444-445, etc. For a more detailed discussion see Chapters VII and VIII in *History of the Second World War, United Kingdom Civil Series*, E. L. Hargreaves and M. M. Gowing, *Civil Industry and Trade*.

[2] Wisely, the British did not proceed with a request for half a million civilian wireless sets, despite the strength of their case in the abstract. At the time no such sets were being made for American consumers.

scarce, in 1942 and the early months of 1943, O.L.L.A. not infrequently questioned whether the supplies requested could actually be shipped, with the implication that if there were any doubt on the matter the requisition ought not to go forward. Now the British argued firmly and successfully against the thesis that production of military equipment on their behalf in the United States should be governed by shipping forecasts. (An exception was made for vehicles, which are unusually bulky in relation to their value and can be economically stowed only in ships of special design.) It was pointed out that the forecasts were notoriously unreliable, and that, since munitions were only a small portion of the total lift, even a small error in the forecast could make a big difference to the volume of stores that could be transported. Deplorable as it would be to have equipment piling up uselessly on the quays, it would be still more deplorable to cut back production and then have to send ships away half empty. Quite apart from this general argument, however, the British insisted that it was for the shipping authorities and not for O.L.L.A., which had no expertise in the matter, to decide whether supplies were eligible in this sense. They also protested strongly against an occasional refusal by O.L.L.A. to approve the supply of material which, according to a combined planning decision, was to be made in the United States rather than in Britain.

PROCEDURES

Even in the difficult later phases of the war, however, the great majority of British requirements were judged eligible for Lend-Lease without serious question. There was hardly ever any doubt about munitions proper, and rarely any about the supply of raw materials or food (except a few items procured from outside the United States, such as Icelandic fish and Caribbean sugar) to the United Kingdom, as distinct from some other Commonwealth countries. Decisions about eligibility, in short, did not have a really serious effect upon the volume of Lend-Lease supply at any time, and in the early stages they had hardly any. A far graver difficulty in the first year or so of Lend-Lease was the sheer mechanical complication of the new system, the interposition of a whole set of new procedures between the customer and the ultimate sources of supply.

British requirements were notified as before to the appropriate mission in Washington by its parent Ministry in London, generally by cable. From the mission they were passed to the Central Requirements Section of the British Supply Council (the new federal organisation which had been superimposed on the missions in December 1940), and filed in the form of a Lend-Lease 'requisition' with the Division of Defence Aid Reports. The latter, having satisfied itself about the content of the requisition, routed it to the appropriate supply department. This was not, however, the first that the department had heard of the matter. Many, if not most, requisitions implemented piece by piece the main Lend-Lease programme which had been submitted to and agreed with the departments concerned before the Appropriation Bill had been drawn up. Even when they represented entirely fresh demands the first step was always to discuss them with officials of the departments; and only when supply was found to be *prima facie* feasible and acceptable was the matter referred to the Division of Defence Aid Reports. Thus the arrival of the formal requisition served, as one official put it, 'as a record rather than a needle', and its approval, if not assured, could at least be presumed.

There remained, however, one final serious obstacle to be surmounted before procurement could begin. In the first few months approval by the Division of Defence Aid Reports did not carry with it an automatic release of Lend-Lease funds. For this, each requisition had to be sent to the White House, where a letter instructing the Treasury to allocate the necessary money was signed by the President with his own hand. Only then was the requisition released to the actual buying offices of the procurement agencies so that contract action could be taken. Mr Roosevelt's signature was again required for the transfer directive which was drawn up when the stores were ready or nearly ready to be handed over. And when he was away from Washington, the papers simply accumulated on his desk. This was clearly to reduce the principle of presidential control over the operation of Lend-Lease to an absurdity. In June an attempt was made to improve the position by setting up small revolving funds which the departments could use to cover the most urgent of the requisitions, but this was hardly more than a palliative.

The new system, indispensable as it had become, had very serious disadvantages. In ceasing to pay for their supplies the British had lost the right to determine what those supplies should be. Before a 'defence aid' contract could be placed they had to win the approval of a series of American authorities. Nor did the placing of such a contract give them any more than a presumptive interest in the material produced. Only when a transfer directive had been signed was the material in any sense 'theirs', and even then, as the immediate sequel of Pearl Harbour was to show,[1] they could not be sure of possession until it was safely on the high seas.

In a sense, all this merely formalised a situation which had existed in practice before the new procedure came into effect. But in addition the British now lost, in theory at least, all contact with the progress of 'their' supplies between the acceptance of a requisition and the notification of transfer. It was a fundamental principle of Lend-Lease procurement that the British missions should have no dealings

---

[1] See below, p. 171.

of any kind with the manufacturers. How rigidly this rule was observed depended on the individual department. The Procurement Division of the Treasury, having at the outset no machinery of its own for the following up of contracts, could not but connive at some progressing by the British Purchasing Commission, which was in fact allowed to establish an elaborate liaison section for this purpose inside the Treasury's buying offices. Moreover, the Treasury invariably placed a separate contract for each Lend-Lease requisition, so that progress was easy to watch. With the War and Navy Departments matters were much more difficult. It was not merely that these departments rigidly excluded the British from direct contact with the suppliers. There was the additional complication that they could make equipment available in three different ways – by placing a specific contract on behalf of the British, by releasing it from stocks, or by diverting deliveries off their own ordinary contacts. Information even about the progress of the special contracts, though promised, was provided only slowly and irregularly at first; and the British were for some time almost completely in the dark about the supplies which they might expect to receive from other sources. In July 1941, they elicited a general statement of the allocations of war material which the War Department intended to make to them over the course of the next year, but only in very provisional terms. Such uncertainty was, of course, a grave handicap to the military and production planners in London, as well as to the shipping authorities, and was calculated to discourage the British Government from making full use of its American arsenal.

Above all, the new system in its experimental phase in 1941 meant serious delay. There were, to begin with, the delays occasioned by the clearance procedure which had to be gone through before procurement could even start. The Division of Defence Aid Reports, whose staff was small and in the main inexperienced, was in itself a narrow bottleneck where requisitions often stuck. There were the delays over the allocation of funds. And there were still more serious delays within the supply departments. The actual process of procurement, after all the special Lend-Lease preliminaries had been completed, was very slow and cumbrous in the period before Pearl Harbour. Lend-Lease, it has to be remembered, was a heavy additional burden upon hard-pressed American agencies which, designed only to provide the modest needs of the federal government of a free-enterprise and pacific country, were now grappling with the huge task of putting the defences of that country hurriedly into order. Treasury Procurement, for example, had never been intended to carry responsibilities remotely resembling in volume or variety those which devolved upon it in 1941. The War and Navy Departments were better prepared, but their more elaborate organisation carried with it a more complex and protracted routine. A 'flow chart', mapping out the course of a Lend-Lease requisition through the War Department mill, listed sixteen separate stages. The Departments were operating at more or less peace-time tempos and with peace-time procedures. Their new clients might be at war, but they were not. It was a general rule of the United States Administration that supplies should be bought by open tender. This procedure, better adapted to prevent corruption than to permit speedy action, was carried on occasion to extreme lengths; one contract was believed to have been put out for tender by the Navy Department to a hundred and twenty-five firms. Again, it must be recorded that officials of the supply departments were, as individuals, no more unanimously in favour of Lend-Lease than was the American public at large. There is, of course, no suggestion here of deliberate wrecking – only of a fairly prevalent feeling that Lend-Lease business was a somewhat unwelcome addition to the main task of strengthening America's defences and could properly be relegated to a secondary place.

Matters would have been relatively simple if Lend-Lease assistance could have been confined to the supply of the major weapons of war. But it was not and could not be so confined. Even on the military side there was a growing tendency to extend the range of American aid, to ask, often with great urgency, for a host of miscellaneous minor stores, each requiring individual attention. It was hoped, for example, that the United States would furnish a large part of the supplies, ranging from workshop machinery to typewriter ribbons, which were required for the establishment of a great military base in non-industrial Egypt. And besides military equipment the British needed, and the Lend-Lease system had to handle, much that had hitherto been purchased, if at all, through commercial channels – not only raw materials, petroleum and food, but also industrial equipment of an infinite variety and a great complex of civilian goods which were essential to the efficiency and the minimum well-being of the Army and people. These miscellaneous needs inflated the numbers of individual requisitions to unmanageable proportions and were the cause of at least ninety per cent. of the difficulties of the transition period. To prevent the system from foundering altogether under the weight of petty orders, an administrative rule was laid down at an early stage that requisitions for stores worth less than $1,000 should not be submitted or accepted. But the complexities of the Lend-Lease procedure were such that British supply officers were sorely tempted to cut through the whole tangle by reverting to cash purchase even for larger orders. In view of the parlous state of British finances this was a temptation that had generally to be severely repressed, at any rate until the last eighteen months or so of the war. On the other hand, the British would not accept the converse ruling that all items worth more than $1,000 must be procured through Lend-Lease. The retention of the optional cash purchase route was essential to the flexibility of the system.

The transition from cash to Lend-Lease procurement was particularly arduous in the case of raw materials, both because United States government agencies were not accustomed to buying these in bulk, as the War Department was accustomed to buying munitions, and because most of them had not hitherto been handled by the British missions. We saw in the previous chapter how the British Purchasing Commission secured control over the purchase of iron and steel, and of copper. But other materials continued to be procured through the most diverse channels. Zinc, rubber, wood-pulp, hemp, ferro-alloys and molasses were bought by the relevant Ministry of Supply Controllers, sometimes through their agents in the United States, sometimes through the producers' agents in London. Other materials were still bought by the trade in the usual way, though in some cases the buyers had been organised into special groups such as the Newsprint Supply Company. The Liverpool Cotton Association was still functioning normally in 1940. Sometimes, as in the case of abrasives and phosphate rock, the American producers and the British users were under the same ownership. For sulphur and for carbon black the users had arrangements of long standing with monopoly export corporations. The marshalling of all this activity into the strait path of Lend-Lease, involving some extension of government control at home and the incorporation of the Controllers' agents within the framework of the British supply organisation in America, naturally took some time to complete. It was not fully accomplished until after the setting up of the British Raw Materials Mission in January 1942. From then on until 1945 practically all the raw materials supplied from the United States were furnished under Lend-Lease. But the majority of those supplied in 1941 were paid for in cash. In part, of course, this fact merely reflects the time-lag between the placing of a contract and the export of material, but administrative difficulties also helped to retard the transfer to Lend-Lease.

The case of iron and steel was particularly instructive. Here there was no special difficulty on the British side, since procurement was already centralised in the British Purchasing Commission. None the less it was some months before the transition to inter-governmental supply was accomplished. First of all there was some dispute as to whether Lend-Lease steel should be bought by Treasury Procurement or the Navy Department; and only when this had been settled in favour of the Treasury could the first requisition, for a million tons of carbon steel, be submitted. This was on 19th April 1941. The Division of Defence Aid Reports raised no objection on the score of eligibility, but it was not until 7th May that the Presidential letter allocating funds was signed and the requisition released to the Treasury. Three days later the Treasury sent out its invitations to bid, and by about the end of the month all the tenders were in. The next stage requires further explanation. The five procurement agencies and the Division of Defence Aid Reports were not the only bodies interested in Lend-Lease supplies. In setting up the National Defence Advisory Commission in 1940 the President had reversed the earlier plan of leaving industrial mobilisation in the hands of the Services. Instead the various problems of preparedness and later of the war economy were entrusted to a series of *ad hoc* bodies, of which the more important were the Office of Production Management and its war-time successor the War Production Board. These agencies performed functions somewhat analogous to those of the British Ministry of Production plus the Raw Materials Department of the Ministry of Supply, although, chiefly because of the lack of a Cabinet system, the analogy was no more than approximate and in some ways misleading. They supervised and co-ordinated but they did not place contracts. From 1943 onwards they allocated materials and scheduled the various production programmes. But in 1941 and 1942 their main instrument was the awarding of priority ratings, and even this function they delegated, in respect of military equipment, to a Service body, the Army-Navy Munitions Board. The demarcation of powers between themselves and the Services was, in fact, a matter of prolonged and at times bitter controversy which never received a fully satisfactory solution. On the non-military side of the war economy, however, their supremacy was much less open to question. Treasury Procurement was a procurement agency pure and simple; it had no great interests of its own to defend, as had the War and Navy Departments. Thus in respect of raw materials, machinery and other non-military Lend-Lease supplies, it was not so much the Treasury's approval as that of the Office of Production Management or the War Production Board which had to be won. These bodies were vitally affected, since they had to consider the effect that Lend-Lease contracts would have upon the other production programmes, including the supply of essential goods and services to the American domestic economy. Nor would such contracts have much chance of making progress without a priority rating from O.P.M. Thus all requisitions had to be approved by that body before a contract could be placed.

As mentioned above the tenders for the first Lend-Lease requirements for steel were all in by the end of May 1941. On 4th June the Treasury forwarded a summary of them to the Office of Production Management. Here there was a further delay while the latter was being persuaded that it was no part of its functions to check the eligibility of a Lend-Lease requisition – it had been attempting to analyse the orders in detail in order to satisfy itself that all the steel was required for military uses. The net result of all this was that three months after the signature of the Lend-Lease Act no Lend-Lease contracts had been placed for steel, and it seemed unlikely that any could come forward until August at the earliest. In order to keep up a flow of the more urgently needed types of steel, such as drop forgings, the British had been obliged to place further cash contracts. The only way they could finance these was by the cancellation of longer-term orders for ordinary steel, and as a result the tonnage of steel coming forward fell so sharply that a gap of at least a quarter of a million tons between the shipping programme and the supplies available was forecast for the end of July. This was a serious matter, because it was during the summer months that the Ministry of Shipping liked to move the bulk of this, its heaviest and most awkward cargo.

Altogether, there was every sign, after a few months of Lend-Lease, that the machinery was becoming dangerously clogged. By the early autumn of 1941 the Division of Defence Aid Reports had on its hands no less than twelve hundred uncleared requisitions. The interval between the submission of a requisition and the placing of a War Department contract was generally in the neighbourhood of three months, and the record of the other departments was little better. For this reason among others the results of Lend-Lease were for some time very disappointing. There was no special cause for dismay in the fact that up to the end of 1941, whereas $12,900 million had been appropriated for Lend-Lease purposes, the value of goods transferred and services rendered was only just over $1,000 million; the provision of finance could not be expected to show immediate results in the form of completed war material. What was disturbing was the fact that considerably less than half the money provided, $5,900 million to be precise, had yet been put to work. $1,800 million had not been allocated to departments; the rest had been allocated, but had not yet been 'obligated', that is to say committed for payment to suppliers in respect of firm contracts. The War Department alone, on 23rd December 1941, had over $3,000 million of Lend-Lease money thus in reserve.

It is not to be supposed that the defects were all on the American side. Both departments in London and the British missions in the United States had to feel their way into the unfamiliar procedure just as had the American authorities. London had to learn, for example, that vague enquiries about the possibility of supply, unsatisfactory enough in the days of cash purchase, would get nowhere at all under the new system; the only way to find out whether the supply of a particular type of material was feasible was to submit a requisition for a specific quantity and see what happened to it.[1] Officials of the missions had to adapt themselves to a new kind of activity, more diplomatic than commercial, in which the 'selling' of a requisition to a government department took the place of the buying of supplies. They had to make and consolidate innumerable contacts with their American counterparts and learn how to make the most of them.[2] Although their personnel grew at a rate sufficient to alarm the British Treasury, the consensus of opinion is that the missions were still, throughout 1941, badly understaffed. The volume of labour was increased rather than diminished by the cessation of contracting (and of course, although few new contracts were placed, the execution of the old ones had still to be supervised). There was far more to the new system than the translation of London's requirements into the form desired by the United States authorities. Supply officers had to be prepared to explain and defend their requisitions (often with far too little information from London to support them), and to 'chase' them from one stage of the procurement machine to the next. It appears that in the latter part of 1941 each of the British Purchasing Commission's supply officers was handling about a hundred requisitions. This was reckoned to be the maximum that could be dealt with efficiently by one man even in the latter part of the war when Lend-Lease procurement had acquired a settled routine. In the experimental conditions of 1941 it was far too heavy a load.

Too much must not be made of these administrative difficulties, which have been described at some length because they form part of an unparalleled development of co-operation between governments. Most of them were mere teething troubles, and the remarkable feature of the period is not the trouble but the achievement. If it still took three months to get a Lend-Lease contract placed, it has to be remembered that in 1940 three months of negotiation had often led to no result whatever. Contracts were being placed, production was growing and American supplies, in slowly but steadily increasing volume, were moving towards the battlefronts. And during the last three or four months of 1941 great improvements were effected in the mechanics of the system. The first step was to clear the most obvious 'bottleneck', the allocation of funds by the President in person. At the end of August the President, anxious to show Congress that Lend-Lease moneys were really on the point of exhaustion, signed a

---

[1] In June 1941, the Ministry of Supply enquired whether the cost of refining Congo copper ores could be borne under Lend-Lease, but only in February 1942, was an actual requisition drawn up. The eight intervening months were time almost wholly lost, for the question of eligibility had then to be re-negotiated with a new set of officials.

[2] Thus they had to learn, to cite a small example, that the word 'demand', even in the semi-technical sense given to it by British supply departments, did not sound sweetly in the ears of Americans who were making available to Britain supplies which, as officials, they knew America needed and which, as taxpayers, they were helping to finance.

'blanket' allocation covering the entire $300 million remaining out of the first appropriation. For the second and all subsequent appropriations the signature of allocations and transfer directives was delegated to the new Lend-Lease Administrator, Mr Stettinius, and this point ceased to give trouble. The establishment of O.L.L.A. also led to a much speedier clearance of requisitions. The procedure was simplified and operated in a less formalistic fashion, so that by early January the number of requisitions uncleared had been reduced from twelve hundred to thirty. The steady accumulation of case-law on eligibility helped to make this part of the process more and more of a swift formality. As for the delays in the actual procurement process, Pearl Harbour was the solvent here. Thereafter the departments had to work fast, and streamline their procedure to that end; and Lend-Lease procurement benefited along with the rest of their work. Thus it may be said that by the end of 1941 the difficult transition period was at an end, and the machine was working smoothly. From then on purely procedural troubles hardly interfered with the flow of war supplies.

Yet the paper work remained formidable enough to necessitate the maintenance of large staffs by the British Commonwealth supply missions. The complications were illustrated by a photostatic collection of Lend-Lease forms which the Australian War Supplies Procurement Mission made in mid-1943. A photograph accompanying the study showed a table covered by the 353 documents weighing 89 lb. which were needed for the procurement of a single lot of automotive spares. The collection reproduced 40 separate and distinct documents involved in Lend-Lease transactions in the following order:

> Incoming Procurement Cable
> Draft Australian Lend-Lease Requisition
> Production Demand
> Official British Lend-Lease Requisition
> Lend-Lease Commitment Letter
> Lend-Lease Requisition Register
> Lend-Lease Transmittal Letter
> War Production Board Application for Priority
> Advance Notice of Treasury Contract
> U.S. Treasury Contract
> Supplier's Mill Report
> Treasury Expediter's Report
> Application for Shipping Instructions
> Ocean Shipping Order
> Consignment Instructions
> B.M.W.T. Space Request
> Forwarding Authorisation
> U.S. Treasury Shipping Instructions

Treasury Bill of Lading
U.S. Navy Store Invoice
Release Note and Certificate
Issue and Receipt Voucher (Navy)
Distribution and Packing Instructions
Supplier's Invoice
Air Corps Depot Shipping Ticket
United Nations Depot Shipping Ticket
Report of Materials Shipped (Navy Air)
Memorandum of Shipment
Lend-Lease Transfer Directive
War Department Bill of Lading
Arrival Notice
War Department Receiving Report
Incoming Tally Sheet
Tally Out Report
Weekly Report of Unallocated Cargo
Allocated Cargo List
War Shipping Administration Dock Receipt
Steamship Company Dock Receipt
Shipper's Export Declaration
Ocean Bill of Lading

(ii)

The Administration and Financing of
Lend-Lease Supply

EARLY FISCAL DIFFICULTIES

The advent of Lend-Lease did not altogether remove the dollar sign from defence. Not merely did the financial embarrassment of the British Government remain acute, in that it had still to find ways and means of paying for deliveries off earlier contracts and for material which, for one reason or another, could not be brought within the framework of the new system, but even within that framework the dollar sign was still very prominent in the early stages. The Act did not give any kind of blank cheque either to the recipient countries or to the Administration. Section 3 (A) 2 began by empowering the President to transfer 'any defence article', but hastened to set limits to his freedom of action. First, the President was not to dispose of any part of the nation's defence equipment without having consulted the Chief of Staff of the Army or the Chief of Naval Operations. Secondly, transfers of equipment 'procured from funds heretofore appropriated' were not to exceed a total value of $1,300 million. This, the so-called Billion-Three provision, was no great matter, for there was nothing like that amount of such equipment available for transfer.

Far more serious was the final sentence of this paragraph, which was an amendment introduced during the passage of the Act and was commonly known by the name of its sponsor, Senator Byrd. This laid down that, 'except to the extent hereafter authorised by the Congress', material procured from ordinary departmental funds appropriated *after* the passage of the Act could not be transferred at all. Therefore, if the Government wished to lend or lease material that was not already in stock or being produced in March 1941, it had to fall back on Section 3 (A) 1, which empowered it to procure defence articles on the especial behalf of Great Britain or other eligible countries, but only 'to the extent to which funds are made available therefor or contracts are authorised from time to time by the Congress'. That was to say, before any new procurement could be initiated for Lend-Lease purposes a separate Appropriation Act had to be passed in which a 'special defence fund' was placed at the President's disposal.

The first of these Appropriation Bills was introduced immediately and duly came into effect on 26th March 1941. It was for $7,000 million. Huge as this sum appeared (it was more than double the entirety of British dollar expenditure to date), it was never intended to be more than a first instalment. The British were told not to worry about finance, to frame their requests in quantitative terms and not to hold back for fear of exhausting the fund too soon. This was encouraging, but with experience of Congressional delays fresh in their minds they could not help but have some hesitation on this score. The very vigour with which the Act was put into effect added to their anxieties; $1,000 million were allocated to departments by the end of April, and by the end of June only about $2,000 million were left. A month earlier, while Hopkins was assuring Purvis that money was no object, at a lower level British officials were being told that certain requisitions could not be proceeded with for lack of funds.

Moreover the distribution of the fund of $7,000 million was hampered by splitting it up into ten separate categories as follows:

		$ *Million*
1.	Ordnance	1,343
2.	Aeronautical material	2,054
3.	Tanks and transport	362
4.	Vessels and marine equipment	629
5.	Miscellaneous military equipment	260
6.	Facilities	752
7.	Agricultural and industrial products	1,350
8.	Repairs, modification, inspection, etc.	200
9.	Services	40
10.	Administrative expenses	10

Now, while the distribution had been influenced by the British

Supply Council's own estimate of requirements, these were not and could not be constant. There was, for example, a steady influx of fresh demands for armoured vehicles and components thereof throughout 1941, so that category 3 was depleted more rapidly than the others. Moreover the appropriation was designed to provide, not for expenditure in any given period, but for deliveries made up to 30th June 1942; and whereas most of the non-military material covered by category 7 was bought only a few weeks or months before it was exported, expenditure on tanks, guns, ships and planes might have to be incurred a year or even eighteen months ahead of delivery. Thus the rate at which the various categories were exhausted was bound to be uneven. True, 20 per cent. of the sum allotted to each category might be transferred to another at the Administration's discretion. But no one account might be thus increased by more than 30 per cent., and the provision was no more than a small mitigation. Despite the maximum use of virement, the military categories 1 to 5 were approaching exhaustion by the early summer.

It was certain enough that more money would be forthcoming – but how soon? The British were at first advised that the Second Lend-Lease Appropriation Act would be voted in August 1941, but prudently determined to lay their plans on the assumption that the original moneys would have to last until the end of October. In this they were justified. Congress adjourned for its summer recess without approving the new bill, and it was not to reassemble until the middle of September. Thus arose a situation that was in some ways reminiscent of the previous winter. On 20th August the unallocated balance of the first appropriation stood at $1,093 million only, and certain categories were practically exhausted. Only $63 million remained in that of tanks and transport, for which demands were still piling up; already several urgent requisitions were blocked for lack of funds. And now it became known that the President required the whole of the balance to be committed by 1st September, leaving nothing for urgent requirements which might arise during the next two months. Once again the British had to be rendered as it were destitute in order that Congress might be convinced that they really needed help. Once again they were forced to a variety of shifts and expedients to eke out their remaining resources until help came. A certain amount of money was recovered from previous allocations, the cost of many contracts having proved lower than the missions' deliberately generous estimates. Outstanding demands were arranged in a rough order of priority and those at the lower end of the list deferred. Balance sheets then drawn up by the missions showed that the worst shortage (about $100 million) would be found, surprisingly enough, in the non-military products category – this because it had been depleted earlier on for the benefit of the munitions programmes.

There was a risk of interruptions in the flow of such supplies as food, petroleum and steel, whose interruption would be most disastrous. The Administration, however, was prevailed on to keep a small balance in hand in other categories in order to cope with such emergencies. Meanwhile requisitions were filed as usual and pushed through the machine up to the point where money was essential. Thus the missions struggled on until 28th October, when the new Appropriation Act finally became law, without a major breakdown but not without delay to some important programmes.

This second appropriation differed from the first in that its term was set not by the date by which supplies were to be delivered but by that at which funds had to be committed. This date fluctuated considerably while the Act was in preparation. It was eventually fixed at 28th February 1942, only four months ahead, and the fund was accordingly restricted to $5,985 million, of which $5,139 million was understood to be earmarked for the United Kingdom. (That four months' contracting should require nearly $6,000 million is striking evidence of the rate at which the demand for American supplies was developing.) The Second Lend-Lease Appropriation Act was, in fact, avowedly no more than an interim measure, and no sooner had it been voted than preparations began on its successor.

A SEPARATE COMPARTMENT OR A COMMON POOL?

The reason was that in the summer and autumn of 1941 the whole question of the financing and administration of Lend-Lease procurement was in the melting-pot. So far, the production of Lend-Lease supplies, other than those covered by the 'Billion-Three' provision, had been carried on in a separate 'defence aid' compartment of American rearmament. In the first few months this had not mattered much, for most of the war material immediately available for transfer had in practice fallen within the terms of that provision, and neither the financial ceiling placed on such transfers nor their limitation to material financed before 11th March 1941, had proved particularly crippling. In the future, however, it was obvious that nearly all Lend-Lease supplies would have to be procured out of the special fund and therefore by special contracts. This was in many ways unsatisfactory. It was not merely that the funds provided were inadequate and in constant need of replenishment, so that the flow of war supplies might be slowed down again and again by the uncertain time-table of Congress. The real objection to the system of the separate compartment was its lack of flexibility. The British would be able to receive only what had been produced on their especial behalf; but since there might be a very long interval between the placing of a contract and the delivery of these munitions, they might not be what the United Kingdom most needed when the time came for shipment. Instead, it was argued on the British side, the American authorities should be free to transfer to them any of the equipment coming forth from the factories, no matter by whom it had been ordered and for what purpose. The War and Navy Departments, in fact, should each have one big appropriation out of which they could place contracts covering both their own needs and those of the defence aid countries with no more than a provisional distinction between the two. Then as deliveries came forward they could be assigned to British, Russian or United States forces according to the needs of the moment. In other words, the separate compartments should be broken down and a common pool created, at least of those munitions which could be used by all the claimants alike.

British opinion was not, however, unanimous on this point. The special Lend-Lease contracts had given the United Kingdom a certain moral claim upon the output of a distinct sector of the American munitions industry. To some it seemed that without such protection they would receive only what was left over after the United States Services had taken what they wanted, and would in fact lose much more than they gained by the creation of a common pool. This argument weighed most heavily with the British Air Commission. British cash and Lend-Lease contracts already guaranteed a substantial supply of American aircraft to the Royal Air Force, and attempts to add to those supplies by arranging for the diversion of planes delivered under United States Army Air Corps contracts had proved an almost total failure. The so-called Slessor Agreement, negotiated by the air staffs of the two countries in March 1941, had broken down within a very few months. Those responsible for aircraft procurement therefore much preferred the continued employment of the capacity already working on their behalf to the prospect of releases, which experience suggested would be arbitrary and inadequate, from a common pool at the discretion of the American authorities. The answer to this objection lay in the system of agreed allocations by a joint authority according to strategic need. Of this there could be no question until the United States was a full partner and ally. Nevertheless the majority of the British favoured the principle of the common pool even if its outlets were to be controlled solely by Americans. The protection afforded by the separate compartment was, after all, a ramshackle affair; it did not prevent, for example, the diversion to Russia and later to the United States air forces of planes produced under 'British' defence aid, and even under British cash contracts.

The United States Administration was moving gradually in the same direction, as became apparent in the summer of 1941 during the negotiations over the Second Lend-Lease Appropriation. The list of British requirements submitted in July amounted, after some trimming and pruning in the Division of Defence Aid Reports, to $10,569 million. The President, however, fearing that this would prove too large a mouthful for Congress to swallow so soon after it had digested the original bill, suggested that the requirements be revised on a new premise, viz., that munitions of 'common' type would be provided out of ordinary departmental funds. The British Supply Council accordingly prepared a fresh list totalling only $6,819 million and covering only non-military supplies and British-type weapons.

This development was in tune with the Administration's growing tendency, remarked on by British observers, to consider the munitions requirements of the democracies, combatant and non-combatant (or not yet combatant), as a single whole. The evolution was immensely stimulated by the preparation of the first consolidated balance-sheet of munitions production and by the formulation of the Victory Programme in October 1941, following joint discussions in London.[1] The Americans were now undertaking to organise and expand their production so as to bridge the entire gap between the output of the Commonwealth and the needs of the Forces required in 'areas of British strategic responsibility', as well as meeting their own needs and their share of the promised supplies in the first Moscow Protocol. The whole discussion in London was couched in terms of global strategy and global supply. No word was breathed of Lend-Lease finance, which was already several weeks before Pearl Harbour, passing into the background of the picture.

Yet there had still to ensue a period of uncertainty before the evolution was complete. The sums provided for munitions in the second Lend-Lease appropriation, when it finally emerged on 28th October ($1,020 million for ordnance, $506 million for aircraft and associated supplies, $319 million for tanks and transport, $811 million for vessels, and $125 million for miscellaneous military equipment) were plainly inadequate, unless the premise suggested by the President was valid. But the premise apparently existed in the minds of the British and of a few persons at the head of the United States Government. The War Department, at the executive level, knew nothing of it; and the British missions, in submitting their detailed expenditure programmes on 29th October, were obliged to include some common as well as British types of armament. Nor, for some time, did anyone appear to know for certain what was to happen in the case of the third appropriation, which was to follow early in the new year. In preparing their estimates for this appropriation a few days after Pearl Harbour the British Purchasing Commission excluded, but the Air Commission and the Admiralty

---

[1] See the discussion on the Victory Programme in *North American Supply, op. cit.,* Chapter VIII, Sections (v) and (vi).

Delegation still included, requirements for military equipment of common type. The matter was discussed with Lord Beaverbrook, then in Washington for the Arcadia Conference. He ruled, and the British Supply Council agreed, that so long as adequate provision was made for British needs the method of financing them was a matter for the United States Government to decide.

One of the chief causes of the uncertainty was the aforementioned Byrd Amendment to the main Act, which appeared to rule out the possibility of using for Lend-Lease purposes any departmental funds appropriated after March 1941. 'How to cope with the Byrd Amendment' was a recurring theme in the discussions of the British Supply Council during the summer and autumn of 1941. The conclusion reached, after soundings had been made with the American authorities, was that it could not be got rid of, at any rate for the time being. Yet the Amendment was not as serious an obstacle to the creation of a common pool as it seemed. Its purpose was simply to give Congress a check on what some of its members feared might otherwise have developed into an indiscriminate transfer of American defence equipment to foreign countries. It forbade the use of departmental funds, certainly, but with the saving clause, 'except to the extent hereafter authorised by the Congress in the acts appropriating such funds or otherwise'. Now such authority had already been given in one instance: the First National Defence Supplemental Appropriation of August 1941 had given the Maritime Commission $1,296 million to spend as it would in implementing the President's recent directive that all-out aid was to be given to the democracies in shipping. Ships were to some extent a special case, in that they could be made available to the British in other ways than by outright transfer. But the precedent was there, and it was followed after Pearl Harbour. The Byrd Amendment was not repealed, then or later, but Congress used its dispensing powers freely. The Third Supplemental National Defence Appropriation, placed at the disposal of the War Department on 17th December, empowered the Department to transfer to the Allies military equipment produced under its 'own' contracts, from whatever funds financed, up to a total of $2,000 million. (By the same Act the original 'Billion-Three' authorisation was cut back to $800 million and restricted to the use of procurement agencies other than the War Department.) Similarly, the Navy Department was authorised to use up to a quarter of its new appropriation for Lend-Lease transfers.

FINANCE AFTER PEARL HARBOUR

The new system of financing, however, applied only to war material in the narrower sense. The Third Lend-Lease Appropriation went forward in the normal way and was duly voted on

5th March 1942, but it and its successors provided only for food, raw materials, petroleum, industrial equipment and other civilian supplies, which together constituted at the time less than a quarter of the total programme.[1] There thus remained, as there had been from the beginning, two forms of Lend-Lease finance: appropriations voted to the President specially for the purpose, and authorisations for the departments to transfer certain proportions by value of the stores which they procured out of their own funds. Only, from December 1941, the scope of the latter was enormously increased. The position may be summarised as in Table 5.

Table 5. Lend-Lease and Transfer Appropriations 1941 to 1945

$ million

Lend-Lease Appropriations	
First (March 1941)	7,000
Second (October 1941) . . .	5,985
Third (March 1942) . . .	5,425
Fourth (June 1943)	6,273
Fifth (June 1944)	3,538
Sixth (July 1945)	2,475
	30,696
Transfer Appropriations	
Lend-Lease Act (March 1941)	800[2]
First Supplemental – Maritime Commission (August 1941)	1,296
Third Supplemental – War Department (December 1941) .	2,000
Fourth Supplemental – War Department (January 1942) .	4,000
Fifth Supplemental – War Department (March 1942) .	11,250
Maritime Commission . .	3,850
Naval Appropriation, 1942 – Navy Department . . .	6,400
Sixth Supplemental, 1942 – War Department . . .	2,220
Navy Department . .	18
Military Appropriation, 1943 – War Department . .	12,700
Second Supplemental, 1943 – Navy Department . .	3,000
	47,534

The Lend-Lease appropriations proper had still to be steered through the eddies of Congressional debate by the Office of Lend-Lease Administration, and were not free from the delays and doubts which that entailed. The exclusion of military supplies, however, meant that the delays had much less serious consequences. The third member of the series, covering deliveries up to the end of 1942, was tagged on to the Fifth Supplemental, and passed, in the prevailing atmosphere of fiscal abandon, almost without debate. The fourth, however, was a more difficult matter. It was originally intended to cover the calendar year 1943. But it was now necessary for O.L.L.A. to acquire fresh powers in the matter of relief and rehabilitation

---

[1] Total requirements for 1942 were put at $24,600 million, those submitted for inclusion in the Lend-Lease Appropriation amounted to $6,000 million.
[2] As amended by the Third Supplemental.

supplies, and these might clearly be the subject of prolonged debate. Moreover, the main Lend-Lease Act was due to expire on 30th June 1943, so that an extension had to be secured before money was voted for the latter part of the year. O.L.L.A. therefore proposed to tackle the problem in three stages: a small interim appropriation bill covering the first six months of the year was to be introduced at the beginning of 1943; this would be followed by a Lend-Lease Extension Act giving the necessary authority for relief supplies; and then a further appropriation would be requested for the fiscal year ending 30th June 1944. Ultimately, however, it was decided that this would overload the legislative time-table, and as existing funds could be made to last until 1st May, the idea of an interim bill was dropped. Whether the Extension Act and the Fourth Appropriation Act could both be pushed through by 1st May seemed very doubtful to the British; and in the event the latter was not signed until 14th June. Yet the six weeks' delay seems to have caused no particular embarrassment. The third appropriation had evidently been based on generous estimates of need, since it could be made to last half as long again as had been intended.

Even in respect of non-military supplies it can be safely asserted that after Pearl Harbour and until the last year of war the financial aspect of Lend-Lease was not at all prominent. The third and fourth appropriations gave the British practically the whole of what they wanted. That of June 1944, however, was about 20 per cent. below the original estimate of British requirements; and in the autumn of that year, when peace and reconversion were in sight, when economy was again the watchword of Congress, and when the extent and even the principle of Lend-Lease were being seriously called in question, negotiations with the United States Government had to be resumed in financial terms.[1] Yet even the sixth appropriation, introduced at a time when the Lend-Lease system was already disintegrating, passed through Congress without any special difficulty or delay.

MILITARY AND CIVILIAN PROCUREMENT

Still more clearly were considerations of finance eliminated from the problem of munitions supply. It is true that some on the British side at first objected to any statutory limitation of the volume of transfers, as being plainly inconsistent with the doctrine of the common pool which was enunciated at 'Arcadia'. So it was, in principle, but the British had little ground for anxiety. The ceilings were a political formality only. In the Fourth and Fifth Supplemental Appropriations which followed in quick succession to the Third they were raised so high as to have no practical effect upon supply. Against the $47,000 million provided in transfer authorisations alone, the

---

[1] See *North American Supply, op. cit.*, Chapter XI.

actual value of *all* Lend-Lease supplies to the British Commonwealth barely exceeded $30,000 million. To this has to be added the $11,000 million worth of goods furnished to the Soviet Union and much smaller sums to France, China and the other Allies; but even so it is apparent that so far as finance was concerned the volume of Lend-Lease could have been very much larger than it actually was. How much the British received after Pearl Harbour depended not on appropriations but on how much was in the pool, that is on the total volume of American production, and on what proportion was allotted as their share. And in theory at least the share-out was based on military considerations alone. It was still of course necessary that some financial provision should be made in advance for British and Allied needs, but the required funds, as a British official put it, were 'provided in Departmental appropriations, defended in Congress by those Departments and subsequently administered by them' as an integral part of their own programmes.

These words point to an important administrative corollary of the change in the method of financing munitions supply. Clearly in the new system there was little scope for the Office of Lend-Lease Administration, since it had lost control over the funds out of which munitions were provided for the Allies. With the whole military sector of supply it had henceforward no direct concern, except for the final recording of the dollar value of transfers. This aspect of the change was the subject of keen controversy within the United States Administration for several weeks after Pearl Harbour, O.L.L.A. itself fighting hard but in the end unsuccessfully to retain a measure of control over Lend-Lease as a whole.

During this debate the British found themselves in an uncomfortable position on the side-lines, not at all sure themselves whether the change would be gain or loss. O.L.L.A., or rather its predecessor, had been a source of tedious delays and on occasion of serious confusion; and although the delays were decreasing, it was still a mechanical improvement to have one stage less in the procurement process. On the other hand, for all its slowness of action, the amateurishness of many of its officers, and what appeared to the British to be its excessive political caution, O.L.L.A. was a much valued friend at court. Having been created for the express purpose of getting supplies moving to the Lend-Lease countries, it served as the advocate with departments whose primary professional duty was to strengthen the defences of the United States; and the British were inclined to fear that they would fare badly if their supplies were entirely at the mercy of the Service departments. Yet the efficacy of the advocate in the munitions sector was really very doubtful. The eligibility of munitions supplies from a Lend-Lease point of view was hardly ever in doubt, and what might be called their military eligibility was a point which the Office of Lend-Lease Administration was hardly competent to determine. A British Admiralty representative later wrote feelingly of 'the somewhat tiresome business of explaining naval requirements in full detail to O.L.L.A's team of energetic but inexperienced lawyers'. And for the same reasons its advocacy could not carry very much weight with the War and Navy Departments. The attitude adopted by these bodies to what they clearly deemed 'interference' by civilian authorities, as evidenced by their relations with the War Production Board and the Combined Production and Resources Board, suggests that it would have paid little heed to representations from the civilians of the Office of Lend-Lease Administration. Indeed, even in 1941 the War and Navy Departments had in practice decided for themselves what military equipment should be procured for or allotted to the British. Such influence as the Division of Defence Aid Reports or O.L.L.A. had exerted, had really been the personal influence of Harry Hopkins; and this was still to be available in another form. Thus the general British view at the time was that while there was a clear need for some sort of arbiter between the British and the American Services, O.L.L.A. was not technically equipped for the role; and that there was much to be said for placing the responsibility for meeting British needs fairly and squarely with those who in practice had to procure and allocate the stores.

Whether the British gained or lost from the virtual elimination of the Office of Lend-Lease Administration from the operation of munitions supply was never very clearly determined. When they had the choice of procuring stores through the War Department or through a civilian agency, usually the Treasury, under the auspices of O.L.L.A., the decision was never easy to make. It must be explained that between the areas of military and of civilian procurement there was a wide indeterminate zone in which the appropriate agency was not obvious. Broadly speaking, it was understood that stores used by the British armed forces, whatever their nature, would be procured by the United States Service Departments; and early in 1943 an attempt was made to establish this criterion of 'end use' as a settled rule. Thus a bulldozer, used to level the ground for a military airfield, would be supplied by the War Department, while an identical machine intended for the preparation of waste ground for crops would be made available through Treasury Procurement. Clearly, it was impracticable to restrict the employment of equipment throughout its life to the work for which it had been procured, so that it could easily happen that machines working side by side on the same task should have had a quite different origin. The 'end use' criterion was not always a satisfactory one. It complicated combined planning and entailed a risk of the duplication of requirements or on the other hand of their total omission. Towards the end of 1943 there was a definite move towards the substitution of a 'commodity-wise' division, that is, to the procurement by the civilian agencies of all stores that were eminently civilian in character, even if the armed forces also had an interest therein. Typewriters were an obvious example. In some instances, commodity grouping had always been applied. All tyres, for example, whether for military or civilian vehicles, had been requisitioned, since the latter part of 1941, from Treasury Procurement. This was really anomalous; since by far the greater number of tyres supplied were for military use. The practice had developed in the first instance because procurement through the Treasury was so much simpler than procurement through the War Department (one early requisition for tyres that was routed to the latter took five months to produce a contract), and it continued because for a long time there seemed no compelling reason for a change.

One class of stores which was the subject of much debate was that of medical supplies. It has already been pointed out that the division of such supplies between military and civilian 'end use' cannot be other than arbitrary. At first Lend-Lease supplies were made available through the Surgeon-General's branch of the War Department. But the British were not satisfied that they were getting fair shares, and in the autumn of 1943 it was agreed that O.L.L.A. should handle all requisitions, have a share in the framing of policy and be given information on the progress of contracts. In reporting this change, the Director-General of the British Ministry of Supply Mission explained that while the re-introduction of O.L.L.A. would complicate procedures it should also mean that greater efforts would be made to meet British needs. O.L.L.A. insisted that the Lend-Lease countries should receive a fair proportion of all material subject to allocation.

The Director-General was opposed, however, to actual transfer of the procurement of British medical supplies to a civilian agency. In general, when the War Department was an important customer for a certain class of supplies, it was found better to leave all procurement in the hands of that Department than to try to compete with it through Treasury Procurement. The later history of tyre procurement underlines this point. By 1944 the supply of tyres fell far short of the demand. In this situation the War Department showed itself a much more successful purchaser than the Treasury. It had greater influence with the Office of the Rubber Director; it secured higher priority ratings and it had, as the Treasury had not, expediters at work in the factories. By the summer a position had been reached in which the War Department held all the stocks and had absorbed all the plant capacity which could be used to satisfy

British requirements. Procurement through the Treasury had manifestly broken down, and the British were compelled for the first time to apply for an allocation of tyres from War Department sources. The allocation was made, not to the British direct, but to the Foreign Economic Administration, which undertook not to release any tyres to the British until the War Department was satisfied as to their operational needs. This, in effect, made tyres subject to assignment like other military stores; and the process was brought to its logical conclusion at the beginning of 1945 when the War Department took over the actual procurement of tyres for the British Army and Air Force.[1]

No general dictum can thus be made as to whether the civilian or the military system of Lend-Lease procurement gave the best results. From a procedural point of view the British missions on the whole preferred to use the Treasury channel, with its simpler mechanisms and less rigid rules, even though it carried with it the additional complication of the scrutiny of requirements by the Office of Lend-Lease Administration. But where the War Department was the main user, the Treasury was liable to be left at the post in a scramble for scarce supplies, and in such cases the munitions assignment machinery was a better protection of British interests than a separate procurement programme. If O.L.L.A's aid could be enlisted as well, as in the case of medical supplies, so much the better; but the opportunities for that were severely limited by the War Department's desire to have Lend-Lease procurement made an indistinguishable part of its total production orders and not something separate undertaken at the request of another organisation, and that civilian.

(iii)

The Procurement of Munitions

NON-COMMON STORES — THE PROBLEM

Over much the greater part of the field of munitions supply, therefore, the British missions, after December 1941, were left face to face with the War and Navy Departments, without intermediary or special advocate. Their relations with these bodies, in their dual capacity of service and supply departments, thus became of paramount importance. In the early days it had been with the Secretary of the Treasury that British representatives chiefly dealt; and the Secretary still took the leading part in the great supply negotiations of the

---

[1] On tyres see *North American Supply*, *op. cit.*, Chapter X, Section (ii).

summer of 1940, notably in those concerning the aircraft programme. But already in June 1940 it had been General Marshall's fiat that made possible the shipment of the 'surplus' arms, for only he could declare them surplus. And as British procurement impinged more and more upon American rearmament it was more and more with the American users of military equipment that the British had to deal. Sir Walter Layton, in the autumn, first approached Mr Morgenthau but was immediately referred to the War Department, and it was with that body that his main negotiations were conducted.[1] In the first phase of Lend-Lease political and financial questions had to some extent pushed problems of strategy and production into the background. Yet even in 1941 the Service Departments had really decreed what types and quantities of munitions should be produced on behalf of the British and what they should finally receive.

The British authorities had therefore given much thought to the establishment of contacts with these Departments. The objective, as Purvis explained it in April 1941, was a relationship so close that no question of priority should arise between British and American requirements and that the British should avoid altogether the position of suppliants for aid, being treated rather as partners in a common enterprise. This was an ideal that could not be fully realised so long as the Americans remained outside the war. And even when they had come in, it would have been too much to expect that the fact that British requirements were being met by supplies made by American hands and paid for with American money should be treated as entirely irrelevant. Nevertheless, even before Pearl Harbour, remarkable progress was made towards the identification of British and American programmes.

Here a fundamental distinction must be drawn between the common and non-common types of warlike stores made in the United States for British use. In the former class amalgamation was theoretically complete. For such stores, once the problem of financing had been cleared out of the way, it was unnecessary for the Departments to place special defence aid contracts, and therefore unnecessary for the British to submit individual requisitions; this procedure was in fact discontinued some weeks before Pearl Harbour. British requirements were made known by means of comprehensive forward programmes, which the War and Navy Departments collated with their own and Russian needs to form a single integral supply programme. During the process of production there was no means of distinguishing British, Russian or American stores. The distribution was made only when the stores were almost ready for shipment, and it was made according to the operational needs then

---

[1] *North American Supply, op. cit.,* Chapter VI.

apparent, without reference to those stated at the time of planning. Thus with regard to standard military equipment, procurement as such became from about the time of Pearl Harbour entirely a matter for the American authorities and ceased to play any part in the story of overseas supply. The processes in which the British and other foreign beneficiaries of American production were interested were forward planning, or programming, and assignment. These will be discussed in the succeeding chapter.

The same procedure, however, could obviously not be applied to stores which the Americans produced only for British use. For such, individual requisitions had still to be filed and individual contracts placed, and with the execution of those contracts the British were vitally concerned. Thus the problem of munitions procurement in the United States resolved itself into the problem of 'non-common' stores.

It was explained in the preceding chapter that from the middle of 1940 onwards the United States authorities had set their faces firmly against the production of equipment which their own Forces could not use. To this general rule, however, a number of exceptions had been conceded. Most conspicuous was the permission to procure one million .303-inch rifles, which was included in the terms of the agreement between Mr Stimson and Sir Walter Layton in November 1940. This was the only complete weapon made in the United States for the exclusive use of the British Army; but, weapons apart, there was an extensive procurement of non-common stores. The American ban had not been applied to ammunition with anything like the same rigour, and several smallish but important contracts had been placed by the British Purchasing Commission, for 2-pounder armour-piercing shot, 2-pounder, 4.7-inch and 15-inch naval shells, 6-inch, 7.2-inch and 9.2-inch howitzer shells, 6-inch and 9.2-inch coastal gun ammunition. Of much greater and more lasting importance, however, was the supply of ammunition for British types of rifle and sub-machine gun. Then there was the class of equipment which was non-standard not because of technical differences in design but because it had no counterpart at all in the American Army, being intended for a tactical role which the Americans did not recognise. Such were the monster tank transporter vehicles, for supplies of which the British Army was almost wholly dependent on the United States. Though it responded promptly to the original call for these vehicles in 1941, the War Department for long regarded them as at most a special requirement for the Desert campaigns and otherwise as an unnecessary luxury. In addition, a large part of the British requirements of miscellaneous signal, engineer, transportation and quartermaster stores – requirements that grew rapidly in volume and variety from 1942 onwards – were classed as non-common.

So also were spare parts even of standard equipment, when requisitioned separately, and, what was far more important, components supplied for incorporation in British-made munitions. This was a problem of major significance. The extreme difficulty of planning a balanced programme of munitions production, of arranging a smooth flow to the assembly plants of all the items which go into the making of such complex implements of war as the modern warship, tank or aircraft, without risking 'bottlenecks' on the one hand or accumulating unneeded stocks on the other, had been greatly mitigated for British planners by the existence of a reserve industry on the other side of the Atlantic. To an increasing extent between 1940 and 1942 American engineering firms were put to work, in effect, as sub-contractors for British munitions plants. It became almost automatic for supply departments in London whenever they saw a production schedule in danger of failure for lack of some essential component to seek the deficiency from the United States. In some instances they had gone even beyond this, planning a whole programme from the outset on the basis of American component supply. Indeed, by the end of 1941 a whole spacious annex of munitions production had been erected in the United Kingdom on the expectation the United States would furnish not only machine tools and steel and other raw materials, but also a wide range of semi-fabricated component parts.

The Admiralty, for example, was seeking supply of the complex diesel engine crankshafts that are essential to the construction of submarines and some types of cargo ship; also a very large number of complete marine engines; also various ammunition and torpedo components. The Ministry of Aircraft Production required not only every possible American aircraft but a large quantity of major components, chiefly engines and propellers, for British-built planes. Even more extensive use of American components was made by the Ministry of Supply, whose purchases and requisitions included shell driving bands, the cores of armour-piercing bullets, liners and loose barrels, some finish-machined, others merely forged, for heavy anti-aircraft guns, and above all tank components.

The Ministry of Supply began to buy parts of tanks from the United States before it thought of ordering complete vehicles. Within a few weeks of the outbreak of war dollars were found for the purchase of 250 sets – about half the total requirement for 1940 – of transmissions, suspension units and gun-mountings for the Infantry Tank Mark III (Valentine). No further steps were taken until the summer of 1940, but then new vistas opened out. The Tank Mission won American approval for the proposition that since the manufacture in the United States of complete tanks to British design had been ruled out, it should at least be allowed to order components. On the Mission's initiative, the Ministry of Supply took the opportunity, so far as the supply of dollars permitted, to clear some of the worst 'bottlenecks' in British tank production by taking up vacant capacity in the United States. Lend-Lease opened the way to further orders; and in the latter part of 1941, when the Russian need for tanks impinged on a British industry that was already strained to the limit of its resources, Washington was inundated with requests for the supply of tank components. By March 1942, orders had already been placed to the value of $111 million, outstanding requirements totalled $50 million, and a further schedule amounting to $207 million was under negotiation for supply in 1943. The total demand was thus $368 million, the equivalent of over 5,000 complete cruiser tanks.

The demand included practically everything that goes into the assembly of a tank. There was a wide variety of semi-fabricated material such as armour plate and castings, and also of minor components such as bearings (also required in large numbers for aircraft production), connecting rods and camshafts. These were of great importance in sum, and often in detail. Armour plate was a critical item in the economy of British war production, its scarcity threatening at one time to disrupt both the tank and warship pro-. grammes. The loss at sea of a consignment of bearings in December 1940, so nearly halted production in British tank factories that replacements had to be rushed across by bomber plane. Then there were the major sub-assemblies of Valentine tanks, which were requisitioned in ever-increasing numbers throughout 1941: it was estimated that in 1942 the makers of Valentines would have to rely on American sources for half their suspension units and three-fifths of their engines. There was also an important series of orders and requisitions for tank and carrier track, of which the British sought to acquire the enormous quantity of 4,000 tons a month in 1942 – about as much as they hoped to be able to manufacture for themselves. Finally, and perhaps most important of all, there were required 3,000 power units for cruiser tanks.

Now it can be stated as a general rule that the British were keener to secure delivery of non-common stores, class for class, than of any other. The point is indeed obvious: the non-common equipment was what they really wanted, while the standard American material, except in the few cases where the United States forces had adopted British designs, was a *pis aller*. Components, in turn, were more precious than finished equipment of any type. A fairly small import of key components could make a very great difference to British output, and the maintenance or expansion of British output was more highly valued than the prospect of an equivalent increase in American production, the fruits of which the British could never be sure of enjoying. American preferences, however, were just the reverse. In allotting facilities for the production of standard equipment on behalf of Britain, the authorities were making only a temporary and revocable grant; they could always take possession of the finished product, although after the assignment machinery had been set up early in 1942 they had first to show that their need was the greater. Factories turning out non-common equipment, on the other hand, were a sort of extra-territorial enclave which could be restored to them only after the expense and delay of re-tooling. Much the same was true of components. In 1940, indeed, orders were not only welcomed by American manufacturers but tolerated and even encouraged by their government. The reason was that there were many firms which could begin making components at once with little additional plant, and which, even if they were eventually to be absorbed into the American rearmament programme, could profitably fill in the interval by working for the British. Three foundries, for example, were allowed to make turret castings for Churchill and Matilda tanks in the winter of 1940-1 and the following spring, while the American tank assembly plants were being built, on the understanding that they would subsequently revert to producing castings for American use. When they did so, they had acquired both plant and experience which made them of infinitely greater value to United States Ordnance. By 1942, however, the situation had completely changed. The manufacture of components for export, acceptable enough in 1940 and early 1941, became a most unpleasant incubus when every foot of factory space, and every pound of raw material, was needed for the gigantic production programmes which the Americans had now set themselves to fulfil.

BRITISH RELATIONS WITH THE SERVICE DEPARTMENTS

In short, while the supply of stores other than those of standard American pattern was often absolutely vital to the British, their manufacture seemed to the Americans, as indeed it was, thoroughly uneconomic and anomalous. The apparent conflict of interest was such that some friction was unavoidable. Left to themselves, the United States authorities, that is to say the executive officers of the Service Departments who actually planned and administered the munitions programmes, would undoubtedly have relegated purely British needs to a very subordinate position in the production scheme. It was therefore of the first importance that British requirements should be discussed and judged in such a way that proper weight would be given to true relative needs, as seen from the point of view of the combined war effort as a whole. This was not wholly a matter of institutions and machinery, but it is of these that we must first speak.

It has first to be recorded that no general solution was found to the problem of the joint planning of American munitions procurement that can stand comparison with that adopted for the distribution of the finished products. Conditions varied greatly from one sector of munitions supply to another. The problem was in many ways simplest in the air sector. Here non-common stores, properly so called, were a very minor element. Even the components supplied for incorporation in British aircraft were mostly standard American products which were manufactured in mass for British and American needs alike. On the other hand, the aircraft produced for the Royal Air Force, though all of American pattern, were regarded as in a sense non-common. They mostly differed in various minor features from those used by the United States air forces; and their production was not merged in quite the same way as was that of, say, tanks. British cash and early Lend-Lease contracts had created a 'separate compartment' of aircraft production which remained distinct. The point is, however, that by the time procurement problems became acute the 'compartment' was already spacious enough to guarantee a fairly ample flow of aircraft to Great Britain. The British Air Commission was reasonably content with the 'continued employment of existing capacity'; additions thereto, chiefly in the form of transport planes and naval aircraft, were a matter of allocation rather than of special new contracting. It may be said, in fact, that the procurement job had already been done, so far as the British were concerned, by the time of Pearl Harbour, and indeed much earlier than that; the British never received more than the thousand planes a month which was the theoretical output of plants contracted for by the middle of 1940.

The job had been done by a unique and remarkable instrument the Joint Aircraft Committee, in which the British were very completely associated with the American authorities in the planning of supply.[1] The Committee overstepped departmental boundaries, containing representatives of the United States Navy as well as of the War Department. Its directive authorised its members to 'act for and obligate' the agencies they represented. Since the heads of the Army Air Corps and of the naval Bureau of Aircraft (or their deputies) sat on the Committee, this presented no difficulty. It covered aircraft supply in both its technical and manufacturing aspects, standardising designs, allocating capacity and scheduling deliveries to the various claimants. Its power to allocate the output of plants, however, was always restricted. In preparing its schedules it had to take account of 'the allocations and differential priorities received from higher authority'; and after Pearl Harbour the Committee lost this part of its functions altogether to the Munitions Assignments Committee (Air), in respect of stores subject to assignment, which included

---

[1] On the Joint Aircraft Committee see also *North American Supply, op. cit.,* Chapter VIII and below Chapter V, Section (i).

all complete aircraft. It remained, however, responsible for the allocation of components. Its powers over production were far-reaching. From April 1941, representatives of the Office of Production Management and its successor sat on the Committee as full members, and for a long time it acted in place of a normal 'industry division' of the War Production Board, as the production planning authority. In March 1943, however, it was directed to exercise its powers in concurrence with the W.P.B's newly-constituted Aircraft Production Board.

The Joint Aircraft Committee had been established at a very early stage in the proceedings. It helped in the expansion of American aircraft production after the R.A.F. had won the Battle of Britain. By the time of Pearl Harbour, with over a year's experience behind it of day-to-day collaboration on all sorts of questions, it was already a working organisation with some sense of corporate identity. Thus while there was strenuous dispute between the Air Staffs over aircraft allocations, there was remarkably little trouble at the procurement stage. Not only were specifically British requirements given a sympathetic hearing by a joint body, but British representatives were able to watch, and share in controlling, the progress made after requisitions had been accepted.

No comparable institution emerged in the ground munitions sector, where there had been no regular liaison before Lend-Lease began. Early in April 1941, after months of effort on the part of Purvis and his colleagues, Mr Stimson set up in the Office of his Under-Secretary, Judge Robert S. Patterson, a special Division of Defence Aid, which was to be the focal point for all Lend-Lease transactions in the War Department. To it requisitions were referred in the first instance, and it decided whether supply was feasible and how it should be effected – from existing stocks or from new contracts. In practice the division acted on the recommendation of 'Defence Aid Requirements Committees' which were established in each of the five main supply arms services, or procurement branches of the War Department – the Ordnance, Chemical Warfare, Engineer, Signals and Quartermaster Corps. The next development came in July, when the Requirements Committees were fused into a single body known as the Defence Aid Supply Committee. This comprised representatives of the several supply arms, of the defence aid section of the General Staff, of the Office of Production Management and of the foreign missions whose needs were being discussed. The composition of the new Committee thus gave it a wide conspectus of Lend-Lease supply in all its aspects, military, economic and manufacturing. In the autumn of 1941 there was a further reorganisation, designed, according to the War Department's explanation, to strengthen the links between the Department and the foreign missions, to speed up the implementation of Lend-Lease and to make for more efficient use of American resources for the satisfaction of combined needs. The Director of the Defence Aid Division, Colonel H. S. Aurand, became chairman of the Defence Aid Supply Committee and the chief point of contact between the Department and its foreign clients. Hitherto the British had almost completely lost touch with the progress of supplies after their requisitions had been approved. Now permanent sub-committees were set up in each of the six supply branches (the five previously mentioned plus the Medical Corps). These bodies, on which there were to be permanent British supply and user repre-sentatives, were intended to 'handle the whole business from requisition to delivery'. At the same time each of the supply arms was to appoint a special Defence Aid Officer whose business was to maintain constant liaison with the foreign missions.

The organisation thus established continued after Pearl Harbour without substantial change. The Committee was given the now more appropriate name of International Supply Committee, just as the Defence Aid Division became the International Division. It should be also noted that the supply arms were reorganised under a single head, Lieutenant-General Brehon M. Somervell, as the 'Services of Supply' (later the 'Army Service Forces'). General Somervell and the head of the International Division, now Major-General Lucius D. Clay, became the key figures in all negotiations over the procure-ment of ground equipment.

It might appear from this description that the International Supply Committee was conceived in the image of the Joint Aircraft Com-mittee. But this was not so. In the first place its functions were significantly narrower. They were defined early in 1942 as being, in general, to review the programmes of requirements furnished by the War Department and, in particular, to pronounce upon the desir-ability of individual requisitions for non-common stores. The Com-mittee did not concern itself with technical matters, nor did it allocate manufacturing facilities. It did not examine or pass judg-ment on the United States Army's requirements, and the British representatives had no detailed knowledge of the way in which the industrial resources at the disposal of the War Department were being distributed. The International Supply Committee, in fact, was not a true combined body, but rather an American committee before which British representatives, along with the Russians and other claimants, came to plead their case for assistance. As such, it tended, in the British view, to act too much as an instrument for the protection of United States Army interests.

The handling of ground munitions supply thus fell a long way short of the ideal of full partnership and equal treatment for British needs. Urgent British requests were not infrequently turned down in 1942 without reference to relative strategic need and merely on the ground that they could not be met without an adverse effect on the main programme for the production of standard equipment. Whether it might not be in the common interest to sacrifice some of the marginal elements in that programme, was a point which the Committee did not generally feel itself called upon to consider.

The crux of the matter, in the first year after Pearl Harbour, was the scarcity of raw materials. The International Supply Committee sought to establish the principle that British requisitions for finished or semi-finished raw materials containing 'critical' raw materials could be accepted only if Britain's allocation of materials in bulk were cut by an equivalent amount. The ruling was hotly contested by the British and was never rigorously applied. But the difficulty persisted as a running sore until the end of the year, when the United States put the principal raw materials under a proper system of allocation so that the total programme of production could be brought into relation with the available supply.

But the approval of requisitions was only the first hurdle which the British had to cross. There was a great danger that orders placed specifically on behalf of the British – and this applied to cash as well as to Lend-Lease contracts – would not be executed at a speed appropriate to the urgency of the supplies or comparable with that of orders for common-type equipment forming an integral part of the American programme. A good illustration can be taken from the procurement of naval ordnance. Admiralty requirements, as formulated in 1940 and 1941, included 1,500 21-inch and 2,500 18-inch British-type torpedoes. Their story was as follows. A contract for 500 21-inch torpedoes was inherited from the French in June 1940, and a further 1,000 were duly ordered by the Navy Department under Lend-Lease. The latter contract, however, was merely a follow-on order, no fresh capacity being set up. Fully two years elapsed before any deliveries were made on the first order, and even afterwards progress was so slow that supplies were superfluous by the time they came forward. The Lend-Lease contract was therefore reduced to 200, and even so was not completed until August 1944. For 18-inch torpedoes, three Lend-Lease orders were placed during 1941 with three different firms, the first for five hundred and the others for a thousand each. The two latter were cancelled by the Navy Department soon after Pearl Harbour on the ground that the resources of the important engineering firms concerned ought not to be dissipated on relatively small-scale manufacture of non-standard equipment. The remaining firm had not delivered a single torpedo by the summer of 1942, nor did it then seem likely that it ever would. In fact it produced fifteen, which were largely assembled by the British inspection staff. The contract was eventually transferred in June 1943, to another firm, which completed delivery in October 1944. This was an extreme example of what was liable to happen to the supply of British-type equipment. Orders were relegated to inferior or unsuitable firms and not supervised by the responsible American departments with the same close attention that they gave to their own orders.

Similarly, for a long time it seemed unlikely that the approval given in principle to the manufacture of a million British-type rifles would have much practical effect. The original idea was that the rifles would be made by the Remington Arms Company with the aid of certain disused plant from the United States Government arsenal at Rock Island. When it came to the point, however, the War Department insisted that Remington should make .30-inch weapons in the first instance, and the proposed later change-over to .303-inch was repeatedly deferred. Meanwhile, after a succession of disappointments the British Purchasing Commission had made firm arrangements with the Savage Arms Company, with whom an initial Lend-Lease contract for 333,300 .303-inch rifles was negotiated in the spring of 1941. It had been hoped that American-made rifles would come forward during the period of really acute shortage in 1941 and early 1942, while British Commonwealth production was being built up. In the nature of things this hope had always been a forlorn one. Results were none the less disappointing. Up to the middle of 1942 only 83,000 rifles had been delivered, and it seemed that several years must elapse before the requirement was met in full. For many months past, therefore, the British had been pressing for additional factory capacity to be allotted for this purpose. In February they had made a formal request in this sense to the International Supply Committee. It was rejected. Now against such decisions the British could appeal to the Combined Munitions Assignments Board (which in addition to its primary function of sharing out finished munitions had been given a somewhat vague responsibility for the supervision of the long-term supply programmes) and even if necessary to the Combined Chiefs of Staff. But this was a time-wasting expedient which could not be used very often or for matters not of the first importance. In this case the British did appeal, and successfully; Mr Hopkins, as Chairman of the Assignments Board, asked the War Department to reconsider its decision. But six weeks later the British Purchasing Commission still had no progress to report.

Experience of this sort soon led the British representatives to a profound dissatisfaction with the International Supply Committee. Both its constitution and the spirit in which it was operated seemed 'contrary to the principle of partnership', and it was widely felt that some radically different form of organisation was required. There was, however, a certain confusion of ideas on this point. The British had before them in the spring of 1942, two distinct though not unrelated objectives. The first was to secure for themselves a greater influence upon the planning of *American* munitions procurement; or more specifically to ensure that their particular, non-common requirements should be considered from a standpoint broader and more rational than that of the fulfilment or non-fulfilment of sacrosanct American programmes. In other words, the aim was to complete the structure of collaboration between the British missions and the United States Service Departments. One side of this structure, the assignment side, had already been completed by the construction of the Combined Munitions Assignments Board in January-March 1942. But on the procurement side there was only a solitary pillar, the Joint Aircraft Committee. It was therefore necessary to add something in the nature of a Combined Ground Munitions Committee and a Combined Shipbuilding Committee. On 7th April it was pointed out in the British Supply Council that apart from the Joint Aircraft Committee there was 'no machinery for the taking of prompt decisions on the creation of capacity for British non-common requirements'. But the discussion ranged much further than this. The second and more ambitious objective was the co-ordination and adjustment of the entire production of the United States and the British Commonwealth, both military and civil, in accordance with global strategy and global supplies of industrial plant, raw materials, labour and shipping. The two objectives were not mutually exclusive, but the second overshadowed and obscured the first. The British Supply Council's discussions issued in the resolve to secure not a Combined Munitions Committee but a general Combined Production Planning (or Adjustment) Board. Later in the month a memorandum was sent to General Somervell expounding the need for 'permanent combined arrangements' for the consideration not merely of questions, such as that of British-type rifles, which were the concern only of the British missions and the War Department, but also of matters of wider import. It was pointed out, for example, that an anti-friction bearing plant was being built in Scotland, and that, since all the material and most of the machinery for it would have to be imported from the United States, there should have been an opportunity for combined discussion of the project before it was launched. The seductive logic of global planning, in fact, had carried the day. A Combined Production and Resources Board was set up in June 1942, but no Combined Ground Munitions Committee.[1]

Now there was reason for this approach, in that British requirements could be given their proper value only when the combined

---

[1] See also *North American Supply, op. cit.*, Chapter IX, Section (v); and Chapter **V** below on the Combined Boards.

military and production strategy had been settled. Nevertheless, there was much weight in the contention, voiced earlier by a high official of the British Purchasing Commission, that the larger scheme was too grandiose, and that there should have been more work on the foundations first. The Combined Production and Resources Board should have formed the apex of a structure of combined planning committees at the executive level. Instead, it was erected separately and in a different place. It was erected, in fact, over the chasm that divided the military and civilian production planners in the United States, and in defiance of the law of gravity, from the top downwards. It started in mid-air, as it were, and threw out committees dealing with specific problems in an effort to reach ground level. But since, as will be shown in Chapter V, it never made effective contact with those who actually controlled the American munitions programme, its influence on supply planning was never great. An official of the British Admiralty Delegation later commented: 'Owing to naval production being in the hands of the United States Navy with little control by the War Production Board, no naval questions of any importance could profitably be handled by C.P.R.B'.

It was not long before it was realised on the Army side also that C.P.R.B. was no substitute for combined organisation within the War Department. On 10th July 1942 the British submitted a specific request for the reconstitution of the International Supply Committee on a regular combined basis. The aim was now 'a permanent joint (i.e., Anglo-American, not international) committee' which should link together the British Ministry of Supply Mission, the British Army Staff, the War Department and the War Production Board and serve as a forum for the discussion of new British requirements and of failures in existing programmes, keeping the production of non-common items under continuous review. But the opportunity to establish such a body had now been lost. In April General Somervell had been reported to be favourably disposed towards the idea, but now he refused to countenance any change in the existing system, and the matter was not pressed further. Thus so far at least as formal machinery was concerned the British failed to secure any real share in the planning of American ground munitions procurement.

It would, of course, have been remarkable if it had been otherwise. At the time when the Joint Aircraft Committee was set up many more planes were being produced in the United States for Britain than for the American air forces; and, although this state of affairs did not long endure, British aircraft requirements were always a sufficiently large fraction of total output to give the British Air Commission a reasonable claim to share in production planning.

But this was hardly true of most other supplies, of which the Lend-Lease element was merely a small marginal addition to the domestic demand.

However that might be, the consequence was that outside the air programmes, British supplies of stores not subject to assignment had to be striven for in piecemeal and unequal negotiations with reluctant American Departments. The gap in the combined arrangements was perhaps most severely felt on the naval side. Here there was no formal machinery of any kind. Officers of the British Admiralty Delegation simply took their requests along to the appropriate section of the Navy Department, the more important questions being discussed between the British Admiralty Supply Representative and Admiral Reeves, the special liaison officer who was also Chairman of the Munitions Assignments Committee (Navy). Here, too, whether British requirements were procured depended in the last resort on a unilateral American decision, and the only remedy was an appeal to Mr Hopkins or to the Combined Munitions Assignments Board (in practice much the same thing).

The Admiralty's requirements included some purely British-type stores, such as the torpedoes whose sad history was related a few pages back. Its greatest worry, however, for most of the war was the supply of escort vessels. Now, although the vessels in question were built to an American design, so much more importance was attached to them by the British than by the American naval authorities that they were in a position almost analogous to that of non-common war equipment. Preoccupied as it was with the prospect of major fleet battles in the Pacific, it was only late in 1942 that the United States Government gave what the British considered adequate priority to the construction of escorts, and the Navy Department was not fully converted until the beginning of 1943. Thus although the original British request for 100 vessels was put forward in June 1941, none was delivered until February 1943. The naval representative's report from which a quotation has already been taken sums up the position, as the British Admiralty Delegation saw it, in the following words:

The fact that large quantities of munitions were obtained did not disguise the fact that the process would have been much more orderly and conducive of mutual trust and confidence if some form of combined production planning board had been set up as a parallel agency to the Combined Munitions Assignment Board. In spite of all our efforts this was never achieved [that C.P.R.B. did not fill the bill has already been explained], and we were forced to rely on the number and variety of our personal contacts to achieve the desired results.

The last words are important. Committees are not everything;

and the lack of formal machinery did not prevent the British representatives in Washington from exercising a considerable influence over the decisions of the American production planners. On the ground munitions side, the Commander of the British Army Staff, General Macready, and the Director-General of the British Ministry of Supply Mission, who from the autumn of 1942 onwards was Lieut.-General Sir Walter Venning, formed with Generals Clay and Somervell a team which worked together, if not always in perfect harmony, at least with an underlying mutual goodwill. Writing in October 1943, the Director-General said of General Somervell that he 'would give me the shirt off his back if he was satisfied that I needed the shirt'. It was perhaps because British relations with the Navy Department were on the whole rather less close and cordial that the lack of machinery seemed in retrospect so important on that side. That this was so was due partly to the purely personal factor but primarily to divergences of strategic thinking between British sailors who thought first of the Atlantic life-line and Americans whose thoughts tended to stray always to the Pacific.

In every sector, indeed, the issue was one of substance rather than procedure. The sharp criticisms of the International Supply Committee that were voiced by British representatives in 1942 belong to the period of acute strain in American industrial mobilisation. The fault lay more in the general strategy of munitions production than in the mechanism of procurement planning. In its struggle to fulfil an impossible programme the War Department had undertaken an inordinate amount of factory construction and had generated a dangerous excess demand for a number of vital raw materials.[1] It could not help, therefore, but adopt a hostile attitude towards British requests whose satisfaction would add still further to the inflationary pressure. The real remedy, as the British soon saw, was the reduction of the United States Army programme to a size which would leave a margin for British needs. This was accomplished during the last months of 1942, and therefore much less was heard about the defects of the machinery which dealt with British requests for special production facilities. That, however, does not alter the fact that the handling of such requests, as distinct from the allocation of standard equipment, though far better than could have been imagined before the event, did not quite reach the ideal of co-operation between allies who had pooled their resources to fight a common enemy.

THE PRIORITY SYSTEM

One of the greatest complications in the procurement of supplies was the priority system operated by the American authorities.

---

[1] *North American Supply, op. cit.*, Chapter IX.

Among the arguments urged in 1940 against the attempt to purchase non-common equipment was that, even if contracts were successfully negotiated, the contractor would find himself at the end of the queue for machine tools, components and raw materials, and would be unable to deliver the goods in reasonable time. The prophecy was not altogether fulfilled, but it was none the less a hard, uphill struggle to secure adequate priority for special British needs.

From the commencement of American rearmament in June 1940, the Army and Navy Board promulgated a series of priority directives, in accordance with which the Office of Production Management attached to all contracts for warlike stores a preference rating entitling the contractors to varying degrees of precedence in the supply of materials and machinery. The ratings ranged from A-1 to A-10, but at a very early stage it became evident that only the A-1 rating, which was divided into sub-classes running from (a) to (j), would have much practical value.

The system had many defects. In the first place, there was the general inadequacy of any system ruled by absolute priorities which give the whole of one class of supplies precedence over the whole of another class. This expedient had been adopted by the British Government to stimulate the lagging production of specially vital items such as aircraft and tanks in the emergency of 1940, but was soon abandoned in favour of the subtler and more efficient system of allocating the factors of production in such a way that the required rate of progress might be achieved, as nearly as possible, in every sector of war production. Conversion to this method followed in the United States rather slowly. Towards the end of 1941 the authorities began to grant high priority only to specified quantities of material, but it was not until early in 1943 that an effective system of raw material allocation came into being.

From the British point of view the priorities system had special disadvantages. The British Supply Council generally saw the directives in draft form, and from July 1941, was allowed to send a representative to meetings of the Army and Navy Munitions Board's Priorities Committee; but the latter's decisions were none the less taken unilaterally. The Board did indeed recognise in principle at an early stage that British and Canadian cash and Lend-Lease orders should be accorded the same degree of priority as domestic orders for similar material. But this did not altogether meet the case. For one thing, the frustrations of 1940 and early 1941 had given most of the American rearmament contracts a lead in point of time over most of the orders on British behalf, so that with merely equal priority these still lagged behind. More important, the structure of British and American needs was quite dissimilar. American strategists were thinking of 1941 in terms of a primarily naval conflict two or three years ahead. They thus gave precedence to warships, even to those that could not be completed till 1943, over land armaments of much nearer date. This was precisely the reverse of current British policy. It did not in any way follow that, because the War Department, in the spring of 1941, was content to see tanks and rifles placed in the low categories A-1-j and A-1-h respectively, British and defence aid orders could fairly or appropriately be given the same ratings; for tanks and rifles were among the most urgent of all British needs. It was essential, therefore, in the view of the British, that their requirements should be considered individually and rated according to their actual urgency, which was obviously greater in most cases than that of comparable American needs. The Munitions Board recognised this to the extent of upgrading the production of .303-inch rifles to A-1-d in August 1941, with the result that the Savage Arms Company was at last able to get some of the machines it needed and so could make a start on its British order just before the end of the year. But it cannot be said that British representations made much impression on the schedule as a whole; long-term naval construction retained its place at or near the head of the list, and tanks did not rise higher than A-1-d.

In the months after Pearl Harbour the American priority system, stricken by a virulent form of the disease to which all such systems are liable, galloping inflation, lapsed into a condition very near to chaos. There was so little attempt to correlate supply and demand that only the highest brackets of the original schedule had any meaning left. In June, therefore, new and drastic measures were adopted. For stores required within the current year a special set of ratings numbered AA-1 to AA-4 was introduced, with AAA for individual items judged to need emergency action. There was much anxiety about the fate of British orders under this new dispensation. The Munitions Board directive was all its own work, and was compiled without reference to the newly-constituted Combined Production and Resources Board. The Minister of Production, Mr Oliver Lyttelton, then paying his first visit to Washington, gave much attention to this problem. He elicited a general directive from the Combined Chiefs of Staff to the effect that British requirements of non-common weapons, components and spares should be awarded the same priority rating as United States requirements 'for forces of equivalent strategic importance'. As usual the declaration of principle at the highest level was at best only a first step. Its implementation was entrusted to a special committee presided over by General Clay. Before long complaints were heard on the British side that the committee was not giving effect to the principle of automatically equal priority for equal strategic needs but was 'merely issuing long lists of ratings' for particular British orders. In reality, however, the lists were more valuable than the principle. Mr Lyttelton and Mr Nelson had assumed that the Combined Chiefs of Staff were about to draw up a combined order of battle from which the relative strategic importance of the various production orders could be deduced. But the order of battle was not forthcoming and without it the principle was meaningless. Before Lyttelton returned home, however, definite agreement had been reached on a schedule of British requirements that were to be accorded either the AA-1 or the AA-2 rating. AA-1 was to be given to the whole series of requisitions for landing craft engines and torpedoes, to half the total quantity of tank components on order, and to specific quantities of other material, for example, to 4,000 tank transporters, 6,200 Universal carriers and 225,000 .303-inch rifles. It was two months or more before instructions in this sense actually reached the manufacturers, and results were not uniformly good. Not even AA-1 priority produced any carriers at all or more than 2,600 tank transporters in the latter half of 1942. On the other hand the output of .303-inch rifles in that period was 242,000; and the negotiations of the summer had at least averted the risk that British orders would be pushed into a corner while the main American programme was rushed through.

Meanwhile steps were being taken to supplement, if not to supplant, the priority system by more direct methods of planning. Machine tools were already guided to their destination by means of allocation, and the War Production Board was experimenting with the allocation of raw materials. Its first essay, the 'Production Requirements Plan', whereby the Board doled out materials to individual manufacturers on the basis of their own estimates of need, was breaking down under its own cumbrous weight; and in the summer of 1942 W.P.B. decided to adopt a version of the well-tried British system, which had been expounded to it by a team of British experts headed by Professor Arnold Plant. Under the 'Controlled Materials Plan', which came into full operation in the spring of 1943, allocations of the four key materials, carbon and alloy steel, copper and aluminium were made to the several 'claimant agencies' (the War and Navy Departments, the War Shipping Administration, the Office of Civilian Supply, the Office of Lend-Lease Administration, etc.) who were then responsible for subdividing the allocation between their various contractors. By Scheduling Order M.293 of February 1943 the War Production Board extended its direct control over some two score key industrial components, such as valves, boilers, heat exchangers.

None of these controls, however, was capable of standing entirely on its own feet, and priority ratings maintained and even enhanced their importance. The directive governing the 1943 production programme did not appear in full until April, interim rulings being promulgated from time to time to keep the most urgent orders moving. When it did appear, British anxieties immediately revived. Here it must be explained that the Army Supply Programme, in which provision was made for all War Department and military Lend-Lease orders, was divided into several sections: Section I contained the main ground munitions programme, Section II the main air programme, while Section III was devoted to special Lend-Lease requirements. The last was commonly described as the 'non-common' section; but this was not quite accurate, for some major non-common weapons such as the .303-inch rifle were found in Section I. Rather, Section III was the home of components and other miscellaneous items procured only for foreign use. Requirements, of course, are not necessarily less urgent because they are 'miscellaneous'. Now it was found that according to the 1943 directive sixty per cent. of the items in Section I were to be rated AA-1 and the rest AA-2X,[1] whereas the highest rating in Section III was AA-2X and twenty per cent. of the items therein were graded AA-3. Against this disparity the British launched an immediate attack, which met with partial success. In June General Somervell conceded that, out of a total Section III programme of $710 million, the British might select items to a value of $200 million which would be given top priority. Nevertheless, the figures of deliveries during 1943 revealed quite clearly the continuing inferior status of non-common stores. Of the total provision made for supplies of ground munitions, common and non-common together, to the British in that year, 86 per cent. was duly liquidated by deliveries. But for tank components the percentage was only 70, for non-common signal stores 78, and for non-common engineer stores 49, whereas the corresponding figures for common stores in these two latter categories were 90 and 84.

NON-COMMON STORES – THE RESULTS ACHIEVED

It should by now be clear that especially after Pearl Harbour all attempts to secure warlike stores of other than standard American type from the United States were made against a strongly flowing tide. This was particularly true of components. The American authorities were naturally very anxious that British needs should be met in the form of complete equipment which was subject to military assignment rather than in the form of either raw or semi-finished material. Nor was this altogether contrary to British interests. A *sudden* shutting off of component supply in the early part of 1942, before America was in a position to make full compensation by way of finished munitions, would obviously have had a catastrophic effect

---

[1] This rating had been introduced in August 1942, to provide a home for essential civilian requirements. It appears to have lost its original significance and merely taken the place of AA-2.

on British output and have resulted in a net reduction of the armaments available to the United Nations at a critical time. But towards
the end of 1942 there was a fair prospect of an immense flow of
American munitions to the battle-fronts in the very near future, and
British production plans had in any case to be modified for lack of
manpower. The supply of many components had already served its
purpose for balancing British production at a critical stage of growth
and could now be dispensed with. The early contracts for 3.7-inch
gun barrels and liners had not been augmented under Lend-Lease,
and supply was allowed to peter out during 1942; and it was accepted
that after the end of that year deliveries of armour plate and of
Valentine tank components need not continue on the same scale.

Tank components were in a rather special category, in that their
export resulted in the production of machines which were fairly
clearly inferior to those then being made in America. The United
States Army was convinced in 1942 that in the Sherman they had a
war-winning weapon with which existing British cruiser tanks could
not compare. This the British could hardly deny, though they
believed that the cruiser then under development, the Cromwell,
would be at least the equal of the Sherman. The whole question of
tank supply in all its aspects, operational, technical and manufacturing, was discussed at a conference in Washington in March 1942,
between the United States Ordnance Corps and a high-level British
mission. Here it was agreed that each country should concentrate on
a single basic design, the United States on the Sherman and Britain
on the Cromwell, with variants to meet special tactical requirements,
and that the British would gradually cut out of their programme the
existing obsolescent or unsatisfactory machines. It followed that the
export of parts for these tanks from the United States could and should
be curtailed in order to facilitate the production of Shermans. The
total British demand was in fact reduced by about a third, from
$368 to $246 million, on the understanding, first, that supplies during
the current year would be maintained more or less at the level
previously planned, and, secondly, that the absolutely vital requirement of components for Cromwell tanks, especially engines and
generators, would be met. In the event, this compromise did not
prove viable. Before many months had passed it was evident that,
except for standard items such as the General Motors diesel engine,
of which a bulk production had been built up to serve both countries,
components for British tanks were simply not going to be forthcoming
on any scale from the United States. The domestic demand was
altogether too strong. A contract for 1,000 Crusader transmissions,
for instance, had been placed with an American firm as far back as
December 1940; by February 1943, when the Crusader was virtually
obsolete, only 73 had been delivered, although the same firm had

shown itself perfectly competent to make Valentine transmissions, on which it started before the American tank programme got under way. This was an extreme case, but not a wholly exceptional one. The value of tank component exports in 1942 was no more than $40 million. In the autumn of that year the Ministry of Supply recognised the facts of the situation by agreeing to a further large batch of cancellations. In the final analysis the value of the components exported to Britain did not exceed $165 million during the whole war. The failure of supplies was partly the effect and partly the cause of the steady decline in the volume of British tank production which set in after about the middle of 1942.

One class of components which was absolutely essential to British war production, and the demand for which persisted long after most others had been dropped, was the internal combustion engine, for installation not only in tanks but also in aircraft and a wide range of the smaller naval vessels. The crux of tank production in the United Kingdom throughout the war was the supply of engines for the fast cruiser type. By the end of 1940 it was obvious that the demand could not be met in full from British sources; and a request for the supply of a thousand Nuffield Liberty engines was lodged in the United States. It was understood that this was to be one of the first charges on Lend-Lease. But, although the prototype of the Liberty was an American aero engine designed in 1918, the search for a supplier, which was apparently restricted to the smaller firms, went on for months without result. This was fortunate rather than otherwise, for the Liberty engine proved hopelessly unreliable as installed in tanks. It was in fact the chief reason for the failure of the early British cruiser models. Towards the end of 1941 the Ministry of Supply found the technical answer to the power plant problem in an adaptation, known as the Meteor, of the Rolls-Royce Merlin aircraft engine. The Cromwell was designed round this engine. It was now proposed that the Packard Company, which was already producing Merlins, should also make Meteors for British use. The Meteor, however, was not acceptable to the United States Ordnance Corps, and at the conference of March 1942, it was decided that the British should instead make use of one of two models then being developed by the Ford Motor Company the V.8 or the V.12. The demand had by now risen to 3,000 engines. Later in the year a Tank Engine Mission led by Mr Miles Thomas (as he then was) settled on the V.8 as being nearer to production, and arranged for the requisitioning of 5,300 engines under Lend-Lease. None of these was actually forthcoming, however, since production was never more than sufficient for United States needs. As a result the output of Cromwells had to be restricted within the narrow limits of Meteor engine supply.

M

The Admiralty and the Ministry of Aircraft Production were more fortunate. The enormous and unforeseen expansion in the United Kingdom programmes of landing craft, motor torpedo-boat and motor launch construction created an insatiable demand, far exceeding the capacity of British manufacturers, for small but high-powered diesel and petrol engines. This was a requirement which American industry was especially well qualified to meet. Engines built by Chrysler, Packard, Hall Scott, Scripps, Gray and other famous American firms made a great contribution to British landing craft and mosquito craft programmes. In all, more than 25,000 engines were supplied. Even greater numbers of American engines came to the support of British aircraft manufacturers. Lend-Lease exports of aero engines to Commonwealth countries amounted to 35,500, of which nearly 24,000 (more than four-fifths of the total in terms of horse-power) were Rolls-Royce Merlins built by the Packard Company. To those must be added 6,000 Merlins which were bought for cash. The beginnings of this venture were described in *North American Supply*. It was a complete success. Not only was the original planned output of 800 a month achieved in reasonably good time, by July 1942, but successive expansions were authorised by the Joint Aircraft Committee after Pearl Harbour and put into effect. By the summer of 1944 Packards were delivering engines at the rate of about 2,000 a month, and a second plant, belonging to Continental Aviation, was coming into production. British aircraft manufacturers drew heavily on American sources of propellers also, to the tune of over 63,000 units. Here too the main development took place after the United States were at war, deliveries rising from 3,649 in 1940–1 to 30,454 in 1944; the latter figure represented about two-fifths of the total British requirement of propellers.

In considering the story of component supply in the Second World War, it is necessary to distinguish its more permanent features, which reflect the differences in the structure of British and American industry, from those which were temporary and accidental, in that they arose from the fact that the United Kingdom was at war two years earlier than the United States. That the United States could be looked to for a surplus of internal combustion engines, which might be used to balance the British output of naval craft, aircraft and possibly tanks, was due to more permanent features of American industry; and the same was true of such basic components as ball and roller bearings of which Britain imported substantial quantities even before the outbreak of war. Such articles, being the regular products of American engineering industry, could be manufactured on an enormous scale for both countries and distributed between them in much the same way as finished munitions of common type. On the other hand, it is in the highest degree unlikely that in any future emergency, Britain and the United States being involved together from the outset, the latter would find it easy to furnish bits and pieces of specific British equipment such as gun barrels or the sub-assemblies of tanks. In the early stages of the Second World War it was both necessary for the British to seek supplies of this kind and possible for the Americans to provide them. Necessary for the British, because complete equipment could thus be made available to their Forces more quickly than in any other way: possible for the Americans because they were not wholeheartedly engaged in armaments production on their own account. But the arrangement was not really satisfactory to either party. It led to a most uneconomic dissipation of the resources of a country whose greatest strength lies in mass production of standard articles; and while it enabled the British to plan a larger volume of munitions output than could otherwise have been attempted, it made the fulfilment of the plan far more uncertain. It was bad enough for the equipment of the British armed forces to be left partly at the mercy of a foreign production schedule, but far worse to have British munitions production thus dependent. The whole United Kingdom tank programme was disorganised by the disappointments over American engines and transmissions and although there was no other breakdown quite like this, too many manufacturers were too often living from hand to mouth upon an erratic supply of American component parts. This seemed to point to two possible conclusions as to future policy. One was that the ideal for the United Kingdom in time of war would be the largest possible measure of industrial self-sufficiency, the manufacture of components being balanced with the capacity for final assembly, even if this meant a small volume of output and, in consequence, either small forces or a still greater dependence on the United States for finished weapons. But a more rational solution might be found in another direction – the making at long last of firm agreements on the standardisation of the design of weapons.

The position of complete non-standard equipment after Pearl Harbour was generally similar to that of components. It is true that early in 1942 the War Department conceded that the Ford Motor Company might make Universal carriers for the British Army in Detroit as well as in Windsor on the other side of the Canadian border. In 1942 also the United States began to make No. 19 tank wireless sets and No. 48 infantry pack sets, continuing with the former until the end of the war. Otherwise no fresh British-type equipment of any importance was introduced in the American production scheme after Pearl Harbour, and those that were already in it were gradually eliminated. Owing to the reduction of War Office scales early in 1941, it had not been found necessary in general to repeat under Lend-Lease the early contracts for British gun

ammunition; and by the beginning of 1943 American supplies of shot
and shell consisted almost exclusively of natures matching standard
American guns. A few items, however, had a considerably longer life.
Of .303-inch rifles we have already spoken. Output reached 50,000
a month at the beginning of 1943 and continued at that rate until
it was stopped in the spring of 1944. Supplies of ball ammunition
of the same calibre were also fairly satisfactory. The Ministry of
Supply hoped for 50 million rounds a month from the United States,
and received on the average about 40 million a month throughout
1942 and 1943, after which supplies ceased to be required. With the
supply of 9-mm. Sten gun ammunition, however, the British did not
fare quite so well. The Ministry of Supply had planned a huge output of this useful little weapon in 1941, but could not arrange for
anything like an adequate supply of cartridges to match it. The
Canadians undertook to do all they could to help, but it still seemed
essential that the small existing output in the United States should be
raised to 100 million rounds a month in 1942 and 1943. The most
the Americans could offer was 35 million rounds a month. British
representatives kept up strong pressure on the War Department to
let production rise to the maximum rate permitted by the capacity
of the plants concerned, which, as the achievement of one particular
month had shown, was of the order of 57 million rounds. But without
success. Raw material was very scarce, and the Americans would not
agree to any compensating cut in the production of their own calibres
of small arms ammunition, although this was planned at a level
which in the British view was fantastically high. It has to be admitted,
however, that the British weakened their case in retrospect by putting
forward no requirement at all for 1944, though in 1943 they had
received much less than half the quantity for which they originally
asked, and both United Kingdom and Canadian production had
been below the forecast. While this seemed to point to an element of
inflation in their earlier requirements it was more due to the fact
(as happened for several items) that when the time came to make the
calculations for 1944 the balance between needs and assets had
changed.

Such success as the British achieved in the procurement of non-
standard equipment as well as of components was due to the special
circumstance that for two years the Americans were not themselves
fighting, so that they could not reasonably avoid paying some heed
to the particular needs of those who were. That a considerable
volume of such supplies continued to be furnished for two years
after the Americans had entered the war was evidence of their
statesmanlike appreciation of combined needs. It was not remarkable
that the British had many disappointments in this field of procurement. What was remarkable was that during these two years twelve

out of every hundred rifles and six out of every hundred rounds of small arms ammunition produced in the United States were of calibres which only the British Army could use; and that in 1944 more than a third of the American production of armoured vehicles, other than tanks, consisted of a type, the Universal carrier, in which the American Army was not interested. It would be most unwise to suppose that anything like this could happen again.

CHAPTER IV

ALLOCATIONS AND PROGRAMMES

(i)

Introduction

ALLOCATION and programming, the two processes that were superimposed on the straightforward procurement of war supplies from the United States by or on behalf of the United Kingdom, were both gradual developments. It is true that the distribution of American arms production by a formal procedure began at a definite moment of time when the Munitions Assignments Board started operations in Washington in March 1942, and that the presentation of forward-looking programmes of requirements became more important, and the programmes themselves more formal and rigid, after Pearl Harbour. But the origins of both processes can be traced back to the earliest days of British procurement. From the first, British purchases had to be collated with the requirements of the United States forces, although it was not until the latter became large and urgent towards the end of 1941 that the problem became really acute. Primitive forms of munitions assignment – that is, the distribution of finished supplies according to relative needs – and of munitions programming, or the forward planning of British procurement, were in evidence as early as the spring of 1940, when the British gave notice of their purchasing intentions and negotiated for the release of aircraft and explosives from American stocks. Both, however, can best be studied by concentrating upon the period in which they were most conspicuous and most difficult – allocation in the months that followed Pearl Harbour and programming at and around the end of 1942.

Both processes were closely related to the work of the Combined Boards which is the theme of the succeeding chapter. The principles and techniques of allocation will indeed be described in the section of that chapter which deals with the Combined Munitions Assignments Board, and only its results in the most critical epoch will be discussed here. The forward planning of supply from the United States to Britain, on the other hand, is something distinct and apart from the more ambitious planning of global supply which was attempted by the Combined Production and Resources Board. The former was an element in the latter, but it would have been necessary even if the latter had not been undertaken at all.

(ii)

The Distribution of Munitions

THE NEW SITUATION AFTER PEARL HARBOUR

A few hours after the news of Pearl Harbour had broken, the word went out from Washington that all war material in process of being delivered to the Lend-Lease countries, whether in depots, at the docks or in the holds of ships still in American harbours, was to be detained 'pending consideration' of urgent United States needs. This was, of course, an entirely natural step for the authorities to take. Not merely was the position of American garrisons in the Pacific desperate, but a Japanese attack on the continental United States, was a real possibility; and the United States Services, from whom a large part of the meagre American arms output had been withheld during the past eighteen months, were not at all well equipped to join in the war themselves. Nor was the freeze order of long duration, or the intervention of Army officers more than a 'quick look-see'. Within twenty-four hours all material for which papers had been signed at the ship's side was released, except aircraft, 1,000-lb. bombs, $1\frac{1}{2}$ million rounds of .30-inch armour-piercing ammunition and four heavy anti-aircraft guns. On 9th December general instructions were given for the release of all non-common ground munitions, and these were followed in the next few days or so by the freeing, item by item, of most common stores as well. In the event, the only actual 'repossessions' of any importance were of small arms ammunition and aircraft, of both of which the Americans were desperately and immediately in need. Besides the .30-inch ammunition already mentioned, the British lost 5 million rounds of .50-inch ammunition from their own contract deliveries. It was at first feared that as many as 1,200 aircraft might be diverted, but actual losses were only 379 planes (and 766 engines) from cash contracts and 200 from defence aid expectations.

The episode was none the less disturbing, not so much because of what it meant in terms of equipment lost to the British forces as because of what it might portend. For Britain (and for Russia) the emphasis was still on immediate reinforcement rather than on long-term development. The Forces in Libya were sadly short of efficient tanks and anti-tank guns and of many types of ammunition. The defences of the United Kingdom were still dangerously thin; shipping losses were mounting alarmingly; and it was essential to step up the pulverisation of German industry by heavy and persistent bombing while the bulk of the Luftwaffe was detained in the east. On the other hand, it was assumed that by 1943, if she survived till then, Britain would be able to equip her land forces with little assistance from the United States. It was assumed also that the problem of shipping and aircraft supply would by then have been solved by the uninhibited expansion of American production. The crux of the matter was how to get through 1942 without disaster. For the time being, therefore, the share-out of currently available munitions was more important than the laying of plans for production in the years ahead.

There was, of course, nothing new in this. The problem of munitions assignment had been very much present in 1941, and there had always been conflict between America's two objectives, the strengthening of her own forces and the support of other anti-Axis nations. But now that the United States was a belligerent and no longer merely an arsenal, the conflict was bound to be greatly sharpened and there was a real risk that the latter objective might be completely eclipsed. In the months before Pearl Harbour there had been, broadly speaking, three groups of opinion in the United States. There were those who believed that America should stay as aloof as possible from the struggle and who therefore regarded the policy of rendering material aid to the democracies with active hostility or at best with tepid acquiescence. Others, more numerous, held that America should help to promote the defeat of the Axis, but held also that it was possible, and if possible, certainly desirable, to achieve this end without the actual committal of United States armed forces. Lastly, there was a small but influential minority, having the Secretary for War, Mr Henry L. Stimson, as its foremost spokesman, which considered this view unrealistic and even somewhat discreditable, and was sure that sooner rather than later, the United States would have to join in the shooting war. Now it was not the first group but the third which had done most to curtail the share of munitions allotted to Britain. If the United States forces were not going to wage war then there was everything to be said for the sending of arms to those who would use them. But if they *were* going to fight, they would have to be made ready. They would have to have planes and tanks and guns, even if the British went short. They would even have to expend in training some of the ammunition which the British desperately needed to expend in battle. Mr Stimson firmly believed that Britain herself stood to gain more in the long run from the creation of strong, well-armed and well-trained American forces than from an immediate increase in the supply of munitions;[1] and now, on 7th December 1941, the Stimson party suddenly came to include the whole

---

[1] Henry L. Stimson and McGeorge Bundy, *On Active Service in Peace and War* (Harper and Brothers, New York, 1948).

Administration. For America was indeed at war, and the contention that American forces should have first claim on American equipment was obviously much stronger than before.

The British authorities recognised that in the new situation they could not look to receive the same proportion of American production as before. A few days after Pearl Harbour a cable from the Ministry of Supply divided the previously stated requirements of army stores into three categories. Some of the stores requested, particularly artillery weapons of American type, were described as 'definitely less urgent'. Others, though urgent, 'could to some extent be replaced by supply here or from other sources', and of these 'some reduction could be tolerated'. But there was a third category of orders whose 'non-fulfilment would seriously impair our immediate fighting effort or gravely interrupt vital production here'. In this class were tanks, tank transporters and heavy trucks, tank and anti-tank gun ammunition, a thousand 37-mm. guns for British-built armoured cars, and most types of small arms ammunition – broadly speaking the munitions needed for immediate use in North Africa. These supplies, together with components and a wide range of machine tools and special materials such as drop forgings and the veneers used in aircraft production, the Ministry of Supply was determined not to forego. Similar urgency attached to all the aircraft on order and to most of the Admiralty requirements, particularly auxiliary aircraft carriers, Oerlikons, torpedoes and engines for small craft. In short, if the inroads made by the American Services went too far, if the flow of the really vital supplies to Britain and to Russia were not maintained during the months after Pearl Harbour, defeat in 1942 was a distinct possibility. The striking of a proper balance between the reinforcement of the points immediately threatened and the development of American strength for future action was the first and most urgent task for the Anglo-American combination. If Suez were lost, if the Red Army were driven into Siberia, if India and Australia fell to the Japanese, if the Battle of the Atlantic were lost or Great Britain successfully invaded, it would be poor consolation to see the American Army emerge a mighty force in 1943.

FAIR SHARES IN FAMINE

The task of distribution was entrusted to the Munitions Assignments Board set up in Washington as a result of the Arcadia conference. It was carried out with a very large measure of success. In September 1942, the British Minister of Production severely criticised the way in which the assignment machinery was being operated at that time, but acknowledged that in the short-term work of dividing up the supplies available in the first four months after Pearl Harbour the assigners had done a good job. How good, from the British point of view, may be inferred from a comparison of the expectations entertained by the British before Pearl Harbour with their actual receipts.

Hopkins, when he attended a meeting of the Defence Committee in London in July 1941, had recognised that the allocation of American supplies was the major uncertain factor in British planning and that the uncertainty ought to be resolved. And at the discussions in London in September, generally known from the protagonists as the Beaverbrook-Harriman conference, some steps were taken in this direction. Two sets of figures emerged from these meetings. One (the Victory Programme) showed the volume of supply, over and above British Commonwealth production, required by the Forces in areas of British strategic responsibility, by March 1943. The other looked less far ahead and implied a more definite commitment. It showed the estimated United States production of the main common-type weapons and ammunition between 1st October 1941 and 30th June 1942, the quantities considered surplus to American needs and the division of the surplus between Britain and Russia.

Table 6 shows for some types of weapons and ammunition the percentages of the total United States production, as estimated in September 1941, which were provisionally allocated to the United Kingdom and the allocations finally made to the United Kingdom, expressed as percentages of actual production.

Table 6. United States munitions production and allocations to the United Kingdom, 1st October 1941 to 30th June 1942

	Per cent.	
	Provisional allocation of *estimated* total production	Proportion of *actual* total production received
Medium tanks . . .	60	51
Light tanks . .	56	16
37-mm. anti-tank guns .	22	8
37-mm. A.P. shot . .	27	38
75-mm. ,, ,, . .	21	31
.30-inch ammunition .	17	25
.50-inch ,, . .	8	25
20-mm. ,, . .	19	51

Thus while there was no close correspondence in detail between expectations and receipts, the general effect was that the proportions were fairly well maintained in respect of the equipment which the British most needed. This result was made possible by the great forward surge of American production. The comparisons which in

Table 6 are shown in terms of percentages are translated into numerical terms in Table 7.

Table 7. Allocations – provisional and actual – to the United Kingdom from United States munitions production, 1st October 1941 to 30th June 1942

	Unit	Provisional allocation from estimated production[1]	Actual allocation[2]	Percentage increase (+) or decrease (−)
				%
Medium tanks . .	number	1,406	2,780	+ 98
Light tanks . . .	,,	1,800	676	− 62
37-mm. anti-tank guns .	,,	1,080	500	− 47
37-mm. A.P. shot . .	thousand rounds	475	3,435	+623
75-mm. ,, ,, . .	,,	350	863	+147
.30-inch ammuniton .	million rounds	242	607	+151
.50-inch ,, . .	,,	33	102	+309
20-mm. ,, . .	,,	2.3	10.4	+452

[1] i.e., column 2 of Table 6 expressed in numerical terms.
[2] i.e., column 3 of Table 6 expressed in numerical terms.

These figures go far to establish the fact that even in the very short run, and even in the narrow field of supply, the British Army gained, after all, far more than it lost by American belligerence.

The Royal Air Force, however, was less fortunate; one reason was that the Americans were able to get into action with aircraft much more quickly than they could deploy their ground forces. From the first day of war, planes were being flown across the Pacific to strengthen the defences of the Philippines; and United States air squadrons were established in England well before the main land forces began to arrive. Thus even in this very early period they had a good strategic case for retaining the bulk of their aircraft production for their own use; and the British were not merely disappointed in their hopes of additional planes from War Department contracts but did not wholly succeed in maintaining the continued employment of their 'own' capacity. In the nine-month period used for the previous comparison they received only 28 per cent. of all the combat planes produced in the United States, instead of the 53 per cent. they had been offered in September. A further reason was that aircraft production in general did not show the same dramatic increase over pre-Pearl Harbour schedules as did that of most army stores. Actual output up to mid-1942 was in fact slightly less than the September 1941 estimate. The aircraft industry was already much more fully developed than most of the defence industries, and new capacity took time to make itself felt. The result was that in the nine months actual British receipts in numbers as well as in proportion to total output, fell far below the allocations promised in September, which had themselves seemed distressingly small.

Table 8. Allocations – provisional and actual – to the United Kingdom of aircraft produced in the United States, 1st October 1941 to 30th June 1942

	Number	
	Provisional allocation	Actual allocation
Heavy bombers	188	171
Medium bombers . . .	831	517
Light bombers	2,710	1,248
Fighters	3,611	2,046
Naval reconnaissance . . .	194	49
	7,534	4,031

The allocation had been revised immediately after Pearl Harbour. The Chief of the Air Staff had accompanied the Prime Minister to Washington in December and had then come to an understanding with his opposite number on the distribution of American aircraft throughout 1942. For the first five months (in June, as we shall see, the terms were radically altered) the Arnold-Portal agreement gave the Royal Air Force 3,800 combat planes. As only 950 had been delivered in the last three months of 1941, this already represented a considerable decline from previous expectations. And in fact the agreement was set aside from the start, actual assignments in the five months totalling only 2,478 combat planes. The reasons were various. A British analysis of the shortfall of 400 planes in the first quarter showed that its main elements were as follows: of 117 Boston light bombers promised all but five had been diverted to Russia; manufacture of the Bermuda bombers, of which 73 were promised, had not yet started; 57 out of 60 Lightning fighters had failed to satisfy British inspectors. In other words (as the Ministry of Production paper put it), bad faith in one case, bad production in another, bad designs in a third – but not as yet any large encroachment by the Americans themselves.

But about the middle of the year the situation began to change. American forces were rapidly expanding and were rapidly getting nearer to action. Before the close of 1942 United States ground troops were committed to battle in the Solomons and in Tunisia. Many others were moving into the United Kingdom, whence American crews were already taking American bombers in operational flights and whence it was still hoped that a great land offensive might be launched early in 1943. Thus the British claims for precedence in the allocation of military supplies was steadily weakening. The dissents registered by the British members of the assignment committees became more frequent, and their appeals to the Main Board more frequently unavailing. The figures in Table 9 are sufficient to show the general trend. Total American production (except of vehicles)

Table 9. Percentage of United States output of certain war stores allocated to the United Kingdom

Per cent.

	July 1940 to Dec. 1941	January to June 1942	July to Dec. 1942
Combat aircraft . .	45	27	19
Medium tanks . .	31	57	23
'B' vehicles . .	13	13	12
Tank and anti-tank gun ammunition . .	61	42	20
Small arms ammunition	56	35	19

was, of course, expanding very fast. Yet the proportionate decline was so sharp that in all these vital categories, except that of small arms ammunition, the actual quantities received by the British were slightly smaller in the second half of 1942 than in the first. Aircraft supply in particular was very seriously affected. In the spring of 1942 the United States Army Air Corps, growing more and more restive at the diversion of the large numbers of American aircraft to assist the expansion of the Royal Air Force, secured from the President a declaration to the effect that no American aircraft should be transferred to another country if there were an American crew ready to fly it against the enemy.[1] In June the British were obliged to assent to a drastic revision, in which very full expression was given to this principle, of the Arnold-Portal agreement. According to the original agreement the Royal Air Force was to receive 5,750 combat planes in the period from June to November 1942 inclusive. The expectation was now reduced by more than fifty per cent. to 2,700 planes. This was to be offset, however, by a nearly equivalent increase in the front-line strength of American air forces operating from the United Kingdom and other British bases. The most serious feature, in British eyes, was a reduction in the allocation of transport planes, which were very badly needed in India and elsewhere, from 850 to 50. Even this agreement could not stand against the tide. Owing to failures in production, by September there were deficiencies of 31 Mustang fighters and 576 light bombers. And at the same time the plan to establish four United States fighter groups in the Middle East had had to be abandoned. There can be little doubt, in fact, that the

---

[1] See also *North American Supply, op. cit.*, Chapter IX.

new American policy was leading to an appreciable loss of immediate impact upon the enemy.

(iii)

The Forward Planning of Munitions Supply

One of the salient features of the history of procurement from the United States during the Second World War was the continuous trend towards rigorous and comprehensive forward planning. Beginning with casual purchases of individual stores, it was marked in its later stages by the framing of detailed programmes in which the whole area of supply from America to Britain was mapped out for as much as two years ahead. This development was the result of continuous pressure from the United States Government, increasing in proportion as tighter administrative control was established over the American economy.

In the first phase of the war the supply ministries in London notified requirements piecemeal to their agents in the United States as the need arose. Only in a few instances was the demand for some class of war material, such as aircraft or explosives, large enough or permanent enough before the fall of France to form the basis of what might properly be called a supply programme. Even at this stage the United States, though content to be treated as a retailer, asked to be given some kind of advance shopping-list, so that it might be sure of laying in adequate stocks. The demand became more insistent when rearmament began in the summer of 1940; and, although a number of British programmes were formulated at this time, even in sum they did not satisfy the Administration's desire, stressed in cable after cable from Purvis, for a really complete forward-looking statement of British needs.[1] The advent of Lend-Lease, however, necessarily brought such a statement into being. It was drawn up by the British Supply Council in February 1941, on the basis of the information about British deficiencies which Purvis had collected in London two months before.[2] This gave the War and Navy Departments and the Office of Production Planning some idea of the provision which they would be called on to make for British needs; but it was primarily concerned with fiscal rather than production planning, and was not in any sense a list of firm orders. These took the form of individual requisitions which were filed from time to time after the Appropriation Act had been passed, and which did not necessarily follow

---

[1] See *North American Supply, op. cit.*, Chapters IV and VI.
[2] Ibid., Chapter IX.

out in detail the original outline plan. Many of them were of the type later known as 'spot' requisitions, covering requirements not foreseen or budgeted for in the initial programme. When, however, the second Lend-Lease appropriation made its appearance in October 1941, the British came under strong pressure to submit at once a detailed programme for the obligation of the entire fund which had been placed at their disposal, in order that the production authorities might correlate British and American needs and plan ahead accordingly. Thereafter, since requisitions were no longer filed for munitions of common type, programmes became not merely a convenience to the American planners but an indispensable part of the procurement process. They were the only means whereby British requirements of such stores could be brought to the notice of the War and Navy Departments at the procurement stage.

On the air and naval aides programming was not particularly arduous. An air programme, the whole of which is closely related to the supply of a single item, the aeroplane itself, is a fairly simple matter. Moreover, since aircraft production was kept at the highest practicable level in the United States throughout the war, British procurement programmes could not affect the issue. The Air Staffs of the two countries met twice a year to decide how many aircraft the Royal Air Force and the Fleet Air Arm were to receive during the next six or twelve months, but this was an example of long-term assignment rather than of production planning. Similarly, Admiralty requirements were confined in the main to a few major items. It was important to the Royal Navy that American production of, for example, escort vessels should be accelerated, but both the production and the allocation of these warships were matters for high-level negotiation and did not call for any special system of programme formulation. The multifarious complex of stores which comprised the requirements of the Army, on the other hand, did call for very elaborate planning; and in what follows it is chiefly of ground munitions that we shall be speaking.

At the end of October 1941, the British Purchasing Commission filed with the War Department a series of documents, known as 'Tabs' A, B, and C, followed two or three weeks later by Tabs F, G, and H. These were first and second instalments of an expenditure programme for each of the three ground munitions categories – ordnance, tanks and transport, and miscellaneous military equipment – of the second Lend-Lease appropriation. It will be recalled that this appropriation was not intended to cover weapons of common type. British requirements of these were listed in a separate schedule, Tab L,[1] of which the War Department took cognisance

---

[1] Tabs D and E were first drafts of Tab L, and Tab J was a list of cancellations. Tab K is not known to history.

when it prepared the estimates for its Third Supplemental Appropriation, voted ten days after Pearl Harbour. In connexion with the Fourth Supplemental which followed hard on the heels of the third, the British Purchasing Commission submitted yet another document, Tab M. This covered all outstanding requirements for delivery by March 1943 – that is, for use in the campaigns of that year. But the plans of the War Department ranged still further ahead, and almost immediately the British were asked to estimate their military needs right up to the end of 1943. The answer was Tab Q, which took its place among the calculations issuing in the Fifth Supplemental of March 1942.

So far, Lend-Lease munitions programmes had been framed in close relation to fiscal appropriations, even though these were no longer voted for international aid as such. But this relation was rapidly becoming inappropriate. Munitions production in the United States was no longer governed by finance but by quite other, physical factors. The crucial question was not how many dollars the Services intended to spend, whether on British needs or on their own, but how many factories they wanted to build and what quantities of raw materials they proposed to consume. By the summer of 1942 the War Department had come to realise that something more was required of it than an expenditure programme for the obligation of congressional funds; and in August it produced the first edition of the formidable document known as the Army Supply Programme. This was a statement of the 'production required', whether under old or new contracts, in each of the calendar years 1942 and 1943 to meet the approved needs of the United States and Allied Armies. The schedule, Tab R, which the British had compiled for this occasion, differed in an important respect from all its predecessors. Like the Army Supply Programme itself, it was not a list of *fresh* requirements but a statement of the total supplies which it was hoped the United States would furnish during the two years in question. Its authors had consolidated Tabs L, M, and Q and added to them the undelivered balance of the cash contracts and of the requisitions filed under the first two Lend-Lease appropriations.

The Army Supply Programme was intended to provide a definitive framework for American munitions production during what remained of 1942 and the whole of 1943. What was included therein would be produced, and very little else. Thus the British Government could no longer put forward claims upon American production as and when the need arose, but had to attempt to estimate at once the whole of what it was likely to require during the whole period of the build-up for the offensive in Europe. The programme was indeed reviewed at roughly six-monthly intervals, but, as the War Department was usually loath to consider important alterations for the current year at the summer revision, British receipts from the United States were for practical purposes settled at least a full year ahead. In theory, of course, nothing prevented the British from bidding for additional supplies at the assignment stage. But unless their operational need was exceptionally clear they stood little chance of getting more than had been provided for them in the programme. They were in fact much more likely to get less. The phrase used by the War Department, 'provided for the British', was not a promise. Indeed, it did not appear in the formal printed document, in which the total 'production required' was broken down into three sections only – Army, Navy and International Aid. The British had to ascertain separately what proportion of the last section was earmarked for them. The figures quoted to them were in practice maxima. As in the past the British would have to bear at least their full share of shortfalls in production.

The new system thus introduced into the planning of Lend-Lease munitions supply a degree of rigidity which, for a number of reasons, was not at all welcome to the British Government. One reason was very simple: it entailed a great deal of additional work. The twice-yearly revision of the Army Supply Programme was always a very hectic time both for the missions in Washington and for the departments at home. War Office requirements had to be hurriedly recalculated, often at a time not otherwise appropriate, United Kingdom and Dominion production forecasts reviewed and the resulting deficiencies worked out afresh in very great detail, that nothing might be overlooked. Nor did the British authorities think much of the value of such calculations. It is a commonplace that the United States is a far more statistically-minded country than Britain. Central planning may not in general be regarded with much favour by Americans, but when they do find it necessary to plan they do so very thoroughly. American firms are required to furnish the Administration with more information about their activities than has been exacted by the Socialist Government of Britain. There was therefore a marked difference of approach to the problems of supply planning. An analogy may be taken from the industrial methods of the two countries. Mr Donald Nelson has described[1] how the American engineers who first saw the Rolls-Royce Merlin engine admired that 'beautiful piece of machinery', but found the accompanying blueprints and manufacturing instructions almost useless. These were little more than a 'gentleman's agreement' between the designers and the skilled craftsmen for whom they were intended, whereas for American purposes every process has to be mapped out beforehand in the minutest detail. In much the same way British administrators regarded the planning of war supply as an art rather than an exact

---

[1] D. Nelson, *Arsenal of Democracy*.

science and tended to condemn 'merely arithmetical' methods. They had little faith in the precision of forecasts, whether of requirements or of production, and held it folly to rely on them to the extent of allowing no deviations from a sacrosanct programme. In connexion with Tab Q the Ministry of Supply protested that it was extremely difficult to estimate marginal requirements for two years ahead; any such calculation 'can have but a limited value and should not determine production planning for 1943'. Again, in June 1943: 'we cannot agree that the war production programmes should remain indefinitely fixed'.

For, quite apart from the general difference of planning method, the British Government had a special reason for desiring flexibility in the American programme. The demands which it made upon the United States represented the marginal element of its requirements and therefore the element most liable to change. Perhaps the most difficult problem of war production planning is how to reconcile the manufacturer's need for continuity in production with the certainty that the user's requirements will fluctuate frequently and widely. In the early part of the Second World War this difficulty had been greatly mitigated by the existence of a reserve arsenal in the United States, which had given British planners a certain amount of room for manoeuvre. When the need had arisen for novel types of equipment such as Oerlikon guns, self-propelled artillery, tank transporters, amphibians, landing craft, auxiliary aircraft carriers, torpedo-bombers or transport planes it had been possible to avoid dislocating British production by passing the whole or the greater part of the new demand on to the United States. Similarly, America had come to the rescue when there was a disproportionate increase in the demand for certain existing weapons, such as tanks and rifles, which British production could not satisfy because its mould was already too firmly set.

It was of great importance to British planners in 1942 that this elbow room should not be lost to them. Towards the end of the year, for example, there was to be a huge and quite abrupt increase in the British Army's demand for vehicles and for signal apparatus, and a wholly new requirement of 20-mm. anti-aircraft guns for ground use. The only hope of satisfaction for these needs was a shift in the balance of American production. The British Government contended that American war industry, being still in the formative stage, ought to be able to accommodate such changes more easily than was possible in Britain, where practically no margins were now remaining. But this was ceasing to be true. It was no longer possible to provide for fresh British requirements simply by adding fresh capacity. Indeed, war production was less flexible in America than in Britain, in that, if they were to make the most of their mass-production techniques, manufacturers there had an even greater need for a long, clear run on a given product at a given rate of output. Thus, so far from being able to use American supplies as a means of softening the impact of changes in requirements, the British were henceforth obliged to calculate their demands upon the United States for longer ahead, and with less chance of subsequent revision, than their own programme.

The severity of the Army Supply Programme was tempered to this extent, that when British demands were too urgent to be deferred until the next revision of the programme, 'spot' requisitions might be submitted for the consideration of the War Department. The concession, however, was so hedged about as to have but very limited value. Such requisitions were subjected to a thorough, hostile, and cumbrous screening procedure by the International Supply Committee. Approval was granted only when the Committee was fully satisfied that the need was genuine and could be satisfied in no other way. The War Department at first insisted that no priority higher than AA-4 (by this time a very low rating) could be recommended unless some previously approved requisition were down-graded, and that the British bulk allocation of raw materials must be cut by an amount equivalent to that used in the manufacture of the stores concerned. These difficulties were gradually mitigated. In the autumn of 1942 it was agreed that 'spot' requisitions, being *ex hypothesi* very urgent, should automatically be rated AA-1; also that a small pool of raw materials (not only the controlled materials, steel, aluminium and copper, but also rubber, zinc and tungsten) should be set aside for this purpose each quarter. The pool, which could be increased only by special dispensation from the War Production Board, was so small, however, that only the very most urgent requirements could be handled in this way. As time went on and the production situation eased, the restrictions were gradually relaxed. The screening process was simplified by delegation to sub-committees; and in the spring of 1943 the War Department agreed that spot requisitions could be freely approved provided that material and facilities were available. At no time, however, was the system more than a small palliative for the rigours of forward planning.

Nor was it possible, after the summer of 1942, to get round the difficulty by stating as a requirement everything that Britain *might* need, allowing a large margin for contingencies. Before Pearl Harbour, and in the first flush of mobilisation, when the firmament itself seemed but a flimsy barrier to the expansion of American war production, British requirements of common-type stores had been accepted for procurement (as distinct from assignment) much as the demands of the United States Services were accepted, with very little scrutiny, question or cavil. But this did not last long. The requirements listed in Tab R for delivery to the British Army during 1942 and 1943 amounted to $10,000 million. They were considered at a series of Sunday meetings presided over by General Clay, and the upshot was that $8,200 million only were accepted for inclusion in the Army Supply Programme.

This apparent hardening of the American attitude not un-naturally gave rise to some murmuring in the British camp. Some among the British representatives in Washington held that as a matter of principle the full British requirement should be stated in the programme as a requirement even if it was not likely to be met in full. This thesis had some justification in that there was no sign as yet of any similar retrenchment on the part of the American Army. Nevertheless it was based on a misconception. American war industry was not a bottomless well from which munitions could be drawn at pleasure. It was not the case that, given only goodwill on the American side, the British could have whatever they chose to ask for. The whole point of the Army Supply Programme was that it was meant to be a statement of the requirements which could, with an effort, be fulfilled. Whether the British share should be greater and the American share less was a matter for argument and negotiation, but to hold out for an unrealistic programme was clearly wrong.

For a long time there had been a marked divergence of view about the proper scope of British programmes of supply from the United States. Purvis and others of like mind had continually urged the Government to set its sights high, to ask for all, and even more than all, the war material that it might be likely to require. Although the Ministry of Supply in particular had not been wholly convinced, there is little doubt that he was right; for during the first two years of war, ambitious British programmes had been the only means of calling the American war potential into being. Such projects as '3,000 aircraft a month' and the ten-division programme, which from a strictly British point of view were flagrant examples of over-provision, had served at the time the essential purpose of inducing the Americans to make for Britain what they ought to have been, but were not, making for themselves. The habit of mind thus en-gendered, however, persisted among the British in Washington after it had ceased to be appropriate. The requirements notified by the Ministry of Supply in December 1941, after Pearl Harbour were stigmatised by its representatives over the water as 'disappointing'. They urged that there would now be plenty of money and in the long run plenty of munitions, and that it would be 'an irretrievable mistake' not to take full advantage of these facts. The Ministry's reply may be paraphrased as follows: This is what we want and this is all we want. True, if we thought that we could get more in 1942 we should ask for more. But in practice we shall now have to wait until 1943 to complete the initial equipment of the Army, and by that time we shall be able to do most of the job ourselves. What the Americans need for their own use they should order on their own account. It is no longer for us to plan their programme for them.

This position was eminently sound. There was no longer any reason to fear that the Americans would underestimate total requirements: the danger in 1942 was quite the opposite. It was no longer true that the more the British asked for the more they were likely to receive. On the contrary, nothing could do more to harm their prospects of getting what was really essential to them than an American discovery that some of their stated needs were *not* essential. This truth was brought home very clearly in the autumn of 1942.

Less than two months after the original Army Supply Programme had been compiled, the decree went forth that it must be drastically revised. This was the result of the high-level reconsideration of the strategy of war production which has been described in *North American Supply*. The procurement activities of the War and Navy Departments, governed as they had been by what its apologists called the 'incentive target' system, had created an intolerable situation. They had been trying to build more new plants than could be built and to use more raw materials than were available. It was now generally recognised that the munitions programmes had to be trimmed in strict accordance with the inexorable limitations of plant and material, particularly the latter. Certain individual programmes of paramount importance to the war effort, viz., escort vessels, merchant ships, aircraft, aviation fuel and synthetic rubber, were singled out by the President as 'musts' and given absolute priority. The remainder of war production had to be fitted into a total of expenditure which was reckoned to be the maximum that the economy could stand without overstrain. For ground munitions the limit was fixed at $22,000 million in 1943. Though expressed for convenience in monetary terms this was not a financial ceiling in the ordinary sense. It had really more to do with the new raw materials allocation system, similar to and inspired by the well-tried British system, which the War Production Board was about to introduce, the Controlled Materials Plan. In the first quarter of 1943, for example, production had to be geared to a total supply of 19.6 million long tons of steel and 0.7 million long tons of copper. Thus the pendulum swung in the United States from *laissez-faire* towards the opposite extreme of rigid forward planning. Long-term programmes, careful balancing of requirement and supply, full justification of every demand upon the productive resources of the United States were now the order of the day. And all this applied at least as much to foreign claims as to those of domestic origin. The American authorities, and in particular the War Department, being no longer under the illusion that everything required could be produced, began to apply a still more critical eye to British programmes. Their new proposals allowed only $4,500 million for supplies of equipment to the British Army in 1943; and as assignments in 1942 seemed unlikely to exceed $1,500 million, this represented a cut of some twenty-five per cent. in the provision previously made for the two years – a cut of the same proportion as the United States Army had been obliged to inflict upon itself. Thus the prospect was that deliveries during the two years would fall short of the stated British need by over $3,000 million.

Once again, there were those who urged that the British should hold out firmly against any such curtailment, pressing the Americans for an intenser effort and more drastic restrictions on the civilian economy. It was true that by British standards the United States were still far from being fully mobilised, and could afford some further paring away of inessentials. But, as one British official sagely commented, 'in the last resort what is essential is what the public thinks essential', and the American public was making real sacrifices in its wonted way of life. In any case, so far as the British were concerned, the division of American resources between civilian and military requirements was a part of the data of the problem. Given that division, it was certain that the military programmes had to be pruned – in fact the British Government had been urging this for months – and only reasonable that in this process British requirements should suffer along with those of the American Army. What was important was that the cuts should not be applied arbitrarily; and the only way to avoid that was for the British to volunteer reductions on their own initiative and according to their own priorities. A searching re-examination of British stated needs was therefore called for. There was fairly general agreement with the view, expressed by various individuals in a rich variety of metaphor, that it was necessary to eliminate both 'water' and 'dead wood' from British demands, to 'get down to operational bedrock' and withdraw all requests that could not be supported by a 'cast-iron' military justification.

That the requirements presented to the War Department in the summer of 1942 did contain much that was obsolete or superfluous, was not open to serious doubt. To understand this, it is necessary to examine the way in which they had come into being. Two main classes must be distinguished. The requirement and supply position of the major ordnance items was subjected to periodic review by the Director-General of Munitions Production, and the demands for such stores that were notified to Washington could therefore be expected to represent genuine, up-to-date deficiencies. This, however, was true only in so far as the War Office requirements on which they were based themselves contained no element of over-provision.

In October 1942, military needs were about to be reassessed; and the Ministry of Supply was confident that when the reassessment was completed substantial cuts would become possible. Moreover, even where there were undoubted deficiencies the case for seeking them from the United States often rested on the assumption that they could be provided thence *early* in 1943. If that were not so, the requirement might well be void inasmuch as British production would have caught up on the demand before American supplies came through. Again, it was to be remembered that Tab R was a compendium, a consolidation of several earlier programmes. These contained a number of items which had been included for special and no longer operative reasons. Such was the 'requirement' of 1,152 105-mm. howitzers, which had come into existence as part of the ten-division scheme of November 1940. That scheme had long since passed into limbo. The British Army did not now want field artillery from the United States, and certainly not 105s. Nor did it want the 1,500 trench mortars, or the 1,155 90-mm. anti-aircraft guns, which had a similar origin. Very few of these were ever bid for by the British representatives on the assignment committee, yet they still appeared in the procurement programme as an unsatisfied British need. Here indeed was 'dead wood'.

There was even more uncertainty about the vast miscellany of requirements which lay outside the main ordnance programme, in particular that wide variety of supplies, ranging from workshop machinery to rubber boats, which are classed as engineer stores, and the even more miscellaneous category known to the British Army as 'general' stores and handled in the War Department partly by the Ordnance and partly by the Quartermaster Corps. To the American authorities it was at least as important that these requirements should be programmed as that others of more individual importance should be. For on being informed of British needs the War Department had to make an analysis of the quantities of scarce raw materials involved, and forward the details to the fourteen Divisional Committees of the War Production Board which arranged the necessary production facilities. Any additional requirements or major variations were therefore, to say the least, highly inconvenient. In the formulation of these programmes the Ministry of Supply Mission and the British Army Staff in Washington had inevitably enjoyed a large measure of discretion. London had generally notified its requirements in individual demand cables, supplemented occasionally by more comprehensive statements such as the Whiteley list of May 1941,[1] and the more recent Ricardo list. During 1942 the Ministry of Supply had done its best to furnish proper forward programmes of engineer stores, but these were so clearly incomplete that the missions filled

---

[1] See above, Chapter I, p. 24.

in the gaps on their own initiative. Moreover, the Ministry's programmes sometimes repeated demands which had been notified separately earlier on. Since the tendency in Washington was to interpret these as additional requirements, there was not always an exact correspondence between the quantities for which London had really asked and those which were submitted to the War Department. A further complication, which made it difficult for London to compile the final programme, was that the Dominions' requirements of engineer and similar stores, unlike their requirements of ordnance, were often transmitted to Washington direct; this again was a possible cause of duplication. It was, therefore, inevitable that there should be some dead wood on the books of the Missions and of the American Departments. The Departments in London did not have at this time either the information or the leisure to make comprehensive periodical reviews.

Now that programming had become essentially a matter of selection rather than of mere compilation, the first necessity was a more thorough consultation between the Ministry of Supply Mission and the British Army Staff on the one hand and their principals in London on the other. Accordingly, the two officers mainly responsible for the preparation of Army programmes were summoned home in September 1942, in order that they might impart first-hand information about the situation in Washington and receive first-hand instructions about London's needs and preferences and the reasons therefor. This helped to straighten out the factual detail of requirements, but these comparatively junior officials were not of course expected to carry the main burden of what were clearly going to be very arduous negotiations with the Chiefs of the War Department. It was no longer enough merely to state British deficiencies, even when these had been thoroughly scrutinised and all superfluities removed. Requirements had now to be backed by convincing and authoritative explanation, if they were to stand a chance of acceptance. When the great strategic decisions of the war had to be taken the Combined Chiefs of Staff organisation in its normal form, containing only *representatives* of the British Chiefs, was not an adequate instrument; the actual military leaders of the two countries had to meet face to face. So now when decisions of supreme importance were about to be taken on supply, no amount of contact through subordinates, however much in the minds of their principals, could take the place of direct discussion between the executive authorities concerned. It was therefore decided that the Minister of Production, who was about to visit Washington for the second time, should be accompanied by two very high-ranking officers of the War Office and the Ministry of Supply, namely, the Deputy Chief of the Imperial General Staff, General R. M. (later Sir Ronald) Weeks, and the Chairman of the Supply Council, Sir William Rootes. These gentlemen embarked on discussions with General Somervell, in whom, speaking very roughly, their joint functions were combined on the American side. Thus 'for the first time' in Sir William Rootes' words, 'a co-ordinated approach was made to the top United States authorities on the problem of British supplies' – for the first time, at any rate, since Sir Walter Layton's mission two years before. These negotiations and the resulting Weeks-Somervell-Rootes agreement have been referred to in *North American Supply* as an example of combined planning, but they have so important a place in the development of the munitions programme system that we make no apology for elaborating the theme here.

The negotiations were of necessity confined to a few, in fact thirty-one, of the many hundreds of items that made up the Army Supply Programme. These, however, were reckoned to comprise about 60 per cent. by value of all British Army requirements. They included armoured fighting vehicles and the principal types of guns and small arms with their ammunition. With one major exception, agreement was reached on all of them rapidly and with little contention, for the ground had been well prepared on the British side. During October the statisticians had been very busy. The War Office had recalculated its requirements for the period from September 1942 to December 1943 inclusive. From these totals had been deducted the revised estimate of output in the United Kingdom, Canada and the Eastern Group in the same period, and also the probable assignments from United States production in the last four months of 1942. The remainder was then the deficit which could be made good, if at all, only from American supplies in 1943. With regard to many of the items covered by the Weeks-Somervell-Rootes discussions, the sums had shown that the true deficit was considerably less than the previously stated requirement. The deficit of all natures of gun ammunition, for example, was under 37 million rounds, although a total of 46 million had been requested from the United States. In some cases the true need was less even than the balance of the provision made in the August edition of the Army Supply Programme. According to that programme almost 24,000 medium tanks were to be assigned to the British in 1943, but only 17,600 were now required; and the deficiency of 6-pounder anti-tank guns was shown to be 1,840 against a provision of 5,760. Even where this was not so, the full requirement was not retained if, as was the case with self-propelled artillery, there seemed to be no likelihood of its being met. Conversely, the demand on the United States was sometimes put higher than the arithmetical deficiency for 1943 as a whole in the hope that additional supplies might be forthcoming when they were most needed, in the first few months of the year. On balance, however, it was established that substantial economies could be made, even apart from the clearing away of the debris of wholly obsolete requirements. The total value of the items requested by the Lyttelton Mission was $2,400 million. Since the provision made for these and similar items in the existing Army Supply Programme for 1943 had been $3,100 million, this represented very nearly the full 25 per cent. cut required by the War Department. In reality, the cut was even more severe, for no allowance had been made for arrears, which amounted to some $600 million, on the 1942 provision.

Even so, the American authorities did not find it possible to satisfy the British on every point. The requirement of .30-inch rifles, for example, still rested at a little over a million, but the British Army Staff admitted that they were lucky to be allotted as many as half a million. The main disappointments, however, were over armoured fighting vehicles. The British asked for 20,000 Universal carriers against a previous provision of 29,750, but were allotted only 15,000. Of armoured cars, by way of exception, they sought an increased provision; an increase was conceded, but not as large an increase as they sought. The most difficult and contentious item, however, was the medium tank. The British were prepared to accept a minimum of 14,000, but the most General Somervell could definitely offer was 10,000, with a possible increase to 12,000 if the supply of raw materials improved. Otherwise there was little difficulty. The upshot was that $1,900 million was provided for the British in the revised programme for 1943 in respect of the major weapons under discussion; and with this the British negotiators were fairly well content. The more important results are set forth in Table 10.

Table 10. Allocations to the United Kingdom, and British requirements of certain war stores for 1943

Number

	Original allocation	Revised British requirement	Revised allocation
Medium tanks . .	23,979	14,000	10/12,000
Armoured cars . .	3,175	5,350	4,000
Carriers . . .	29,750	20,000	15,000
Field guns . . .	1,152	—	—
S.P. artillery . .	3,597	3,150	2,207
Anti-aircraft guns . .	2,550	1,570	1,570
Gun ammunition (thousand rounds) .	34,000	25,000	21,000
Anti-tank guns . .	5,760	5,000	5,000

This, however, was only the first round of the negotiations, and not the most arduous. An essential feature of the Weeks-Somervell-Rootes Agreement was a clause to the effect that the War Department would make every effort to incorporate in the Army Supply

Programme additional British requirements still to be discussed. The discussion started in December 1942, after Lyttelton, Weeks, and Rootes had returned home, and it did not proceed smoothly. One reason was that it was conducted at a lower altitude, where the atmosphere was always more oppressive. Mr Lyttelton had realised that in order to make his agreements stick he would have to go 'down the line' and impress the British arguments not merely on the group of broad-visioned statesmen at the top, but also on the more nationally-minded officers who controlled the actual working of the supply machinery. An official with long experience of Washington had remarked that this would be 'a very tough assignment', and so it proved.

The crux of the matter, however, was that whereas the British had more or less willingly accepted reductions in the items covered by the main agreement, in the remainder of the programme they were seeking an increased provision. The 'additional' requirements, in fact, amounted to much more than the 40 per cent. of the total previously assigned to them. They amounted to no less than $4,100 million, whereas the provision allowed for them in the August programme had been $2,100 million only. As its minimum needs were met, the British Army's standards naturally became higher. The nearer it approached to satiation in weapons and ammunition, the more insistent became the claims of the supporting arms and services. Requirements of mechanical transport, for example, showed towards the close of 1942 what British officials themselves described as an 'astonishing' increase of more than 50 per cent., and the requirements of some types of signal equipment were almost doubled. Manpower in the United Kingdom (and in Canada) was so scarce that most of this new demand had to be diverted to the United States. Now, the United States Army being still at an earlier stage of growth, the American planners had not so far given very high priority to these classes of equipment. In the British view, indeed, they were gravely under-rating their own needs. However that might be, it was obviously not going to be easy to persuade them to furnish the British forces with war material on a scale much more lavish than they were allowing for their own. If the British Army had received its full requirement of vehicles it would have enjoyed considerably more carrying capacity per head than the United States Army. The Chairman of the British War Supplies Committee urged that it would be 'the worst possible tactics' even to let the Americans see such figures, and they were in fact scaled down to a more reasonable and politic level before they were submitted. Even so they were far in excess of what America could supply from her existing facilities. Similarly, the stated British requirement of signal stores (including Air Force communication equipment) amounted to

$850 million. It was something of an understatement to describe this as 'a very large slice' of the capacity of the industries concerned, which at the time was about $2,000 million a year. The War Production Board was persuaded to increase the potential output of the radio and allied industries to $3,000 million a year and more. But such compliance was rare; nor, even when industry was expanded, did the War Department necessarily look with greater favour upon expanding British claims. At first, it took the line that the 25 per cent. cut must be applied over the whole field of British requirements. This position abandoned, it insisted that nothing which had not appeared in the August programme could be accepted for the revised edition, unless a corresponding reduction were made elsewhere. Reasons given were the scarcity of raw materials, the restriction on the construction of new plants and the dollar limit that was imposed on the ground munitions programme as a whole.

Long and complicated negotiations ensued. It has been explained that the Army Supply Programme contained four sections, of which the two relevant here were Sections I and III. It was sometimes said that the former covered common and the latter non-common types of ground equipment, but this was not quite accurate, since .303-inch rifles, for example, were included in Section I. Rather, this section comprised the main ground munitions programme, while the miscellaneous, minor stores produced primarily for International Aid[1] were relegated to Section III.

For this section, which contained some of Britain's most pressing requirements, including tank components, a large quantity of clothing for British forces in the Middle and Far East and an important part of the signal and engineer stores, the outlook did not appear at all promising. The British negotiators were at first told that they could have in 1943 only the unexpended balance of the provision made in the August programme for the two years. This was found to amount to $500 million, whereas the residue of requirements not included in Section I was estimated at $1,160 million. During February, however, the gap was gradually narrowed. First, the War Department conceded an additional $124 million. Then it was agreed that certain miscellaneous items to a total value of $150 million, could be dealt with outside the main military programme, either by 'spot' requisitions (with a special extra allowance of raw materials) or through Treasury Procurement. An attempt to get similar treatment for $100 million worth of clothing, however, failed, and the British seemed to be faced with the necessity of cutting out some $300 million worth of badly needed supplies, chiefly signal and engineer stores. But in the meantime important changes had occurred in London. Owing to the prevailing scarcity of manpower

---

[1] See above, p. 163.

and raw materials the British Government had been obliged to make a fundamental revision of its own army supply programme. Heavy cuts had been effected in the domestic production of ground munitions, and some of these made consequential reductions possible in overseas supply, especially of ammunition. The balance of requirements was therefore altered: a smaller provision of ordnance could be accepted if that made it possible to secure more signal and engineer stores. The British therefore took $80 million out of the provision for ordnance in Section I in order to expand Section III, in which their maximum allowance thus rose, with some minor adjustments, to $711 million. Meanwhile re-calculation had shown that the total value of requirements properly belonging to this section was less than had been thought, in fact $937 million. The gap had thus narrowed to $226 million, of which $151 million were to be taken care of in other ways, so that in the end the British secured provision for all their Section III requirements save only $75 million.

The negotiations over Section I had been completed earlier, and on the whole had gone more smoothly. There had, however, been one major setback in the matter of mechanical transport. The requirements stated by the British for delivery in 1943 amounted to 217,000 vehicles. This was less than half the arithmetical deficiency, but nearly double the number which the War Department could see its way to provide. The trouble here was sheer lack of production capacity, which in its turn could be traced back to the extreme scarcity of shipping. In general, the British had argued firmly and successfully against the thesis that production on their behalf in the United States should be governed by shipping forecasts, on the ground that, since munitions were only a small fraction of the total lift, even a small error in the forecast could make a big difference to the volume of such stores that could be moved. Deplorable as it would be to have military equipment piling up uselessly on the quays, it would be still more deplorable to cut back production and then have to send ships away half empty. Vehicles, however, were a special case; they were very bulky in comparison with other equipment of the same value, and could not be stowed economically except in special ships. In this one instance, therefore, it had seemed reasonable to restrict production on behalf of the British to the number which they were likely to be able to ship. Allowing for large Canadian deliveries, this appeared in the summer of 1942 to be 10,000 a month. The British had at first acquiesced in this ruling, but now sought to have it modified, urging – quite correctly as it turned out – that the supply of ships was sure to improve in the latter part of 1943. The War Department, however, would not agree to make provision for more than 10,000 a month throughout the year, though it was understood that the question would be considered again in the summer.

The upshot was that in addition to the items covered by the Weeks-Somervell-Rootes Agreement $2,600 million was provided in Section I of the revised Army Supply Programme. The results of the whole series of negotiations may be tabulated in round figures as in Table 11.

Table 11. British requirements of ground munitions and provisions made for them in the U.S. Army Supply Programmes

$ million

Ground munitions for delivery in:	1942	1943	1942-3
June – August 1942			
British requirements submitted, June 1942			10,000
Provided in Army Supply Programme, August 1942	3,000	5,200	8,200
December 1942 – *February* 1943			
British requirements submitted, December 1942:	(1,500)	6,500	8,000
of which; Items in Weeks-Somervell-Rootes Agreement . . .		2,400	
Other items in Section I . .		3,200	
Items in Section III . . .		900	
Provided in Army Supply Programme, February 1943:	(1,500)	5,200	6,700
of which; Items in Weeks-Somervell-Rootes Agreement . .		1,900	
Other items in Section I . .		2,600	
Items in Section III . . .		700	

On the face of it, therefore, the outcome was very much the maintenance of the status quo. In broad terms, the shortfall on assignments in 1942 had to be considered as a dead loss, but the British had averted any further cut in the total value of ground munitions being procured for them in 1943. The final provision for the two years represented only two-thirds of their original request, but well over four-fifths of the more searchingly examined requirements put forward at the end of 1942. This was by no means an unsatisfactory outcome.

One large question-mark, however, hung over the above presentation of the situation. Of the provision made in Section I no less than $1,200 million was still uncertain. It would indeed have been more accurate to say that the total provision for 1943 was $4,000 million, with a possibility that $1,200 million would be added later. In point of fact it was not added. The item in doubt was the British Army's request for very large numbers of quick-firing light anti-aircraft guns of 20-mm. calibre, similar to those which had proved so successful in the defence of ships. The story is a complicated one. When the need for a weapon of this type became apparent early in 1942, there was no immediate prospect of Oerlikons becoming surplus to naval requirements. On the other hand, a larger output of 20-mm. Hispano-Suiza aircraft cannon had been arranged than was required by the combined air forces. The British therefore appealed successfully to the War Department to keep production at the maximum level and release the surplus to the Army. The Hispano, however, could not be regarded as more than an understudy in this role. For one thing, it lacked a mounting for ground use; and although one was designed and production laid on in the United Kingdom, Canada and Australia, deliveries could not be expected in any quantity until late in 1943, by which time supplies of a special land version of the Oerlikon, the Polsten, would be coming forward from the same sources. The demand for Hispanos was therefore dropped in the spring of 1943, after some 40,000 had been assigned. Thus the supply of a suitable weapon early in 1943 depended on there being, after all, Oerlikons to spare. At the time of the Lyttelton Mission there seemed a good chance that this would be the case. But in the event, although the production of Oerlikons rose very fast,[1] the requirements of the United States Navy rose even faster. Not only did the British Army receive none in 1943 (or later) but assignments to the Royal Navy had to be curtailed.

Thus in practice the provision made for supplies to the British in the revised edition of the Army Supply Programme was $4,000 million only, and fell short of the provision made in August by very nearly the full 25 per cent. originally proposed. It represented, moreover, little more than sixty per cent. of the well-screened minimum requirements put forward in December. It must not be concluded from this, however, that the negotiations had been in vain. Superfluous and obsolete requirements having been eliminated, what was now included in the programme was, as far as care and forethought could provide, what the British Army really needed most. Not only had the true economic value of the supplies to be furnished by the United States been greatly enhanced, but there was a much greater likelihood that they really would be furnished. The British Government had given an assurance, and supported it with factual argument, that the supplies for which it asked were no more than were absolutely necessary, and that it was not trying to amass more material than it could profitably use. Satisfied on this point, the United States War Department had formally recognised the principle that its acceptance of British requirements carried with it an obligation to procure and make available the stated quantities

---

[1] Mr Donald Nelson has used the Oerlikon as a striking illustration of the way in which the problems of war supply were solved by mass-production methods. The first gun was made in July 1941. Within a year output was at the rate of 3,000 guns a month, and by the summer of 1943 it was 4,600 a month.

in the stated time – an obligation equal to that which was attached to its own programme. Any shortfall in production was to be shared in due proportion; nor were alterations to be made in the programme unless the strategic situation changed, and then only by mutual agreement. Thus the term 'provided for the British', from being a mere prognostication, had become something very like a promise.

The promise was not of course absolutely binding: if it had been, the munitions assignment organisations could have been dissolved at once, and no one suggested that. Nevertheless the change was very marked. In 1942 the British Army had received only about half the total value of the provision made for it, although the provision had been calculated as late as August, and although total production of ground munitions fell only 17 per cent. behind schedule. In other words the British had been compelled to suffer quite disproportionately from the shortfall. By contrast in 1943, 86 per cent. of the total provision was duly delivered. The main reason for the improvement was admittedly the tremendous upsurge of American production and the consequent general easing of supply and allocation problems, together with the fact that the worst shortages of the American Army had been remedied in the previous year. None the less, it was undoubtedly easier to get British requirements accepted and the acceptance honoured now that the American authorities knew beyond all reasonable doubt that the requirements stated were absolutely sound.

The general picture, however, still contained some dark patches. British receipts of vehicles (armoured and other), artillery, small arms, clothing and explosives were all within ten per cent. of the scheduled quantities. The percentage satisfaction of gun ammunition, on the other hand, was only 60, of 20-mm. ammunition 62, of tank components 70, of engineer stores 75 and of signal stores 86. Deliveries of gun ammunition were short, partly because of technical difficulties in production, but partly because of a declining demand for certain natures. The story of 20-mm. ammunition was very similar to the story of 20-mm. guns. Oerlikon ammunition could not be extracted from the Navy Department in sufficient quantities, and the alternative Hispano-Suiza type was not regarded with favour by the Army. The other three classes were of more general interest. Significantly, all of them belonged wholly or partly to Section III. Moreover 90 per cent. of the signal stores provided in Section I, but only 78 per cent. of those in Section III, were actually delivered, while for engineer stores the figures were 84 and 49. This confirms what has been said earlier about the inferior status of non-common stores. For such stores procurement still did not follow automatically from the acceptance of a programme. Individual requisitions had to be filed; and they could be, and sometimes were, rejected. The

British, however, recognised that this was a reasonable corollary to their own right to submit 'spot' requisitions. More serious was the fact that whereas 60 per cent. of the items in Section I was accorded AA-1 priority, the highest rating given to any item in Section III was AA-2X. The War Department tended to assume, it seemed, that 'miscellaneous' requirements could not be particularly urgent. The delays caused first by the requisitioning process and then by the placing of a special contract with a low rating, were such that the Ministry of Supply had been warned not to expect delivery of non-common engineer stores within twelve months of the time when the programme was accepted.

These disappointments did not alter the fact that in the main there was a far closer correspondence between procurement programmes and actual deliveries in 1943 than there had ever been before. And the correspondence was maintained at any rate for the first half of 1944. The British provision in the Army Supply Programme for that year was settled, provisionally in the summer of 1943 and definitely a few months later, not indeed with perfect accord but with far less excitement and upheaval than in the previous year. Not the least important of the gains that emerged from that upheaval was the firm establishment of the principles and technique of munitions programming. As a matter of principle, the British authorities had learnt that nothing, or very little, could be obtained from the United States unless it had been included in a programme; and that nothing would be included in the programme unless it was vital to the British war effort, and had been shown to the Americans to be so. General Somervell, it will be recalled,[1] was prepared to give his British colleague the shirt off his back *if he was satisfied* that otherwise pneumonia might set in. The need for full and convincing justification of British requests became not less but more acute as the war proceeded. Throughout 1943 and the early part of 1944 two conflicting tendencies were at work. On the one hand the volume of production increased so rapidly that the needs of the United States Army were apparently met much sooner than had been expected and there was therefore more and more capacity to spare for employment on British behalf. Indeed, quite early in 1943 the British Government found itself in the unfamiliar situation of being pressed to take more war material from the United States than it really wished. The opposing tendency, which quickly gained the upper hand, was the American desire to use the redundant munitions factories and the labour and material that went with them for purposes other than the reinforcement of the British Army. The Ministry of Supply was accordingly warned by its representatives in Washington that onerous as the task might be, it would have to be

---

[1] See above Chapter III, p. 159.

o

prepared to document its requests with a still stronger array of supporting facts and figures, remembering all the time that Lend-Lease was a real burden upon the American public, and that American officials were exposed to public scrutiny and censure to a degree unknown in England. In the latter part of 1944 the first tendency was reversed. The war in Europe was clearly going to drag on for some time yet, and the American Services found that they had under-rated their needs. Munitions production had been cut back too far, and surplus again gave way to shortage. Thereafter both tendencies worked together and in opposition to the satisfaction of British needs. Assignments were curtailed so sharply in the last few months of 1944 that over the year as a whole deliveries of the British Army reached only 75 per cent. of the provision; and there was great difficulty in securing provision in the 1945 programme even for Stage I requirements – that is, those which were based on the assumption that the war in Europe would continue.

As for the methods of programme formulation, the procedure developed at the end of 1942 into a regular drill. The twice-yearly revision of the Army Supply Programme was always a very hectic period both in London and Washington, in which a mass of calculations had to be completed at very short notice, since it was obviously desirable that the primary calculation of War Office needs should be made as near to the time as possible. The United States War Department was only gradually and incompletely won over to a more continuous and piecemeal review of requirements and provision. The form of the calculation was well established. As we have seen, for the negotiations in 1942 documents had been prepared showing first, War Office requirements, then the estimated production in the United Kingdom, in Canada and in the Eastern Group, then the resulting deficit, then the balance outstanding from the provision made in the existing programme, and finally the suggested provision in the new programme. Documents of this type, known later as 'B' tables, became a regular feature of all subsequent negotiations, though the Ministry of Supply was never wholly reconciled to the use of such arithmetic as a sufficient basis for the planning of supply. It became a matter of routine also that the officials who actually submitted the programmes should come home for consultation beforehand, and that a team of experts should be sent out to help in the negotiations. The negotiations, however, were conducted in the main at a lower level than in 1942. The main outlines of American supply to Britain having been determined then, it was not again found necessary to make a special intervention at the highest level on the Army programme[1] – until, that is, the autumn of 1944, when

---

[1] The Minister of Supply himself visited the United States at the close of 1943, but more as a matter of courtesy and general liaison than for purposes of negotiation.

Mr J. M. (later Lord) Keynes and Sir Robert Sinclair went out to discuss the principles of supply in Stage II, i.e., after the defeat of Germany. Their negotiation is dealt with in *North American Supply*. It covered a much wider field than the mere programming of Army supplies, which was overshadowed by considerations of high national policy, political, strategic and financial.

(iv)

The Forward Planning of Civilian Supplies

'Civilian supplies' was a term covering an immense miscellany of manufactured goods not obviously military in character. The main constituents were capital equipment (other than machine tools, which received special treatment) for British industry and agriculture, such as ploughs, tractors, industrial power plant and coal-cutting machinery and consumer goods such as textiles, office equipment, torch batteries and pen nibs.

A certain amount of normal trade in such commodities persisted in 1940 and in January 1941 the Ministry of Agriculture transmitted a request for the supply from the United States of a large quantity of farm equipment. But in the main, it was not until 1942 when the diversion of British industry to direct war production had been completed and stocks had run down, that the British were forced to rely to any large extent upon the United States for goods other than munitions (and machine tools) on the one hand and the bulk primary commodities on the other. Even then the requirements of the United Kingdom itself were less important than the requirements of the Dominions and Colonies, which were no longer able to continue their normal imports from Britain. The considerable task of gathering together all the requirements of the other civil departments, including not only their own direct needs but also those of industries and organisations 'sponsored' by them, fell to the Ministry of Supply.

About the same time formidable obstacles began to be raised against procurement from the United States, which, apart from the financial aspect, had hitherto been a simple matter; even if requirements could not be met out of trade stocks, there had been ample manufacturing capacity available for civilian-type goods so long as America was at peace. But in 1942 war mobilisation was proceeding apace and the War Production Board, through its thirty-six 'industry divisions', was scheduling one section of manufacturing industry after another for conversion to war production. This process clearly involved the danger that production of civilian goods would be cut back so far that really vital needs, both domestic and foreign, would be left unsatisfied and so it raised a 'combined planning' problem of the first importance, to which the Combined Production and Resources Board gave close attention from the outset. While the Board promised the Combined Chiefs of Staff that civilian requirements would be reduced everywhere to a bare minimum, it also set out to ensure that enough capacity would be left in being to provide for the essential needs of the United States, and those minimal needs of Britain and the other United Nations that were not met by British or other production.

With the wider combined planning which sought to reconcile global requirements with global supply we are not here concerned. But one essential component of such planning was the construction of forward-looking programmes of British Commonwealth requirements from the United States, which became necessary in the course of 1942 even for straightforward procurement, even if no combined planning adjustments were to be attempted. Until the spring of 1942 the only programme required from the British in respect of civilian supplies was that which the Office of Lend-Lease Administration exacted from them each time Congress had to be asked for a new appropriation. These programmes covered food, petroleum and raw materials as well as civilian goods, and, being required for budgetary rather than production planning purposes, were framed in broad categories and justified only in fairly general terms. But something more now became essential. In order to assess the extent to which industry could safely be converted, the War Production Board set up an 'End Products Committee' (which later became the Standard Products Committee and later still was broken up into several Divisional Requirements Committees). This body's task was to collect statements of requirements from fourteen claimant agencies representing the various users, to decide how much production capacity could be left undisturbed, and, since this was invariably less than the total stated requirement, to allot the estimated output between the several claimants. The principles and techniques, in fact, were similar to those applied to the allocation of raw materials under the Controlled Materials Plan. The interests of America's foreign customers were represented by the Office of Lend-Lease Administration, which received a bulk allotment of each commodity from the End Products Committee and in turn allocated it to its various clients. In this process the British Commonwealth was treated as a unit: the allocation received from the Office of Lend-Lease Administration was 'apportioned' between the United Kingdom, the Dominions and the Colonies by a special committee of the British Supply Council. Now the Office of Lend-Lease Administration could obviously not serve its clients efficiently without exact knowledge of their requirements and the reasons therefor: and for this purpose the ordinary 'appropriation programmes' were not nearly detailed enough. Accordingly, in May 1942, the British were requested to furnish a comprehensive statement of 'requirements for the United Kingdom and for each Dominion and major Colony for all highly manufactured goods . . . to be programmed now for shipment in the calendar year, 1943'. The original deadline for this task, 1st July 1942, was impossible of achievement and it was not until September that enough data were received from London to enable the British Supply Council to submit the so-called Five Quarters Programme, covering the last quarter of 1942 and the whole of 1943. Meanwhile interim statements had been called for on several individual commodities as they came up for review by the Standard Products Committee. There was thus much confusion and duplication of effort in 1942 which was somewhat mitigated by the centralisation of all non-munitions programming in a new division and sub-committee of the British Supply Council. At the London end the Ministry of Supply had gallantly undertaken the task of co-ordinating and presenting the whole programme of civilian requirements, collecting from the other civil departments – the Post Office, the Ministry of Transport, the Board of Trade, the Ministry of Agriculture, the B.B.C. and others – statements covering not only their own direct needs but those of all the industries and organisations which they could be regarded as sponsoring.

Munitions programming was complicated enough, but its complexities were far excelled by the planning of non-munitions procurement. The mere range of commodities almost defies imagination. Programmes were requested for over twelve hundred separate items, the catalogue of which resembles one of those bizarre lists on which Mr Paul Jennings' fancy likes to play. Among more familiar and more evidently important items were such things as cream setter cans, joy loaders, getters, amplidynes and selsyns, bachelor buttons, tournapulls and broom corn de-seeders. Whereas those responsible for military supply were dealing with the relatively specialised needs of definite numbers of men grouped into organised units, civilian supply embraced the entire range of all manufactured goods required by civilised society. Munitions procurement had been centralised from the start, and here the introduction of programming merely meant that requirements had to be calculated for longer periods and with less opportunity for revision. The trade in civilian goods, on the other hand, was normally carried on by a multitude o more or less specialised buyers and suppliers; and the canalisation of all this activity through governmental planning offices was a more formidable task than any administration had ever attempted.

One of the basic problems was that of definition and classification.

A heroic effort was made by the United States Government's Technical Committee on Standard Commodity Classification to frame a standard terminology which would be used by all claimants and all agencies for all purposes. But the 'Kolesnikoff Code', so named after the Committee's chairman, did not win universal acceptance, and for certain purposes other classifications continued to be used with much resultant confusion and loss of time in translating requirements from one code to another.

A further complication from the British point of view was that, whereas most military demands upon the United States originated from London, Dominion and Colonial needs being merged with the United Kingdom's own deficit, the several members of the Commonwealth could not be expected to agree to a similar arrangement for civilian supplies. London was the focus of the Commonwealth's war strategy, but there was no comparable centralised co-ordination of its economic life. All the Dominions and India individually, and the Colonies collectively, procured non-munitions through their own missions in Washington. At the same time the United States authorities insisted that the Commonwealth should act in this matter as in others, as a unit; and it was clearly undesirable that each country should present its own requirements, based on its individual ideas of what was or was not really essential, without some kind of central scrutiny. The question was, how and where were programmes to be collated and checked. Now there was in London already a Commonwealth Supply Council, whose Non-Munitions Committee seemed the appropriate body for the formulation of Commonwealth programmes; and London Departments clearly had much easier access than anyone in Washington to the kind of knowledge required for intelligent judgment of total needs. On the other hand practical exigencies often demanded quick action which could not wait on the deliberation of a body on the other side of the Atlantic. It was not merely a question of compiling a programme, but, quite often, of being forced to modify it at the request of the United States authorities. Moreover, certain of the Dominions looked askance at the Commonwealth Supply Council and preferred direct action through their Washington missions. The upshot was that a parallel body representing the United Kingdom and other Commonwealth missions was set up in the United States and a complicated compromise procedure worked out whereby the London body would have a chance at least to express its views at each stage from the framing of draft programmes to the apportionment of the quantities allocated to the Commonwealth by the Office of Lend-Lease Administration.[1] In practice it was impossible for London to carry out any effective

---

[1] See below, Chapter VII, Section vi.

scrutiny of the immense volume of requirements submitted and the Washington missions were perforce given a pretty free hand.

The worst complication of all, however, arose from the need to justify requirements in the sight of the United States authorities, to provide the background information which might convince them that the domestic market and the armed forces *ought* to be deprived of commodities which became progressively scarcer as the war proceeded. The Five Quarters Programme gave very little such information, which had therefore to be provided separately. For this purpose a document known as the Office of Lend-Lease Administration Requirements Branch Form 1 was devised on which each Lend-Lease country was asked to state by calendar quarters its stocks, home production, necessary home consumption, exports and resultant deficiency of each of some twelve hundred commodities, together with its proposed imports from the United States, the United Kingdom or from third countries, the end-use of the commodities and any other supporting information. The completion of these forms – fifteen thousand of them altogether – was a staggering task for the governments concerned. Part of the information contained on them might duplicate that which had already been furnished in ordinary demand cables sent through the normal procurement channels: other parts might require research. Thus, although the Office of Lend-Lease Administration attached much importance to having the forms ready in time for the preparation of the 1943 Civilian Requirements Programmes, and threatened that it would not be responsible for any breakdown in supply if they were not ready, it is not surprising that submissions were not complete until the end of August 1943. Meanwhile the original Five Quarters Programme, much revised as a result of the Standard Products Committee's work and of further consideration in London, had been allowed to stand as the basis of 1943 procurement.

It is hard to resist the conclusion that here was a case of planning run mad. Clearly, foreign countries could not be allowed to take just what they wanted from a tightening American market. Clearly, also the United States authorities had to have a reasonably clear idea of the total requirement of commodities whose production they were proposing to curtail, and had to satisfy themselves that the requirement was genuine. Serious damage might have been done to the war effort if either domestic or foreign needs of important capital or consumption goods had been left unsatisfied, and damage almost as serious might have resulted from the uncritical acceptance of maximum demands. But almost certainly programming and apportionment were carried in respect of civilian supplies to a point where the paper work involved yielded no proportionate return. At first it was laid down that forms must be submitted even if the requirement from the United States was nil. The British representatives managed to get this altered and also to secure the elimination of some of the less important items; but the number of commodities subjected to the procedure still exceeded a thousand. War experience has shown that modern administration can devise and work reasonably efficient and equitable systems of rationing for bulk commodities of real importance, but that the effort breaks down if it is applied too widely. Often it may be better to let people scramble, go short or get too much. This is still more true of international supply planning. Even the most elaborate system could not make the calculations of miscellaneous requirements other than arbitrary. It was not easy, for example, for the New Zealand Government to decide exactly how many pen nibs it would really need to import in the next twelve months, and for the Board of Trade in London, the British Supply Council or the Office of Lend-Lease Administration to check its findings was virtually impossible. It has to be stressed that British Commonwealth requirements of civilian goods were rarely a significant fraction of American production. No great harm would therefore have resulted, and much time and effort would have been saved, if the United States authorities had abandoned the quest for perfection in planning, and had allowed their foreign customers to buy or requisition as many drawing pins, within reason, as they wished. Programming and detailed justification might well have been applied to the major items, say to the twelve groups of important industrial equipment and consumer goods which were the subject of full-dress combined planning. For such items as tractors, textiles, generators and office machines, programming was very necessary and much credit is due to those who, with a fair measure of accuracy, carried out that arduous task.

CHAPTER V

THE COMBINED BOARDS

(i)

The Teamwork of Kindred Societies

NO DISCUSSION of the constitution and authority of the combined bodies can explain the success of the network of British-American war-time machinery. Its constitutional and legal structures were woolly and imprecise. A British member of the staff of a Combined Board commented after the war as follows: 'the organisational arrangements and frontiers of responsibility, both within the British organisation in Washington and within the American organisation, and within and between the Combined Boards were always misty in the extreme, and were the subject of continuing controversy. Anyone who reads the papers is bound to come to the conclusion that this could not work. Yet it worked with great success. . . . The effect of this network of organisations and contact was that by 1944 the two countries' economies were in fact completely integrated. We had a top priority list – called the Designated List. If a particular item was on this list it had special facilities for getting labour which was, of course, the scarcest of the resources. The Americans likewise had a top priority list of the things on which *they* concentrated their resources. These two lists were pretty well identical in 1944. This really meant that there were no unused resources in either country for producing the things which the combined military effort most required'.

All this, of course was merely part of the wider British-American Combination which extended from the highest political level, through the Combined Staffs and Commands down to the work of innumerable teams great and small working together on many aspects of the common war effort. Ultimate explanations of the success of the combination must be looked for not at the level of constitutional forms but in the deepest springs of the national being of free societies.

The British people in their Island and the Americans on their Continent worked as teams under the same compelling necessity. Their free societies fostered in their citizens the self-reliance and initiative and the sense of social responsibility which made effective teamwork possible with a minimum of formal rules and direction from above. These qualities were heightened and concentrated when the common emergency brought together into combined teams some of their ablest, most devoted and energetic public officials. Common ways of thinking and doing things, common language and historical traditions, played a highly important part.

This was something which British officials were more inclined to take for granted than were some of their American colleagues. They had a long and wide experience of working successfully with other countries of the British Commonwealth without any formal machinery. This new experience of working in the same kind of way with Americans was to them neither new nor surprising. They concluded from the experience that any attempt to work out and impose a more centralised and precise organisation would have produced less satisfactory results. The important thing, they concluded, was to bring together experienced and responsible officials and let them work together with the minimum of formality. They gave much weight at the time and in retrospect to several facts the importance of which they felt to be very great but which cannot easily be documented. One is the fact that the British Government sent on mission or stationed in Washington some of their best experts in war production and requirements – men who perforce had gone through a much longer training in war production than the American teams which were recruited in large measure after Pearl Harbour. Of the catalytic – or speeding up – effect, of the presence of such men, of their experience and disinterested help and advice at critical phases in the development of the American war programmes, there is much evidence in the cables and correspondence that crossed the Atlantic and above all in the critical year 1942.

These results were due in no small measure to the very informality of their presence and functions at innumerable Combined meetings.

(ii)

The Four Civilian Boards

'We use the word "combined",' the Minister of Production said in June 1942, 'to relate to any body representative of both American and British interests'.[1] The term was not used for bodies like the Pacific War Council or for international bodies like the United Nations Relief and Rehabilitation Administration and other United Nations organisations.[2] The latter were fully international. They

---

[1] Mr. Oliver Lyttelton, speech in the House of Commons, 24th June 1942. H. of C. Deb., Vol. 380, Col. 1986.

[2] After the war, however, the term 'combined' was still used for the committees on tin, hides, and rubber although they had been enlarged by the admission of other nations. See below, Chapter VI, Section (v).

were based on international agreements, had international governing bodies, international budgets, and international secretariats
whose allegiance was international. A combined body on the other
hand stood somewhere between national and international; it was
a mechanism for bringing together two or more departments of the
British and American Governments. The officials in the combined
bodies continued to be national officials, and to form an integral
part of their respective national Departments; yet they performed
international functions and acquired the ability and the habit of
looking beyond national interests.

The British-American combined organisation served the United
Nations. But there was no direct participation by other United
Nations in the Combined Boards until towards the end of the war
when problems of the transition to peace began to come to the fore.
The participation was limited to taking part in the work of committees of the Boards; there was no increase in the membership of
the Boards themselves. 'British', it should be noted, tended in
practice to mean British Commonwealth. Not only were the interests
of the Commonwealth as a whole taken always into account, there
was also in some degree representation of other members of the
Commonwealth. Canada was represented on a number of the combined bodies, civil and military. Representatives of other Commonwealth countries sat on combined committees, especially on the
military side.

Set up by the President and the Prime Minister by virtue of their
war powers, the Boards were unfettered in most cases by formal
directives. The Boards were so designed that they could rely upon
the full authority of national departments at a time when these were
working under conditions of more or less unlimited war-time concentration of powers. Since in the main the consent of only two
governments had to be obtained, the Combined Boards were able to
act quickly and decisively. Thus the history of international organisation can show nothing comparable to the swift action – on a wide
variety of important matters affecting interests in many parts of the
world – by which the Combined Raw Materials Board in its first
year of operation brought order into the supply of the raw materials
for war production. In the words of its American member, Mr
William L. Batt, in 1944, 'the smoothness with which these world
problems of supply have been solved has been a revelation'.[1]

The accent in this and the next chapter will be on the Combined
Boards in so far as they were concerned with war production and the
supply of munitions and raw materials. The emphasis will thus be on

---

[1] Speech by W. L. Batt, 2nd June 1944. W.P.B. Release O.W.I., 2560. Mr Batt
spoke as United States member of the Combined Raw Materials Board and deputy
member of the Combined Production and Resources Board.

the Combined Raw Materials Board and the Combined Production and Resources Board; but some reference will also be made to the Combined Board which dealt with the final phase in the process of supply, that of Munitions Assignments. Since the history of the Combined Raw Materials Board best illustrates the conditions which led to the setting up of the Combined Boards, their structure and functions, their general character and methods of operation, a separate chapter is devoted to it. Shipping and food fall outside the scope of this study; but several references must be made to the Combined Boards dealing with these matters, to illustrate the nature and working of the other Boards.

The general character of the combined organisation which centred round the Combined Chiefs of Staff is outlined in *North American Supply*, Chapter IX. The history of the idea of combination, of the use of combined methods and the growth of combined organisation before the full system of the Combined Boards came into existence, indicates that combination came whenever and wherever experience showed it was needed for the handling of particular problems. Historically, British-American combination was expressed in Lend-Lease and developed with it. Whilst the terms of the Lend-Lease Act were general and applied to other nations, the Act itself originated as a movement for 'aid to Britain'. China was far away and Russia at the time of the enactment of Lend-Lease was still regarded as closer to the Axis than to the Allies. As soon as Russia became a partner in the war she bore her own load in her own way; her interests were faithfully served, however, by the combined machinery. But neither Russia nor China ever became – or sought to become – a member of any part of the combined organisation. The British-American combination remained unique and unchanged until the end of the war. As an American writer said, 'It could be said that there are three, not four, major allies – Russia, China and Anglo-America'.[1]

Until Pearl Harbour the relations of Britain and America were in no sense those of an alliance between two belligerents who could move forward together in step as they developed their common war plans. Thus the combination which did develop before Pearl Harbour could follow no logical order. Between allies at war the first step in such a logical order might have been taken on the military side in the form of a general plan of strategy; whilst the second step might have been a general plan for war production, followed by more specific plans for the main constituents of production: factories, machine tools, raw materials and manpower. This in turn could have led to the fixing of schedules of production for the main munitions. The last

---

[1] *Fortune*, October 1942.

step would have been the assignment of the finished munitions. In practice no such orderly development was possible. The whole relationship was fluid and informal. One party was a belligerent, the other a friendly neutral. Both were preparing for future campaigns, but the circumstances and timing of their war preparations and arms production were quite different. The first important signs of combination came in connection with strategic materials and their denial to the Axis countries. Then came the large Allied orders in the United States, before Dunkirk, for aircraft and machine tools which led to the beginnings of some sort of combined planning and assignment for these parts of American production. The Joint Aircraft Committee (J.A.C.) was set up during the Battle of Britain, on 13th September 1940, for the assignment of the output of American aircraft and as a means of taking the first tentative steps towards joint planning of design and production. The J.A.C., which had certain subsidiary bodies such as the Joint Radio Board, was the forerunner of the Combined Boards.[1] The J.A.C. retained its peculiar constitution to the end. The Minister of Aircraft Production on the occasion of its winding up in September 1945 praised its contribution to 'combined planning'. Its directive gave it wide authority over allocations: 'to consider and decide . . . aircraft delivery schedules', and also power to deal with 'aircraft standardisation'. 'Each group of members of this Committee', the directive stated, 'is authorised to act for and obligate the agency it represents'. The Joint Aircraft Committee was not a fully combined body. In form it was an American inter-agency committee, set up by the Secretary of War, Mr Stimson. But it was established with the 'concurrence of the Chairman of the British Supply Council'; and both countries were represented on it. The British members (the heads of the British Air Commission and the Royal Air Force Delegation) continued to be appointed throughout the war by Mr Stimson.

Also in the autumn of 1940, a less formal committee – in which the British had less say – began the allocation of machine tools. The beginnings of combination for raw materials are referred to in Chapter VI. For food, also, combination developed quickly after the Lend-Lease Act. Conferences between the British Food Mission and the United States Department of Agriculture on supplies of food to the United Kingdom led to the setting up in May 1941 of the Anglo-American Food Committee out of which the Combined Food Board emerged a year later to deal more effectively with the now world-wide problem of food.[2]

---

[1] See above Chapter II, Section (iii), and *North American Supply, op. cit.*, Chapter VIII.
[2] See *History of the Second World War, United Kingdom Civil Series*, R. J. Hammond, *Food* (Vol. 1), *The Growth of Policy*, p. 255 *et seq.* Also S. McKee Rosen, *The Combined Boards of the Second World War* (New York, Columbia University Press, 1951), p. 193 *et seq.*

On the side of high policy, however, combination came more slowly. There were no serious military Staff talks until February 1941; and these were not renewed until the Atlantic Conference in August. For war production as a whole there was no serious joint planning before Pearl Harbour, although the Victory Programme of September 1941 was a first tentative step in that direction.

It was only after Pearl Harbour that the President and the Prime Minister were able to consolidate all these informal and tentative elements of combination into the full combined system: consisting of the Combined Chiefs of Staff, the Combined Munitions Assignments Board, and the civilian Combined Boards for raw materials and shipping, and the already existing Joint Aircraft Committee. Civilian boards for production and food, for which logic had seemed to call already in January, were finally set up in June 1942.

A comprehensive account of the British-American combination would have to discuss the subject under three main headings: first, the combined organisation on the military side; secondly, the combined organisation on the civilian side; thirdly, the unorganised combination, both military and civilian, which spread in waves in all directions from the central activities of each of the regular combined bodies.

The first of these aspects is outside the scope of this book. Since one military body, the Munitions Assignments Board, has to be referred to (since it straddled the line between civil and military) the reader should remember that it was merely one of a complex organisation of Combined Committees and Boards serving the Combined Chiefs of Staff.[1] Some of these bodies, like the Combined Intelligence Committee (Washington) and the Combined Communications Board (Washington) were rooted in the joint Staff talks of the early spring of 1941. The Combined Communications Board, suggested in March, was set up in its first form in November 1941. It dealt with communications of all kinds – radio, wire, visual and sound – affecting the armed services and the mercantile marine of the two countries.[2] The other combined committees, set up by the Combined Chiefs of Staff at the outset, were the Combined Staff Planners (Washington), and the Combined Military Transportation Committee (Washington). A Combined Meteorological Committee

---

[1] See *North American Supply*, *op. cit.*, Chapter IX, Section (iii).

[2] A reorganisation in June 1942 resulted in the setting up of the Combined Communications Board in its final form. The corresponding London body became the British Joint Communications Board with which American communications staffs in the United Kingdom were linked. The communications organisation was a highly complex system with many technical committees and ramifications extending over land and sea in all the war areas. The Combined Communications organisation included representatives of the Royal Canadian Navy, Air Force and Army, as well as representatives of the Australian and New Zealand Governments, and later South Africa. A Combined Joint Communications Committee was set up later in Washington to co-ordinate British Commonwealth problems.

(Washington), mooted already in 1941, was set up in April 1942.[1] Other combined bodies on the military side included the Combined Administrative Committee (Washington), the Combined Civil Affairs Committee (Washington),[2] the London Political Warfare Co-ordination Committee and the Oil Rehabilitation Sub-Committee.

No adequate account of unorganised combination – the wider fringes of combination in the office or in the field outside the regular combined machinery – can ever be written since most of it was never recorded. 'The Anglo-American war management', as an American writer has said, 'is one huge interlocking committee that never stops meeting. . . '. The functioning of the Combined Boards, as he noted, rested 'not so much on specific grants of authority as on a complex interlocking of British and American officials'.[3] Only part of this interlocking took place within the Boards and the other recognised combined bodies. Thus the national departments, which composed the Boards, dealt regularly with each other outside the Boards. Action which began within a Board might continue outside it. The Boards were important pieces in the game of combination played daily by British and Americans, but there were many other pieces. Thus in Washington it was impossible to draw any sharp line between the work which was being done all the time with American agencies by the different British Supply Missions and the work of the British sides of the Combined Boards. The staffs of the Boards themselves might play a dual role; at times they acted as if they were members of a supply mission, pressing for something Britain needed, rather than as Combined Board officials acting in a combined capacity. Though it must go unrecorded much of this combination outside the Boards was essential to the smooth working of the Boards themselves.

Some Combined Board patterns were reproduced in this unorganised combination – especially the characteristic two-member arrangement of the Boards. The practice whereby each country entrusted special powers of liaison, negotiation and decision to a single representative was already a familiar expedient in Washington long before the Combined Boards were established. From the autumn of 1940 onwards the allocation of machine tools was handled by such a two-man 'working party'. The expedient continued to be used at a number of points throughout the war. An example on the

---

[1] Attempts to secure the attendance of a Soviet meteorological representative were fruitless. The first meeting of the Combined Committee was attended by representatives from Australia, New Zealand and other parts of the British Commonwealth, and it became the regular practice for a Commonwealth Joint Meteorological Committee to meet just before the meetings of the full Combined Committee.

[2] See p. 222 below.

[3] *Fortune*, October 1942.

civil side was its use for the orderly relaxation of controls over imports into the Middle East towards the end of the war. An example of its use on the military side was the permanent two-man working party which dealt with military government matters under the Combined Civil Affairs Committee.[1]

The combined 'working party' was more often than not a larger body with a number of members representing different departmental interests. It was a common administrative device in the United Kingdom long before it became a widely used combined device. The peculiar nature of the Combined Boards is perhaps more understandable if they are regarded as a more highly organised and permanent kind of working party. Each Board tended to become the nucleus round which other less formal working parties grouped themselves.

The four civilian Combined Boards had a certain amount in common. Each had the characteristic two-man pattern. Each worked on the principle of bringing together opposite numbers from two national departments, thus gearing them for combined action. The staffs of each Board were composed of national officials engaged on combined activities for all or part of their time. Each Board had the nucleus of a central secretariat in the form of two or more officials who acted as executive officers of the Boards, but were paid from the funds of national departments. All the Boards were engaged to some degree in the allocation of supplies or services. Two of them promoted on an extensive scale the co-ordinated purchasing of supplies. All were sources of or channels for combined statistics. In the case of each of them systematic, exact, comparable data, speedily assembled, gave some solid basis of fact for planning and the carrying through of plans. The British teams on the Boards had to learn how the complicated American political system worked and how to get on with the Americans; and the Americans had to learn, and to unlearn, about the British.

Some of the Boards dealt with simpler and more manageable problems than the others. The path of wisdom for the Boards was to let well alone. Thus steel, which was mainly a problem of shipping and of Lend-Lease – British needs being only a very small fraction of the American output – was left by the Combined Raw Materials Board to direct negotiation; as was aluminium for which less combined methods sufficed. The Combined Raw Materials Board concentrated from the outset on the most critical materials in short supply for most of which the United States depended largely on British controlled sources. The Board set its face against any attempt

---

[1] The working party in this case consisted of the Chief Planner of the United States War Department's Civil Affairs Division and an opposite number on the British side.

to make anything in the nature of theoretical surveys of the whole field of the raw materials essential to war industry. A combination of factors made it perhaps the most successful of the Combined Boards.[1] It shared with the Combined Food Board the advantage of a limited and comparatively simple field of operation – that of primary commodities.[2] The staffs of these two Boards on the British side drew strength from the fact that they were part of larger British Supply Missions. Such Supply Missions had many direct links with London. They were engaged on the practical task of procurement of supplies from the United States. They were long established in Washington and skilled in its ways. They commanded more technical knowledge than the small staff of a Board, made up in part of newcomers, could possess. The small staff of the Combined Production and Resources Board did not have such advantages. It had the misfortune to be saddled with the impossible task of supervising and co-ordinating the whole field of war production. Something might have been done in this field if the Board had had a large staff, a long span of time and united departmental support on the American side; but it had none of these. Like all the Boards, it learned that it could function best by dealing with problems as they arose rather than by attempting to make systematic plans for the future.

Some reference is made in *North American Supply* (Chapter IX) and in a later section of this chapter to the chequered history of the Combined Production and Resources Board. It suffered from the fact that it was given by the two Governments a much more ambitious and vague function than was assigned to any of the other Combined Boards. It was conceived as a kind of Chiefs of Staff for Production. The British Ministry of Production and the United States War Production Board seemed to regard it as an opportunity to create a super board which would co-ordinate the other Boards. Since the other Boards were concerned with aspects of war production – while the concern of the Combined Production and Resources Board was war production as a whole – their roles would be subordinate to that of the new Board. Nothing came of these plans; but they did nothing to improve the relations of the Combined Production and Resources Board with other Boards. It lost any hope of playing a dominant role after its failure at the outset to make headway with its primary task of combining the war production programmes of Britain and North America.

This episode was followed by a period of many months in which

---

[1] On steel see Chapter VI. See also *North American Supply, op. cit.,* Chapter IX; and *The Combined Boards* by Courtney C. Brown, Department of State Bulletin, 1st July 1945.
[2] On the other hand, food involved problems of mass distribution and manifold sources of supply which made control inherently more difficult than in the case of raw materials. See R. J. Hammond, *op. cit.,* Chapters XVIII–XIX.

P

the Combined Production and Resources Board – with its main road barred and its leadership weakened – fell back on its secondary role of making adjustments within the war production programmes. It was able, however, to recover some of its lost prestige by developing still another function, which is referred to later in its charter, that of dealing with the 'essential needs of the civilian population': in other words the field of non-military supplies. Problems in connection with relief and rehabilitation became one of its main activities from 1943 to 1945. But even in these tasks it was hampered by the weakness of its position in the matter of allocating supplies. The only Board on which Britain was more a giver than a receiver was the Combined Raw Materials Board.[1] Only on that Board did the United Kingdom have any substantial powers in the matter of allocation of supplies and even here its powers related to foreign raw materials within its control rather than to those produced in the United States over which it had no control whatsoever. Since the United Kingdom had very little surplus to offer by way of manufactured goods it had no effective lever by which it could influence the allocation of American supplies. The real power of allocation of such supplies, including many raw materials to foreign countries, was retained by American agencies.[2]

The Combined Food and Shipping Boards lie outside the scope of this volume. But a very brief reference to them is necessary for a better understanding of the structure and scope of the other civilian Boards and the difficulties encountered by all the Boards. The Combined Food Board shared with the Combined Raw Materials Board the advantage of being firmly rooted in North American supply from the beginnings of Lend-Lease.[3] It also had the advantage that it dealt largely with a permanent peace-time agency of the American Government – the United States Department of Agriculture. But in this case also the United Kingdom was in no position to exercise any great influence over the allocation of American food since it was itself so largely dependent on food supplies from across the Atlantic. American agencies retained the substance of the power of allocating American foodstuffs. But the United Kingdom controlled directly or indirectly important sources of foreign food supplies and in respect of these it could claim and exercise a major voice in allocations. It was indeed because of the increasing difficulties of obtaining food supplies from third countries that the Combined Food Board was set up in June 1942. The main difficulties were twofold: first, problems of shipment; and secondly, the need

---

[1] See Milton Katz (Executive Officer of the Combined Production and Resources Board), 'A Case Study in International Organisation', *Harvard Business Review*, 1946.

[2] Largely the Foreign Economic Administration in the later stages of the war.

[3] On the Combined Food Board see R. J. Hammond, *op. cit.*, Chapters XVIII and XIX.

to hold prices steady by avoiding undue competition for limited supplies. The Board sought to ensure the strictest economy in the use of ocean-going tonnage for international movements of foodstuffs. To secure price stability Great Britain and the United States shared the responsibility for the purchase of food in third countries. The sharing was arranged largely on the familiar hemisphere pattern. The supplies which were purchased were allocated by the Combined Food Board. Thus schemes were worked out in 1942 for the co-ordinated purchasing and allocation of supplies of oil and fats, sugar, tea, canned fish and South American canned meats. In its approach to problems the Combined Food Board was largely influenced by the practice of the Combined Raw Materials Board. Like the latter it dealt with problems as they arose and avoided from the outset anything in the nature of long-term planning of food supply in general. As food became shorter in the later stages of the war, the field of action of the Board was widened to cover most of the important foodstuffs except wheat for which special machinery existed. Some of the main difficulties of the Combined Food Board, like those of most of the Boards, sprang from conflicts of jurisdiction between the different American agencies dealing with food and agriculture – mainly the United States Department of Agriculture, the War Food Administration, and the Foreign Economic Administration.[1] Major discussions on food tended to take place directly between London and Washington rather than through the Board itself. Like the Combined Production and Resources Board, however, the Combined Food Board found fresh fields of activity in connection with relief and rehabilitation in the later stages of the war.[2]

Only in the case of munitions and shipping were there parallel Combined Boards both in Washington and London.[3] In each case the United Kingdom had important assets to contribute to the common pool of war supply; and the allocation of these assets could best be dealt with in London. In the case of shipping the charter of 26th January 1942 began with the statement that:

1. In principle, the shipping resources of the two countries will be

---

[1] R. J. Hammond, op. cit., Chapters XVIII and XIX. American accounts of some of these conflicts are to be found in War Production Boards, *Industrial Mobilisation for War*, Vol. I, Program and Administration, Historical Reports on War Administration, War Production Board (Washington: United States Government Printing Office, 1947), and S. McKee Rosen, op. cit.

[2] Because of the continued shortage of food supplies the Combined Food Board remained in existence until the end of June 1946, six months longer than the Combined Raw Materials Board and the Combined Production and Resources Board.

[3] The Combined Production and Resources Board and the Combined Food Board had subordinate London committees (see below pp. 238–9); but there was no counterpart of any kind in London for the Combined Raw Materials Board. The idea of parallel Boards in London for shipping, food, raw materials and oil was favoured on the British side at the end of December 1941 (see *North American Supply*, op. cit., Chapter IX, p. 348); but there is no basis in the British records for the suggestion in one well-informed American account (see S. McKee Rosen, op. cit., pp. 20–21), that a parallel London Board for raw materials was seriously considered in London early in 1942.

deemed to be pooled. The fullest information will be interchanged.

2. Owing to the military and physical facts of the situation around the British Isles, the entire movement of shipping now under the control of Great Britain will continue to be directed by the Ministry of War Transport.

3. Similarly, the appropriate authority in the United States will continue to direct the movements and allocations of United States shipping, or shipping of other Powers under United States control.

The charter then went on to provide for parallel shipping boards which were to make adjustments between the two sections of the pool of ships. It ended with a statement that:

In both cases the executive power will be exercised solely by the appropriate shipping agency in Washington and by the Minister of War Transport in London.

The London Board consisted of the Minister of War Transport (or his deputy) and the head of the United States Mission in London (or his deputy). On the Washington Board the Minister of War Transport was represented by a deputy.[1] Only the Minister on the Board in London, not his deputy in Washington, could allocate British tonnage to a non-British service.

In a general sense it was true of all the Boards that executive action in respect of American-controlled supply was lodged in Washington, and in the case of British-controlled supply in London. But this was true in a special sense for shipping and munitions. The point was emphasised for shipping in a memorandum by the Ministry of War Transport at the end of 1942. Notwithstanding this fact the memorandum emphasised that the two shipping Boards still had important tasks to perform. The 'chief tasks of the Boards' as it defined them were:

(a) to ensure by full exchange of information that executive action on both sides of the Atlantic is based on an agreed and accurate appreciation of the world shipping problem;

(b) to bring together the thought of both controlling centres so that similar cases may be decided on similar lines, and similar problems may, where necessary, be handled through similar mechanisms; and

(c) to ensure that world shipping responsibilities may be performed by one or other Board (or by both in concert) with a minimum of gaps on the one hand or of overlapping on the other.

The memorandum went on to state that combined statistical returns were

gradually becoming available over the whole field, and provide the foundation for combined shipping policy. The task of bringing together the policies of both controlling centres is performed by constant contact between the M.W.T. (Ministry of War Transport) and

---

[1] Cmd 6332, 1942.

W.S.A. (War Shipping Administration) representatives in London and Washington, which supplements the formal Board meetings. Routeing of shipping correspondence between the Ministry and the British Merchant Shipping Mission, Washington, through the British side of the Board Secretariat ensures co-ordinated action in accordance with Board decisions.

Thus the tendency to conduct the day-to-day negotiations on shipping outside the Washington Board was already strong in the first year of its existence. From the end of 1942 the importance of the Washington Board dwindled. Its meetings were a forum for general discussion and for the exchange of information rather than for the negotiation of important issues of policy. More and more the latter tended to be discussed directly between the national shipping authorities. Even more than the other Combined Boards it suffered from jurisdictional difficulties on the American side.[1]

The three civilian Combined Boards were organised on the common pattern of the two-man Board with one British and one American member, each flanked usually by a deputy. Each of them was served mainly if not exclusively by civilian personnel. The Combined Munitions Assignments Boards, on the other hand were multi-membered military bodies. Both on the American and British side they were composed of representatives of the three armed services; and their staffs were mainly Service officers. The parallel Munitions Boards in Washington and London were subordinate to the Combined Chiefs of Staff. They acted under their general instructions and the Combined Chiefs had final jurisdiction in the event of disagreement in the Boards. The multi-member pattern for both the Washington and London Boards was set by the British view that a two-man Board was not sufficient. In this view the General Staffs of both sides must sit in with the Boards that had to assign munitions.[2] But a civilian chairman, Harry Hopkins in Washington and Oliver Lyttelton in London, presided over each of the Boards. Variations between the history of the Washington and the London Boards were due to three main factors; first, the long established tradition in London of the subordination of the armed services to civilian authority; secondly, the much greater quantities of munitions which the Washington Board had to assign; thirdly, the advantage which the Washington Board had of operating beside the Combined Chiefs of Staff. A brief account of the Combined Munitions Assignments Board is given below.[3]

RELATIONS BETWEEN THE COMBINED BODIES

It was assumed, when the combined organisations were set up in

---

[1] For an American account, see S. McKee Rosen, *op. cit.*, pp. 126–130.

[2] See *North American Supply*, *op. cit.*, Chapter IX, pp. 349–350.

[3] In Section (vi). See also *North American Supply*, *op. cit.*, Chapter IX, Section (iii).

January 1942, that since the Combined Boards were concerned largely with what might be called the strategy of supply, they would work in close contact with the military side, in particular with the Combined Chiefs of Staff. At the London end relations between the civil and military sides of the war organisation had always been close and remained so in the combined bodies operating in that capital. But there was no counterpart in London for the completely combined organisation which functioned continuously as the Combined Chiefs of Staff in Washington. It was housed in a single building with a combined secretariat and a complex system of combined committees. This form of organisation was not the first thought of the national staffs, when they came together for the first time in Washington for staff discussions from January to March 1941. Their idea at that stage was that, if the United States entered the war, the strategic control of the joint war effort should be double-headed – with a joint body in both London and Washington. In the year that followed, however, the British Combined Chiefs of Staff came to the conclusion that the American Joint Chiefs would not find it possible in practice to make any real delegation of authority to representatives in London. They concluded that if there was to be a combined organisation, it must be set up in Washington. This coincided with the view of General Marshall that there could not be duality in the higher direction of the war on the military planning side.

Situated as it was in Washington the Combined Chiefs of Staff was strongly influenced by the marked aversion of the American Services – partly on grounds of security – against working through civilian channels. Largely for this reason none of the Combined Boards (except the Munitions Assignments Board which despite its civilian head was a military board directly under the Combined Chiefs) succeeded in establishing very close working relations at any period of the war with the Combined Chiefs of Staff.[1] For the Combined Production and Resources Board a relationship of a peculiarly close kind was envisaged – with the negative results described in *North American Supply*.[2] In the early period the Board invited to its meetings representatives of the Munitions Assignments Board and of the Combined Chiefs of Staff. The attempt to maintain relations through liaison officers continued even when the main

---

[1] See also *North American Supply*, *op. cit.*, Chapter XI, pp. 23–24.

[2] Ibid., Chapter IX. The charter of C.P.R.B. provided that the Combined Chiefs of Staff and the Combined Munitions Assignments Board should keep it 'currently informed concerning Military Requirements' whilst it should keep these bodies 'currently informed concerning the facts and possibilities of production'. The first of these provisions was not carried out effectively. The charter further provided that C.P.R.B. should utilise the Combined Raw Materials Board and the Joint Aircraft Committee and other existing committees or national agencies for war production, as it deemed necessary. Here the liaison was not as effective as it might have been, but it was perhaps enough for the limited purpose and the functions of C.P.R.B. as they developed in practice.

centre of interest of C.P.R.B. had shifted to non-munitions. A closer contact was maintained when the Board was dealing with military supplies of special importance, such as escort vessels, the production of which was lagging. Military representatives were present at meetings of C.P.R.B. or its sub-committees from time to time when it was dealing with items of supply in which there was a considerable military as well as civilian interest, such as tyres and tubes, textiles, trucks and coal.

The Combined Raw Materials Board had even less contact with the Combined Chiefs. But, as the first annual report of the Board noted, its executive secretaries met regularly for informal discussions with executive officers of the Combined Chiefs.

The Combined Shipping Adjustment Board noted that its task – the adjusting of demands on shipping to the ships available and the settlement of priorities – would require liaison with the other Boards in Washington. An attempt was made in March 1942 to secure such liaison through a short-lived Priorities and Allocations Committee composed of representatives of the different Boards and the Office of Lend-Lease Administration. The Committee itself soon died; but liaison was continued by an exchange of papers, as well as by the normal interdepartmental liaison in London and Washington.

Such informal relationships were of vital importance in the working of the combined organisation as a whole; but relationships of a more formal character were difficult to maintain in the constantly shifting current of Washington. On the British side in Washington, however, relationships between all parts of the British organisation, civil and military, were hardly less close than those normally maintained between departments in London. Thus the British members of the combined bodies in Washington gathered together regularly at a weekly meeting and a fortnightly dinner. The latter was attended by Sir John Dill, Sir Clive Baillieu, Mr R. H. Brand, Sir Arthur Salter, and Sir Robert Sinclair. M. Jean Monnet also attended regularly, as did the British Resident Minister for Supply after his appointment at the end of 1942. The Heads of all the British Missions, military and civilian, attended the regular meetings of the British Supply Council to discuss matters of common interest. In addition they met on a more informal basis at meetings called at frequent intervals by the British Ambassador throughout the war. As in London British officials and Service officers in the various combined bodies in Washington spent much of their time in committee meetings and working parties dealing with common problems.

The fluid interplay of British and American officials of the Combined Boards makes it difficult to sustain the criticism sometimes voiced that the Combined Boards worked in separate compartments without effective liaison. They shared what was in fact a common telephone switchboard. Most of them, British and American, even shared adjoining offices in the same building as was the case with the Combined Raw Materials Board and the Combined Production and Resources Board; these two bodies indeed used a combined registry for all their common 'Board' papers, although separate registries were kept for 'national' papers and records. Relations between the two Boards became closer in the later stages of the war. Thus W. L. Batt, the American member of the Combined Raw Materials Board, became also deputy member (the active head) of the Combined Production and Resources Board. Finally in December 1944 both Boards were headed by the same American and British members, W. L. Batt and Sir Henry Self.

At the outset the members of the different Boards were acutely aware that they were working with undefined frontiers in relation to each other. An early example of such apprehension was the fear of the Munitions Assignments Board in Washington that the Combined Raw Materials Board was rushing ahead in its allocation of raw materials without proper consideration of strategic requirements.[1] Later the need was felt to supplement informal contacts by setting up combined committees linking two Boards. The first example was the Combined Fertiliser Committee which linked together the Combined Raw Materials Board and the Combined Food Board. This Committee, like the Combined Rubber Committee which also dated from the autumn of 1942, was for practical purposes a subsidiary Combined Board for a particular raw material.[2]

---

[1] Thus it was pointed out in March 1942, that a general cut of 25 per cent. had been made by the Combined Raw Materials Board in the use of rubber without reference to the Assignments Board. Attention was drawn also to the fact that whilst the United Kingdom was allocating to the aircraft industry 93 per cent. of its available aluminium, the American aircraft industry was receiving less than three quarters of American supplies of this metal.

[2] Though the Combined Fertiliser Committee was in effect a separate Combined Board for fertilisers, its recommendations were channelled through the Food and Raw Materials Boards. Its decisions were always unanimous, and it came to be regarded as an autonomous allocating body. The United Kingdom presented in the Committee the claims of all British Commonwealth countries (save Canada), as well as the Middle East (including Turkey), and also the colonies of France and Belgium until these countries became members. The United States presented the claims of Latin American countries. Claims of European neutrals were presented jointly as were those of liberated areas under military jurisdiction. Rubber was dealt with by the Combined Raw Materials Board until September 1942, when the Office of Rubber Director was set up under Mr William Jefferies. He possessed almost unlimited powers over rubber and was averse to sharing them with the American side of the Board. To get over this difficulty the Combined Rubber Committee was set up. It was not a Committee between two combined Boards, but between the British side of the Combined Raw Materials Board and the Office of Rubber Director. The Committee had four members: two from the staff of the Combined Raw Materials Board (one British and one American), a member of the Office of Rubber Director and a member of the British Raw Materials Mission. Recommendations and documents of the Committee went direct to the Board itself without passing through the Advisory Operating Committee of the Board; but since no recommendation was ever questioned the Combined Rubber Committee like the Combined Fertiliser Committee was in effect a separate Combined Board for rubber. Even after the Office of Rubber Director disappeared in September 1944, the Combined Rubber Committee, which had become a highly efficient body, was continued.

The Combined Food Board also established with the Combined Production and Resources Board a Combined Agricultural and Food Machinery Committee. From January to August 1943, seven combined C.R.M.B./C.P.R.B. committees were set up for steel, copper, aluminium and magnesium, coal, conservation, footwear, leather and hides, pulp and paper.[1] The combined committees on copper, aluminium and magnesium tightened the relationship of Canada with the Combined Raw Materials Board and replaced for these materials the Materials Co-ordinating Committee of the United States and Canada.

The possibility of a more far reaching co-ordination between the combined bodies in Washington seemed to open up for a short time at the turn of the year 1942–3, with the setting up of a body called the Committee of the Combined Boards. The Committee was set up by the State Department in December 1942 on the recommendation of the Combined Chiefs 'to handle combined civilian economic matters regarding North Africa'. The Allied landings had been made earlier in that month before the procedure for dealing with liberated areas had been decided. The Supreme Commander found himself faced from the outset with problems arising out of relations with the civilian population and the answer was found in the Committee of the Combined Boards. The Committee contained representatives of the State Department and the Board of Economic Warfare on the American side and on the United Kingdom side, officials from the Foreign Office and the Ministry of Economic Warfare. The Executive Secretaries, British and American, of the four civilian Combined Boards were also members of the Committee; and the Combined Chiefs were represented on its secretariat. The Committee of the Combined Boards dealt with matters of a civilian character referred by General Eisenhower to the Combined Chiefs of Staff. The Committee discussed the possibility of securing export surpluses of food and raw materials from North Africa and recommended allocations of such commodities. Its main concern, however, was the supplying of civilian commodities needed in the territory. Its last meeting was held at the end of January 1943. The day-to-day work was then undertaken by various informal combined committees convened by the State Department; for these the Committee of the Combined Boards continued to serve as an umbrella. The Committees dealt with French North Africa, French West Africa, French Equatorial Africa,

---

	Date of first meeting
[1] Combined Steel Committee	5th January 1943
Combined Copper Committee	1st February 1943
Combined Aluminium and Magnesium Committee	6th August 1943
Combined Coal Committee	25th August 1943
Combined Conservation Committee	27th August 1943
Combined Footwear Leather and Hides Committee	18th August 1943
Combined Pulp and Paper Committee	24th August 1943

the Belgian Congo and Madagascar. The informal committees were attended by representatives of the United Kingdom and of the American agencies concerned with economic questions relating to these areas. Although the Committee of the Combined Boards remained amongst the lists of the combined organisations until it was dissolved in the spring of 1944, it had been described in a British memorandum of October 1943 as already an 'ancient ghost'. The possibility of using it as a central co-ordinating body for civilian affairs in all liberated areas was mooted on the military side in March 1943. It was suggested that it should be reorganised with the addition of representatives of the United States War and Navy Departments and that officers of the Combined Chiefs of Staff's organisation should serve permanently on its secretariat. The idea was not favoured, however, by the United States Chiefs of Staff on the ground that a body under the leadership of the Foreign Office and the State Department might confront the Supreme Commander with orders from two different authorities – civilian and military. Moreover it was recognised that whilst the Combined Boards could advise they could not operate effectively as operating agencies for handling the multitude of detail arising in connection with liberated areas. Finally in the summer of 1943, at the suggestion of the United States Joint Chiefs, a Combined Civil Affairs Committee was set up under the Combined Chiefs of Staff. Its function was to undertake the general responsibility for the planning and administration of civil affairs in occupied areas. The Committee consisted of representatives of all interested civilian departments as well as representatives of the British War Office and Admiralty and American officers from the War and Navy Departments. The British Joint Staff Mission in Washington supplied the British Service members. The Foreign Office was represented by a member of the British Embassy staff. One branch of the Committee dealt with military government questions and another (C.C.A.C.(S)) with supply. The primary task of the latter was to assess civilian requirements, but it also played a part in determining sources of supply and the financial implications involved.[1]

(iii)

Constitution and Authority

The authority of the members of the Combined Boards continued throughout their existence to derive directly from the war powers of the President and the Prime Minister, supplemented by those of the

---

[1] See below, Section (v).

national departments to which the British and American members of the Boards looked for instructions and the carrying out of decisions. Any changes in the heads of the Boards required the consent both of the Prime Minister and the President. A change in either the British or the American representative was often a matter of considerable concern to the other Government. The United Kingdom Government learned to attach great importance to the personality and weight in the Administration of the American opposite number on a Combined Board, or on any other combined body. There were well established procedures for seeking the consent of the other country in case of a change in representation on a Combined Board. Usually on the British side the Ambassador wrote to the Secretary of State asking whether the nomination of a new British member had the approval of the President, and on receiving a reply in the affirmative executed a document certifying the new British member on the Board.

The main charters of the Boards were contained in statements which in form were simple agreements between the Prime Minister and the President. The texts were of a very informal character, apparently in each case without signatures or initials. The texts were usually published simultaneously by the two Heads of Government. On the American side the text was usually forwarded by the President with a memorandum or letter to the American agency concerned. Thus the statements of 9th June setting up the Combined Production and Resources Board and the Combined Food Board were sent by the President in the form of memoranda to Mr Donald Nelson, head of the War Production Board, and Mr Claude Wickard, Secretary of Agriculture.

In the case of the Combined Raw Materials Board the charter provided that the Board should 'make the recommendations necessary to execute' the plans which it was enjoined to prepare for the 'best and speediest development, expansion and use of the raw material resources under the jurisdiction or control' of the two Governments. 'Such recommendations' the charter added 'shall be carried out by all parts of the respective Governments'. The British member, the charter noted, would 'represent and act under the instruction of the Ministry of Supply' (later the Ministry of Production). In recording its 'decisions'[1] C.R.M.B. always spelt out the 'decision' in a series of 'recommendations'. The imperative ('shall be carried out') was not used for any of the other Combined Boards.

---

[1] See the illustration given in *North American Supply*, *op.cit.*, Chapter IX, pp. 369–371. The decisions or recommendations of the Combined Raw Materials Board were numbered serially and reached the total of 457 during the life of the Board. Each side of the Board circulated the decisions to the operating Departments in its own capital with a letter pointing out the kind of action desired from each Department. Each side of the Board remained responsible for seeing that action was duly taken and for reporting progress to the Board.

(A similar phrase had been used, however, for the Joint Aircraft Committee.) The Combined Munitions Assignments Board, according to its charter, was to 'advise' on assignments in accordance with strategic needs; under a later directive issued by the Combined Chiefs of Staff it was to be 'responsible for making assignments', but subject to policies and agreements made by the Combined Chiefs of Staff. In the case of the Combined Shipping Adjustment Board the charter provided that 'the executive power will be exercised solely by the appropriate shipping agency' in each capital. It was made clear that each representative would act under the instructions of his national authority to which he remained responsible. Thus while the Board was called upon to 'adjust and concert in one harmonious policy' the two national shipping authorities, its task was confined to discussion, the formulation of joint agreements and the pooling of information, rather than executive action. The memorandum of organisation (signed by Admiral Land and Sir Arthur Salter, the two members of the Washington Board, on 19th February 1942) added detail, but no further point of substance, in regard to the authority of the Board.

The charter of the Combined Production and Resources Board (as modified with the admission of Canada) provided that the 'Board shall . . . combine the production programmes of the United States, the United Kingdom and Canada into a single integrated programme . . . assure the continuous adjustment of the combined production programme . . . arrange for . . . conferences . . .'. It was also to 'utilise' various other combined bodies and national agencies. But there was no implication that the Board was to have any power of action except through the Ministry of Production in the United Kingdom and the War Production Board in the United States.

The duties of the Combined Food Board, according to the joint announcement of the Prime Minister and the President on 9th June 1942, were to 'consider, investigate, enquire into and formulate plans . . .' in matters of common concern regarding food and material used in its production, and to 'make recommendations to the Governments of the United States and United Kingdom'. The Head of the British Food Mission in Washington, who was the British member of the Board, was to represent and act under the instruction of the Minister of Food. The Secretary of Agriculture himself was the American member of the Board. It was quite clear that the Board as such could act only through the Governments of the two countries.[1]

Such studied informality had its disadvantages; and it created some trouble for the Boards in their relations with American governmental agencies. But no trouble occurred within the far more unified British system of cabinet government. Since the understandings and

---

[1] R. J. Hammond, *op. cit.*, pp. 238–240.

agreements had behind them the authority of the Prime Minister and the War Cabinet they were unlikely to be questioned by any department of the British Government. In the view of American agencies, however, the constitutional basis for the Combined Boards was weak. The Boards depended merely on letters, memoranda or orders of the President. Thus their authority was regarded as not comparable to that conferred by an Act of Congress. An agency such as the Office of Lend-Lease Administration (or its successor the Foreign Economic Administration), which was based on an Act of Congress and was accountable to Congress, tended to look askance at the recommendations of a Combined Board which was in no way accountable to Congress and was half foreign in its composition. If a Board was to function at all the American representative on the Board, and its American staff, had to be drawn from some one agency and it was bound therefore to be involved in inter-agency friction.[1]

The imperative used in the charter of the Combined Raw Materials Board ('Such recommendations shall be carried out by all parts of the respective Governments') had meaning in London. This was not because the text had the force of law, but because the British system worked in such a way that effect was easily given to any international agreement, whether formal or informal, made by the Prime Minister, or by another Minister of the Crown, or by a responsible official acting under instructions. In Washington, however, the imperative had little weight. The Combined Raw Materials Board had only just begun to function in Washington when a British message warned London that the Office of Lend-Lease Administration was the 'organ of the United States Administration which decides whether particular supplies can be Lend-Leased and in that capacity it cannot be overruled by decisions of the Combined Raw Materials Board'. London was still unconvinced:

> We understand it will be for the Board to make final decisions, subject only to appeal to the President and the Prime Minister, on allocation of raw materials available for United States and British Empire and to make recommendations as to expansion of existing resources or development of new resources.

---

[1] Thus the Combined Raw Materials Board and the Combined Production and Resources Board were both based on the United States War Production Board. Although they worked through committees, on which the different American agencies were represented, both were affected by friction between the War Production Board and the Office of Lend-Lease Administration (and its successor the Foreign Economic Administration). Allocations by the War Production Board of American supplies to foreign Governments had to be financed out of Lend-Lease funds for which the Foreign Economic Administration was responsible to Congress – and F.E.A. also controlled licences for export. On the other hand if the British or Canadian sides of a Board allocated British or Canadian supplies they could count with some certainty on the allocation not being challenged in London or Ottawa. There was some initial friction between the War Production Board and the Combined Raw Materials Board, but that was quickly overcome. War Production Board, *Industrial Mobilisation for War*, *op. cit.*, pp. 222–224.

The message was duly delivered to the American member of the Board, but it had little effect. In practice 'decisions' of the Board were merely recommendations made to the departments responsible for action.[1] This did not mean there was any serious failure to carry out such recommendations. For the usual practice was that a recommendation was worked out in advance and agreed to by the departments before it was adopted. Here the public testimony of the American and British members of two of the Boards might be cited: 'The Board', Mr Batt stated early in 1943 in reference to C.R.M.B., 'provides a meeting ground where all can go and get a decision – a decision which will be accepted and implemented'. Sir Clive Baillieu said in mid-1943 that all the Board's recommendations had been 'accepted and carried out by the Governments concerned'.[2] The record of the Combined Production and Resources Board was also clear in this respect. 'This is the first occasion', the Minister of Production wrote in February 1944 to the head of the War Production Board, 'on which member countries have been unable to reach agreement'. The trouble was over the cotton textile programme for the second quarter of 1944, and the Minister intervened personally to secure an agreement which had not been possible at lower levels. Whilst these statements were broadly true, there were no doubt a certain number amongst the many hundreds of recommendations which were not carried out. Some of the recommendations were vague in their assignment of responsibility for action, being little more than general admonitions that the two Governments should do this or that. Moreover the carrying out of a recommendation was often a long process of which it was difficult to keep track. In general the texts of recommendations were recorded in the combined series of documents issued by the Boards. Officials were enjoined to watch over the execution of recommendations; but situations changed rapidly and a certain number of recommendations were bound to fall by the way.

Yet in this respect the record of the Combined Board system was impressive. It would surely not have been improved by giving the Boards authority and powers which the Departments alone were in a position to exercise. The Boards could not operate as a Department. They had no budgets and handled no funds. They could not make contracts. They could neither buy nor sell nor store.[3] In short they could act only through the Departments which possessed all the necessary instruments of executive authority with which the legislatures had armed them for war. The national departments

---

[1] See *North American Supply*, *op. cit.*, Chapter IX, Section (vi), pp. 368–372.
[2] W. L. Batt in commenting on the Annual Report of the Combined Raw Materials Board; Sir Clive Baillieu in a broadcast, Washington, July 1943.
[3] *British Year Book of International Law*, 1944. Note on the Combined Raw Materials Board by H. Duncan Hall.

continued to do all the things they had done before the Boards were created. They had large staffs in close touch with industry. They made contracts at home and abroad for supplies. They issued licences, regulated the import, use and distribution of raw materials, food and shipping; they enforced measures of conservation. Moreover they were responsible to the Parliaments for their action and their use of funds. They could not also be responsible to the Combined Boards. Thus whatever the charters might say, the Boards could not command nor could they issue instructions. They could, however, make recommendations, and if these had been cleared with the departments they acquired force – the force that came from the war-time powers of the departments themselves, and of the Prime Minister and the President.

In the long run the Boards had much more to gain than to lose from modesty. If they had been more pretentious, they could hardly have survived national and international jealousies . . . on the one hand the jealousies of the national departments, on the other Allied jealousy of exclusive British-American machinery of international allocation.[1]

Yet it was to be expected that the informal and fluid system of the Boards would be looked at askance by officials brought up in the legal traditions of American administration. Thus attempts were made in Washington to provide more precise directives for some of the Boards. The point arose on the American side at the outset in connection with the Combined Raw Materials Board. Its operations involved relations between the American member, who was based on the War Production Board, and other American agencies such as the Board of Economic Warfare. A draft executive order by the President 'delegating to the representative of the United States Government on the Combined Raw Materials Board certain functions and duties', was under discussion in Washington in February 1942. It was abandoned, however, because the agencies could not agree on its text. Hopkins, to whom the President looked in such matters, disliked hard and fast directives and gave it no support. Later in June he was said to have pushed aside as unnecessary a draft 'Executive Order' by the President, which had been prepared for the Combined Food Board.[2]

The Combined Production and Resources Board likewise had no executive order or directive, other than the statement issued by the President and the Prime Minister on 9th June. The planning staffs of the United States War Production Board and the United States Bureau of the Budget tried their hand at drafts of a comprehensive

[1] cf. R. J. Hammond, *op. cit.*, pp. 254–6.
[2] War Production Board, *Industrial Mobilisation for War, op. cit.*, pp. 222–4; S. McKee Rosen, *op. cit.*, pp. 16–19; 204–5.

directive. This was to provide the new Board with the powers
necessary for it to carry out the task of acting as a combined 'chiefs
of staff for production', which seemed to be the role for which the
Board's charter had designed it.[1] These drafts called for the abolition
of the Combined Raw Materials Board, and the subordination of the
other Combined Boards to the Combined Production and Resources
Board. The plans also called for a redistribution of powers and
functions amongst the American agencies dealing with matters of
concern to the C.P.R.B. The Combined Boards were to have a single
combined secretariat, and the responsibilities of the agencies dealing
with them were to be redefined. Thus the proposals involved nothing
less than a recasting of the whole civilian side of the combined
machinery. Nothing, however, came of all this discussion. Its lack of
realism was demonstrated immediately by the failure of the War
Production Board to secure the collaboration of the armed services
without which the Combined Production and Resources Board
could not begin to carry out its main function.

The problem of securing a clearer legal basis for the operations of
the Boards was purely an American problem; it was neither a British
nor an international problem. Its core was the perennial question of
the relations between the agencies of the American Government.
The whole history of federal administration in the United States
during the war showed the wisdom of the decision of the Prime
Minister and the President to set up the Combined Boards by means
of informal agreements couched in general terms. A combined
organisation was hardly possible on any other basis without fundamental changes in the American system of government. The
Combined Boards themselves could not be the instrument of such
changes.

The very nature of war – certainly of this war – and the relationship which it imposes on a war-time coalition of powers, seems
incompatible with any exact definition of the powers and functions
of their common organs. The security which such legal instruments
might seem to give involves the kind of illusion that the witches
employed to bring about the downfall of Macbeth: 'Security is
mortal's chiefest enemy'. International bodies, with powers and
functions closely defined by international agreements, tend, because
of their closely defined legal structure, to be pushed aside in time of
war – whether cold or hot; they are replaced by organisations less
trammelled by legal boundaries and therefore able to act more
swiftly. Thus the extraordinarily close and intimate combination
built up between the United Kingdom and the United States (which
at least equalled while it lasted even the intimate informality of the
British Commonwealth of Nations) made no use of legal instruments

---

[1] S. McKee Rosen, *op. cit.*, pp. 138–145. See also below, Chapter VI.

of any shape or kind, save for lesser matters and these mostly of a technical nature. The lack of legal structure was a measure of the closeness of the relationship. There could hardly be a more impressive contrast than existed between this intimate combination and the war-time relations, political, military and economic, with Moscow.[1] The contrast was reflected at a number of points in the arrangements made for supplies to the U.S.S.R. 'It has not been found necessary', a British memorandum noted in December 1942, 'to provide a link between the (Combined Production and Resources) Board and Russia. . . . The essential task of combined planning', the paper noted, 'is to share scarce resources between the military and non-military programmes of the countries concerned: this implies elasticity of programmes and frequent adjustments. . . . The programme of supplies to Russia is laid down by protocol as a first charge upon combined resources, and is not subject to change.' As between Britain and America such fixed relationships were avoided. London in times of disappointment, when expected supplies were not forthcoming, might yearn for long-term assignments. Once indeed – during the Stage II negotiations when peace was not very far ahead – it suggested that a fixed protocol arrangement should be adopted for supplies to be furnished from the United States. But there can be no question that the United Kingdom fared better during and after the war by relying on what its partner in the combination was able to offer. For its partner gave more than it could have pledged itself by protocol in advance to give. The uncertainty added often to the difficulties of planning production and supply; but it was largely unavoidable.

To some extent the above discussion has been concerned with matters of small interest to a British official, but of greater interest to American officials and experts in public administration. The difference between the British and American approaches is of some importance for an understanding of the nature of the Combined Boards. The British approach to such questions tends to be pragmatic and inductive, with little or no trace of the deductive or legalistic thinking which may be detected in some American accounts. For British thinking on such matters tends to begin with particular problems; its starting point is not the rules and principles of a written Constitution which provides the legal basis for government and the criterion for judging the validity of inter-governmental agreements.[2]

In the British view a Combined Board was not much more than a 'working party', to which unusual authority had been given in the form of a solemn pronouncement by the President and the Prime Minister. The more pretentious it was in the matter of titles and

---

[1] J. R. Deane, *The Strange Alliance* (New York: The Viking Press, 1947).
[2] cf. L. S. Amery, *Thought and Language*, English Association, November 1949.

powers the more likely it was to run into trouble. A Board differed from the usual kind of working party by being much better organised and possessing offices and a staff. There was little or nothing of the characteristic American concern for better legal definition. An attempt to suggest this difference of approach was made (perhaps in an exaggerated form) in a conversation at the end of the war by a British official of the Combined Raw Materials Board:

> British officials begin to notice a problem; they put Brown to work on it. He collects bits of it here and there and outlines its shape. He discusses it with others. When it becomes important enough there is a meeting about it and finally a working party is set up.

The American approach, the official thought, was something like this:

> They begin to see a problem and begin to define it under various heads; they decide that a Body is needed to deal with it. A Body must have a Directive. The Directive must define the scope of the problem and the relations of the Body with the various Government agencies. Round the Directive develops case law. In the event of a dispute between agencies it is fought out on a much more legalistic basis than could ever happen in London.

The administrative history of the war – American, Combined and British – is strewn with discarded committees and working parties, which functioned for a short time on the crest of some problem and then were lost in the trough. More often than not the reason was that the problem itself had been solved, or had changed, or had merged into some wider problem which other bodies were better able to handle. It was not surprising therefore that the Combined Boards had their ups and downs, and that they tended in some degree to shrink in their functions and activities as the war progressed. In a capital in which the life expectation of war-time government agencies was short and uncertain, the Combined Boards managed to survive well into the peace; and this was one of their little recognised achievements.

The Combined Boards could hardly have survived if they had attempted to engage in institutional warfare. As the official history of the War Production Board notes[1] the Combined Raw Materials Board, because it had no directive, 'relied heavily upon informal personal contacts and personal good will to develop a web of working relationships with the various United States agencies. These relationships, though unregularised and devoid of any fixed pattern, were reasonably satisfactory'. And the unpublished American history of C.R.M.B. noted at the end of the war that the Board's operations

---

[1] War Production Board, *Industrial Mobilisation for War, op. cit.*, pp. 222–224.

'met the all-important pragmatic test, in that they had in fact worked successfully'.[1]

It follows from what has been said that the Boards were never intended by the Prime Minister and the President as super agencies which would eliminate the need for conferences between Heads of Governments or direct negotiations between Cabinet Ministers. The criticism was sometimes made, inside and outside the Boards, that the two Governments tended to by-pass their own Combined Board machinery by resorting to direct negotiations on policy matters of special importance. Thus no direct use was made either of the Combined Production and Resources Board, or of the Combined Shipping Adjustment Board, by the Lyttelton Mission in November 1942, although it was discussing with the American Government important matters of policy of considerable interest to both Boards. Likewise the Combined Shipping Adjustment Board in Washington was by-passed in connection with the subsequent negotiations in the first half of 1943.[2] On several occasions important questions of food policy were discussed between the food authorities of the two Governments instead of through the Combined Food Board.[3] Direct negotiation outside the Boards (the Keynes-Sinclair Mission) was also the method used for the Stage II agreements in the second half of 1944. Little use was made of the Combined Boards on matters of higher policy in 1945. On the whole the Combined Boards were not very suitable bodies for the settlement of policy issues of the first importance. For such matters it was advisable to appoint special negotiators possessing special authority or rare knowledge – or a combination of both, such as Lord Keynes possessed. All such missions profited much, however, from the advice and help given them by the heads and staffs of the British sides of the Combined Boards in Washington.

THE STAFFS OF THE BOARDS

The charters of the Boards had little to say on staff or secretariat. Only two in fact mentioned staff. The American text for the Combined Raw Materials Board stated that: 'The Board shall have the power to appoint the staff necessary to carry out its responsibilities.'[4] The charter of the Combined Production and Resources Board stated that 'to facilitate continuous operation, the members of the Board shall each appoint a deputy, and the Board shall form a combined staff'. The charters of the Combined Shipping Adjustment Board

---

[1] Cited by S. McKee Rosen, op. cit., p. 67; Industrial Mobilisation for War, op. cit., p. 222.
[2] See North American Supply, op. cit., Chapters IX and X.
[3] R. J. Hammond, op. cit., Chapter XIX; S. McKee Rosen, op. cit., pp. 227 and 242.
[4] This sentence slipped out of the London text in Cmd 6332.

and the Combined Food Board were silent on staff; but this merely meant that the matter was taken for granted.[1]

The 'combined staff' referred to in the charter of the Combined Production and Resources Board meant in practice a small group of officials, directly appointed by the Board, and a wider group drawn mainly from the War Production Board and the British Supply Mission. The immediate staff of the Board itself was headed for its first few weeks by a high American army officer (General Aurand); his transfer at the end of August 1942 by the War Department to another post dealt a severe blow to the Board. The Board was served by three executive officers, British, American and Canadian, who were responsible for seeing that decisions were carried into effect; and by a Joint Planning Staff.[2] It had also two secretaries who were jointly responsible for documentation and for the recording of the Board's activities.

The staff arrangements of the Combined Raw Materials Board were somewhat similar. Each of the two Board members had his Chief of Staff – the United Kingdom and the United States Executive Secretaries. They in turn were assisted by a small staff, more or less equivalent to a central secretariat, dealing with administrative matters and general questions affecting several commodities, such as shipping, co-ordinated buying and relations with third countries. The main working staff of the Board on the British side consisted of officials of the British Raw Materials Mission. These 'commodity officers', fifteen or more in number, were organised within the British Raw Materials Mission in some five commodity divisions each under a senior officer as chief of division.

The staff and working arrangements of C.R.M.B. were organised on a commodity basis. It was assumed that a certain number of commodities, which were giving trouble or threatened to do so, would remain difficult and would require regular attention. Each

---

[1] Thus the Memorandum of Organisation of the Shipping Board (19th February 1942) outlined a plan of organisation providing for the appointment of staff as well as of advisers to sit with the Board. The Board was to be organised in five sections, each under British and American representatives. The advisers were appointed, but not all the 'sections' materialised. The memorandum provided further for a joint economic analysis section of which the Board was to name the chief. Economic analysts were appointed later to work in London or Washington as circumstances might require. There was also to be an Executive Officer of the Board who was to 'supply Secretariat as required for all sections'. The Board as organised had joint secretaries and an American Executive Officer; later, in 1943, a British Executive Officer was added. The Combined Food Board provided itself with a British and American adviser and with joint British and American Executive Officers (each with a deputy). For most of its staff work, however, it used officials of the British Food Mission and the American Office of Foreign Agricultural Relations of the United States Department of Agriculture.

[2] For a time, March 1943 to September 1944, an American Executive Director was made responsible to the Board for its combined secretariat. As originally constituted the Joint Planning Staff consisted of a member of the British Joint War Production Staff, the Statistical Officer of the British Supply Council and three American statisticians and economic experts from the War Production Board.

member of the staff had to look after one or more such commodities. He worked on each commodity with his American opposite number; both worked in adjoining rooms and with the utmost informality. Together they assembled and analysed the data, framed recommendations by the Board, and negotiated on any difficult points with the interested departments. The outcome was the commodity report which was submitted to the Operating Committee and formed the basis of the Board's action. The commodity officers were thus engaged both in work of a statistical kind and in what could be called the 'diplomacy of supply'. This accorded with the British civil service tradition that its officials should be able to undertake diverse functions of this kind, and the calibre of the small body of officers on both sides made the combination of tasks effective. The main staff on the American side, roughly corresponding in numbers to the British staff, were officials of the War Production Board. Their work was centred round the inter-agency Requirements Committee, which assembled American data for each commodity and made allocations between the different American agencies.

All these officers were also national officials, with a good deal of work to do which was of little direct concern to the Board. It was customary, at least on the British side, to speak of the Board as having a 'combined secretariat'; this included not only the Executive Officers and central staff, but also the body of commodity officers, British and American, who were engaged on work of a combined nature for the Board.[1]

THE GEARING TOGETHER OF NATIONAL ADMINISTRATIONS

The Boards thus were a means of gearing together the two national administrations in order to deal more efficiently with matters of common interest. When this process of intermeshing was complete, as in the case of the Combined Raw Materials Board, a Board worked effectively – as the official history of the War Production Board testified.[2] Where it failed, or was incomplete, the working of the

---

[1] The Combined Chiefs of Staff went rather further than the Boards in the direction of a Combined Secretariat. A group of officers, appointed by the Combined Chiefs of Staff, served it as secretariat, maintained its records, prepared essential papers and carried out such other work as was required by the Combined Chiefs.

[2] 'A great impetus to co-operation was supplied by the decision of Batt, the United States member, to keep the American staff of C.R.M.B. small and rely primarily upon W.P.B. for staff work, for information and for implementation of C.R.M.B. recommendations. The result was that the facts and recommendations submitted to C.R.M.B. and the Requirements Committee were in almost all cases identical. This arrangement worked especially well during the first half of 1942, when Batt was both C.R.M.B. member and chairman of the W.P.B. Requirements Committee. Even after he ceased to hold the latter position, he continued to rely heavily on the Requirements Committee staff for assistance on C.R.M.B. matters.' War Production Board, *Industrial Mobilisation for War, op. cit.*, pp. 222–3.

Combined Board system was seriously impeded.[1] The process as it affected raw materials was described thus by Sir Clive Baillieu in a broadcast in Washington in July 1943:

> We worked out a method of gearing the two administrations together at every operational level, so that when a problem finally got to a meeting of the Board it had behind it agreement on the essential points right back down the line. . . . The mainspring of this standing machinery for maintaining regular contact with all the principal departments concerned with the use or the production and distribution of raw materials, is the Advisory Operating Committee of the Board on which these agencies are represented. This Committee prepares in advance the agreements which finally emerge in the recommendations of the Board. Recommendations are followed up by the Committee to see how they are being carried out. Through this Committee we have direct links with the other United Nations. This organisation works smoothly, and in fact most day-to-day problems are solved by informal agreement.

The experience of the British side of the Boards showed the special importance of the words 'right back down the line'. The gearing together depended on the daily work of each commodity officer with his opposite number. The British Missions learned from experience that negotiations begun low down the line and carried up to higher levels by the American officials themselves were more likely to be durable. Except where matters of high policy were involved, interventions at a high level were more likely than not to backfire, causing a hardening of opposition at lower levels.

The Combined Raw Materials Board itself was an entirely informal body consisting of the two Board Members, the Executive Secretaries, the staff responsible for the various commodities under review at that particular meeting, and occasional visitors. Meetings took place in the personal office of the American Member. In general, as a result of the preceding staff work and inter-departmental discussion, recommendations were ready for approval without serious amendment and discussions were normally confined to broader matters of supply and policy. Only formal minutes were kept.

The two sides of the Board were not thus in the same position as regards direct contacts with their own departments. American departments were on the spot, and their officers were available on the telephone or for meetings. The United Kingdom side of the Board was briefed through a continuous telegraphic correspondence with the Ministry of Production, supplemented by periodical visits to

---

[1] An American official analysis in mid-1943 of the difficulties of the Combined Food Board made the point that 'the primary difficulty hampering combined planning and operation is a failure to integrate the American side of the Board with the War Food Administration. Without such integration the whole combined machinery breaks down'. Cited by S. McKee Rosen, *op. cit.*, p. 228.

London by the British Member and his senior staff. On the British side all recommendations were 'cleared' by telegram before being issued by the Board, except in rare urgent cases where the British Member had to act on his own initiative. Whether this closeness to its base was a source of strength to the American side is an open question. It had obvious advantages, but the process of consultation was so easy and so many people could be consulted so often that an agreed view was often slow in emerging. On the British side the process of telegraphing took time, but the London departments were subjected to the discipline of putting down on paper under pressure a coherent and lucid summary of their position which helped to speed up negotiations in Washington.

The Advisory Operating Committee, referred to above, was the main organ of the Combined Raw Materials Board. The Board's two executive secretaries, British and American, were members of the Committee. On the British side it was attended also by representatives of the Foreign Office and the Ministries of Production, Supply and Economic Warfare (through officers in each case of the British Raw Materials Mission and the British Embassy), on the American side the following agencies were represented: the State Department, the War Production Board, the Department of Commerce, the Office of Foreign Economic Administration (Economic Warfare and Lend-Lease).[1] Thus the Committee brought together at its weekly meetings high officials from the main government departments in London and Washington on which the successful carrying out of the work of the Board depended.

Each of the other Combined Boards made free use of committees which were attended by representatives of the principal American agencies; but none of these major Board committees played such a steady and vital part in the work of a Combined Board, from the beginning to the end of its existence, as did the Advisory Operating Committee of C.R.M.B. One of the main reasons for its success was indicated by Sir Clive Baillieu in the passage cited above. The Committee was the master hand that shaped all reports and all actions before they came formally before the Board. The Combined Raw Materials Board refrained from creating lower level commodity committees like those set up by the other Boards. Its flexible working arrangements and the absence of a rigid committee structure contributed to the Board's efficiency. Attempts made by the Combined Production and Resources Board and the Combined Food Board to work through inter-agency committees, modelled more or less on the Advisory Operating Committee, were frustrated by the existence of the system of commodity committees used by these two

---

[1] The Foreign Economic Administration absorbed also the Federal Loan Department, the Metals Reserve Corporation and the Defence Supplies Corporation.

Boards. Thus the co-ordinating functions of the main inter-agency committee became dispersed amongst the separate commodity committees which themselves contained representatives of the different agencies.[1]

(iv)

Relations with the United States and
the United Kingdom

The experience of the war seems to show that no such intermeshing with American agencies would have been possible if the Boards had been located in London instead of Washington. The choice of Washington as centre was due to several factors. One was the importance of American production and Britain's dependence on the United States for part of her requirements. It was an advantage to have small staffs of British officials housed with certain American agencies in Washington. But the benefit was not all on one side. The presence in Washington of British Combined Board staffs had a favourable effect (as the official history of the War Production Board noted) on the 'provincial commodity outlook of some of the industry branches' of that agency; they learned from the daily contacts 'the importance of the British Empire as a source of materials'.[2]

But there was also another factor, which (as mentioned above) had been recognised in 1941 by the British Chiefs of Staff, namely, the strength of the resistance within the American system to the

---

[1] The main committees of the Combined Production and Resources Board were:

Committee	Date of First Meeting
Truck Committee	17th November 1942
Non-Military Supplies Committee .	22nd January 1943
Medical Supplies Committee . .	28th January 1943
Internal Combustion Engine Committee .	25th September 1943
Machine Tools Committee . . .	14th October 1943
Tire and Tire Fabric Committee . .	9th November 1943
Textile Committee	5th January 1944
Public Utilities Committee . . .	31st January 1944
Transportation Equipment Committee .	30th June 1944

In addition there were the seven combined committees (C.P.R.B.-C.R.M.B.) set up in 1943 which are listed above on page 221. For the date of termination of the Combined Production and Resources Board, and of the Combined Committees, see Chapter VI, Section (v).

[2] War Production Board, *Industrial Mobilisation for War, op. cit.*, p. 223. There were other effects of a more subtle kind. One was the 'catalytic' effect on inter-agency meetings which the presence of one or two British officials seemed to have. Their presence seemed to help to promote agreement on the very frequent occasions when representatives of the different agencies came to combined meetings without having worked out amongst themselves any Administration policy on the subject under discussion. The British officials were impressed by the tolerance with which their silent presence was accepted whilst such American domestic issues were being discussed.

delegation of authority to American representatives abroad.[1] The authority and influence of an American official abroad tended to be in inverse proportion to the length of his absence from Washington. It was much easier, therefore, for the American Government to work through combined machinery located in Washington. Being on the spot the American representative on a Combined Board could keep his place in the competitive struggle of the Washington agencies.

Many of the difficulties encountered by the Combined Boards arose from the tangle of political and administrative problems which the American Government faced in its first year of war. 'The tasks were unique, the problems not well understood, the resources not well inventoried, the necessary objectives not always clearly visualised, the methods to attain them untried.'[2] Thus, with little in the way of a solid core of career officials, the War Production Board had to digest, and to train into a team, a staff which rose to 23,000 persons at its peak in 1943. It had also to contend, as its official history noted, with an almost chronic division of authority at the higher levels.[3] Part of its difficulty stemmed ultimately from the lack of anything in the nature of a war cabinet in the United States. Mr Stimson dwelt in his book on the need of such a cabinet; it might have included, he thought, the President's 'most trusted personal adviser, Harry Hopkins, and perhaps the Secretaries of State, Treasury, War and Navy'. He envisaged it as 'organised like the Joint Chiefs of Staff, with a secretariat of top quality and a continuing record of the policy decisions made or approved by the President. . . .' The regular Cabinet meetings, he noted, had become a formality. Thus differences between Departments – particularly, in his experience, between the Army and Navy – could only be overcome in the last resort by the direct intervention of the President himself.[4] British officials frequently reported to London on the effects on their work of competition between the different American agencies. Few things impressed them more than the lack of a tradition of collective responsibility and the profound way in which it affected all parts of the Administration. But they also noted many instances in which the spirit of individualism worked to their advantage. Thus a well disposed, able and energetic official, armed with authority at some key point, could make all the difference between success or failure in the work of a Combined Board where it touched his field of responsibility. Perhaps the most striking example in the history of

---

[1] See above p. 218.
[2] *The United States at War, op. cit.,* p. 506.
[3] War Production Board, *Industrial Mobilisation for War, op. cit.,* pp. 975–6.
[4] Henry L. Stimson and McGeorge Bundy *On Active Service in Peace and War* (New York: Harper & Brothers, 1948. London: Hutchinson, 1949), p. 562 and Chapter XX. From the time of its creation, in mid-1943, the Office of War Mobilisation, under Mr James F. Byrnes, played an increasingly important part in co-ordinating the work of the different war agencies.

the Boards was afforded by the work of Mr William L. Batt, to whom the President paid a special tribute on 19th January 1945, when he announced that the Combined Boards would be maintained until the end of the war. At the outset in 1942 Mr Batt was the Chairman of the Requirements Committee of the War Production Board and later Vice Chairman for International Supply. As the American member of the Combined Raw Materials Board throughout the war, and the American member for most of the war of the Combined Production and Resources Board, he was able to gear these two Boards very closely to the War Production Board.[1]

THE TWO CAPITALS OF THE BOARDS — LONDON AND WASHINGTON

Although Washington was the main centre of the Combined Boards some machinery was needed in London to ensure the smooth working of the system. The British sides of the Combined Raw Materials Board and the Combined Production and Resources Board were responsible to the Minister of Production. The British side of C.P.R.B. had as its London counterpart the Joint War Production Staff of the Ministry of Production. The Minister himself was the British member of the Board in Washington although he normally acted through a deputy. The task of the Joint War Production Staff was to relate munitions requirements to production possibilities; to co-ordinate the allocation of manpower with programmes of requirements and to take any action necessary as a result of decisions by the Board in Washington. The Ministry of Production co-ordinated action between the Supply Ministries on the one hand and Service Departments on the other. Liaison between the Ministry of Production and the two Boards in Washington was maintained by a continuous stream of cables supplemented by an exchange of documents and by personal letters, and in the case of C.P.R.B. by a Weekly Letter sent by the Minister's deputy to the Minister in London. The text was not circulated in Washington; but it was seen each week by the American member, and later by the Canadian member of the Board. The fact that in the organisation in London no one official in the Ministry of Production was named to act as opposite number of the British Executive Officer of the Board in Washington may have looked untidy on paper, but was probably a source of strength rather than weakness.

A London Committee (L.C.P.R.B.) of the Washington Combined Production and Resources Board was set up in July 1942. It consisted of the Minister of Production and his deputy, and on the American

---

[1] War Production Board, *Industrial Mobilisation for War, op. cit.*, pp. 571 and 587. Mr Batt was also the American member of two United States-Canadian bodies, the Materials Co-ordinating Committee and the Joint War Production Committee.

side of representatives of the American civilian and military mission in London.[1] The London Committee carried out work on the Board's recommendations which could be more conveniently done in London than in Washington. One function of the London Committee was to help the Board by considering and making recommendations on 'proposed adjustments in United Kingdom production programmes which arise in connection with Combined Production Planning by C.P.R.B.'[2] Another function was to secure the utmost economy in shipping. The London Committee examined from this point of view the supply requirements of American forces in the United Kingdom. The Combined Coal Committee (Washington and London) was set up on its initiative; and it established a number of working parties on particular problems, such as the supply of tyres and tubes and public utilities equipment. It also took an active part in developing the interchange of technical information. Moreover it linked the Combined Production and Resources Board in Washington with the Commonwealth Supply Council in London on which Commonwealth countries were represented.[3] By this means the scope of C.P.R.B. was extended indirectly to cover the various minor segments of war production outside the three principal countries directly represented on the Board. The terms of reference of the London Committee were framed 'to safeguard the position' of the Washington Board as 'the only body capable of decisions in principle'. This was to ward off any suspicion of attempts to shift the centre of the Board's power from Washington to London.

(v)

The Boards and Other Countries

The relations of the British-American combination to other countries involved a series of complex problems. Only a brief reference can be made here to some of these problems, namely, the question of extending the membership of the Combined Boards, the relations with other countries in general, and the question of exports to such countries.[4]

---

[1] Including the American Mission for Economic Affairs, (M.E.A.L.) which developed out of the Harriman Mission of 1941. This was a small Mission of some 25 administrative officers who kept in close touch with British supply authorities and the Ministry of Production.

[2] An informal interdepartmental committee to co-ordinate work on the Combined Boards met each week in London for a number of months from the autumn of 1942. It was convened by the Joint American Secretariat of the North American Supply Committee. The latter was no longer an active body but served from the end of 1942 as the channel through which communications passed between the Ministry of Production and the Combined Boards in Washington.

[3] See below, Chapter VII.

[4] On the Munitions Assignments Board and third countries see the final section of this Chapter.

The agreement of 26th January 1942, between the Prime Minister and the President, setting up the Combined Boards, stated that these bodies would: 'confer with representatives of the U.S.S.R., China and such others of the United Nations as are necessary to attain common purposes and provide for the most effective utilisation of the joint resources of the United Nations'. In general the British and American Governments adopted the principle of pooling their own resources under the Combined Board system; but they could not take for granted that the resources of other nations would be thrown automatically into the common pool. The charters of the Boards stated the principle of pooling very clearly in connection with munitions and shipping. In both cases the United Kingdom had important resources to contribute to the Pool. Between them, the two countries controlled directly or indirectly the greater part of the shipping and munitions production of the United Nations. In the case of raw materials, however, the United Kingdom had almost nothing that could be contributed from its islands. It was dependent almost wholly on overseas supply largely within different parts of the Commonwealth. Even the United States, which had far greater internal resources, was also dependent for many strategic materials on supplies from abroad. It was for this reason that the charter for the Combined Raw Materials Board made a pointed reference to 'others of the United Nations'. The Board, on the one hand, was to deal with raw material resources 'under the jurisdiction or control of the two Governments'; on the other hand, it was to collaborate with others of the United Nations to secure the 'effective use of their raw materials'.[1] The same situation existed for food, and exactly the same wording was used in the charter of the Combined Food Board. Of all the Combined Boards the Combined Production and Resources Board, as originally conceived, seemed to have the least direct concern with other United Nations. Its main field was to 'combine the production programmes of the United States, the United Kingdom and Canada in a single integrated programme. . . .' In doing this however, it was to take into account the 'maximum utilisation of the productive resources available to the United States, the British Commonwealth of Nations and the United Nations'. In the later stages of the war, however, it was to become just as much concerned as any of the Combined Boards with the other United Nations.[2]

Nevertheless there was an undercurrent of concern in some American circles, including the State Department, that the Combined Boards might be regarded as an Anglo-American monopoly. From

---

[1] The charter enjoined the Board 'in collaboration with others of the United Nations to work toward the best utilisation of their raw material resources and, in collaboration with the interested nation or nations, formulate plans and recommendations for the development, expansion, purchase, or other effective use of their raw materials'.

[2] See below, Section (vi).

the sheer force of circumstances however the Boards (save for the admission of Canada) remained American and British to the very end. The 'circumstances' were the greater efficiency in time of war of the principle of combination as against a multi-national organisation.[1] The difficulties of working on a multilateral basis, involving agreement between many countries, were demonstrated in the last months of the life of the Boards. In the war years, the Boards had to work against time. They had to secure speedy agreement on short-term allocations, many of them quarterly, some even monthly. If figures were not ready on time interim decisions had to be made. The addition of even one or two countries would have meant a considerable slowing down of the speed of operations. And if the additional member lacked the ability or the will to co-operate the system would become unworkable. The combined system depended on the whole-hearted co-operation of the two (or three) partners in every field of common interest. Moreover full combination required the sharing of secrets and the most complete exchange of information. For these reasons Washington and London agreed that the admission of the U.S.S.R. or China could only diminish the efficiency of the system. All attempts to obtain statistical information of any sort from Russia on her raw materials and war production were a complete failure. Thus when the question of the admission of the U.S.S.R. to the Combined Boards was raised by the head of the War Production Board, in September 1943, the outcome of the discussion was the agreement 'that membership . . . would be extended to additional countries only upon certain conditions: that there be a complete exchange of information . . . and complete willingness to pool their resources'. Again when the Combined Boards at the end of 1945 were dissolved into international commodity committees the conditions of effective membership were defined as follows by the British side in Washington:

> These committees can work effectively only if the countries which participate are prepared both to disclose their production capacity fully or to justify their requirements, as the case may be, and to execute any relevant recommendations which the committees agree.

The Protocol arrangements, covering definite quantities of supplies for the U.S.S.R. to be furnished by the United Kingdom, Canada, and the United States, were brought within the scope of the Combined Raw Materials Board in 1942. The second and third Protocols were cleared by the Board; and the fourth, which proved abortive, was also referred to it.[2] The requirements submitted by the

---

[1] The reasons for the original decision to put the organisation on a combined rather than an international basis are indicated in *North American Supply, op. cit.*, Chapter IX.

[2] The first Protocol, from 1st October 1941 to 30th June 1942, was concluded before the Board came into existence. Canada became a signatory of the 1944–5 Protocol.

U.S.S.R. for the Protocols were never accompanied by any justification or explanation of the figures – even to the extent of indicating what proportion of their total requirements were being used for other than direct military purposes. This absence of data was one of the factors in the final breakdown of the Protocol arrangements.

THE POSITION OF CANADA

Canada was the only country apart from the United States and the United Kingdom with an appreciable surplus of war production. Moreover her contributions in the matter of raw materials and food-stuffs were greater than those of any other part of the British Commonwealth. Already in 1941 Canada had established close working relationships with the United States in matters relating to raw materials, war production and economic issues arising out of the war. The joint committees which were set up between the two countries anticipated in some ways the structure of the Combined Boards. Thus for raw materials there had existed since the summer of 1941 something like an informal Canadian-American Combined Board in the shape of the Materials Co-ordinating Committee (United States-Canada). This body served as Canada's link with the Combined Raw Materials Board and was the reason for Canada not becoming a member of that Board.[1]

Indeed the old and well established channels for consultation between Ottawa and London, and the new Canadian-American combined machinery, seemed at first to make it unnecessary for Canada to become a member of any of the Combined Boards. The view taken in London and Washington was that: 'The production of Canada is already integrated'.[2] This view seemed to be shared at first in Ottawa. When Mr W. L. Batt informed Mr C. D. Howe, the Canadian Minister of Munitions and Supply, of the arrangements which were being made for the organisation of the Combined Raw Materials Board, the latter replied (on 10th February 1942): 'Two-man direction could only be improved by making it one-man direction'. But Mr Howe thought that Canada ought to be represented on the Advisory Operating Committee of the Board; Ottawa was 'somewhat disturbed' because it had not been consulted in the setting up of the Boards, although their jurisdiction seemed to 'extend to the disposition of our raw materials and finished products'. In the end the existing machinery, the American-Canadian Materials Co-ordinating Committee, of which Mr Batt was the American member,

---

[1] *Canada's Relations with War-Time Agencies in Washington,* by S. D. Pierce and A. F. W. Plumptre, *Canadian Journal of Economics and Political Science,* Vol. II, No. 3, August 1945 and R. Warren James, *op. cit.*

[2] Statement by Mr Oliver Lyttelton in House of Commons on the setting up of the Combined Production and Resources Board, 24th June 1942. H. of C. Deb., Vol. 380, Col. 1987.

was accepted as a sufficiently close link with the Combined Raw Materials Board. No Canadian claim was made for membership of the Combined Shipping Adjustment Board. Canada desired at one stage to join the Washington Combined Munitions Assignments Board. But it was felt in Washington that the Board, which had six members and a chairman, was already too large. Moreover it was feared that acceptance of Canadian membership would lead to claims by other countries.[1] This fear was at first an obstacle to Canadian membership of the Combined Production and Resources Board and the Combined Food Board. By the time these two new Boards were set up the Canadian Government had come to the conclusion that it should be a member of both of them. In July 1942 a suggestion was made by the Canadian Government that Canada should become a member of the Food Board in view of her large contribution in the matter of food.[2] To avoid creating a precedent by enlarging the membership of the Board London and Washington agreed with Ottawa on a compromise, namely, that Canada should be represented on the Commodity Committees of the Food Board. (Membership of the Board itself followed a year later in October 1943.)

The question of Canadian membership of the Combined Production and Resources Board was mooted as early as April 1942. A suggestion was made by the Australian Minister of External Affairs in the Pacific War Council that Canada should act on the new Board as a representative of all the Dominions. Mr MacKenzie King however thought that if Canada became a member she should represent herself. The matter was brought to a head at the end of August by a suggestion made by Mr Howe to Mr Donald Nelson that a Canadian-American Production Board should be established. A discussion on this idea in the British Supply Council showed a general feeling, shared by the Canadian member, that a much better solution would be simply to add Canada as the third member of the Combined Production and Resources Board. A separate Canadian-American Board, it was felt, would merely add an unnecessary piece of machinery, since the relations of Canada with the United States were already sufficiently close.[3] London and Ottawa concurred in this view. Messages received from Ottawa showed that the question of Canadian membership of the Combined Production and Resources Board, of the proposed Post War Relief and Rehabilitation Board, and if possible of the Food Board, had now become a matter of principle. Canadian membership was regarded

---

[1] The sequel is told at the end of this Chapter, p. 259.
[2] R. J. Hammond, *op. cit.*, pp. 241–247.
[3] The American member of the Combined Production and Resources Board was in fact the Chairman of the Joint American-Canadian Defence Production Committee.

as not only necessary in itself, but desirable for another reason – to prevent a possible alienation of smaller powers on the ground that too much authority was concentrated in the hands of the United States and the United Kingdom. The matter was discussed in mid-September with the authorities in Ottawa by the British Heads of the Combined Food Board and C.P.R.B. and in Washington by British, Canadian and American representatives. The result was full agreement that Canada should join C.P.R.B. There was still some misgiving that this step might open the way to claims by other countries. Thus when London, at the end of October, informed the other members of the Commonwealth of the decision to admit Canada as a full member of the Board, it emphasised the unique position of Canada. Indeed no other country had this combination of qualities – close relationship with the United States, and a considerable war production which dovetailed with that of the United Kingdom.[1]

From this point onwards the question of the composition and future of the Combined Boards began to be discussed from a somewhat different angle. Whilst the superior efficiency in time of war of the two or three-member Boards was never disputed, it was agreed that towards the end of the war the situation might change. In order to prepare for the transition to peace it might become necessary to associate other countries more closely with the work of the Boards. Serious combined discussions on the matter began in the first half of 1944 as a result of a telegram from the President to the Prime Minister on 24th February. The President invited an exchange of views on the future of the Boards and the possibility of associating other countries with them, and the Prime Minister agreed. Informal talks began in March and continued intermittently until the end of the year. One of the points under discussion was the functions of the Boards in Stage II; and when in the autumn it became clear that Stage I was unlikely to end in 1944 interest in the question slackened. In the announcement finally made by the President and the Prime Minister on 19th January 1945 it was agreed that the three Boards for raw materials, food and production should continue in their existing form until the end of the war with Japan, but that they should begin to associate other countries 'increasingly' with their work. The announcement encouraged an extension of the existing practice of several of the Boards of inviting representatives of other United Nations to be present at meetings of Combined Board committees when matters of immediate concern to a particular country were under discussion. The arrangements were on a very informal basis.

---

[1] The entry of Canada into the Board was announced on 7th November. The Canadian Minister of Munitions and Supply became the Canadian member of the Board, his place being normally taken by his deputy.

Experiments which were made in the summer of 1944 with Tripartite Committees of a more formal kind showed that they served no very useful purpose.[1]

THE PROBLEM OF EXPORTS TO THIRD COUNTRIES

The continued import of essential supplies by the United Kingdom was dependent in some degree on the maintenance of a minimum of exports. Lend-Lease diminished the need of exports to pay for a large part of British imports from the United States. This made possible a higher degree of munitions production in the United Kingdom and the cutting back still further of the production of civilian goods for export. The same process began in the United States in 1942, and by November of that year the amount of civilian-type goods available for export to third countries had shrunk to the point where some combined programming of British and American exports to importing countries had become necessary. Through the Boards (C.R.M.B. and C.P.R.B.) and the national machinery for regulating procurement and for licensing and controlling exports, London and Washington did their best to assure minimum supplies of essential commodities to third countries. The supervision of the production and distribution of manufactured goods to third countries became one of the main functions of the Combined Production and Resources Board from 1943 onwards.[2]

The moment the Combined Raw Materials Board began to allocate supplies to the United Kingdom and the United States it had to face the problem of exports to what were known as 'third' countries. The import requirements of most other countries as regards raw materials were usually very small. In the case of the five European neutrals it was important to prevent even limited amounts of critical materials from reaching the enemy; at the same time it was necessary to sustain the economies of these countries in order to prevent them from drifting into the orbit of Germany and Italy. The supply to the neutrals both of raw materials and manufactured goods, and the purchase from them in return of any strategic materials which they produced, were regulated by special purchase or war trade agreements made with them early in the war.[3] Negotiations under the agreements were conducted by the British and American diplomatic representatives in each country. Data on both supply and requirements were submitted to the Combined

---

[1] Tripartite Committees (in which the British and American members of a Board met the representatives of another country) were tried out in 1944 with France and Belgium.

[2] See Section (vi) below.

[3] W. N. Medlicott, *The Economic Blockade*, Vol. I, Part I (London: Her Majesty's Stationery Office, 1952).

R

Boards.[1] The requirements were usually small enough to be met out of a 'contingency reserve' for which the Board provided in many of its commodity reports. Exports to countries other than the neutrals and the U.S.S.R. were not regulated by special agreements. For exports to the British Commonwealth, machinery was provided at the London end (through the Empire Clearing House – later the Commonwealth Supply Council) which ensured that the requirements of all parts save Canada were included in the claims for allocation presented in Washington by the United Kingdom.

The most difficult part of the problem was not the exports of raw materials themselves, but how to make proper allowance for the raw material content of manufactured goods exported by the United Kingdom and the United States. Although C.R.M.B. recognised the need to make provision in its allocations for exports, no very consistent line was followed in its commodity reports. In some cases the reports indicated that requirements as presented by the United States and the United Kingdom included the raw material content of exports of semi-manufactured or finished goods for export. In that case due allowance might be made in the allocations (e.g., in the early part of 1942, in the allocations of tungsten, nickel, antimony and graphite). In most cases, however, the reports merely assumed, without definitely stating the point, that exports were included in the allocations. The provision for copper illustrated the complexities of the problem. The report accompanied the allocations with the recommendation that:

> import requirements in Copper, semi-manufactures of Copper, and Copper Alloys, and manufactured products other than military, consisting wholly or principally of Copper or Copper Alloys, be met normally: Western Hemisphere, U.S.S.R., China and Iceland, by the U.S.A.; other British Empire, Africa and European neutrals, by the United Kingdom.

The Board's report early in 1942 on jute and burlap and manila-sisal also assigned responsibility for supplying third countries.[2] Most of the other reports of the Board left the problem hanging in the air. If no really serious supply problem were involved it was not necessary to define export responsibilities. But it was necessary to have some co-ordination between the exporting countries to ensure that some importing countries did not get more than a reasonable share of a commodity in short supply. This was not a serious problem in the

---

[1] The data were cleared by the Commodity Officers who presented them direct to the Board – an unusual procedure which was adopted also in the case of the Russian Protocol figures. Normally all such proposals passed through the Advisory Operating Committee.

[2] An attempt was even made to protect the importing countries from possible shortage if they attempted to re-export either to the United Kingdom or the United States.

case of raw materials as such. The feeling in the Combined Raw Materials Board was definitely against any elaborate attempt to find a combined solution for a problem which by its nature was incapable of precise regulation and was in any case of merely marginal importance.

There the matter might have rested without further ado, if it had not been for the complications caused by the theory and politics of Lend-Lease. It was these complications which had led earlier to the self-imposed restrictions on British exports – particularly in respect of their Lend-Lease raw material content – which had been provided for in the British White Paper of September 1941.[1] In a letter of 31st December 1941 the Lend-Lease Administrator had suggested the idea of substituting export-programmes for the previous method of case by case consultation and clearance by the United Kingdom before export could take place.[2] Meanwhile, for a temporary period, he suggested that the United Kingdom could export without such advance clearance. The idea was to link export programmes with allocations of raw materials by the United States to the United Kingdom. The suggestion was welcomed in London as a possible means of escaping from the onerous restrictions of the White Paper. Such restrictions no longer seemed to be justified on the new theory of pooling supplies which underlay the system of the Combined Boards.

Moreover it was foreseen in London that with the growing shortages of essential civilian supplies, the real problem was not that of competition between American and British exports, in which Lend-Lease might have given the latter an unfair advantage. It was rather the growing difficulty of meeting the essential civilian needs of third countries out of greatly diminished supplies. For political reasons, however, the United States opposed any relaxation of the actual terms of the White Paper.[3] A proposal from the American side, at the end of April 1942, that the Combined Raw Materials Board should draw up joint export programmes to cover as much as possible of the export trade of the two countries, led to the setting up in June of an informal Combined Exports Markets Committee under the chairmanship of the American Executive Secretary of the Board. The main purpose of the Committee was to secure agreements between the two countries on the quantities and types of supplies of

---

[1] This is discussed in greater detail in *History of the Second War, United Kingdom Civil Series*, E. L. Hargreaves and M. M. Gowing, *Civil Industry and Trade*, Chapters VII & VIII.

[2] See *North American Supply, op. cit.*, Chapter VIII, p. 296.

[3] The political reasons sprang partly from a widespread misunderstanding in the United States of the nature of the Sterling Area, the function of British exports in that area, and the effect on the Sterling Area as a whole of Lend-Lease supply to a particular country in the Area. See *North American Supply, op. cit.*, Chapter VII and Appendix IX, and a volume on Financial Policy to be published later in this series of histories.

raw materials and semi-manufactures to be exported to third countries. London was anxious that at least British Commonwealth countries should get the supplies they needed; but there was no certainty that the United States would be able in fact to supply them. Moreover with South American countries there was a growing currency problem. The heavy fall in British exports to South America since 1939 had resulted in the accumulation of sterling balances to a point where there was an increasing reluctance to make further exports to the United Kingdom.

Thus from the outset several elements were mingled in the problem of export programming: one was the restrictions on British exports under the White Paper; another was the shortage of some strategic raw materials; a third was the growing scarcity of certain kinds of civilian goods. This scarcity was due to the shrinkage of British production for export and a lesser shrinkage which began in the United States in 1942 as the American economy was placed on a war basis. Actually the process of curtailment in the United States was much less drastic than anticipated. The War Production Board set up a Standard Products Committee to supervise the process of cutting back the production of finished goods. In calculating minimum requirements of such goods the needs of export markets were taken into account. The detailed work of drawing up export programmes for particular commodities was left to the Combined Exports Markets Committee. At the end of the year, the Committee was split into two committees, one dealing with raw materials and the other with finished goods. In most cases responsibility for supplying markets was apportioned roughly on a hemisphere basis: the Western Hemisphere to the United States and the Eastern Hemisphere (including the British Commonwealth, except Canada) to the United Kingdom. In actual practice, although a number of export programmes were submitted by one side or the other, final agreement on combined export programmes was reached in very few cases. One of the limiting factors was the extreme difficulty of securing adequate statistical information as to the future requirements of importing countries and their alternative sources of supply, including their domestic production.[1] Attempts to secure such data from the importing countries by means of a standard form, drawn up by the Office of Lend-Lease Administration, produced little result. White Paper restrictions on

---

[1] The problem was less difficult in an area of combined responsibility such as the Middle East. The existence of the Middle East Supply Centre, a fully combined organisation composed of British and American officials, made it possible to provide countries in the area with a more elaborate system for assuring their import requirements. The Centre drew up detailed import programmes for the various countries. These were screened by area committees in London and Washington which made recommendations as to sources of supply (loading areas). The latter were recorded in a Commodity Index which was used by the import licensing authorities in the territories concerned. Some commodities were pooled or procured on bulk indents from sources of supply agreed between London and Washington.

British exports were also largely responsible for the failure to agree on export programmes.[1] Thus in the case of bicycles, and agricultural hand tools – particularly matchets – a United Kingdom proposal at the end of 1942 for joint export programmes, was met by an American argument that the United States should supply world requirements of these items. An appeal was made in both cases to the Combined Production and Resources Board; but the Board refused to adjudicate. It explained its refusal by pointing out that there was no shortage of world production capacity and that the amount of steel and labour involved was inconsiderable. 'It seems obvious to us that the combined war programme would not be affected by any transference of production from one country to another'. Although few fully combined export programmes finally emerged from all this activity, it helped to safeguard the interests of importing countries. Progress was made on copper sulphate, cinematograph film, sewing machines, steel pen points, crown corks, electric lamps and lamp-making materials. Even when joint export programmes had been worked out they were not necessarily adopted finally by the Combined Exports Markets Committee.

(vi)

Essential Civilian Supplies and the Combined Production and Resources Board

From early in 1943 the question of planning exports to third countries became merged in the wider problem of planning the production and distribution of essential civilian supplies for the United Kingdom and the United States as well as for the other United Nations. Until mid-1942 the output of civilian supplies in the United States was adequate for domestic needs and to meet deficits in Allied countries. The problems were those of transport and payment rather than of any lack of goods. But as the mobilisation of American industry began to near its peak, London and Washington recognised that shortages of essential civilian goods were likely to become serious enough to impair the Allied war effort. Thus towards the end of 1942 a serious problem was created by a world shortage of textiles; this was due in part to the concentration of industry in the United Kingdom, in part to the heavy demands of the armed forces and in part to the disappearance of textile exports from Japan. Increased production in the United States failed to meet the deficit,

[1] As indicated in *North American Supply*, *op. cit.*, Chapter XI, the problem of the White Paper continued to be discussed in a desultory fashion until the air was cleared by the Stage II agreements at the end of 1944.

because any increase was absorbed immediately by the demands of the war agencies and by civilian demand inflated by increased earnings. Another series of shortages was developing at the same time in connection with the supply of certain types of machinery used both in the production of war goods and essential civilian supplies. Even a seemingly minor item such as flashlight bulbs could cause serious difficulties. The war-time requirements for such bulbs were considerable; and the normal source of most of the world requirements, the Far East, was closed by war.

The general nature of the problem which now had to be met was indicated in the terms of reference of the Non-Military Supplies Committee.[1] Set up in January 1943 by the Combined Production and Resources Board, the Committee was to make recommendations to the Board on various aspects of the problem. The first was how to reduce to the barest minimum the production of non-military supplies in the United States, the United Kingdom and Canada. The combined output of such supplies was to be treated as a common pool. In the second place the Committee was to make recommendations as to how much productive capacity should be allocated to each article and how the output should be distributed. The problem of fair distribution was complicated by the high consumption levels in the United States (as compared with the United Kingdom) and the difficulties in the way of reducing them.

Non-military supplies as defined by the Combined Production and Resources Board covered several categories of goods. One was goods for civilian consumption, including civilian-type goods used by the armed forces. Another was equipment for the 'maintenance and repair of the public utility, transport and essential industrial system and facilities for health, education, etc.'[2] The recommendations of the Non-Military Supplies Committee were to cover also the essential requirements of other United Nations, which they could neither produce themselves, nor import from sources other

---

[1] The members of the Committee were drawn from the War Production Board, the British Supply Mission, the Board of Trade Delegation and the Ministry of Production. The Canadian Wartime Prices and Trade Board was also represented. The Committee under its terms of reference was to work through Commodity Sub-Committees.

[2] In order to assure the American share of foreign requirements of non-military supplies, the War Production Board and the Office of Lend-Lease Administration needed programmes of requirements. Programming for non-military supplies, at its height, covered about 1,200 commodities ranging from earth-moving machinery to crown corks. Actually foreign requirements of most of the 1,200 items were only a minute fraction of United States production. The War Production Board (through its Standard Products Committee) allotted a share of United States production to the Lend-Lease Administration. The latter allocated in turn to the different countries. In the case of the British Commonwealth a single allocation was made to the 'British Empire'. This was apportioned by the Apportionments Committee of the British Supply Council on which sat representatives of the Commonwealth countries and colonies. Throughout the history of the Apportionments Committee all such apportionments were made by unanimous decision. The decisions were subject to approval by the American authorities, but were rarely questioned. See above Chapter IV, Section (iv).

than the United States, the United Kingdom and Canada. At the London end a Non-Munitions Committee of the Commonwealth Supply Council was set up; it worked with the Non-Munitions Division in the Ministry of Production which served it as secretariat.

Towards the end of 1943 the commodity sub-committees which the main Committee had created supplanted it. They became full committees reporting direct to C.P.R.B.[1] They covered medical supplies, internal combustion engines, machine tools, tyres and tyre fabrics, textiles, footwear and leather products, coal and coal-mining machinery, agricultural equipment and machinery, public utilities equipment, transportation equipment and trucks.

Problems connected with the relief of liberated areas began to play an important part in the work of the Combined Boards from the end of 1942.[2] The requirements for relief and rehabilitation fell into two periods. First, the period of military responsibility, when goods were needed for the prevention of disease and unrest. Second, the period of civilian control in which suffering had to be relieved and steps taken to restore a stable economy. During the 'military' period the Combined Civil Affairs Committee, operating under the direction of the Combined Chiefs of Staff, had the primary responsibility for civilian relief and supply in a conquered or liberated area. It submitted requirements to the various Combined Boards. On the basis of information received from the departments in London, Washington or Ottawa, the Boards then made recommendations as to sources and distribution of supplies. The military period ended in the various liberated territories at dates fixed by the military commanders. It was succeeded by a period in which the United States and the United Kingdom combined to help the liberated countries to organise their own procurement of supplies. Apart from the special case of Italy, most of the liberated countries proved able to take over the management of their own economic affairs rather more quickly than had been expected. In the second stage military programmes were replaced by national relief programmes. But even in the earlier stages of relief there was much work to be done by the Combined Boards and the civilian Missions in Washington.[3] In mid-1943 a British Mission Relief Committee was set up. As national programmes began to replace military programmes detailed work had to be undertaken on more than two score of relief programmes for food, raw materials, manufactured goods and shipping. The requirements for the period of military responsibility decreased

---

[1] See above, Section (ii), final paragraph.

[2] See *North American Supply, op. cit.*, Chapter XI, Section (v), and above Section (i), final paragraph.

[3] See above, p. 222. To co-ordinate supply arrangements a combined committee to deal with policy matters (C.L.A.C.) was set up in the State Department with a supply sub-committee (C.L.A.C. (S)) housed in the Foreign Economic Administration.

rapidly from the end of 1944, whilst national import programmes, including those presented by UNRRA and the so called 'paying countries' (Norway, Denmark, Belgium, Holland, France, Italy, the Far East) increased in volume and urgency.[1] By the second half of 1944 it was clear that most of the requirements listed in the relief programmes were of little interest to the Boards. In November 1944 the commodities of interest to them were defined in a Reserved Commodity List.[2] This list, a composite one for the several Boards, was part of an agreement on the procedure for handling requests for relief supplies presented by the United Nations Relief and Rehabilitation Administration and Paying Countries.

Under the agreed procedure it was the duty of the Combined Production and Resources Board and the Combined Raw Materials Board to examine estimates of requirements received from these and other sources. The Boards made recommendations as to the production of supplies, the sources of supply, the availability of goods and their distribution amongst claimants. These recommendations were generally acted upon by the national agencies. The long disputed question as to who allocated American supplies was settled by an agreement between the different American agencies signed on 16th January 1945. The agreement gave the Foreign Economic Administration the substance of allocation in respect of goods mainly supplied by the United States. The Foreign Economic Administration was given the right to take the initiative in claiming these requirements before the War Production Board; the Combined Boards retained the initiative only in dealing with manufactured goods and raw materials for which other countries were the main sources of supply.

The Reserved Commodity Lists were gradually narrowed in 1945. Thus in September 1945, when the Combined Production and Resources Board reviewed the situation, it decided that the only commodities falling within its jurisdiction which still required combined planning were: coal, coal-mining machinery, textiles and footwear. The handling of requirements from liberated areas marked an important transition in the history of the Combined Boards. Up to this stage the primary interest of the officials of the Boards was in securing priority for direct war requirements. Supply for liberated

---

[1] Requirements approved and supported by UNRRA formed an element which the Combined Boards had to take into account in framing allocations of available supplies. Although UNRRA was the first of the organs of the United Nations on a full international scale, it was essential that it should be tied in rather closely with the combined supply and shipping machinery. A chaotic situation would have been produced if UNRRA had begun to compete with the armed forces and civil authorities by entering the market for such supplies as boots and shoes, farm machinery and fertilisers, cf. R. J. Hammond, *op. cit.*, pp. 247–248.

[2] See also *North American Supply, op. cit.*, Chapter XI, Section (v).

areas educated officials in a new set of factors, those involved in the transition to peace.[1]

(vii)

The Problem of Assignments — The Combined Munitions Assignments Boards

The final process in supply – the assignment of munitions as they came off the assembly lines in the factories – was the responsibility of two military Boards in Washington and London, each with a civilian chairman, Mr Harry Hopkins and Mr Oliver Lyttelton. Little information as to the nature of the Combined Munitions Assignments Boards and their functions was given in the agreements of the President and the Prime Minister as published on 26th January 1942. The text began with the words: 'The entire munitions resources of Great Britain and the United States will be deemed to be in a common pool, about which the fullest information will be interchanged'. It went on to speak of bodies in Washington and London 'under the Combined Chiefs of Staff' which would 'advise on all Assignments both in quantity and priority, whether to Great Britain and the United States or other of the United Nations, in accordance with strategic needs'.[2] The appointment of a civilian chairman and the setting up of a combined secretariat were also mentioned.[3]

Three and a half years later, at the Potsdam Conference in July 1945, the Prime Minister gave the President a summary in retrospect of the operations of the Assignments Boards, on the eve of their dissolution:

> ... the Munitions Assignments Boards in Washington and London were established to operate the common pool of production for war purposes of the United States and Great Britain. Their duty was to study the combined resources and to assign the output under directives from the Combined Chiefs of Staff in accordance with strategic needs. It was the wholehearted pooling of resources which governed the production programmes of the two countries and led to the concentration of production of certain items in one country or the other. Under the Boards was established a considerable machine for the collection and presentation of information, and for carrying out the detailed work of assignment.

---

[1] See below, Chapter VI.
[2] For reference to the subordination of the Combined Munitions Assignments Board to the Combined Chiefs of Staff and its dependence on the latter for strategical guidance, see *North American Supply, op. cit.*, Chapter IX, Section (iii).
[3] Cmd 6332, January 1942.

The Washington Board held its first meeting on 31st January 1942, but its organisation was not complete until March. Its draft directive, prepared by the Combined Chiefs of Staff, was finalised in that month. The delay was due to various factors including the difficulties of drafting by cable, the differences between American and British drafting habits, and the already divergent procedures of London and Washington in respect of the assignment of munitions.

The directive as completed in March 1942 consisted of four texts: (1) The Order Establishing the Board, (2) Procedure for Making Assignments, (3) Organisation of Staff, (4) Preliminary Assignments Directive. The Washington Board, working in close collaboration with the corresponding London organisation was set up to maintain, for the use of the Combined Chiefs of Staff, 'full information of the entire munitions resources of Great Britain and the United States'. It was to translate such resources 'into terms of combat forces and their material reserves'. For this purpose the Board was to maintain an effective liaison with supply authorities. It was to recommend to the Combined Chiefs of Staff 'measures necessary that land requirements programmes may be in line with (a) strategic policy, (b) changing operational conditions in their effect on war material, (c) the realities of production'. This in effect charged the Board with the maintenance of the Consolidated Statement of Production which had emerged in the months before Pearl Harbour.[1] But the wording was so wide that the main task of the Board might have seemed to be the co-ordination of production; and for a time there was a strong emphasis on this aspect in the discussions of the Board, and in the Planners Committee of the Combined Chiefs of Staff. In June 1942, this function was given to the Combined Production and Resources Board.

The second task of the Combined Munitions Assignments Boards under their directive was the assignment of munitions. They were to be 'responsible for making assignments of stocks and production of finished war materials to the United States and Great Britain and to others of the United Nations'. This was to be done in accordance with 'strategic policies, directives and priorities as approved and in agreement with the corresponding London organisation'.

It was the task of the Munitions Assignments Board, Washington, to assign United States production to all claimants. It was responsible for presenting the requirements of the American group, i.e., North and South America (other than Canada), China, and later French North Africa. It also allocated bulk assignments made to the United States from British and Canadian production.

The main traffic between the two Boards in the matter of bulk

---

[1] See *North American Supply, op. cit.*, Chapter VIII.

assignments was, however, from Washington to London.[1] The traffic in the other direction was nevertheless important, e.g., the supplies of British radio and radar equipment furnished to the United States.[2] To economise shipping in the maximum degree, Britain furnished the United States forces in the United Kingdom with very large supplies of general engineering stores, building material, accommodation stores, clothing and miscellaneous equipment. This formed ultimately a large, but incompletely recorded, element in the account of Reciprocal Aid.

The London Combined Munitions Assignments Board, under the Combined Chiefs of Staff, assigned United Kingdom production. It also allocated to various theatres of war bulk assignments made to the United Kingdom in Washington, Ottawa and Canberra, for use in its spheres of responsibility. The London Board dealt with the requirements of the British areas of responsibility, namely, the British Commonwealth, European Allies and neutrals, Africa (excluding French North Africa), Middle East, Persia, Iraq, and Turkey. The aircraft and motor vehicle requirements of Canada, Australia and New Zealand, however, were dealt with in Washington. It was a rule – though it was not rigidly applied – that requests by a nation for assignments should be made either in London or Washington, but not in both. The importance of such a rule was shown by the fact that there were in all some forty claimants on the Washington-London munitions pool.

The London C.M.A.B. took over a going concern. Machinery for allocating munitions of British manufacture amongst the large number of countries in the British sphere, had already been operating satisfactorily in London for many months. It was essential, the Combined Chiefs of Staffs pointed out in a telegram to the Joint Staff Mission in February 1942, that all these countries should continue to channel their requirements through the London Munitions Assignments Board. Complete confusion could only result if they were permitted to apply for arms in both Washington and London. This was part of the problem of third countries referred to above in connection with the other Combined Boards; its munitions aspect is mentioned at the end of this section.

The assignments work of the Washington Board was delegated in the first place to three Munitions Assignments Committees: M.A.C. (Ground), M.A.C. (Naval), M.A.C. (Air). Naval assignments caused little difficulty. Air assignments were more controversial and at times

---

[1] *North American Supply, op. cit.*, see the tables given in Chapter X. The London Munitions Assignments Board functioned with six sub-committees – Naval, Army, Air, Small Arms Ammunition, Radio Stores and Engineer Stores.

[2] For some figures showing the two-way traffic in bulk assignments, see W. K. Hancock and M. M. Gowing, *op. cit.*, pp. 294–295 and note C on p. 300.

raised large questions of policy.[1] Ground assignments were multi-
tudinous and complex.[2] Liaison between these three Committees
and the three British Service Missions was maintained by giving
membership in the appropriate Committee to the Principal Requirements Officer of each Service Mission. The Board itself had three
British and three American Service representatives under its civilian
chairman (Harry Hopkins). It had a secretariat headed by an
Executive (Major-General J. H. Burns, United States Army). The
Executive was responsible for the administration of the combined staff
of the Board and the carrying out of the Board's decisions. The
civilian chairman was appointed as much to mediate between the three
Services of his own country as between the United States and Great
Britain.[3] Apart from the chairman the British and American representatives on the Board were drawn from the Armed Services.[4]

After Pearl Harbour the dualism whereby the Lend-Lease
Administration as well as the Service agencies was concerned with
the distribution of American munitions came to an end. The procurement of munitions was finally centralised in the War and Navy
Departments. The War Department combined the functions of the
British War Office and the Ministry of Supply. For this reason, and
on grounds of security, the War Department preferred to deal with a
single British organisation under army control.[5] The system under
which the civilian British Supply Mission dealt with 'requirements'
whilst the British Army Staff dealt with assignments, came to an end
with the amalgamation of the two missions late in 1942. By this time
requirements had lost much of their earlier importance, for it was
the final process of assignment which decided whether the United
Kingdom received any particular requirement from the United
States. Requirements figures still had to be submitted as a basis for
the United States Appropriation Acts. But these programmes were
merely advance sketches of a most general kind required by the
United States for planning purposes. They were incorporated in the
United States Army Supply Programme which itself was rather a
general target than a plan of production.[6] Acceptance of such a

---

[1] On the crisis in aircraft assignments in 1942, see *North American Supply, op. cit.*,
Chapter IX, Section (iii).

[2] Thus in May 1942 M.A.C. (Ground) dealt with 449 items of American production;
228 of them were solely for the American army; 221 items were shared with the United
Kingdom and other countries.

[3] See *North American Supply, op. cit.*, Chapter IX, Section (ii).

[4] The British representatives were supplied by the three Service missions in Washing-
ton: the British Army Staff, the Royal Air Force Delegation, and the British Admiralty
Delegation. The Commander of the British Army Staff acted as British Military
Member of the Board up to April 1944.

[5] See below pp. 328–9.

[6] The United States Army Supply Programme (A.S.P.) covered a 24-month period.
It was revised from time to time up to the end of 1944. Deficiencies in the British Army
home programme, which were not taken care of in the United States A.S.P. were
treated as spot items. See above Chapter IV, Section (iii).

British programme, and even of requisitions based on it, was no guarantee of supply. Neither the programme nor the requisitions could earmark in advance any particular sector of production. As was indicated in *North American Supply*, the attempts which were made from time to time to agree on the allocation in advance to the United Kingdom of a fixed quantity of production within a definite period of time (such as the Slessor and Arnold-Portal agreements for aircraft) rarely succeeded.[1]

In practice as supplies were produced they went into the pool for assignment. In effect they were put up to auction, and bids were made by the different claimants on the strength of their need.[2] When the actual assignment was made current needs might be very different from needs as foreseen in an Order of Battle made many months in advance. Between this starting point and the final stage of assignment stalked a host of uncertainties – uncertainties of production as well as of war. In the early period, for a year or more after Pearl Harbour, the acute shortages of munitions, and the reverses in the field, made it necessary to assign on the basis of one month firm and two months tentative. This hand-to-mouth arrangement complicated British production and shipping plans. The desirability of long-term assignments was recognised in theory on the American side, but they proved to be very difficult to obtain in practice.

The main difficulties in the process of assignment occurred in the year 1942, a year of small production and large shortages. The United States War Department in 1941 had encouraged the placing of large British requirements as a means of increasing the total output of war supplies. But the real spurt of production, which British orders (together with American Army orders) were to produce, had hardly begun when the United States found themselves at war, with a large army still lacking most of its equipment. The British Army was already better equipped, and there was a natural tendency in the United States to put the needs of their own Army above those of countries to which they supplied arms under Lend-Lease. In the early months of 1942 backlogs in the filling of British requirements tended to accumulate until the deficiency became serious. When supply was not forthcoming the assignment was likely to be cancelled. An attempt to remedy this situation (as regards certain British needs for 1943) was made late in 1942 under the Somervell-Weeks-Rootes

---

[1] An exception was the Russian protocols by which fixed quantities of munitions and supplies within a definite period were made a first charge on production. Supply to Russia was made by the United Kingdom-Canada and by the U.S.A. on a fifty-fifty basis.

[2] The channel for a British (or Commonwealth) bid was: British War Office (Admiralty etc.) through the appropriate Service mission in Washington, to the U.S. Service Department. It was there considered, along with other bids, by the body dealing with that particular type of equipment, and submitted to the appropriate C.M.A.B. committee. The Board itself gave formal approval or arbitrated differences.

Agreement referred to in Chapters IX and X of *North American Supply*. Under a 'block system', bidders were assigned a certain percentage of a block of supplies; claims on one block were to be met before issues were made from the next block. A block was roughly a third to a half of the estimated production for the month. This complex system was difficult to administer and it was abandoned in the spring of 1943. In its place the original system of straightforward quantitative assignments based on production forecasts was substituted. By that time forecasts tended to be more accurate. Supplies were becoming more plentiful and assignments could be made further ahead.[1]

ASSIGNMENT AND THIRD COUNTRIES

The London and Washington Boards met the needs of third countries and thus were interested in any surplus the latter might have. The theory of a single pool of all United Nations production, which London and Washington Boards would assign, was never fully realised. Apart from the production of Russia, which was unamenable to any Allied co-ordination, there was only one country in 1942 with a real surplus over domestic need. This was Canada. Some surplus would come later from some of the other Commonwealth countries, particularly Australia.[2] But for the moment Australia was caught with most of her stocks held abroad for the supply of distant fronts. It was not until towards the end of 1942 that production in Australia had built up to the point where assignment became a possibility. An Australian Assignments Committee, Canberra, was then established. Its chairman was the representative of the Australian Chief of General Staff. The three Australian Services and the Australian Ministry of Munitions were represented on it. It had also a member appointed by the British War Office and an American representative appointed by General MacArthur.

The Canadian surplus was far more important. It also presented a simpler problem from the point of view of assignment. Production was organised on the basis of long-term programmes to meet the requirements of the Canadian forces, and certain specific requirements of the United Kingdom. By 1942 it was possible to forecast Canadian munitions output with considerable accuracy. Types of

---

[1] During the period of scarcity strenuous attempts were made by the United States Services to prevent the accumulation of munitions at any point along the supply line. The policy was first applied in mid-1942 in relation to aircraft. (See *North American Supply, op. cit.*, Chapter IX.) The United States War Department then introduced a 45-days' stock rule by which stocks not shipped within 45 days were to be repossessed. As supply eased the period was lengthened to 60 and then 75 days and the rule finally fell into abeyance. From a shipping point of view it was necessary for the British Missions to maintain a certain level of stocks at seaports so that ships could be kept constantly filled; but lack of ships resulted in the piling up in some cases of excessive stocks.

[2] See Chapter IX on the Eastern Hemisphere.

weapons were largely standardised with those of Great Britain, and the output was earmarked for Canadian and British use in the field where Canadian and British troops were training and fighting side by side. The relations between Canadian production and the Canadian armed forces, and those of Britain were so close that they were not likely to be disturbed by the adoption of any particular method of assignment. There were two possibilities, (1) assignment by a Canadian Board or (2) the assignment of Canadian production by either the London or the Washington Assignments Board. If the latter alternative were adopted there was a clear case for Canadian representation on the Board that made the assignments.

Because of the very close relations, built up in the two years of war together, between the British and Canadian armies and industries, the preference in London was for the Canadian output to form part of the British pool. Canada, however, preferred to pool supplies in Washington in view of the close relations established with the United States during the war in the matter of war production policies. (This arrangement also fitted in with the view that Canadian troops should have the first claim on Canadian munitions.) The two countries now had all the machinery necessary to do business speedily between Ottawa and Washington. Moreover both countries had the same shipping problem. Thus Canada, with the full support of Britain, sought membership of the Washington Board – already a seven-man Board. But the latter saw difficulties in admitting a third country; to grant the application of Canada would not only increase the size of the Board, but also might open the door to still other countries. Any increase in the size of the Board, it was felt, would slow down the speed of assignment.

The upshot was that Canada made her own arrangements for the assignment of Canadian production. During an interim period assignments were made by an *ad hoc* committee which worked within the British Army Staff in Washington, and was known as the Department of Munitions and Supply Allocation Committee. Finally, in November 1942, a separate Canadian Munitions Assignments Board was set up in Ottawa. It was under the control of the Canadian Minister of Munitions and Supply who appointed a civilian as Chairman. The latter was advised by the Canadian Chiefs of Staff.

A Committee of the Ottawa Board (C.M.A.C. (A)) met monthly in Washington for the assignment of army supplies. Its meetings were held in advance of the monthly meetings of the main Washington Munitions Assignments Committee (Ground). Thus despite the absence of any formal direct responsibility to the Combined Chiefs of Staff the Ottawa Board was able to maintain close liaison and to avoid overlapping.

. Part of the Canadian assignments, particularly those arising from American orders placed in Canada with War Supplies Ltd., were made to the United States. The bulk of Canadian assignments, however, went to the London Board for use by the United Kingdom or for allocation to other countries in British spheres of responsibility. In the latter case a simple notification of the allocation was made to Ottawa through the British Army Staff, Washington. On occasion special assignments were made direct by Ottawa to another country, e.g., Australia. After the adoption of Mutual Aid in May 1943, orders for war equipment from Canada for countries other than the United Kingdom or the United States were channelled through the Joint War Aid Committee in Washington. This included amongst its members the Director of the International Division of the United States War Department and the Chief of the Canadian Joint Staff. The latter, in close consultation with the Commander of the British Army Staff, acted as a representative of the whole British Commonwealth. This helped to prevent overlapping between the spheres of responsibility of the British and American Boards.

The rule that third country bids had to be made either to the London or the Washington Board was not easy to keep. The Office of Lend-Lease Administration had direct relations with countries in the British sphere of responsibility which received Lend-Lease and these countries were thus clients both of the London Board and of the Office of Lend-Lease Administration. The latter claimed a say both at the requirements stage and in the final accounting for Lend-Lease supplies, even if they were assigned to the London Board for allocation to other areas such as Turkey and the Middle East. Turkey was the subject of much discussion and difference of opinion in 1942. The Combined Chiefs of Staff were called on for a decision which they gave early in 1943 as follows:

> The Combined Chiefs of Staff recognise that Turkey lies within a theatre of British responsibility and that all matters connected with Turkey should be handled by the British in the same way that all matters connected with China are handled by the United States of America. In particular, under the general directive of the Combined Chiefs of Staff, the British should be responsible for framing and presenting to both Assignment Boards all bids for equipment to Turkey. The onward despatch to Turkey will be a function of the British Commanders-in-Chief in the Middle East.

Since the property claims under the Lend-Lease Act remained unaffected by this procedure, Washington had to be notified of all United Kingdom transfers to Turkey of Lend-Lease supplies.

Here there was no doubt that the area was in the British sphere of strategical responsibility. Other cases, such as the Free French territories and Australia, fell partly in British and partly in American spheres, and a rough dividing line based on practical considerations had to be found. In the case of Australia, whilst General MacArthur and the Government wanted to bid direct in Washington, there were very strong practical objections to such a course. For there was no part of the Commonwealth so closely intermeshed, in training, equipment and tradition, with the Army, Navy and Air Force of the United Kingdom.

As the United States were in any case almost the sole source of supply for Australia and New Zealand as regards aircraft and motor vehicles a general ruling was finally adopted whereby they submitted their bids for such equipment to the Washington Board and all other demands to the London Board.

CHAPTER VI

THE COMBINED RAW MATERIALS

BOARD

(i)

The Genesis of a Combined Board

THE HISTORY of the Combined Raw Materials Board illustrates the processes which created the Combined Board system. The general background of that system was the reassertion in the darkest year of the war of the natural family feelings of the English-speaking peoples. Common language, a common inheritance, and common interests made it possible to work together without interpreters. Many of the forms and methods, the bilingual staffs and other impedimenta of a normal allied relationship, were absent. The rejection at the Arcadia Conference of a Supreme War Council of the traditional type came from the final realisation that America and Britain could build their entire war machinery on the intimate informality to which they had grown accustomed and which had stood the test of experience since Dunkirk. An important part of that experience was gained in the field of raw materials. Like each of the other Boards, the Combined Raw Materials Board was the product of new methods of co-operation which British and American officials had shown to be practical and efficient – as between Britons and Americans.

This was not because the experience of inter-allied organisation in the First World War had been forgotten. On the American side Mr Baruch, in a book published in 1941, with the title *American Industry at War*, had revived American memories of allied organisation in 1917–1918. In the raw materials field that organisation included co-ordinated purchasing of raw materials on a large scale which was extended still further after the United States entered the war in 1917. Extensive plans for Commodity Boards for jute, rubber, manganese, tungsten, platinum, flax, leather, wool and other materials, were cut short by the ending of the war. On the British side in Washington in 1941 there were two men – Sir Arthur Salter and M. Jean Monnet – who played important parts in and had reflected deeply upon the inter-allied organisation in the latter part of the First World War and the first part of the Second.[1]

COMBINED ACTIVITY BEFORE PEARL HARBOUR

Already by the end of 1940 and increasingly during 1941, the personalities who were later to play the major parts on the British and American sides of the Combined Raw Materials Board had sought out each other and had learned to work together. Although in a less organised way than became possible later under the Board, team work had begun. Its field was mostly raw materials from foreign sources. At first the direct raw material requirements of Britain from the United States – apart from steel and timber – were relatively unimportant, less important in fact than from Canada.[2] But the situation changed with the adoption of Lend-Lease; it then became possible, and essential from the point of view of shipping economy, to draw increasing supplies of raw materials from the United States. Lord Beaverbrook, in a paper written on board the *Duke of York* in December 1941, foresaw that Britain would need from the United States in 1942 steel, aircraft timber, certain chemicals, nickel alloy products, copper and zinc. In fact the copper was only a fraction of the amounts Britain was importing from other sources; but a third of British requirements of zinc would have to come from the United States. Such shifts in British requirements did not alter the broad fact of American dependence on the British Commonwealth for many essential raw materials. Thus, the Mead Committee of the United States Senate looking back over the war from 1946 concluded that ' The United States did not have the world's best natural resources even for World War II'. They were dependent on outside sources, many of them in the British Commonwealth, for such vital materials as chromium, industrial diamonds, mica, graphite, cobalt, manganese, lead, tungsten, nickel, tin, natural rubber, jute and sisal, asbestos, bauxite.[3]

In the months before Pearl Harbour British and American co-operation made its greatest advances on the borderline between economic warfare and supply. This followed mainly from the shifting of the accent of economic warfare in 1941 from control at sea to control at source.[4] This made it necessary for the two countries to

[1] Sir Arthur Salter, *Allied Shipping Control, op. cit.* Also Brigadier General Charles G. Dawes, *Report on the Military Board of Allied Supply* (1924), and Sir Alfred Zimmern, *The League of Nations and World Order*, 1937.

[2] Canada's contribution towards the war-time requirements of the United Nations included nickel, 95 per cent.; asbestos, 75 per cent.; aluminium, 30 per cent.; zinc, 20 per cent.; lead, 15 per cent.; copper, $12\frac{1}{2}$ per cent.

[3] *Fifth Annual Report of the United States Senate Committee investigating the National Defence Programme*, 79th Congress, Second Session, Report No. 110, Part 7, page 15. See also Report of the President's Materials Policy Commission: *Resources for Freedom*, 5 volumes (United States Government Printing Office, Washington, D.C. 1952).

[4] W. N. Medlicott, *The Economic Blockade, op. cit.*

co-operate more closely in order to secure strategic materials for their war industries and to deny them to the enemy.

The two officials who formed the British raw materials team in Washington from early in 1941, one from the Ministry of Supply and the other from the Ministry of Economic Warfare, became respectively the British Executive Secretary and Deputy Secretary of the Combined Raw Materials Board. Opposite them were an American team which included the future American Member of the Board, William L. Batt and its future American Executive Secretary, Howard Sykes, as well as W. L. Clayton and T. K. Findletter of the State Department and S. D. Straus of the Metals Reserve Corporation. Most of them had been working closely with the British on raw materials since July 1940. The first joint task undertaken in that month, as was noted in a British minute, concerned mica; the task was to secure the 'supply and blockade requirements of both governments'. The American idea of a joint mica pool, to be held in the United States as a means of safeguarding the joint supplies of Indian mica, was discussed at great length. From January 1941, the co-operation broadened to cover co-ordinated purchasing of mica supplies in Latin America. Arrangements for a joint purchasing programme covering a number of strategic materials in Brazil, including mica and quartz crystal, took shape after a visit to Latin America early in 1941 by the British economic warfare officer in Washington.

As the year advanced pre-emptive purchasing in third countries was accompanied by more emphasis on the long-term planning of British and American supply, and co-operation in securing supplies abroad. Information was exchanged on supplies from other countries; joint purchases were made and the supplies obtained were allocated on an informal basis. With these activities went more careful programming of British supplies from the United States. Examples of adjustments in supply began to occur which were similar to those soon to be made regularly by the Combined Raw Materials Board. One example was zinc; a shortage of zinc had long been foreseen. In January 1941 British and American supply requirements data on zinc and brass were exchanged. A report was prepared which was much like those done later by the Board.[1] Manila hemp, a vital war commodity, already in short supply before Japan seized the Philippines, afforded another example of combined action. A large British requisition for 10,000 tons under Lend-Lease brought the commodity into combined discussion in May, 1941. Surprise was expressed at the size of the British requirements, but these were justified as 'the absolute minimum essential for the conduct of the

---

[1] This was in the form of a memorandum sent by the British Embassy to the United States Defence Commission.

war'. In August, both sides had become anxious about supplies of hemp and at the end of the month the United States were recognised as the sole purchaser. The British Government withdrew from the market and the United States bought up all stocks available in the Philippines. British hemp supplies thus became dependent on American allocations. In the first days of January 1942, London was told that the whole hemp-sisal position was ' under active joint consideration', and on 14th January a 'first review of the joint position' was received from Washington. At the beginning of the month, the British Government had given the United States a priority on the shipment of 50,000 tons of East African sisal; it asked for manila hemp in return to bring up its stock level, which had fallen to the dangerously low level of three months' supply. Thus, without the loss of a single step or any essential change of methods the informal joint arrangements of 1941 for manila hemp and other commodities passed under the control of the Combined Raw Materials Board.

Meanwhile, combined action had been increasing rapidly in the second half of 1941 in the handling of Latin American raw material surpluses. A Ministry of Economic Warfare programme for pre-emptive purchase of wool, rubber, industrial diamonds, several ferro-alloys and other raw materials had been drawn up in May, following discussions with the United States. The emphasis shifted rapidly, however, from economic warfare to supply. British pre-emptive purchasing was inextricably tied up with American and British supply interests. Total Allied requirements might be less than the output of a strategic material, but the whole output might have to be bought in order to deny the remainder to the enemy. The market itself knew no division between supply and pre-emption and the closest liaison was necessary to prevent the two governments from bidding against each other. If by agreement one of the countries stepped in as sole purchaser of a commodity it then found itself saddled with the problem of allocation to other users. There were many combined meetings in Washington on this kind of problem in 1941. Thus in mid-July the United States undertook by a purchasing agreement with Mexico to buy the whole of that country's exportable surplus of antimony, cobalt, graphite, copper, lead, mercury, non-ferrous metals, ferro-alloys and fibres. Similar agreements were being made with other South American countries, such as Brazil (bauxite, chromite, industrial diamonds, mica, quartz, rubber, etc.); and Bolivia (tin and antimony).

On the British side, as the Embassy pointed out in a message to London at the end of September 1941, the action taken by the United Kingdom to secure control over supplies of 'wool in Australia, over graphite in Ceylon, over cobalt in Canada, by the Indian

Government over mica, by the Australian Government over lead, etc., has had the effect both of securing supplies for the United States Government and of getting them at favourable prices'.[1]

But this implied the imposing of restrictions on private purchases by the United States to ensure that the market was kept stable. Thus the Metal Reserve Company decided to undertake all United States graphite purchases in order to prevent a rise in prices through unrestricted competition in Ceylon by private American buyers. This decision to adopt 'centralised American buying' was warmly welcomed by London. In the end the Ministry of Supply agreed to purchase the graphite requirements of both countries from Ceylon and to allocate supplies in a fair ratio, in agreement with the United States and Russia. Similar typical Combined Raw Materials Board procedures – regular joint meetings between the supply representatives, agreement on combined supply-requirements, the drawing up of a balance sheet, and the principles of pooling and allocation – were in existence in 1941 for burlap, cotton linters and antimony.

THE ORGANISING OF INFORMALITY

So far, however, this was a purely commodity approach without any central machinery or carefully worked out policies. It was now becoming necessary to organise the informality. Numerous piecemeal anticipations of Combined Board procedures could not add together to make the full combination achieved by the setting up of the Board. Many joint meetings were taking place, but there was no continuity between them. There was no common Secretariat to record decisions, to follow them up and to see that they were executed. Moreover, on the American side, the agencies concerned had very inadequate powers of control. There was still much uncertainty as to departmental frontiers and responsibility for action. Departments competed with each other for any new sphere of power opened up by a new agreement on a particular commodity. Thus from October to December 1941 several American departments were engaged in drawing up their own programmes of total raw material requirements, American, United Kingdom, British Commonwealth.

Already in mid-October 1941 British officials in Washington recorded their view that the time was ripe for 'the creation of a standing joint committee which could handle problems relating to the supply of raw materials and could be a focal point through which information could be collated as regards statistical information,

---

[1] Another example of British action was the purchase in October of the Egyptian flax crop, of which Great Britain undertook to resell a quarter to the United States at cost price.

arrangements for purchasing and also for the exchange of information regarding methods of control'.

In November, London put to the British Supply Council what it described as 'an issue of first strategic importance' – the need for combined action on raw materials in relation to shipping. The question London posed was: how, with the present concentration of shipping in the North Atlantic, Britain could rely on getting the necessary tonnages of raw material drawn from areas outside the North Atlantic. The Ministry of Supply alone drew from such outside areas 7.5 million tons a year. It suggested using American ships to form halfway-house stockpiles in the United States of chromite, copper, lead, manganese ore and a number of other materials. The question raised three central issues handled later by the Combined Raw Materials Board: joint stockpiles, combined purchasing, and supply in relation to shipping.

In December 1941 and early January 1942, during the meetings of the Prime Minister and the President in Washington, work proceeded at two levels on the designs for combined machinery in production and supply. The military planners and the supply officials worked independently without either being fully aware of the planning by the other.

There were national and combined discussions on the problem amongst groups of high officials on both sides. Their sense of urgency arose from their recent work on the Victory Programme and their knowledge of its vast implications in the matter of strategic raw materials. It was urged in a British memorandum drawn up in Washington on 10th December 1941, that supplies should be regarded as a common pool and should be dealt with by a joint co-ordinating committee with half a dozen technical sub-committees corresponding to the principal groups of raw materials. Using this and other data as basis, Monnet some days later sent a memorandum to W. L. Batt. With it was a table showing for the main strategic materials, the supply available to the United States, and the combined requirements under the Victory Programme. Monnet suggested that for each commodity in short supply there would be set up 'one central statement continuously kept up to date by information supplied by each Government'. These 'basic running statements' would present all the relevant facts including requirements, supply, substitution and so forth. There should be, Monnet added, 'one single organisation centralising all this information, and at the same time receiving both the United States and British requirements and analysing them with fully competent United States and British representatives'. But instead of suggesting a fully combined board, Monnet proposed that this 'central work' should be done by an inter-departmental committee centred in the Office of Production Management with Batt as

Chairman and with a single British representative. His remark about analysis by competent American and British representatives suggested, however, a wider British collaboration on the staff level.

THE INTERNATIONAL RAW MATERIALS CONFERENCE

For the next three weeks British and American thinking on the official level was built round this idea of 'Mr Batt's Committee'. The thought of Harry Hopkins and the President seemed to be running on the same lines. On 15th December, Hopkins sent a personal message to Lord Beaverbrook. It referred to the setting up of a combined Raw Materials Conference on the 'production and allocation of the world's raw materials' and suggested that Lord Beaverbrook should be represented in the discussions. Two days later, the President sent a letter to Batt, proposing that he should set up a 'working conference on raw materials of the world'; it was to be attended by eight high American officials whom the President named.[1] This body, which was referred to as 'Mr Batt's Committee' or the 'International Raw Materials Conference', met on 18th December. It held two further meetings at the turn of the year, which British officials attended, Lord Beaverbrook being present at one of them. Amongst the matters discussed were the statistical data required and the form of joint recommendations to be made on raw materials. According to an Office of Production Management note of 2nd January the action recommended included 'allocating all joint supply by areas to respective users in order to make most effective use of shipping and processing facilities . . . allocations of new processing facilities . . . allocations of individual national responsibility for division of labour in development of new supply arrangements for control of purchasing'.[2] Here was an advance sketch of the main field of action of the Combined Raw Materials Board. A British brief for Lord Beaverbrook noted some days earlier that the new body would cover both 'expansion of production and restriction of consumption' and 'all raw material questions whether main source of supply is inside or outside U.S.A.'. Work would begin on the most critical materials drawn from dangerous areas. It was assumed on both sides that steel would be covered. The body, the brief suggested, would have a 'joint operations Committee'. On 5th January, Sir Clive Baillieu was appointed British member of the new body.[3] It was still regarded at this date, as he noted later, as a large Committee, 'nine-tenths of which would be Americans'.

---

[1] W. L. Batt (O.P.M.), E. R. Stettinius (O.L.L.A.), Will Clayton (R.F.C.), James V. Forrestal (Navy), Robert P. Patterson (War), T. Findletter (State Department), Milo Perkins (B.E.W.), Donald Nelson (S.P.A.B.). A representative of the Maritime Commission was added later.

[2] Note by Dr William Yandell Elliott addressed to the British side.

[3] On 14th January, the British Raw Materials Mission was set up on the verbal instructions of Lord Beaverbrook with Sir Clive Baillieu as head.

On 8th January 1942 – three days before the last talks began between the Prime Minister and the President, W. L. Batt made a report at the President's request on the carrying out of the directive of 17th December. The letter, which Baillieu saw in advance, was accompanied by an organisation chart. It showed how literally the officials on both sides had been following the President's directive to set up 'a working conference on raw materials'. Provision was made for attendance of the American departmental heads mentioned by the President. British representation was to consist of Sir Arthur Salter and Lord Portal in addition to Sir Clive Baillieu. But at this point, 'Mr Batt's Committee' dropped into the limbo of rejected alternatives. No trace of it is to be found in the text of the agreement setting up the Combined Boards which the Prime Minister and the President concluded six days later, on 14th January, as a result of their final discussions with their military advisers at the White House.[1] The general background of these discussions is referred to in *North American Supply*, Chapter IX. The Combined Boards were planned as an integral part of the organisation grouped round the Combined Chiefs of Staff. The scheme as a whole emerged from the thinking of the Prime Minister and the President and their military planners. What emerged for raw materials was not an unwieldy International Raw Materials Conference of at least thirteen people but a streamlined two-man Combined Board. Such a Conference would inevitably have been slow in action. The one British member might have found himself swamped by the nine American departmental heads; and he probably would have had to listen whilst they thrashed out their domestic differences. As if to emphasise the difference between a Combined Board and an International Conference the agreement commanded (in words not used in connection with any of the other Combined Boards), that the Board's recommendations 'shall be carried out by all parts of the respective Governments'.[2]

The text of the agreement of the Prime Minister and the President was not circulated to officials in Washington until after its publication on 26th January. The Prime Minister wished first to consult the War Cabinet on the text and to inform the other British Commonwealth countries. (He cabled to the President on the 23rd that arrangements were being made to set up in London an Empire

---

[1] The British text of the agreements as published on 26th January (Cmd. 6332) is appended to *North American Supply*, *op. cit.*

[2] See Chapter V, p. 225. The difference of wording was not important; nor was the omission for raw materials of the principle of pooling which is expressly mentioned in the agreement in connection with munitions assignments and shipping. The conception of a common pool of resources governed in fact every provision of the British American agreements. 'In all our recommendations', Batt had said in his letter to the President, 'we shall think of the world's available raw materials as a joint pool, to be allocated to the United Nations according to where they can best be used for the joint effort'.

Clearing House to deal with Empire supplies and requirements.)
The absence of the actual text of the agreement at the operational
levels in Washington led to the use of a variety of names for the
Board. The word 'combined' was not yet in use and Batt still called
it 'the Joint Materials Conference'.

Meanwhile all through these constitutional discussions the combined teams of officials had been hard at work on critical raw
materials since early in January. Batt's letter to the President on
8th January indicated that there were already in existence two draft
recommendations – an increase in the capacity of the Texas tin
smelter, and an exchange of British steel against American manila
hemp. A number of other agreements were made during these early
days and the governments put them into effect without waiting on
the formal ratification by the Board which was to follow in its
opening meetings.[1]

Existing Canadian-American joint machinery for raw materials
probably influenced the setting up of the Board, although Canada
never became a member of it.[2] The organisation chart with Batt's
letter of 8th January showed Canada under the heading: 'U.S.A./
Canada Joint Co-ordinating Committee for Raw Materials'. The
Materials Co-ordinating Committee (United States–Canada) was in
effect a Canadian-American Combined Board. It consisted of four
men, two from each country. Regular information on requirements,
production and stocks, were exchanged for a considerable number of
raw materials. The Committee allocated scarce materials between
the two countries and dealt with problems of new production. Thus
nickel was regarded as a common stockpile – the stock being maintained in Canada. The supply of crude rubber was also considered
as a common stockpile – maintained in this case in the United States
which procured for Canada as well as for themselves. Likewise for
synthetic rubber:

> The synthetic rubber programme which was begun at about the same
> time in both countries was treated as one continental programme.
> There was the closest consultation on engineering; equipment for
> plants in both countries was scheduled as for one programme.[3]

---

[1] The first formal meeting of the Board was on 17th February; its first business meeting
on 20th February. The first formal meeting of the Operating Committee was on 2nd
March; but the staffs had been operating informally long before these dates.

[2] The machinery consisted *inter alia* of (1) the Joint Defence Board (set up as a result
of the Ogdensburg Agreement on joint defence in August 1940); (2) the Canadian-
American Materials Co-ordinating Committee (set up ten days after the Hyde Park
Agreement of April 1941); (3) the Joint Economic Committees (set up on 17th July,
1941 to study the use of the combined resources of the two countries for defence) and
(4) the Joint War Production Committee of Canada and the United States, set up at
the end of 1941.

[3] S. D. Pierce and A. F. W. Plumptre, *op. cit.* For a reference to correspondence in
February 1942 between C. D. Howe and W. L. Batt, see above Chapter V, p. 242.

There was an exchange of ingredients across the border from both sides to expedite the production of synthetic rubber in each country.

(ii)

Combined Allocation of Raw Materials

The Combined Raw Materials Board more than any other Combined Board had to face at the very outset in January 1942 a series of crises in relation to specific materials. The crises were due to two main factors: the cutting off of supplies by Japan and the sudden vast increase in the demand of American industries for strategic materials. The Board coped with shortages by other methods besides allocation, but allocation remained its most characteristic activity. All the typical methods used by the Board to solve shortages emerged within its first few months of intense activity. They were set out in its series of decisions and recommendations based on commodity reports on particular materials. By means of 'comprehensive formal reports', or 'less detailed working surveys', it had handled by June 1942 twenty out of the thirty critical commodities which it covered in its first twelve months. In its four years of activity from January 1942 to December 1945 the Board held 71 formal meetings and promulgated 457 decisions, or series of recommendations, dealing with the supply, purchase, distribution and use of some 50 important war materials.[1] The field of the Board's work was immense and this chapter can only refer briefly to a few of its typical activities.

Allocation was the central activity of all the Combined Boards since all of them were built round the problem of shortages. Their aim, and those of the Ministries which they served and through which they operated, was to assure enough strategic raw materials, food, shipping, factories, machine tools, and manpower to win the war. Shortages could occur at any point along the line from raw materials to finished munitions, and could shift backwards and forwards. Thus in the case of copper the main problem was usually the shortage of refined copper, as in 1942 and early 1943; and again at the end of 1944. But in between there were 'bottlenecks' in fabricating capacity[2]. Many factors entered into shortages of raw

---

[1] The series of annual reports of the Board for the years ending 26th January 1943, 1944 and 1945 were published by the Ministry of Production as White Papers (H.M.S.O. London) and by the War Production Board in Washington.

[2] e.g. the shortage in communications wire early in 1944. Requirements were less than 90,000 miles a month in January, but with the approach of the Normandy invasion they moved sharply upwards to reach a peak of 270,000 miles by May 1945. *Wartime Production Achievements and the Reconversion Outlook: Report of the Chairman of W.P.B.*, 9th October 1945.

materials. There were the more obvious ones of the cutting off by the enemy of regular sources of supply, the loss of cargoes at sea, or the lack of sufficient productive capacity in the shape of mines or plantations. Seasonal factors played an important part in the case of agricultural raw materials. Sea transport was a vital common factor. Shipping was of special importance for commodities involving very large tonnages such as manganese. Inadequate rail transportation – as across India, or the chronic example of the Beira Railway, the outlet from Rhodesia – could cause shortages. Another factor, of special importance in some cases like tin, could be a deficiency in refining capacity. The speed with which production could be expanded, or economies could take effect, varied greatly from material to material. And even in war, margins of cost continued to play their part, since ultimately cost meant competition for other factors in short supply, such as manpower in the case of lumber, or steel in the case of synthetic rubber and high octane gasoline. But no matter what factors were involved allocation remained the permanent core of the Board's work. It retained its primary importance until towards the end of 1944 when one commodity after another began to show a surplus.

In theory allocations were the result of a simple calculation, in which combined requirements were totalled against total supply available or in sight. If there was enough to go round there was no problem of allocation – although there might be other difficulties such as transport. If supplies were appreciably less than requirements then the Board had to allocate to the claimants in proportion to their need. The process was rarely as elementary as it sounded. Allocations could hardly ever be determined by a simple mathematical formula. It was rarely possible to take the figures of requirements from the two sides at their face value and apply an equal percentage cut. Some categories of need were more important than others, and while this was sometimes self-evident it was often a matter for argument. The same uses were not of equal importance in all countries. The differences were usually in the character of industry, in the economies and substitution, in the levels of working stocks in each country. There was also the factor of the distance of each country from the producing areas and the amount of the supplies which were produced within its own borders and the extent to which it depended upon imports from overseas. Very few of these factors were capable in practice of mathematical assessment. As good a judgment as possible had to be made in the light of argument and counter-argument round the table. There had to be give and take. An error could still be remedied in the next allocation, or, if very serious by a reopening of the allocation during its currency. Such miscalculations became less frequent as time went on. In the first two years, when time pressed and the maintenance of the flow of materials was the first consideration, decisions were often made which seemed to involve some unfairness for one side or the other. But in the long run rough justice was done; and it was immeasurably better for both sides than no justice at all.

Many examples of the difficulties involved in allocation could be culled from the commodity reports of the Board. An allocation by the Board of shellac (C.R.M.B. Decision No. 144) illustrates the difficulty of securing clear cut figures. In this case two requirements figures were definite: (1) the United Kingdom and British Commonwealth requirement which was given as 8 million lbs.; (2) a Soviet requirement which had been fixed in the Second Protocol at the figure of 8 million lbs. a year. The main requirement figure, however, that of the United States, was variable. The American side indicated that the United States must have a minimum of 15 million lbs., but could use to advantage in their war production up to 40 million lbs. But after deducting the fixed charge for the U.S.S.R. the total available supply was only 42 million lbs. The higher American figure, together with the British requirements, would result in a figure 6 million lbs. in excess of the available supply. Since the United States were unable or unwilling to commit themselves to a precise figure of requirements, there was no alternative but to arrive at a figure by a complicated process of bargaining. The British side suggested that the figure for the United States should be fixed by splitting the difference between their maximum and minimum proposals. This gave a figure of $27\frac{1}{2}$ million lbs. The American side countered with a figure of 30 million, which was accepted after some discussion. Although it was an arbitrary figure, it still left an unused margin between estimated requirements, which would then stand at 38 million, and estimated supply which was 42 million lbs. Thus the United Kingdom was not likely to get less than its minimum needs and might easily get more. The outcome of all the bargaining, as happened often enough in such cases, was an allocation which corresponded roughly to the relative populations and industrial strengths of the two countries. For the year 1st April 1943 to 31st March 1944 purchases of shellac were allocated by the Board in the proportion of 3.75 to the United States and 1 to the United Kingdom.

The tendency to arrive at some such ratio, no matter how different the approach might be, was due to a number of factors, including considerations of equity. In practice the plea of equity – the idea that allocations should be roughly proportionate – was a potent argument. It was easy to elaborate on differences of efficiency, real or imagined, between the industry of the two countries. But the argument was difficult to sustain; because although efficiency might be less in the United Kingdom in some cases, the differences were rarely great enough to justify wholesale shifts in the war production programmes of the two countries.

But even if it were agreed that the allocation should be 'fair' and in proportion to population, it might still be difficult to agree on precise figures. Hides, skins and leather proved particularly difficult from this point of view. The attempt of the Board to use a simple supply-requirement formula broke down completely. It gave two decisions, in fact, on this basis, but neither side was satisfied. Neither had any effective check on the other's requirements, because of factors like the use of substitutes and the different types of leather goods, especially boots and shoes, produced in each country. The two sides therefore agreed, after a period of some tension and much discussion, to fix allocations on an 'historical' basis. A base year was taken for each country, 1940 for the United Kingdom and 1942 for the United States – in each case the first complete calendar year of war. The number of hides, both from domestic production and imported, put into process (wettings) by each country were calculated; this gave a ratio of 3.5 for the United States to 1 for the United Kingdom. This became the ratio for total supplies of hides and the ratio for the purchase of foreign hides was worked out after deduction of each country's domestic supplies by the process described in Section (iii) below.

Combined allocation was only one part, and not always the most important part of a complex process. The complexities differed from material to material. In the case of rubber 80 to 90 per cent. of the world's supplies had been cut off by Japan. No remaining sources could possibly fill the gap. The main answer had to be not so much allocation as new production on a vast scale by chemical processes – the building of synthetic rubber plants in the United States. By a major decision of policy the new synthetic rubber plants were to be confined to North America. Meanwhile the United States lived on their stockpile, on economies from civilian use, and on some natural rubber released by the United Kingdom from its supply in Ceylon. The Board allocated supplies and co-ordinated development in all rubber-producing areas.

THE CASE OF TIN

Or the difficulty might be not so much lack of a raw material as lack of plants to refine it. Tin was a case in point; and since it illustrates the complex factors involved, a diversion may be permitted. Bare statistical tables, showing chronologically year by year how the Board allocated tin from 1942 to 1945 (such as were prepared for the Mead Committee of the United States

Senate at the end of the war) tell little of the real nature of the problem.[1]

There was no real problem of tin metal until after Pearl Harbour. An agreement in mid-1940 between the Metals Reserve Corporation and the International Tin Committee, had increased tin production almost to maximum output. This had enabled the United States to acquire large quantities of tin metal for its stockpile. The seizure by Japan of the tin-producing areas in Malaya, the Netherlands Indies and Siam eliminated also the smelters in this area. The only remaining smelters were those in the United Kingdom and the Belgian Congo. Up to this point there had been no allocation of tin metal. Informal combined discussions in 1941 had been concentrated on (1) the maximum production of tin ore and concentrates, and (2) the problem of replacing the tin smelters lost in the summer of 1940 in Holland and Belgium – a loss which had cut in half the smelting outlets available for Bolivian production. Low and medium grades were those mostly affected, since most of the high grade Bolivian production had been smelted for many years in the United Kingdom. The United States, which had not smelted tin since the early 1920's, decided in the summer of 1941 to re-enter the tin smelting business. A contract was entered into by the Reconstruction Finance Corporation with the Billiton Company for the design and management of a smelter to be constructed at Texas City.

The Texas City smelter was still unfinished when the Japanese attacked. The remaining smelters in the United Kingdom and the Belgian Congo could refine only about 50 per cent. of the needs of the Allies and were unable to handle the world's production of tin concentrates. Completion of the Texas smelter was the first of the Combined Raw Materials Board's interim decisions in January 1942. Other early decisions on tin included allocations of tin metal and concentrates, the drastic curtailment of tin consumption throughout

---

[1] The tables show the allocations of tin metal or tin concentrates made from 1942 to 1945 to the United States, the United Kingdom, the U.S.S.R., Canada, New Zealand, India, Ceylon, the Union of South Africa, Southern Rhodesia, Switzerland, Sweden and the Middle East. Other countries received tin from their domestic production. The allocations (in terms of contained metal) were made largely by dividing up sources of supply on a yearly basis. The production of areas with a small output were assigned in most cases wholly to the United States or to the United Kingdom. Only one source, Bolivia, was important enough to be regularly divided between the United States and the United Kingdom. Thus in an allocation made by the Board in August 1942 the United Kingdom was allocated 18,500 tons for a year from Bolivia. The United States were to receive the Bolivian production in excess of this amount. The United States received also all the production, or the exportable surplus, from the French Cameroons, Alaska, Mexico and part of the production of the Belgian Congo. The United Kingdom received its own domestic production and all the exportable surplus from Nigeria and other African sources as well as from Portugal. Canada was assigned its own production and 1,250 tons from the Belgian Congo. New Zealand was assigned 450 tons from Australia. The U.S.S.R. was assigned 9,000 tons, made available by the United Kingdom, as well as the exportable surplus of China.

the Allied world, the use of tin substitutes, such as silver solder, the reduction of the tin content of solder and bronzes and the thinning of the coating on tin plate. Development missions were sent out to tin producing areas – a British Mission to Nigeria and an American Mission to the Belgian Congo. The United States undertook responsibility for increasing production in Bolivia. An attempt was even made to increase the production of tin in the ancient tin mines of Cornwall.

With the provision of tin smelting capacity in the United States it became necessary for the Combined Raw Materials Board to allocate tin concentrates as between the smelters in the United Kingdom and the United States. A first distribution of the concentrates was made by a decision of the Board in August 1942. This created a pattern of allocation which was adhered to more or less until the end of the war. The American contract with the Bolivian producers, calling for all the tin that could be produced over and above the amount earmarked for the United Kingdom, provided for a distribution of ores between different grades. But in practice the contract did not produce enough high grade material to meet the needs of the Texas City smelter. Most of the high grade concentrates were under a long-term contract, running from 1940 to 1950, between the principal Bolivian producer (Patino) and a British firm (Williams, Harvey). The British Government was asked by the United States to divert part of these high-grade concentrates to the Texas City smelter. The Combined Raw Materials Board worked on the principle that its decisions overrode all such contracts. But in this case there were practical difficulties to be overcome. This was a legal contract made between private interests in the United Kingdom and Bolivia, and neither the writ of the Board nor that of the British and American Governments ran in the latter country. It was only with considerable difficulty that the Bolivian firm was persuaded to agree to the diversion. Its agreement was subject to two conditions: that its contract remained unbroken and that the English firm suffered no loss. The arrangement involved months of negotiations before the final terms of the contract could be fixed. A diversion was authorised by the Board in 1943, but there was no shipment in that year. In 1944 the United States received 8,000 long tons (contained metal) of concentrates from this source as against 9,039 tons supplied to the United Kingdom. A request early in 1944 for the diversion of half of the Patino production in that year was withdrawn after several months of negotiations on the understanding that the United Kingdom would agree to divert 50 per cent. of Patino concentrates in 1945. The negotiations were not completed until April 1945. This diversion was the most important transaction on tin handled through the Board from 1943 onwards. In effect the

Board acted as a procurement agency to procure high-grade Bolivian concentrates for the United States.[1]

ELEMENTS IN THE BALANCE SHEET

The examples given above show the difficulty of generalising about the process of allocation. They show the importance and limitations of the statistical element. They indicate the existence of a number of different types of allocation; they show how the process could be complicated by technical factors. Each of these aspects may be examined in turn. On the statistical side the Board sought to secure what was called – not very aptly – a balance sheet. The threat of a shortage was known usually to the national authorities before it could be known to the Board. The departments kept a running check in such cases on production and imports and watched consumption, conservation and stocks. The purpose of the Board's balance sheet was to show as authoritatively as possible whether the combined position was better or worse than the various national departments had separately estimated. It was the function of the Board to collect and to co-ordinate all figures, available to each side, of production, consumption and stocks, and of estimated requirements and estimated supply. The figures provided the basis for a commodity report which was prepared in combination by the commodity officers on the two sides of the staff. The report presented the balance sheet and gave the basis for a critical forecast of requirements and supply over as long a period as was feasible. The reports were working documents in the true sense of the term and were not composed with an eye to publication. They analysed the main elements involved in keeping supply in balance with requirements and they drafted recommendations on the allocation of existing supply and any necessary measures for expansion of output or economy in use. The material for these periodical staff reports and balance sheets was provided by a regular system of statistical reporting from London, Washington and Ottawa. The statistical returns were made monthly for commodities under quarterly review; and quarterly in most cases for materials under annual review.

Each item on the balance sheet had its own pitfalls – even the commodity itself was often difficult to fix from a statistical point of view. The regular statistical returns formed the basis of the allocation; and then served as a check on its execution. The exchange through the Board of figures of stocks, consumption and new supplies by origin, showed each side how far forecasts were proving to be accurate. Each staff report had a section on progress. From day to

---

[1] The United States share of the 1945 diversions was shipped in the second half of the year and in the early months of 1946. The Texas City smelter had by this time a stock of concentrates and its output of tin early in 1946 was at the rate of about 40,000 tons of tin a year.

T

day, as information on the carrying out of recommendations was received by a Commodity Officer, it was promptly made available to his opposite number. Forecasts could never be certain; shipping might fail to move supplies; output might be more or less than anticipated; consumption might show unexpected variations. But the system of the Board enabled a much closer watch to be kept than is normally possible.

In general the Board tried to express its allocations and statistics in terms of the product as covered by the returns of the national controls which usually followed commercial practice. Metals could be expressed in terms of metal content, or of concentrates, or of ore. The product as used might be semi-refined; e.g. molybdenite (concentrates) was used in the form of ferro-molybdenum with a molybdenum content of 60 to 70 per cent. by weight; the Board's figures were therefore in terms of ferro-molybdenum. In other cases, e.g. manganese, the weight of 'ore' was used. Figures for tungsten and tin were expressed in terms of weight of metal contained in concentrates. Some minerals such as mica, and agricultural products such as hides, could be highly variable in quality and grades and therefore difficult to measure. Whether the Board's allocations recognised the existence of grades and qualities was a matter of convenience. Thus the Board made separate allocations for a number of grades of mica with some provision for substitution between them. The reason was that supply requirements were not identical for each grade, and some of the grades could only partially, if at all, be substituted for each other. In the case of hides the variations of type, quality, source and time of arrival on the market were so great that the Board's allocation was made in three groups governed largely by weight. The detailed work of distribution within the groups involved a great deal of give and take and was left to the Joint Hide Control Office in Washington.

Both sides tended to overestimate their requirements in the first year or so. But the tendency diminished with time, since quarterly figures of consumption were usually available and an over estimate could be corrected in subsequent allocations. Apart from the obvious temptation to play for safety there were several difficulties in estimating future consumption. Estimates were often based on production programmes which might fall short for a variety of reasons, such as lack of some other raw material or labour difficulties or simply the weather. Some sudden war need might cause an unforeseen change of programme. Or more rapid progress than anticipated might be made in substitution or conservation – a field in which estimating was notoriously difficult.

At first there was a good deal of difference between the two countries as regards standards of conservation. High standards of civilian consumption – e.g. in such commodities as leather and shellac – were more difficult to prune in the United States than in the United Kingdom. Moreover, the United Kingdom had been longer at war; the stocks in the hands of private firms and individuals were nearer exhaustion, and needed more rapid replacement than in the United States. In some cases, for technical or other reasons, the United States were rather more economical than the United Kingdom in the use of particular materials, such as ferro-alloys. Another factor was the wider range of materials available in the United States which made substitution easier than in the United Kingdom. The existence of groups of substitute materials complicated the problem of allocation since allowance had to be made for substitution. Examples were shellac and synthetics, nylon bristles and natural bristles; and various ferro-alloys, such as nickel, molybdenum and tungsten.

Forward estimates of supply tended to be more accurate than those of requirements. But the output of new munitions factories was often less easy to calculate than the output of well established mines or plantations or other peace-time sources of raw materials. Where expansion of an existing mine was involved calculations and forecasts could be relied on with some degree of certainty. In the case of new and untried development schemes, such as new mines in places where mining had not been tried in time of peace, output was difficult to forecast and usually disappointing. But even where total supply could not be foreseen, an allocation could still be made by dividing actual supply on the basis of an agreed ratio.

All systems of international control over the distribution of commodities have encountered difficulties in the treatment of stocks. The points at which stocks could be measured satisfactorily differ with different materials. Usually the importing country has to take into account stocks at the port, stocks in government stockpiles, if any, and stocks in factories and warehouses. There is also the problem of stocks afloat and stocks in producing countries which have already been bought or are being accumulated under long-term contracts with producers. Difficulties of statistical measurement and the uncertainties of transport usually made it necessary to count only stocks in the importing country. But on occasion during the war, when the stock level was abnormally low, stocks afloat might have to be taken into account. An allocation could reasonably take into account a low stock level, particularly in a country like the United Kingdom which depended almost wholly for its raw materials on imports brought from afar by long sea voyages. The need of the United Kingdom to maintain a stock level equal to a certain number of months' consumption was usually recognised in the discussions in Washington. But the strong stockpiling tradition in the United States made for still higher stocks in that country. Thus where the United States depended on imports, as for manganese and chrome ores, it maintained stock levels equal to 12 months' supply. Stocks for these and other commodities in the United Kingdom rarely rose above six months and were frequently less. In view of the complexities involved it is not surprising that the Board always refrained from attempting to set up any agreed criteria as to what were reasonable stock levels for critical materials.

The higher levels in the United States were a reserve from which the United Kingdom as well as the United States might benefit in case of need. Thus the American stockpile of some 800,000 tons of natural rubber at the time of Pearl Harbour averted possible disaster. With the continuing supply from Ceylon it made possible an orderly transition to synthetic rubber. Mica was also stockpiled by the United States in large quantities in 1940 and 1941. It was urged on the American side that, for reasons of safety, mica stocks should be concentrated in the United States rather than in the United Kingdom. Thus the Board found in 1942 that mica stocks in the United States were much higher than in the United Kingdom. The latter approached the Board in mid-1942 with a plea that allocations should be used to equalise stocks in the two countries in proportion to consumption. It was not however until the mica allocation for the second quarter of 1943 that an approach began to be made towards stock equalisation for groups and grades and qualities where relative equality seemed desirable.

METHODS OF ALLOCATION

The many differences between materials as regards their mode of production, sources and uses, were reflected to some extent in the different methods of allocation used by the Board. Broadly speaking, supply from third countries was allocated on a hemisphere basis.[1] With some notable exceptions supplies from Latin America were allocated to the United States, whilst supplies from the British Commonwealth and Eastern Hemisphere countries were allocated to the United Kingdom. The division was little more than a convenient means of allocation which corresponded roughly to shipping requirements and the division between sterling and dollar areas. Certain supplies in each hemisphere were shared, as in the case of

---

[1] The practice of hemisphere division was not an arbitrary arrangement. It was the outcome of existing financial and trading relations, and was common to several of the Combined Boards. It was implicit in some of the raw material arrangements made in 1941. At the beginning of March 1942 the British Government suggested that both requirements and allocations of raw materials should be stated on the hemisphere basis. London would be responsible for gathering and submitting requirements for the Eastern Hemisphere. The United States would be responsible for Western Hemisphere countries.

tin from Bolivia, mica, shellac, manganese ore and jute from India, sisal from East Africa and hides from many areas. There were often cases in which the quantities produced were in excess of British or American requirements, so that a quantitative division became necessary. Another type of area allocation occurred when certain areas such as Madagascar and French North and West Africa were liberated. Here it was necessary for political and economic reasons to assign quickly the surplus production of all strategic materials in the area. In the case of French North Africa the whole of the supplies of particular commodities was assigned to the United Kingdom or the United States. Thus all supplies of cork, manganese, copper and cobalt ore were allocated to the United States; whilst the United Kingdom received all supplies of zinc, lead, tungsten and molybdenum, together with such amounts of iron ore and phosphates as it could ship. Any residue of these two materials went to the United States. In one case, tantalite, in May 1943, the Board allocated to the United States the whole of world supplies.

Quantitative allocations were made either for specified amounts or in accordance with an agreed ratio. The latter method was specially useful where, as in the case of Indian mica, it was difficult to make very accurate estimates of supply. If necessary, sharing by ratio could be made to begin after one country had received a certain minimum amount of the output. Allocations of specific amounts were more useful where supply was assured either by the steady nature of the production or by the existence of buffer stocks at the source which could be used to maintain a steady flow of supplies. If supplies fell short of the allocation, as happened in the case of shellac, it was assumed that the parties would not take more than their proportionate share of the reduced output. As is shown in the example of tin given above, a quantitative type of allocation could be combined with an area allocation. Manganese ore was another example. Thus in the first half of 1944 the Combined Raw Materials Board (Decision No. 213) allocated supplies from British West Africa in the following amounts: 36,000 tons to the United Kingdom; 90,000 tons to Canada and 100,000 tons to the United States. The United States was also allocated manganese ore from India at the rate of 15,000 tons per month; supply to the United Kingdom from this source being confined strictly to whatever was essential for ships ballast or deadweight. The Board's decision also assigned to the United States the whole of the manganese ore from French North Africa, the Belgian Congo, Brazil, Cuba and other Latin American countries.

Still another type of allocation was that made to a group of countries such as the Middle East; the British Commonwealth of Nations, excluding Canada; the United States with Canada; the

United States with Latin America, or Latin America as a separate group.

Some care had to be exercised in defining the terms by which allocations of the sources of supply of raw materials were made to particular countries. At first the tendency was to express allocations in terms of 'availability'. The term implied that supplies from a particular source were to be made available to the consuming country if it desired to purchase them. Sometimes the allocation was in the nature of a permit to purchase up to a certain amount. In the case of hides each country could purchase hides abroad in a fixed ratio to purchases by the other. Thus a Board decision (No. 210) provided that 'for the month of November 1943, purchases of foreign cattle hides (should) be allocated in the following ratio: 45 per cent. to the U.S.A. and 55 per cent. to the United Kingdom'. The United States had some difficulty in controlling such purchasing arrangements, since there was no general prohibition in that country against the transfer by its nationals of funds abroad. In the United Kingdom an importer had to secure in each case approval both of the order and of the transfer of funds; an American buyer, however, was free to use dollars to purchase supplies abroad, even though he might not yet have obtained an import licence.[1]

Exports by third countries were used on occasion as a convenient basis for allocation. They had the advantage that national export statistics provided a reliable means for checking allocations. An example of an export allocation was afforded by Ceylon rubber. Mica was also dealt with at first by an export allocation, but this proved difficult to administer. In the case of mica the Board in effect delegated its powers of allocation to an American-British Joint

---

[1] See below, Section (iii). In general the Combined Raw Materials Board took the view that it was not concerned with financial questions. Its allocations were regarded as overriding contracts (see tin above). It was not directly concerned with the question of how payment would be made for American or Canadian raw materials allocated by it to the United Kingdom, or for British-controlled materials which the Board allocated to the United States. Most American raw materials supplied to Britain were paid for by the United States out of Lend-Lease up to the end of 1944. The United States on the other hand paid in dollars for most materials obtained from British Commonwealth sources. Even after the beginning of Reciprocal Aid only a proportion of the raw materials from the Commonwealth were furnished to the United States on a Reciprocal Aid basis. The question as to how payment was made was less important than the fact of supply. As mentioned above the Commonwealth supplied a substantial proportion of many of the important materials which the United States had to import, such as rubber, jute, sisal, nickel, chromite, cobalt, lead, manganese, tin, graphite, asbestos, mica, shellac, industrial diamonds and a number of others. On the other hand the United States was the principal source of exports to the United Kingdom of munitions and manufactured goods. Financial complications arose in connection with supplies to the U.S.S.R. under the Protocols at a late stage in the war. Thus in connection with the Fourth Protocol (1944–1945) the Soviet desired substantial amounts of raw materials under Lend-Lease from the United States which could also be supplied from within the sterling area. The United States was by this time anxious to limit their obligations to the U.S.S.R. which involved the expenditure of dollars. The United Kingdom was willing to supply, but the negotiations in London to persuade the U.S.S.R. to take these materials, e.g. copper, from British-controlled sources, on normal cash and credit terms, proved exceedingly difficult.

Mica Mission which was established in India in the summer of 1942. The Mission acted on behalf of the Board and channelled supplies, as they came forward, to the United States and the United Kingdom.

In the case of nickel, produced almost wholly in Canada, and molybdenum produced mainly in the United States, the allocations by the Board were based partly on export quotas, and partly on maximum releases for consumption in certain countries in accordance with quantities specified by the Board. Whilst Canada used only a small part of the nickel which she produced, the United States could have consumed much more than their reasonable share of molybdenum. Since they were by far the largest producer, and also the largest consumer, the only method of control was by an allocation covering consumption. The arrangements in the case of nickel were complicated by constitutional as well as practical considerations. The most convenient method of watching usage in Canada and the United States was by means of an allocation based on consumption. Nickel produced in Canada was under statutory control by the Canadian Metal Controller, so that there was an easy check on releases for consumption in Canada and the United States. The addition of the United Kingdom to the list of countries subject to consumption control was due to constitutional reasons. Canada was not a member of the Combined Raw Materials Board and the Metal Controller was not obliged to release supplies in accordance with the amounts fixed by the Board. In practice the Controller decided the quantities of nickel to be made available to the United Kingdom (nickel matte to be refined in the United Kingdom). The Combined Raw Materials Board protected its power over allocations by fixing the amounts which the United Kingdom might consume.

(iii)

The Allocation of Hides

Such was the diversity of raw materials that no one example could be regarded as 'typical'. Hides though one of the most complicated of the Board's materials gave a good cross section of its work.

ELEMENTS OF THE PROBLEM

Raw materials from which leather is made are produced, processed and consumed to some extent in all parts of the world. Almost every country is in some degree both an exporter and an importer of such materials, and they enter into international trade at all stages from the raw state to finished consumer goods such as

footwear. The three groups of major importance are:
  (i) Cattle Hides and Calf and Kip skins, including Buffalo Hides
    and Skins
  (ii) Goatskins
  (iii) Sheepskins (including Hair Sheepskins).

Since animals are not killed merely for their skins, the total supply of hides and skins depends on other factors than the demand for them. Thus the primary supply of the raw material is relatively little affected by changes of price. On the other hand, in a free market small increases in demand may cause rapid and substantial increases in the price of raw hides and skins. In the immediate pre-war years the range was about 50 per cent. above or below the average price.

Raw hides and skins show wide variations of weight and quality and are sold by description. The actual quality of a parcel of hides or skins is a matter of opinion and in normal times differences of opinion are settled by an elaborate system of arbitration. Unless the buyer insists on maintenance of standards, it is very easy for sellers to obtain hidden increases in price by including inferior material or by 'up-grading' in description or, in the case of wet hides, by declaring excessive shipping weights.

War brings an immediate demand for large quantities of high-grade leather since military footwear requires far more and better quality leather than ordinary civilian footwear, and military requirements in pairs per capita are also much higher than civilian standards. Clothing and gloving leathers are also required in large quantities and special requirements such as chamois leather for petrol strainers, shearlings for flying suits and hair sheepskins for high altitude gloves also become important.

Quantitative and qualitative allocation were necessary to ensure that essential military requirements were met and to secure equitable distributions of supplies for civilian use. No less important was price control to prevent unnecessary increases which would have occurred in a freely competitive market. On the American side the War Production Board allocated imported and domestic materials to consumers, whilst the Foreign Economic Administration procured imported materials purchased by the United States Government. The Office of Price Administration set internal price ceilings, including the resale prices of such imported materials as were purchased through ordinary commercial channels. Private American importers could only import quantities specified in import licences but since they were free to export currency they could buy and hold a material overseas for speculative purposes even at a time when there might be a complete ban on private imports. Thus the withholding of an import licence did not prevent continued purchases in the overseas markets in anticipation of future licences. This inability to prevent continued purchases by United States nationals overseas caused difficulties in connection with implementing allocations of East India tanned skins and, still more seriously, of hair sheepskins. The Office of Price Administration's internal price ceilings could be evaded with comparative ease by such practices as up-grading the description of material, by making hidden payments to related supplying firms in the country of origin, or by 'tie-in' sales under which excessive prices were paid for uncontrolled material, e.g., an excess payment for hair sheepskins was charged against a purchase of leopard skins. The difficulties arising from such evasions became particularly acute in the latter part of 1945 and 1946 when importers began to speculate on the ending of control.

The United States and the United Kingdom purchased abroad at mutually agreed prices. The United Kingdom was the sole purchaser of Nigerian, Mombasa and Middle East hides and resold certain quantities to the United States, but with this exception each country maintained its own independent procurement system and there were no joint purchasing arrangements. When in the later stages of control it became desirable to make various price modifications, these could be secured quickly for materials on public purchase by the appropriate United States agency. The modification of internal ceiling price orders was in general an extremely slow process, often taking months from the time that a decision was reached in principle until the amended order was issued.[1]

When any agreement regarding the sharing of supplies was reached, it was implemented through the rate at which import licences were granted by the two countries. Statistics were exchanged periodically to keep track of the respective rates of purchase. For materials on private purchase, British import licences were generally issued in respect of specific parcels; the rate of purchase could be controlled in detail because British importers could not transfer funds until an import licence had been granted. Control of American importers was much looser and for some materials they were given a block of licences to cover imports for a quarter. Allocations could be implemented much more effectively when the material was on public purchase in both countries. As the result of pressure from the United Kingdom, where hides and calfskins were on public purchase, the United States brought them also under public purchase in December 1943. On the other hand the United Kingdom brought goatskins under public purchase in December 1944 on the insistence of the United States which had already taken this step.

By December 1943 the controls in each country were sufficient to

---

[1] But when the United Kingdom raised its purchase prices of East India tanned goat and sheepskins on 19th June 1946, the Office of Price Administration put up a record by following suit within two days.

make it possible to set up the Joint Hide Control Office in Washington. Thereafter every individual offer of foreign hides and calfskins received by either country was cleared through the Joint Office. Thus purchases could, if necessary, be kept in line from day to day.[1] The Joint Office enabled the system of allocation to work with a high degree of efficiency. The range and detail of its activities were impressive, especially during the period when it was screening the day-to-day purchases of ten European countries in addition to the United States, the United Kingdom and Canada. The high technical knowledge of the United Kingdom representatives, and the frequent changes of personnel on the American side, placed the main burden of running the Office on the British team.

HIDES BEFORE C.R.M.B.

In the United Kingdom, hides, skins and leather were brought under control immediately on the outbreak of the war. Until the middle of 1941 there were no particular problems of international significance. There was no immediate increase in United States demand. The enemy countries and, gradually, the occupied countries, were cut off from overseas supplies. Overseas purchases by the United Kingdom itself were limited by shortage of shipping. Consequently during this period, prices tended to fall rather than to rise; and the United Kingdom had no difficulty in procuring all the material for which shipping could be provided. Until 1941 there was no official contact with the United States except in connection with the procurement of footwear, but in that year the first quantitative arrangements were made in connection with supplies of hides from overseas. Cattle hides were at all times the most important element and provide the main thread for the events from 1941 onwards. Early in 1941 increases in United States requirements led to substantial American purchases in foreign markets. The purchases of the United States, the United Kingdom and Canada in that year reached about 14 million foreign cattle hides compared with normal pre-war imports of less than 10 million. This was only a prelude to far higher American purchases when the United States entered the war. Already in June 1941 the danger of uncontrolled increase of prices, as a result of these three main purchasers bidding against each other in foreign markets, led the Ministry of Supply to send a representative to the United States to discuss the possibility of joint arrangements. At the end of October 1941, the Deputy Leather Controller was sent over with instructions to work out with American Government agencies a scheme for the quantitative sharing of the world hides and an agreement on prices. At the same time steps

---

[1] A corresponding office to screen raw goatskin purchases, the Joint Skin Office, was set up in December 1944. This detailed method of control, the only one that could be fully effective, was not, however, extended to other materials in this field.

were taken in the United Kingdom to suspend private purchases and to transfer to a new Imported Hide Division and Imported Tanning Materials Division of the Leather Control the whole of the buying of hides and tanning materials. At first the situation in the United States was not favourable to the adoption of controls. Money was free and very high prices were being paid for imported hides. But the attack on Pearl Harbour on 7th December changed the atmosphere overnight. During the next two days meetings were held at the State Department between representatives of the British Embassy and all the important United States agencies. It was decided to suspend trading in hides from 10th December until further notice to enable the United States and United Kingdom representatives to agree on prices and on the means of dividing supplies. Trading began again on 21st January 1942. The aim of the negotiators was to fix intrinsic prices for hides. The strong position of the United States and the United Kingdom as virtually sole buyers was not to be used to force low prices on the producing countries. Thus Buenos Aires Frigorifico hides were priced at 106 pesos. This was higher than pre-war levels; but below the immediately preceding market level of 118 pesos. The price remained unchanged at 106 pesos from the early days of 1942 until May 1946. It was in line with the price adopted by the Office of Price Administration for United States domestic packer hides.

At the same time (December 1941) it was agreed that purchases of foreign wet-salted hides should be in the ratio of 65 per cent. to the United States and 35 per cent. to the United Kingdom. The United States, itself a large producer of raw hides, had purchased less abroad before the war than the United Kingdom; and it found some difficulty in purchasing up to its ratio. This first sharing arrangement was limited to wet hides. It was not yet thought necessary to have any sharing arrangements for dry hides or for calfskins. From March 1942 onwards, the United Kingdom was anxious for a more favourable ratio. At various times both sides requested the other country to take a 'buying holiday'. A formal agreement was reached finally on 8th January 1943 (the Thompson-McKendrew Agreement) which included dry hides and altered the basis to:

Wet-salted hides   40 per cent. United Kingdom to
                                 60 per cent. United States
Dry hides   50 per cent. United Kingdom to
                                 50 per cent. United States

Calf and kipskins were still excluded. The division was based upon 'known requirements' including the Second Russian Protocol. The agreement assumed a supply of 18 million hides. (This figure should be compared with the 13 million actually purchased in 1943 and the

5¾ million to which foreign supplies had dwindled by 1945.) In February 1943 there began the practice of issuing a series of chronological order numbers for Argentine and Uruguay Frigorifico hides. Thus each purchase of these hides by the United States or the United Kingdom was made in accordance with a previously agreed rota. The co-operation of the Frigorifico companies in this arrangement had been obtained early in 1943 by American and British visiting experts. The system worked successfully until 1946; and it was extended to cover all the countries which became members of the Combined Committee. In May 1943, a situation foreseen in the agreement of 8th January – the inability of the United Kingdom to secure enough hides to meet its requirements – came to a head. For various reasons, including losses at sea, the British position had become very serious. The number of hides secured proved to be totally inadequate. The United Kingdom therefore invoked the escape clause of the agreement and asked for a substantial increase in its allocation.

THE FIRST COMBINED ALLOCATIONS

Up to this point combination on hides had taken place outside the Combined Raw Materials Board. Since negotiations on a new allocation between the British Raw Materials Mission and the War Production Board produced no result, an appeal was made finally to the Combined Board. This was a step which the War Production Board had wished to avoid. Its opposition was based partly on fears regarding American domestic supplies of hides (since there had been a serious slump in production) and partly on the plea that there was not sufficient statistical information to serve as basis for a Combined Raw Materials Board allocation. Agreement was reached, however, in July, with the United States side of the Combined Board, to bring the matter before the Board with a view to allocation. An allocation recommended by a combined staff memorandum at the end of July proposed that foreign cattlehides (wet and dry) should be shared in the ratio of 40 per cent. to the United States and 60 per cent. to the United Kingdom for August and September. This was to be an interim arrangement to give time for full information on requirements and supply to be collected as a basis for a longer term allocation. The proposed allocation was refused, however, by the War Production Board. The refusal raised an important constitutional point, since the Combined Raw Materials Board's decisions were usually agreed decisions in the sense that they were not normally made over the opposition of the national departments. After a prolonged struggle the American member of the Board managed to secure the agreement of the War Production Board to allocate on this basis for the month of August alone.

One result of the discussions was the setting up on 4th August 1943, of a Combined Footwear, Leather and Hides Committee (under the Combined Raw Materials Board and the Combined Production and Resources Board) to report on the position as regards each of these commodities. One of the most important functions of the new Committee was to make recommendations to C.R.M.B. on the allocation of hides and leather. The new Committee took over formally the duty of preparing reports and allocations of hides and leather. Actually the work was done as before by the staff of C.R.M.B. Before the Combined Committee could get to work, the problem of the September allocation came up and the staff had to prepare a report and draft recommendations for the September and October allocations. The United Kingdom was extremely dissatisfied with the previous allocation of 60 per cent. of foreign hides and sought to obtain 80 or 100 per cent. Finally, C.R.M.B. on 2nd September made an allocation for September and October of 70 per cent. to the United Kingdom (excluding supply for European neutrals) and 30 per cent. to the United States. The two months were to afford a breathing spell during which a Technical Mission could visit the United Kingdom to exchange information on the situation, and a Joint United States/United Kingdom/Canadian Hides Mission, then in South America, could report back on supplies in that area.[1] The allocation by C.R.M.B. provided that either side could ask for a review – which the War Production Board promptly proceeded to do. It appealed to the Board to fix the allocation at 50 per cent. for the United Kingdom and 50 per cent. for the United States. The appeal was rejected by C.R.M.B. on 23rd September 1943.

THE HIDES AGREEMENT

The virtual deadlock which had now been reached was ended by the adoption of the new 'historical' approach referred to earlier in this chapter. The suggestion was made by the British Raw Materials Mission in August and renewed again in September. The new Combined Committee incorporated the idea in the instructions which it framed for the American Technical Mission about to visit

---

[1] Technical missions played an important part in connection with hides and leather. Two British Missions in 1941 are referred to above. A second American Mission to the United Kingdom, on goatskins, followed in June 1944. Three Joint British and American Missions were sent to South America in 1943, 1944 and 1945. The first of these Missions (on which there was also a Canadian representative) was of special importance. Its proposals played an important part in stabilising supply from Latin America and in the setting up in Washington of the Joint Hide Control Office. A Joint Mission was also sent to South Africa in the early winter of 1944 to discuss the price basis of hides exported from that country. The ceiling prices which it recommended for export were adopted as a basis for internal ceiling prices in South Africa. There was also a Joint United Kingdom United States Mission to the liberated areas in Europe in January 1945.

the United Kingdom. The Mission was instructed to include in its investigations 'the proposed approach to hides allocation on the basis of cattlehide wettings over an agreed past period'. The Mission returned in November with an agreement worked out in London to adopt this 'simplified approach'. The basis was to be 'wettings' (hides put into process) in the United Kingdom in 1940 and in the United States in 1942, the first full year of war in each case.

An allocation for November 1943 had to be made before the Mission returned. It was accordingly decided in London in consultation with the Mission, to adopt for November the 'simplified' basis for cattlehides. The supply of cattlehides (domestic and foreign) was totalled and divided in the ratio 3.5 to the United States (basis 1942) to 1 to the United Kingdom (basis 1940). From these gross amounts each country's domestic supplies for November were deducted. The resultant quantities were the amount of foreign hides each country was allowed to purchase. The quantity of foreign hides for each country was then expressed in the form of a percentage of the estimated supply of foreign hides for November; this gave 45 per cent. to the United States and 55 per cent. to the United Kingdom. The formula was worked out in the report of the Technical Mission which was agreed with the Ministry of Supply. The Combined Board adopted these proposals at the end of October on the recommendation of the Combined Footwear, Leather and Hides Committee. From this point onwards the new formula was used as the basis for the allocation of hides. It was accepted by both sides and was relatively simple to operate.[1] Attempts to work out a full text for the so-called Hides Agreement came to nothing and its documentary basis remained the recommendations as set out in the report of the American Technical Mission. No serious difficulties arose in carrying out these recommendations insofar as they applied to raw hides and skins, or even with regard to the charging of purchases of South American sole leather. In spite of the absence of any formal document or even formal ratification by the Combined Raw Materials Board, the new basis of allocation continued to work smoothly.[2]

It soon became clear that an attempt to keep the distribution of hides and skins exactly in line with the ratio each month would

---

[1] Under the formula total supplies of cattlehides (domestic and foreign) were shared by the United States and the United Kingdom in the ratio of 3.5 to 1. Raw calf and kipskins were shared in the ratio of 5.8 to 1, but with recognition of the prior claim of the United Kingdom to all East India tanned kipskins up to 500,000 pieces per month. The formula operated cumulatively from 1st July 1943 and the appropriate allocations of foreign supplies were made monthly. Ratios were agreed with Canada on a similar basis.

[2] In February 1945, however, the Board formally recognised the existence of the ratios and recommended that they should be continued.

involve constant and substantial alterations of the proportionate division of foreign supplies between the United States and the United Kingdom. The arrangements were therefore interpreted in the light of forward estimates over several months. This made it possible to maintain the division of foreign supplies on a relatively stable basis without diverging too far from the agreed ratio.

HIDES IN RETROSPECT

Over the two and a half years from 1st July 1943 to 31st December 1945 there was a steady increase in American domestic supplies and a steady decrease in foreign supplies. The result was that the United Kingdom's share of foreign supplies increased steadily throughout the period. In the later stages it was 90 per cent. of both foreign hides and foreign calf and kipskins. From the autumn of 1945 it became clear that the division of hides could only be kept in balance if the United States became a net exporter. Although it did not admit formally any obligation to export, the United States limited its foreign purchases to the nominal figure of 30,000 hides per month and exported substantial quantities of domestic hides (up to 200,000 per month).

By 31st December 1945 when the Combined Raw Materials Board came to an end, over 72 million hides and 46 million calf and kipskins had been divided in accordance with the agreed ratios. The division of these totals was within half of one per cent. of the ratios for the whole period. It is doubtful whether any other allocation covering comparable quantities of material was implemented over so long a period with anything approaching this degree of accuracy.

The 3.5 to 1 ratio of hide supplies between the United States and the United Kingdom came to have many uses in addition to the primary division of hide supplies. It was used, for example, as a basis for determining the relative contributions of leather to the liberated countries in the latter part of 1944 and the early months of 1945. Even after the dissolution of the Combined Raw Materials Board, the ratio had become so much a habit that it continued in 1946 to regulate the substantial contributions of domestic hides made by the United States to European countries.

Amongst the commodity officers of the Board it was agreed that 'hides are different'. The chief differences arose from the fact that for this raw material there was no general control over the sources of supply. It was not possible, for example, to obtain the kind of control which was secured by long-term contracts for metals. All procurement was essentially on the basis of spot purchases of small quantities offered daily from the exportable surplus of the various producing countries. Thus, there was no assured supply and no means of increasing the quantity of raw material available as demand increased. It was in fact extremely difficult to estimate the supplies likely to become available even over relatively short periods. Purchases by countries which did not co-operate in the distribution scheme could not be controlled. Nor could there be any control of purchases by the nationals of the co-operating countries unless these countries had the necessary exchange control regulations to prevent their nationals from exporting currency. Nor could there be any complete check on exports of hides from many of the producing countries. The British Commonwealth countries and colonies had export licensing systems. The navicert system prevented shipments to the small group of European neutrals. But there was no means of preventing other shipments, such as those, for example, to ex-enemy countries. Nevertheless, during the war serious leakages of hides were prevented by the lack of ships other than those controlled by London and Washington. After the war such leakages steadily increased. Even during the war Mexico was a very substantial purchaser of hides and for two years pre-empted virtually all the exportable surplus from Colombia by bidding above the ceiling prices set by the United States and the United Kingdom.

Such success as was achieved depended on the voluntary co-operation of the consuming countries. Even then success was only possible where those countries had complete control of imports (both as to quantity and price). Success was most complete where the government concerned made all purchases. This degree of efficiency was only achieved in the case of hides, calfskins and raw goatskins. For the other materials there were leakages and evasions in varying degrees. Shippers and importers showed great ingenuity in diverting materials from controlled to uncontrolled forms; for example, there was a great boom in 'Paprah slats' from India, which diverted the raw material which normally went into East India tanned sheep-skins. The means of implementing allocations were limited. There was little difficulty if all the countries concerned received offers in excess of their allocation so that the allocation was automatically carried out if they limited their purchases to the approved quantities. This was the case with hides and calfskins. In order to ensure that all orders were taken up, the United Kingdom, as the largest buyer, was authorised to purchase any balance available. Any such excess purchases were subject in theory to redistribution.[1]

Yet in the main the efficiency of the distribution of hides between the three countries – the United States, the United Kingdom and Canada – was remarkable. The system was extended with no less

---

[1] For some of the minor skins, such as pickled pelts and tanned skins, when the shippers for one reason or another were unwilling to make offers to some of the European countries, no method was devised by which the allocations could be enforced.

success to virtually all the major European importers. And for a year after the war stable prices were maintained and a reasonably fair distribution of supplies.

(iv)

Expansion and Development of Supply

Allocation – which was a temporary stabilisation of the position – was not enough in itself. The Board was established because of shortages, present or anticipated, which for many materials could not be cured by the sharing of supplies, by economies in use and by substitution. Indeed the charter of the Board put the emphasis first on development and expansion: the Board was to 'plan the best and speediest development, expansion and use of the raw material resources . . . of the two Governments . . .' Development and conservation belonged to fields which were much more technical than that of allocation. Many technical considerations entered into conservation and economy in use and the substitution of one material for another – such as factors of time and cost; variations in established manufacturing techniques and practices necessitating experiment and trial runs; the testing out of new specifications. A range of questions no less technical was involved in development: where should increased production take place? Who should undertake it? What were the prospects in terms of cost and output? What equipment or incentives were needed? Would price premiums be required? Should there be tax concessions? Moreover there was the factor of time; if increased production was to be of use before the war ended it had to be available within two years, or at the outside, three.

The only satisfactory guide to development and expansion of output was the situation revealed in the statistical balance sheet; in the long run, for development as for allocation, the most important function of the Board was to secure adequate statistics. If the balance sheet for a particular material showed for a sufficiently long period ahead that requirements were outrunning supplies, then it was the Board's duty to take steps to secure an increase in production in order to raise output to the level of demand and to provide a reasonable margin of safety.   The determining factor was thus primarily the statistical outlook at a particular point of time for a particular material, not omitting, of course, other materials which might be substituted for it in certain circumstances.

The process was described thus by a British official of the Board:

When the relevant data had been assembled on both sides and the Board's machinery had secured an agreed total view of the position, the result might show that supply/requirements were so close as to provide no margin of safety in an emergency, or that requirements had overtaken or were overtaking supply. The figures themselves would largely determine how far development measures had to be pushed by the two Governments or their allies in order to maintain and foresee a safe production level. In some cases the compilation of the combined view showed for the first time the need of energetic action on the part of the Governments. In others the total statistical picture merely confirmed the policies, based on less complete data, already adopted by the operating agencies. In other cases the Board's recommendation lent support to measures already under favourable consideration by the responsible agencies. Or the recommendation might tip the scales one way or the other when the operating agencies, making the best estimate they could of the overall position, were hesitating whether or not to embark on certain marginal projects (e.g., in nickel and tin), or when they were trying to make up their minds as to the degree of importance which should be attached to increasing the output of a new war material like balsa wood.

Decisions on development were amongst the earliest acts of the Board. The earliest decision – that on the Texas City tin smelter referred to above – was taken early in January some three weeks before the Board was formally established. A more elaborate interim decision on manila hemp, sisal and other fibres was made on 16th January 1942 and confirmed by the Board on 3rd March. It was largely the result of the Japanese invasion of the Philippines which had cut off the source of manila hemp. The full text of this interim decision is given in an Appendix to this book.[1] It illustrates how development was interwoven with the other main strands of the Board's work. It shows also how well the two raw materials teams in Washington had already learned the business of combination, and how clearly they envisaged the main factors in the work of the Board and the methods by which it was to operate. The decision covered the development of substitute hemp crops – hemp, sisal, abaca and New Zealand flax – in new areas, or their expansion in existing areas. The countries in which expansion of output was to be sought included the United States, Panama, Costa Rica, Haiti, Mexico, British East African and Portuguese African Territories and New Zealand. Measures were recommended for cutting down the use of the more valuable fibres, such as sisal in rugs, and in wrapping and binder twines. The manila rope specifications in the United Kingdom, United States and Canada were to be revised and sisal substituted where possible. Manila hemp and sisal were allocated to these three countries for the whole of 1942. The stock of manila fibre, held

---

[1] Appendix 3. With it is annexed a decision made by the Board early in January 1943 on copper which illustrates also this inter-relation of factors.

largely in the United States, was to be shared with the United Kingdom in return for British East African sisal.

CASES AND METHODS

Many other decisions on development followed in the first six months of the Board's activities. A few of these may be mentioned.[1] Decision No. 3 (3rd March 1942) aimed at the maximum development of the production of nickel in the existing mines in Canada and the maintenance of production in New Caledonia which was threatened by a shortage of coal. It called also for an examination of the possibilities of production in Cuba – out of which nothing came. Decision No. 6 (4th March) on tungsten provided:

> The United States and Canada to be responsible for development in the Western Hemisphere, and the United Kingdom for the Empire.

Another decision (No. 16 of 26th March) made the same hemisphere division of responsibility in connection with the expansion of crude rubber:

> U.S.: the Western Hemisphere and Liberia
> U.K.: the remainder of the world.

A decision (No. 44 at the end of May) on copper recommended maximum increase of copper production in 1942 and 1943 'in all producing countries', the areas mentioned being Canada, United States, Chile, Belgian Congo, Rhodesia, South West Africa and Australia. The lack of ships to move ores and concentrates from Latin America led to a recommendation that a possible increase in the smelting and refining of copper in that area should be investigated. A decision on vanadium called for the hurrying into production in two other mines. There were a number of such recommendations relating to particular enterprises amongst the decisions of the Board. Thus one called for the maintenance of nickel matte production from the continuous operations of two smelting furnaces in New Caledonia and the operation of a third in so far as fuel could be obtained from Australia. In the decision on copper cited in Appendix 3 the United Kingdom was made responsible for more than doubling the output of copper in an African mine.

The majority of the Board's reports in 1942 contained recommendations on development which were fairly specific, mentioning not only the places in which development should be undertaken, but also the methods and steps which should be taken. In later years the Board's recommendations tended to be of a more general character. Its main function became the assembling of figures which usually

---

[1] Others related to manganese, chromite, balsa wood, rubber, etc. There was some reference to development in the commodity reports on almost every critical material.

indicated plainly enough to what extent expansion and development were necessary and it refrained from attempting to specify with any exactness where, when and by whom. Such general recommendations were usually sufficient. The Board was not in fact equipped to give detailed guidance to the governments on highly technical matters of this kind which called for the staff and resources of a fully organised government department. Its business was to state the need clearly and to see that it received proper attention from the governments.

The Board and its member Governments were not always right in their forecasts. Thus by a decision in September 1942 (No. 77) the Board recommended that no further steps should be taken towards construction of a cobalt metal plant in the Belgian Congo. The reasons were that at the time the supply of cobalt seemed fairly satisfactory; whilst construction of the new plant would draw on scarce materials. Therefore, it recommended that neither the United States nor the United Kingdom should release materials for the project. But the decision proved to be wrong. A large and unforeseen expansion took place in the use of cobalt for jet propulsion engines. Belgium, however, was not a member of the Board; and the Belgian company had proceeded with the construction of the plant despite the withholding of materials by the British and American Governments. The plant turned out to be a valuable war asset, since, without it the demand for cobalt could hardly have been met.

NEW OUTPUT FROM OLD SOURCES

Directly or indirectly government finance played a large part in the expansion of raw material production for war purposes. The Governments themselves rarely undertook direct responsibility for particular enterprises. Expansion of production could often be secured only by the payment of higher prices to cover the high cost of production of marginal supplies. Usually each country undertook responsibility for the extra cost involved in development in its hemisphere area of responsibility. This involved both countries in considerable expenditures abroad.[1] As far as possible the British Government used the method of long-term guaranteed contracts with particular producers. Under such contracts the Government took the whole output for the duration of the war and a period after it, at a price which was either fixed in advance or adjustable in accordance with factors mentioned in the contract. The United States paid premium prices for marginal production within its

---

[1] Thus the United Kingdom had to meet the cost of expanding the production of the best quality Indian mica by purchasing, much beyond its needs, the inferior grades, the production of which was inseparable from that of the better grades.

territory of copper, lead and zinc.[1] Such premium prices rarely squeezed from the marginal mines what might perhaps have been obtained with a lesser expenditure from existing mines – at the cost, however, of their earlier exhaustion. But in the case of copper, the premium price plan was largely responsible for increasing the production of copper in 1942 by 19 per cent. over that of 1941.[2]

The division of financial responsibility between the two countries was not of course clear cut. It was necessary in a number of cases to obtain supplies, such as railway and mining equipment, needed for particular projects; since the United States was then the only possible source of supply they had to be obtained under Lend-Lease. Development schemes in various parts of the Commonwealth could often be undertaken only if the necessary equipment could be obtained from the United States. The Combined Board drew the attention of the Commonwealth Missions in Washington to the help it could give them in such matters by endorsing their requests for Lend-Lease equipment.

With some exceptions the necessary expansion of output for war needs came largely from existing rather than new sources of supply. This was especially true of the metals. The experience of the Board once more emphasised the limiting factors of geology and climate. Whilst raw materials are produced all over the world, the great proportion of the total output of most individual commodities comes from a few particular sources, particular deposits of ores and minerals, or areas with particular climatic conditions, such as those necessary for the production of rubber and tropical fibres. The difficulty of discovering new sources of supply, and developing them quickly enough to be of use during the war, was demonstrated time and time again. But spectacular increases in production from new sources occurred where production could be put on an industrial basis by means of the application of chemical or metallurgical processes combined with large scale capital expenditures. The well known examples were aluminium and magnesium, synthetic rubber and nylon.

The difficulty of exploiting new sources was particularly marked in the case of the non-ferrous metals and ferro-alloys. Thus in the case of nickel all the efforts of the Board produced no change in the existing pattern by which 90 per cent. of the world's production came from the two existing Canadian nickel-mining companies. Nearly all the lead came from the United States, Canada, Australia

---

[1] For a history of United States premium price policy, see *Evolution of Premium Price Policy for Copper, Lead and Zinc, January 1940 to November 1943*. (Historical Reports on War Administration, War Production Board, Special Study No. 4, February 1946.)

[2] *Wartime Production Achievements and the Reconversion Outlook : Report of the Chairman of W.P.B.*, 9th October 1945, p. 45.

Peru and Mexico. Most of the copper came from the United States, Canada, Chile, Rhodesia, the Belgian Congo and a small part from Australia and South Africa. Cobalt came almost entirely from Rhodesia and the Belgian Congo; molybdenum almost entirely from the United States; graphite from Ceylon and Madagascar; mica, particularly the most important grades, largely from India, with Brazil as the main secondary source.

This concentration of supply simplified the problem of the Board in the matter of development as well as of allocation. It could look to the known larger producing sources as the most likely places to secure a large and rapid expansion of output. On occasion it might be worth while to try to expand smaller sources, producing, say, a useful one or two per cent. of the world's output; but usually they could not be counted on to yield enough extra output to justify any large expenditure of effort and money. In the case of mica a premium price as high as $6 a pound, paid to producers in the United States, failed to produce much new mica; and what was produced was mostly inferior in quality.

In developing new sources of supply the Board sometimes made use of special missions of investigation. It did not itself create such missions but merely recommended their appointment by the appropriate British or American government departments. The reports of the Missions were made in most cases to these departments rather than direct to the Board. Thus in May 1942 the Board recommended that a Mission composed of one American and one British expert should be sent to the Belgian Congo to examine with the competent authorities the possibilities of increasing the production of strategic raw materials. The territory was a source of cobalt, copper, rubber, tin and other materials. The Mission was asked to report on the prospects of increased output and to indicate what mining or other equipment was needed for this purpose. The Mission reported later in the year and steps were taken by the Advisory Operating Committee of the Board to ensure that its recommendations were carried out. A Mission was also sent to Nigeria to investigate the possibilities of increasing the production of tin. A Joint Wolfram Mission was also despatched to West Africa early in 1943. Before it could leave, molybdenum, which was also included in its terms of reference, had become more important than tungsten. The terms of reference for this mission, as suggested by London, illustrated the factors of time, price and other conditions involved in development. As regards wolfram London pointed out it was doubtful 'whether exploration of a backwoods country, in which development in any case may be expected to be difficult, could be justified except on exceptionally favourable and definite indications'. The mission was to confine itself to the more promising prospects and to pay particular attention to the factor of time. Efforts were to be made to reduce the intervention by British and American nationals to a minimum by using as far as possible local firms.

(v)

From 'Combined' to 'International'

The transition from war to peace, from combined to international, brought out clearly the unique character of the combined Boards – the 'novel experiment in economic collaboration' which had 'unquestionably hastened the moment of victory'.[1] The transition involved steps of two kinds. The first was the gradual removal of raw materials from allocation and other controls as supplies became more plentiful. The second was the broadening of the basis of the Combined Boards by associating other countries with their work. A number of steps towards these goals were taken during the twelve months before the end of the war. The drawing up of the Reserve Commodity List in November 1944 was a move in both directions. The list enumerated the commodities on which the three Combined Boards concerned (Raw Materials; Food; Production) desired the co-ordination of war requirements with the new requirements of the liberated countries of Europe and of the United Nations Relief and Rehabilitation Administration. The Reserve Commodity List contained some thirty raw materials. These were mostly materials drawn by the United States and the United Kingdom from overseas sources. The list did not include some of the basic materials needed for economic reconstruction such as steel, cotton and wool. Programmes for most of the thirty were presented to the Board by UNRRA and by France, Belgium, Norway and Denmark. By the early spring of 1945 the Board had allocated enough of the main commodities to enable industries in these countries to get under way. In a number of cases, e.g. the non-ferrous metals, the Board authorised the United Kingdom to draw on its stocks in order to meet the immediate needs of Europe. Less progress was made in the supply of the most critical of the materials, e.g. cordage fibres, forest products, and hides and leather. By the spring of 1945 the Allies had available, by allocation or purchase, a greater tonnage of raw materials than they could ship.

The drawing up of the Reserved Commodity List was accompanied by recommendations made by a Joint Committee of the three Boards concerned on the future work of the Combined Boards.[2]

---

[1] Statement by the President of the United States and the Prime Ministers of the United Kingdom and Canada on the dissolution of the Boards, 10th December 1945.

[2] The recommendations of the Committee (which was attended also by representatives of the British and Canadian Embassies and the State Department) summed up the results of discussions that had been going on since the summer of 1944.

These recommendations became the basis of the joint statement of the President and the Prime Ministers of the United Kingdom and Canada, on 19th January 1945, announcing the continuation of the three Boards, without change of membership, until the end of the war with Japan. The Boards were to 'collaborate increasingly with representatives of other United Nations in the common interest', and to continue to add representatives of other countries to their working committees when this seemed necessary. The criterion was to be the importance of these countries as producers or consumers of particular commodities in short supply. The policy of both governments, the statement indicated, was to maintain allocation by the Boards for commodities which continued to require combined planning in order to meet military and civilian requirements. Allocation was also to continue in cases where a removal of controls would create serious shipping difficulties. The Boards were not encouraged to deal directly with problems of surplus supply; but they were to study such problems and to inform the member governments of any commodities likely to become 'in burdensome excess supply'. The Combined Raw Materials Board was to direct its work on particular raw materials so that it could be fitted into any international scheme which might later be adopted.

The association of representatives of other countries with the work of committees of the Combined Boards was a step in this last direction. On the raw materials side representatives of other countries had been taking part for some time in joint discussions on the distribution of hides and leather and lead; and also on textiles. In February 1945 there were inconclusive discussions on how to extend this collaboration, at joint meetings between C.R.M.B. and C.P.R.B., together with representatives of the State Department and the British and Canadian Embassies. In April steps were taken by the United Kingdom and the United States to set up in London inter-allied working groups on pulp and paper, and on timber. Both groups reported to the Combined Raw Materials Board. The object of the groups was to co-ordinate the purchase, price and distribution of these commodities as they became available in Northern Europe.[1]

From V-E Day the process of removing controls began to gain speed. The first revision of the Reserved Commodity List was issued in April 1945. From June to August controls were relaxed in the United States with extreme rapidity. The decision of January 1945 continued the Combined Boards until the end of the war with Japan. With the surrender of Japan on 14th August 1945 both governments recognised the need of an immediate decision to extend the life of the

---

[1] Since it was recognised that other countries might have requirements for these supplies, lists of requirements were sought through London and Washington from the British Commonwealth, Latin America and UNRRA.

Boards for a further period, but without formal change of membership. Under the new directive as issued on 29th August the President and the Prime Ministers of the United Kingdom and Canada announced that the three Boards would continue for the time being to operate 'on the present basis in order to ensure that there is no interruption in combined machinery which is handling various supply questions of critical and immediate importance'.

The nature of the problems that would arise in this further period was foreseen by the British side in Washington at a joint meeting on raw materials held on 21st August. Irrespective of its formal membership the Combined Raw Materials Board would have to conduct its operations on a multilateral basis with the principal producers and consumers brought into international commodity committees. In theory, if not in practice, the United States and the United Kingdom would have no prior claims in such committees. 'A round table conference of up to ten countries' would find great difficulty in attempting to make short period allocations. Some new 'rough formula' – such as division of supplies on the basis of pre-war consumption – would have to be found for allocations in the new period. There would be no time for the investigations needed to secure agreement on criteria of comparative need. (How, it was asked on a later occasion – could Dutch need of lead for housing be measured against American need of lead for automobile batteries and leaded gasoline?)

The problem was simplified somewhat by the announcement by the Combined Raw Materials Board on 11th September 1945 that all outstanding recommendations of the Board were annulled in respect of nearly a score of raw materials. This revision left only 13 raw materials on the Reserved Commodity List, namely copal gum, cordage fibres, hides, skins and leather, hog bristles, jute and jute goods, lead, lumber and timber, mica splittings, newsprint, pine resin, rotenone rubber and tin. The Board continued to allocate most of these commodities up to the end of December. At the end of September the machinery was further simplified by the termination officially of the Combined Committees, with the exception of the Combined Coal Committee (C.R.M.B./C.P.R.B.), the Combined Footwear, Leather and Hides Committee (C.R.M.B./C.P.R.B.), and the Combined Fertilizers Committee (C.R.M.B./C.F.B.).[1] Any continuing work in connection with the fields covered by any of the dissolved Committees was handled henceforward on a staff basis.[2]

Even though both sides were agreed on the principle of removing

---

[1] The committees of the Combined Production and Resources Board except Textiles came to an end formally on the same date.

[2] Several of the Combined Food Board committees were wound up at the same time but most of them continued until the Board ended on 30th June 1946.

as soon as possible war-time controls on international trade, there still remained a hard core of commodities for which combined control would continue to be needed after the ends of the Boards. These were commodities for which there was serious world shortage which was likely to continue far into 1946, or even longer. It was necessary to find for them some means whereby allocations could continue without Boards. The effectiveness of any such arrangements would depend, it was agreed, on the continuation in the United States of authority to control imports of these commodities, to make public purchases abroad, and to control and to give priority assistance to exports from the United States.

THE SEQUEL TO THE BOARDS: THE COMBINED COMMITTEES

Tripartite discussions between London, Washington and Ottawa, from September to the end of November 1945, on the arrangements needed after the dissolution of the Boards, centred on the list of commodities still in 'global short supply' and the question of the machinery needed for their continued control. The list of commodities was finally narrowed down to four: rubber, tin, hides, skins and leather, and textiles. This left some doubtful cases such as lead, copper and hard fibres, for which some special and less formal arrangements might be needed. On the matter of machinery there was agreement from the outset that allocations should be by small international commodity committees. For each of the four commodities, save tin, combined committees under the Combined Boards were already in existence. On each Committee were several Allied countries as well as the States members of the Boards. Thus the problem might be solved by dissolving the Boards into these committees and setting up a similar committee for tin. But there still remained a number of practical points to be settled, such as: whether the Committee should be set up before or after the end of the Boards? and what should be their membership, powers, organisation and relations with each other?

Final agreement between the three Governments was not reached until the end of November. A statement was drawn up by the two Prime Ministers and the President to announce (on 10th December) the termination on the last day of the year of the Combined Raw Materials Board and the Combined Production and Resources Board.[1] The statement indicated that the four commodity committees for cotton textiles, tin, rubber, and hides and leather already existing under the Boards would continue with 'representation . . . on an appropriate international basis'. In most cases, it was pointed

---

[1] The Combined Food Board was to be terminated at the latest on 30th June 1946, but here too some commodity committees might have to be continued on an international basis.

out, membership already included countries having 'a major interest' in the particular commodity.[1] For 'some additional commodities in uncertain supply', the statement intimated, the Boards 'may make suitable distribution arrangements before the end of the year to extend into 1946'.

As soon as agreement was reached between London, Washington and Ottawa it became necessary to explain the arrangements to the Allied countries represented on the commodity committees. For this purpose a joint meeting of the Combined Raw Materials Board and the Combined Production and Resources Board was held on 6th December with representatives of UNRRA and of Belgium, Denmark, France, the Netherlands and Norway. The meeting began with plans for 1946, and ended with a tribute by the heads of the two Boards to the patience, co-operation and understanding of 'their customers', the Allied Nations, and a vote of thanks by the latter to the Combined Boards. The French representative expressed the gratitude of France to the Combined Boards. France's most essential needs had been covered, and in most cases on time. The text of the statement terminating the two Boards was given to the meeting by the Chairman, Mr W. L. Batt. He explained the necessity of retaining intergovernmental allocation arrangements into 1946 for the five commodities, four of which the Boards had been allocating on the basis of recommendations of the respective combined committees. For the fifth, tin metal, the Combined Raw Materials Board had set up a few days earlier a similar combined committee. He emphasised the importance of continuity. By continuing the present five combined committees on an independent, international basis, the setting up of new machinery could be avoided. Existing allocations and international agreements in respect of the five commodities would be maintained, and the collaboration between the members of the Boards and the other countries already represented on the combined committees would be preserved. The combined Committees would be essentially short-term organisations which would make allocations only as long as the extraordinary supply shortages continued. They would have to take their own decisions as to membership, in particular whether additional states should be invited to become members of the Committees.[2]

---

[1] The statement also referred to coal for which there existed an 'organisation in respect of Europe but special considerations make it desirable that for the time being the coal committees in Washington and London now under the Boards continue in their present form'.

[2] The meeting was informed that the U.S.S.R was being notified by the United States, the United Kingdom and Canada, through diplomatic channels, of the termination of the Boards and the continuation of the commodity committees. The notification indicated that the three Governments would be glad to receive any observations by the U.S.S.R. and to be informed of any interest which it might have in the work of the Committees. It did not in fact seek membership of any of the committees.

As Mr Batt pointed out the committees followed different patterns in the matter of membership. The Rubber and Tin Metal Committees consisted of the four or five major producers and consumers. Their work was therefore of a trustee character; they were responsible for allocations to non-member as well as member countries. The Hides Committee, on the other hand, would consist of the consuming countries which normally purchased hides and leather entering international trade.

The initial membership would be[1]:

Combined Rubber Committee:

United States, United Kingdom, France, Belgium, Netherlands, Canada.

Combined Tin Metal Committee:

United States, United Kingdom, France, Netherlands, Belgium.[2]

Combined Hides, Skins, and Leather Committee:

United States, United Kingdom, Canada, Belgium, Denmark, France, Netherlands, Norway, Spain, Sweden, Switzerland. (Later Portugal, Turkey and Finland joined the Committee. UNRRA had access to the Committee on behalf of the countries, including Italy, which looked to UNRRA for supplies.)

Little was said on organisation at this meeting, this being a matter for the committees to decide; but the Board members had already agreed that the committees should continue to meet in Washington and should carry on as far as possible with their existing British and American officers. For the Tin Committee a Dutch chairman and a British secretary were chosen. The Combined Raw Materials Board by some last acts, Mr Batt said, would ease the transition into 1946 as regards the other nine raw materials on the Reserved Commodity List. For *copal gum* the Board was trying to arrange with Belgium, the sole supplier, a distribution pattern for at least part of 1946. It was working on the possibility of similar action for *cordage fibres*. As for *jute and jute goods* when the last allocations by the Board

---

[1] The members of the Textile Committee were composed of producers: the United States, the United Kingdom, Canada, India and France, with other producers such as Brazil and Mexico associated where necessary. The Combined Fertilisers Committee (C.R.M.B. and C.F.B.) was also mainly a body of consumer states with some producers. It continued in existence during the life of the Combined Food Board. The Committee consisted originally of the United States, the United Kingdom and Canada but before the end of the war France and Norway were added. After the war ended the Committee was enlarged by adding Belgium, the Netherlands, Denmark and Chile, UNRRA being represented by an observer. Later Australia and New Zealand, followed by India, were added. The Committee during the first half of 1946 managed to secure enough agreement to continue the allocation of fertilisers. It then became a Committee of the International Emergency Food Council.

[2] The Combined Tin Metal Committee continued allocations long after the termination of the other two committees. China was invited to become a member during the second half of the year and took part in the final allocation for the remainder of the year.

were fulfilled, India, as sole supplier, would decide whether to continue allocations by a system of export quotas.[1] *Timber, newsprint* and *pine resin* were being reviewed by inter-allied groups in London. A United States allocation for the latter would bridge the first quarter of 1946. For *rotenone* the Board would make a last allocation which the national supply departments would carry out in 1946.

Lead presented special difficulties. Towards the end of the war it had become much more critical than copper. The shortage affected not only the United States and the United Kingdom but also most European and many non-European countries. It was not possible to set up a committee for lead on the lines of other combined committees since the lead producers in several countries were opposed to the continuance of government controls. The problem was handled by means of informal arrangements between the United States and the United Kingdom. They drew up a quarterly balance sheet for 1946 showing estimated supplies and estimated requirements for lead; and they voluntarily agreed to restrict their purchases from overseas sources within limits which would leave a balance available for the other countries.[2] For copper there was also an informal arrangement of a simple kind. The two countries merely kept each other informed of their purchases of copper in various countries. Whilst there was no co-ordination as to the amounts purchased some attempt was made to keep in line in respect of prices.

THE COMBINED RUBBER COMMITTEE

The history of the Combined Rubber Committee illustrated the problems, particularly the economic issues, involved in attempting to continue controls on a multilateral basis in time of peace. Under its terms of reference the new committee was to: 'Keep the rubber position under review and to allocate supplies of rubber to member and non-member countries. . . .' It had in fact been operating since June 1945 as an international allocating body advisory to the

---

[1] In the case of *jute* the Combined Boards allocations ended in the middle of the jute year on 31st December 1945. Jute and jute goods continued to be in short supply throughout 1946 but the Government of India maintained controls which regulated supplies and prevented prices from getting completely out of hand. As regards *hard fibres*, difficulties had arisen in the autumn of 1945 as a result of the termination by the U.S.A. of public purchase of Mexican manufactured cordage. This decision meant in the British view putting an end to the basis of Combined Board allocation of hard fibres, including sisal. Nevertheless the United Kingdom undertook to continue allocations of sisal and the hard fibres (as apart from manufactured cordage) until the end of the year. By this time the basis for effective allocation no longer existed, but there was some co-operation between the United States and the United Kingdom during 1946 by the exchange of information on production and on shipments of fibres.

[2] The figures were adjusted quarterly but the final agreement was that the maximum amount of lead that the United States would buy from overseas sources in 1946 was 120,000 tons, whilst the United Kingdom would purchase up to 234,000 tons. This left an estimated balance for other countries of 120,000 tons.

Combined Raw Materials Board.[1] In the last quarter of 1945 it had allocated natural and synthetic rubber to a score or more rubber consuming countries. In the new independent committee the United Kingdom continued to present the requirements of the British Commonwealth, and of such Eastern Hemisphere countries as were not separately represented on the Committee or whose claims were not presented by UNRRA. Likewise the United States continued to present the rubber requirements of Latin American countries. On the procurement side the Committee carried on the Combined Board's principle of dividing responsibility for procurement between the United States and the United Kingdom on a hemisphere basis; the only change was that France, Belgium and the Netherlands were now responsible for procuring from their colonial territories.

The main problems which the Combined Rubber Committee faced were: (a) the continued world shortage of natural rubber and uncertainties of supply from South East Asia; (b) the rate at which reconversion should take place, i.e., the rate of increase in the proportion of usage of natural to synthetic rubbers. Linked with (b) was the question of the relative price levels of natural and synthetic (or dollar) rubber. The first allocations by the Committee in its new form were suspended to the end of January 1946 until the price of natural rubber was fixed by negotiations held outside the Committee, between the governments of the United States, the United Kingdom, the Netherlands and France. (This matter of price was to be re-opened again in June.) Supplies of natural rubber for 1946 were estimated at not much more than a third of total estimated requirements of rubber (natural and synthetic). The basis of allocations was fixed as follows: in the first place, countries were not to receive more than half of their requirements for one quarter of their average annual pre-war imports of natural rubber; but an additional allowance was made for depleted stocks. The balance of their requirements could be made up by synthetic rubber from the United States. In the second place, a rate of reconversion from synthetic to natural rubber was fixed.

The assumption that countries could continue to count on supplies of synthetic rubber from the United States proved to be incorrect for two reasons: first because production was not fully maintained and second because the lifting (in November 1945) of internal controls in the United States led to a sharp increase in domestic consumption. In the third quarter of 1946 the United States Government decided to allow no further sales of synthetic (GR-S) for export. To

---

[1] The original 'Combined Rubber Committee' set up in 1942 was replaced in June 1945 by a new committee, the C.R.M.B. Rubber Committee which advised the Board on rubber allocations. The following new governments were then invited to become members: France, Belgium and the Netherlands. Canada was added when the new Combined Rubber Committee was set up at the end of 1945.

meet in part the deficit thus caused in supplies of synthetic rubber, the Committee found it possible to make the third quarter allocations of natural rubber on a more generous scale. An agreed increase of the price of natural rubber in June led to much greater supplies from Malaya in the third quarter than had been expected. Rubber was now in fact becoming available from this source at a rate far in excess of allocations. Thus allocations for the fourth quarter could be approved without limitation. It was agreed therefore that international allocation should cease at the end of the year, and that the Combined Rubber Committee should be dissolved on 31st December 1946.

During the life of the Combined Rubber Committee all the more significant proposals adopted by the Committee were made either by the American member, who was Chairman, or by the British member. They were in a position to participate more actively in the work of the Committee than the other four members. They were usually consulted by their respective staffs not only on matters which could be dealt with at the staff level, but also on general questions of procedure and policy; and their staffs worked together closely. Their countries had a considerable interest in the Committee's work; since the United States was the largest consumer of rubber and the source of synthetic, and the United Kingdom was the largest supplier of natural rubber. Little natural rubber was coming as yet from French, Belgium and Dutch sources; in fact during the greater part of the year the United Kingdom was the only supplier of natural rubber. The other members therefore played inevitably a less active role, their interest being largely directed to ensuring that their own countries received satisfactory treatment as regards allocations. The French, Belgian and Dutch members were also somewhat handicapped by the fact that they were not kept well informed by their Governments on the supply position in their own countries. In practice the attempt to speed up action by giving the members of the enlarged committee some discretion in agreeing to decisions was a failure. This did not prevent the reference back to Governments of the recommendations, which held up the action of the Committee. On several occasions during 1946 the operations of the Committee were affected by important decisions, such as those on prices, which were made outside the Committee. Thus the subsequent recommendations of the Committee merely reflected agreements made between certain of the member countries. The policy of the United States regarding the rate of reconversion from synthetic to natural rubber depended not only on supplies of natural rubber but also on the settlement of price questions with which the Committee was not concerned. The Committee was handicapped also by the inadequate supporting data which accompanied the demands of most countries.

Figures for stocks and consumption in a particular quarter were often difficult to reconcile with information available to the Committee from its records of allocations in previous years, and from the regular reports which it received from London of the exports which had been made from supplying areas against allocations. That this was only a transitory difficulty seemed to be shown by the much more satisfactory returns which the Committee received in the third quarter of 1946 as the basis for its final allocations.

THE COMBINED HIDES COMMITTEE

The Combined Hides Committee faced a more complex set of problems than either the Rubber or Tin Metal Committee and its life was the shortest of the three. Its large size (eleven states as well as UNRRA) was a sign of the conflicting interests which had to be harmonised. Its initial membership was made up from the members of three former Hides Committees with the addition of three new members, Portugal, Finland and Turkey. The main body had been the Footwear, Leather and Hides Committee (C.R.M.B. and C.P.R.B.) which recommended allocations direct to the Boards on behalf of all claimants. Its members were the United States, the United Kingdom and Canada, which together controlled directly or indirectly most of the supplies of the free world. The other five members were neutral and liberated states of Europe.[1]

The general formula devised in August 1945 for these groups of countries was modelled roughly on the Hides Agreement referred to in Section (iii) above. In calculating the percentage of the allocation of foreign hides due to each country, its pre-war consumption was taken as a basis; its current domestic production of hides was then deducted. From August the neutrals and the 'paying countries' began to undertake their own procurement directly, screening their offers through the Joint Hides Control Office. Since navicert control over the neutrals was now reduced, the control of purchases rested with the individual countries. How much they could procure, within their quotas, depended on the efficiency of their administrative systems and their ability to transport and process hides. As their capacity in this respect increased, the question of the formula became more important. So long as the war lasted there was general recognition of the need to give priority to the military requirements of the United States and the United Kingdom. But after the war

---

[1] These were drawn from the two former subsidiary hides committees: (a) the Liberated Areas Committee (Liberated States of Europe and UNRRA) set up in October 1944 and (b) the European Hides and Leather Committee, consisting of the neutrals, Spain, Sweden and Switzerland, set up in May 1945. Both bodies were concerned with the allotment of hides released to them by the United States, the United Kingdom and Canada. The neutrals agreed to control their purchases of foreign hides in accordance with agreed quotas. Their quotas were made comparable as far as possible with those of the liberated countries and UNRRA.

there was increasing pressure to put the allocations for all countries on a uniform basis.

The issue came to a head in the Combined Hides, Skins and Leather Committee in the early months of 1946. One of the difficulties in getting any agreement on a single formula for all countries was the absence of adequate statistics for most of the members of the Committee. Early in the year a decline in the supplies of foreign hides threatened to diminish the number of hides available to European countries. The situation was eased somewhat by the decision of the United States to take two steps: first, to limit their consumption of domestic hides to 1,800,000 a month out of a monthly production of 2,000,000 and to make the residue available for export; and secondly, to restrict their purchases of foreign hides to 30,000 hides a month – a figure appreciably lower than that set by the formula under the Hides Agreement. Within the United States however, commercial interests were pressing for the abolition of controls; and there was a conflict of policies on this point between several American agencies. The State Department desired to end controls; but other agencies, especially the Office of Price Administration and the War Production Board wished to maintain them in the interest of price stabilisation. The State Department objected to the representation on the Committee solely of importing countries. The Committee therefore invited the Argentine, Brazil, Uruguay and the U.S.S.R. to discuss co-operation with it, but none of these countries showed any eagerness to become members.

Thus in the first months of its existence the Committee was unable to make any progress towards agreed principles of division. For several months, indeed, it was unable to secure unanimous agreement on allocations. Usually in the absence of full agreement, allocations had to be made by the Chairman; and in practice the members did not carry their dissatisfaction to the point of refusing to accept their allocations.

Membership of the Committee was voluntary and there was already speculation on its dissolution. No commitment had been undertaken by any of the members to continue their membership. As a British official attached to the Committee commented after its dissolution: 'Every nation maintained its right to leave the Committee if its supplies fell below its own ideas of the essential minimum; as speculation on the end of control increased, supplies diminished and the Committee was killed by slow strangulation'. Attempts were made to improve supplies by price increases, in the hope of overcoming the resistance of sellers who were holding back in anticipation of the ending of price controls. The increases brought no lasting improvement in supply. In June supplies of all kinds of hides and skins dried up almost completely. The United States and the United

w

Kingdom came to the conclusion that the committee was on the point of collapse and they obtained the consent of the other members to its dissolution on 28th June 1946.

CONCLUSION

Thus the attempt to carry forward into the peace some degree of control over a few remaining raw materials, on a multilateral rather than a combined basis, encountered many difficulties. There no longer existed the single common objective of victory, an objective so imperative in its demands that all lesser interests were subordinate to it. War demanded unquestioned priority for military requirements. Unity was its sign; but diversity was the sign of peace. There were no agreed principles upon which peace-time allocations could be made. Divergent national views and aims pulled against each other. Some countries thought it was enough merely to state requirements without making clear their basis. One formula battled with another as the chosen basis for allocations: pre-war consumption, urgency of need, capacity to use, ability to pay, the confining of distribution to export surpluses, merit acquired by the strictness with which a country economised in its use of materials. The more countries there were on a committee the more difficult it became to secure agreement on the kind of issues with which the combined committees had to deal. An adjustment made to satisfy one objector was likely to result in dissatisfying some other country. In a multi-member committee it took longer to clear decisions with member Governments since the pace had to be adjusted to the slowest. It was not very useful for some Governments to give their representatives a large margin of discretion to agree on decisions unless all did the same. The more agreement was impeded by such difficulties the greater was the tendency of Governments to take their own decisions without waiting on the slow and uncertain processes of the Committee. Where many countries had an important interest in a commodity, as producers and consumers, even a large committee – as in the case of hides – might still be too small to placate all the interests that could wreck it.

The efficiency of the Combined Boards had depended in a very large measure on the accuracy, regularity and swift preparation of their statistics. But this was a result that was achieved only with difficulty under the pressure of the war and over a fairly lengthy period of time. Most of the new countries represented on the combined committees – even some which had had efficient statistical systems before the war – were not able to reach in time the high level of accurate and speedy statistics necessary for the efficient working of the controls.

From the outset the American and British members took the lead in the combined committees despite their desire to avoid the appearance of anything in the nature of an Anglo-Saxon bloc. Their leadership was due to other factors besides their greater purchasing power and control over large sources of supply. Their representatives usually had the advantage of a wealth of training and experience in combined planning and combined action not possessed by any of the newer members of the committees. Moreover they had acquired for the same reason a degree of expert knowledge of the commodity rarely possessed by the others.

Most of the Combined Board officials in Washington, accustomed to the simplicity and efficiency of the Boards, were not enthusiastic about their replacement by international commodity committees. They had no illusions that international committees could be as smooth running and efficient as combined bodies had been during the war. They recognised that the time had come when it was necessary to substitute international commodity committees for two of the Boards; but they preferred, as did the British and Canadian Governments, to maintain the Combined Food Board itself for a further period of at least six months, rather than to dissolve it prematurely into a series of independent commodity committees. American doubt, especially that of the State Department, as expressed in combined discussions in November 1945, as to whether allocation could continue any longer in time of peace on 'a purely Anglo-Saxon basis', was met by the argument that there was no real evidence of any serious pressure from non-member countries – even from France – either to join or to dissolve the Combined Food Board. The British and Canadians argued successfully that it seemed unwise to replace the Board by some international co-ordinating committee 'with shadowy authority and untested by experience at a time when food shortages in many claimant countries were as grave as at any time during the war'. The shortages involved so many interchangeable foodstuffs that only the continuance of the Combined Board could provide the necessary co-ordinating authority.

Yet despite the limitations of the international commodity committees which were set up to replace the Boards, it could not be denied that they made a useful contribution while they lasted. Without them available supplies would have been less well distributed. Prices were maintained at more reasonable levels than would otherwise have been possible. There was indeed some rise in prices, but nothing like the complete break which might have been expected if there had been unrestrained competition. Such a break in fact occurred with the disappearance of the Hides Committee.

CHAPTER VII
BRITISH WAR
ORGANISATION IN THE
UNITED STATES

(i)

The Control of an Overseas Whitehall

WHEN THEY crossed the Atlantic British missions and officials came as explorers into a strange New World of government and administration. It was a world, as one of the war-time officials put it, 'as different from ours as anything could be'; so different, indeed, for those who carried with them the fundamental assumptions of British politics that it could only be learned from experience on the spot and not from documents.

Some reference is made to this factor in *North American Supply*.[1] Here it is sufficient to mention only a few of the aspects of the strange new political environment which the visiting official found in the United States. (In Canada of course he was at home with a system of government closely modelled on that at Westminster.)

In the United States the British official discovered that words like 'Cabinet' and 'Minister' had a quite different meaning: they were used for a form of Government in which 'Ministers' were neither members of Congress nor elected, like the President, by the people. Nor did Ministers form a 'Cabinet' in the British sense; for one of them (Secretary Morgenthau) could describe them as 'the President's hired servants'. Moreover the President did not sit with them as a 'Prime' Minister – *primus inter pares* – but as Head of the State. The President and his Cabinet did not possess any financial initiative, as Government does in the British Parliament; since that initiative, as indeed, all legislative initiative lay with Congress. And the senior officials unlike those of the United Kingdom did not form part of the permanent civil service. For the British official discovered that – in the words of one of them – American senior officials tended to be 'political nominees apt to be replaced as new personalities acquire influence (especially when war-time needs are developing

---

[1] See e.g., *North American Supply, op. cit.*, pp. 139, 466–471 and 491.

rapidly) so that no sooner has one got on terms with one man than one has to start afresh with another'. An 'Agreement' made with one would not necessarily be valid with another. Nor would an agreement with one Department of Government necessarily be accepted by any other. Nor would an agreement by the Executive necessarily bind the independent Legislature. Did indeed the word 'agreement' mean the same thing in the vocabularies of the two systems: for on the American side it meant so often in practice something of a much more preliminary kind – an agreement to try to get an agreement.

In short here was a new and 'immensely complex set-up'. The initial impression was one of unregulated competition and disorder – within a much more precisely defined legal framework of order than existed in Whitehall. If in the end, as the British official acknowledged, things got done and often with surprising speed he remained convinced that the system was costly and wasteful. But that was not his business. His first task was to understand how the system worked, and the first step towards such understanding was to put aside his own political assumptions and to learn the assumptions and vocabulary of the American system.

The theme of this chapter is not administration in the narrower sense. It deals with several major problems caused by the building up in the United States of a large-scale British war organisation. Beginning with the small and simple Purchasing Mission set up by Purvis in New York in November 1939, the organisation developed into a complex administration of over a score of autonomous British Missions.[1] The total staff grew from under 40 at the end of 1939 to over 9,000 at the peak in June 1943. To house these Missions the British Government leased, either in whole or in part, 31 buildings in Washington and several in New York.[2] This complex structure was co-ordinated by a dual system of control. On the spot, in Washington, co-ordination was secured by the British Ambassador, the British Supply Council, and a British Resident Minister for Supply. In London, co-ordination was secured by the operation of the Cabinet system and by the parent Ministries with the help of interdepartmental committees. Close liaison between London and Washington was maintained by a vast amount of cabling, by the circulation of documents, by correspondence between opposite numbers, by visits and missions, and above all by the strong tradition of the civil service that officials must work as a team and keep each other informed. Some of the issues of policy involved in controlling

---

[1] In addition there were six Missions set up by other countries of the British Commonwealth of Nations.

[2] In Washington this meant approximately 626,000 feet of floor space at a rental of about $892,000 per year. Several of the British Missions were housed free of charge in United States Government buildings. The total staff had declined to 7,000 at the end of the war.

and co-ordinating this miniature overseas Whitehall are dealt with in this chapter. It is not concerned with the host of administrative questions falling roughly under the headings of establishment and financial control.

On the general principle that there must be co-ordination at the policy level there could be no disagreement. The difficulties arose in applying the principle in the unprecedented and unforeseen conditions produced by the war. At the beginning of the war it would have seemed an intolerable situation that there should ever be a score of British Missions in Washington, talking directly on supply and other matters to agencies of the American Government. The first plans for British war organisation in the United States were based on two assumptions: first that there must be a single British Purchasing Commission and second that this Commission would have little to do with matters of policy. Its function would simply be to buy on the market, leaving questions of policy to be settled by the Embassy or the Government in London. Both assumptions were short-lived. The second collapsed at once when the President and Secretary Morgenthau decided in December 1939 that Purvis was the man with whom they must work on matters of policy affecting economic warfare, and soon after on all major questions of war production and supply. The undermining of the other assumption – that of a simple British purchasing agency – began soon after Dunkirk. No sooner had Purvis secured the concentration through the British Purchasing Commission of all independent buying, whether private or departmental, than there were signs of the sprouting round the Commission of a crop of separate departmental missions. By December 1940 the assumption of a single purchasing agency had been abandoned. Already by that time the principle of the autonomy of a number of departmental missions was well enough established to withstand all later assaults.

The idea of a single British high command for supply lingered, however, until well after Pearl Harbour, and several half-hearted efforts were made towards its realisation. The interest of these episodes, which are referred to below, lies in the apparent discrepancy between theory in London and facts on the spot in Washington. There was a not unnatural tendency to try to apply overseas the traditional system of co-ordination which operated in London. There departmental autonomy was kept within reasonable limits by the existence of the War Cabinet and its collective responsibility to Parliament. So long as the overseas operations of departments were limited to one or two missions, co-ordination could still be maintained by long distance methods – by cable, telephone, the exchange of documents, and personal visits – as well as by the working of the normal machinery of inter-departmental committees. The problem was what to do when the number of missions overseas was multiplied into a large-scale organisation. Whenever the authorities in London faced this kind of issue their thinking tended to begin with the assumption that Cabinet control overseas could only be exercised effectively by a Minister of State or by a Resident Minister of Cabinet rank.[1] Such a Minister would speak for the Government as a whole on all important matters of policy and thus ensure unity of action between the different British missions. The expedient of a Resident Minister was applied successfully in various theatres such as Cairo, West Africa and Ottawa.[2] The British Missions in the United States, however, opposed any such solution for their problem of co-ordination. The heads of the Missions maintained successfully that any attempt to interpose a resident Minister of State between themselves and their Ministers in London would be unworkable. They argued that they could not be responsible to two masters; and that to carry out effectively in Washington the tasks assigned to them they must continue to have free and direct access to the agencies of the American Government with which they had to do business. There was full agreement that there must be co-ordination; but it was felt that it could only be secured effectively by informal and voluntary means such as inter - mission committees, the meetings of the British Supply Council, the still less formal meetings summoned by the Ambassador, and perhaps most of all by keeping the rule that everybody must keep everybody else concerned fully informed. When finally at the end of 1942 a Resident Minister was appointed he was given no overriding powers.

It would be easy – but probably wrong – to conclude that this was just one more example of the strength of administrative vested interests. The logic of theory in London was strong, but the logic of experience in Washington was more compelling. The judgment of the British officials on the spot was strongly influenced by their practical experience of working with American Government departments. In the British tradition to which they were accustomed departments were bound together closely under the authority of the Prime Minister and the Cabinet. They found that in the United States, under the American presidential system, departments were more independent. They concluded that if a mission was to succeed it had to have direct channels of approach to each of the American departments with which it wanted to do business.

The theory of a *single* channel on the British side broke down

---

[1] During the First World War Lord Northcliffe was appointed (in 1917) to look after all British supply interests in the United States as head of the British Mission. The arrangement of a Minister for Supply in New York and a British Ambassador in Washington proved unsatisfactory and Lord Reading was appointed in February 1918 to fill both roles.

[2] Mr Malcolm MacDonald when appointed High Commissioner of the United Kingdom at Ottawa retained his Cabinet rank.

because of the unsolved problem of finding any comparable American channel. This was, indeed, one of the most baffling problems of the British supply organisation in the United States, as *North American Supply* has shown.[1] The only direct channel to American departments in theory was through the President; and this could be used only on rare occasions. The experience of the British missions showed that if a mission were to succeed its officials had to have a multiplicity of channels of communication with opposite numbers in American agencies. The emphasis in the American system was on the individual. The individual British official had to prove himself in two ways: in the first place he had to overcome the initial suspicion with which a British official tended to be met. In the second place he had to make his way to the right individuals on the American side. As a British diplomat commented after the war 'Until a British official found the right stairs to go up and the right person at the top he got nowhere'. Because of the initial prejudice with which a British proposal tended to be regarded, officials learned (he noted) that it was 'unwise for the "British side" to present the Americans with a ready-made and completely worked-out plan. There was an immediate unfavourable reaction whatever the merits of the plan. If the British had one, the only way of getting it accepted was to hide its existence, start at the first stages of it with the Americans, bring them gradually along step by step, until it was almost a case of their considering it their own and securing *our* acceptance'. It was at any rate necessary that they should be brought to regard it as being as much their plan as ours.

The main stages in the development of the British supply organisation in the United States have been mentioned in *North American Supply*. Until the fall of France co-ordination was secured largely through the working of the Allied machinery – the Anglo-French Co-ordination Committee in London under Monnet and the Anglo-French Purchasing Board in the United States under Purvis. In the United States unity of action as between the Allied governments in the matter of government purchases was secured by the rule that in all matters of any importance the Anglo-French Purchasing Board, through Purvis its chairman, was the sole channel of communication between the British and French Purchasing Commissions, and American Government departments. The two Purchasing Commissions were housed together; office supplies and furniture were purchased jointly. The British Purchasing Commission used the photostat equipment already installed by the French Commission. The purchasing and shipping programmes of the two Missions were co-ordinated; they had a joint credit investigation department; and

---

North American Supply, op. cit., pp. 72-80.

as far as possible their contract procedures were made uniform. Information as to prices, new inventions, and so forth, was pooled. Common policies were adopted in such matters as public relations, prevention of sabotage, and United States taxation. Procedures were worked out for apportioning deliveries on contracts as between the two governments, with proportionate payments in cases where both governments participated in an order. This disposed of questions involving priorities as between the Allies for goods in short supply.

When this whole Allied organisation was dissolved in July 1940, Purvis fell back upon the British Purchasing Commission. Its staff at this time was still very small and still almost exclusively commercial. Until July Purvis did not have on his staff a single permanent British civil servant. He then received several young British civil servants by transfer from the British Supply Board in Ottawa; but he had to wait until November for a senior British civil servant who, as Secretary General of the Commission, could take over the responsibility for administrative matters. Apart from several experts on explosives, machine tools and small arms ammunition, who had been sent direct from the United Kingdom, there was an almost complete lack of technical staff on the Commission. Most of the British technical advisers in North America up to July 1940 had been stationed in Ottawa. Some of these were now transferred to the Commission. The staff at this time was made up mostly of locally recruited persons of British or American nationality with commercial experience. The nucleus of the original staff had been provided by the New York office of the British Cunard White Star Company. Most of the senior officers of the Commission, however, were recruited from large American commercial concerns. From this point until the end of the war Americans – working sometimes for almost nominal salaries – were to play an important part in the British supply organisation.

There were some difficulties at first in reconciling traditional practices and conceptions of British administration with the conditions and standards current in the United States. When early in 1940 Purvis complained of the limitations imposed on him in the matter of recruitment he was told by a British Treasury official in Ottawa that the powers already delegated to him 'would be the envy of the head of any Department in London'. His task, however, was of a very different kind; he had to recruit on the open market in order to build up a purchasing commission to carry out novel tasks in a foreign country. The cautious policy dictated by the British civil servants in the mission at Ottawa and their departments in London meant that when the crisis came after Dunkirk the British Purchasing Commission had far too little staff to cope with the enormous increase in the volume of work. The shortage of trained and expert staff led departments to send visiting missions from the United Kingdom; and also to set up permanent departmental missions. This involved a departure from the principle of a single purchasing commission and created the problem of co-ordination which forms the central theme of this chapter.

Meanwhile in London the gap caused in July 1940 by the dissolution of the Anglo-French Co-ordinating Committee had been met by the setting up of a new interdepartmental North American Supply Committee. Amongst its duties was the co-ordination of programmes of the three armed services. Monnet at the personal invitation of the Prime Minister had left London on a British passport in order to work with Purvis in Washington. The chairmanship of the new committee was undertaken by Sir Arthur Salter, then Parliamentary Secretary of the Ministry of Supply. The committee was assisted by a small permanent secretariat. This was called the Central Office for North American Supplies, was attached to the offices of the War Cabinet and was composed of British officials who had served the Anglo-French Co-ordinating Committee. The North American Supply Committee itself was composed of high officials from ten different ministries, which had some concern, direct or indirect, in supply from North America. The function of the Committee was to co-ordinate policy and action as between these ministries. Most of the work, however, fell upon the Chairman and the Central Office since the meetings of the committee itself were irregular and infrequent. It met only twice after the end of August and held in all only six meetings. Since it was not attended by Ministers, the Committee was not effective in dealing with the more serious clashes of interest between departments such as occurred over the allocation of machine tools. A sudden flurry of cables from Washington early in October 1940, showed the close connection which existed between such diverse matters as machine tools, pilot training, and the production of munitions and of aircraft. The Committee was ineffective as regards aircraft since the Ministry of Aircraft Production did not co-operate closely with it. In December when the War Cabinet decided to set up the British Supply Council in North America with Purvis as Chairman, it took the opportunity to reshape the North American Supply Committee by making it a committee of the three Supply Ministries. The War Cabinet directed that communications from London with the British Supply Council should be directed through a new North American Supply Committee in London 'domiciled in the Ministry of Supply'. The Minister of Supply was named Chairman; and the other members of the Committee were the First Lord of the Admiralty and the Minister of Aircraft Production. To ensure that the interests of other Departments, with a less direct concern in North American supply, were not forgotten, the War Cabinet provided that they should receive the relevant papers of the Committee and have the right to attend its meetings when they considered that their interests were involved. The new North American Supply Committee, however, promised to be no more active than the old. In February 1941 Purvis was told by the head of the Central Office that the Committee was 'not a very active body; in fact it has never formally met and it is quite conceivable that it never will'. Nevertheless, although it met very rarely, it served as an umbrella for action. Cables and papers were exchanged in its name with the British Supply Council and its papers were circulated by officials of the Central Office. Problems of a more important kind were settled informally by the officials with the individual Ministers who composed the Committee.

(ii)

The Victory of Autonomy

The problem of co-ordination in Washington had meanwhile come to a head, and had been solved for the time being by the concentration of still greater authority in Purvis as Chairman of the new British Supply Council created in mid-December 1940. Already in October Sir Arthur Salter, Chairman of the North American Supply Committee in London, had referred to Purvis as a 'kind of Economic Ambassador', and had compared his position with that occupied by Lord Northcliffe and Lord Reading in the last war. Purvis and the Ambassador were now 'the two outstanding British personalities in the United States'.[1] The setting up of the British Supply Council, whilst it strengthened the hands of Purvis, also reinforced the tendency of departments in London to set up their own independent missions in the United States. The creation in October 1940 of an independent British Air Commission was the opening wedge. Already in June 1940 the Minister of Aircraft Production, Lord Beaverbrook, had sent Mr Morris Wilson to Ottawa and the United States to act as his personal representative. The Minister corresponded directly with his representative and sent orders for aircraft through him. Close relations were maintained between Morris Wilson and Purvis and the latter took the leading part in all important negotiations. But, as the trouble over machine tools had shown, the existence of two major supply Missions was bound to create complications. Moreover the contracts for aircraft were on

---

[1] See also *North American Supply, op. cit.,* Chapter IV.

a much larger scale than those for munitions.[1] In the autumn the growing independence of the Air Commission was already becoming a source of embarrassment in Washington. A third but smaller permanent mission was already in existence in the shape of the British Admiralty Technical Mission at Ottawa. It conducted some supply operations through the British Purchasing Commission, but was soon to be subordinated to the British Admiralty Delegation in Washington.

Besides these permanent missions a flock of temporary visiting missions had descended on Washington after the fall of France. Before the summer of 1940 was out there were no less than eight or ten separate British missions operating in North America. The Ambassador reported some bewilderment amongst the Americans and the Prime Minister called for a list. 'I should like', he commented, 'to clarify and simplify this network of commissions'. The list showed, in addition to the three permanent missions mentioned above, three separate military missions which had been sent over to assist Purvis in dealing with types of weapons to be produced in the United States. There was also an Admiralty merchant shipbuilding mission engaged in negotiations with American shipbuilders. An important scientific mission had also been sent to the United States and Canada under Sir Henry Tizard; and there was an important *ad hoc* mission led by Sir Walter Layton. When he received the list the Prime Minister called for 'a considerable tidying up'. Some of the missions were to be brought back as quickly as possible, and the general control of Purvis was to be strengthened. Sir Walter Layton was instructed to look into the question of British organisation in the United States. 'It is one of the objects of your mission', the Prime Minister wrote, 'to put Mr Purvis fully into the picture'.[2] The upshot was Sir Walter Layton's proposal in mid-November for the setting up in Washington of a British-North American Supply Council which should co-ordinate the requirements of the three Services and be responsible for dealing with matters of general purchasing policy. The three existing missions representing the three Services would be members of the Council.[3] Purvis as Chair-

---

[1] On 1st November 1940 British aircraft contracts of all kinds totalled $1,262 million as against $883 million for all other products – munitions, ships, machine tools and raw materials.

[2] The Prime Minister agreed at the same time that Purvis should come to London – he would be delighted to have a chance to see him. The visit was not possible, however, until mid-November – after the fateful American election was over.

[3] It was also suggested that representatives of the Ministry of Shipping, of the Canadian Department of Munitions and Supply and of any missions visiting the United States from time to time should serve on the Council as associate members. In practice the responsible heads of various British supply organisations in Washington were already falling into the habit of meeting regularly each week in the late autumn of 1940 to discuss questions of common interest. These meetings were attended by Purvis, Morris Wilson, Monnet, Sir Henry Self and Sir Walter Layton after his arrival. See *North American Supply*, *op. cit.*, Chapter VI.

man should be the sole spokesman on matters of policy with the United States administration. The 'direct responsibility of the missions' to their London ministries and their direct access to the corresponding agencies of the American Government should be safeguarded. Sir Walter Layton noted in a covering letter to Purvis that without such safeguards the scheme would 'go to shipwreck in London', in the opinion of all the responsible heads in Washington. But the emphasis on autonomy and direct contact made it all the more vital, he pointed out, 'that the work of the missions should be co-ordinated, that they should pursue a common line of action in matters of general policy and that British requirements should be presented to the United States administration through a common channel'.

Purvis left just after for London and negotiated these proposals with the Ministries in London; and he did not find their passage easy. The Ministry of Supply and the Admiralty felt that the right course was to set up a single supply mission representing all departments. The Ministry of Aircraft Production on the other hand thought that the proposals went too far and might infringe upon its complete control over all matters relating to air supplies. The result was a temporary deadlock in the North American Supply Committee which Purvis had to break by direct discussions with the three Supply Ministers. He secured the approval of Lord Beaverbrook to the scheme in substance and the War Cabinet adopted it with minor drafting changes on 12th December. Under the scheme as explained to the missions in Washington in a cabled message:

> The three Supply Ministries were to retain separate organisations in the United States for the purpose of dealing with their supply requirements. The head of each of these organisations would be a member of the British Supply Council in North America. The Supply Ministries would communicate with their representatives direct, and complete information about these communications would be at the disposal of the Council. The Council in harmony with H.M. Ambassador would deal with all issues of policy concerning supply including all representations made to the United States Administration.

In practice these instructions gave the Council no overriding authority. Harmony with the Ambassador was secured by consultation and by his attendance at meetings of the Council. Press releases in London and Ottawa on the occasion of the first meeting of the British Supply Council on 15th January 1941 made clear some further points. Purvis was now to devote himself entirely to his new duties as Chairman of the Council, the role of Director General of the British Purchasing Commission being assigned to Sir Clive

Baillieu who would be a member of the Council. Monnet was co-opted as a member at large at this first meeting and remained a member until June 1943 when he resigned from British service in order to serve again in his own country. Morris Wilson, Lord Beaverbrook's personal representative, became Deputy Chairman of the Council. The Canadian Minister of Munitions and Supply became a member of the Council 'in view of the close interconnection between Canada and the United States programmes'; but the agreement of Ottawa was secured only after the British High Commissioner had explained that there was no intention of disturbing the direct relations between the Canadian Department of Munitions and Supply and the Departments in London.[1]

The setting up of the British Supply Council was thus a victory – won in the War Cabinet itself – for the policy of decentralisation in Washington. The idea of a single Minister of State, or Ambassador for Supply, was rejected in favour of a system of autonomous missions loosely linked by a Supply Council. The members of the Supply Council were the Directors of the Missions. Each Director remained responsible solely to the Minister of the parent Department in London, and each spoke for the Minister in direct negotiations with the corresponding agency of the American Government. The victory of departmental autonomy could hardly have been more complete.[2]

Nevertheless, limited though they were, the powers and functions of the British Supply Council were of some importance. The importance of the role of the Chairman is indicated in *North American Supply*. The distinct and permanent character of the new body was marked by separate premises; and by the possession of its own Secretariat, independent of the staff of the missions. Its administrative costs were carried on the votes of the Ministry of Supply. The Council was empowered under its charter to deal with 'all issues of policy concerning supply'. It was also to handle 'all representations made to the United States administration'. Thus it spoke for the British Government and was its channel for communications on all matters of general policy, especially those affecting more than one Ministry. The Council was careful to recognise and safeguard the autonomy of the Missions. Thus in March 1941, when the new Food and

---

[1] Canada's membership of the Supply Council in fact linked the Department of Munitions and Supply even more closely with the London Departments. Canada submitted statistical returns on all Canadian programmes to the Supply Council. The personal relations of the Minister with Purvis remained very close. The Minister remained a member until towards the end of the war; he very rarely if ever attended meetings of the Council.

[2] The Missions, indeed, were not always masters in their own fields. Thus during 1941 agents of the British Raw Materials Controls still continued to purchase on the American market, on direct instructions from the Ministry in London, and more often than not without the knowledge of the British Purchasing Commission.

Shipping Missions were to be set up, the Council noted that 'the new Missions should be independent as to their own activities as in the cases of the British Purchasing Commission and the British Air Commission, though similarly subject in matters of general policy to the Supply Council'. At the same time the Supply Council under its charter had the right to receive 'complete information' about communications between the Supply Ministries in London and their representatives in Washington. This was assured in large measure by the circulation to the Council of all the cables received or despatched by the Missions. To ensure that the Council was also informed of important correspondence exchanged between the Missions and the United States Government, the Council requested the heads of the Missions to forward to it copies of such correspondence. In practice this request was more honoured in the breach than in the observance. But the members of the Council made verbal reports at its weekly meetings, and the circulation of cables kept it in touch with any important communications to American agencies.

Whilst the Council sought to confine itself strictly to policy matters, leaving administrative detail to the Missions, it was forced at the outset to undertake certain administrative functions. These related mostly to matters closely linked with policy which affected all the Missions, such as legal issues, questions of priority, and many matters relating to the application of Lend-Lease, including programmes and the filing of Lend-Lease requisitions.[1] All Lend-Lease requisitions – United Kingdom, Commonwealth, and Allied – passed through the Supply Council where they were scrutinised, recorded and transmitted to the United States Government. A record was maintained of all subsequent transactions, e.g., amendments and transfers. The Supply Council (through its Records and Statistics Branch) forwarded to the American Government all British as well as Dominion and Allied Lend-Lease requirements programmes. The Records and Statistics Branch also prepared general statistical reports, including the data required in 1941 for the Victory Programme.

The necessity of the co-ordinating function of the British Supply Council became more and more clear as the British Missions continued to expand in number, size and complexity. The list of British Missions is given below with the dates of their formation.[2]

November 1939   British Purchasing Commission (initially a branch of the British Supply Board,

---

[1] Priorities were dealt with by a Supply Council Priorities Committee consisting of the heads of the Missions. The British Secretary of the Committee was the representative of the Supply Council on the United States Army Navy Munitions Board Priority Committee.

[2] The British sides of the combined bodies are not mentioned since these were mostly drawn from the Missions themselves.

	Ottawa; name changed to British Ministry of Supply Mission in July 1942).[1]
November 1939 and November 1940	Inspection Board (at first part of the British Purchasing Commission; absorbed in November 1940 in the Joint Inspection Board of U.K. and Canada).
September 1940	Exchequer and Audit.
October/November 1940	British Air Commission.
December 1940	British Supply Council.
January and May 1941	British Merchant Shipbuilding Mission (absorbed by the British Merchant Shipping Mission set up in May).
January and June 1941	'200 Military Mission' (advisory to the British Supply Council, absorbed by the British Army Staff in June).
January and June 1941	The British Army Staff (set up in June, absorbed various military missions including the '200 Military Mission').
March 1941	British Central Scientific Office (previously known as the Sir Henry Tizard Mission, merged in the British Commonwealth Scientific Office, midsummer 1944).
May 1941	British Food Mission.
April 1941	British Information Service (absorbed the British Library of Information – a pre-war organisation – and the British Overseas Press, set up in October 1940).

---

[1] After the dissolution in the summer of 1940 of the 'British Supply Board in Canada and the United States' its place was taken by small British Missions concerned with technical matters and liaison. Most of the business of procurement for the United Kingdom was undertaken by the Canadian Government. British requirements were notified by the Supply Ministries in London direct to the Canadian Department of Munitions and Supply. A small United Kingdom Technical Mission, made up of some of the officials of the British Supply Board, was attached to the office of the British High Commissioner. An Admiralty Technical Mission arrived in Ottawa in July 1940. It dealt with supply matters in the United States through the British Purchasing Commission. Aircraft matters were dealt with in Canada by Lord Beaverbrook's personal representative, Mr Morris Wilson, who arrived in Canada in June 1940. Other organisations which operated in Canada at various times included:

The United Kingdom Air Liaison (concerned with the British Commonwealth Air Training Plan).

The Joint Inspection Board of the United Kingdom and Canada covered inspection other than shipping and aircraft for both governments; Canada paid 70 per cent. and the United Kingdom 30 per cent. of the cost.

The British Army Staff, Canada (set up in September 1941; worked under the British Army Staff, Washington).

ATFERO (later Air Transport Command, R.A.F. and R.C.A.F.; responsible for ferrying aircraft across the North Atlantic).

British Ministry of Supply Mission (set up in December 1942; worked in close contact with the British Supply Mission and the British Raw Materials Mission, Washington).

British Food Mission, Ottawa Office (set up in February 1942; under the supervision of the British Food Mission of North America, Washington).

May 1941	British Petroleum Mission (merged in the Merchant Shipping Mission in January 1942).
June 1941	British Admiralty Delegation.
June 1941	Royal Air Force Delegation.
July 1941	British Colonies Supply Mission (at first called Colonial Supply Liaison).
August 1941	United Kingdom Commercial Corporation.
January 1942	British Raw Materials Mission.
Early in 1942	Board of Trade Delegation.
March 1942	Joint Staff Mission (set up as a separate Mission linking the three British Service Missions).
September 1942	Security Co-ordination.
1943	United Kingdom Treasury Delegation.[1]

Several of the countries of the British Commonwealth had representatives working with the British Purchasing Commission in the early part of the war. Separate offices were set up as follows:

March 1940	Dominion of Canada: Department of Munitions and Supplies in New York (Washington Office set up in October 1940).
July 1940	Union of South Africa Government Supply Mission.
April 1941	New Zealand Supply Mission.
August 1941	Indian Supply Mission (first in New York, later in Washington).
January 1942	Southern Rhodesia Mission.
January 1942	Newfoundland Supply Representative.
January 1942	Australia War Supplies Procurement Mission.

The British-American staff talks early in 1941, followed by the stationing in Washington of representatives of the British Chiefs of Staff and the setting up of the three British Service Missions, widened the problem of co-ordination. There were now three main British centres in Washington – the Embassy, the British Supply Council and the Joint Staff Mission, each separated from the other

---

[1] A representative of the United Kingdom Treasury, Sir Frederick Phillips, was stationed in Washington from November 1940. He was assisted from time to time by other officials from the Treasury. The Treasury Delegation – never more than 5 or 6 officials – dealt with matters of financial policy in relation to the United States Government and advised the British Missions on such matters. A subordinate Treasury establishment branch, dealing with administration and establishment matters, was created early in 1942. This step followed the despatch by the War Cabinet of a Treasury official to investigate the problems created by the rapid expansion of British staff. An establishment Offices Committee, composed of establishment officers of all the missions, was set up in March 1942 to co-ordinate establishment matters, including questions of recruitment, conditions of service, salary scales and many other matters of common interest. A Directorate of Common Services was set up under the Treasury Establishment representative. Services centralised wholly or in part included mail room, car pool, transportation, telephones, mimeographing and typing services, security guards, staff records.

by a distance of several miles. The British Supply Council seemed to be too limited for efficient co-ordination. The original plan of the War Cabinet confined the Council to the three Supply Missions representing the three Supply Ministries. Apart from the Chairman and Vice-Chairman, and the member at large (Monnet), all the members of the Council (including its Canadian member) had administrative responsibility for some aspect of supply from North America. The Council was to work 'in harmony with the Ambassador'; but he was never formally a member, although he began to attend meetings towards the end of April 1941. The British Treasury representative (Sir Frederick Phillips, whose influence on the supply side in the years ahead was to be second only to that of Purvis) attended meetings of the Council from the beginning; but he, too, was not formally a member. No provision had been made for the attendance of representatives of the armed services.

Early in April 1941, the Ambassador spoke to Purvis about the steps needed to pull the different British activities more closely together. The Ambassador saw a 'danger of real confusion and waste of time and effort. There are now so many different British Missions over here, many of them dealing with questions more or less closely related'. The need of co-ordination on the British side was all the greater, he noted, in view of 'lack of co-ordination among the American authorities and their tendency to dispose of matters by "off the record" conversations rather than through the normal channels'. This led to two results: first, the regular attendance by the Ambassador at meetings of the British Supply Council; secondly, an arrangement whereby the Ambassador summoned occasional meetings at the Embassy attended by the Chairman and members of the Supply Council and the heads of the Service Missions and the Service Attachés.[1] Co-ordination between the British civil and military missions was discussed early in May between the British Supply Council and members of the Military Missions. A British Staff Mission, consisting of representatives of the First Sea Lord, the Chief of the Imperial General Staff and the Chief of the Air Staff, had recently been organised in Washington; and a similar Staff Mission, representing the United States Chiefs of Staff, had been set up in London. The functions of the two Staff Missions, the Supply Council was informed on 7th May, were 'to represent jointly their own Chiefs of Staff vis-à-vis the Chiefs of Staff of the country in which the Mission was situated, for the purpose of collaborating in the formulation of military policies and plans.' In addition the British Staff Mission in Washington was available to advise the British Supply Council on the strategical aspects of supply matters.

---

[1] The meetings continued to be held from time to time throughout the war. They were never formally organised and a record was very rarely made.

One important matter of this kind was referred to in this meeting of the Council. A senior British officer representing General Wavell was in Washington to present to Hopkins as Lend-Lease Administrator an important document. This was a statement of war supplies needed from the United States by the British forces in the Middle East theatre over the next three or four months. It was agreed that in such a case British Naval and Military Officers should first prepare the ground by discussing the operational side with the United States Joint Chiefs of Staff; they would indicate what war supplies the United Kingdom itself was providing for this theatre. It was an unusual procedure for a theatre commander to make a direct approach to Washington for military supplies. It was agreed that the memorandum indicating in detail British requirements should be signed by General Wavell's representative; it should then be presented to the United States Secretaries of War and Navy by Purvis, as Chairman of the British Supply Council, jointly with the Washington representatives of the Chief of the Imperial General Staff.[1]

Early in June 1941 the question of a further major step to co-ordinate the military and supply side was raised by the Foreign Office with the Ambassador. The Joint Staff conversations earlier in the year had recommended – the Foreign Office pointed out – that each country should set up in the capital of the other a 'central agency to supervise and co-ordinate the activities of all its own non-military councils, missions or commissions. . . .' It was further recommended that when these non-military bodies needed military advice they should seek it through the military missions. Some machinery of a slightly more formal kind than then existed might meet the need of a 'central agency'; and it was suggested that the Ambassador and Purvis might discuss the matter with the British Military Mission. The alternatives seen by London were 'some cut and dried scheme' or to let the organisation 'develop gradually'. Neither the Ambassador nor Purvis, however, saw any use for a new central agency. The Ambassador saw 'obvious practical difficulties' in an agency which would co-ordinate the many British civilian organisations – including the Embassy and the Consulates – already functioning in the United States. All that seemed necessary, he suggested to Purvis, was to ensure that the different missions and agencies kept each other informed of the main lines on which they were working and on their progress in their day-to-day relations

---

[1] See page 24. The memorandum was accompanied by a Schedule of Requirements in the form of a 'Balance Sheet' showing:
 Total estimated requirements.
 Anticipated U.S. production on British contracts and Lend-Lease.
 Estimated shipments of material from United Kingdom during period involved.
 Deficiency to be supplied by United States if possible.

with the American authorities; and this simply meant continuing to see that 'papers of common interest are circulated to the different Missions and having regular meetings between the heads of the different Missions'.[1] Purvis thought that the meetings should be both regular and frequent. But the Ambassador was inclined rather to 'let them develop naturally . . . I am still afraid of them tempting those who attend to try to do one another's work'. He agreed, however, on fortnightly meetings.

The suggestion of a 'central agency' was discussed from the military angle in July and August 1941 by the British Joint Staff Mission. The result was a scheme, of which nothing came, for a British War Board over which the Ambassador would preside and on which the heads of the civil and military missions would sit. The Joint Staff Mission agreed that there were serious objections and dangers in the idea of a British Minister of State in Washington to co-ordinate the civil and military sides. Thus the whole idea of a 'central agency' on the British side in Washington fell by the way-side.[2]

The question of supply arrangements came up in the renewed Joint Staff discussions held during the Atlantic Conference of the President and the Prime Minister. The American Staff representatives complained that the British Joint Staff Mission in Washington and the 'Purchasing Commissions' did not work hand in glove. American authorities were receiving conflicting requests for material through more than one channel and without proper indications as to the relative importance of the different requirements. If British requirements could come through the British Joint Staff Mission there would be clearer indications as to the military grounds on which the figures were based. The same problem was discussed in Washington by the Ambassador, Lord Beaverbrook and the heads of the civil and Service missions in a meeting held on 17th August 1941 to examine the consequences of the death of Purvis a few days earlier. It was agreed at this meeting that the Supply Council should remain the supreme authority in supply matters. There should be no approach to the War and Navy Departments on supply by the

---

[1] The existing routine for papers was that the British Supply Council gave copies of all its cables to the Embassy and received in return all relevant Embassy cables. The Embassy circulated political telegrams to the Joint Staff Mission which sent copies of its own telegrams to the Embassy.

[2] The same fate was to befall the second piece of machinery suggested as a result of the Joint Staff talks in March 1941. This was the idea of an Anglo-American Supreme War Council to be set up if the United States entered the war. Already by August the British Joint Staff Mission had come to the conclusion, after studying the United States machinery of government, that here too the only wise course was to let any war machinery 'develop more or less automatically from the ever increasing contacts' between the authorities of the two countries in Washington. The final decision against a Supreme War Council was taken in Washington in January 1942. See *North American Supply, op. cit.*, Chapter IX.

British Service chiefs except on the terms and conditions defined by the Supply Council. The Service chiefs, however, would be independent of the Council on questions of strategy. Lord Beaverbrook reported later to the Prime Minister that General Marshall himself had given the advice that the British organisation for obtaining supplies in Washington should remain under civilian direction. There was an advantage to the United Kingdom, Lord Beaverbrook pointed out, if the control of supply remained in civilian hands since the balance was then more likely to be held even, as between British and American claims on American war production. The British Chiefs of Staff in London concurred; they held that if the Joint Staff Mission in Washington were to deal directly with the American political authorities, the American Chiefs of Staff would be by-passed. It was essential that there should be a 'channel of political approach' to the American authorities.

This line was taken by the War Cabinet when it discussed supply arrangements in Washington on 1st September 1941. The War Cabinet rejected the idea of submitting British requirements to the United States through military rather than civilian channels. Experience had shown, the Prime Minister noted in a memorandum, that representations to the United States should continue to be made by the British Supply Council. In order, however, to secure closer co-ordination between the Council and the Joint Staff Mission the following arrangements would take effect:

1. The Council would look to the heads of the Joint Staff Mission in Washington for advice on all technical and military matters.
2. The heads of the Joint Staff Mission would be responsible for making such representations as may be necessary to the War Department and the Navy Department on the strategical aspects of our supply needs.
3. The heads of the Joint Staff Mission would not initiate representations on supply matters without prior consultation with the Council.

At the same time the Service Ministers were to become members of the North American Supply Committee in London to ensure that the instructions which it gave to the British Supply Council and the Missions in Washington were based on strategic as well as supply considerations.

(iii)

The Defeat of Centralisation

The second problem facing the War Cabinet on 1st September 1941 was the appointment of a successor to Purvis. His death in a plane accident was referred to after the war by Mr Churchill in 'The Grand Alliance': 'Purvis was a grievous loss, as he held so many British, American and Canadian threads in his hands, and had hitherto been the directing mind in their harmonious combination'. A British member of the Supply Council Secretariat set down later his sense of the 'immense diminuendo' that followed the death of Purvis. In the years of war that were still to run no single person on the British side in Washington ever commanded in an equal degree the same prestige with the United States Administration, the British Missions in Washington and the Governments in London and Ottawa.

The problem was how to restore again something of the 'harmonious combination' which Purvis had achieved by his personality, and his unrivalled knowledge of the whole background. The co-ordination which his leadership produced was of the kind which no mere machinery could achieve. Lord Beaverbrook (then in Washington as Minister of Supply) and the Ambassador were asked on 16th August to consult and advise on a successor. At their meeting next day, with Mr C. D. Howe and the heads of the Service Missions amongst others, it was agreed that the danger of losing ground on the supply side through the loss of the unique connections and personal authority of Purvis could only be countered by the appointment of a Minister of State. It would be the business of such a Minister to carry on all negotiations on supply matters with the leaders of the United States Administration; he would have as his advisers the heads both of the civil and Service missions. The solution of a British Minister of State had the support also of the British Chiefs of Staff, who saw in it a better means of harmonising civilian and Service missions. Nevertheless, it was rejected by Ministers in London.

Lord Beaverbrook himself favoured appointing a Canadian or an Australian. He reported to the Prime Minister that the organisation in Washington was altogether too large: 'It has too many branches. Too many voices are speaking to the American Government'. What was needed, he suggested, was a 'central authority ruthlessly controlling supply staffs and confining representations on supply subjects to a single channel. This job requires a two-fisted man with a wallop'. To this the Prime Minister replied: 'You have not told me who your double-fisted giant is'. Discussions a week later in London between Ministers, in which Lord Beaverbrook played a leading part, resulted in the proposal to make two appointments to replace Purvis: that of Chairman and a new officer to be called 'President of the Supply Council'. The Prime Minister regarded this arrangement as unbusinesslike; but it was adopted in a modified form. On the recommendation of Lord Beaverbrook and the Ambassador,

Mr Morris Wilson (previously Vice-Chairman and Lord Beaver-brook's personal representative in the United States) was appointed Chairman and Mr E. P. Taylor (then the supply representative of the Canadian Government in Washington) 'Vice-Chairman and President'; the latter title, the Prime Minister was assured, was 'in common use on the American continent'. The allocation of duties between the two heads of the Supply Council was arranged in London in discussions between them and Lord Beaverbrook. 'The Vice-Chairman and President' was to be 'the chief executive officer of the Council responsible for the day-to-day business relating to supplies'.

The cabled news of the appointment of the Vice-Chairman and President, with powers that seemed at first sight to infringe on the autonomy of the Missions, created a minor crisis on the British side in Washington. The head of the British Purchasing Commission in a cable to the Minister of Supply assumed that his general responsi-bilities to the Minister would remain undisturbed. There was plain speaking at a meeting between the heads of the Missions and the two new officers of the British Supply Council. The new Chairman upheld the independent character of the Missions, whilst the 'Vice-Chairman and President' thought that his position gave him certain overriding responsibilities. The heads of Missions asserted their direct responsibility to their Ministers in London both for 'the function-ing and administrative conduct of their Missions'. Within these limits they welcomed the functions of the Council 'as co-ordinator and stimulator of the Missions'. The episode was a decisive victory for the principle of Mission autonomy; it might be challenged again, but the challenge was never very serious.[1]

The problem of co-ordination was still further complicated by the setting up of the Combined Boards and the Combined Chiefs of Staff in January 1942. This meant a large expansion of British and combined organisations in Washington, but without any personality to direct their 'harmonious combination', in the way Purvis might have done if he had lived. Once more the idea of a Minister of State was put forward. This time the War Cabinet made the suggestion in a message to the Prime Minister at sea.

> We hope [the message said] that all the British Missions in Washing-ton and all U.S. Missions in London, civilian and military alike, will be placed under the direction of a single Head who can speak with authority on behalf of His Majesty's Government. We are thinking in terms of someone of ministerial standing and responsible to his Government as a whole but without derogating from the position of the Ambassador.

The idea had some support from the British Chiefs of Staff. It

[1] The position of 'Vice-Chairman and President' was abolished at the end of 1942.

seemed to envisage a Joint Ministerial Defence Committee in each capital composed of the British and American Minister of State in that capital. But the scheme was regarded as impracticable and was dropped. On the American side General Marshall pointed out that it would be very difficult for an American Minister of State to function effectively in view of the fluid and shifting character of the American inter-departmental structure.

Moreover the proposal was rejected in no uncertain terms by the heads of all the British Supply Missions in Washington. The classical statement against it was made by Sir Arthur Salter in a letter to the Ambassador:

> The present organisation consists of separate technical missions, which (*a*) are under the *Ambassador's 'general supervision'* and so responsible to him as regards any aspects of their work which involve the political relations of the two countries; (*b*) are *co-ordinated*, on questions of principle and procedure which are common to the several Missions (but are *not* instructed on their specialised policies) through a Supply Council of which the head of each Mission is a member; (*c*) are *instructed* on their specialised policies by their respective Ministers at home; and (*d*) subject to the above, negotiate directly with the respective technical departments of the U.S. administration. The general principle of this organisation is to place combined shipping and supply arrangements between two countries engaged in a common war effort on an *administrative* as distinct from a diplomatic basis. Instead of a request, e.g. for ships, having to be made by the specialist Ministry of War Transport through first the Embassy and then the State Department before it reaches the 'opposite number' of the British Ministry – (i.e. going through two offices, which are not specialists in shipping) – it goes direct.

The basis of this system, he pointed out, would be impaired, if not destroyed, by the appointment of a Minister of State with overriding authority. The efficiency of each Mission would be undermined. 'The authority of the Ambassador, of the Departmental Ministries in London, and of the Heads of Missions here, would all be displaced or impaired'. The new system would probably break down 'through a collision of authority between the Minister here and the Departmental Ministers in London'. He gave a concrete illustration:

> In deciding whether I should ask for more tankers, I should ask for the new Minister's authority and not Lord Leathers'. Will he decide? If so, Lord Leathers is displaced. Will he refer to Lord Leathers? If so, the only effect had been to interpose a new unspecialised Minister between myself as Parliamentary Secretary and my own Minister. A similar result would follow as regards relations with the U.S. Departments – i.e. an unspecialised intermediary would be interposed.

The only trace which the proposal left in the combined structure set up in January 1942 seems to have been the position assigned by the Prime Minister to Sir John Dill, whom the Prime Minister left in Washington as his representative in his capacity as Minister of Defence. Sir John Dill was to have certain undefined civil functions, the general idea being that he should promote better co-ordination between the civil Combined Boards and Missions and the Combined Chiefs of Staff. For this purpose he was given a civilian assistant with the rank of permanent under-secretary. These functions never developed. Sir John Dill served, however, as Vice-Chairman of the Ambassador's informal meetings between the heads of the civil and Service missions; and these meetings now became more important. The continued inability of the Supply Council to close the gap between the civil and military missions diminished its usefulness as a co-ordinating body. Sir John Dill made it clear in March that he was opposed to the Supply Council having any formal responsibility for co-ordination outside supply matters. The tendency was, therefore, to turn back to the Ambassador. An understanding was reached between the civil and military sides early in April that the Ambassador's informal meetings would discuss policy matters above the level of supply; whilst 'co-ordination at the supply level, that is between the Ambassador, the Joint Staff Mission and the Supply Council (was) effected by attendance at weekly Supply Council meetings of the Ambassador and the representative of Sir John Dill as well as by the heads of the Joint Staff Mission. . . .'

(iv)

The British Supply Council and the Combined Boards

Some of the discussions in the first half of 1942 leading up to the creation of the Combined Production and Resources Board have been referred to in the preceding chapter.[1] The setting up of the new Board complicated matters by seeming to create a fourth candidate for the role of co-ordinator: the other three being the Ambassador, the Supply Council and the military side. It also threatened frontier conflicts between several of the Boards. The preliminary discussions in Washington up to early June pointed to a continuation of the Supply Council on its existing basis, but with the Ambassador playing a stronger part as co-ordinator; more frequent meetings – if

---

[1] See also *North American Supply, op. cit.,* Chapter IX.

possible weekly – were to be held at the Embassy. The Ambassador himself continued to be reluctant to act as co-ordinator; this he regarded as mainly the business of the Supply Council. On the other hand he gave warning that anyone coming from the United Kingdom expecting to exercise control over the heads of the Missions, themselves appointed by and responsible to their respective Ministries in London, might find himself in serious difficulties. (Here it should be noted that the heads of the Missions in a number of cases were not civil servants. They were men drawn from business and public life, accustomed to independence, and ready to defend the autonomy of their Missions by threats of resignation.) After examining the situation in Washington in June 1942 the Minister of Production, Mr Oliver Lyttelton, reported to the War Cabinet that there was no room in Washington for a Minister of State with overriding powers. Such a Minister would be liable, he thought, to become a fifth wheel of the coach. The heads of the Missions must argue their own cases before the United States Administration and they could do it better than any Minister could do it for them.[1]

The Minister reported also on the need for better co-ordination between the Missions and the Boards. To this end he suggested several steps: first, visits by the Minister of Production several times a year to the United States; second, reorganisation of the North American Supply Committee in London. The latter, he wrote, 'has not been functioning as a live and effective body'. Thus it had failed to furnish the Supply Council with information on matters of general policy.[2] The changes made in the London Committee, however, proved to be of a minor character and it still continued to be a body which rarely met. Its Secretariat was strengthened and membership was extended to the Canadian Government since a Canadian Minister was a member of the British Supply Council in Washington. The terms of reference of the Committee were widened, since its field was no longer one merely of supplies from the United States, but of the better distribution of combined resources. It could now deal with questions of Anglo-American economic and supply policy outside the scope of any one department, including matters

---

[1] The Chairman of the Supply Council in a minute despatched to London at this time pointed out that whilst a Cabinet Minister fresh from London carried great weight, because he represented the latest views of the British Government, such special authority decayed rapidly in Washington and would be lost in a month or two.

[2] The Chairman of the Supply Council complained that he was receiving neither information nor papers from the War Cabinet; he had no background reports and was therefore hampered seriously in carrying out the work of co-ordination which the Council had to perform in Washington. Steps taken to remedy this situation included the preparation in London from August onwards of a document entitled 'Anglo-American Weekly Notes' designed to give the members of the British Supply Council background information on matters of policy affecting the work of the Supply Missions. Various London papers, including those of the North American Supply Committee and the Allied Supplies Executive, were also circulated to the Chairman of the Supply Council.

arising out of the work of the various Combined Boards. Whilst the British Supply Council in Washington was now expected to be more active in co-ordinating the British sides of the Combined Boards, the final authority in such matters continued to rest with the North American Supply Committee.

In the third place Mr Lyttelton proposed that his deputy on the Combined Production and Resources Board in Washington (Sir Robert Sinclair) should be appointed Chairman of the British Supply Council.[1] This combination, however, was regarded in Washington as impracticable. One reason was the feeling that the two positions were too distinct in character and covered too much ground to be combined by a single person. The work of the Chairman of the British Supply Council involved a considerable amount of detail; whilst the role assigned to the Combined Production and Resources Board, under the directive of 9th June, was on such an ambitious scale that its British Head was expected to have his hands more than full. Moreover the proposal, combined with the special position which the War Cabinet seemed to assign to the Minister's deputy in Washington, appeared to threaten the autonomy of the Missions and the British sides of the Combined Boards. According to the War Cabinet decision, as communicated to the British Missions in Washington:

> The Heads of the Supply Missions (other than the Food Mission), while remaining responsible in their procurement work to their respective Ministries in London, should follow any directions which Sir Robert Sinclair, under his (the Minister's) authority, might find it necessary to give them in the fulfilment of his functions.

The members of the Joint Staff Mission were also enjoined to co-operate with Sir Robert Sinclair in his task. In the end the proposal to appoint the Minister's deputy as Chairman of the British Supply Council was dropped. He became an ordinary member of the Council. Mr Robert Brand (later Lord Brand) was to carry on as Chairman 'for the time being'. For six months, therefore, there was an element of uncertainty in British organisation on two points, the status of the Chairman of the Supply Council and the frontiers between the Combined Production and Resources Board and some of the other Combined Boards. The British head of the Combined Raw Materials Board noted a little later that there were now three high British officials in Washington 'all heading up to the Minister of Production; and with rather moving frontiers'. The three were himself, the Minister's deputy on the Combined

---

[1] The post of Chairman had been held since the resignation of Mr Morris Wilson in April by a temporary chairman, Mr R. H. Brand, who in fact continued to hold the position until his place was taken in December 1942 by the new Resident Minister for Supply.

Production and Resources Board and the Chairman of the British Supply Council.

Several more months were needed to fix the 'moving frontiers' between C.P.R.B. and C.R.M.B., and to remove the fear that the latter might be absorbed by the former.[1] This account deals only with the problem as seen by the British sides of two Boards. The British correspondence from Washington with London had much to say about the difficulties with which their American colleagues on the Boards had to contend: e.g. the tense fight for raw materials between the agencies, and the difficulties encountered by the American side of the Combined Production and Resources Board in attempting to carry out the Board's charter. A high officer of the British Raw Materials Mission noted in a letter to London in October 1942, that the United States were 'still somewhat chaotic in their war organisation'. But he prophesied correctly that in three or four months the situation would have improved greatly: '. . . we will find that they are not short of raw materials at all, and . . . are amassing munitions at a much faster rate than they can use them anywhere near the enemy'. Meanwhile British officials on both Boards and their opposite numbers in London were concerned about the undefined frontier between the Boards and the danger of conflicts of jurisdiction. '. . . We have not yet got a proper understanding', the same official added, 'about whether the relations on common subjects are to resemble those in the Athanasian creed or whether they (i.e. C.P.R.B.) are to be in the end predominant; or whether it will be possible to divide the labours'.

The head of the Raw Materials Department in the Ministry of Production had reported a few days earlier that the Minister 'was very anxious for the two Boards to function in parallel and with equal responsibility'. The allocation of raw materials should be a function not of C.P.R.B., but of C.R.M.B. – a point on which W. L. Batt the American head of the latter was in complete agreement. Any jurisdictional difficulty was in fact between the two Boards as a whole rather than between their two British sides. The British Executive Secretary of C.R.M.B. noted that . . . 'things are probably more difficult on the American side than ours'. In November the Minister was advised by the head of his Raw Materials Department that it was important to maintain intact the work of the C.R.M.B. It had acquired an effective 'operating technique',

---

[1] The likelihood that the fitting of the new Combined Production and Resources Board into the existing context of the Combined Boards would cause some disturbance had been foreseen for some months. The British heads in Washington of the Joint Aircraft Committee and the Combined Raw Materials Board (who were also the heads of the corresponding supply missions) both pointed out that it was unwise to interfere with successful existing combined bodies which had a clear jurisdiction and good connections with the American agencies. They had the full support in this matter of their American opposite numbers.

whilst C.P.R.B. as yet had 'not succeeded in developing any operating methods at all . . . The United Kingdom simply cannot afford for some months to come for the operational wires to be crossed on raw materials. At present no decisions of the Combined Raw Materials Board have been challenged and the materials have continued to flow'.

The most critical point on the frontier between the two Boards was steel; and here the powers of the two Boards were clarified, so far as the British side was concerned, by an exchange of notes between Sir Clive Baillieu and Sir Robert Sinclair towards the end of November. Steel, it should be noted, was not under the Combined Raw Materials Board.[1] But the procurement of steel from the United States was the responsibility of the British Raw Materials Mission under Sir Clive Baillieu who was also the British Head of C.R.M.B. 'My responsibility for steel in the B.R.M.M.', Sir Clive wrote in the exchange of letters, 'is such that I cannot, except under the express direction of the Minister, allow it to be dealt with operationally by the Combined Production and Resources Board'. The way out of a possible clash of jurisdiction between the two Boards was found by the device of the Combined Steel Committee, which reported to both Boards and on which both were represented.[2] This was the forerunner of half a dozen other combined committees set up in 1943 for other raw materials. These were frontier devices of the same kind as the Combined Steel Committee. The frontier agreement between the two Boards on steel, which formed part of the exchange of letters, provided that the production of steel and the maintenance of the general flow of steel supplies was the concern of the Combined Raw Materials Board. The Combined Production and Resources Board on the other hand was concerned with the flow of manufactured steel to manufacturers, i.e. 'the review and co-ordination of end product programmes'. Direct negotiation by the United Kingdom on steel supplies from the United States was the peculiar concern of the British Raw Materials Mission.

(v)

The Mature Organisation

Between August and December 1942 the British War organisation in North America became stabilised in its final form. The main

---

[1] The British Executive Secretary of the Board wrote in October that to have attempted in the early days to cover steel would 'probably have killed the Board'.

[2] The War Production Board (Steel Division), the Minister of Production and the Department of Munitions and Supply (Ottawa) were also represented on the Committee. It was set up first as an interim body on 2nd October 1942.

element in the process of stabilisation was the restoration of the
British Supply Council to something like its original importance as
the chief co-ordinating authority on the British side in Washington.
Its directive was redrafted to define its role more clearly. The
relations between the British Supply Council and the Embassy on
the one hand and the Service Missions on the other were strengthened. The process was completed by two developments at the end
of the year. One, which had been under discussion for some time,
was the creation of a civil secretariat – modelled on the lines of the
War Cabinet Secretariat in London – which was attached to the
British Supply Council. The other, which is referred to below, was
the sudden and unexpected step taken by the War Cabinet in
appointing a Resident Minister for Supply in Washington.

As one after another of the possible competitors was eliminated,
the choice was narrowed down to the Supply Council as the main
co-ordinating body on the British side in Washington. A Minister of
State with overriding powers found no favour. The idea that the
Combined Production and Resources Board might play a large part
in co-ordinating the Combined Boards was soon abandoned, partly
because of opposition from both the British and American sides in
Washington and partly because C.P.R.B. itself failed to secure the
co-operation of the American Army and Navy in carrying out its
principal task. For a time there were still lingering hopes that the
Ambassador might be induced to act as a co-ordinating authority.
He still held ministerial rank as a member of the War Cabinet and
was regarded by all the missions, civil and military, as neutral enough
to refrain from attempting to infringe their autonomy; and he was
already playing a limited part as co-ordinator in the Supply Council
and by means of informal meetings which he held from time to time
at the Embassy. For a time the latter seemed to contain a germ of
something bigger. Plans to set up a body of a more formal kind to be
called the Ambassador's Council, with a central secretariat linking
the civil and military sides, were suggested at various times in
Washington during the summer of 1942 and they found some favour
in London. The idea was a body somewhat like the Minister of
State's Council in the Middle East. It was to be composed of Sir
John Dill (representing the Combined Chiefs of Staff and the
Combined Munitions Assignments Board) and the four heads of the
civilian Combined Boards. It was to have a joint civil and military
secretariat drawn from the British Supply Council and the Joint
Staff Mission and was to report direct to the North American
Supplies Committee in London. To the British Supply Council
would be left merely the task of co-ordinating the civil missions and
handling Lend-Lease and area questions. The failure of this line
of approach was marked by a War Cabinet Office minute at the

end of September 1942: 'The Ambassador has consistently declined to act as a Minister or High Commissioner overseeing the activities of all British representatives'. If, the minute pointed out, there had been some one on the British supply side whom all accepted as a leader, 'it would have been possible to attach to him a central secretariat, embracing military and civil, modelled on War Cabinet lines'.[1]

Thus by a process of elimination the British Supply Council, nearly a year after the death of Purvis, emerged again as the only body which could play an important part as an organ of co-ordination. The decline of the Council after the death of Purvis was commented on in a War Cabinet minute in December 1942: 'Under Arthur Purvis the Supply Council was the Board of Directors of the British Supply Missions, with Purvis as both Chairman and Managing Director'. After his death, however, the Council became merely a 'weekly forum at which the Heads of Missions discussed as much or as little of their major problems as they felt like bringing up'. By the time a new Chairman took over in the spring of 1942, the minute noted:

> the position had been altered by the United States entry into the war and the creation of the Combined Boards. The latter development automatically made it impossible for the Supply Council to be the channel for negotiations with the United States Government on a large range of important supply problems even had the status of the Council vis-à-vis the Missions allowed it. The Heads of the Missions were, however, most suspicious of any attempt on the part of the Supply Council to get back into an executive position and if the Supply Council was to perform a useful function it was necessary to gain the confidence of the Missions by letting them come to the Council with their common problems rather than by trying to force them to do so.

This was the policy which was now being adopted successfully. Since experience had shown that neither the civil nor the military side would accept supervision by the other, and both rejected with equal firmness the idea of a Minister of State with overriding powers, the only thing left was for the two sides to work together as equals.

---

[1] The idea of a central secretariat was not abandoned, however, and was eventually achieved at the end of the year in the form of the civil secretariat attached to the British Supply Council. In August a step towards linking the British civil and military sides in connection with the planning of war production was taken by the setting up of the British War Supplies Committee. This was a Committee of the British Supply Council. It considered any major question of policy affecting supply in so far as it concerned the Combined Production and Resources Board. The Minister's deputy on the Board was its Chairman. It had a joint secretariat, the civil side of which was supplied by the Supply Council and the military side by the Joint Staff Committee. The British War Supplies Committee corresponded to the Joint War Production Staff in London and exchanged papers with it. See also *History of the Second World War, United Kingdom Civil Series*, J. D. Scott and Richard Hughes, *Administration of War Production* (Part V, Chapter III, iii).

Steps were taken in August 1942 to make the heads of the three
Service Missions full members of the Supply Council. In October
the Secretary of the Joint Staff Mission reported that things were
running much more smoothly between civil and military missions.

In order to strengthen the Supply Council its terms of reference
were redefined in August by the North American Supply Committee and the War Cabinet. As the new terms of reference governed
the activities of the Supply Council until the end of the war, and with
one additional clause became in December 1942 the terms of
reference of the Resident Minister for Supply, the full text may be
given:

1.   The Supply Council, in harmony with His Majesty's Ambassa-
     dor, will consider questions of policy or procedure arising out of
     the work of Civilian Combined Boards or Committees estab-
     lished in Washington and deal with matters of common interest
     to the various British Missions in North America. The Supply
     Council will be responsible for seeing that action is taken on other
     Anglo-American economic and supply problems which are not
     covered by the existing machinery.

2.   The various British members of the Civilian Combined Boards
     or Committees established in Washington will keep the Chairman
     of the Supply Council informed on the activities of the Board or
     Committee on which they represent the British Government.
     Questions concerning more than one Board and general matters
     of procedure and the relationship between the various Boards
     will be discussed at the Council. Thus, without derogation from
     the responsibility of the British representatives on the Board to
     their several Ministers, it will be the Council's function to secure
     the requisite co-ordination between the activities of the various
     British representatives on the Boards.

3.   The Chairman will report at regular intervals to the Chairman
     of the North American Supply Committee on the progress made,
     will make such suggestions as he deems wise, and will submit to
     him any questions arising on general policy.

4.   It will be the duty of the Chairman of the Council, by keeping
     in close touch with the Ambassador and the head of the Joint
     Staff Mission, to assist in ensuring proper co-ordination between
     all the civilian, military and other British representatives in
     Washington.

5.   The Chairman will be provided with the information necessary
     for the full discharge of his duties. This will include such informa-
     tion:

     (*a*) From London on matters of general economic and supply
          policy.

     (*b*) From other British representatives in Washington on the
          work of the Missions and of the Combined Boards or Com-
          mittees.

(c) Drawn from communications between London and the British Missions. The Chairman will impart to the British Missions any of the information referred to in (a) above which is necessary to their work.

The terms of reference of the Resident Minister, who was made Chairman of the Supply Council, were defined in identical terms except for the substitution of the words 'the Minister' for 'the Supply Council' in various parts of the text and the addition of a new paragraph:

6. In addition the Minister will be the Minister of Production's deputy in the United States of America except that he will not personally serve either upon the Combined Production and Resources Board or upon the Combined Raw Materials Board.

The new terms of reference thus extended the Council's field of co-ordination to the Civilian Combined Boards in Washington, and required the British members of each of the Boards to keep the Chairman of the British Supply Council informed on its activities. The Council was to co-ordinate; but without derogation from the responsibilities of the members of the Boards to their several Ministers. The Chairman of the Supply Council was to keep in close touch with the Ambassador and the head of the Joint Supply Mission; and he was to *assist* in ensuring co-ordination 'between all the civilian, military and other British representatives in Washington'.

The text bears the marks, in several of its qualifications and omissions, of objections raised by the Embassy and the Foreign Office that the terms as originally drafted were so wide that they infringed on the functions of the Embassy. The Embassy, as a minute by one of its staff pointed out, was 'the only constitutional representative of His Majesty's Government as a whole and . . . the only body charged with the management of Anglo-American relations in this country'. It was the Ambassador, who was also a member of the War Cabinet, who should deal with any questions of general economic policy rather than the Supply Council. Slight changes in the wording were made, therefore, in the terms of reference to preserve the constitutional position of the Embassy and to make it clear that the Supply Council was a forum for discussion rather than an executive body to which the British members of the Combined Boards were bound to report. The Foreign Office quoted the assurance given by the Minister of Production in the North American Supply Committee that 'it was not intended that the Supply Council should be regarded as the body to represent His Majesty's Government in negotiations with the United States Government on economic matters in general, e.g., post-war planning. Their interest in questions of general economic policy would be

Y

limited to those which bore on the work of the Missions and the various Combined Boards'. The Council and the Missions, the Ambassador pointed out, were primarily administrative bodies of limited range. He agreed that there was bound to be some overlapping, since it was not possible to draw any hard and fast lines; and he pointed out that the Missions and the Embassy had worked together smoothly enough in the past. It was the regular working practice of the Missions, as the Chairman of the Supply Council noted, to discuss with each other and with the Embassy any question which involved interests other than those of a particular Mission. On the other hand the complexities of American Government and the need of speed and efficiency made it essential in his view that the Missions and the British representatives on the Combined Boards should be free to approach directly their American opposite numbers.

A report by the Chairman of the Supply Council to the Minister of Production in mid-November 1942 showed definite progress in co-ordination. He was keeping in close touch with Sir John Dill and the British Ambassador. The military members and the Ambassador came regularly to the meetings of the Council. Thus all important British interests in Washington had now a regular clearing house for the discussion of matters of common concern. Relations between the Council and the civil and military missions were very harmonious. The civil and military sides were working together on matters of production in the British War Supplies Committee. A British-American 'Committee of the Combined Boards' had been set up to co-ordinate matters relating to North Africa; and the Council itself had a civil and military committee on North African questions as well as several other area committees. The responsibilities of the Chairman were being increased by putting various bodies under his direction. An example was the British Central Scientific Office whose secretariat was 'responsible administratively in Washington to the Chairman of the British Supply Council'.

In December 1942 the very rapid increase in North African business brought a further and final step in the organisation of the Supply Council, the decision to set up a Central or 'Civil Secretariat', as it was to be called. This step had been under discussion for several months. Thus an Embassy minute in November had referred to the need of a 'Civil Secretariat' which would co-ordinate the exchange of information between the Embassy, the Supply Council and the civil and service missions – 'some sort of more or less neutral body on the lines of the Cabinet Secretariat at home'. The suggestion had the support of the Joint Staff Mission. On 9th December the Ambassador reported that an impossible situation was arising on the administrative level as a result of the flood of work in connection with North and West Africa. A similar situation, he pointed out, would arise as the Allied armies liberated one territory after another. All the interests in Washington, including the British Supply Council, agreed that the situation called for a civil secretariat headed by a high official from the Embassy; he would be attached to the British Supply Council and would be responsible to the Ambassador, the Chairman of the Council and the heads of the civilian missions. A similar arrangement, the Ambassador noted, existed already on the military side where the Senior Military Secretary of the Joint Staff Mission was responsible to the Ambassador, the head of the Joint Staff Mission and the heads of the Service Missions.

By its terms of reference drafted in February 1943:

> The Civil Secretariat will occupy a position in relation to the Ambassador, the Resident Minister for Supply and the Heads of the United Kingdom Civil Missions in Washington analogous to that of the Civil War Cabinet Secretariat in London in relation to Ministers. It will work in close touch with the Embassy, the Joint Staff Mission and the United Kingdom Civil Missions.

Members of the staff of the British Supply Council whose functions were of a secretarial nature became part of the Supply Council Secretariat whilst officials with executive functions carried on as a small administrative secretariat known as the Supply Council Executive. The civil secretariat itself had no executive functions. It was a clearing house of information. All telegrams and papers affecting more than one British organisation in Washington passed through its hands. Its main task was to co-ordinate the day to day work of the civil missions and Combined Boards. In co-operation where necessary with the Joint Staff Mission, it served existing committees, or if necessary set up new committees to deal with matters of concern to more than one mission, such as particular areas and questions relating to relief and rehabilitation.

The increasing role of the staff of the British Supply Council and the growing number of Supply Council Committees serving the different missions and in turn served by the staff of the Supply Council was one of the reasons for the increasing use made of the Council and its growing influence. Without counting *ad hoc* committees, or working parties representing different missions, the British Supply Council Secretariat (i.e., the Civil Secretariat and the Supply Council Executive) was serving by 1943: the British War Supplies Committee, the Civil Supplies Committee, the Principal Commonwealth Supply Committee and its four separate sub-committees and seven 'area' Supply Committees (Committee on Supplies for Liberated and Conquered Territories, Committee on

African Economic Affairs, and Committees on Supplies to China,
Latin America, Middle East, Russia and Turkey).

Just as the civil secretariat was being initiated from Washington,
a sudden and unexpected development occurred late in November
1942 in London. As part of a reshuffling of a number of Cabinet
posts, the War Cabinet decided to appoint a Minister for Supply in
Washington. It was announced on 23rd November that Colonel
J. J. Llewellyn, then Minister of Aircraft Production, would fill 'the
post of Minister Resident in Washington for Supply and will be
responsible to Mr Lyttelton as Minister of Production under the
general aegis of H.M. Ambassador for work in relation to British
Missions and Combined Boards in Washington concerned with
supplies'. The appointment, according to private messages received
in Washington, was not the outcome of any careful consideration of
the need for such a post or of its scope and duties. When the terms
of reference were framed some weeks later it was decided – in
accordance with advice rendered from the British side in Washington
– that the only role which the Resident Minister could usefully fill
was that of Chairman of the British Supply Council. He was therefore made Chairman of the Council, with terms of reference identical
with those of the Council itself, except for the slight differences noted
in the text given above (p. 341). He was the Minister of Production's
deputy in Washington, but without any derogation from the position
of the heads of the Combined Raw Materials and the Combined
Production and Resources Boards. Moreover, in accordance with the
explanation given to the War Cabinet when it approved the appointment, the Minister Resident was not to intervene in regard to the
work of the Food Mission, or the British Merchant Shipping
Mission, except at the request of the Heads of these Missions. In the
case of all the Missions the direct responsibility of the Head of the
Mission to his Minister in London was not to be impaired. At least
one Head of a Mission sought private assurance on this point;
namely that 'the underlying responsibility (of the Missions) to their
respective Ministers will be preserved'. Apart from the new Resident
Minister's function of co-ordinator, and the exercising of a 'general
oversight' over the work of the three Supply Missions, the one specific
field which the War Cabinet mentioned as specially suitable for co-
ordination by him was 'area problems' such as North Africa.

Even with these safeguards for the Missions the terms of reference
of the Resident Minister still left him an important role; and he was
able to play it more effectively because the safeguards encouraged
the Missions to co-operate freely. Since the British Supply Council
was now headed by a Minister of War Cabinet rank its position was
strengthened. The British organisation in Washington had now
reached the form which it was to preserve almost unchanged until

the end of the war. The charts at the end of this chapter show the organisation in its earlier and later phases.

(vi)

The British Commonwealth in Washington

Parallel with the supply organisation of the United Kingdom a British Commonwealth organisation was built up gradually in Washington. The final step was taken in June 1943 when the Principal Commonwealth Supply Committee was set up parallel to the Commonwealth Supply Council in London. The supply organisation of the British Commonwealth as it stood in London and Washington was summed up towards the end of the war in the following statement made in the House of Commons:[1]

The special conditions created by the war have led to the setting up of new machinery to facilitate the discussion of supply and other problems arising out of the dislocation of normal trade. The most important of the bodies established for this purpose are the Commonwealth Supply Council and the London Food Council. The Commonwealth Supply Council was established to co-ordinate, within the framework of the combined war planning of the United Nations, problems arising within the British Commonwealth in regard to the production and requirements of raw materials (other than fuel and foodstuffs) and of finished goods, including plans, components and other things necessary for their manufacture. The London Food Council was set up, as a parallel body, to formulate in conjunction with the appropriate authorities plans of common concern to its members regarding the production, supply, movement, allocation and utilisation of foodstuffs and related products and of agricultural materials used for the production of such foodstuffs. Canada, because of her special position in relation to North American production and supply problems, does not take a direct part in the proceedings of these Councils, which are otherwise fully representative of the Commonwealth and Empire. The Commonwealth Supply Council and London Food Council carry out their detailed work mainly through Committees, dealing in the case of the former with broad categories such as raw materials, machine tools, railway equipment and non-munition supplies and in the case of the London Food Council with each of the principal foodstuffs in short supply, e.g., meat, oils and fats, and cereals. Joint Committees of the two Councils have been established to consider questions relating to such matters as fertilisers and food and farm machinery.

---

[1] Statement made on 2nd February 1945 in the House of Commons by the Under-Secretary of State for Dominion Affairs. H. of C. Deb., Vol. 407, Cols. 1747-48.

A Committee known as the Principal Commonwealth Supply Committee has been set up in Washington to deal with supply problems of concern both to the United Kingdom and other Commonwealth and Empire Supply Missions. The Committee, under the chairmanship of the United Kingdom Resident Minister for Supply, includes the heads of other Commonwealth and Empire Missions. It works in close conjunction with the Commonwealth Supply Council in London. In addition consultation on various war-time supply questions had been facilitated by bodies such as the Eastern Group Supply Council at Delhi (which does not however deal with supplies for civilians). Moreover certain supply departments here have had permanent Missions in some of the Dominions, such as the British Food Missions in Ottawa and Canberra, while Dominion Supply Departments have also arranged for special representatives in London.

During the war most of the normal machinery of the Commonwealth centred on London continued to function. Communications between the Governments by their High Commissioners in the various capitals and by documents, cables, correspondence, missions, visits and conferences of ministers and officials, were never interrupted. As always in the past most of the lines uniting the different parts of the Commonwealth continued to run through London. The war, however, made Washington an important, though still secondary, centre of Commonwealth communications. This was due to the importance of the United States as a source of armed strength and of war supplies, and to the concentration in Washington of the weight of the combined organisation. Since all parts of the Commonwealth had important business of a political, military and economic character to transact with the United States all the different members of the Commonwealth established their supply as well as diplomatic missions. Between these Commonwealth missions, diplomatic and economic, there were close links. Information was exchanged and there were regular consultations on problems of common interest. The senior member of the Commonwealth – the United Kingdom – acted freely for other members at their request in dealings with the United States Administration. In some matters Canada acted for the United Kingdom and occasionally for other parts of the Commonwealth. Visits by the British Prime Minister, and by members of the War Cabinet, to Washington were regularly the occasion of meetings and consultations with representatives of the other Commonwealth countries. Thus when the Prime Minister landed in Washington after Pearl Harbour, for his conference with the President, his first act was to go over the whole ground of the conference in advance with the representatives of the other members of the Commonwealth. Such visits usually included Ottawa and were the occasion for important consultations between the British and Canadian Governments. The routine, common in foreign capitals wherever countries of the British Commonwealth have missions, of regular meetings and consultations between their heads and staffs, became of special importance in Washington during the war.[1]

At the beginning of the war there was no clear evidence as to the attitude which the Administration would take towards the Commonwealth, especially towards any manifestations within the United States of group action by the members of the Commonwealth. The principle of direct and independent relations between the American Government and the different members of the Commonwealth had long been established. There was standing evidence of it in the separate legations maintained in Washington by some of the Dominions; and before the war was ended all parts of the Commonwealth were represented by their own diplomatic missions. The entry into the war in September 1939 of all members of the Commonwealth (save Eire) was a demonstration of unity. Moreover, the war was to afford in the national capital of the United States a continuous demonstration of the unity in diversity of the British Commonwealth of Nations. But at first the policy of the Administration towards the Commonwealth as such was obscure. Would the United States prefer to deal separately in all matters and at all times with each member of the Commonwealth? Would it foster the unity of the Commonwealth, or simply ignore it? Or would it on the contrary seek to weaken the relations between the United Kingdom and the overseas members in the hope perhaps of drawing them individually more closely to the United States? This latter possibility seemed to find some support in the well known phenomena of the rash of headlines across the country at any hint of disagreement between the United Kingdom and some overseas member of the Commonwealth.

The earlier chapters in *North American Supply* showed how steadily and strongly Administration leaders pressed from the outset for Commonwealth unity in the matter of supplies from the United States. This policy was continued throughout the war, despite occasional fleeting signs of a tendency in some agencies (e.g., in the matter of Lend-Lease supplies towards the end of 1941) to encourage purely bilateral supply relations. Outward manifestations of this policy of maintaining the Commonwealth as a force in world affairs, in the interest of the United States, were given from time to time in

---

[1] Some of the Commonwealth supply missions far outnumbered the small Embassies or legations maintained by their countries in Washington. These Supply Missions had their own direct relations with their home Ministries. The largest, the Australian Supply Mission, at its height had a staff of 600; and its relations with the small staff of the Australian Embassy were loose and distant.

official acts and proclamations.[1] Supply relations during the war
furnished innumerable proofs of the great administrative convenience, and the political and economic advantage to the United
States of the existence of the Commonwealth and Empire. Their
existence and their machinery for handling group relations greatly
facilitated global supply arrangements. The advantages were twofold. On the one hand Commonwealth machinery assured a steady
stream of supplies to the United States from all parts of the Commonwealth. On the other hand the machinery solved the problem of
securing the most economical distribution of essential supplies from
the United States to the various parts of the Commonwealth.

The fall of France strengthened rather than weakened the desire
of the Administration that the Commonwealth should use a single
channel in making demands for supplies from the United States.
Thus the British Embassy in Washington warned London in July
1940 that the Administration was insisting that 'the requirements of
the Commonwealth should be co-ordinated and presented as a
whole and dealt with through the British Purchasing Commission,
expanded into a Commonwealth Commission'. The fall of France
and the entry of Italy into the war brought the war much closer to
all parts of the Commonwealth and increased their supply pressures
on the United States. Since supplies from the United Kingdom
seemed likely to be cut off for a considerable time, fresh enquiries
and orders began to come to the United States from all the southern
Dominions as well as from India and Canada. The demand from the
United Kingdom, however, was far greater than that of the rest of
the Commonwealth put together. Moreover, the overseas members
of the Commonwealth, apart from Canada, had neither the volume
of requirements, nor the purchasing power, nor the direct and
influential connections with the Administration, nor the staff, to
operate effectively on the American market.

The British Government was willing and eager to meet the wishes
of the Administration for centralised purchasing. Purvis was told by
London in July 1940 that he should act as the spokesman for all the
Commonwealth countries, just as he had formerly acted for France
in negotiations with the Administration. But a 'Commonwealth
Purchasing Commission' would be open to objection, not merely
because it would be unwieldy in size, but also because it might
mean that questions of priority for supplies of munitions might tend
to be settled in the United States rather than in London. The
British Government was anxious that supplies from the United States
should be programmed in London, and when they became available
should be allocated there as between the different members of the

---

[1] For examples see H. Duncan Hall, 'The British Commonwealth as a Great Power',
Foreign Affairs, New York, July 1945.

Commonwealth. Purvis was instructed, therefore, that the British Purchasing Commission should not be transformed into a full Commonwealth Purchasing Commission, but that the close relations already established with the Canadian and Australian representatives in New York should be extended to include the Missions for South Africa, New Zealand, India and Eire, which had been set up in, or were about to be despatched to, the United States. The procedure which London desired was as follows: the Dominions should communicate their full requirements to London where they would be examined in relation to the general strategy of the war and if necessary included in a combined North American supply programme.

It was recognised that the Dominions could not be debarred from sending some at least of their requisitions direct to the United States, but if such orders seemed likely to endanger the main programme Purvis was to ask for guidance from London. This policy was based on a general view of strategy. The War Office held that the most grave and immediate menace was to the British Isles and the Suez Canal, both vital to the continued existence of the Commonwealth. Therefore supplies needed for these points should not be diverted to the outer parts of the Commonwealth. Examples of the danger of diversion were the requests by the southern Dominions, e.g., New Zealand and South Africa, for substantial quantities of artillery; yet all available guns were urgently needed at that time in the United Kingdom and the Middle East. The British Government was also anxious that purchasing by the Dominions in the United States should not prejudice the important principle of standardisation of British types of weapons and equipment as far as possible throughout the Commonwealth.

On receipt of these instructions Purvis immediately held meetings early in August 1940 with representatives of the different Commonwealth countries and secured their collaboration. He also set up within the British Purchasing Commission a new office of Coordinator of Empire and Allied Requirements.[1] He seized the opportunity to ask London for a comprehensive Empire programme for North America. The need for co-ordinating requirements in London was then explained by the British Government to the other Governments of the Commonwealth. All agreed, except Canada which was not prepared to participate in any central allocation of supplies in London. The British Government recognised the force of this objection, particularly in view of the very close relations which had been built up between the Canadian Department of Munitions

---

[1] To this post an American businessman, Mr W. J. Davidson of General Motors, was appointed. The policy of co-ordination on the Allied side continued to be pressed from London. The common interest of the United Kingdom and the Allies in this matter was emphasised by the Foreign Office in a letter addressed to the Allied Governments on 28th December 1940.

and Supply and the British Purchasing Commission in New York. But the special situation of Canada in relation to the United States increased the difficulties of strengthening Commonwealth machinery in London for consultation and central planning; and little progress was made in this direction until 1942.

The case for co-ordination was reinforced by the fact that all parts of the Commonwealth save Canada drew on the common dollar pool. This continued to be an important factor long after the Lend-Lease Act was passed.[1] The Act itself increased the pressure from the American side for the use by the Commonwealth of a single channel in the matter of supplies. In mid-February 1941 the Administration asked – as a matter of extreme urgency – for a single Lend-Lease programme for all Commonwealth requirements. In informing the Governments of the southern Dominions of this request, the British Government referred to the arrangements previously made, whereby 'all Dominion orders for warfare stores . . . have been placed through or in conjunction with the British Purchasing Commission and the British Air Commission'; it was able, therefore, to include Dominion requirements for 'warfare stores' with its own estimates, and pointed out the advantage of including also 'non-warfare stores'. Here it may be pointed out that the supply missions of the Dominions and India in the United States were concerned mainly with supplies other than military. Under the agreed arrangements applications for munitions and military and naval equipment were concentrated in the United Kingdom. The procurement in the United States, of any munitions requirements which could not be met in the United Kingdom, was usually carried out directly by the British missions in the United States on express instructions from London.[2]

In August 1941, as a means of strengthening Commonwealth co-ordination through the British Supply Council, the Office of Co-ordinator of Empire and Allied Requirements was brought under the Council itself, which henceforward supplied its secretariat. The Office of the Co-ordinator was divided into two parts, one dealing with Commonwealth affairs and the other with the Allies. The staff of the latter part was larger, since much of the work for the Allies was done in the Co-ordinator's office whereas in the case of the Dominions much of the detailed work in connection with Lend-Lease requisitions was done in their own missions. The Co-ordinator's office now became the centre of a group of Commonwealth committees functioning below the level of the Supply Council but under its auspices. The committees included a general Commonwealth

---

[1] See *North American Supply, op. cit.,* Chapter VII.
[2] The arrangements for inland and seaborne transportation were also made by the United Kingdom missions; the other Commonwealth missions were kept informed of the movement of military stores to shipboard.

Committee which met weekly. Other committees dealt with Requirements, Priorities and Apportionment of supplies allocated by the United States.

The procedure for co-ordinating the Commonwealth in connection with Lend-Lease supply was briefly as follows: programmes – detailed statements of requirements for supplies under Lend-Lease– were submitted by all parts of the Commonwealth and filed with the Administration by the British Supply Council.[1] The Commonwealth countries (and certain of the Allied missions) procured what they needed under Lend-Lease mainly by 'transfer' from the United Kingdom. Consequently the process of procurement and shipment was carried out mainly by the supply missions of the United Kingdom. The first step was the receipt by the Commonwealth mission concerned of instructions to requisition. The Mission prepared a draft requisition which was then discussed with the appropriate supply officer in the United Kingdom supply mission dealing with this particular commodity. The latter prepared the requisition in the final agreed form, obtained a British Supply Council number for it and filed it through the British Supply Council with the Office of Lend-Lease Administration.[2] The long process of following the requisition through the American agencies concerned (Office of Lend-Lease Administration, Treasury Procurement, War Production Board) was primarily the responsibility of the United Kingdom supply officer who had prepared the requisition. Although he was in constant touch with the Commonwealth mission concerned, the officers of the latter frequently made their own direct contacts with the United States agencies. The final placing of the contract was notified direct by the United States Treasury Procurement Division to the Commonwealth mission concerned. The Commonwealth missions made their own cash purchases independently; but they were assisted by the United Kingdom in the matter of priority ratings and export licences, these being common services provided by United Kingdom missions. The United States Government required that export licences for all Commonwealth missions should be issued through one central British Office.

The procedure of the United States in respect of the final allocation of supplies under Lend-Lease afforded a still more striking illustration of the treatment of the British Commonwealth as an entity.

---

[1] Under Reciprocal Aid, given by the British Commonwealth to the United States, the latter was also requested to submit a single co-ordinated programme covering its requirements from all parts of the Commonwealth. In other words the United States were not to make piecemeal approaches to the different parts of the Commonwealth, but were to use a central channel.

[2] The British Supply Council was furnished at each meeting with a cumulative list of all requisitions for all parts of the British Commonwealth filed through it by the different missions. Requisitions for military stores were mostly filed direct by the Service missions with the War and Navy Departments.

The group approach of the Commonwealth to the United States for raw materials, munitions and manufactured goods greatly facilitated the work of the Combined Boards. As time went on the United States showed an increasing disinclination to deal with matters on a country by country basis; it looked more and more to the British Commonwealth group to do its own planning and co-ordination. In this way production within the Commonwealth could be taken fully into account before any approach was made to the United States. The practice of a single allocation to the 'British Empire' may be illustrated from the first allocation of finished products made in the autumn of 1942. The Office of Lend-Lease Administration then made allocations of some 45 such products, for varying periods, to the 'British Empire' as a whole. Since in many of these cases the amounts allocated were less than the total requirements submitted by the different members of the Commonwealth a regular procedure for apportionment had to be devised by the Supply Council. The work of apportionment was undertaken by the Apportionment Committee of the Supply Council composed of a representative from the British Supply Mission and one from each of the Supply Missions of the other Commonwealth countries. The Committee established from the outset a tradition of unanimous agreement on the apportionment, between the different members of the Commonwealth, of the global 'British Empire' allocations. The tradition of unanimity was maintained unbroken by the Committee and its successors until the necesssity for apportionments died at the end of the war.[1]

A somewhat similar procedure of apportionment of 'British Empire' allocations had already been established at the beginning of 1942 for strategic raw materials in short supply. Steel afforded one of the best examples of the persistent habit of the Commonwealth countries of working together as a group in relation to the United States. Co-ordination included: the drawing up of a Commonwealth programme of steel requirements, a Commonwealth approach to the United States, allocations of steel to the Commonwealth as a whole and apportionment by its members of supplies amongst themselves, and finally co-ordination of shipping arrangements. The process began in London in meetings of the Empire Clearing House (later Commonwealth Supply Council) attended by High Commissioners of the Commonwealth countries and representatives of United Kingdom departments (Iron and Steel Control, Ministry of Production, Board of Trade, Dominions Office, India Office, Colonial Office). The quantity of steel which each part of the Commonwealth would require from the United States each quarter was calculated.

---

[1] The Apportionment Committee frequently kept a portion of the global allocation as a British Supply Council reserve to meet emergencies. In such cases the amounts held in reserve, as well as the amounts apportioned, were notified to the Office of Lend-Lease Administration.

The requirements in respect of the different kinds and shapes of steel were then submitted to the War Production Board by the Steel Division of the British Raw Materials Mission.[1] When the steel allocation was finally made by the War Production Board to the 'British Empire' the Board asked the British Supply Council to inform W.P.B. and the Office of Lend-Lease Administration of the division of the global allocation amongst the different countries of the Commonwealth. The Steel Division then suggested through the Co-ordinator of Empire and Allied Requirements the allocation to be made to each of the Commonwealth countries. In the family discussion that followed unanimity was always reached. The proposed apportionment was submitted in each case to the American authorities and was rarely, if ever, challenged by them. Nor indeed was there any reason for challenge since the United States had much to gain from a system by which they shared advantages of unity which were similar in kind to the advantages secured from their own union of 48 states.

The entry of Japan and the United States into the war gave the southern Dominions and India a much more lively interest both in supplies from the United States and in matters of policy in the fields of supply and strategy. For these countries the first six months of 1942 were a period of anxiety and disappointment in the matter of supplies. They were unable to obtain much-needed supplies either from the United States or the United Kingdom. But this was due to the shortage of munitions rather than to any defect of organisation. They did not participate formally in the new British-American war organisation set up in January 1942 by the President and the Prime Minister, but their voices could nevertheless count effectively through other channels. On the political level their membership of the Pacific War Councils in London and Washington seemed to give them a more direct voice, but the limited value of these bodies was shown by their short life.

The setting up of the Combined Boards, centred largely in Washington, raised the question as to how far Washington should now become a centre of co-ordination for the Commonwealth in supply matters other than munitions. Thus the issue was raised for raw materials in February by the British Raw Materials Mission. London replied that the work of supervising the carrying out of recommendations of the Combined Raw Materials Board should be centred in London which should also remain the centre for the

---

[1] The programme as submitted indicated the different kinds of steel required for each Commonwealth country; separate headings were shown not only for each member of the Commonwealth but also for the Middle East Supply Centre, for the Fighting Forces and for petroleum production. Steel required for ship repairs throughout the Commonwealth was co-ordinated for all its territories by the Admiralty which then requisitioned in Washington for all the different kinds required (plates, sheets, angles, bars, tubes, etc.).

co-ordination of information as to supplies and requirements of Commonwealth countries for all non-munitions supplies, including raw materials. The Empire Clearing House (later absorbed into the Commonwealth Supply Council) had been created for this purpose. Its function was 'to construct for the purpose of the Combined Raw Materials Board composite and co-ordinated pictures of the actual and potential resources and of the requirements of raw materials of the Empire and Allied countries in the Eastern Hemisphere'.[1] Each Dominion Mission in Washington was kept fully informed at all times by the British Raw Materials Mission of data relating to its country requested from or received from London. Whenever, as happened not infrequently, the British Raw Materials Mission received data direct from Commonwealth Missions in Washington, it always passed on the information to London and asked for instructions.

As a means of giving the heads of the Commonwealth Missions in Washington a share in the formulation of policy, the British member of the Combined Raw Materials Board set up an Empire Advisory Committee consisting of the heads of the Commonwealth Missions and of the Dominion Ministers in Washington. For the same reason similar co-ordinating bodies were set up in connection with other British supply missions. Thus the heads of the Commonwealth Missions became members of the British Purchasing Commission's Requirements Board and of the Priorities Committee of the British Supply Council. A further step in the same direction was taken by the Chairman of the British Supply Council in mid-summer 1942 by the setting up of what was known as the Chairman's Commonwealth Committee. In theory this was to have been a high-level body to facilitate consultation with the heads of the British Commonwealth Missions on matters of longer term policy; but in practice it met very rarely.

Thus by the summer of 1942, as was noted in a British Supply Council report in July, the southern Dominions and India had been given a direct voice in the formulation of policy, but only 'below the level of the Supply Council'.

A suggestion that the British Supply Council should be broadened into a British Commonwealth Supply Council by the addition of Dominion members had been made at the first meeting of its Commonwealth Committee in September 1941. The Council, however, rejected the idea. The argument against such a step was still that, if a British Commonwealth Supply Council were to be set up, London was its logical centre.

It was true that Canada had been made an original member of

---

[1] Similar co-ordination for the Western Hemisphere in the case of raw materials was the task of the Requirements Committee of the War Production Board.

the British Supply Council; but the position of Canada was quite exceptional. The name given to the Council from the outset was 'the British Supply Council in North America'. It seemed essential that Canada should be a member, not only as a major source of British supply, but because of Canada's unique relationship with the United States. For the same reason Canada was the only overseas member of the Commonwealth to receive separate representation on several of the Combined Boards; again for the same reason Canada was the only part of the Commonwealth which did not participate in the Commonwealth group arrangements described above. In practice, however, Canada's membership of the British Supply Council was little more than nominal. Her supply role was played in the joint Canadian-American supply bodies and in the two Combined Boards, C.P.R.B. and C.F.B., of which she became the third member. Thus for Canadian supply Washington was at least as important as London as a co-ordinating centre; in fact Canada played little direct part in the Commonwealth co-ordinating machinery in London. In actual practice the great bulk of the work of the British Supply Council in Washington concerned the United Kingdom. As its Chairman noted in August 1942, 'at least 99 per cent. of the business' that came before it 'directly concerned only the United Kingdom or the United Kingdom and the United States'. The occasion of the remark was a hint from the Australian side in Washington that Australia might like to attend meetings of the Supply Council. The Council agreed that if necessary a matter affecting a particular Dominion could be brought before it, in which case the head of the Dominion Mission concerned would be asked to take part in the discussion. This, however, was an exceptional procedure which was not often used.

London remained throughout the war the natural planning centre for the British Commonwealth countries in the eastern hemisphere. Its role was facilitated by the setting up in London late in 1942 of the Commonwealth Supply Council. The Council co-ordinated for its members their supply requirements by means of three Committees; Raw Materials (which absorbed the Empire Clearing House), Non-Munitions and Munitions. The latter worked in close touch with the Joint War Production Committee. As Chapter IX explains, the military programmes of the Commonwealth countries in the southern hemisphere were centralised through the Eastern Group Supply Council in New Delhi, which had direct links with the British War Office and the Ministry of Supply. Military requirements which could not be met from the local production of the Eastern Group were treated as part of the requirements of the armed forces of the United Kingdom.

The Non-Munitions Committee of the Commonwealth Supply

Council worked in close contact with the Non-Munitions Supply Division of the Ministry of Production.[1] The attempt to plan and collate in London the non-munitions requirements of the Commonwealth (apart from Canada) was less successful than for munitions. For one thing the range and variety of commodities was greater. Moreover, whilst both the United Kingdom and the United States, as the principal producers and exporters of finished products in short supply, had a common interest in ensuring a fair and economical distribution, the Dominions were accustomed to order American supplies direct; and since they had Missions in the United States for this purpose it was natural for them to send copies of their requirements direct to these Missions. The point that mattered was that the same requirement should not be duplicated by being presented both in London and Washington.

To facilitate co-ordination in Washington the new British Resident Minister for Supply made it one of his first and main tasks to set up a Commonwealth body known as the Principal Commonwealth Supply Committee composed of the heads of the Commonwealth and Empire Missions in Washington. As Chairman of the Committee he represented the Minister of Production in the latter's double capacity. As Chairman of the North American Supply Committee – a British departmental committee dealing with British supplies – the Minister of Production was represented in Washington by the Resident Minister in the role of Chairman of the British Supply Council. In the Minister's second capacity, that of Chairman of the Commonwealth Supplies Committee in London, he was represented by the Resident Minister as Chairman of the Principal Commonwealth Supply Committee. The Resident Minister could thus speak not only for the United Kingdom but also for the Commonwealth as a whole.

Apart from the Principal Commonwealth Supply Committee the only body in Washington which could be described as specifically an organ of the British Commonwealth was the British Commonwealth Scientific Office. The Office remained in existence after the war. It was set up in mid-summer 1944, on the initiative of Dominion scientific missions in Washington and comprised the British Central Scientific Office and the Scientific Missions of Australia, New Zealand and South Africa; there was also a close relationship with the National Research Council of Canada. At the outset, twenty-three scientists – mostly chemists, physicists and metallurgists – from these countries made up the staff of the Office. In structure it followed the pattern of the Commonwealth. The separate missions maintained their identity but worked together

---

[1] See above page 251 and J. D. Scott and Richard Hughes, *op. cit.*

BRITISH SUPPLY ORGANISATION IN THE U.S.A.

January 1943

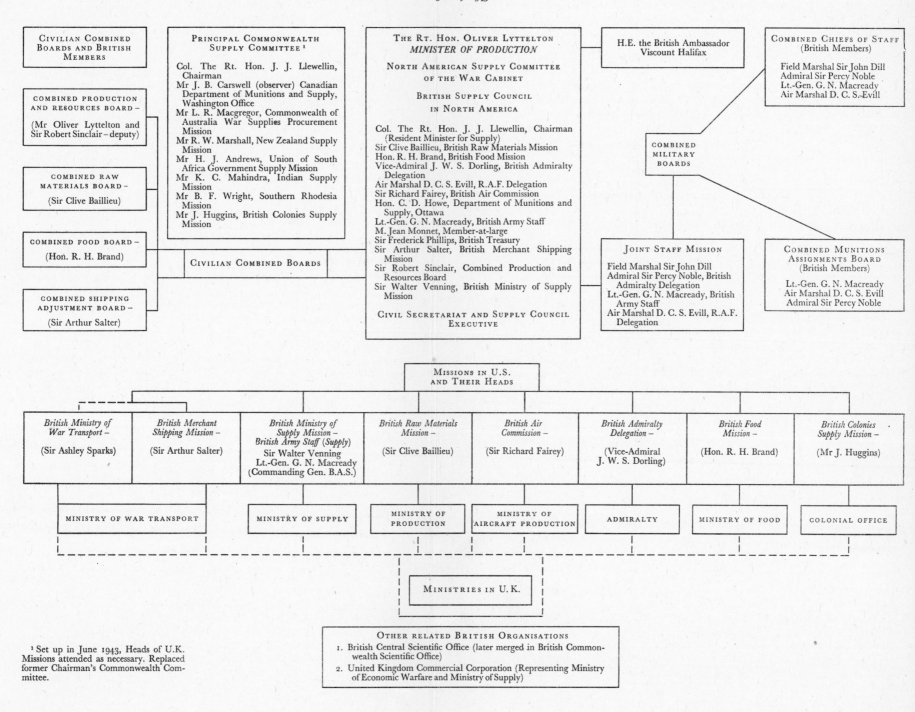

CIVILIAN COMBINED BOARDS AND BRITISH MEMBERS

COMBINED PRODUCTION AND RESOURCES BOARD –
(Mr Oliver Lyttelton and Sir Robert Sinclair – deputy)

COMBINED RAW MATERIALS BOARD –
(Sir Clive Baillieu)

COMBINED FOOD BOARD –
(Hon. R. H. Brand)

COMBINED SHIPPING ADJUSTMENT BOARD –
(Sir Arthur Salter)

PRINCIPAL COMMONWEALTH SUPPLY COMMITTEE [1]

Col. The Rt. Hon. J. J. Llewellin, Chairman
Mr J. B. Carswell (observer) Canadian Department of Munitions and Supply, Washington Office
Mr L. R. Macgregor, Commonwealth of Australia War Supplies Procurement Mission
Mr R. W. Marshall, New Zealand Supply Mission
Mr H. J. Andrews, Union of South Africa Government Supply Mission
Mr K. C. Mahindra, Indian Supply Mission
Mr B. F. Wright, Southern Rhodesia Mission
Mr J. Huggins, British Colonies Supply Mission

CIVILIAN COMBINED BOARDS

**THE RT. HON. OLIVER LYTTELTON
*MINISTER OF PRODUCTION***

NORTH AMERICAN SUPPLY COMMITTEE OF THE WAR CABINET

BRITISH SUPPLY COUNCIL IN NORTH AMERICA

Col. The Rt. Hon. J. J. Llewellin, Chairman (Resident Minister for Supply)
Sir Clive Baillieu, British Raw Materials Mission
Hon. R. H. Brand, British Food Mission
Vice-Admiral J. W. S. Dorling, British Admiralty Delegation
Air Marshal D. C. S. Evill, R.A.F. Delegation
Sir Richard Fairey, British Air Commission
Hon. C. D. Howe, Department of Munitions and Supply, Ottawa
Lt.-Gen. G. N. Macready, British Army Staff
M. Jean Monnet, Member-at-large
Sir Frederick Phillips, British Treasury
Sir Arthur Salter, British Merchant Shipping Mission
Sir Robert Sinclair, Combined Production and Resources Board
Sir Walter Venning, British Ministry of Supply Mission

CIVIL SECRETARIAT AND SUPPLY COUNCIL EXECUTIVE

H.E. the British Ambassador Viscount Halifax

COMBINED MILITARY BOARDS

COMBINED CHIEFS OF STAFF
(British Members)

Field Marshal Sir John Dill
Admiral Sir Percy Noble
Lt.-Gen. G. N. Macready
Air Marshal D. C. S. Evill

JOINT STAFF MISSION

Field Marshal Sir John Dill
Admiral Sir Percy Noble, British Admiralty Delegation
Lt.-Gen. G. N. Macready, British Army Staff
Air Marshal D. C. S. Evill, R.A.F. Delegation

COMBINED MUNITIONS ASSIGNMENTS BOARD
(British Members)

Lt.-Gen. G. N. Macready
Air Marshal D. C. S. Evill
Admiral Sir Percy Noble

MISSIONS IN U.S. AND THEIR HEADS

British Ministry of War Transport – (Sir Ashley Sparks)	British Merchant Shipping Mission – (Sir Arthur Salter)	British Ministry of Supply Mission – British Army Staff (Supply) Sir Walter Venning Lt.-Gen. G. N. Macready (Commanding Gen. B.A.S.)	British Raw Materials Mission – (Sir Clive Baillieu)	British Air Commission – (Sir Richard Fairey)	British Admiralty Delegation – (Vice-Admiral J. W. S. Dorling)	British Food Mission – (Hon. R. H. Brand)	British Colonies Supply Mission – (Mr J. Huggins)
MINISTRY OF WAR TRANSPORT		MINISTRY OF SUPPLY	MINISTRY OF PRODUCTION	MINISTRY OF AIRCRAFT PRODUCTION	ADMIRALTY	MINISTRY OF FOOD	COLONIAL OFFICE

MINISTRIES IN U.K.

OTHER RELATED BRITISH ORGANISATIONS
1. British Central Scientific Office (later merged in British Commonwealth Scientific Office)
2. United Kingdom Commercial Corporation (Representing Ministry of Economic Warfare and Ministry of Supply)

[1] Set up in June 1943, Heads of U.K. Missions attended as necessary. Replaced former Chairman's Commonwealth Committee.

CHART OF ALLIED PURCHASING

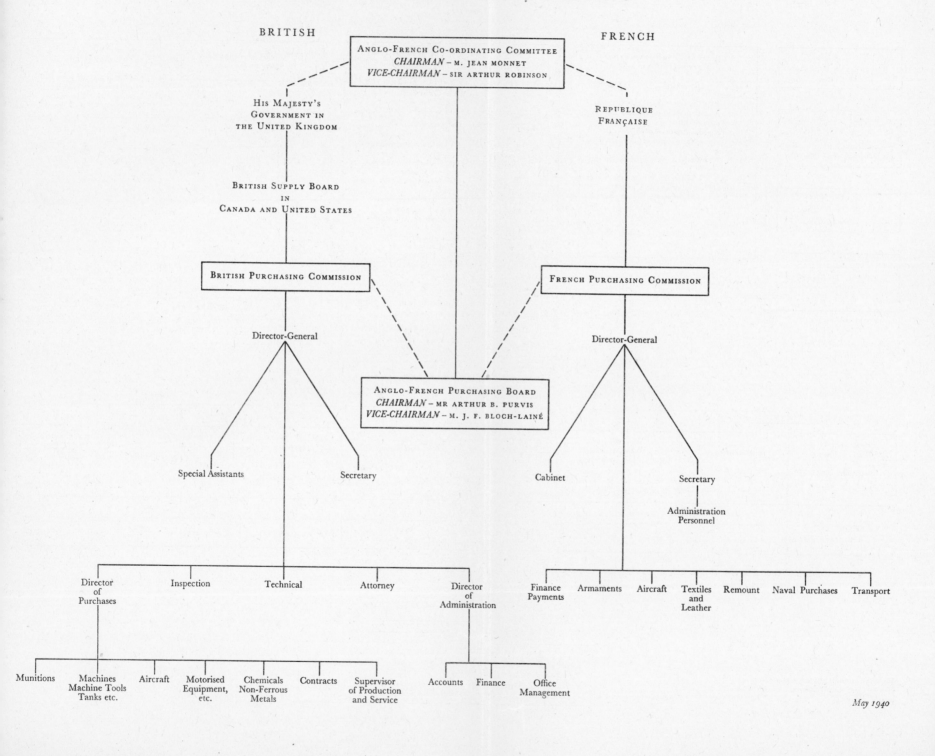

BRITISH

FRENCH

ANGLO-FRENCH CO-ORDINATING COMMITTEE
CHAIRMAN – M. JEAN MONNET
VICE-CHAIRMAN – SIR ARTHUR ROBINSON

HIS MAJESTY'S
GOVERNMENT IN
THE UNITED KINGDOM

RÉPUBLIQUE
FRANÇAISE

BRITISH SUPPLY BOARD
IN
CANADA AND UNITED STATES

BRITISH PURCHASING COMMISSION

FRENCH PURCHASING COMMISSION

Director-General

Director-General

ANGLO-FRENCH PURCHASING BOARD
CHAIRMAN – MR ARTHUR B. PURVIS
VICE-CHAIRMAN – M. J. F. BLOCH-LAINÉ

Special Assistants

Secretary

Cabinet

Secretary

Administration
Personnel

Director
of
Purchases

Inspection

Technical

Attorney

Director
of
Administration

Finance
Payments

Armaments

Aircraft

Textiles
and
Leather

Remount

Naval Purchases

Transport

Munitions

Machines
Machine Tools
Tanks etc.

Aircraft

Motorised
Equipment,
etc.

Chemicals
Non-Ferrous
Metals

Contracts

Supervisor
of Production
and Service

Accounts

Finance

Office
Management

May 1940

with a common headquarters, maintained common files and exchanged data. The benefits were mutual, but the Dominions secured a special advantage from the far larger resources of the United Kingdom on the scientific side. The effectiveness of the different missions was increased since a scientist in a specific field could act where desirable for all parts of the Commonwealth. The Office was established for mutual aid and to facilitate a group relationship with the United States.[1]

Looked at broadly, co-ordination within the Commonwealth was a system of five triangles erected on the London-Washington base with their apexes in Canberra, Wellington, New Delhi, Pretoria and Bulawayo. Some confusion was inevitable in such a complex system despite the British Government's long experience in operating large international networks of this sort. One source of confusion was that Dominion heads in London and Washington sometimes reported to different departments in their national capitals. In practice the repeating of all important cables to the third capital, and the close liaison maintained between London and Washington, kept confusion to a minimum and the system worked with a reasonable degree of efficiency.

---

[1] See Chapter VIII, Section (iii).

Z

CHAPTER VIII

SCIENTIFIC COLLABORATION BETWEEN THE UNITED KINGDOM AND NORTH AMERICA

(i)

International Science and Military Security

THE TRADITIONS of scientific research require of the scientist that he should make the results of his work freely available throughout the world. Scientific practice has provided easy and convenient means for him to do this. Provided with an abundance of journals, the research scientist is also frequently in direct touch by personal correspondence with colleagues in other countries, and has reasonable opportunities to meet them personally at international conferences, or by exchange visits, or on other occasions. In the decade before the outbreak of war there were nearly a hundred international scientific conferences a year. With such opportunities for meeting it is not surprising that the leading workers in a particular field, whatever might be their country of origin or settlement, were generally familiar colleagues and often personal friends.

The links between British scientists and scientists in the other Commonwealth countries were naturally peculiarly close. Among the countries outside the Commonwealth none was more closely associated with British science than the United States, where a large number of scientists born and educated in Britain had made their careers. Writing in *The Times* in 1941[1] Professor A. V. Hill, in referring to the reasons for this close association, mentioned the practice of American scientists since the First World War of coming to Britain instead of going to Germany for advanced degrees; the influx of American Rhodes scholars; the temporary emigration of British Commonwealth Fund scholars; and the assistance to British Universities from the Rockefeller and other foundations. Friendly relations existed between learned bodies; Berkeley College, Yale, for example, had an *amicabilis concordia* with King's College, Cambridge;

---

[1] *The Times*, 17th June 1941.

an arrangement existed between the Royal Society and the National Academy of Science for lectures in alternate years in London and Washington; and there were arrangements for joint membership between the two national Associations for the Advancement of Science. In 1941, when the Royal Society elected the President of Harvard, the Secretary cabled him: 'Greetings foreign member Royal Society, but not very foreign'.

This neighbourliness was not limited to the world of academic science. It was not uncommon for official scientific bodies to have a close liaison with their opposite numbers in other countries. Thus the British Aeronautical Research Council had, almost from its inception, contact with the United States and other countries. Such contact was a feature of the First World War, and particularly of its closing phase, when there was a continuous exchange of information with the American National Advisory Committee for Aeronautics through the Scientific Attaché of the American Embassy. In peace the exchange continued, and the Committee came to regard the comparison of the facilities and work of its own country with those of others as a part of its normal function.

This free exchange of information is in fact the well-accepted background of scientific research, and until the outbreak of the Second World War the exceptions to the general rule of free interchange of information were equally well-accepted. Each country guarded a class of secrets which were specifically and recognisably military, and which usually lay rather in the field of technical advance than in the field of scientific research. The British explosive RDX and the American Norden bombsight were characteristic examples in the pre-war period.

The need for imposing restrictions on the publication of scientific or technical matter which possessed military interest had some influence on the organisation of science in all the countries concerned. A scientist who considered a career in the field of military science – using the phrase in its widest sense – had a poorer chance than another of achieving either the stimulus of international contacts or the international repute which might follow. This was a marked discouragement to those who conceived themselves to have any chance at all of such distinction, and in any case, 'security' apart, conditions of work in government establishments were not so favourable to active and advanced research as they were in the Universities. The result was that, in peace-time, governments did not, except in a few cases, succeed in recruiting the most brilliant research scientists for military work; their strength lay rather in the inventiveness of their technicians. In the Second World War, however, all the principal belligerent countries, with varying success, attempted to utilise the general body of their scientific personnel for war purposes, and both in Britain and America large numbers of academic scientists of the highest standing became leaders in such work. These men carried over into war the international habit of mind which they had acquired in time of peace, and although of course authority to collaborate or exchange information could come only from their respective governments, it was a factor that the disposition and ability to collaborate effectively were already in existence.

Secrecy about military science and invention is never, in any case, absolute. Military inventions, however secret, are based upon knowledge and processes available to scientists in all countries. Moreover, secrets which may be kept from the world at large are shared with allies or well-disposed countries. In the pre-war period, and up to the disasters of 1940, the British Government made its scientific and technical advances freely available to the French. We are here however, concerned mainly with North America, and it was, naturally, with Canada that the British Government first began to arrange a specially close war-time contact. Professor (later Sir Ralph) Fowler, a member of the Scientific Advisory Council, went to Ottawa as a semi-permanent liaison officer with the National Research Council, and was very active there for some months. The value of Professor Fowler's work in bringing about what Dr (later Sir Edward) Appleton, in the autumn of 1940, described as the 'close and completely happy relations that now existed between this country and Canada in the scientific field', was very great, and was based from the outset on free disclosure by both sides.

Scientific liaison with the United States was not of course at this period upon the same basis of formal military alliance as in the case of France, or Commonwealth partnership as in the case of Canada. A visit made by Professor A. V. Hill to Washington in 1939 had shown that great friendliness to the Allied cause existed among American scientists, but that their willingness to collaborate was ineffective in the face of official security regulations. Yet Professor Hill formed the view, which was shared and advocated by his scientific colleagues, that if the British made proposals for a complete sharing of secret information, the higher authorities in America would respond. In London, when it was put forward, the official view was one of reserve, or perhaps it would be more correct to say that lack of interest had so far prevented any real policy from being formed. However that may be, the practice of the various departments at this time was less cautious. Although in the absence of interdepartmental co-ordination the freedom with which information had been given to the Americans had varied, within limits, from department to department, they had in fact been told a good deal about what British scientists were doing. The War Office had given information about all equipments in the production stage, passing this information through the various missions in the United States to the Military Attaché, or to the American Army officers who had visited Britain from time to time. The Admiralty had also made information available to United States visitors, but had systematised the whole matter of the exchange of technical information by setting up a committee for the purpose. In the Ministry of Aircraft Production requests for technical information and prototypes of secret equipment were centralised in a special department.

The return of Professor Hill from America had the effect of bringing high policy into line with departmental practice, and indeed to take a step ahead of it. The vital step was the sending to America of the Tizard Mission of August 1940. It was this Mission which brought about a very extensive, indeed a practically complete exchange of scientific information. More will be said about the details of these interchanges later in this chapter. Here we are concerned with the evolution of high policy. The policy laid down for the Tizard Mission was, in the words of Sir Henry Tizard himself, 'to tell them what they want to know'. Sir Henry's terms of reference were in fact as broad as they well could be; in a form of words which was approved by the Prime Minister they were 'to give all assistance I can on behalf of the British Government to enable the armed forces of the U.S.A. to reach the highest level of technical efficiency'. But to give information to the Americans was not of course the sole object of the Tizard Mission. It was equally charged with obtaining information, though it was specifically stated in the terms of reference that this was not to be a bargaining point. In fact, British frankness made bargaining unnecessary: Sir Henry Tizard reported, as we shall see below, that the Americans had displayed an equal frankness.

The understanding reached by the Tizard Mission with the Americans was satisfactory so far as it went but towards the end of 1940 it seemed to the British Government that the time had come to put matters upon a stronger basis of organisation. Scientific and technical information, although the only kind of information with which we are here concerned, was not the only kind of secret which it might be of mutual advantage for the Americans to share, but which it was vital to keep out of enemy hands. America, as a supplier, and as a friend if not yet formally as an ally, was already being given a great deal of information about British production, consumption, and stocks, and the more complete was the picture presented the more clearly would Britain's needs emerge. When, therefore, the whole question of imparting secret information to the Americans came before the War Cabinet, the decision was to give information with complete freedom unless general or particular obstacles prevented it. There was indeed one obstacle of a general nature, and when the views of the War Cabinet were conveyed to the British Ambassador at Washington it was pointed out that while we wished to deal with the Americans 'on [a] basis of complete trust', it must be borne in mind that America, as a neutral, had not established the same security precautions in offices and industries as had Great Britain after fifteen months of war. While therefore it would be necessary to disclose technical secrets to firms making equipment for the British Government, it would be desirable in the case of specially secret apparatus, to break the knowledge up into small units by having the components manufactured by different firms. There was also a general, and natural, ban upon disclosing technical matters intimately associated with forthcoming operations.

The Ambassador – Lord Lothian, whose death occurred very shortly after this – displayed uneasiness about these instructions. He deprecated any suggestion, however distant, that new difficulties were being put in the way of passing on secret information, and the inference might be drawn by the Americans that this was the real meaning of any attempt, however well-intentioned it might be in fact, to place arrangements upon a more formal footing. The Government, however, felt bound to move at least some way in this direction, and in December a ministerial committee 'on the disclosure to the U.S.A. of secret information relating to supply matters' was set up. It consisted of the three ministers responsible for supply matters. This committee, at its first meeting, laid down some guiding principles for departments. In the first place, if equipment was being manufactured for us in the United States information and prototypes must be given. If Britain did not require any manufacture of her own account, then the committee considered that 'our attitude should depend on the attitude the United States Authorities were at the time adopting towards us on supply matters'. If in doubt, departments were to consult the committee.

Prompt as the committee was in laying down those guiding principles, however, they were overtaken by events. In January 1941 the Lend-Lease Bill was submitted to Congress. If there had been a tendency in the principles laid down by the committee, to maintain, or reintroduce, an element of bargaining about secret information, it seemed in these new circumstances wholly inappropriate, and a revised set of principles was issued. These, in effect, did away with all restrictions save only those of the security of imminent operations and the handing over of immature devices or ideas.

Thus it may be said that by the beginning of 1941 the British Government had evolved a complete policy about the disclosure of scientific and technical – and in fact all other – secret information to the Americans. So far as the matter was subjected to political examination at a high level this was practically a final step. The entry of America into the war was not in this field a matter of great significance, since for at least a year before Pearl Harbour British and American scientists had been treating one another on very much the same basis as they treated scientists working in different government research establishments in their own countries, withholding from one another in effect only immature ideas, which in scientific as in other work are normally a subject for professional reticence. Something remained to be done in increasing the intimacy of the contacts, and more in extending them into new fields, systematising them and devising means to render them more fruitful. The administrative measures involved form our next subject. From the point of view of high policy, however, the sharing of secrets had, save for one episode, ceased to be an issue by 1941.

That episode,[1] however, was an important one which caused the most grave concern in Britain. Late in 1942 a position had been reached in the development of the atom bomb which enabled work to be put in hand for the building of the vast plants required for manufacture. In June it had been decided that this work should be carried forward in America only, since neither British industrial resources nor scientific manpower could stand the great additional strain. The transformation of the project in America from a research task to a military and industrial project involved a shift in authority from scientific to military hands, and it became the policy to restrict the passage of information to those 'who need it now and can use it in the furtherance of the war effort'.[2] A strict interpretation of this policy resulted in a complete cessation of American information passing to Britain. The Prime Minister expressed his anxiety to Mr Hopkins, supplied him with full information about the course of events and referred to the possibility of the 'sombre decision' having to be made that Britain should go ahead separately on the project.

It was not until the Quebec Conference of 1943 that measures of co-operation were once more agreed upon. An account of these steps will be given in the section of this chapter which deals in detail with the atomic bomb. Here we may note that this departure from the policy of free disclosure was associated with the assumption of control of the American side of the project by the United States military authorities, and that the principle evolved by the Americans was generally recognised, open though it might be to different interpretations in particular instances.

---

[1] See Robert E. Sherwood, *Roosevelt and Hopkins* (New York, Harper and Bros. 1948). (This work was published in two volumes in the United Kingdom: London, Eyre and Spottiswoode, 1948, under the title of the *White House Papers of Harry L. Hopkins* – see Vol. II). Also Sir John Cockcroft, *The Development and Future of Nuclear Energy* (The Clarendon Press, Oxford, 1950).

[2] Sherwood, *op. cit.*, Vol. II, p. 707 (U.K. edition) quoting memorandum from Dr Bush to Harry L. Hopkins, dated 31st March 1943.

(ii)

The Machinery of Collaboration

Looking back on the abolition of secrecy which has just been described, we see that this step, which appeared bold and even revolutionary at the time, was a mere preliminary, a clearing of the decks for action. It removed one of the administrative obstacles to full co-operation; but full co-operation could not be achieved simply by removing obstacles. Co-operation between scientists may have been a natural process; full co-operation between British and American science was not. It required organisation, and that organisation is our present subject. It required organisation, moreover, not only in the international sphere, but within each country. Both Britain and the United States had of course an official framework of organisation in being before the war, and both greatly extended and strengthened this in war-time. To understand the international organisation it is necessary to have some idea of the national organisation existing in each country.

At the outbreak of war many British Government departments were responsible for scientific investigations involving work in research establishments, and those that were not were often intimately concerned in scientific activities of various kinds, employing for actual investigations the facilities provided by the Department of Scientific and Industrial Research, the Medical Research Council, or the Agricultural Research Council. Although a number of departmental research and development establishments had been founded before the First World War, and specialist committees had been set up in various fields of science, the modern organisation of science by the British Government – outside the field of medicine – may be said to date from the establishment, in 1915, of the Department of Scientific and Industrial Research. The D.S.I.R., as it is generally known, is a department of the Privy Council with the function of organising and developing scientific and industrial research. Broadly speaking its scope included all branches of natural science, and all industries except agriculture, fisheries and forestry (although it included the fish trade and forest products). The Department's research programme and the allocation of funds at its disposal were made on the recommendation of an Advisory Council consisting of scientists and industrialists experienced in these fields, and operating normally through sub-committees dealing with particular subjects. The Department was responsible for directing the activities of many research institutions including the National Physical Laboratory and the Chemical Research Laboratory, and it also interested itself, as occasion arose, in certain investigations carried out in university departments or in industrial research institutions, as well as making research and maintenance grants to individual scientists. Its staff was composed not of established civil servants, but rather of scientists engaged on the same basis as the scientific staffs of university departments, a system which, it was maintained, allowed for free movement of scientific staff between the Department and universities and industry. The main development in the history of the D.S.I.R. up to 1939 was the extension and enrichment of its contacts in the industrial and other fields.

The Medical Research Council, set up in 1913, exercised an analogous function in medicine – understood in the widest sense as a concern in all problems affecting health and efficiency – to that of the D.S.I.R. in natural science. Its members were drawn from the various medical fields and by 1941 it controlled forty-five subsidiary committees, thirteen of which were set up to deal with problems arising directly from the war. The Council's principal research establishment was the National Institute for Medical Research. Like the D.S.I.R. it was responsible to the Lord President, who was Chairman of the committees of the Privy Council concerned with medical, scientific and industrial research. The Agricultural Research Council, the third of these great bodies, was for various historical reasons much less free and unfettered than the other two, and even within its own sphere of agricultural research its functions were mainly advisory. Its position was complicated by its relations to the Ministers responsible for Agriculture and to the Development Commissioners.

Leaving this group of organisations we turn to those departments whose scientific activities were subsidiary to and determined by their administrative functions. The defence departments, which had a rudimentary scientific organisation before the First World War, each acquired during the inter-war period a more extensive and elaborate organisation headed by a distinguished scientist who had the title, in each department, of director of scientific research. On the foundation of the Ministries of Supply and Aircraft Production, the directors from the War Office and Air Ministry went over to the new departments with their staffs.[1] Each Director of Scientific Research controlled a number of research establishments, and had freedom to consult outside scientists. But there were differences between the three directorates in this respect. Any consultation of outside bodies by the Admiralty director was taken on his own initiative, and there was no independent advisory panel which he was expected to consult – a feature which was to occasion a certain amount of criticism in war-time from the senior scientific committee. The

---

[1] For an account of these directorates see J. D. Scott and Richard Hughes, *op. cit.*

Ministry of Supply on the other hand did maintain such a consultative body – an Advisory Council of Scientific Research and Technical Development – of which all three Directors of Scientific Research were members as well as many outside scientists and industrialists, operating in as many as twelve sub-committees. Although this committee was advisory its terms of reference enabled it to initiate new proposals for research and development. The Ministry of Supply made free use of the extra-mural activities provided by the research departments of engineering, chemical, and other producing firms. The Ministry of Aircraft Production had the advice of the Aeronautical Research Council and its various sub-committees. This body, which has already been referred to, was established in 1909, and consisted partly of official, partly of unofficial members. It was an authority on aerodynamics, engines, fuels, and aeronautical science generally. The Director of Scientific Research, Ministry of Aircraft Production, could also consult the Committee for the Scientific Survey of Air Warfare set up in 1935 under Sir Henry Tizard. This committee advised the Air Ministry on all scientific matters of air warfare other than those dealt with by the Aeronautical Research Committee, but it ceased to function in June 1940.

To complete the picture of the research organisations of the defence services mention must be made of two other bodies: first, the Ordnance Board, an inter-service body ancient in origin, now acting under the Ministry of Supply, and exercising executive functions in regard to trials and calculations concerning firearms and their equipment; secondly, the Ministry of Home Security which used research facilities of various kinds.

Although in this brief account of the British Government's organisation for science we have ventured here and there across the frontier of the war period, what has been described was essentially a peace-time organisation. The transition to an appropriate wartime organisation was not a smooth one, and in the early months of the war a good deal of criticism was levelled at the Government by scientists and others for their alleged neglect of science. This criticism had two main themes. The first one was that the recruitment of scientists was inadequate. The official machinery depended mainly upon what was called the Central Register, an inter-departmental recruiting agency. A Central Register Advisory Council of the Ministry of Labour existed to advise specifically on the utilisation of people with scientific and professional qualifications, and its opinions had not been disregarded in the drawing up of the Schedule of Reserved Occupations. Institutions such as the Royal Society also took it upon themselves to compile a register for scientific research, and the joint Recruiting Boards of the universities helped to conserve the supply of technically trained men. Despite all these provisions there was, during the first nine months of the war, a strong feeling that scientific personnel were not being brought into the war effort in sufficient numbers or in the right places. By 1941, however, the Central Register Advisory Council had been placed under a Director with special university connections and disquiet over this problem was beginning to die away. The second and more powerful criticism of the Government handling of science was that it kept it in too dependent and subordinate a condition. This criticism took various forms. One, strongly stressed by one of the eminent British scientists concerned, was that only one or two of all the government departments had adopted the principle on which the work of the three Research Councils was based, of having advisory councils or committees to help, guide, and criticise the work of the department. 'When a specific need arises', he said, 'a Scientific Committee is frequently appointed *ad hoc*, but none was there to anticipate the need before it became obvious, sometimes painfully obvious to the public outside: consequently our use of science had often been slow and timid where it should have been quick and confident'. He went on to say that few of the political leaders of the country had any personal acquaintance with scientific and technical developments and got little help from their higher civil servants, which meant that either the permanent scientific and technical staff had it all their own way in technical matters or else that they were merely the servants of the administration. His solution was the setting up of more bodies for independent critical advice on scientific and technical subjects. Such a function was in his opinion carried out in the Ministry of Supply by the Council for Scientific Research and Development, formed in 1940. Its various committees had the duty and the right to visit and advise upon the work of all the establishments of the Ministry and to offer advice through the Council and its Chairman directly to the Minister. Also (as we have seen) until June 1940 the Tizard Committee for the Scientific Survey of Air Warfare helped in collaboration with the Director of Scientific Research to guide scientific developments in the Air Ministry.[1] Apart from the Aeronautical Research Committee and the special Radio Committee neither the Air Ministry nor the Ministry of Aircraft Production was after 1940 accessible to any independent scientific advice or criticism.[2] The scientist also complained that in the Admiralty since the last war, and after the rather unsuccessful experiment of the Board of Invention and Research under Lord Fisher, no place had been found for independent scientific advice.

---

[1] The Tizard Committee came to an end soon after the formation of the Ministry of Aircraft Production.

[2] It should be pointed out, however, that a number of well-known scientists were engaged in the Air Ministry and the Royal Air Force for operational research, scientific intelligence and other aspects connected with aerial warfare.

The allocation of proprietary rights in design and development to selected individuals or establishments had blocked the way to the valuable assistance which the Admiralty could readily have secured by more direct association with scientific people outside. Similar criticisms were made of the Ministries of Agriculture, Health and Food.

These criticisms may be taken as representing a view widely held by responsible senior British scientists – by the very men, in fact, who were later to occupy the most prominent positions in the official hierarchy. At this period they were in the main private citizens, or had at best a foot in the camp of official science by reason of their membership of one or another specialist Advisory Committee. Their feelings were, however, shared in at least some government quarters. Mr Churchill, when he was First Lord of the Admiralty, had expressed the view that the Government was not getting the best out of its research organisation. What he and his supporters had in mind was the necessity of a central authoritative review of technical progress – some means of deciding on the relative priority of researches in progress or of new proposals. A short list of 'war-winners' should be selected by the head men concerned with technical development, for submission first to the Chiefs of Staff and then to the War Cabinet. Possibly there should be a Minister without Portfolio to carry out these functions. These proposals, embodied in a memorandum, were considered in May 1940 and won widespread acceptance, but the pressure of political events was such that they had to be laid aside. In September the matter was raised again, not in the specific form outlined above, but as a general enquiry into the use of scientists. The suggestion was now officially made that a committee should be set up 'if only to keep scientific people quiet'. Finally, the Lord President recommended the setting up of such a committee with Lord Hankey as president and with the following aims – to advise the Lord President on any scientific problem referred to it; to advise government departments when so requested on the selection of individuals for particular lines of scientific enquiry or for membership of committees on which scientists were required; and to bring to the notice of the Lord President promising new scientific or technical developments which might be of importance to the war effort. Membership of the committee was confined to a small number of the most eminent scientists.

The new committee – the Scientific Advisory Council – appears to have decided that it would achieve greater effect by using its critical powers sparingly. It declared at its first meeting that it would only consider scientific problems referred to it by government departments, recognised scientific bodies and scientists of repute. With regard to staffing it did not intend to interfere in any way with subordinate staff, but only with the recommendations about the appointment of scientific advisers on a high level. Nor did it represent sectional interests. Requests from the British Association and the Institute of Electrical Engineers that they should be represented were not granted. As Lord Hankey was to say later, 'The Government envisaged a small body with contacts over the whole range of science but not representing any particular section so as to ensure the utmost use of science and scientists in the prosecution of the war'. The next important step, taken in October 1940 was the formation of a panel from the members of the Committee – Lord Hankey, Dr Appleton, Professor Hill and Professor (later Sir Alfred) Egerton, and Sir Edward Mellanby – to advise the defence departments.

Meanwhile there had occurred – there was still developing – a feature of the British organisation of science for war purposes which it is not easy to pin down in the pages of a narrative mainly concerned with formal organisation, but which was nevertheless of great significance. From the time when he took office Mr Churchill relied greatly upon the advice of Professor Lindeman – later Lord Cherwell – a distinguished Oxford physicist whose connection with 'defence' science went back to the very active part which he played in the First World War. As Paymaster General, Lord Cherwell became the head of a small group of scientists, with a particular interest in statistics, who were in effect a private staff working for the Prime Minister. Thus wherever the massive personal authority of the Prime Minister was exerted, it was supported by the advice of an eminent scientist. Whether or not ministers, officials and scientists were always happy about this arrangement, the scientists were constrained to admit that the voice of a scientist was constantly heard in the most exalted quarters.

By 1941, then, most of the criticisms made about the Government's use of science had received an adequate answer. Some reservations of course were made. Professor Egerton thought that government departments, through lack of initiative rather than reluctance, were still not making enough use of science. Service departments, he said, often stated their requirements too specifically: 'It is not enough to use science to solve problems which are evident but it should be used to discover what the problems are, the order of their importance and also to forestall the incidence of difficulties and to invent methods of attack and defence'. Professor Egerton recommended that operational staffs and certain selected scientists should work in close collaboration. He believed that the old charges about the lack of advisory committees still stood though in an abated form.

In February 1941 the Scientific Advisory Committee, in a very full report on its activities and the general progress of science in war-time, declared that the main conclusion it had drawn from its survey was that the scientific activities of government departments were far more extensive and effective than was commonly realised, and much of the criticism offered on this score had been due to a lack of knowledge of the facts, itself resulting in some degree from the often necessary secrecy that obscured so much of what was being done. The way in which individual scientists were used, though not ideal, reflected no discredit on anyone and was unlikely to be improved by any change in organisation. The D.S.I.R. and the Medical Research Council were given a clean sheet, but the Agricultural Research Council was thought to be weakened by having to serve too many masters. It was thought that the research facilities of the defence services would be improved by more outside contacts and that security should never lightly be accepted as a bar to the use of such contacts. The range of subjects covered by government science was wide enough, with the exception that insufficient attention had been paid to problems affecting the efficiency of fighting personnel.

This report was undoubtedly influential. Contacts between the scientists, the user, and the production expert became closer. The Ministry of Aircraft Production asked the Air Ministry to grant honorary commissions to a number of scientific workers employed by it in order that they might see in actual operation the scientific devices in which they were interested. The Admiralty encouraged its scientific staff to go to sea, and also set up a Scientific Advisory Panel under the chairmanship of its Director of Scientific Research.

Public knowledge naturally lagged behind these changes, and a debate took place in the House of Lords in April 1941,[1] in which Lord Hankey, defending the government use of scientists, used many of the arguments propounded by the Scientific Advisory Committee in its report. A similar criticism was made again in the next year, July 1942, when Lord Strabolgi and Viscount Samuel put forward the idea of a Scientific General Staff.[2] This was rejected on the grounds that ministerial responsibility had to be preserved. If the supply ministers were to be responsible for the efficiency of their equipment they had to retain the right to reject advice offered them. The step was taken, however, of appointing to the Ministry of Production three eminent full-time Scientific Advisers, to advise the supply departments. This did not, however, completely satisfy the critics, who were convinced that the words of the Scientific Advisory Committee did not carry the weight they deserved with the supply departments. So there was still criticism; but it is significant that few expressions of serious discontent about the use of science as

---

[1] H. of L. Deb., Vol. 118, Cols. 973–999, 2nd April 1941.
[2] H. of L. Deb., Vol. 124, Cols. 75–104, 29th July 1942.

a whole seem to have been made by government-employed scientists after 1941. Nor should it be assumed that a mere sense of official propriety would have kept them quiet upon so serious a matter, since it did not silence them upon less serious issues. It is therefore largely upon negative evidence that the conjecture is based that, by 1942, the British scientific effort was satisfactorily organised both within departments and at the supra-departmental level. In this case negative evidence appears acceptable.

The main distinction between government-sponsored scientific research in Britain and the United States was that in the latter country, until the outbreak of war, such research was cut down to a minimum, private industry doing most of the work and paying for its own mistakes.[1] This was particularly true of the armaments industry. Various attempts to carry out technical development were made by the Government in the inter-war period, but there was no obvious advantage over the privately produced article and the policy was dropped during the thirties; although it is true that the Government sometimes found itself sponsoring projects which did not interest private firms. One economic historian[2] has described how private firms did not greatly welcome development contracts from the Government, since they disliked technical interference and were by no means sure of a good prospective market. According to this historian's view, there was a marked lack of stability in United States development programmes which was partly due to frequent changes in government personnel. The Services also complained that their experimental funds were appropriated for only one year in advance, and that they could not even carry money already appropriated over to another year because of the rule that money unexpended at the end of the year reverted to the Treasury.

The career prospects for scientists in government establishments were not encouraging, for many of the disadvantages that repelled recruits to the Government Scientific Service in Britain existed in America also. Salaries in the higher ranges compared unfavourably with those offered by industry. The dependence by the Government on research by industry with its tacit assumption that the competitive spirit should prevail in all fields led to another striking difference between American and British research. In the United States there were two separate agencies for sponsoring the development weapons – the Army and the Navy. Such a system possessed, of course, the

---

[1] It was equally true of the United Kingdom that a great deal of the initial experimental work was often done by private industry. This was especially the case in connection with the radio and armament research.

[2] For general background see Robert Schlaifer and S. D. Heron, *Development of Aircraft Engines and Aviation Fuels*. (The Graduate School of Business Administration, Harvard University, 1950.)

advantages of private enterprise but American critics remarked that each Service was often disinclined to accept the verdicts of the other upon particular projects,[1] with the result that the same work was often done twice.

This then was the general picture of American science under Government aegis. What were the actual institutions set up to encourage, garner and present the fruits of research to American officials? Official organisation of science was a long established factor in American public life. The first step was taken in recognition of science by the United States Government in 1862, when Lincoln, in association with a group of scientists, founded the National Academy of Sciences. The Academy was, when occasion arose, consulted by the Government on scientific and technical problems, and such aid was sought by President Wilson in 1916. When America entered the First World War, however, it became clear that the Academy was not an appropriate body to advise the Government on scientific problems of defence; and in 1918 the National Research Council was set up for this purpose. In 1940 the American Council of National Defence and its National Defence Advisory Committee, became the nucleus for important further developments.

By the end of 1940 very important executive bodies had been set up. The first of these was the Committee of Health and Medicine. It was composed of the three Surgeons-General in charge of the State Medical Services – the Army, the Navy and Public Health – with the President of the American Medical Association and the Chairman of the National Research Council. The Committee of Health and Medicine had powers to co-ordinate the activities of the Army, Navy and Public Health Medical Services. The National Research Council, in its advisory capacity, also played a part in the co-ordination of scientific activities. Its Medical Division had already, at the request of the State Health Services, set up thirty-two advisory committees which, in addition to attacking particular problems of medical defence, were attempting to secure uniformity in record-keeping and to prevent overlapping. By far the most important body, however, was the National Defence Research Committee (N.D.R.C.) formed in June 1940 for the purpose of supplementing the work of the Army and the Navy in the development of weapons. It had become obvious that the Army and Navy would be seriously hindered in their treatment of scientific problems of modern warfare if some civilian organisation were not at hand to supplement their efforts. The new committee was placed under the chairmanship of Dr Vannevar Bush, President of the Carnegie Institution of Washington, and from the first it was given a liberal hand with

---

[1] Robert Schlaifer and S. D. Heron, *op. cit.*

money. An account of its activities was given by Dr Bush himself in October 1941.[1]

He described N.D.R.C. as a civilian organisation formed as an operating part of the emergency governmental machinery, in contrast with the position of the National Academy of Sciences, which was an independent organisation operating under a Congressional charter which defined its obligation to render advice when called upon by government agencies. The N.D.R.C. consisted by 1941 of six civilians (including the President of the National Academy of Sciences and the Commissioner of Patents), an officer of the Army and one from the Navy. Initially it was organised in four divisions with two heads with high technical experience and two with scientific experience. There were about sixty sections in these divisions, composed of voluntary part-time and full-time workers plus a few technical aides who were paid by the Government. Altogether there were about 500 individuals in the N.D.R.C. organisation who served as members of sections, consultants, and so on. About 2,000 scientific men were engaged in defence research in connection with N.D.R.C. contracts and there were probably an equal number of helpers. The N.D.R.C. tried to carry out its work with a minimum of interruption to the regular affairs of the universities. Nevertheless by the autumn of 1941 the majority of American scientists were engaged in war work of one kind or another. Dr Bush said that of the available physicists whose names were starred in 'American Men of Science' about 75 per cent. were engaged in war research in one way or another, and of the chemists about 50 per cent.

The committee operated primarily by means of contracts with universities, colleges, research institutes and industrial laboratories, the contracts being drawn up with the intent that the contractor, whether university or industrial laboratory, should neither gain nor lose financially through participation in defence research activities. The ten million dollars, which it spent in each of its two first years of life, accordingly went so much the farther.

The special function of the N.D.R.C. was to supplement the work of the Army and Navy in the development of devices and what were called instrumentalities of war, and to effect this there was very close liaison with the Army and Navy, each section of the N.D.R.C. having its own liaison officers. Interchange of scientific and technical information with Britain was effected by a London Office of N.D.R.C. in charge of Mr Hovde.

---

[1] 'Science and the National Defence' by Dr Vannevar Bush – an address delivered at the joint luncheon of the Acoustical Society of America, the Optical Society of America and the Society of Rheology in New York on 24th October 1941. Published in *Science*, 19th December 1941.

In June 1941, after one year of operation by the N.D.R.C., the President, by an Executive Order, established the Office of Scientific Research and Development (O.S.R.D.), of which Dr Bush became director, with the object of co-ordinating all defence research wherever need might occur and initiating it when necessary. The O.S.R.D. had two major divisions, one being the N.D.R.C. which continued as before, save for a change of chairman and the addition of a business office and a liaison officer with the task of handling American relations with Britain. The second major division of O.S.R.D. was the Committee on Medical Research described above. The committee shared with N.D.R.C. the funds of O.S.R.D. in order to conduct medical defence research. The O.S.R.D. had an Advisory Council which included the chairman of the two main groups and the chairman of the National Advisory Committee for Aeronautics, a body which had been in existence for twenty-five years, and which as we have seen had established relations with its opposite number in Britain. Also on the Advisory Council was a Special Assistant to the Secretary of War and a Co-ordinator of Research of the Navy.

The terms of reference of the O.S.R.D. were that it was to advise the President on the status of scientific and medical research relating to national defence and the measures necessary to assure continued progress; to serve as the centre for the mobilisation of scientific personnel and resources of the United States to ensure their most effective use; to co-ordinate, aid and where desirable, supplement the experimental and other scientific and medical research activities relating to national defence carried on by government departments; to develop broad and co-ordinated plans for the conduct of scientific research in the defence programme in collaboration with representatives of the War and Navy Departments; to review existing scientific research programmes formulated by government departments and to advise them on the relationship of their proposed activities to the total research programme; to initiate and support scientific research on the mechanisms and devices of warfare with the objective of creating, developing and improving instrumentalities, methods and materials required for national defence; to initiate and support scientific research on medical problems; to initiate research in any country if it wishes it and whose defence is vital to U.S.A.; and to perform such duties relating to science as the President might from time to time assign to it.

O.S.R.D., although the dominating feature of American scientific organisation in war was not the only agency working for the purpose of mobilising all the scientific resources of the United States.[1] The National Roster of Scientific and Specialised Personnel and the

---

[1] Dr Vannevar Bush, *op. cit.*

National Research Council were responsible for locating competent personnel. The National Inventors' Council was formed under the Department of Commerce for the purpose of evaluating the very large number of suggestions coming in from the public and where appropriate passing them on to the Army and Navy for development. These agencies together constituted the national machinery.

Since effective scientific collaboration with America was a main object of the British scientific organisation, it is not surprising to find that the bodies and individuals which moulded the internal organisation also played the leading part in determining the nature of the collaboration. Thus, in Britain, as it was the Royal Society which gave the impetus that resulted in the founding of the Scientific Advisory Committee, which in turn became the guiding body of British science in war-time, so it was the Royal Society and the Scientific Advisory Committee which in the early days of the war did much to foster the close relationship with America. Professor A. V. Hill, joint secretary of the Royal Society, who as we have seen, acted as a spokesman for British scientists in their approaches to their own Government, played an equally prominent role in the external relations of British science. It was from this quarter that there came, at the outset of the war, expressions of concern about the inadequacy of the British liaison both with the United States and with Canada. Canada held a place of particular importance in the minds and discussions of influential British scientists at this time. There was not only the scientific and industrial strength of a country bound in the Commonwealth tie, but also the peculiarly intimate relationships which existed between Canadian and United States scientists. To scientists in Britain it seemed important that the peacetime scientific association of the three countries should be made a war-time alliance.

The first formal step was taken very shortly after the outbreak of war. In November 1939 a proposal was made that a British scientist should go to Washington in the role of adviser to the Air Attaché. This proposal was backed by Sir Henry Tizard, then scientific adviser to the Air Ministry, and Professor Hill accepted an invitation to fill the post. It was not, of course, expected or intended that Professor Hill, who as well as being a Member of Parliament was a member of two of the most important official committees dealing with aspects of military science, should confine himself to the limited role that was nominally assigned to him. He was being provided with an opportunity to meet and influence American scientists, and it lay with him to make what he could of the opportunity. Of all this Professor Hill was very well aware. Nor was he thinking only of collaboration between British and American academic scientists. He foresaw 'that certain scientific developments might play a major part in determining the issue of the war', and that tremendous advantage could be derived from the close association which existed, in America, between 'pure' science and the research organisations of industry.

On arrival in Washington, Professor Hill found that the American scientists were as anxious to co-operate as he had expected. Lord Lothian, the British Ambassador, was interested in the idea and did all he could to forward it. Mr Richard Casey, then Australian Minister in Washington, also saw the significance of the plan and was very helpful. It soon became evident, however, that the restrictions of secrecy imposed by the Navy and War Departments would prevent any but minor help from reaching Britain unless some formal plan were accepted by both Governments to make possible an exchange of technical ideas. Professor Hill was convinced that the British Government should offer a complete interchange of scientific and technical information with the United States and he was assured on very high authority that the President would agree to such an offer. The Ambassador cabled the Foreign Office asking permission to make such an approach to the President; and separate communication was made on the subject by the Air Attaché and by the British Purchasing Commission. The Foreign Office, however, showed little interest. After waiting vainly seven weeks for a reply, Professor Hill realised that little progress would be made before he returned to England; he accordingly turned his attention to the urgent question of making possible an intensive technological collaboration with Canada. These discussions eventually led to the appointment of Professor R. H. Fowler as British liaison officer in Ottawa, a most significant step in the development of Anglo-American as well as Canadian relations.

An account has already been given of Professor Hill's return to Britain and of the way in which the Government abandoned a policy of caution in favour of the bold proposal of the scientists for a complete exchange of information. It is time now to examine in greater detail what was involved in this proposal in the way of actual projects and devices. Although, in 1940, the most important single class of British scientific secrets was the radar devices either in being or projected, the list which Sir Henry Tizard took with him to the United States included a wide selection of projects and items from all fields of warfare. The Admiralty, for instance, was ready with full information about the various devices and weapons for the protection of surface ships from submarines and air attack. The combined Air Ministry-M.A.P. list included, as well as the jet propulsion project about which more will be said later, communications equipment; the gyro-predictor gun sight; the automatic oxygen separator with its compressor and power unit; cable cutters and balloon barrage technique; the gliding torpedo; and catapults and accelerators. The Ministry of Supply and War Office offered details of new anti-aircraft equipment; information about chemical warfare; in the field of explosives, details of the manufacture of R.D.X., Penthrite, and flashless propellant; and in the field of metallurgy, centrifugal casting applied to guns.

The suggestions made by the departments to Sir Henry Tizard also gave a picture of the information which it was hoped that his mission might obtain. The list does not suggest that the British authorities concerned had learned or deduced anything more than a general idea of American achievements. Their requests were neither detailed nor specific, but were apparently based upon an assumption that the Americans had been pursuing much the same objects and had traversed similar ground. Thus the Admiralty asked simply for 'reciprocal information' about R.D.F. (as radar was then called) and Asdics, and out of a dozen or so requests the Air authorities mentioned specifically only the Norden sight.[1] For the rest the Air authorities asked in general terms about American radar work – although they did go so far as to mention specifically centrimetric waves – about 'new guns between .5-inch and 22-mm., or any other weapons'; about turbo-superchargers and de-icing equipment; and for 'information concerning development of new aircraft and engines'. On the whole they seemed more interested in assessing the possibilities of future collaboration, and in American industrial potential, than in the concrete information that the Americans might have to offer. The Military authorities displayed the same lack of exact information about American progress. They were unaware whether the Americans had developed a radar fire-control system giving accurate elevation and bearing; if so it would be important to obtain sets to supplement the British production of G.L.II. Among other anti-aircraft equipment the Military authorities enquired about power control systems; new types of projectiles; proximity fuses; 'any projectiles of the rocket type', and so on. Their enquiries about chemical warfare, explosives, metallurgy, and coast defence equipment were all of the same kind, that is to say general enquiries based upon the idea that if a thing had been investigated in this country, something along the same lines had probably been investigated in America. The Military authorities displayed the same interest as the Air authorities in the prospects of future collaboration and particularly in the further development and manufacture in America of British radar devices and valves.

All examinations of the British list, as it was approved by the Prime Minister, makes it quite clear that the British Government,

---

[1] On the Norden sight see *North American Supply, op. cit.*, Chapter III, Section (i).

in sending the Tizard Mission to America, had committed itself to a complete revelation of its scientific and technical secrets. Although, as we have already seen, there followed moments when a more cautious attitude was displayed, the die had in fact been cast.

This was clearly understood by the American scientists in the Army and Navy Departments and others with whom the Tizard Mission had contact. They were, Sir Henry reported, deeply impressed by the British willingness to give them all the information they wanted, and they had reciprocated with an equal generosity. Discussions with American operational and research staffs had disclosed an eagerness for British suggestions on operational problems, and the help which they had been given had convinced them of the desirability of close liaison between scientific and operational staff. Sir Henry Tizard and his colleagues, on their side, were convinced of the need for maintaining in America a number of first-class scientists, capable of dealing with problems as they arose. They also had proposals to make about scientific liaison with Canada, which General McNaughton said he considered to be somewhat ineffective. They thought that Britain should dispatch to Canada such R.D.F. experts as could be spared from this country; that sample sets of all new equipment should be sent to Canada and the United States; and that Canada should be asked to test all new equipment under operational conditions.

It remained to set up an organisation, under the general control of the British Supply Council, for carrying out this policy. Ideas for such an organisation had been under discussion by the British scientists – notably Sir Henry Tizard, Professor (later Sir John) Cockcroft and Professor Fowler – for some time, and in November 1940 Professor Cockcroft had submitted to Sir Henry Tizard a memorandum which was the basis of the proposals finally approved. By these proposals there was to be set up in Washington a Central Technical Office under the direction of a highly qualified scientist. This Office was to collaborate with United States research bodies and to act as a channel for exchange with the United States authorities, and in particular the National Defence Research Committee. It was, in addition, to serve as the headquarters for the United Kingdom liaison officer with Canada – at the time Professor Fowler – when visiting the United States, and to ensure that all information given to the United States was also given to Canada. The fact that the business of the Office would be restricted to scientific and technical matters, and that professional military matters would continue to be handled by the appropriate attachés, was stressed at more than one point in the proposals.

Thus there came into being the most important single institution, on the British side, of Anglo-American scientific collaboration. It did not, of course, render other kinds of contact superfluous. Exchanges of visits continued. For example an important one took place when Dr Conant, the President of Harvard, came to Britain in the spring of 1941 at the head of a group of American scientists, and left one of them, Dr Hovde, behind him as an attaché at the American Embassy. But despite the importance of the visits of Dr Conant and others the main administrative burden of liaison from January 1941 onwards was borne, on the British side, by the British Central Scientific Office (B.C.S.O.) in Washington. We have already seen its formal terms of reference; it had before it a clear principle of full disclosure, and the example of the Tizard Mission to show how successfully this principle could be applied. Much however was obscure. How would the Office really work? There remained in London some lingering scepticism about the whole project; the question of commercial rights and of patents was foreseen, even by the enthusiasts, to be an awkward one, and Dr (later Sir Charles) Darwin, the newly appointed director, and Dr Webster, the secretary, had it brought home to them in the course of their leave-taking tour that they were going to America as pioneers in a new and highly experimental method of the international organisation of science.

That the problems which Dr Darwin and Dr Webster encountered in Washington were not even more severe than they proved to be was largely due to the fact that an office had already been established there by Professor Fowler, and although its organisation was naturally elementary it gave a start to the new institution. After an initial settling-down period under Professor Fowler's guidance, Dr Darwin and Dr Webster were able to work out their own method of operation. As Secretary, Dr Webster became in effect the resident manager of the office, and he conducted its day-to-day enquiries. Dr Darwin, as director, took over from Professor Fowler the activity of 'showing the flag', taking advantage of every opening to American laboratories and committees directing scientific war work to which British entry was appropriate. Dr Darwin, unlike Professor Cockcroft and Professor Fowler, had had little opportunity for sustained contact with secret war work in the United Kingdom before setting out for Washington. While, therefore, he was setting himself to mastering what new knowledge was available in America, he had also the task of familiarising himself with the knowledge from Britain which he could make available to the Americans.

Dr Webster saw from the beginning that the establishment of an efficient internal organisation in the office was a matter of importance. The more uncertain and unpredictable was the course of scientific research and technical development, the more essential it was that the office should be able to cope with it. The chief objective of the system which he evolved was that it would be capable of expansion in any specialised direction, and yet within the capacity of a single person to comprehend. He had to cater, not only for these obvious lines of subject classification of scientific and administrative matters, the varied and at times complex lines of interest of different departments in the United Kingdom and the United States, but also for the needs of perpetual expansion in almost any direction in science and technology.

While Dr Webster was putting this task in hand, Dr Darwin was seeing more clearly the nature of his role. Broadly speaking he reached the conclusion that breadth was more important than depth. He could not learn everything; he therefore attempted to learn as much as possible about a very large number of things. If his knowledge of peripheral subjects was little more than gossip, the gossip might nevertheless be useful to an enquiring mind in Britain. Dr Darwin accordingly and deliberately followed a policy of writing reports which were sometimes a medley of precise detail, of vague descriptions of things seen, and of hearsay.

As the work of the Office came to develop further, a tacit agreement was reached whereby the London office of the O.S.R.D. became mainly responsible for obtaining details of British work required by the Americans, while the British office devoted itself mainly to the corresponding task of seeking American information for British use. Each office soon acquired, however, the very natural tendency of handing out some of its national information as a sort of bait for the attraction of what it sought from the other country.

Following the practice established by the Tizard Mission, the British Central Scientific Office continued to correspond direct with the various departments of the Government in London interested in the technical knowledge which they supplied. The chief recipients of scientific information obtained from the Americans by B.C.S.O. were the directors of scientific research of the three supply departments, the Ministry of Home Security, the Medical Research Council, the Department of Scientific and Industrial Research, and other departments were also furnished with technical reports where appropriate. Many instances of parallel and even overlapping interests between British departments became apparent, and it became part of the B.C.S.O. task to point out such cases to the people concerned. The Americans themselves had similar cases in their domestic activities reported to them by B.C.S.O. It was not uncommon for Dr Webster to bring together representatives of the War and Navy Departments and the National Defence Research Committee in early stages of projects, while Dr Hovde in London sometimes performed a similar function.

A reference has already been made to the misgivings which were entertained both in London and Washington about the obstacle of commercial rights. The fact that the question of commercial rights was not frequently raised in regard to specific cases of information given by no means disposed of the problem. On the contrary, it had the effect of building it up as something vague but menacing in the distance. The situation was aggravated by the difference in effective war powers which the two countries could exercise at this time over their firms. Generally speaking the powers of the United Kingdom Government in this respect were much greater than those of the United States Government. American industry was in a position to resist even quite strong Government pressure.

The most effective device for avoiding such troubles was to make use of the normal affiliation between firms in the United States and the United Kingdom, allowing the use of normal commercial channels for the passage of information of commercial value. In daily practice, and as experience was gained, the British authorities were impressed by the willingness of the United States firms to impart information. In some cases they obviously had little to fear from subsequent British competition, in others they no doubt counted on being able to reap sufficient reward from a rapid general development of a whole new field. In many cases, however, there existed a genuine and obvious desire to help to win the war – even before the United States had joined the Allies. American business men, when supplying the British Central Scientific Office with information, often expressed the belief that America was bound to get into the war. Nor had they any illusions about the difficulty of winning it. There was, however, one field in which the misgivings proved to be all too well justified. In the case of process information, chiefly in heavy chemical manufacture in the United States, the B.C.S.O. failed completely to learn what it wanted to know, in spite of sustained and well-supported efforts.

There is a good deal of evidence about another kind of difficulty which the British Central Scientific Office experienced during its first year of life. Enthusiasm for collaboration with American scientists manifested itself at the beginning of the war, as we have seen, mainly in the distinguished research scientists who were accustomed to moving on the international plane. It was some time before the general run of British scientists and technicians acquired the same experience of the benefits of this collaboration, and during the running-in period interest was rather slow in building up. Scientists in Britain were now, as a class, overworked, and their work was being disrupted by air raids and other factors. There was in any case a general lack of appreciation on the part of scientists working for the Government in Britain of the potentialities of

American scientific and production efforts. Britain had been at war for two years before Pearl Harbour, and her research programmes were much in advance of those of the American laboratories. British scientists accordingly often failed to understand how important the American potential was. The feeling grew in Washington that even at the higher levels support for the Office was not what it had been initially. The administrative position of the Office, being responsible in a general way to the Scientific Advisory Committee, a body which possessed no executive authority and no technical secretariat, was also a source of some dissatisfaction. The looseness of the Office's hierarchical links, and the replacement of the customary Government method of working to an opposite-number office in London by an uncertain collection of responsibilities conveyed at first a welcome freedom to act with speed and effect, although it imposed on the Office at the same time a responsibility for dealing fairly and quickly with all its many correspondents in London. But when real support and policy decisions were required this absence of an opposite number in London was felt to be unfortunate. A complicating factor was that financial responsibility for the Office was in the hands of the Ministry of Supply. Of the various views which were now emerging about the proper functions of the Office, it was believed in Washington that the one held in the Ministry of Supply was, so to speak, the lowest. There was undoubtedly a point of view held in London – and perhaps in some quarters of the Ministry of Supply – that the Office in Washington should perform a restricted role of technical post office.

It seemed at one time that this view would prevail. Dr Darwin had originally been appointed as Director of the Office for a period of six months. As soon as that time had expired he was recalled to London, and Dr Webster, the Secretary, was thus left to carry on with the assistance of Dr Wolfenden, an Oxford chemist who had been sent out to look after the chemical side of the Office's activities. The period which followed the recall of Dr Darwin, that is to say roughly the first half of 1942, was a difficult period for the Office. Dr Webster felt that it was being allowed deliberately to decline from its high beginning, and a combination of overwork, frustration, and sense of neglect descended upon it, with the result that London was eventually stimulated to undertake an enquiry into its running and the whole question of its future.

The real question at issue was whether Dr Darwin should be succeeded by another British scientist of the highest rank, or whether the Office should continue with a secretary of less seniority. The question was an anxious one. Dr Darwin himself at first thought that the senior position which he had occupied need not be filled; a little later, however, he changed his opinion and came round to the view that the continuance of this appointment was in fact a very important matter. Eventually, however, the Scientific Advisory Committee decided that there was no need to appoint a senior man and that the Office might conveniently carry on under its Secretary with occasional temporary appointments as director of eminent scientists from Britain. This decision was in line with the practice which the Americans had adopted for their equivalent office in London, and reflected the views of Dr Bush and other American leaders of war science. That there were disadvantages in the situation, however, is indicated by the long discussion which took place before it was finally resolved to agree upon it.

The return of Dr Darwin to London left the Office without a representative in physics at a stage in the war in which the United States had just got into its research stride, particularly in physical applications such as radar, the proximity fuse and fire control equipment. Even as early as September 1941, Dr Webster was concerned about the position in physics, which he did not feel was being fully covered. When, in March, a physicist was appointed – Dr Moon of Birmingham – the appointment was restricted both in time and in the specialised nature of the work.

The next step was the appointment, in June 1942, of Dr A. C. Egerton, Secretary of the Royal Society and a member of the Scientific Advisory Committee, as a temporary director of B.C.S.O. with the special task of enquiring into the usefulness of the Office and deciding whether it should be continued. At the same time an informal enquiry was held in London by Sir Henry Dale and other members of the Scientific Advisory Committee into the value which was placed on the B.C.S.O. by British scientists. In July 1942 Dr Darwin submitted his report. In it, he recognised that the Office had been understaffed, and the inference may be drawn that Dr Webster's sense of frustration had been justified. Dr Egerton now recommended that there should be four permanent officers of Principal Scientific Officer grade, a chemist, a physicist, a radar expert, and an administrative officer. On the question of whether a senior director was required, Dr Egerton was influenced by American advice that it was best not to have such a director, because if his appointment were continued very long, he would inevitably tend to turn the work of the Office more and more into the track of his own special subject. The advice which Dr Egerton received in America, and his own opinion as expressed in his report, could leave no doubt in London that the Office was fulfilling a very useful function. Dr Egerton was, however, unfortunately unable to persuade Dr Webster that these views would prevail, and Dr Webster, to whom the Office owed much, resigned at this juncture. Meanwhile, the London investigation, which has already been referred to, had taken place. Dr Egerton's report to London was followed by further discussions which resulted in the end in full approval for Dr Egerton's proposals.

These discussions coincided with the reorganisation of the government scientific war effort to which reference has already been made. One of the first tasks undertaken by the new Scientific Advisers to the Ministry of Production was the reform of the B.C.S.O. as part of the general scheme for Commonwealth and foreign scientific liaison. Effect was given to the proposals in September 1942. First, for financial and administrative purposes the Office was transferred from the Ministry of Supply to the Ministry of Production, a move which more clearly established its independence of the various supply and other departments to which it provided information. The Ministry of Production was not itself responsible for scientific projects, but was interested in the co-ordination and progress of scientific and technical work throughout the whole war effort. The Office thus preserved its right of direct correspondence with all government departments wishing to use its services. The interest of these technical departments in the facilities offered by the Office was ensured by the appointment of a Scientific Sub-Committee of the North American Supply Committee of the War Cabinet. The Chairman of this committee was the Permanent Secretary of the Ministry of Production, and its members consisted of the directors of scientific research of the three supply departments, the three scientific advisers of the Ministry of Production, the Secretary of D.S.I.R., a scientific representative of the Army Council, and the Chief Scientific Adviser of the Ministry of Home Security. The Committee was made responsible for liaison on the research level with the United States, particularly through B.C.S.O. It thus became the body responsible for discussing the main problems of policy and operation of the Office and which approved the appointment of staff. The strong representation of the Ministry of Production on the Committee ensured a close link between it and B.C.S.O. There seems little doubt that, in fact, the new arrangement was what was wanted, and that it afforded the B.C.S.O. the support in London which members of the Office had thought to be lacking.

The fact that by the beginning of 1943 the experimental period of the B.C.S.O. was over did not, however, mean that its development was at an end. What it meant was that it was now free to develop along the lines thought to be best for it by the London authorities and by its own senior personnel. Yet the general shape had now been evolved and was not widely departed from. Although the title of the head of the Office was elevated from secretary to director, the directorship was an appointment for an energetic scientific administrator of the middle rank rather than for one of the most eminent leaders of British research. And although adequately staffed by comparison with the thin days of 1941, the Office never became very large. At its maximum the staff consisted of a secretary, a director, two chemists, two chemical warfare officers, two physicists, one radio-physicist, one chemical engineer, and one medical research representative.

By now the general shape of scientific liaison with the United States had become a stable pattern. The Washington Missions of the three Services had their own technical groups and possessed, for example, their own radar experts. The work of reporting to the United Kingdom on new American devices and instruments, which had played such an important part in the early days of the Office, had, therefore, more or less disappeared, and little by little the Office had settled down, first, to reporting on research trends in the United States of longer range interest; secondly, undertaking liaison on materials, industrial processes, standardisation, insect control, new drugs and medical technology, all of which were of immediate interest for the war effort but did not fall to any of the other Missions; thirdly, provision of expert scientific help to the Service Missions in connection with projects essentially their responsibility (for example help to the Army Staff on scientific aspects of the development of proximity fuses); and finally, co-ordination of technical activities of common interest to all three Services and particularly initiation of new work of this type (an outstanding example of this function was the leadership of B.C.S.O. in Washington in the initiation of intimate liaison with the Americans on the development of guided weapons).

Perhaps the most significant development of the Office which occurred in the last years of the war was the way in which it acquired a comprehensive Commonwealth character, and the formal recognition which was in due course given to this character. This move was largely a spontaneous and natural one on the part of all concerned; partly a process deliberately fostered by particular United Kingdom and Commonwealth scientists; and partly an accident of accommodation in Washington. The organisation which was finally approved by London was a *fait accompli*, and was a somewhat unorthodox confederation of United Kingdom and Commonwealth Missions, working more or less as a unit, and acknowledging – again more or less – the leadership, or at least the guidance, of the director, although the Missions remained formally responsible to their own Ambassador or Minister. In this form the Office – known latterly as the British Commonwealth Scientific Office – completed its work in the war and entered upon a field of post-war relations with American scientists with which we are not here concerned.[1]

---

[1] See above Chapter VII, Section (vi).

(iii)

The Fruits of Collaboration

If the effectiveness of the machinery described in the last section is to be measured, this must be done in terms of the results achieved. What devices or weapons were produced by Anglo-American collaboration which would have been delayed, weakened, or perhaps not produced at all if this collaboration had not existed? This is a question which it would hardly be possible to answer. So pervasive was the collaboration which existed, so intimate and so informal, that it resists an attempt to map it. We are driven instead to consider certain fields of activity in which collaboration was particularly intimate, in which it is believed to have been particularly successful, and by examining these, to gain some idea of the wider measure. Some such fields of activity thrust themselves upon the attention.

RADAR

The first is radar. From the days of the first war-time contacts until the end of hostilities radar is the subject most frequently mentioned in the papers dealing with Anglo-American scientific collaboration. The contacts were close and continuous; the results from the very beginning played an important part in the war. Radar in fact might be described as the bread-and-butter of our subject. The jet engine is another case. Here the striking feature is the magnitude of the original British contribution. When, in the spring of 1941, General Arnold was informed that a gas turbine had been built in Britain, and was actually on the point of being flown, the stimulus applied was one, not so much of friendly competition, but of complete shock. Such an episode could not, of course, have occurred in a later epoch of free exchange of information, but partly for that reason – if also for other reasons – the story of co-operation in the design of gas turbines is an outstanding one. There remains the most spectacular achievement. The development of the atomic bomb sprang with a startling directness from the disinterested work of physical research; it was conceived in the pre-war atmosphere of free international scientific intercourse, and any account of the war-time scientific collaboration between Britain and America must include a study of the manner in which this peace-time intercourse was developed for war purposes. It is in these fields, then, that we propose to pursue our subject.

The development of radar in Britain from 1934–45 is one of the best-known stories of war-time science, and it need be only briefly recalled here. Up to the date of the outbreak of war in 1939 development had been concentrated almost entirely on the great defensive system which was called the Home Chain. The Home Chain owed its origin to the first of a series of very fruitful contacts between scientists and military planners, which had taken place in 1934. In that year there had been set up the Committee for the Scientific Survey of Air Defence (more commonly called, from the name of its chairman, the Tizard Committee) which had the widest terms of reference to bring recent advances in science to bear on aerial defence. Among the first possibilities considered was that of the so-called death-ray, that is to say the use of a beam of radio waves to kill or disable men or destroy or damage aircraft, and the man to whom the Committee turned for an explanation of it was the Superintendent of the Radio Department of the National Physical Laboratory, Mr (later Sir Robert) Watson-Watt. Mr Watson-Watt had no difficulty in producing a few figures which relegated the death-ray idea once again to the realm of Wellsian fantasy. But his mind was now engaged upon defence possibilities, and he suggested as an alternative that of detecting aircraft by radio echo. He was asked to submit his proposals in some detail, and the result was a paper entitled 'The Detection of Aircraft by Radio Methods'. The title of this paper to be considered as an historic document is considerable. The technique which it described, that of transmitting very brief pulses of radio energy, and measuring from the time which they take to return in the form of an echo from an impenetrable object, the distance of that object from the transmitter, was well established. It was in fact a principal technique in the study of the ionosphere in which Mr Watson-Watt had been engaged. What was remarkable in Mr Watson-Watt's paper was the faith which it displayed in the defence possibilities of the technique, although these possibilities were based only upon a few fairly simple calculations. The Committee shared his faith, and after preliminary experiments work was put in hand which, in the course of the next four years, provided the British Isles with a chain of radar stations, covering the coast from Netherbutton in the Orkneys to Ventnor in the Isle of Wight.

The period 1939-42 saw the second stage of British radar development. In this period the purposes for which radar was being developed had moved from the defensive to the offensive. By the date of the outbreak of war several devices had already been considered, but work upon them had been very largely postponed in the interests of the Home Chain, and it was only in this second period that they were developed. The most important of these devices (apart from variations in the C.H. type of station and a Naval adaptation thereof) were a radar gun-laying device for anti-aircraft guns, known as G.L.; an air interception equipment to be carried in night fighters, called A.I.; and a device for the identification of aircraft, called I.F.F. (Identification Friend or Foe). Even with these devices in being, however, and other devices on the horizon, it was still not possible, in 1940, for anyone except a small number of scientists to foresee the effects of a revolutionary technical advance – described by Sir John Cockcroft as having 'contributed more to the success of the war than the atomic bomb'[1] which was then in course of being made.

This was the development of centimetric radar, which permitted the transmission of radar pulses to take place, as it were, along a narrow beam instead of the 'floodlighting' of the Home Chain station or the comparatively broad beam of the early A.I. This remarkable technique, which became possible as a result of the invention of the cavity magnetron early in 1940, opened up new possibilities, and was instrumental in allowing radar to play the great part which it did in the bomber offensive of 1943 onwards, and also in the war against the submarine. Long before this period however the American work had been amalgamated with the British.

In the United States the first consideration to be given to radio methods of detecting aircraft was in 1930, when the Director of the Naval Research Laboratory, as a result of observations on the reflections of continuous waves from aircraft, submitted to the Navy Department a detailed report on radio echo signals on moving objects. The Laboratory was directed to investigate the matter. During the same period the United States Army Signals Corps Laboratory was conducting similar investigations. In 1934 the two laboratories pooled their results and thereafter exchanged information. All this work was with continuous signals. It was in 1934 that Mr L. C. Young of the Naval Research Laboratory proposed that the pulse principle be applied to the problem of radio location. Work on this method was pursued during the next year, and in 1935 the first funds for the specific development of radar were allotted by the Naval Appropriations Committee of the House of Representatives. The sum allotted was 100,000 dollars.[2]

In June 1936 a demonstration was given of detecting equipment on land, and in the following April a shipboard early warning station was demonstrated for the first time. The next two years were spent in designing a practical shipboard model, and in 1939 a 1.5 metre early warning radar was given exhaustive sea trials in the battleship *U.S.S. New York*. Results were so satisfactory that in

---

[1] Sir John Cockcroft, *The Development and Future of Atomic Energy*, The Romanes Lecture for 1950 (The Clarendon Press, 1950).
[2] The account of the development of Radar in the U.S.A. in this and the succeeding paragraph is based upon that in the publication *Radar* of the United States Joint Board of Scientific Information Policy – reprinted in London, H.M. Stationery Office, 1945.

October 1939 the first contract was given to a commercial company for the manufacture of six sets of aircraft detection equipment.

In the meantime the Army Signal Corps Laboratory was pursuing a similar line of investigation. They demonstrated their first pulse radar against a bomber aircraft early in May 1937, the equipment being intended primarily for use with searchlights: the demonstration resulted in the first substantial allocation of army funds particularly for radar development. In November 1938 an approved 1.5 metre equipment, suitable for gun laying as well as searchlight control, was given extensive tests by the Coast Artillery Board. This set was considered sufficiently satisfactory for 18 pre-production models to be built in 1940/41 by the Signal Corps Laboratory, in order that equipment should be available for troops whilst commercial quantity production was getting under way.

This Signal Corps set was, of course, a short range device. The demonstration of it was witnessed by the then Deputy Chief of the Air Corps, General Arnold. As the result the Air Corps shortly afterwards asked the Chief Signal Officer to undertake the development of a 'long range detector and tracker'. The resulting equipment was demonstrated in November 1939, when ranges of 100 miles were obtained, and in August a contract was placed for positive production of this equipment for use by the Air Corps. From this beginning the United States Army Air Forces came to be the largest Service users of radar. Their interest included blind bombing devices similar to the British H_2S, short range navigational equipment and technical control equipment.

The development we have described so far was done in time of peace, directed wholly by the research laboratories of the two Services. As the war developed in Europe and the United States began their tremendous expansion of defence activities in 1940, there began a new phase in American radar work. The National Defence Research Committee set up a Microwave Committee in June 1940 to explore the possibilities of the radar field.

In its preliminary investigations the Microwave Committee concluded there were many important possibilities in the use of centimetre waves, but that none could be realised until a sufficiently powerful generator was devised. It was at this stage that the Tizard Mission visited the United States and revealed to the American authorities the British invention of the cavity magnetron, a device which had at one stroke lifted centimetric radar from the realm of the speculative to that of the accomplished. Immediate steps were taken to develop the magnetron in the United States, particularly by the Bell Telephone Corporation. The Tizard Mission urged the National Defence Research Committee to specialise in the microwave field and establish a large laboratory. The Mission also suggested that the United States should undertake the development of certain specific centimetre projects. These suggestions met with the approval of the Microwave Committee, which unanimously recommended the establishment of a special laboratory for the development of centimetre technique, staffed by university physicists. The N.D.R.C. as we have seen, was not empowered to build and operate laboratories of its own, but only to make contracts with others to do so. A contract was accordingly placed with the Massachusetts Institute of Technology (M.I.T.) to provide and administer the new laboratory. M.I.T. was chosen as fulfilling the requirements suggested by the Tizard Mission as being particularly important, viz. proximity to the sea, proximity to an airfield, and possession of a nucleus of scientists familiar with centimetre problems. This Radiation Laboratory, as it was named, was opened in November 1940, and a British Liaison Officer was appointed to its staff. This officer, Dr E. G. Bowen, exerted a profound influence on the development of the laboratory in its formative stage, and outlined the specification for the proposed centimetre A.I.[1]

Radiation Laboratory is of particular interest inasmuch as it filled in the American scene very much the same role that the Telecommunication Research Establishment (T.R.E.), the great British radar establishment, occupied in the United Kingdom. The staff was recruited from similar sources and it worked in a similar way. It had the advantage of more commodious buildings and better equipment, and was never disturbed by evacuation. Like T.R.E. the Radiation Laboratory grew rapidly; in fact from a total strength of 450 at the end of 1941 to 2,700 at the end of 1943, reaching a peak of 4,000 in 1944. During its life the laboratory was responsible for the design of no fewer than 150 distinct radar sets, all working on centimetre waves. In addition it designed the equipment for Loran, the long range navigational aid. As the war progressed the emphasis of the work of the Laboratory shifted, just as it did at T.R.E., from fundamental research to development, assistance to manufacturers, and field service.

From its inception Radiation Laboratory had close contact with T.R.E. and there was a very free interchange of information between the two establishments. This collaboration reached its peak with the establishment of a branch of the Laboratory within the precincts of T.R.E. This branch, known as B.B.R.L. for British Branch of the Radiation Laboratory, was responsible for advising on the use of American equipment in the European theatre and for undertaking such modifications to it as were found necessary. It played an important part in the co-ordination of American and British scientific

---

[1] J. P. Baxter 3rd, *Scientists Against Time* (Boston, U.S.A., Little, Brown & Co., 1946), p. 145. This book is a brief official history of O.S.R.D.

efforts in the later stages of the war. The close similarity between the Radiation Laboratory and T.R.E. is less surprising when one recalls that it was founded with the example of T.R.E. in mind and that its constitution was deliberately designed to resemble that of T.R.E. The fact that it subsequently developed along the same lines as the British establishment is a comment on the similarity of the scientific ways of working in different countries, and the similarity of the trend of war in both countries.

There were differences, of course. The most important was in contact with the Services. On the whole the contact between Radiation Laboratory and American Services was less direct than between their British counterparts, and it was not until fairly late in the war that a comparable degree of collaboration with the Staff authorities, particularly in the U.S.A.A.F., was established.

The two particular fields of radar work in which collaboration was closest were those of I.F.F. and what was called 'Beaconry'. I.F.F. stands for 'Identification, Friend or Foe'. From the earliest days of radar it was realised that it was essential to enable the operator of a radar set to determine whether the indications which he was receiving were caused by friendly or hostile craft, whether air or seaborne. It was realised that this identification should be quick (preferably instantaneous) and certain. The earliest mark numbers of the British I.F.F. were crude. In late 1940, that in use was Mark 2. The next development, which came to be known as I.F.F. Mark 3, was more than a new development. It was really a new system. It was based on a proposal first discussed at the Bawdsey Research Establishment in 1939, the development of which had not then been considered to be practicable by the Air Ministry. It was intended to be comprehensive and universal. The principle involved was that the function of location (i.e. the true radar function) should be separated from that of identification, at the detecting station. Experimental work on this proposal had been going on at T.R.E. since early 1940, and it was known that the possibility was technically a sound one. In September 1940 the Air Ministry decided that development of the scheme should proceed. Whilst, of course, the main consideration in pressing on with the Mark 3 programme was the most urgent operational requirement, another factor had also to be taken into account. This factor was the possibility of the United States coming into the war, in which event it would be necessary to have an I.F.F. system common to both British and American forces.

The Americans had been impressed with the need for radar identification and had developed a system of their own, which was for convenience called Mark 4 in the British, and subsequently in the combined discussions. In the British opinion this American system contained certain features which (either for operational or technical reasons) were undesirable. In June 1941 discussions in Britain brought the realisation that as the Americans were much concerned with I.F.F. policy, and might develop a system which would not fit in with our own radar services, a clear indication of our policy should be given. In the circumstances it was agreed that there should be no deflection from the policy of I.F.F. Mark 3, and accordingly that nothing should be allowed to hold up outstanding developments. In September a high level meeting was held between representatives of the United States Army and Navy and the British radar authorities, and at this meeting the new British system was described. The possibility of using both systems together was discussed. It was pointed out that such a course would involve considerable technical difficulties, and it was suggested that the United States Navy might find it impossible to use the British Mark 3 in its ships. The meeting was not qualified to decide the matter but it was agreed that it should be discussed again between British and American experts. In the meantime a T.R.E. scientist had flown to America with a model of the airborne Mark 3 set.

It had already been decided that a large-scale trial of the Mark 3 was necessary, to test particular facilities, and generally to demonstrate its suitability for use by all three British Services. Added urgency was now given to the requirement by the need to show a working system to the Americans. In August a newly formed Committee decided upon a programme of inter-Service trials to be held in Pembrokeshire as soon as possible. These trials, which were held in September 1941, were exceedingly elaborate and thorough-going. Some difficulties were inevitably experienced, owing to the experimental nature of part of the equipment, but the results were in general very satisfactory. The report made to the appropriate committee stated 'that all observers agreed that the trials amply demonstrate that the I.F.F. Mark 3 system should be made the basis of a universal identification system, employing R.D.F. means.' To quote from the report submitted to the United States Embassy, 'it has been urgently and jointly recommended that this system be adopted in its entirety by the United States War and Navy Departments in all geographical areas.' The following July the appropriate American committee recommended that a common identification system for radar was essential, and that the British Mark 3 should be adopted as standard for United States and British forces. This was the final stage in the acceptance of I.F.F. Mark 3 for use in the Allied Services.

I.F.F. Mark 3, however, was by no means the end of the identification story. It was realised at an early stage that this system would probably not last out the war, for two main reasons, namely its inability to function satisfactorily in very high aircraft densities, and the ease with which it could be interrogated by the enemy, so giving him a cheap long-range warning system. These considerations relating to I.F.F. Mark 3, had also been a source of concern to the Americans. Indeed, within a month of accepting I.F.F. Mark 3 the United States authorities had written a paper describing the system which they thought should replace it. A few months later, in June 1942, they began preliminary work on the development of such a system. This I.F.F. was known as Mark 5. At this stage they had not decided on the wavelength to be used, but shortly afterwards, as the result of a visit to the United States of a British radar scientist, they were persuaded to consider the possibility of using the same wavelength as the British were using for what was called S.B.B., Single Band Beaconry.

It will be convenient here to insert a brief explanation of the nature of radar beaconry. The Radar Beacon was in a sense the inverse of the I.F.F. set: that is, it provided a means by which an aircraft carrying an appropriate radar set might identify a point on the ground by means of a transponder placed at that point. The importance of this in guiding an aircraft, or homing it to a given point, needs no explanation. By the spring of 1942 the multiplication of types of beacon and associated equipment had led to a situation as confused and complicated as that of I.F.F. had been in 1941. There were in existence the A.I. and A.S.V. Beacon network operating on two different wavelengths in the 1.5 metre band, and each including two different types of beacons. In April 1942, therefore, proposals were made for a new system, together with suggestions for an interim scheme to cover the period that must elapse before the comprehensive system – called S.B.B. for Single Band Beaconry – could be put into operation. It had four major features: first, it was to use a separate and exclusive band of short waves; secondly, it was to offer greatly increased security against imitation by, or interference from, the enemy; thirdly, it offered more facilities than were provided by existing Beacon-Interrogator systems, including the H method of bombing, and in certain cases blind bombing and torpedoing; fourthly, a small number of standard units was proposed by means of which any aircraft or ship could be provided with any, or all, the facilities.

This illustrates the importance of the United States having been persuaded to consider the possiblity of using the same wavelength for their Mark 5 as the British were proposing to use for S.B.B. Moreover, the Americans suggested that should I.F.F. become universal it was desirable that the new system should be developed by an international group. This suggestion was welcomed, and British representatives joined the group, which was working at the

Naval Research Laboratory, Anacostia, during the latter part of 1942. This was the first occasion in the field of radio upon which the British and Americans had engaged in a combined research effort, and very great political importance was attached to it.

Thus, by the end of 1942, two lines of research were proceeding, one (a purely British effort) in this country towards S.B.B., one on a combined basis in America towards Mark 5. Inevitably the question arose of combining the two efforts, especially in view of the British conviction that beacons and identification were inseparable. After considerable discussion on both sides of the Atlantic it was finally agreed that development of the two projects should be combined. An important factor in reaching this decision was the insistence of the United States Navy upon the vital importance of beacons and I.F.F. to its operations, especially in the Pacific. It was further decided to transfer the whole of the development work, and the T.R.E. team engaged upon it, to Washington. This decision was made partly in pursuance of the idea of combined research already embodied in the international I.F.F. Mark 5 group, and partly because it was realised that in view of the tremendous magnitude of the programme involved, it would be impossible for the heavily loaded British radio industry to undertake production.

In the spring of 1943 the T.R.E. team went to the United States to join the Combined Research Group in a laboratory specially built for the purpose, to undertake a programme of work upon what, at the suggestion of the British, was now renamed United Nations Beacons. The project was given highest priority by the Americans. It would be out of place in the present narrative to pursue the history of the United Nations Beacons any further; it will suffice to know that it reached an advanced stage of development, and that the contracts for production had been placed by the end of the war. With the end of the war the development was stopped and the Combined Research Group wound up in October 1945.[1]

So much for I.F.F. and 'Beaconry'. Another important field of collaboration between British and American radar scientists was that of radio counter-measures, or R.C.M. as they came to be known. By R.C.M. was meant devices, systems, or operational signals technique designed to hinder or prevent the use by an enemy of his own radio signals or radar system. The most obvious counter-measure is jamming, that is to say radiation of suitably modulated signals on the same wavelength as that used by the enemy, the jamming signals being much stronger at the enemy's receiver than those that he desires for it. Other counter-measures include the radiation of signals so as to cause his direction-finding equipment to give false indications, the emission of 'spoof' signals intended to

---

[1] See *North American Supply, op. cit.*, Chapter XI.

divert his attention from one's own operational system, and the discharge of reflecting objects capable of producing misleading echoes in his radar set. The story of what might be called the counter-measures war in radio is in itself elaborate, and we need only note here that a very great deal had been done, and many outstanding successes obtained on the British side, before the Americans entered the field in the spring of 1942. At that date they established at Harvard the Radio Research Laboratory (R.R.L.) solely for the development of counter-measures. As the result of a visit of the Compton Mission to the United Kingdom, at about the same time, it was agreed that the new laboratory should concentrate on longer term problems, while the British establishments, situated as they were near to the main theatre of operations, should undertake projects of more immediate applicability.

In the autumn of 1942 the Americans decided to set up a forward section of R.R.L. in England. As a first step scientists were sent, in the spring of 1943, to work with their opposite numbers at T.R.E. By the autumn buildings had been erected within the precincts of T.R.E. and the Group was established there. This American Group was, of course, in no way controlled by T.R.E., but there was the closest technical collaboration between it and the British and it was represented at meetings of the appropriate British committees. During the last eighteen months of the war the British benefited directly from the long-term projects sponsored by the R.R.L., particularly the development and production of critical components such as noise-generating valves. American designs, therefore, were used in operations by the R.A.F. in 1944.

The counter-measures war, which may be likened to a game of chess, continued until the end of hostilities. During the last phase the most important element in it, on the Allied side, was the defence of the bombers. The enemy's methods of attack varied and improved in many respects. In the summer of 1944 Germany introduced a new kind of A.I., similar in principle to the Allied A.I. Mark 4 and much better suited to free lance operations than the existing German equipment. To counter this, airborne electronic jammers, based on American equipment, were used. The availability of this American equipment was a consequence of a policy of encouraging long-term research at the R.R.L. in the United States. Many different methods, some very crude, of communicating with their fighters, were tried by the Germans in their efforts to overcome British jamming; and to neutralise the effects of interference with his ground control of inter-ception, new methods of fixing his fighters were developed by the enemy.

The Germans, indeed, fought the counter-measures war to the bitter end, and despite the shorter distance over enemy territory which Allied aircraft had to cover as our troops advanced in Europe, the threat was by no means disposed of at the end of the war. The idea that the Germans might have up their sleeve a counter-measure – or counter-counter-measure – which would prove dramatically successful against the great armada of Allied aircraft then regularly in the air, remained a kind of nightmare possibility. Against the threat of disaster in the radio war the integration of British and American science was a necessary measure; its completeness and its almost complete lack of serious discord was impressive.

THE JET ENGINE

The striking parallel which existed between the British and American development of radar was not reproduced in every field. The possibility of using jet reaction as a means of propelling aircraft had been considered for many years by scientists and engineers in many countries, but the story in Britain and in America was very different. In England it was Air Commodore Sir Frank Whittle who pioneered jet propulsion as a practical scheme, and the first definite proposal to use a gas turbine for jet propulsion was contained in a patent taken out by him in 1930. Whittle had first become interested in jet propulsion in 1928 as a young R.A.F. Cadet when he realised that a gas turbine working on the internal combustion cycle would be an efficient means of providing compression, combustion and expansion for jet propulsion. The Air Ministry, however, although sufficiently interested in Whittle himself to send him to Cambridge, first to take a degree, and then to work upon his project, was not interested in his project. Accordingly, in 1935, a private company known as Power Jets Ltd. was formed from sources quite outside the aviation industry to develop his inventions. The firm's assets were very small; indeed, apart from Whittle's ability they had scarcely any. However, a contract was given to the British Thomson Houston Company to manufacture an experimental jet propulsion unit to Whittle's designs and instructions. Throughout this period Whittle experienced great difficulties. Although he had the constant support of Sir Henry Tizard, the Air Ministry still thought his problems virtually insuperable. It had a certain interest in the results of his experiments and paid a contribution towards his running costs, also offering him such limited resources on gas turbine work as the Royal Aircraft Establishment (R.A.E.) could offer. Dr Griffith of the R.A.E., however, who had done pioneer work on gas turbines independently of Whittle, was not now actively pursuing it. In any case Griffith and his colleagues, by contrast with Whittle, were much more interested in collecting certain scientific and theoretical data than in building an engine. But although his theories met with considerable appreciation with the Aeronautical Research Council (A.R.C.) in the twenties, for various reasons direct work on the gas turbine at the R.A.E. ceased from 1930 to 1937, and Griffith, a man of multiple scientific talents, turned his attention elsewhere. In 1937 interest was greatly revived at the R.A.E., particularly when Mr Hayne Constant put forward the view that a turbine unit could be built at that time without further research. The interest of the authorities was excited and maintained, and work on such a unit and its variants continued from this period.

Whittle's single-stage centrifugal compressor with single-stage turbine was, compared to the elaborate multi-stage axial flow compressor and turbine designed at the R.A.E., almost elementary and perhaps potentially less efficient. But it was relatively cheap to build and although mechanical failures did occur and it never in fact achieved its designed performance, it worked from the first moment it was completed. It was not. however, until 1937, when Dr Griffith made a generally favourable report on the experimental unit, that official interest really quickened. The Engine Sub-Committee of the A.R.C. then declared that it thought 'the time was ripe for departures in power plant design of this type'. Accordingly, in 1938, a research contract was given to the firm by the Air Ministry, and after several setbacks the unit was, in 1939, run successfully up to 17,000 r.p.m. The Air Ministry then invited the Gloster Aircraft Company to design an experimental airframe for the installation of Whittle's engine.

The 'jet engine' was now, at last, an official development project, a project of acknowledged importance and of high promise, something to be pulled right out of the 'back room' and given a place in the sun. The small firm of Power Jets, precariously if bravely financed, was turned, at the expense of the Ministry of Aircraft Production, into an adequate development unit with its own small factory, and Whittle and his team were given a free hand for the speedy development of his engine. By the end of 1942 Power Jets was firmly established and eleven firms had taken on commitments involving aspects of gas turbine engineering. What was equally important was the fact that, largely as a result of Government policy, most of these firms agreed to form a committee – the Gas Turbine Collaboration Committee – for the purpose of pooling information and giving assistance to each other, the patents question being shelved until after the war. The Chairman of this Committee was Dr Roxbee Cox, the Deputy Director of Scientific Research in M.A.P. The Director and General Manager of Rolls-Royce declared that 'as the Americans were being given all information British firms might as well receive it'. In its activities the Gas Turbine Collaboration Committee was given much theoretical help by the R.A.E. It is now appropriate to consider the course of turbine development in the United States and the impact of the work of Whittle and Griffith upon it.

The indigenous development of the gas turbine in America has been described in an American history.[1] Although design studies of a preliminary character for gas turbine for jet propulsion had been undertaken by various firms in America by 1941 under official encouragement, little progress had been made. It would be fair to say that by this date American jet pioneers were in much the position of Whittle in the thirties – talent and zeal were not lacking but government and industrial interest were at best tepid. Furthermore, while Whittle had had in mind the whole time one constant and limited aim, namely the construction of an engine for the propulsion of aircraft, the Americans seemed undecided as to where the jet principle could best be applied. Engineers in the United States had been interested for a long time in the gas turbine and its related projects such as the turbo supercharger – a gas turbine with the combustion chamber replaced by a reciprocating engine. Wright Field and the General Electric Company concerned themselves during the thirties with such projects, but obstacles were discussed in terms of airframes, speeds, and so forth still appropriate to the reciprocating engine. The higher authorities in the Army were not forthcoming with much support and although the nature of some of the problems that faced the jet engineer were well realised – the difficulty for example of finding a material capable of withstanding high temperatures, a task that delayed Whittle's progress for a long time – the resources were not there for experimentation. Hence it was not until 1939 that a serious attempt was made to prepare a design of an aircraft gas turbine with active support from a government quarter.

Such a design was produced by the Northrop Aircraft, Inc., with the support of the United States Naval Bureau of Aviation, the United States Army also displaying a more distant interest. An Army-Navy development contract was eventually placed with Northrop in June 1941 for design and manufacture of the unit but little interest was shown in long-term development, testing facilities were inadequate and in particular no engine appears to have been built in order to test the compressor, although the engine in question was of 25,000 h.p. Another scheme was attempted in 1940 by the Lockheed Aircraft Corporation, whose designer, Mr N. C. Price, unlike Northrop's, designed his turbine to be used for jet propulsion, not to drive a propeller. Moreover, his firm decided that what was

---

[1] The source for turbine development in the United States is *The Development of Aircraft Engines and Aviation Fuels*, by Robert Schlaifer and S. D. Heron of Harvard University, 1950.

necessary was a fundamentally new attack with the purpose of attaining radically higher speed and altitude than with the conventional engine.[1] It was not, however, until 1942 that the plans were formally submitted to the Army for an appropriate airframe and engine and it is symptomatic of the isolation in which each firm was working – partly as a result of Government policy – that it was not until 1943 that Lockheed heard that other companies had been working since 1941 on jet engines of both American and British design. It would appear that the first firm to take a deep interest in Whittle's experiments was the Wright Aeronautical Corporation, which made no study of gas turbines on its own, but heard in 1940 of Whittle's experiments and in 1941 entered into negotiations for an American licence to manufacture the Whittle engine. These events were all to be thrust into the background, however, by the direct deal, described later, between the American Army and the British Government with regard to the Whittle engine, but at least the negotiations showed that Americans generally were now beginning to take a greater interest. The Navy entered into a contract with the Turbo Engineering Corporation in 1942, its head engineer having already devised a turbo-supercharger shelved for lack of Government or private interest. From this time until at least about 1943 the Navy investigated very seriously the possibilities of turbojets, in particular a turbo-jet booster engine as a means of obtaining short bursts of very high speed.

In the meantime jet propulsion had seized the attention of the military authorities. The Army set up a committee known as the Special Committee on Jet Propulsion, officially to investigate rockets as primary power plants for aircraft but with an interest in jets of all kinds. It included representation from the universities, turbine firms and the Services. As a result of the vigorous activities of this Committee it was decided that three turbine companies should each go ahead with a detailed study of an engine of the type it preferred, the other two firms criticising each design. The regular aero-engine companies were intentionally excluded at the request of General Arnold and those companies received no official information whatever about the development of gas turbines at any time before 1945. After an analysis by the committee it was decided that the three proposals, all of them for axial compressors, were promising enough to justify design studies being made, and the committee then submitted a report to the Bureau of Aeronautics, recommending that contracts should be given for the development of all three engines.

The indigenous development of the turbine in America was, however, bound to lose much of its significance when it was realised

---

[1] Robert Schlaifer and S. D. Heron, *op. cit.*, p. 450.

in the United States how far Whittle had gone, and the time for this realisation was ripe. Sir Henry Tizard had already given some intimation of British work on gas turbines to the National Advisory Committee for Aeronautics in 1940, and General Arnold[1] in the course of his visit to England in the early months of 1941, was informed 'to his great astonishment', as it is recorded, that gas turbines had actually been built and were on the point of being flown. It is not surprising, therefore, that the American Government should have asked the British Government in June of the same year for information on the Whittle project, posing several detailed questions about the state of development and the behaviour of the unit on flight tests. The matter was referred to the North American Supply Committee under the chairmanship of Lord Beaverbrook, and in July 1941, it was agreed that information on the Whittle engine should be released to the United States Government, with the recommendation that the General Electric Company, the pioneer of this work in the States, on the grounds of their previous experience of turbo-superchargers, should undertake development. An American committee was then set up under General Arnold to arrange with M.A.P. about collaboration. Dr Roxbee Cox, one of the foremost names in the history of British jet propulsion, and chairman of the Gas Turbine Collaboration Committee, was placed in direct control of the release of information and by October a general agreement was reached between the two Governments as to the nature and purpose of the disclosure, by which it was agreed that the chief object would be to assist the joint defence plans. For this commendable, but somewhat vague purpose, the W1X engine, one of Whittle's earlier types, was to be sent to America by air, and educational orders for W.2 engines were to be placed in the United States. It was decided that the Whittle project should be the basis of a jet propulsion development programme, the United States by agreement concentrating on production. Subsequently the U.S.A.A.F. was furnished with production drawings, including material specifications of current Rover W2B drawings, and the W1X engine was despatched with the loan of the services of three Power Jets engineers, who assisted General Electric in the early stages. Information was also released to the United States Embassy in London about the jet projects of Metropolitan Vickers (the unit F.2), De Havilland (the H.1 engine), and Rolls-Royce, and, after the formation in England of the Gas Turbine Collaboration Committee minutes of all the meetings and progress reports were sent to the United States.

In addition much information on British projects was sent to

---

[1] Robert Schlaifer and S. D. Heron, *op. cit.*, p. 461.

America during the months immediately following the original disclosure to assist General Electric in their manufacture of Whittle type engines, and British representatives were appointed in both countries to transmit information. The number of American departments sharing the benefits of turbine information increased. Thus in June 1942 it was decided that all information about gas turbine projects should be in duplicate, one copy being sent to the U.S.A.A.F. and the other to the Bureau of Aeronautics Navy Department. In the same year Whittle himself went over to America and spent two months with the General Electric Company and the Bell Aircraft Corporation, giving them all the assistance he could in the development of the projects, and this precedent set by Whittle and his Power Jet engineers in visiting America was followed by exchange visits of American and British experts which continued throughout the war. Also, from the end of 1942 onwards the submission of designs by British firms to the United States for possible manufacture in that country became a regular feature. Thus in September 1942 Major D. J. Keirn, who was at that time in charge of the gas turbine projects in the United States Army, accompanied by a U.S.A.A.F. colleague, visited Britain to investigate the possibility of the manufacture of the De Havilland H.1 engine in the United States. It is interesting to note that he reported that the British were far ahead in four respects: the development of the engines themselves, research on the possible applications of the engines, the study of the design and possible performance of turbine-driven planes, and the co-ordination of the development of the planes and the engines.[1] As a result of the visit installation drawings and other data of these engines were sent over to the United States and Dr Hawthorne of the R.A.E. took over similar data on the Metropolitan Vickers F.2 unit, as well as visiting the General Electric Company to inform and advise them.

In May 1943 a conference was held at the Bureau of Aeronautics, Washington, with representatives from the United States Navy and Army and the British Air Commission to discuss the use of a fighter aircraft incorporating a reciprocating engine driving a propeller of a De Havilland H.1 unit installed as a booster. After some abortive negotiations this idea was replaced by that of a new fighter powered by one De Havilland H.1 unit, the contract being placed with the Lockheed Aircraft Corporation. Full specifications of the aircraft were sent to M.A.P. and a mock-up of the De Havilland engine was sent by air to the United States in July 1943.

In the meantime, in the middle of July 1943, a United States Mission, consisting of members of the U.S.A.A.F. and United States

---

[1] Robert Schlaifer and S. D. Heron, *op. cit.*, p. 466.

Bureau of Aeronautics, together with representatives of the General Electric Company and the Bell Aircraft Corporation, came to Britain to make a complete tour of the British gas turbine industry. The party was given free access to every firm and establishment in the United Kingdom working on gas turbines. Shortly afterwards another Mission sponsored by the Bureau of Aeronautics, with strong industrial representation, followed it. During the visits of these two Missions the manufacture of the De Havilland H.1 unit by Allis-Chalmers was discussed at some length and a provisional agreement was made between the two companies and sponsored by the respective Governments. It was agreed that Allis-Chalmers should be given a non-exclusive licence to manufacture the H.1, no changes to be introduced without permission of De Havilland, and that the latter firm would supply complete manufacturing drawings, material specifications and in addition sufficient parts to enable Allis-Chalmers to manufacture the engines called for in their original contract from the Bureau of Aeronautics. They proceeded with their preparations for the manufacture of this unit and by the end of the war had manufactured several engines, the performance of which was comparable with those manufactured in Britain by De Havilland. The firm of Lockheed's also did some work on the De Havilland H.1, and the United States Army and Lockheed's gained valuable performance data from the two H.1 units sent over from England. In addition to this, drawings and a considerable amount of data were sent to the United States on the following units – De Havilland Goblin H.1, Power Jets W2/500 and W2/700, Rolls-Royce Welland B.23 and Derwent B.37, Metropolitan Vickers F.2 and F.3 and Armstrong-Siddeley ASX.

At the beginning of 1943 a special branch was set up in the Ministry of Aircraft Production to act as the channel for interchange of information on gas turbines. Through this channel up-to-date details of the various engines were sent, day-by-day queries were dealt with, and any difficulties experienced by the Americans were passed to this country through the British Air Commission for advice and assistance if possible. The Americans on their side made available copies of progress reports issued weekly by General Electric and monthly by both Westinghouse and Northrop, who were working on gas turbine projects. Engine and aircraft brochures were sent as they became available. Early in 1944 the Bureau of Aeronautics sent a representative to London to act in the United Kingdom on gas turbine projects. From that time until the end of the war this representative was given very complete facilities to visit such British firms working on gas turbines as he liked and to collect information on British gas turbine projects. At the same time it became apparent that a visit to the United States by a British expert of the same standing as Whittle was desirable in view of the frequency of the visits of American experts. Hence Group Captain Watt and later a party consisting of Constant and Griffith and representatives from the main British gas turbine firms toured the United States with great success.

As far as interchange on the material side was concerned, in addition to the supply of units described above the United Kingdom sent over seven De Havilland H.1 units for flight testing or test bed running, and for a short time a Meteor was sent for flight testing. From the American side Britain received a number of forged turbine blades, of particular use at that precise moment, a Bell P.59 aircraft, sent in 1943, and a Lockheed P.80 with a Rolls-Royce B.41 engine. Until the end of the war all releases of technical information between the two countries had been covered by the Patent Interchange Agreement which specified that either Government could request from the other full details of any items of war equipment likely to contribute to the war effort of the United Nations. At the end of the war this arrangement was replaced by normal commercial procedure.

So far little has been said of the actual work carried out in the United States on gas turbines. American firms were concerned, as were British firms, with the two types of engine – centrifugal and axial. Work on the former had the closest connection with this country, General Electric having an almost complete monopoly of it, all details of the earlier Whittle engines having been released to them. The only other firm manufacturing the centrifugal gas turbine in America was Allis-Chalmers, who were manufacturing the De Havilland H.1 under licence. The firm experienced many of the difficulties of Power Jets as well as combustion trouble of their own. The firm of General Electric made great strides during the four years of the war they were at work on centrifugal engines, with the aid of their enormous resources and a spirit of initiative and interest, but they appear to have been hampered by their lack of experience on aero-engine manufacture and the general difficulties, inherent in many war-time projects, of putting an entirely new design of engine into production before development had gone far. They built several designs except for the combustion equipment, almost entirely on the power jet W2B, W.2500 and W.2700 designs, their versions being known as the I.14 and I.16, and the I.20. The I.40 version was a larger engine similar in principle to recent centrifugal engines in Britain the designing of which began in June 1943. This was perhaps the most promising of the American engines. The I.40 engine by the end of the war had an average rating of 4,000 lb. thrust for a weight of 1,820 lb., with a maximum over-all diameter of 48 inches. This may be contrasted with the Rolls-Royce Nene,

the design of which was begun in March 1944 (ten months after the
I.40), and which had in 1946 obtained a rating of 5,000 lb. thrust
for a weight of 1,580 lb. and a maximum diameter of 49½ inches.
The design of axial flow compressors used in America represented
one of the greatest differences in gas turbine practice between the
two countries, and was probably to some extent influenced by the
National Advisory Committee for Aeronautics which had designed
and ran an axial flow compressor of its own. By the end of the war
General Electric had two axial flow gas turbine units under development, one of which, the TC.180, was designed to give a 4,000 lb.
thrust. Neither of the units was in a fully developed state and for
some time they were both overshadowed by the enormous amount
of work which was being carried out on the centrifugal type of
engine. There was apparently no connection in General Electric
with the centrifugal work being carried on in the same firm.
Failures of cast turbine blades delayed development for a time,
forged blades having to be used, and it was clear that a great deal
of development had to be done before the engines would be ready
for production in any numbers. Difficulties of a similar kind were
experienced by Westinghouse which succeeded in constructing units
with a far lower weight than corresponding units of other firms, but
found combustion as serious a problem as General Electric had done.

A comparison between the gas turbine activities in Britain and
in America would stress the fact that in Britain after the setting up
of the Gas Turbine Collaboration Committee in 1941 all manufacturers engaged on gas turbines, together with specialists on various
associated subjects, had worked in collaboration. The necessity of
disclosing useful information to the other members of the committee was accepted. But no parallel organisation existed in
America, and the American Government maintained as of old that
the firms were likely to progress more quickly when working entirely
independently of each other and as strict commercial competitors,
although the American manufacturers of conventional aircraft
engines had been exchanging every sort of information since 1940[1].
As a result of this there were no concerted efforts to overcome
particular problems inherent in gas turbine design. The differences
over security regulations and their effect were another source of
difficulty when the American tradition of maintaining the strictest
security is contrasted with the British notion of 'no secrets within
the main secret'. The Americans occasionally found fault that
information they sent over to Britain was handed out to all the big
firms. This, of course, was part of a difference of procedure between
the two countries by no means confined to jet problems.

---

[1] Robert Schlaifer and S. D. Heron, *op. cit.*, p. 467.

So a project first conceived as practicable by a young Air Force Cadet in 1930 became during the war a vast Anglo-American industrial venture and laid the foundation for the post-war jet industry in the United States based largely on British jet engines manufactured under licence. Throughout, the venture owed much to the intensely practical approach of Whittle, his resolute insistence upon it as an engineering project whose end was to get an engine flying. There could be no greater contrast with the story to which we now turn.

THE ATOMIC BOMB

Of all the scientific achievements of the Second World War the atomic bomb sprang most directly from disinterested scientific research. The history of the achievement has become familiar,[1] and it is not proposed here once again to cover all the ground from Becquerel's discovery of radioactivity in 1896 to the dropping of the first atomic bomb on Japan in 1945. The intention is rather to illustrate the nature of the international co-operation than to give an account of its results, and it will be assumed that the reader has at least an outline knowledge of the general history.

The series of discoveries in the field of nuclear physics which marked the period from 1896 to 1945 provide as striking an illustration as could be wished of the international character of scientific research. The work of J. J. Thomson and Rutherford, Chadwick, Cockcroft and others in England, was woven into a fabric in which other strands were supplied by Bohr and his colleagues in Denmark; by Joliot Curie and others in France; by Fermi and his school in Italy; by Einstein, Planck, Hahn, Strassman, Meitner, and others in Germany; and by Wheeler, Lawrence, Urey and others in America. Nuclear physics had in fact followed the normal pattern of international co-operation. During the thirties, however, abnormal developments had occurred which were to have very important effects. Both Nazi Germany and Fascist Italy, by the policy which they pursued, lost some of their most distinguished nuclear physicists, and their loss was their future enemies' gain. Thus Halban and Kowarski left Germany first to work in France with Joliot Curie and later in England; in 1939 Frisch and Meitner went to Denmark to work with Bohr; in 1934 Fermi left Italy for America; Simon, Peierls and Fuchs came directly to Britain. When, in January 1939, Bohr paid a visit to America, he came fresh from discussions with Frisch and Meitner as well as with his Danish-born colleagues, and

---

[1] See *Statements Relating to the Atomic Bomb* (London, H.M. Stationery Office, 1945) and *Atomic Energy* (United States Government Printing Office: reprinted in London, H.M. Stationery Office, 1945).

CC

entered into further discussions with Fermi, as well as with the American-born scientists whom he would normally have met there.

Without going into details it may be as well to give a brief indication of the state of nuclear physics at the time of this important visit. The discovery of the neutron by Chadwick in 1932 provided physicists with a fresh and powerful means of examining the nature of atomic nuclei, which in the following years were systematically subjected to slow-neutron bombardment. Particular interest attached to the bombardment of the heaviest elements, and above all to uranium. A characteristic result was the formation of new isotopes – that is to say materials differing in atomic mass but not in physical or chemical properties – which then normally decayed by radiation. The radioactive products which resulted from the bombardment of uranium, which certainly could not be identified with any of the elements immediately below uranium in atomic number, were at first taken to be laboratory creations, since they did not exist in nature. In 1939, however, Hahn and Strassman showed that one of these products was identifiable as an isotope of barium, an element with an atomic number only about half that of uranium. What had occurred in fact was a splitting of the uranium nucleus into two, a phenomenon which came to be known as 'nuclear fission'. This phenomenon was comprehensible in the light of a theory of nuclear reactions which had been propounded by Bohr some time previously.

The visit by Bohr to America early in 1939 was thus more than merely an interesting illustration of the especially close contacts which Nazi and Fascist persecution had brought about among nuclear physicists in the democratic countries. The discussions which then took place on the subject of uranium fission, Fermi's suggestion that multiple neutrons might be emitted in the process, and the successful and almost simultaneous completion of fission experiments in France, Denmark and America, brought about the situation in which the new development became a subject of legitimate interest to military authorities.

The circumstances which made nuclear fission a matter of practical interest was, of course, the emergence of the possibility of a chain reaction. The principle of a chain reaction is simple and well-understood. Briefly, the condition, as applied to uranium fission, is that if, in the bombardment of a fissionable element by neutrons, each fission releases more than one new neutron, then a process is involved which rapidly releases a vast amount of energy. Knowledge of the theoretical possibility of deriving energy from mass was widely spread outside scientific circles long before 1939, and interest had been stimulated by works of popular science in which considerable ingenuity had been displayed in devising illustrations of the amounts of energy involved. In scientific circles in 1939, however, there was no disposition to be optimistic about the realisation in practice of the possibility which had just been revealed. The theoretical problems were complex and severe; even if they could be solved there were immense practical difficulties whose very nature was obscure. Yet the possibility of utilising atomic energy for military purposes did exist, and both in Britain and in America steps were taken at least to initiate a liaison between the scientists concerned and the military authorities.

In America it was Pegram of Columbia who in March 1939 brought about a meeting between Fermi and representatives of the Navy Department. The Navy Department expressed interest, but at this period the initiative remained in the hands of the scientists, and in particular the group of foreign-born scientists of which Szilard was a prominent member and which operated to some extent under the auspices of Einstein. It was this group which Mr Alexander Sachs of New York represented when he drew the attention of President Roosevelt to the importance of the subject and the desirability of Government support. The President accordingly appointed a committee, the Advisory Commitee on Uranium, with Briggs as chairman and representatives of the Army and Navy Ordnance Organisations as its members.

Official recognition was a very important step, but it did not in itself mean any great acceleration of the preliminary steps which were then being made. These moves in fact were rather hesitant. The American committee first met in October, and in November submitted to the President a report which proposed a modest experimental programme, for which a first allocation of $6,000 was made by the military authorities. No second meeting of the committee was held until April 1940, and although important progress had been made as a result of which interest was now centred upon the U-235 isotope exclusively, disturbing intelligence had arrived from Germany about work on uranium being undertaken at the Kaiser Wilhelm Institute in Berlin. A renewed sense of urgency was experienced and voiced by the scientists, but before we examine the effects that this was to have in the United States we must consider the state of affairs in Britain, where a very important step was taken in the same month of April 1940.

It may be assumed that at the time of the outbreak of the European war in September 1939, and for at least some months afterwards, almost all that was known in the field of nuclear physics was known internationally. There was also the likelihood that scientists everywhere would follow certain lines of thought and investigation which had already suggested themselves. British, American and German scientists started level. We may therefore concentrate on the organisation in the United Kingdom and the United States and the steps that were eventually taken to co-operate. In Britain there already existed, as we have seen, a fairly elaborate framework for the organisation of scientific work for war purposes, and when it was decided to give official recognition to nuclear research in this respect the work could be fitted into this framework. In fact it was a body known as the Committee for the Scientific Survey of Air Warfare, an Air Ministry organisation, which originally took this research into its province. This Committee had already had, in 1940, a distinguished career. It was the successor of the Committee for the Scientific Study of Air Defence – generally known from the name of its chairman as the Tizard Committee – which had done much to guide and further the radar work which had been the most important single scientific contribution to defence in the immediate pre-war period. It was in April 1940 that the Air Warfare Committee set up a sub-committee 'on the U-bomb'. This sub-committee, which was presided over by Professor G. P. (later Sir George) Thomson was, from the date of its first meeting on the 10th April, a very active body. Attendance was elastic, being made up of some six to twelve of the most eminent university physicists, and the fact that meetings were held, not in the offices of a department of state, but at the Royal Society, tended to emphasise that this was a project which depended peculiarly upon academic science. All the early research, which was from the outset pressed forward upon the assumption that a uranium bomb for use in the current war was a reasonably practical proposition, was done in the various university laboratories, and the raw materials required were obtained directly from industrial firms by the scientists concerned.

Thus despite the markedly practical aim which the work now had it was carried on in very much the same way, and in rather the same atmosphere, as the pre-war research had been. The note of personal responsibility was very marked and the independence of the official government machinery was also noteworthy. The work was spread by personal contacts, and while it was necessary to refer to Military Intelligence for information about work being done in Germany the first mention of the United States, made as early as the second meeting, was a reference to Professor G. P. Thomson asking Professor Hill 'to find out whether anything of interest is being done in U.S.A.'. America also figured in the early discussions as a possible source of uranium. In July it was decided to approach Professor Fowler, who was about to set out for Canada, 'so that he could make informal overtures with regard to Canadian and American co-operation'.

Events were, in fact, moving towards a pooling of knowledge. It was specifically proposed at a meeting of the British Committee (now called the M.A.U.D. Committee) in August; at the same meeting a note by Professor Hill on the American work was produced. In January 1941, Professor Cockcroft, reporting on activity in America, said that the work for the National Defence Research Council was mainly concerned with isotope separation; the Naval Laboratory at Washington was working on hexafluoride production. This report was brief, but took account of the work of many American nuclear physicists working in different centres. At the third meeting of the M.A.U.D. Technical Committee – for the main committee had now been divided into two – Professor Bainbridge of the N.D.R.C. was invited to discuss the production of heavy water. At this point – April 1941 – the United States were considering embarking upon an extensive production programme, and wished to have a report from Halban. This report, Professor Fowler thought, if accompanied by a critical study by Chadwick, might have great influence in America. At this meeting both Professor Bainbridge and the British scientists emphasised the inadequacy of exchanging reports and the desirability of visits and close personal contacts. Dr Halban's report was duly sent to America, and the design of plant for the manufacture of heavy water was taken up by the N.D.R.C.

Information flowing the other way was contained in two reports, from Darwin in July 1941, and from Oliphant in September. These together gave an adequate outline of activity, thought, and possibilities in the United States. One or two major distinctions between the American and the British approach were already well appreciated. The Americans were less interested in heavy water as a moderator; their hopes lay rather in graphite. In the field of isotope separation the British emphasis was on the diffusion process; the Americans had given at least equal attention to the centrifugal and electromagnetic methods of separation. An exchange of scientific information upon such matters was a benefit of the highest importance, but it was not perhaps the most beneficial result of the interchange of visits which took place in the summer and autumn of 1941. In July of that year the British M.A.U.D. Committee had produced a report in which it was stated that the scientists concerned having 'entered the project with more scepticism than belief' had since become 'more and more convinced' that the release of atomic energy could be achieved in circumstances which would make it a powerful weapon of war; they now believed moreover that this could be achieved during the current war. This as we shall see was to be a powerful stimulus to international action.

Events thereafter moved rapidly. The Scientific Advisory Committee endorsed the report of the M.A.U.D. Committee, and in consequence the Prime Minister, with the concurrence of the Chiefs of Staff Committee, invited Sir John Anderson to supervise the whole project of the uranium bomb as a matter of great urgency and importance. In this task the Lord President had the support of a Consultative Council consisting of the Chairman of the Scientific Advisory Committee (Lord Hankey and later Mr R. A. Butler), the President of the Royal Society (Sir Henry Dale), the Secretary of D.S.I.R. (Sir Edward Appleton), and Lord Cherwell. Lord Brabazon, Minister of Aircraft Production, also served on this Council at the beginning. At the same time there was created, in D.S.I.R. the celebrated 'Directorate of Tube Alloys', presided over by Mr Akers of Imperial Chemical Industries, who was assisted by a technical committee consisting of some of the leading atomic scientists. Accordingly, by the late summer of 1941, the British scientists were embarking with determination and practical optimism upon a new phase of the uranium bomb project, with all the weight of Government authority behind them.

Things had not moved quite so far in America. In the spring of 1941 Briggs had appointed a committee, known as the National Academy Reviewing Committee, and over the year this committee submitted three reports. The first two of these reports, although pressing for the work to be pushed on vigorously, were as much or more concerned with atomic power as with a bomb, and were at any rate more cautious than the – roughly equivalent – British report of July. The National Defence Research Committee was sufficiently impressed to make a grant of over a quarter of a million dollars, and to discuss the possibility of much larger grants, but it remains the case that at the time of the missions of Darwin and Oliphant which have already been referred to, America was not deeply or decisively committed to the bomb project. It may be said that at this point the British scientists made a contribution to the joint Anglo-American project which went beyond the contribution – of undoubted importance in itself – of their scientific achievements and views. They had a faith in the realisation of the project as a whole, which was the more impressive in that it was carefully measured and expressed with traditional scientific reserve. They had convinced their own Government that it was something urgent and practical; they had caused it to be put upon a new official basis. It now rested with the Americans to do the same.

This the Americans very soon did. Even before the third report of the National Academy Reviewing Committee was presented (in November), Bush saw the President and Vice-President Wallace and convinced them that the time was rapidly approaching for a more aggressive attack on the uranium bomb project. The first result was the formation of an august body called the Top Policy Group, consisting of the President himself, the Vice-President, Secretary of War, Chiefs of Staff, Bush and Conant. The third report of the National

Academy Reviewing Committee showed the way more clearly. It was on the whole in line with the British Report of July; it envisaged the manufacture of bombs as a project still hazardous in its chances of success, but as being on the whole a calculable risk, a risk which the calculations suggested as being bold but acceptable.

A considerable reorganisation of the American effort now took place. The section of the N.D.R.C. which dealt with uranium problems now came under the direct control of the superior body, the Office of Scientific Research and Development, coming under the chairmanship of Conant (representing Bush) and being enlarged in numbers from 9 to 13. There was also set up a Planning Board to take charge of the industrial aspects of the project. Contracts for scientific work were to be recommended to Bush by Briggs and Conant, and for the various separation processes by the Planning Board, which also took charge of the heavy water programme. The project as a whole thus bifurcated into a scientific and an industrial side, and when this organisation was approved by the Top Policy Group the way was clear for administrative action.

Under a new organisation on both countries Anglo-American co-operation became rapidly closer. The visit of Pegram and Urey to England in November 1941 was returned by Akers, Halban, Peierls, and Simon in the spring of 1942. These visits, backed by a constant interchange of papers, were making certain vital points clear. The existing American technical facilities, and the potential American industrial facilities, were ahead of anything that Britain, so heavily committed elsewhere, could provide. In some fields at least, however, British thought was ahead of American. After a great deal of discussion about the best form for a fully-integrated Anglo-American project, a joint programme was decided upon which gave to Britain a heavy task of theoretical work and to America both theoretical work and industrial – or pre-industrial – development. Two of the principal British tasks were the determination of essential nuclear physical data and the study of a chain-reaction, its explosive effect, and the design of a bomb to utilise this effect. Another responsibility was the gaseous diffusion separation process for U.236. This involved both study of the theory and also the design and manufacture of the materials and machines involved. The further study of slow neutron physics was another British responsibility, particularly with heavy water as the moderating agent; this involved the production of both uranium metal and heavy water.

It was at this stage in the project that there occurred the hiatus in Anglo-American collaboration to which reference has already been made in this chapter. The efforts to bring it to an end took place at the political level, indeed at the highest political level, and in this account of the scientific work we may pass directly to the point at which, after the Quebec Conference in August 1943, collaboration was resumed. The nature of the collaboration now envisaged was a complete fusion of British and American work upon certain aspects of the project.

A prototype scheme was already in being in Canada. It was indeed inevitable that the ability of Canadian physicists, in whom the influence and tradition of Rutherford's work at McGill University was still potent, should play an important part in the project, and towards the end of 1942 the team which Halban was leading moved from Cambridge to Montreal. While the great majority of the 340 scientists who were employed on this Montreal part of the project were Canadian many British scientists, and many scientists who, like Halban, had passed through Britain and made a contribution to the work there, were brought in. The Montreal research project was associated with the pilot plant which was set up at Petawawa, Ontario,[1] for the extraction treatment of the Canadian uranium deposits.

This transfer to Canada may be looked upon, as has been suggested, as a prototype of a process which was to end with the transfer to the American continent of almost all the British theoretical work and also almost all the work on the electromagnetic isotope separation process. In August 1943 Sir John Anderson, who was responsible for superintending the British side of the project, visited America and discussed proposals for the final stage of unified effort. This stage took place under the guidance of a Combined Policy Committee set up by the President and the Prime Minister, and was co-ordinated by Sir James Chadwick, who late in 1943 represented the Government in Washington on the project as a whole. Within the United States the British contribution may be divided into three components, those at Berkeley in California, at New York, and at Los Alamos.

These three components of the British contribution differed in respect of organisation as well as in their scientific content. Thus the party which, under the leadership of Oliphant, went to Berkeley in November 1943 to work on the electro-magnetic separation plant, continued in America to work as a team. The work at Berkeley was organised upon a team or group basis, each group attacking a problem or aspect of a problem, and the group-leaders reporting to the supervisory authority for the Berkeley work as a whole. Thus although in fact some Americans were added to the British team, it remained an essentially national component – a group of some 15–20 British scientists who were working for convenience on American soil. In New York different arrangements were made.

---

[1] See *Canada's Role in Atomic Bomb Drama* (National Research Council, Canada, 1945.

When, at the beginning of 1944 a mission led by Akers of I.C.I. visited the United States to discuss the best arrangements for diffusion work, two members of the mission – Kearton and Peierls – remained in New York to collaborate in the design of the diffusion separation plant. There was, however, no British 'team' in New York. Kearton and Peierls, and the other scientists who joined them – there were only about half a dozen British scientists in all on this part of the project – worked in New York as individuals, an arrangement which owed something to the relative eminence of the individuals.

The British contribution to the work at Los Alamos resembled more closely that made at New York than that at Berkeley. Here again there was no team: British scientists worked as individuals. Some, for instance Penney, were resident members of the staff of the Los Alamos project; others such as G. I. Taylor, were visitors. The contributions were, again, very different in content: G. I. Taylor's great knowledge of the physical effect of blast, for instance, enabled him to make suggestions for elucidating data with a view to determining how the optimum effect should be achieved. Other British scientists, however, were directly concerned with the actual design of the weapon, and although a knowledge of physical theory was a *sine qua non* in this work, it possessed a character which made engineering ability and experience indispensable. Thus in the process of giving practical application to the thought and observation of scientists – a process in which Americans rightly believe themselves to excel – British scientists made their contribution, as they had done to the thought and observation itself, upon which the project rested.

CHAPTER IX

THE EASTERN HEMISPHERE

(i)

Introduction

THE MAGNITUDE OF THE CONTRIBUTION

ALTHOUGH the greater part of this volume, as well as the whole of its predecessor, has been devoted to supply from North America, it must not be supposed that this continent held any kind of monopoly in 'overseas supply'. On the contrary, other countries, more especially the three southern Dominions and India, played a valuable and significant part. This account can touch only on their part in munitions supply, and must omit their extremely important contributions in the matter of raw materials and food. Statistically, indeed, their munitions contribution does not bulk large: between them they supplied only 1.6 per cent. by value of all the munitions which accrued to the British Commonwealth forces during the war, whereas North America supplied no less than 28.9 per cent.[1] The proportion of space devoted to the latter, however, has been dictated less by statistics than by the special difficulty and complexity of the problems associated with supply from the long-neutral and always foreign United States. On the other hand the contribution of the countries which we shall henceforth call collectively the Eastern Group deserves in many ways more attention than the bare figures in themselves would warrant. First there is the time factor. Munitions production both in the United States and in Canada started late and supply therefrom was very largely concentrated in the years 1942–44; in the period of greatest need they contributed least. But in most of the eastern countries the production of some warlike stores was well established before the outbreak of war and developed *pari passu* with that of the United Kingdom. In 1940, when supply from North America represented only eight per cent. of total Commonwealth receipts, supply from the Eastern Group was already over one per cent. of the total. This wider spread in time naturally added enormously to the true value of the eastern contribution. Each shipload brought to Liverpool or Suez in 1940

---

[1] See *North American Supply, op. cit.*, Chapter X.

or 1941 was worth the freight of a whole convoy in 1943. 'There was a time', a high official of the war-time Ministry of Supply has written, 'when a few million rounds of small arms ammunition from India or Australia meant more to us than all the later billions from North America'. Most readers of this book will be able to judge for themselves whether the six modern anti-aircraft guns shipped to England from Australia in 1940 were not as valuable as the hundreds which began to arrive from North America in 1942.

Moreover, figures of total production and supply do not always give an adequate picture. When the eastern contribution is analysed more closely, it emerges that the Commonwealth depended on these countries for a really appreciable proportion of its supplies of many important stores. These were in the main the simpler types of munitions which could have been provided elsewhere without difficulty. But they were not less valuable on that account, for the existence or the prospect of an eastern surplus of these 'easy' items freed labour and factory space in Britain and North America for the more complex forms of production.

Many of the munitions which occupied the foremost place in the story of North American supply were necessarily much less conspicuous in that of supply from the eastern hemisphere. The wonder is that some of them appeared at all. The manufacture of mechanical transport, for example, which was so prominent a feature of the Canadian war effort, was not established in any of the eastern countries, except in the form of the re-assembly of imported chassis and some body production. Tanks, supplied in tens of thousands by the United States, were represented here by fifty machines built by Australia in 1943. Aircraft production, also confined to Australia, never did more than meet local needs, though this was in itself a great thing. To have built some 3,500 military aircraft in the course of the war was an achievement of which, considering the rudimentary state of her aviation industry in the 'thirties, Australia has every reason to be proud, even though well over two-thirds of the planes produced were trainers, and the rest were fighters or light bombers. (Australia supplied, in fact, about four and a half per cent. of the British Commonwealth's trainers, but only one per cent. of its Service aircraft.) In shipbuilding also, though it had a part to play, the Eastern group could not, of course, rival other parts of the Commonwealth. The completion, towards the end of the war, of ten ocean-going cargo ships was a more notable event in the industrial history of Australia than in the general history of the Second World War. However, the eastern hemisphere as a whole did supply more than 100,000 gross tons of merchant shipping – a small but useful entry on the credit side of the British Commonwealth's table of gains and losses; and it was a fact of great importance that

Australia went a long way and India a little way towards making their considerable navies self-supporting.

As in the case of Canada, sixty per cent., or rather more, of the warlike stores produced in the Eastern Group were for Army use. In this field eastern production was not only a notable achievement when measured against the resources of the countries concerned but formed a substantial increment to imperial supplies. The analysis of overseas supply already quoted in relation to Canada showed that at the beginning of 1944 the output of ground munitions in the Eastern Group was equivalent to the output of 100,000 additional workers in the United Kingdom and represented three per cent. of supplies from all sources.

In some individual cases the proportion was much higher. The assembly of the lighter armoured fighting vehicles, given generous importations of components and materials, was a task which the industry of the southern Dominions was well able to tackle; the Bren gun carriers made in Australia and New Zealand represented six per cent. and South African armoured cars fourteen per cent. of total Commonwealth supply. Among ordnance weapons the trench mortar was an obvious choice for manufacture on a large scale in countries whose industrial development was incomplete and whose experience of armaments production was slight; and no less than thirty-seven per cent. of the Commonwealth's supplies of the 3-inch mortar were made in the Eastern Group, in South Africa and New Zealand as well as in Australia. So also were fourteen per cent. of its grenades – another fairly simple product.

The assistance of the Eastern Group was by no means confined, however, to the more elementary types of armament. It contributed in general about five per cent. of the Commonwealth's artillery equipments, and in particular was the sole source of supply of the light 'mountain' gun, the 3.7-inch howitzer, which went into action in country that no other gun could penetrate. It is also worthy of note that Australia was the only country other than the United Kingdom to manufacture even a few of those highly efficient tank destroyers, the 17-pounder guns. Rifle production is not a simple art, but it was established in India and Australia long before the outbreak of war and greatly expanded during its course. Between them, these two countries produced almost a million rifles – rather more than Canada, and seventeen per cent. of the Commonwealth's supplies from all sources, including the United States. The Eastern Group also furnished the Commonwealth with fourteen per cent. of its small arms ammunition, a store which can be economically made only in large factories elaborately equipped.

These were the highlights of eastern hemisphere production, and the figures given are sufficient to confirm that in the equipping of the imperial armies other countries besides the United Kingdom, Canada and the United States played a very considerable part. This book, however, is not concerned, strictly speaking, with imperial supply as a whole but only with the supplies received by the United Kingdom from overseas. We are bound to enquire, therefore, how much of the total Eastern Group production can be credited to the latter account. The question is a difficult one to answer. It is easy to establish that Australian-built aircraft flew only in southern skies and that there were none to spare for the Royal Air Force; also that, except for five cargo ships delivered at Hong Kong to Admiralty order in 1941, all the ships built in the eastern hemisphere sailed under the ensign or remained on the register of their country of origin. But the distribution of ground munitions was intricate and obscure. There were some actual shipments to the United Kingdom, but for obvious reasons these were few. Far more munitions stores were moved to the Middle East, to Singapore and to the Eastern borders of India, where they might or might not be used by the troops of the producing country. For a while the Ministry of Supply statisticians sought to distinguish between stores thus shipped to 'War Office-controlled theatres' and stores retained by local defence forces. But the distinction was ultimately found tenable only in the case of Australia, which from 1942 onwards was strategically separated from the rest of the Commonwealth, forming part of a United States command. The whole output of Indian, South African and New Zealand factories, less certain small allocations to foreign countries, was classed as 'supplies for Empire' without further analysis. Thus it is not possible to establish how far the Eastern Group as a whole was able to do more than contribute to its own needs. In the case of Australia, shipments to British theatres of war were only a small part of total Australian production. For few stores was the proportion much more than a quarter and for most it was considerably less.

What can be established is the proportion of munitions production in the eastern hemisphere which was the result of United Kingdom orders. The proportion varied widely from one country to another and from one item to another, but the following general conclusions may be stated for the Group as a whole. With the exception of South Africa's armoured cars, more than half the output of every important munitions store was in fulfilment of orders from the local governments. There were certain types of munitions of which the Ministry of Supply definitely sought substantial quantities from the eastern countries in aid of its own requirements, and so built up production much in excess of local needs. Thus London orders accounted for between twenty-five and forty-five per cent. of the eastern hemisphere production of Bren gun carriers, 3.7-inch anti-aircraft guns,

6-pounder anti-tank guns, mortars, mortar bombs, grenades and small arms ammunition. At the other end of the scale there were weapons which countries concerned, particularly Australia, produced on a limited scale solely in order to make themselves independent of external supplies, without receiving any orders from London and without creating a surplus. These included Bofors guns, 17-pounders, Brens and Sten sub-machine guns. Intermediately, there were 3.7-inch howitzers, 25-pounders, 2-pounder anti-tank guns and .303-inch rifles, of which a small proportion (less than a quarter) was produced at the direct request of the Ministry of Supply. These were mostly weapons which the Ministry had hoped to receive in much larger quantities but had been thwarted by the intensification of local needs which followed the Japanese intervention. For example, only 266 25-pounders were actually delivered in Australia to the Ministry against a United Kingdom order for 480, only 31,600 rifles against orders for 130,100, the balance being diverted to the growing Australian Army.

From the foregoing it is at least clear that the United Kingdom was only to a fairly small extent the direct beneficiary of Eastern Group production. The latter thus differed markedly from Canadian war production, the greater part of which was undertaken on United Kingdom account. Since the eastern countries raised, in total, much larger forces of their own than Canada, and produced far fewer munitions, this was only to be expected. Indeed the whole enquiry is not perhaps very profitable. The entire production of the Eastern Group, however it might be disposed, was very definitely an asset to the United Kingdom. For each Australian-built Beaufort aircraft patrolling the eastern seas, one more could be safely spared for operations across the English Channel. If India had not made rifles for her own troops, British Army stocks would have had to be depleted in order that they might be armed. In helping themselves the nations of the Commonwealth were helping Britain almost if not quite as directly as if they had sent all their output to equip United Kingdom forces.

GEOGRAPHY AND SUPPLY

In measuring the contribution of the Eastern Group it is, of course, important to remember where the contribution was made. Their relative proximity to certain of the main theatres of war gave the output of the southern Dominions and India a real value out of all proportion to its size. Nowhere indeed did geography and strategy have so profound an influence upon munitions production. From a purely economic point of view there was much to be said for concentrating war production in the countries which could most readily undertake it. Production of munitions in the eastern hemisphere was generally more expensive than in Britain and took more time and effort to develop than in either Britain or North America. It may be thought that, since for most of the war the need for munitions was practically unlimited, the question of comparative cost was irrelevant, that a maximum industrial effort was needed everywhere if victory were to be won. Unfortunately, however, production in the eastern hemisphere was not independent from production elsewhere. Outside quite narrow limits, expansion of the output of armaments in India, South Africa, New Zealand and even Australia could be achieved only by diverting, either from Britain or from North America, machinery, components and materials which could generally produce more munitions more quickly if they were retained in the west. Thus the establishment of an arms factory in the east was liable to mean a net *loss* of production in the short run – and it was always the short run that counted most. If therefore the war had been a purely European one, there would have been little pressure upon the eastern countries to do more than provide for their own local needs. But when the war spread there was another factor in the sum. From Liverpool to Suez by the Cape route is 10,700 miles, and from New York 11,700 miles. But Karachi is only 2,750 miles and Durban only 4,600 miles away. Stores shipped to Suez from Australia had indeed nearly as far to go as those sent from Britain, but the waters they had to traverse were in the main much safer. When the destination was Singapore, Chittagong or Port Moresby the disparity was, of course, even greater.

Thus the function of Eastern Group munitions supply was fundamentally altered from time to time according to the way the tide of battle flowed. Up to the summer of 1940, though the prospect of a Far Eastern and a Mediterranean war was never far from the thoughts of those responsible for Commonwealth defence and Commonwealth supply, the immediate threat was in Europe and the role allotted to the Eastern parts of the Commonwealth was therefore a minor one. London was anxious that they should as far as possible reduce their dependence on the United Kingdom for the equipment of their own forces. It welcomed any small contribution that they might be able to make in the near future to the building up of military stocks in Britain or in the very subsidiary Egyptian supply centre. But time, cost and remoteness combined to exclude them from playing a major industrial part in the development of imperial strength. The Italian intervention, however, entirely transformed the picture. Egypt now became an operational base second in importance only to the United Kingdom, and it was now separated from British factories by 11,000 miles of perilous sea. Any supplies that could be produced locally were therefore of immeasurable value, and 'locally' in this context meant anywhere from Tel

Aviv to Sydney. Even now the authorities did not lose sight of the economics of munitions production: it was still only within fairly narrow limits that they were prepared to sacrifice production in the United Kingdom or North America for the sake of creating eastern arsenals. But within these limits every effort was now made to assist the expansion of output in the eastern countries, which were urged to provide between them the maintenance of no less than fourteen Commonwealth divisions. The words 'between them' are to be noted. The events of 1940 and the necessary limitations of United Kingdom aid imposed a new unity of mutual help and co-operative endeavour upon countries which had hitherto had little in common save their membership of the British Commonwealth. The 'eastern group', previously little more than a geographical expression, became a real collective noun with capital letters and a novel piece of administrative machinery, the Eastern Group Supply Council located in New Delhi.

The second great revolution in the war, the intervention of Japan, had effects equally far-reaching but of a rather different order. In the first place the swift advance of the new enemy split the Eastern Group asunder; Australia and New Zealand passed into the American sphere of strategic responsibility and in consequence the organisation of eastern hemisphere supply as an integral unity was crippled just as it was getting into its stride. At the same time the whole situation of the constituent countries was altered. The function of India, Australia and New Zealand was no longer to provide men and stores for campaigns in a distant theatre; they were themselves threatened with immediate invasion. India had to send her newly-trained divisions not to Egypt or Persia but to her own eastern frontier. The Australian division in the Middle East was recalled (though not until after it had helped to save Egypt) for the defence of its homeland. By the same token these countries no longer had supplies to spare for other theatres but were in desperate need of reinforcement from without. For Australia this meant that for a while shipments of munitions to British-controlled theatres practically ceased; United Kingdom orders had to be left unfulfilled until Australia's own growing forces were ready to take the field fully equipped. Indian supplies were not affected in the same way, for the defence of India was no less a British responsibility than the defence of the Middle East and Indian-made munitions were a British asset whether they moved westward or eastward from the factories. But production in India was very grievously affected by the new turn in the war. The direct and indirect consequences of the Japanese occupation of Burma were such that the expansion of munitions output planned in 1940-41 had to be largely abandoned. The economy of India was sufficiently strained by the services which she had to render as an operational base for the armies massing within her borders, and to have gone ahead with an intensive mobilisation of her industrial resources would have meant complete collapse. Thus after 1941 only South Africa was able both to develop war production without impediment and to contribute the products to the British pool.

In the final phase of the war, as the Far East gradually became a major and in the end the sole theatre of operations, the importance of the eastern countries in global planning was naturally still further enhanced. On the other hand, the demand for the land armaments which had been their staple products was universally declining, and only Australia could provide the ships and aircraft for which there was a continuing and even an increasing need. In the main, the emphasis was now on the supply of textiles and general stores and on the provision of services, such as ship-repair, victualling, railway transport and the construction of bases rather than on a further expansion of munitions production. Indeed the latter declined sharply in the Eastern Group as a whole during 1944, rather more sharply than in the United Kingdom.

THE CONTRIBUTING COUNTRIES

The Eastern Group comprised all the British territories which lay to the east and south of the Mediterranean theatre of war, and had any significant resources for war production, that is to say, the three southern Dominions, India, Ceylon, Burma, Hong Kong, Singapore and Malaya, Palestine, the East African dependencies and the two Rhodesias. Even if raw materials and foodstuffs are left out of the account, most of these countries had some part to play. Hong Kong had two large shipyards, from which, as we have noted earlier, five ocean-going ships were delivered to Admiralty order, as well as five more on private account. Singapore constructed some of its own harbour craft. Burmese workshops supplied a few components for Indian-made munitions. Palestine was a not unimportant source of military stores, other than munitions proper, for the Middle East forces, and East Africa supplied the Army with mortar barrels, anti-tank mines and even reconnaissance cars as well as clothing and general stores. To all intents and purposes, however, the production of munitions of war was concentrated in Australia, New Zealand, South Africa and India, and it is of these that we shall henceforth be speaking.

The combined resources of these four countries were by no means small. Their population, even if we exclude as we must the subsistence farmers of India and South Africa, greatly exceeded that of Canada; and much of that population was exceptionally vigorous, well-educated and adaptable. They produced in 1937 more than three times as much coal as Canada, nearly three times as much pig-iron and over sixty per cent. more steel.[1] It is, however, significant that the achievement was relatively greatest in the primary activity of coal-mining and least in the production of finished steel. None of these countries, in fact, had achieved the widespread and high development of secondary industry which was the foundation of Canada's success in war production. Not merely was there no manufacture of automobiles but engineering industry in general was weak and immature when the Second World War began.

New Zealand stood rather apart from the other countries under discussion, not merely in being smaller but in being predominantly an agricultural and pastoral country. She had only such industry as was necessary to the performance of her main task of food production and export and to the way of life of a prosperous western-type people. There were several efficient railway repair shops; re-assembly of imported cars and commercial vehicles was an extensive and flourishing business; a number of small factories and workshops turned out farm implements, churns, lawn mowers, water heaters, electric cookers and so on; and in connexion with this there was a little brass and iron founding. But there was no steel production or large-scale industry of any kind, and all the activities described were heavily dependent on imported machinery, components and raw materials. This was a slender basis for munitions production.

In the other three countries the previous half-century, and more especially the previous quarter-century, had seen considerable industrial development. In all of them steel production had been established, and this basic step had been accompanied or followed by a certain proliferation of manufacturing industry. But progress had been on the whole slow and halting, and success was not yet assured. Much of the development had been sponsored or encouraged by Governments; most of it still relied on Government support in the form of protective tariffs and other aids. There was much head-shaking by economists and others over the economic structure of these countries in the inter-war years. In Australia and in South Africa a single specialised form of primary production was relied on to provide the wealth which nourished the growth of many other agricultural and industrial undertakings unable, because of their high costs and limited internal markets, to make a competitive living for themselves. The South African economy has been likened to an inverted pyramid insecurely balanced on the profits of the Rand mines.[2] Similarly the industries and even the wheat and dairy-

---

[1] *United Nations Statistical Bulletin*, August 1947.
[2] *Overseas Reference Book of the Union of South Africa* (Todd Publishing Co. Ltd., London and New York, 1945), Article on 'Secondary Industry' by C. S. Richards, p. 69.

farming of Australia have been described as clinging desperately to the fleece of an enormous sheep.[1]

Nevertheless Australia was on the whole better fitted than any of the others for munitions production. The intensified protectionism that followed the onset of the world depression gave a further stimulus to industrialisation, reflected in the fact that, after a temporary setback at the beginning of the period, steel output more than doubled in the ten years after 1929. In 1937 it was already 900,000 long tons, more than in any other eastern member of the British Commonwealth. Whether or not this growth of industry was strictly economic is less important for our study than the fact that it took place. There were obvious quantitative limits to the output of munitions from a country of seven million people who were still highly dependent on their exports of primary products, and who still possessed no mass-production plants comparable to those of the United States or Canada. But technically there were few things that Australia could not do. Under the stimulus of the First World War she had built not only small warships but ocean-going merchant vessels. Efforts to establish the latter form of production as a permanent peace-time activity had not been successful, but the experience and certain of the shipyards remained. By the late thirties there were the rudiments of an Australian civil aviation industry in being. There were Australian factories outside the government arsenals which needed only capital and 'education' in order to turn out guns and shell. Above all, Australia was far less dependent on imports of industrial equipment than were the other eastern countries. Machinery, including many of the special-purpose machine tools essential to armament production, were or could readily be made within her borders in considerable quantities.

For South Africans, almost alone among the primary producers of the world, the thirties were a period of great and growing prosperity; the national income increased by eighty-four per cent., in monetary terms, between 1933 and 1939. The main reason was the high world price of gold, but there was also a large expansion of industrial activity; the gross value of manufacturing output more than doubled in the same period.[2] Even so the industrial resources of the Union were slender at the outbreak of war. Annual steel production was about a quarter of a million tons. Certain industries ancillary to the Rand mines were flourishing greatly; of particular importance to the present story was the very large output of explosives. But all South Africa's vehicles and nearly all her farm implements and industrial machinery still had to be imported. In other respects also the South African war potential did not appear

---

[1] See W. K. Hancock, *Australia* (Ernest Benn, Ltd., London, 1930), p. 98.
[2] *Overseas Reference Book of the Union of South Africa, op. cit.*, p. 69.

promising. Owing to the social structure of the Union there was a serious dearth of the type of labour which either was or could readily become skilled.

The obstacles to industrial progress in India are well-known. Capital was scarce and shy; men with technical and managerial skill were rare; labour was ill-fed, unhealthy, ill-educated and untrained, and in general had not yet been fully inured to the disciplines of regular factory employment.[1] Neither the old-established textile industries nor the minor industries which had grown up since the beginning of the century were likely to be useful in the production of munitions, though textiles themselves were to be one of India's most important contributions to the war economy of the United Nations. The output of metal goods was very small and as yet of very poor quality. Such articles as nuts, bolts and wire were nearly all imported, as were most hand tools and all machinery and vehicles. Thus while the peace-time output of armaments in the Indian ordnance factories was relatively large and diverse, there was little scope for expansion into the domain of civilian industry. The railway workshops were naturally numerous, and though they were for the most part repair shops only, they had been used for armament work in the First World War and could, it seemed, be so used again. There was some machine capacity at the disposal of the Posts and Telegraph Department and the Mints. But the Government could count only fourteen private engineering works which could undertake munitions production, and these were capable only of the simpler types of manufacture and repair. The real limitation upon India's capacity to make munitions, however, was not the specific deficiencies of Indian industry but rather, as appeared in the event, the general poverty of the country, the inability either to avoid inflation or to endure it without utter collapse. European, North American or Australasian peoples could divert a large part of their resources to the purposes of war because they lived normally far above the subsistence level; Indians did not.

So much then for the industrial potential of the Eastern Group. It is perhaps necessary to complete the picture by rehearsing a few well-known facts about the political background. Australia and New Zealand were clear-sighted in their appreciation of the danger of war and wholehearted in prosecuting it when it came. South Africa's declaration of war, on the other hand, came only after a reconstruction of the Government and a close parliamentary vote. Although the people endorsed the war policy by giving the United Party an impressive majority at the general election of 1943, it is still true that a strong minority of South Africans would have preferred to

---

[1] See, e.g., V. Anstey, *The Economic Development of India.*

see the Union neutral. India was brought into the war by a government containing a preponderant British element and not fully responsible to the legislature. There is no reason to doubt that its action was supported by many millions of Indians of all classes. But the main Indian political movement was opposed, in the existing circumstances, to Indian belligerence, and the mass of the people, preoccupied with the struggle for individual survival, was neither hostile nor enthusiastic but indifferent and indeed for the most part uncomprehending.

(ii)

Progress up to June 1940

THE PEACE-TIME NUCLEUS

When the disasters of mid-1940, in particular the Italian intervention and the closing of the Mediterranean sea-route, brought the southern Dominions and India into the forefront of the strategic and supply pictures, both the actual production of war supplies and preparations for its expansion were much further advanced in these countries, in proportion to their resources, than in Canada, and compared not unfavourably with the progress made in the United Kingdom itself. For this most of the credit must go to the Governments concerned. The extent of their preparations prior to the war naturally varied. The industrial resources of New Zealand were so slender that it was manifestly uneconomic to attempt to establish armaments production there on any scale when supplies could readily be drawn from the United Kingdom or from Australia. Thus there were in New Zealand no government arsenals and only one arms factory of any kind when war broke out. In Australia, however, and in India and to a lesser extent in South Africa considerable industrial preparations were made during the years of peace. In all these countries Principal Supply Officers' Committees on the model of the London organisation were at work by the early thirties and by 1939 a nucleus production of many types of warlike stores had been started.

Throughout its history the Commonwealth of Australia had been fully aware that it lived in an unsafe world and that the Royal Navy was no sure guarantee of its continued survival. First the presence of Germans in New Guinea (one of the main reasons for federation) and then the rise of Japan had kept Australians in a state of continuous unease. As a result they had early set before themselves and steadily kept in view the ideal of making themselves as nearly as might be self-sufficient not only in military and naval forces but also in the means of their supply. The first important steps were taken to this end during the 1914–18 war. In that period, which also saw the first successful ventures in steel production and in shipbuilding, Australian factories, notably the workshops of the Victorian railways, undertook the manufacture of guns, ammunition and some other military stores. In the main these projects matured too late to be of real value at the time, but they had sufficiently demonstrated that Australian industry was technically capable of armament work. The lessons of the war were deeply pondered in the following years, and a strong desire became manifest that Australia should be provided with a permanent government arsenal or arsenals similar to the Royal Ordnance Factories of the United Kingdom. Such a project was not easy to push forward in the relative tranquillity of the twenties or in the financial stringency of the early thirties. Nevertheless by the mid-thirties, when the threat of a new war made itself seriously felt, an impressive achievement was on view. Three government factories were in operation in addition to one which made uniforms for the Services: a small arms ammunition factory at Footscray, Victoria; an ordnance, explosives and filling factory, or rather group of factories, at Maribyrnong, near Melbourne, which was turning out complete 3-inch anti-aircraft equipments and army and naval shell up to 6-inch calibre; and a small arms factory at Lithgow in New South Wales, where Vickers machine-guns as well as rifles were manufactured. Current output was extremely small, but visitors from the United Kingdom were uniformly impressed by the keenness and ability of managers and men, and at least at Maribyrnong, by the quality of the plant. Stores were made strictly to United Kingdom specifications and occasional samples of naval ammunitions and cordite sent to England for proof had fully satisfied the Admiralty. In short the authorities had every reason to claim that 'the foundations of a munitions supply base (had) been well and truly laid in Australia'.

In South Africa the development of armaments production up to the middle thirties was much less advanced. After the elimination of Germans from the African continent during the First World War, no obvious threat to the security of the Union emerged until the Italian intervention in Abyssinia in 1935. During the years of untroubled peace the Government had not considered it necessary to establish an armaments industry either in government arsenals or otherwise. Early in 1935, however, it responded to the general stir of fear throughout the world to the extent of starting investigations into the possibility of making munitions. But the investigations were confined to the simpler types of stores: the initial list comprised small arms ammunition, cordite, 3-inch mortars and their ammunition, 18-pounder shell, rifle barrels, rifle grenades, aerial bombs (minus the fuses), gas masks, steel helmets and bullet-proof tyres. They were also for the most part preliminary in character. The idea was to ascertain to what extent production could be undertaken on the outbreak of war; it was assumed, quite correctly, that some months would elapse before South Africa was heavily engaged. There were certain exceptions to this. It was proposed that the great explosives firm, African Explosives and Industries, Ltd., should proceed at once to set up a small plant for the manufacture of cordite; and since it had been established that almost all the necessary raw materials were present in Southern Africa, three English firms had been invited to tender for the construction and operation of a small arms ammunitions factory. Otherwise preparations were to be confined to the acquisition and study of War Office process manuals, the manufacture (by the Artillery Depot at Robert's Heights) of jigs and gauges and the testing out of the process by selected engineering firms.

Like Australia and unlike South Africa, India possessed a regular peace-time establishment of armaments factories which were designed to meet the bulk of her Army's needs both in peace and war. Six government ordnance factories, capable of making several types of guns, small arms and ammunitions and propellants were in being in 1936 and the authorities were reasonably confident that in the main adequate capacity existed therein for the Indian Army's war requirements. There were, however, still a number of important deficiencies. Thus the manufacture of artillery did not include the optical accessories; for pistols and machine guns the Army was wholly dependent on the United Kingdom; cordite was made in India, but high explosives had to be imported. Many of the weapons for which the plant had been designed were obsolescent and efforts at modernisation during the next two years unfortunately coincided with a transitional phase in British design. Thus the modified 18-pounder field gun and the Vickers Berthier light machine gun were introduced into Indian ordnance factories at a time when they were about to be superseded by the 25-pounder and the Bren, so that the replanning and re-tooling were largely wasted. Moreover, the war of which the Indian authorities were thinking was a 'war for the defence of India'. No provision had been made for the despatch of expeditionary forces, for which higher scales of equipment would be required. Again, local supply had been arranged only for the Service which had hitherto been overwhelmingly predominant in the defence of India, the land army. The very small but growing naval and air forces were as yet wholly dependent on supplies from the United Kingdom not only of ships and aircraft but also of ordnance and ammunition. Nevertheless with all these limitations India, if only because of her relatively much larger peace-time forces, was endowed at the beginning of the rearmament period with much more extensive and comprehensive facilities for armaments production than any other part of the Commonwealth overseas.

UNITED KINGDOM WAR PLANS AND THE EASTERN WAR POTENTIAL

Active interest in the present and future capacity of the Dominions and India for the manufacture of war supplies awakened in London early in 1936, very soon after the launching of the United Kingdom rearmament programme. Hitherto the Dominions had been acting on their own initiative. The authorities in London had neither inspired their endeavours nor even knew very much about them. It is true that the Principal Supply Officers' Committees in Australia and South Africa had for a number of years been furnishing the corresponding United Kingdom organisation with annual reports on their activities. But the information contained therein and in other communications does not appear to have percolated very thoroughly into the Service departments. A grand tour of the Dominions carried out in 1934 by Sir Maurice Hankey (as he then was), Secretary to the Cabinet and to the Committee of Imperial Defence, opened a good many eyes in the inner circle of government to the resources available and in particular to the actual capabilities of the Australian munitions factories. Nevertheless, when active enquiries were started at the beginning of 1936, it was still possible for an eminent personage in the War Office to remark that the information thus obtained was 'extraordinarily interesting and very much more hopeful than anyone here could have hoped'. With India relations were naturally closer, since the ultimate responsibility for the defence of the country rested with the Imperial Government. But local autonomy in defence and supply was a natural part of the general constitutional development that had been going on since 1909 and more especially since 1919. Supply for the Indian Army was quite distinct from and independent of supply for the forces administered directly by the War Office.

Rearmament had not long been in progress before it was realised that the balance sheet of requirements and supply was incomplete if it was confined to the United Kingdom alone. It was pointed out in the War Office at the beginning of 1936 that planning had so far taken into account neither those needs of the Dominion forces which would have to be met from United Kingdom production nor the supplies which the United Kingdom might be able to obtain from the Dominions. On the latter point, two distinct questions were raised. Could the Dominions help in any way to remedy the present deficiencies in the equipment of the United Kingdom forces? On a longer view, was it desirable and feasible to assist the Dominions so to increase their capacity that when war came they would at worst be more self-sufficient than at present seemed likely and at best would have a surplus to spare for United Kingdom use? Though distinct, these questions were evidently closely related. The only practical way in which the United Kingdom Government could induce the Dominions to extend their war potential was by placing definite orders for material in time of peace; and conversely any such orders given for the primary purpose of securing an immediate reinforcement would have the effect of increasing war potential. It was, however, the short-term needs that weighed most heavily with the authorities in London; and in practice the decision as to whether orders should be given turned largely on the question whether they would result in supplies coming forward within the rearmament period, that is, within the next two or three years.

Assistance in so near a future could clearly be looked for only from the two countries, India and Australia, where a nucleus production of armaments had already been established. Now both these countries were very anxious to execute United Kingdom orders. Australia in particular had been pressing for orders for some years past. The reason was simple. In normal times the local market for munitions was altogether inadequate to maintain an armaments industry of an economic size. Only with very great difficulty had the government factories been kept ticking over, plant maintained and a minimum labour force held together during the depression period. The Munitions Board had been forced to bear the cost of production on its own vote, supplying stores to the Services free of charge. No funds were available locally for increasing the size and efficiency of the plant to anything like the extent that would be needed in time of war, and peace-time orders from the United Kingdom seemed to offer the only solution to the problem. The case for such orders had been strongly represented by the authorities in a letter to the High Commissioner in London in 1932. It was put to Sir Maurice Hankey in 1934 and to a visiting representative of the Dominions Office (who forcibly supported it) in the spring of 1936. Later in that year, the Controller-General of the Munitions Supply Board, Mr N. K. S. Brodribb, came to England in person to study recent technical developments such as the Bren gun and to explore the possibility of orders. London was supplied with detailed figures showing the surplus capacity then available for United Kingdom use. Thus the theoretical capacity of the small arms plant was 50,000 rifles and 300 machine guns a year but the current output was only 1,000 rifles and 100 machine guns; only 18 million rounds of small arms ammunition were being made in a plant capable of 40 millions a year under peace conditions; there was a potential surplus of 100,000 rounds of light shell a year and of several hundred tons of T.N.T. and cordite. If the United Kingdom could be induced to take up these surpluses, machinery could be tuned up and additional workers recruited and trained, with obvious benefits to Australia's and the Commonwealth's capacity to wage war when it came. There was a further psychological point, on which the Dominion Office representative laid much stress: orders from the United Kingdom would serve as final recognition of Australia's successful efforts to establish the production of armaments and would do much to encourage her to further endeavours.

India's position was not dissimilar. Here, too, there was a wide gap between the actual and the potential output of the ordnance factories, which gap the United Kingdom Government was invited, for the same reasons, to fill by placing production orders in time of peace.

The United Kingdom authorities were, however, very doubtful whether from their point of view such orders would serve a useful purpose. The primary responsibility of the Service departments in London was to remedy the known deficiencies of the British forces as quickly as possible, and, since the funds at their disposal for this purpose were extremely limited, as cheaply as possible. Australian production costs were high, partly because of the dearness of labour, partly because of the small scale of the undertakings; and to these would have to be added the heavy cost of transporting the finished stores to Britain. Nor was it thought likely that really up-to-date material could be obtained quickly from either India or Australia. The munitions in current production there were mostly of types which dated from the last war and many of which were now being superseded in the United Kingdom by improved equipment. To establish production of the latter in overseas countries would mean both heavy expense and a long wait. Generally, the conclusion was that so far as the deficiency programme was concerned there was little that the Dominions or India could do to help, that any supplies that they could furnish could be obtained at least as quickly and as cheaply within the United Kingdom. At this time the United Kingdom authorities were not in a position to place enough orders even to build up an adequate war potential in the home country.

One class of stores above all others occupied the anxious attention of the War Office in 1936 – anti-aircraft guns, and to a less extent the ammunition therefor. Indian and Australian supply of these stores, which were also being sought vainly from Canada and the United States, was very seriously considered and was in fact the acid test of the practicability of overseas assistance in rearmament. It was the main concrete proposal discussed with Mr Brodribb. Unfortunately, however, the anti-aircraft gun was not one of the items for which the Australian Government had capacity ready and to spare. Domestic requirements would absorb the very small current output (eight guns a year) for at least three years ahead. These guns were not, of course, the 3.7-inch equipments (which were not yet in production anywhere) but the obsolescent 3-inch model. Mr Brodribb, however, estimated that if the War Office were to place long-term contracts with the Commonwealth Government, the Australian factory could be made to produce fifty 3.7-inch guns a year together with their quota of ammunition. The proposal seemed attractive, but on closer study became less so. Capital expenditure to the tune of £375,000 would be required, and this would have to be borne in the first instance by the Imperial Government; the Australians would be in competition with the United Kingdom manufacturers for machine tools and steel forgings; and production could not start for at least twelve months. So while Mr Brodribb received all possible encouragement and advice he returned home without any definite prospect of War Office orders for Australian arsenals.

An Indian mission led by the Director of Ordnance Factories visited London about the same time and met a similar lack of success. Again attention focused on the 3.7-inch gun, and again the United Kingdom authorities saw little point in providing money, machinery and in this case technical assistance, in order to obtain from overseas guns which could be produced at home probably at lower cost and certainly in a shorter time. (Two years were likely to elapse before the first complete Indian equipment could be delivered.) There was also the further objection that anti-aircraft guns did not figure prominently in India's own defence requirements.

Thus although supply from the eastern parts of the Commonwealth was by no means ruled out in principle, the 1936 discussions in the main confirmed the authorities in London in their first impression that little if any assistance from that source could usefully be invoked during the rearmament period.

There remained the much more important question of Australia's war potential. This was discussed intermittently during 1936, but without much positive result. It was decided, although there were some who felt that this was delaying matters rather long, to await the Imperial Conference which was due to assemble in May 1937, before taking any definite action. It was not in dispute that large and efficient munitions industries in Australia and India would be to the general advantage of the Commonwealth. The only question was how far the United Kingdom could or should help to create such industries. At first a certain parochialism manifested itself in the discussion of this subject; it was implied that the United Kingdom had no direct interest in financing the development of munitions plants overseas whose whole output was fairly certain to be absorbed, in the event of war, by the local governments. Before long, however, it was generally recognised that even if the development did no more than make other members of the Commonwealth self-supporting it would still be very much to the United Kingdom's benefit. But there was still the dominant problem of finance to be faced. The funds available being barely sufficient (in retrospect we should say quite insufficient) to create a war potential in the United Kingdom, any expenditure on making the overseas members better prepared for war could only mean that the United Kingdom would be worse prepared. The question thus resolved itself into one of priorities; and there could be no serious argument but that the first claims upon the British Government's resources must be the building up of production facilities in the country which had most experience and was nearest to the main probable theatre of war. In so far as there was any money to spare for overseas development it went, not to the southern Dominions but to Canada. For this there were many and valid reasons. For one thing Canada was much closer. For another, the Canadian Government, unlike the Governments of India, Australia or even South Africa, was doing as yet very little on its own account, so that if Canadian resources were to be used at all the United Kingdom Government had to take the initiative. Moreover, those resources, as we have seen, were much larger and more easily adapted to munitions production than the resources of the eastern countries. Canada provided phenomena which had no parallel anywhere in the eastern hemisphere – private engineering firms which from 1936 onwards actively solicited United Kingdom orders and offered convincing proof of their ability to execute them.

The Imperial Conference of 1937 was dominated by the problems of imperial defence, and amongst those problems the co-ordination of supply figured prominently. Summarily speaking, the Dominions came to the Conference with the objective of securing from the United Kingdom, firstly, financial help in the form of production orders covering the cost of capital expansion in the creation of a largely self-sufficient armaments potential, and secondly, the supply of such armaments as they could not economically make for themselves. The United Kingdom, on the other hand, was concerned to preach to the Dominions the necessity of the largest possible measure of self-sufficiency, and at the same time to avoid any definite financial commitment. In the circumstances it was to be expected that the recommendations which emerged from the Munitions Committee of the Conference should be somewhat lacking in precision. The United Kingdom gave no guarantee that it would be able to meet the Dominions' needs; it merely undertook that 'to the utmost extent practicable, having regard to the difficulties involved' it would endeavour to give them priority over those of foreign countries. Nor did it hold out any definite promise of assistance in the attainment of self-sufficiency. It accepted the Committee's advice to give early and intensive consideration to the placing of orders for munitions in the Dominions and India, but so far as the southern Dominions were concerned such orders, with one important exception, did not materialise.

REARMAMENT IN THE DOMINIONS AND INDIA

The effect of the Conference was thus to throw the Dominions back upon their own resources, in a double sense. They could not count upon having their own deficiencies made good from the United Kingdom surplus, for there was not nor was likely to be any large surplus to draw on; in practice they were already finding it difficult to secure early delivery of many badly needed stores. Neither could they rely upon United Kingdom help in making themselves self-supporting in matters of supply. Henceforward it depended on themselves alone how well prepared they were to be when the emergency arose. These developments, coupled with a certain necessary vagueness on the part of the United Kingdom representatives as to the disposition of the Royal Navy in the event of war, marked a change of some importance in the defence position of the more isolated parts of the Commonwealth. The mother country was now too closely beset and not strong enough to cast its shield over them with the same assurance as of old. In 1937, Australia and New Zealand (and perhaps even South Africa) felt the first breath of the chill wind of isolation that was to blow so bleakly upon them in 1942.

To this challenge they responded well. From New Zealand little could be expected in the way of supply, though one factory there had begun to assemble small arms ammunition out of imported materials before the outbreak of war. In Australia on the other hand rearmament was undertaken on a big scale. Work had begun even before the Imperial Conference. The Defence Resources Board had been given in 1936 a 'basis of enquiry' consisting of the war establishments of the three Services for which provision was, if possible, to be made. The peace-time strength of the Navy was to be doubled; the Army was to comprise the equivalent of seven divisions, including one which might be sent overseas; and a seventeen-squadron Air Force was to be raised. The Board's third report, composed early in 1937, showed that certain fundamental truths had been faced: namely, that equipping the Forces was not a once-for-all transaction which could be completed in time of peace, but that the aim must be to create a production capacity from which initial equipment together with war wastage would be provided as soon as possible after the outbreak; that the gap between the capacity required and the capacity in existence was almost ludicrously wide; that it could not be bridged by mere expansion of government factories, but that the whole industrial resources of the country would be needed in war; finally, and perhaps most importantly, that if these resources were to be effectively and speedily deployed when war came, the Government would have to provide private firms with technical advice and 'educational' orders and help them to acquire the necessary specialised equipment, in time of peace. These were already commonplaces in the United Kingdom, but they were an almost revolutionary development in Australian thinking. A note of urgency ran through the whole report, and from thoughts the Government was proceeding rapidly to action. A three-year programme involving the expenditure of £3,616,000 on the development of government munitions capacity was launched in 1936. Progress at first was slow; up to the spring of 1938 only a few hundred thousand pounds had actually been spent. It accelerated somewhat during the fiscal year 1938-39 at the end of which the value of new factories built and building, together with machinery and some stocks of key materials, was £2.8 million, and the men employed on munitions work numbered nearly 6,000. Even so, expansion was not yet spectacular: the value of munitions output, £0.6 million in 1936-37, was not expected to exceed £2 million in 1939-40. More important were the steps taken towards the mobilisation of civilian industry. On the recommendation of an advisory panel of industrialists a sum of over one million pounds had been provided for the creation of twenty-five armament annexes to private engineering works and the railway workshops of certain States, which were being educated in the production of such stores as gun ammunition components.

On the eve of war Australia could look forward to attaining in the near future a very large measure of self-sufficiency in armaments supply. For the time being, however, she was actually in a sense less self-supporting than ever. The reason for this was the recent introduction into the Commonwealth armies of a large number of novel weapons and stores, some being improvements on older models, others new types designed to meet new tactical needs. In addition to the established production of standard munitions such as rifles, Vickers machine guns, artillery shell and small arms ammunition, Australia expected to begin producing, at various dates in 1940, Bren guns, Bren gun carriers and armoured cars, and to change over from the obsolete 3-inch to the 3.7-inch anti-aircraft gun. But in the meantime she had to rely on the United Kingdom for supplies of many of these latter stores and also of Bofors and anti-tank guns. When all allowance is made for the advantages of hindsight and for the real difficulties of the War Office in this matter, there could be no more pointed commentary on the United Kingdom's failure to order 3.7-inch guns from Australia in 1936 than the fact that, desperately scarce as anti-aircraft guns were in Britain in 1939, some had to be exported thither at that time, and that supplies of guns from Australia, which might well have been available before the outbreak of war, did not actually begin to arrive until late in 1940.

The most striking features of Australian preparations for war were in the spheres of shipbuilding and aircraft production. The Cockatoo Island dockyard, more or less derelict since the early twenties, was put into operation and had actually completed two escort sloops and one 'local seaward defence' vessel before the outbreak of war. Plans provided for the future construction not only of more of these types but also of two Tribal class destroyers, the first of which was laid down in November 1939. Thus while the Royal Australian Navy had still to procure its cruisers from the United Kingdom its smaller warships were beginning to be provided from local sources.

The development of aircraft production in Australia, a project which the Commonwealth Government had been nursing for some years, was inaugurated in 1937. Hitherto the Australian aviation industry had consisted of a small branch of the De Havilland Company which had been set up to sell, service and repair civil aircraft. But early in this year the Government concluded an agreement with a group of big industrial interests, which had formed a new organisation called the Commonwealth Aircraft Corporation, for the construction of a fully-fledged factory capable of turning out light military planes. A United States model, the North American Aviation Company N.A.16 powered by a single-row Pratt and Whitney Av. Wasp engine, was to be manufactured under licence. This plane was the prototype of the Harvard trainer but as adapted for production in Australia it was known as the Wirraway. This choice of plane was criticised by some sections of opinion in Australia and caused some misgiving in London but it was judged to be the simplest military type and so the most suitable for initial production in a new country. A first order for 40 machines was soon expanded to 132 and deliveries were just starting when war was declared. The most striking feature of the undertaking was that the Corporation was preparing to make not only the complete airframe but also, ultimately, the engine – a remarkable venture for a country which had not made automobile engines; but a successful one.

Just before the war the Australian Government placed orders with De Havilland for 50 Moth primary trainers and 200 Gypsy engines. The engines and almost all the components of the airframes were to be made in England, but it was intended that as experience was gained the Australian branch of the firm should eventually manufacture the complete frames. Meanwhile, however, a much larger project was taking shape. It was a natural corollary of the steps taken in the summer of 1938 to secure additional supplies of aircraft from Canada and the United States that the United Kingdom Government should consider whether Australia also might not be able to contribute something to the ever-increasing needs of the Royal Air Force. At the same time the Commonwealth Government, finding it more and more difficult to buy planes from Britain, was more than ever desirous of establishing indigenous production of Service aircraft as well as trainers. From this identity of interest there emerged a plan to co-operate in creating Australian capacity for the manufacture of aircraft for the joint use of the Royal Air Force and the Royal Australian Air Force. The type chosen was the twin-engined Bristol Beaufort, which met Australia's primary need for a general reconnaissance landplane to keep watch over her northern approaches and which could also serve as a medium bomber. An Air Ministry mission went out to settle the details in January 1939. Though an ultimate output of perhaps a thousand planes a year was envisaged, initial orders amounted to only 180 planes, to be divided equally between the two countries. To undertake this venture a new organisation, the Aircraft Production Commission, was set up, in which the Commonwealth Government was associated with representatives of certain big industrial and Commonwealth interests, notably General Motors-Holdens Ltd., and the great steel firm Broken Hill Proprietary Ltd. The organisation was placed under the tutelage of the English makers of the Beaufort, the Bristol Aeroplane Company, which was to provide technical instruction, materials, components and in the first instance Taurus engines, though in due course these last were to be made in Australia.

Thus when war came the ground had been prepared in Australia for a very extensive and comprehensive war production, which included nearly all classes of military, naval and air force stores except mechanical transport, tanks and the largest types of warships, planes and guns. Quantity was as yet less well assured than quality. The Government had been obliged to accept an interim objective of three divisions in lieu of the seven which it hoped to equip eventually. But the arrangements made for enlisting the aid of civilian industry held out a good prospect that, given time, Australia would be as nearly as might be self-supporting in munitions supply. Certainly her preparations were more ambitious and more energetically pressed than those of any other part of the British Commonwealth overseas.

The measures towards preparedness that were taken by South Africa were on an altogether smaller scale. Less well equipped industrially than Australia, less obviously exposed to attack and less certain that it would participate in a general war, the Union was content to follow out the modest programme sketched in 1935. The

Government did not seek United Kingdom orders, nor did it aim at self-sufficiency in any but the simpler types of armament. A contract for a small arms ammunition factory was signed with Imperial Chemical Industries on 1st June 1937, and the buildings were completed towards the end of 1938, as was a small plant for the manufacture of rifle cordite. Otherwise no specific war plants were set up in peace-time, but technical preparations were put in hand and trial orders given to civilian engineering firms for mortars, grenades, aircraft and mortar bombs and several natures of gun ammunition. Production of 3.7-inch and 4.5-inch howitzers and of Bren light machine guns was also envisaged, though in the event only the first-named was undertaken. Thus here also there was the potential for a fairly wide range of armament production in time of war, but the range was less than in Australia – there was no question of shipbuilding or of aircraft production and little prospect of the manufacture of small arms or of anti-aircraft guns – and more time would be needed for industrial deployment after hostilities began. There were no government arsenals to bridge the gap while mobilisation was taking place or to provide a reservoir of the relevant skills; even in 1941 there were said to be no more than two or three really experienced armament engineers in the country.

While the Dominions were in the main left to make their own industrial preparations for war with no more than encouragement from London, the situation of India made a more positive intervention imperative. The Imperial Government and Parliament recognised that the meagre revenues, the dependent status and the chilly political climate of the country made it impossible to leave the defence of India entirely to local initiative, especially if 'defence' was to be interpreted, as London desired, in an active sense which would include the despatch of men and stores into the Red Sea area. Up to the time of Munich very little progress had been made, and indeed India was falling further behind, as more and more of the standard products of her ordnance factories became obsolescent. In September 1938 the situation seemed so disquieting that the British Government set up an expert committee under the chairmanship of Admiral of the Fleet Lord Chatfield, to examine the existing organisation and make recommendations for its improvement. The Committee soon came to one very important conclusion: private engineering industry was not large enough or skilled enough to be included in the munitions potential, and efforts had therefore to be concentrated on expanding and improving the government ordnance factories. To this end it recommended a series of measures which were estimated to cost £2,760,000 and which were financed out of a grant of £5 million authorised by Parliament for Indian defence in general. Only one new plant was to be set up for the manufacture of T.N.T. But each

EE

of the six existing factories was to be expanded and adapted for the manufacture of new types of equipment. Certain stores, such as pistols and aircraft bombs, which had hitherto been imported were now to be made locally and obsolescent weapons were to be replaced by their modern equivalents, for example the Vickers-Berthier by the Bren light machine gun.

The 'Chatfield Measures' were not finally approved by the British Government until August 1939. Their implementation would need time, and meanwhile a large part of India's initial war requirements would have to be supplied from the United Kingdom. India would also need plant, machinery and technical skill, all scarce commodities which would have to be furnished by the United Kingdom. And even when they were completed, the measures would still leave India without facilities for the manufacture of aircraft, ships, vehicles (armoured or unarmoured), anti-tank or anti-aircraft guns; the plan definitely excluded provision for stores so complex or so little used by India that production would be manifestly uneconomic. Already it was becoming apparent that India, easily the Commonwealth's largest producer of armaments outside the United Kingdom in 'normal times', was far less capable of war-time expansion than Canada, Australia or South Africa. Eventually, and with considerable help from Britain, she could hope to become self-supporting in most kinds of munitions; but she was never likely to have a large surplus, and at the outset she was in the matter of armaments supply on the whole a liability rather than an asset to the United Kingdom.

THE FIRST NINE MONTHS OF WAR

For the eastern members of the Commonwealth even more than for the United Kingdom the interval between the outbreak of war and the crisis of mid-1940 was rather an extension of the preparatory period than the beginning of intensive war production. It gave a breathing space in which they could test out the machinery of war organisation, carry through the first stages of military mobilisation, ease their economies gently – more gently even than the United Kingdom – from a peace to a war footing, and proceed with the initiation of civilian industry into the production of warlike stores. All of these made substantial progress in this period, though all were gravely hampered by the general and much accentuated shortage of machine tools and plant. New Zealand, though most dependent of them all upon imported industrial equipment, not only took steps to increase the output of her one pre-war munitions product, small arms ammunition, from two and a half to five million rounds a month but inaugurated the production of several other types of stores. Included among these new projects was the manufacture of

Bren gun carriers – an ambitious scheme in appearance but never-theless quite soundly based. The heavy machining was to be carried out by the New Zealand Railway workshops, the assembly by the local branch of General Motors. Manufacturing drawings, machine tools and most of the material were to be provided by arrangement with the Australian Government and Canada was to supply Ford power units and some other components. Hand grenades and 3-inch mortar bombs were to be produced by the expedient of breaking-down the process of manufacture into stages and distributing the contracts among a number of small engineering firms, none of which could have undertaken the whole product.

For South Africa the main business of the period was the transla-tion into action of the plans which had been matured during the past four years, the conversion of experimental orders into quantity pro-duction. The pre-war technical preparations now bore fruit; by the middle of 1940 the production of 3.7-inch howitzers and 3-inch mortars, of shells, small arms ammunition and grenades, of aerial and mortar bombs, of cordite and high explosive, was either estab-lished or in sight, and plans were well advanced to introduce new items such as anti-tank guns and armoured cars.

The Australian scene presented a similar picture on a larger scale. During the first months of war the existing government ordnance factories were enlarged, the tempo of production quickened and the change-over to modern types of equipment was completed. New plants were set up to make additional items such as the 25-pounder field gun and the 2-pounder anti-tank gun. The construction of government armament annexes to commercial firms, chiefly for bomb and shell components, proceeded apace: all the twenty-five originally projected came into operation during 1940 and a number of others were rising by the end of the year. In addition, general commercial industry was gradually drawn into the war production network by means of large government contracts for clothing and general stores. Industrial mobilisation was hampered as elsewhere in the Eastern Group by a grave shortage of supervisors and tech-nicians, and by the difficulty of importing adequate supplies of machine tools and other equipment. The latter problem, however, was resolutely tackled despite the lack of experienced toolmakers. Australia set to work to remove this initial obstacle to munitions production by making herself as nearly as possible independent of external supplies of machine tools.

In India also progress was steady though unspectacular. The 'Chatfield' modernisation schemes were pressed forward, but less rapidly than had been hoped, because under war conditions the United Kingdom found it harder than ever to make available the necessary machinery and the equally necessary technicians. Meanwhile the output of the existing plants in their existing form was brought up to full war capacity and was supplemented by substantial contracts placed with civilian industry for ammunition components.

Up to the outbreak of war, as we have seen, the Dominions, and to a large extent India also, had built up their armaments production and laid their plan for war-time expansion more or less independently of the United Kingdom. Their aim was the equipment of their own Forces and the contribution of a surplus to a Commonwealth pool did not enter into their plans. With the exception of the Australian Beaufort aircraft scheme and the Indian modernisation programme the United Kingdom had not helped to establish a war potential in the eastern hemisphere, nor had it attempted to secure war supplies thence, again except for the ninety Australian Beauforts, which were merely to offset the supply of aircraft to Australia in the immediate future. The actual advent of war naturally raised again the question, whether some part of the new munitions capacity which obviously had to be brought into being somewhere should not be brought into being in the east. The main argument against such a course was now largely removed: finance in general was not the impediment that it had been in time of peace. At the same time some of the arguments in favour were stronger than before. Since Britain was now committed to raising a very much larger army and a considerably larger navy and air force than had been contemplated before 1939, it was more than ever clear that her own resources would not suffice and more than ever desirable that the reserves of labour, materials and industrial facilities in the Dominions and India should be brought fully into play. There was also the very potent argument that factories there would be virtually secure from enemy attack. In one case these arguments were decisive. The outbreak of war having revealed a very serious deficit of small arms ammunition, it was decided to create seven new factories, with a total capacity of 260 million rounds, and one of these was to be built 'east of Suez' – in fact, in India – where it would be safe from air-raids and well placed to serve the Commonwealth forces already being assembled in the Mediterranean area. But this, in the period before Dunkirk, was the only example of such action. Otherwise, first priority in the building up of fresh munitions capacity was given to the United Kingdom itself and second priority, notwithstanding the grave problem of dollar finance, to North America. The reasons were two-fold. First, production was needed as close as possible to the main centre of war in Europe. Secondly, production was needed quickly; and it could almost always be obtained more quickly if plant and equipment were retained at home rather than shipped to the east. A single example will suffice. At the outbreak of war the Australian Government had an order in Britain for a large rolling mill and extrusion press with which it hoped to fabricate aluminium for its aircraft programme. The Air Ministry, however, withheld this plant (promising to send finished aluminium in lieu) on the ground that if it were shipped to and set up in Australia five months' badly needed production would be lost. In general the British Government at this stage could not afford to add further to the sacrifice of plant and equipment entailed by the existing Dominions and Indian production programmes.

But if it could not help with long-term schemes of expansion the Government was exceedingly glad to take up any current output that the eastern hemisphere countries might be able to spare. Although the main current flow of munitions supply was still in the reverse direction, the Dominions and India had already surpluses of certain stores to offer, more especially of ammunition. Even New Zealand sent some very welcome .303-inch cartridges. South Africa could not yet provide complete rounds but sent several million brass cups and bullet caps to the United Kingdom in return for the release of the plant which it needed in order to begin balanced production. Naturally, however, Australia and India were by far the most promising sources of supply. Close co-operation, as direct and informal as letter, telegram and interview could make it, was established from the outset between the Ministry of Supply and the Australian Ministry of Supply and Development, which showed itself eager to do all it could to help. As early as November 1939 the authorities in London were furnished with a complete account of the present state and the future prospects of Australian production and of the quantities available for supply to the United Kingdom; and orders were promptly placed in Australia for a number of very badly needed stores, notably 50 3.7-inch anti-aircraft guns, 30,000 rifles, over half a million rounds of filled shell together with some additional empty components, and 85 million rounds of small arms ammunition. As between the United Kingdom and Australia the procedure was one of formal request and formal acceptance; relations were those of independent authorities engaging in mutual assistance at the margin, as it were, of their own needs and resources. The links between London and Delhi were much closer. The British Government's acceptance of partial responsibility for the planning and financing of Indian expansion and the direct interest of the War Office in the despatch of Indian troops with their equipment to the Middle East, helped to make Indian production an almost integral part of London's supply planning. Ministry of Supply orders placed in the first few months of war, which included 600,000 rounds of filled shell and 150 million rounds of small arms ammunition, absorbed the greater part of India's existing capacity for ammunition production. The available surplus of weapons was much smaller, but

75 3.7-inch mule-pack howitzers, an equipment made only in India, were ordered in view of possible operations in mountainous country.

Most of these orders bore fruit in 1940 or the early months of 1941. Even before Dunkirk, the Indian ordnance factories, whose performance was noted in London as being exceptionally reliable and prompt, had supplied the United Kingdom with 124,000 filled shells for field and medium guns, and 66 million rounds of small arms ammunition. From Australia there arrived in the latter part of 1940 30,000 rifles and six heavy anti-aircraft guns, the remaining forty-four being shipped a little later to the Middle East. By June 1941 Australia had delivered to United Kingdom order 100 million rounds of small arms ammunition, 36,000 filled and 146,000 empty mortar bombs. Total supplies of munitions from the Eastern Group in this period were not large, but coming as they did at a time when the British armies at home and in Egypt were facing desperate perils with desperately inadequate resources, and when supplies from North America (except for the 'emergency' shipments of June 1940)[1] had hardly begun to appear, they were of immeasurable value. Many of them, too, were just the kind of stores that, if such items as tanks and aircraft are excluded, were most grievously scarce. The 30,000 Australian rifles take on a new importance when it is recalled that total production in the United Kingdom in 1940 was only 81,000, that the Army was drilling with dummies and that no .303-inch weapons arrived from North America until 1942. Since supplies of small arms ammunition were so short in the summer of 1940 that a special report on the stock position was rendered weekly to the highest authority of all, the Defence Committee (Supply), it can be judged how welcome were the 142 million rounds shipped in that year from India and Australia to the United Kingdom. Together with the 58 millions shipped to the Middle East, the eastern supplies represented an increment of very nearly fifty per cent. to United Kingdom production of small arms ammunition in 1940. Indeed it was probably in 1940 and the following winter that the Eastern Group countries made their most valuable direct contribution to United Kingdom munitions supply. Nor was the contribution made at the expense of their main task of equipping their own Forces: by the summer of 1941 an Australian, a New Zealand, a South African and two Indian divisions were in action or ready for action in the Middle East, all partly, and the Australian and Indian formations very largely, equipped from domestic production.

---

[1] See *North American Supply, op. cit.,* Chapter V, Section (ii).

(iii)

The 'Eastern Group' Phase,
June 1940–December 1941

THE ORGANISATION OF THE GROUP

Meanwhile a great change had come about in the strategic situation. In June 1940 the French Army was broken and the Italian Government declared war. In August British Somaliland was overrun; enemy forces began to deploy against the frontiers of Egypt, Kenya and the Sudan; and the British Government determined that Suez must be held at all costs, thus making the Middle East a major theatre of war. The temporary closing of the Burma Road revealed acute British fears of the opening of the second eastern theatre of war. The effects of all this upon eastern hemisphere supply were obvious and profound. Even if the United Kingdom had had supplies to spare for the much larger forces which would now have to be located in the east, it could not have despatched the supplies thither, the Mediterranean passage being now virtually closed, except at inordinate cost in time and shipping space. Very much therefore depended on how far the countries near at hand could relieve it of the burden. The role of these countries was no longer to provide a smallish increment to United Kingdom stocks of certain stores but to form one of the main pillars supporting the whole structure of resistance to the eastward expansion of Axis power. Thus, in the first place, the destination of their supplies was altered; while emergency shipments to the United Kingdom continued for a few months, it was obvious that in the future their surplus production as well as their troops would be directed either to the actual Middle Eastern or to the prospective Far Eastern theatres of war. It was also evident that every effort would have to be made to increase the quantity of the surplus. At the end of June a rough indication of the scale of assistance now required from the Eastern Group was given by the War Office, which suggested that supplies should be sought thence for about one-quarter of the total Commonwealth land forces, that is, for the twelve or fourteen Commonwealth divisions which, it was now expected, would be operating in the Middle or Far East; this in addition to local garrison and home defence forces. This was not the impossible target it might appear. It did not relate to the initial equipment and reserves of the divisions, which they would bring with them from their country of origin, but to their subsequent maintenance, that is, the replacement of equipment lost or destroyed and of expendable stores such as ammunition. Furthermore, the twenty-five per cent. applied only to those items which were being or could readily be made in one or other of the eastern countries, and not to tanks, transport or heavy artillery. Even so it was evident that a very strenuous effort would have to be made if the plan were to be even approximately fulfilled.

It was natural that in this new situation the British countries in the eastern hemisphere, sharing a common peril, should draw closer together and should begin to consider replacing in some measure their several links with the United Kingdom, now physically more tenuous and strategically less appropriate, by a network of mutual assistance. The idea of a more or less self-supporting eastern zone of supply, based primarily on co-operation between India and Australasia, was not new. It had been prominently in view when the main threat was considered to come from Japan, and had formed one of the strongest elements in the case for the peace-time expansion of munitions capacity in the eastern countries. As such, it had been made much of by the Australian Government at the Imperial Conference and in principle it had the benevolent approval of the United Kingdom authorities. So far, however, co-operation had not been practised to any marked degree. Since the early thirties New Zealand had drawn most of her military supplies, and more recently the means of making them also, from her immediate neighbour. But apart from this each country's relations with the United Kingdom were far closer than its relations with any of the others. Each was working on its own initiative to supply its own Forces, wherever situated, and to meet its separate Commonwealth commitments, without any co-ordination except such as was applied by the War Office and the Ministry of Supply in London. Neither the requirements nor the resources of the Eastern Group as a whole had ever been collated. Clearly, there was a possibility that by co-ordination much economy of effort could be obtained. Shipping could be saved to the extent that, for example, Australian forces in Egypt might be supplied from India and Indian forces in Malaya supplied from Australia. The risk of over-production or under-production of particular items could be minimised. Total production might be increased by the exchange of surplus components. It was thought that Australia might be able to provide some of the machine tools and presses required by India and South Africa, thus reducing their dependence on imports from much remoter sources. The need for the greatest possible interchange of raw materials had hardly to be insisted on.

These points were not overlooked in London. Though India seems to have been expected to carry the main burden, the expansion of supply referred to above was regarded as a collective task for the area 'east of Suez'; and the mission, which in July 1940 the Ministry of Supply decided to send out to investigate the possibilities of expansion in India, was instructed to bear in mind the need for tying this up with any help that Australia or South Africa might be able to give. It was, in fact, to break its outward journey in South Africa (at the request of the Union Government) and it hoped to make contact with Australian representatives in Delhi.

Meanwhile, however, a larger plan had taken shape as a result of an initiative taken by the Government of India. In July 1940 the Viceroy invited the Governments of South Africa, Australia, New Zealand, Ceylon, Burma, Malaya and Hong Kong, the East African Governors' Conference and the Ambassador at Shanghai to send representatives to a conference in New Delhi to 'settle the division of the joint war supply policy'. The Conference, at which the United Kingdom was represented by the above-mentioned Ministry of Supply mission, assembled on 25th October 1940, and produced its final report just a month later. From its deliberations there emerged an ambitious new production programme for the Group, to which we shall refer later, and an equally ambitious scheme for the administrative direction of supply throughout the area. Co-ordination was discussed under two heads, corresponding to the division of functions between the War Office and the Ministry of Supply – provision and supply. 'Provision' is a military function, comprising the estimation of military requirements, the placing of demands upon the supply organisation and the holding and distribution of stocks. Under this head the Conference recommended first that 'local provision offices' in each of the five actual or prospective operational areas, viz. Africa south of Abyssinia, the Middle East (Egypt, the Sudan, Palestine and Syria), India (covering Iraq and Burma), Malaya and Hong Kong. These, together with the existing internal provision offices in Australia and New Zealand, were to place demands for such of their needs as could not be met locally upon a new organisation to be established in Delhi, the Central Provision Office, which was to be responsible for supplying all the eastern theatres. For this purpose it was to pass on the demands to an Eastern Group Supply Council, also in Delhi, which in turn would make arrangements for new production, 'allocating' the necessary order to one or other of its member countries, or, if none of these could undertake it, referring the requirement to London.

Neither the United Kingdom nor any of the Governments concerned raised serious objections to this new machinery, except that at the instance of the War Office the local provision offices were rearranged so as to correspond with the structure of operational command. The East African colonies together with Northern Rhodesia and Nyasaland and also Iraq, were associated with the Middle East office; South Africa and Southern Rhodesia were t have internal provision offices like those of Australia and New Zealand; Burma was separated from India and joined with Hong Kong and Malaya in the Far East provision office. It was agreed that the Central Provision office should be located in Delhi and that it should be directed by an officer of the Imperial General Staff. Major-General W. C. Holden received this appointment, with which went the title of Controller-General, Army Provision. The Eastern Group Supply Council was to be a representative body comprising nominees of the United Kingdom, Indian, South African, Australian and New Zealand Governments, together with the head of the Central Provision Office. The United Kingdom appointed as its representative, and as Chairman of the Council, Sir Archibald Carter, lately Secretary of the Admiralty. It was proposed at first that the non-self-governing territories represented at the Conference should not be full members of the Council, but should send 'advisers'. It was decided, however, that according to normal constitutional practice, the Colonial Governments, while not being debarred from sending advisers, should actually be represented on the Council by Sir Archibald Carter. To preserve continuity of action on munitions matters, the Munitions Adviser of the Ministry of Supply Mission was appointed Munitions Adviser to the Council.

While there was little dispute about the structure of the new institutions, the Conference report left much room for discussion as to their powers and functions. Opened by the Viceroy in person, presided over by the Supply Member of the Governor-General's Executive Council, attended by large delegations with leaders of not dissimilar standing and by observers from the Netherlands East Indies, the Colonial Office and the Middle East Command, heralded by wide and impressive publicity, the Delhi Conference was a political event of the first magnitude, and its recommendations were correspondingly bold and far-reaching. On one interpretation of the report, the 'Eastern Group' was conceived as a real political entity, the Supply Council as a kind of federal Ministry of Supply with executive powers. The members were to be 'men of the highest ability having the confidence of their governments', which suggested that the Council would be able to take decisions in some degree binding upon the several governments. There was a similar implication in the recommendation that the Colonial advisers would be entitled 'to a hearing but not to a vote'. The Council was to be empowered to purchase and to hold stocks and to 'make arrangements' for new production. Though primarily concerned with military provision it was also to act as a clearing-house for information on supply matters generally, and would be entitled to advise the governments concerned on matters affecting the needs of the civilian populations of the region.

All this went a good deal beyond what the governments concerned, or some of them, were prepared to accept. The South African Government immediately entered a caveat against being debarred from preferring its demands directly upon London. To the United Kingdom Government, co-operation between the eastern countries was highly desirable, but an autonomous supply organisation east of Suez was quite another matter. It was of vital importance that nothing should be done to disturb the unity of imperial strategy and imperial supply which was based on central direction of both from London. In the summer of 1940 this unity was gravely threatened. Despairing of having their urgent needs met from the United Kingdom, the Dominions had begun to seek supplies independently from whatever source was open, that is, mainly from the United States, where they were in danger of competing with the British Purchasing Commission. There was even a threat to the vital principle that all the Forces of the Commonwealth should be equipped with weapons of the same type. Unity was gradually restored, as the Dominion missions in America were brought within the framework of the British supply organisations there, and the Dominion Governments were persuaded to place all their demands for munitions upon the War Office which, in consultation with the Ministry of Supply, decided whence and to what extent they should be met. But in this context it is easy to see that the authorities in London would consider co-ordination within the Eastern Group dearly bought if it were at the expense of co-ordination of Commonwealth supply as a whole; and of this the first draft of the new organisation, even though it was to be headed by United Kingdom representatives, seemed to afford some danger. Moreover, the Delhi Conference report clearly envisaged and was based on the assumption of a much larger volume of production in the east than the United Kingdom authorities, on whom the feasibility of expansion depended, were prepared to consider. As London saw it, Middle East supply was not and could not be a purely Eastern Group matter. Britain would have to bear the main financial burden and, together with North America, the major part of the manufacturing burden; and it was thus essential that eastern supply should be tied up closely with global supply plans.

Discussions in London during November and December 1940 established that the Eastern Group Supply Council would not be a federal executive but rather, in one aspect, a kind of permanent conference of the eastern countries' supply organisations and, in another aspect, a Ministry of Supply mission covering the eastern hemisphere as a whole and taking the place of the separate missions which would otherwise have had to be established in each country. On receipt of demands from the Central Provision Office the Council, in the light of the knowledge which it would acquire of the supply position in each country, would allocate the necessary production order to one of its members. But the decision would have to be unanimous – there was no question of voting – and the 'allocations' would be a request which the Government of the country concerned was, of course, perfectly entitled to refuse. Nor would the Council actually purchase stores, as the Conference had suggested. In allocating an order it would authorise the Government concerned to incur expenditure which the latter would recover from the Government of the country from which the demand originated – in the great majority of cases, the United Kingdom (the final settlement being adjusted according to the terms of the separate financial agreements in force between the United Kingdom on the one hand and the Dominions and India on the other). The Council was not, however, empowered to authorise capital expenditure without reference to London. Furthermore, its operations were to apply to those types of military stores which could be provided wholly or mainly from within the Group. The Ministry of Supply drew up a list of 'excluded' stores which would be demanded from London directly as before. This comprised, roughly speaking, all 'munitions' in the narrower sense of the term, that is to say, weapons, ammunition, vehicles, explosives and most of the important classes of signal and engineer equipment. Also excluded were petroleum, coal and most raw materials, for the procurement of which existing arrangements were judged adequate.

Thus the actual functions of the Eastern Group Supply Council were comparatively modest. It was definitely excluded from the sphere of civilian supply, except in so far as this might form an incidental part of military provision. In the military sphere, it performed three main functions. Its main sphere of active operation lay in the field of the miscellaneous stores which make up a large part of the equipment of an army (stores classified by the War Office under Votes 7, 8 and 10). For such stores India was already marked down as the main source of supply for the Middle East theatre of war. What the new organisation did was firstly, through the Central Provision Office, to introduce order and system into the flow of demands from the operational commands, and, secondly, to relieve the burden on India by investigating the possibilities of supply from other countries in the area. In respect of munitions proper ('Vote 9' stores) the Council, or rather its Munitions Committee, which was in the nature of a separate enclave with the United Kingdom Munitions Adviser as special representative of the Ministry of Supply, acted as the channel through which United Kingdom claims upon the surplus production of the eastern countries were distributed. Finally, while the primary responsibility of the Dominion and Indian Governments for meeting the requirements of their own Forces was not affected by the new arrangements, the Council helped by arranging an interchange of components and, in a few cases, of complete munitions.

Even in these more limited spheres it was some time before the Delhi organisation began to function effectively. Sir Archibald Carter and Major-General Holden arrived in February 1941, and the other members of the Council followed in the next two months. On 25th March the Council announced that it was ready to operate. In respect of two of the functions just described, action proceeded smoothly enough. A considerable number of orders for munitions were received from the Ministry of Supply in the latter part of 1941, and duly allocated to participating governments. In the same period several useful arrangements were made for mutual assistance in munitions production within the Group. Thus fuses were ordered from New Zealand and Australia to match Indian and South African production of other shell components; Australia was asked to supply India with mortar barrels and India to furnish harness for the mortars being made in South Africa; supplies of South African cordite were arranged for India, while the South African production of demolition explosives was facilitated by supplies of glycerine from India and New Zealand. Some of these adjustments, however, had been initiated by the Ministry of Supply mission which toured Australasia before the Supply Council came into being.[1]

For the main task of co-ordinating the supply of stores other than munitions, however, the existence of the Central Provision Office was essential. The latter took longer to organise than the Supply Council; it was not in full operation until October 1941, though it began to transmit a few demands to the Council from July onwards. The delay did not mean that nothing was done to supply the Middle East before this. In so far as they were available stores were already being shipped from India according to arrangements made through ordinary G.H.Q. channels in the previous year. Nor did the new institutions effect much immediate change, for they were not yet really in a position to carry out their allotted tasks. Since there was as yet little data about the resources of the other countries, the great majority of the Central Provision Office demands were still referred automatically to the Indian supply organisation as the nearest source of supply, and in order to avoid the delay of enquiry and re-enquiry. Nor could much be done yet to systematise requirements or to prepare the long-term forecasts urgently needed by the suppliers. In 1941 the situation was frankly chaotic. The number of individual demands was enormous – over thirty thousand were transmitted in the last three months of 1941. There was much duplication, much confusion over differing specifications and Service vocabularies.

[1] See pp. 453 and 456.

The demands were mostly for immediate delivery for urgent operational needs, and there were no data for any but the most conjectural forward planning of production. By the end of 1941, as a result of the laborious endeavours of the Central Provision Office and the Supply Council staff, all this was beginning to be sorted out. The picture of Group resources was becoming clearer, and long-term military needs were taking shape. The Central Provision Office managed to draw up a rough forecast for the year 1942, though this was too late to influence production in that year, and it was not until 1943 that the production authorities had a firm basis of requirements to work on. Meanwhile, however, changes in the strategic sphere had, as we shall see, grievously restricted the developing activity of the organisation and confined it to a much narrower scope than had been intended.

Nevertheless the volume and value of the work done was very considerable. A final analysis made when the organisation was wound up early in 1946 showed that orders had been allocated to and accepted by Eastern Group governments to a total value of £286.5 million, of which more than half had been ordered in 1941-42. Of this total 'munitions' accounted for only £43.1 million, of which the greater part, £30.3 million, were ordered at the direct request of the United Kingdom. On the other hand the great majority of the remaining orders, £224.9 out of £243.4 million, were placed to meet Central Provision Office demands, chiefly on behalf of the Middle East Command. This remainder comprised £131.4 million worth of general stores, £80.8 million worth of textiles and clothing and £24.1 million worth of engineer and transportation stores, the small balance being made up of medical stores, R.A.F. stores and stationery and office equipment. The distribution of the orders is of some interest. Leaving aside munitions, the supply of which was especially affected by the strategic factors, India was very much the most important source of supply, receiving over three-fifths of the total value of orders, or £151.9 million. Next came Australia with £41.2 million, and South Africa with £36.3 million. Orders were placed on New Zealand to the value of £8.3 million, on the Rhodesias for £2.3 million, and on East Africa for £1.4 million, and on Hong Kong, Malaya, Palestine, Ceylon and Burma for a combined total of £1.9 million. India was a principal supplier of paints, varnishes and dopes, steel sections, timber and woodware, tentage and camouflage, acids and chemicals, clothing and footwear, web equipment, sandbags and hessian, ropes, brushes, asbestos sheets, linseed oil, dubbin, soap, sera and vaccine, batteries, hand tools and above all of cotton textiles, of which she was one of the world's major producers. Australia's most important contribution was in the form of steel products such as steel billets, steel rails, barbed wire, pipes and fittings and particularly railway equipment, but she was also the main source of woollen textiles, tyres, sulphuric acid, sulpha drugs and sera. South Africa specialised in aircraft hangars, bridges, floating barges, cement and firebricks, steel wire rope, electric motors and generators, power pumps, heavy steel tubes and fittings, aircraft and vehicle tyres, rubber and canvas hose, boots and shoes, steel helmets, electric cable and electrodes, and in a number of important chemicals. New Zealand led the field in the supply of broadcast receivers, accumulators, electric cable and insulators, wallboard, and water-bottles, besides making important contributions in various types of clothing. Palestine was a large supplier of electric cable, dental burs and razor blades. Though available for so short a time, Hong Kong was the leading supplier of mess tins and web equipment and a large supplier of many other stores. The contribution of Malaya, Burma and Ceylon was largely confined to raw materials including some of crucial importance. The African colonies provided considerable quantities of clothing and equipment as well as large quantities of timber and other materials.

The above is sufficient to indicate the range of supplies ordered by the Eastern Group Supply Council from its member countries. Some idea of the quantities may be obtained from the following figures: 937 million yards of cotton cloth and canvas, 245 million articles of clothing, 26 million towels, 330 million sandbags, 20 million pairs of boots and shoes, 2 million steel helmets, 46,000 tons of barbed wire, 7 million dry batteries, 36 thousand field cookers. This small selection, which takes no account of the supplies rendered by each country to the Forces operating within or near its own borders, is perhaps enough to indicate the magnitude of the production effort in the Eastern Group, involving many commodities hitherto made there on a very small scale or not at all, the relief afforded to United Nations shipping as well as to the manufacturing resources of the west, and the size and complexity of the tasks undertaken by the planning and distributing organisation in New Delhi.

THE DEVELOPMENT OF MUNITIONS PRODUCTION

Besides setting up administrative machinery for the co-ordination of eastern hemisphere supply, the Delhi Conference of October 1940 made far-reaching recommendations on the expansion of munitions production. Its starting point was an estimate drawn up in London of the additional capacity required in India for the manufacture of weapons and ammunition in order that the proposal to maintain fourteen Commonwealth divisions east of Suez might be implemented. The Conference correlated this estimate with the increased local requirements of the Dominions and allocated the total additional capacity between the several countries represented in Delhi,

India's share of the whole being as a result somewhat reduced. The total increase required was very large. The planned output of rifles, for example, was to be doubled, from 200,000 to 400,000 a year. The Eastern Group was to manufacture each year not 6,000 but 10,000 Bren guns, not 3,461 but 6,011 artillery equipments. The output of gun ammunition was to be approximately doubled, making the ultimate objective about 1½ million rounds a month, and that of small arms ammunition raised from 91 to 135 million rounds a month. Considering that in that year the United Kingdom with its vastly greater manufacturing resources actually achieved output figures only two or three times greater, in most cases, than those now projected by the Eastern Group, the delegates certainly did not approach the problem before them with any undue timidity or caution.

The whole programme was based on the assumption that the new strategic situation, not only the prospect of intensive fighting in the east but also the more obvious vulnerability of factories in Britain, would compel the Government of the United Kingdom to revise its whole thinking about the proper distribution within the Commonwealth of the factors of production, particularly machine tools and skilled labour. The Conference report stressed that the fulfilment of the new plans, and indeed of the plans in force before the Conference met, was absolutely dependent on plant and personnel being made available by the United Kingdom. Very far-reaching ideas were entertained in the East on this subject. A few days after Dunkirk the Viceroy had put forward a suggestion, now repeated, that British munitions plants should be transferred to India bodily, machines, managers and men. The State Government of Victoria later made a similar proposal about British shipyards. This sort of scheme never had any real chance of acceptance. It had implications which the authorities in London were not prepared even to consider. It will be recalled that the Prime Minister asserted that 'if this island were subjugated and starving, the British Dominions beyond the seas would carry on the fight . . .' but it will also be recalled that this was a contingency in which he did 'not for a moment believe'.[1] The possibility of subjugation apart, there was no case even for a partial evacuation of British war industry, for bombing would have had to be heavy indeed to have done more damage to the Commonwealth's war effort than the loss of six months' production during the removal.

But this did not mean that the Government was not far more anxious than before that eastern munitions production should be expedited and enlarged, and rather more ready to spare machinery and technicians for that purpose. Thus the Government of India's

---

[1] H. of C. Deb., Vol. 361, Col. 796, 4th June 1940; reproduced in Winston Churchill's *War Speeches, Into Battle* (Cassell & Co. Ltd., 1941).

representations were met by the proposal that a mission should be sent forthwith to study the Indian potential.

Sir Alexander Roger, chairman of many industrial companies and of the recently constituted Tank Board, was appointed leader of the mission, which was despatched by the Minister of Supply in consultation with the Secretary of State for India, and a numerous team of experts was recruited from industry and the government service. The mission sailed in August 1940, and after a brief stay in South Africa, acted as the United Kingdom delegation at the Viceroy's Conference; and then, in consultation with the Supply Department of the Government of India, made a thorough survey of Indian resources and submitted a series of recommendations as to the reorganisation and expansion of Indian war production. From India, sections of the mission went on in the spring of 1941 to visit Australia, New Zealand, South Africa, Hong Kong, Malaya, Burma and Palestine before returning home.

In Australia the role of the Ministry of Supply Mission was not to make recommendations or to stimulate fresh expansion but rather to see what was being done and to seek Australian aid for Indian progress. It found the Australians in little need of stimulation, but pressing vigorously ahead with their own large programme and with the large additions made thereto in Delhi. The Mission's impression was that 'the present and planned programme for production of armaments and war supplies generally in Australia far exceeds the possibilities of any other country in the Eastern Group'. Australia alone possessed the sturdy stem of general industry whereon ambitious schemes for munitions production could be safely grafted. Far more than any other eastern country she had both the will and the ability to fulfil her plans without external aid. The Prime Minister, Mr Menzies, told London that to the utmost possible extent Australia would refrain from asking the United Kingdom for technical staff or machinery. 'Managements are not frightened by the obvious difficulties', the Ministry of Supply Mission commented, 'and if they cannot obtain plant they make it wherever possible'. Australia was not only self-supporting in machine tools except for a few highly specialised items, but could offer a considerable surplus in relief of deficiencies elsewhere in the Eastern Group, particularly in India.

The Australian munitions programme made great headway in 1941. Production of Bren guns, Bren gun carriers, 25-pounder field guns and 2-pounder anti-tank guns, all started during the year. Construction of a new rifle factory encouraged and partly financed by the United Kingdom was in progress and due to come into operation early in 1942. Manufacture of shells and small arms ammunition was going forward according to schedule, though the former was hampered by a shortage of explosives. But while production was expanding rapidly the surplus available over and above Australian needs was if anything contracting. In 1941 Australian eyes could not but be increasingly fixed upon the smouldering volcano that was Japan; and just as they could not afford to add to the division that they had sent to the Middle East, so the Australians felt compelled to give the strengthening of their local defences, including the Malayan outpost, the first call upon their output of munitions. London was warned that the whole capacity of the Bren gun factory would be required by Australia for two years to come, that no further deliveries of rifles, over and above the 30,000 already shipped, could be made for the time being, and that there was little chance that 25-pounders or their ammunition could be exported during 1941. Nevertheless, Australia did accept several important additional orders from the United Kingdom in this period – for example, for 150 more 3.7-inch A.A. guns, of which she undertook to raise the export rate from two to four monthly, for 100,000 more rifles from the new factory, for 2,000 Bren carriers and for 700 2-pounder guns, 575 of them complete with carriages. The only reinforcements that British forces in the Middle or Far East received in 1941 as a result of these new orders, however, were 125 2-pounder anti-tank guns, and the execution of the remainder was, as we shall see, imperilled by the strategic changes at the end of the year.

Meanwhile important developments were proceeding outside the Ministry of Supply field. The Beaufort aircraft scheme had been delayed by the outbreak of war, which made it much more difficult for the Air Ministry and the Bristol Aircraft Company to make available the technical assistance, the plant, components and materials on which the scheme depended. Two days before Germany invaded Poland, indeed, the Commonwealth Government had enquired whether the plan should not be abandoned; it wished to proceed, but did not want to find itself saddled with a task which would be impossible if the United Kingdom could not play its allotted part. London's reply was reassuring, and with some inevitable delays the shipment of plant and material and the training of Australian technicians did proceed reasonably smoothly. There was one important change, however: the Bristol Aircraft Company could no longer do what was necessary to initiate Australian manufacture of Taurus engines. Shipment of complete engines to match Australian frames was promised in lieu, but the Australians were determined to establish engine manufacture and accordingly decided to adopt the American Pratt and Whitney Wasp instead. The first Australian Beauforts were completed in September 1941, and ten were delivered before the end of the year. Up to that date Australia had also made 367 Wirraways and several hundred smaller trainers.

Shipbuilding also was making great strides, seven naval shipyards being in operation by the end of 1940 compared with one at the outbreak of war. Ships under construction included Tribal class destroyers and large numbers of patrol vessels equipped for anti-submarine and minesweeping duties; of these latter the British Admiralty ordered thirteen in June 1940. Australia was also proceeding with the long-cherished project of establishing or rather re-establishing a local merchant shipbuilding industry, although she had failed to secure British orders for cargo ships, the Admiralty taking the view that priority should be given in Australia to naval construction.

For South Africa the Delhi Conference was a revolutionary event. Hitherto the Union had been proceeding quietly towards a limited objective, the equipping of its own Forces with the simpler types of armament and warlike stores. Now it found itself called upon to shoulder a very large part of the burden of supply undertaken by the Eastern Group, to produce a much wider range of stores in quantities which went, as the High Commissioner's Office in London put it 'immeasurably beyond the requirements of South Africa and of anything which the Union Government had contemplated'. The Union, which had not intended to make small arms at all, was now asked to make 4,000 Bren guns a year. It had not intended to make field artillery, but the Conference suggested a yearly 240 25-pounders. It received an allocation of 1,000 2-pounder anti-tank guns, of which it had been planning to make about a hundred. It was asked to add capacity for a monthly output of 24 million rounds of small arms ammunition to the 16 million which it needed for its own purposes, to make 3.7-inch anti-aircraft and 25-pounder shell, to assemble tracked carriers as well as armoured cars and to make large additions to its output of mortars, mortar bombs and grenades. Clearly such a programme raised formidable problems of finance, plant and personnel. The machine tool situation was easier in South Africa than elsewhere in the Eastern Group (except Australia), but personnel, both skilled artisans and armament engineers, were even scarcer than elsewhere. The Union Government estimated that the full Delhi programme would require capital expenditure to the tune of £4½–£5 million, and over three thousand technicians, both of which it looked to the United Kingdom to provide. The Government, however, was quick to appreciate that of the latter there was no chance whatever, and therefore it did not accept the Delhi recommendations in full. It declined to make anti-aircraft shell or 25-pounder equipments. The Bren gun scheme had to be dropped, since it depended on the establishment in the Union of a team of refugee Czech experts who in the event were allotted to India instead. The planned output of anti-tank guns was cut down to five hundred a year and was to be deferred until the completion of existing orders for 3.7-inch howitzers and 3-inch mortars, so that new plant was not required. London advised that in view of the number of Bren carriers scheduled for production in the United Kingdom, Canada and Australasia, production in South Africa would be superfluous. These modifications reduced the capital cost of expansion to £3½ million and, what was more important, the number of British technicians required to two hundred and fifty. Even this was more than the United Kingdom could afford and there had to be some further scaling down of the South African programme. The Union did not, in fact, undertake any new weapons in addition to those already planned. What it did undertake was an output considerably in excess of its own needs of items already included in the programme, such as armoured cars, mortars, shell, aircraft bombs, mortar bombs and grenades. The prospect of such a surplus raised for the first time the question of the United Kingdom's placing orders on South African production; and orders were in fact placed during 1941 for over a thousand armoured cars, a thousand 3-inch mortars, half a million 25-pounder shells and a million hand grenades, and a wide range of aircraft bombs. Thus within a limited range of munitions South Africa was allotted a substantial part in the maintenance of the Middle East forces.

An important consequence of the Delhi Conference and the Roger Mission, was that for the first time the smaller eastern producers, among which must be included New Zealand as well as Hong Kong, Burma, Malaya and Palestine, were drawn into the framework of supply planning. From the last three little could be expected in the way of munitions except a few simple components. Hong Kong might have been asked to do more if it had not been for its exposed position. But New Zealand was now recognised to have, within obvious limitations, a valuable potential which could be exploited to the benefit of the United Kingdom and the Eastern Group. The Ministry of Supply Mission which visited New Zealand early in 1941 was chiefly concerned to arrange for the production of fuses to match Indian and Australian shells. This item had been chosen as peculiarly suitable for New Zealand in that it required skilful workmanship but not large plants or large imports of raw material; and production was duly initiated. But the Mission also found that, the normal imports of motor-cars having been suspended, there was considerable unemployed assembly capacity which was not utilised or going to be utilised by New Zealand's own very small munitions programme. Moreover, the requirements of the Dominion's armed forces for Bren carriers, hand grenades, 2-inch mortars and their ammunition would very soon be met, and if external orders were not placed production would have to stop. United Kingdom orders were not readily forthcoming, for items which were within the capabilities of New Zealand were 'easy' for British, Indian and Australian producers also. If the Dominion's resources had been thoroughly assessed sooner, production of such items might have been delegated to New Zealand on a substantial scale. As it was, more or less adequate production had been built up elsewhere, and there was no pressing demand for additional supplies. Nevertheless after much discussion substantial orders were placed in 1941 for all these stores, and as a result some specialisation was achieved; New Zealand became the Eastern Group's largest producer of hand grenades, 2-inch mortars and their bombs.

It was in the development of Indian munitions production, however, that the Government of the United Kingdom had the most direct and urgent interest. India was regarded as the key to the Middle East supply problem. She was closer to the scene of operations than any of the Dominions and more closely integrated with imperial supply planning; and in some quarters both in India and at home very large ideas of her war potential were entertained. At the same time it was clear that, more than in any of the Dominions, progress would depend on United Kingdom initiative and help, in finance, plant and personnel. The object of the Ministry of Supply in sending out Sir Alexander Roger was to ascertain precisely what, within the real limitations of time and of the available machinery and technical skill, India could achieve in the way of munitions production, and what degree of assistance would be necessary. The Mission's terms of reference and instruction were carefully composed with this object in view. Its function was to advise the two Governments concerned whether India's present output could be expanded 'by the discovery and adaptation of existing capacity'. The creation of fresh capacity was not ruled out, but no schemes were to be adopted which would not yield results before the middle of 1942 at the latest, and stress was laid on the primary need for projects which would need little additional plant.

The Mission set about its task with great energy. Having served as United Kingdom delegation to the Delhi Conference, it joined forces with the Indian Supply Department in translating the Conference recommendations, in so far as they affected India, into concrete production schemes. In a remarkably short time it produced a series of twenty-five reports in which were set forth both certain recommendations as to the structure and methods of the Indian war production organisation and its detailed proposals for the expansion of munitions capacity. The latter were far-reaching indeed. Chief among them were the following. By extending the existing gun and carriage factory the output of artillery equipments was to be raised from the previously scheduled 30 to 110 a month. By similar means the output of shell was to be raised from 114,000 to 530,000 rounds a month. A new rifle factory was to be created with an annual capacity of 80,000 rifles. Another new factory, to be operated by the above-mentioned Czech technicians,[1] was to turn out 3,000 Bren machine guns a year. Capacity for the production of small arms ammunition was to be increased from 28 to 40.5 million rounds a month. Associated with all this were plans for a vast increase in the production of alloy steel, cordite and high explosive. Altogether the 'Roger' proposals entailed the construction of six new factories, ten enlargements of existing factories and the conversion of three railway workshops as well as the extension of private engineering works, the whole to cost £15½ million. The magnitude and audacity of the proposals most clearly emerge when it is recalled that the initial cost of the 'Chatfield' measures, which had not proved by any means easy to implement, was only £2¾ million.

The programme was, in fact, designed to establish in India the maximum munitions output of which India's industry was capable. Unfortunately, it entailed two basic assumptions, neither of which was altogether correct. One was that India could be mobilised industrially in much the same way as Britain, Canada and Australia were being mobilised. In fact, this was neither politically nor economically feasible. The Government of India had rarely been in a more uncomfortable position than it was at this time. On one side the European business community was publicly castigating it for its allegedly dilatory and half-hearted prosecution of the war; on the other were Indian business men, lukewarm for the most part in their support of the war and profoundly suspicious of any extension of European industrial activity, and in the background the National Congress, formidably murmuring against the war effort and against any addition to the country's burden. The Government had therefore to steer a course between doing too little and doing so much that economic and political stability would be imperilled. For the present the former danger seemed the greater, but the Government had none the less to go carefully. While it fully associated itself with the expansion schemes put forward by the Roger Mission, it could not accept certain of the Mission's other recommendations, for instance, that strict financial control be relaxed, which were more appropriate to British than to Indian conditions.

The other assumption on which the programme depended was that Indian production could be considered independently of production elsewhere. The cables and letters emanating from the Mission show that it believed either that the United Kingdom could contribute the necessary assistance without undue sacrifice of its own war effort, or that the development of the maximum Indian production was so vital as to justify any such sacrifice, however heavy.

---

[1] See p. 455.

This belief stemmed from a certain misunderstanding about the function of the Mission. Sir Alexander Roger regarded himself as being charged with the task of finding ways and means to establish in India the capacity which London wanted to see established there. His proposals were designed to produce outputs not greater than those which the War Office and the Ministry of Supply had suggested before the Mission sailed. But these outputs were regarded in London as a desirable objective, not as a firm programme which was to be implemented at any cost. The United Kingdom Government did not baulk at the purely financial cost of the projects, high though it was. What worried it was the cost in terms of the scarce factors of production. The projects entailed the acquisition of some 3,000 machine tools, about half of which, including most of the more elaborate types, would have to come from outside the Eastern Group. It entailed also the loan from the United Kingdom of 26 supervisors and 284 skilled armament workers. It was not less true than it had ever been that every machine tool and every technician made available to India meant a loss of output at home, so that in spite of the strong new reasons for helping India there had still to be a very careful weighing of benefit and cost.

As a result of this misunderstanding an awkward situation developed in the early months of 1941. In order to save time while the full details were being worked out, summarised versions of the various projects were telegraphed to London during November and December 1940; and a quick Yes or No was clearly expected. But this was just what the Ministry could not provide; for it was precisely on the details that its assessment of the practicability, as distinct from the intrinsic desirability, of the projects depended. On many of them it could not make a firm decision without knowing what numbers and types of machine tools, what numbers and grades of technicians it would have to provide; and for this knowledge it had to wait for the full reports which were not available in London until the beginning of April. The delay much disquieted both the Mission and the Government of India; and as their anxieties were communicated to the Governments of Australia, New Zealand and South Africa, the feeling spread throughout the Eastern Group that London was not treating its problems with the urgent attention that they deserved, and that India was going to be allowed to remain a weak link in the chain of imperial supply.

Such fears were exaggerated and so unjust. Most of the schemes had been promptly sanctioned in principle, and planning staffs had been approved so that preliminary work could go forward but the detailed reconciliation of the projects with imperial needs on the one hand and imperial resources on the other inevitably took longer, and when it was completed the Indian expansion programme emerged in a much modified form. The scheme for the new rifle factory was cancelled almost immediately, on the ground that it could not be completed until 1943, by which time additional Australian, not to mention British and North American capacity, would be in full operation. The Bren gun factory was approved in March 1941, but negotiations with the Czechs were unhappily so protracted that it eventually had to be abandoned as superfluous, after much preliminary expense had been incurred. The artillery scheme was drastically revised, the required output of anti-tank guns being halved. The proposals relating to gun ammunition were affected by the current scaling down of requirements; less production was needed in India and plant was more readily available. Consequently, far less explosives and filling capacity was required. Small arms ammunition was in a rather different category, for here a definite decision had been taken before the Roger Mission began its enquiries. In August 1940, the Ministry of Supply had obtained Treasury sanction for the construction of a factory 'east of Suez' capable of producing 40 million rounds a month, and had budgeted for the necessary plant in its programmes of purchases from North America. The Delhi Conference decided that this was too heavy a burden for any one country to carry and distributed the 40 million between

Munitions programmes for India: plans and achievement up to 1942

Table 12   *Units unless otherwise stated*

	Period	Output planned before July 1940	Proposed additional output			Total planned output (Col. 3 plus Col. 6)	Actual output 1942
			Original M.O.S. proposal	'Roger Reports'	Approved by M.O.S.		
Column 1	2	3	4	5	6	7	8
25-pounder guns		—	240	—	—	—	—
3.7-inch howitzer		63	60	61	79	142	—
2/6-pounder A.T. guns	per annum	250	950	950	150	400	—
Rifles (thousands)		100	60	100	20	120	122.4
Brens (thousands)		—	n.a.	3	3	3	—
Gun ammunition (thousand rounds)	per mensem	114	450	426	164	278	112
Small arms ammunition (million rounds)		28	40	12.5	18.4	46.4	20.3

India, Australia and South Africa, India being allotted 12.5 million. This scheme went forward; indeed, after discussions between Delhi and London, India's target was raised to 18.4 million.

These adjustments reduced the cost of the total programme to £8.8 million and the number of personnel from the United Kingdom to 17 gazetted and 176 non-gazetted staff. The whole story can best be summarised in tabular form. (Table 12).

The last column in Table 12 shows that, in so far as it was intended to be fulfilled in 1942, the programme of Indian expansion worked out at the close of 1940 was an almost total failure. The Japanese advance had so far disorganised production that actual output hardly exceeded, and at some points fell short of the output which had been scheduled before ever the Roger Mission sailed or the Delhi Conference conferred. And although it was in India that the disappointment was most severe, none of the countries of the Eastern Group managed to perform in full the task which the Conference set it. For the Group as a whole the picture was as shown in Table 13.

Munitions programmes for the Eastern Group: plans and achievement

up to 1942

Table 13   *Units unless otherwise stated*

	Period	Output planned before the Delhi Conference	Delhi Conference programme	Total output planned	Actual output 1942[1]
Column 1	2	3	4	5	6
25-pounder guns		1,040	—	1,040	848
3.7-inch howitzers		364	—	364	216
2/6-pounder A.T. guns	per	1,850	2,350	4,200	1,372
3.7-inch A.A. guns	annum	150	100	250	204
Rifles		200,000	200,000	400,000	234,400
Brens		6,000	4,000	10,000	6,944
3-inch mortars		6,271	—	6,271	4,436
Gun ammunition (thousand rounds)	per	1,008	821	1,829	525
Small arms ammunition (million rounds)	mensem	91	44	135	85

[1] Highest quarterly output expressed as an annual or monthly rate.

No elaborate reasons need be advanced for this relative failure. The programme was simply too ambitious. There was no parallel at all between the situation of the eastern countries and that of North America in 1940. In the former area there was no large reservoir of resources waiting to be drained off by intensive industrial mobilisation. On the contrary, the plans already laid by the Dominions and India were sufficient or nearly sufficient to occupy their whole available strength. They could not successfully undertake heavy additional burdens without, on the one hand, a more stringent war economy than, for various reasons, they were able to contemplate, and on the other a much larger injection of machinery and technical skill than the United Kingdom could afford to give them.

Was it then a mistake to set before the Eastern Group the large objectives which were set before it in 1940? Certainly the Delhi Conference, by its ready acceptance of London's requirements, raised expectations, both in the east and at home, which were not destined to be realised. (One of the supreme virtues of the British civil servant, however, is the sceptical habit of mind which renders him, if not always his masters, fairly proof against undue exercise of faith and hope.) On the other hand it may be argued that here, or later in the United States, the statement of impossible aims served as a stimulus and so extended the area of the possible. But so far as India was concerned at least, it seems fairly clear that results equally good could have been attained at much lower cost if the sights had been set lower at the start. This is not a criticism of the able and energetic men in the Indian Supply Department and the Ministry of Supply Mission who framed the larger projects, except in so far as the latter, carried away by their enthusiasm, stepped outside the role of technical advisers working out the means of fulfilling a given plan and made themselves advocates of the plan itself.

At all events it was tolerably clear before the end of 1941 that the idea of maintaining the Commonwealth forces in the Middle East to any large extent from production east of Suez was a chimera, so far as armaments were concerned. Australia was easily the largest producer in the Eastern Group, but even in 1941 it was apparent that Australia's main interests lay much nearer home. Up to the time of Pearl Harbour only a small fraction of total Australian production had been sent to the United Kingdom or the Middle East, and the proportion was not increasing. From South Africa, whose resources had hardly been counted in London's supply planning before Dunkirk, substantial assistance could be expected, but only in a rather narrow range of warlike stores; and India was manifestly unfitted to play her role of corner-stone. It would be as much as she could do to meet the main requirements of her own Army, with perhaps a considerable surplus of ammunition.

This account has perhaps been too much dominated by the visions which took possession of men immediately after the collapse in Europe, and so appears unduly negative in tone. To say that the eastern countries failed to hit their target may be to condemn the judgement of those who set it up, though the emergency atmosphere of the period and the Japanese intervention must not be forgotten; it is not proof of the weakness of the archers. What was remarkable was the unprecedented fact that these countries were not only supplying the main needs of their own considerable Forces but were able to make a contribution, however small, to the general pool; and it was not so very small at that. Up to the end of 1941 the Eastern Group had already delivered to United Kingdom order 240 guns, 710 armoured cars, 556 trench mortars, 30,100 rifles, 818,000 filled shells and 300 million rounds of small arms ammunition.

(iv)

After the Intervention of Japan

THE DISINTEGRATION OF THE EASTERN GROUP

The opening of a new theatre of war in the Far East, though it had long been foreseen as a possibility, none the less entailed sudden and painful readjustment of all the plans laid for the organisation of supply east of Suez. For a short while it seemed that the importance of the Central Provision Office and the Eastern Group Supply Council would be enormously enhanced. With the creation of a new international command based on Singapore and controlling Indian, Australian, and Netherlands East Indian as well as British and American forces, a still closer unity was imposed upon the countries bordering upon the Indian Ocean. If the command had endured, the organisation in Delhi might well have become one of the focal points in the direction of global war supply. But the command foundered beneath the swiftly flowing tide of Japanese military triumph, and when the flood reached its limits and was stayed the Eastern Group emerged in a much weakened and truncated form. Hong Kong, Malaya and Burma were lost to it for ever; from Australia, which from March 1942, formed part of a United States command, few supplies could be expected until the menace of invasion was lifted; India, compelled to make an abrupt about-turn and face her eastern frontier, had a yet smaller surplus to spare for the Middle East.

Australia was not only almost isolated physically by the onrush of Japanese power, but her leaders, unable to take part in the higher direction of global strategy and global supply in Washington, felt themselves, and made little secret of their feeling, to be morally isolated as well. This feeling was gradually dispelled, on the diplomatic plane by the creation of the Pacific War Councils in London and Washington, on the military plane by the arrival of United States land, sea and air forces, whose presence was made dramatically manifest when Australian and American warships fought side by side to gain the saving victory of the Coral Sea. Nevertheless in the early months of 1942 Australia was transformed from a surplus to a deficit country in the matter of war supplies. Faced with an imminent threat to their survival, widely compared with that which confronted Great Britain after Dunkirk, the main preoccupation of Australians was the quest for immediate external aid, more especially in aircraft, tanks and anti-aircraft guns. It was only in the nature of things, though the step is said to have been taken at the specific request of the Supreme Allied Commander, South-West Pacific, that the Commonwealth Government should have laid an embargo on the export of munitions to other areas. As a result, while production rose rapidly in 1942, as the facilities planned earlier on came into full operation, and the stimulus of pressing danger made itself felt, shipments to War Office-controlled theatres were virtually suspended and not resumed till 1943. Australia could neither accept further United Kingdom orders nor, for the time being at least, execute those which she had already undertaken. Outstanding orders for 575 anti-tank guns, 100,000 anti-tank mines and 1,100 army wireless sets were cancelled. Against an order for 100,000 rifles, only 1,500 were ever delivered, and those not till 1943. At the end of 1941 Australia held a United Kingdom order for 150 heavy anti-aircraft guns; none were delivered until late in 1943. It was only on the small arms ammunition orders that deliveries continued, even on a much reduced scale, through 1942. Much the same applied to supplies other than munitions; the Eastern Group Supply Council had to search hurriedly for alternative supplies of the multifarious military stores which were no longer forthcoming from Australia. However, the stores which had been produced and were in C.P.O. stores were invaluable to Australia. Much the same applied also to New Zealand, which made no deliveries until 1943, against the munitions orders received from the United Kingdom in 1941. The 'Eastern Group' was thus virtually confined for the time being to India and South Africa and India's power to help in the achievement of the Group's original objects was very limited.

For India the advance of Japanese forces was a many-sided and heavy calamity. An invasion being threatened and air-raids having actually taken place, tiny in scale but devastating in their moral effect, it became necessary to transplant to safer areas most of the munitions plants located on the east side of the country. In at least one case this meant dismantling the steelwork of the buildings and re-erecting them 400 miles away, together with the equipment and machine tools. The smouldering political discontent broke into open flame, and the Government was faced in many parts of the country with the threat of a grave and widespread breakdown of internal order. It was not surprising therefore that the curve of munitions production rose in 1942 much more slowly in India than elsewhere in the eastern hemisphere. Moreover, since India was now itself a theatre of war, there was a far smaller surplus available for external use; hardly any orders for warlike stores were placed in India by or on behalf of the United Kingdom after the end of 1941.

Thus the central organisation of the Eastern Group found its sphere of activity severely contracted after the intervention of Japan. With the provisioning of the new theatre of war it had little direct concern, and of its member countries only South Africa could continue to provide supplies on any large scale for the Middle East. The record of the volume of stores shipped by the Central Provision Office told the story clearly, the tonnage falling from 125,000 tons in January to 87,000 tons in February 1942, and 45,000 tons in March 1943, at about which level it remained constant until the end of 1944. So does the distribution of munitions orders. Of the total value of £43.1 million placed by the central organisation from 1941 to 1946, nearly half, £19.5 million, went to South Africa. Next came Australia with £14.5 million, practically all ordered before the end of 1942 (and most, it is fair to assume although evidence is lacking, before the spring of that year). New Zealand accepted orders for £8.6 million, but from India, which had been intended to be the corner-stone of the whole supply system, and was so as far as other stores were concerned, the value of munitions ordered by the Eastern Group was barely half a million pounds sterling.

Out of these developments there soon arose a question as to the future of the Eastern Group Supply Council, whose status was now much reduced. In the spring of 1942 the Government of Australia and New Zealand withdrew their original eminent nominees, leaving their remaining Eastern Group interests to be represented on the Council by their Trade Commissioners in Delhi. It was now open to doubt whether there was sufficient work to justify the maintenance of the elaborate organisation which had been built up in 1941. The Council's main function had been the distribution of orders, and distribution was now virtually reduced to a simple choice between India and South Africa. Other organisations were emerging to steal the Council's thunder. An Australian Munitions Assignments Committee with Australian, British and United States Army representatives, was set up in December 1942, to allocate Australian production of certain ground munitions on the orthodox lines laid down in Washington and London, and a similar body was established in India a little later. But a more immediately relevant development was the establishment towards the end of 1942 and the beginning of 1943, of Commonwealth Supply Councils in London and Washington. United States supplies of munitions, machinery, raw materials and civilian necessities were of such rapidly growing importance to

all the Commonwealth countries that close co-ordination of requirements, military and otherwise, through a single channel was more
necessary than ever. The work of these Councils did not duplicate
or cut directly across that of the Eastern Group Supply Council, but
their creation was evidence of the extent to which the regional unity
of the Eastern Group was being merged in the wider unities of
Commonwealth and combined planning. From 1942 onwards, when
leading representatives of the eastern countries met, they met in
London or in Washington rather than in Delhi.

Sir Archibald Carter and Major-General Holden went to London
for consultations in April 1942, and did not return. From that date
until March 1943, there was a long-drawn out discussion in London
upon the fate of the Eastern Group Supply Council. Broadly
speaking, the United Kingdom and South African Governments
were in favour of keeping the existing machinery ticking over, in the
belief that the disintegration of the Eastern Group was only temporary and that the future course of the war would once more give
the Delhi organisation a big part to play: the Indians and Australians
preferred that the Supply Council should be abolished. And broadly
speaking it was the latter view that prevailed. But the Council could
not simply be abolished without anything being established in its
place. The military side of the organisation had a much greater
vitality than the supply side, and the War Office had no intention of
dismantling the machinery whereby the requirements of the Forces
under its control in the eastern theatre of war were assembled and
collated in a central focus east of Suez. The machinery was now
beginning to function effectively. Large stocks had been built up,
the mechanism of distribution perfected and long-term programmes
formulated. Whatever happened to the Supply Council, centralised
military provision was to stay, and therefore centralised supply
planning had to continue in some form. An Australian suggestion
that the residual functions of the Supply Council might devolve upon
the Indian Supply Department was understandably not welcomed
by the latter. An alternative was that the Central Provision Office
should take over the allocation of orders in addition to its existing
function. Up to a point this was a satisfactory solution, but it presented certain difficulties. The jealously guarded constitutional
division of functions between the War Office and the Ministry of
Supply might be imperilled if a single regional organisation were
allowed to do the work of both. Nor had the Provision Office the
right kind of expertise to handle the new tasks without guidance on
production matters. It was therefore decided that, while the routine
work of supply should be dealt with henceforth by the Central
Provision Office, the Ministry of Supply should establish in Delhi a
small mission which would be technically responsible for the allocation

of orders and for the financial aspect of supply operations. As head of the mission the Ministry appointed Mr I. F. L. Elliott, who arrived in India in April 1943. A year later he was succeeded by Mr F. H. Harrison, Munitions Adviser to both the Roger Mission and the Council who remained until the Council closed down in March 1946. The two organisations were closely linked by the occasional meetings of a Supply Policy Committee and the daily meetings of a Supply Executive Committee. The Eastern Group Supply Council survived in a rather insubstantial form, inasmuch as meetings of representatives of the Eastern Group countries might be convened when required by the head of the Ministry of Supply Mission.

This development was quite logical. We have described the Eastern Group Supply Council as a compound of a standing conference and a Ministry of Supply Mission. Since the diplomatic and co-ordinating functions of the Council had lost their former importance, it was natural that the Council itself should be reduced to a shadow and that the active body should become in name as well as in fact a Mission linking the United Kingdom and Indian supply organisations and keeping a general watch over Ministry of Supply interests in the other eastern countries.

The Eastern Group never attained the integral unity of the Delhi Conference ideal, not did the Eastern Group Council wield the influence that had once been expected of it. One turn in the fortunes of war had drawn together the British countries of the eastern hemisphere, but the next drove them apart: and the concentration of global planning in Washington and London inevitably reduced regional organisations to a secondary position. Nevertheless the Supply Council was an instrument of international co-operation almost as novel and in some ways hardly less significant than the Combined Boards; and the entity which it represented, though ephemeral, did not dissolve without leaving a mark on history. The peoples linked together in Delhi had previously had little in common save their membership of the British Commonwealth and their location in the same quarter of the globe. Indeed, as is well known, political relations of India and South Africa had often been acutely strained, and between India and Australia there had been little knowledge of each other and no great cordiality. Their close association, even though confined to certain of the abnormal activities of war, left its traces in their peace-time relations. Above all, amid the many war-time influences which turned Australian and New Zealand eyes towards and across the Pacific Ocean, here was one factor which made for the strengthening of their ties with the Commonwealth and with Asia. It is perhaps not fanciful to see a tenuous link between the Delhi Conference of 1940 and the Colombo Conference of 1950, between mutual assistance in war supply and the plan of economic development in the framing of which the Australian Government played so prominent a part.

PRODUCTION AND SUPPLY 1943—45

The general situation in the Eastern Group at the beginning of 1943 was broadly similar to the situation in Britain. Except in India, where some of the 'Roger' and even some of the 'Chatfield projects' had yet to be completed, the production of warlike stores had reached or was rapidly approaching the maximum capacity of the countries concerned. At the same time the end of the main industrial task, the provision of initial equipment and reserves for the ground forces of the Dominions, was now in sight, and it was possible to look forward to a scaling down of many individual programmes. The object of future planning was not the further expansion of total production, but on the one hand the fixing of permanent rates of output at the level required for maintenance and on the other the adjustment of the programme as a whole so as to provide for the items which were still scarce at the expense of those which were now plentiful. London, however, was anxious that the revision of eastern hemisphere production should be considered, not in isolation, but in close connexion with the general reassessment of global requirements and supply that was taking place in London and Washington. Hitherto, the Dominions, especially Australia, had framed their plans very much on the basis of local needs, and London was neither always consulted nor even very perfectly informed about what they intended to produce. So long as the aim everywhere was the largest possible output of every kind of stores, this had not mattered so very much. Now, however, when requirements were becoming selective rather than comprehensive, it was essential to make sure that the eastern countries should make the right things in the right quantities, 'rightness' being determined not simply by their own individual needs, nor even by the collective needs of the Eastern Group, but by the total needs of the Commonwealth and indeed of the United Nations. It was essential to make sure that Australia, for example, should not shut down capacity which from her own point of view had become superfluous but which might well be used to remedy a grave British Commonwealth deficiency. The point was underlined by the manpower crisis in the United Kingdom, which was enhancing the importance of all overseas supply, and by the prospect that in the not distant future, South-East Asia would become a major theatre of war, which added a special importance to production in the Eastern Group.

It was thus necessary that the United Kingdom should have full and exact knowledge of the eastern countries' capabilities and intentions, and that they in turn should not take decisions without full and exact knowledge of United Kingdom needs. For this, discussions carried on directly by cable, or at one remove through Delhi, were not sufficient, and the Ministry of Supply therefore decided to send out Mr W. L. Kearns, a prominent member of the Roger Mission who had since served as Chairman of the Ministry's Eastern Group Requirements Committee, to make direct contact with the several supply authorities. Mr Kearns, accompanied by the Munitions Adviser of the Eastern Group Council, visited Australia and New Zealand in the early spring of 1943, South Africa in the summer, and India in February-March 1944. In each country he acquired first-hand up-to-date knowledge of the production scene, arranged for improvements in the flow of statistical information and represented the Ministry of Supply's views upon the planning of future output.

Australia, as we have suggested, was the remotest, the most autarkic as well as being by far the most prolific of the eastern countries. Since the end of 1941 very few external orders had been accepted, and those placed earlier had been either cancelled or had been given a very low priority. Normally, the only way in which the United Kingdom could take advantage of Australian surplus production was by entering 'bids' for finished stores at the meetings of the Munitions Assignment Committee – a procedure which was satisfactory in respect of urgent operational needs, but which gave the Australian Ministry of Munitions no help in framing forward programmes. That Ministry, indeed, was finding it difficult to elicit the future requirements of the Australian Army, and was already embarrassed by surpluses of certain stores; consequently it was ready to welcome any guidance that its visiting representative could give.

But the working out of an agreed programme which would take full advantage of Australia's resources was not an easy task. For one thing, the Ministry of Munitions was still bound by the Australian Government's ruling, referred to above, that production was not to be undertaken for export. Thus actual United Kingdom orders seemed to be ruled out, and the most that could be done was to establish the general lines on which it was desirable from the British Commonwealth point of view that Australia should be working. Kearns' instructions were that besides doing all that was necessary to attain full self-sufficiency, Australia should be urged to accelerate production of certain items, notably rifles, Bren guns, .303-inch tracer and incendiary bullets and Sten gun ammunition, of which there was still a general shortage. In addition, it was considered desirable to maintain production of some other items, such as 25-pounder and 6-pounder guns, although these were not generally scarce, in order to preserve in being a source of supply close to the scene of future operations. Now the position in Australia was that the total volume of munitions production could not be much further increased, and there were great practical obstacles to expansion at the key points where expansion was most needed. Theoretically, for example, the small arms factories were capable of producing five thousand rifles a week, but shortage of labour in the tool-rooms prevented the actual output from rising much above three thousand. The fact that Australia's requirements of some other stores were virtually exhausted did not help much: machines and labour set free from the manufacture of cartridge cases in Western Australia did not readily become available for the production of small arms in New South Wales, nor could the facilities no longer required by Australia be kept in employment for imperial purposes, for what was superfluous in Australia was generally superfluous elsewhere too. Thus the Kearns discussions did not prevent Australian output of most types of munitions, except aircraft, from falling off sharply after the middle of 1943, and still more sharply in 1944, partly for lack of demand and partly because of production difficulties. The structure of Australian war industry was, in fact, on the whole less capable of the adjustments demanded by the changing needs of the last years of war than was that of British, United States or even Canadian industry. On the other hand, the satisfaction of the more pressing needs of her own Forces, and the eastward shift of the war, enabled Australia to emerge in these years from the isolation which had encompassed her in 1942. Shipments to theatres under War Office control were resumed on a considerable scale in 1943–5, partly as a result of the belated fulfilment of earlier United Kingdom and Eastern Group orders, partly as a result of successful bidding by the British Army representatives on the Assignment Committee.

The New Zealand and South African programmes presented a much simpler problem, in that they were already far more closely integrated with United Kingdom planning. For these countries the virtual completion of their own Forces' equipment did not entail a sharp curtailment of production, for by 1943 they were already working mainly on United Kingdom and Eastern Group orders. The question was to what extent these orders would continue. Some items, it was clear, would no longer be required. South African production of armoured cars lost most of its value when the war moved away from North Africa, and New Zealand's Bren carriers were becoming superfluous as world production at last caught up with demand. On the other hand, for many of the stores manufactured by one or both of these countries – aircraft bombs, mortars, mortar bombs, hand grenades, light artillery – the demand remained rather unexpectedly steady throughout 1943 and 1944, and the production of some other stores was maintained here although the general demand was declining, the main cut being borne by the United

Kingdom; thus the output of .303-inch ball ammunition fell by thirty per cent. in Britain between 1943 and 1944, but rose by thirty per cent. in South Africa. Thus it was possible to provide both South Africa and New Zealand with a steady flow of continuation orders for most of the munitions which they were able to make, and to arrange that the general level of war production, after rising steadily up to the end of 1943, should fall off thereafter so gradually as to avoid any abrupt dislocation or any feeling that their services were no longer valued.

Once again, however, India was the problem child of the Eastern Group, both because most was required of her by the United Kingdom and because her difficulties were greatest. The execution of the projects planned in the autumn of 1940, and indeed of those approved earlier than that, had been extremely slow, for reasons both internal and external. The promised supplies of plant from Britain and the United States had not all been delivered at the promised dates, and some of them had been sunk on the way over, while deliveries from local sources were often still further behind schedule. Owing to the flimsiness of the general structure of industry and the lack of stringent controls, there were recurrent shortages of such basic necessities as nuts and bolts, bricks and cement. Moreover, in India more than elsewhere, the actual construction of a factory and the installation of machinery was only a part of any new industrial project; often it was necessary to build what amounted to a new town, with houses, waterpipes, power-lines and all other essential services.

Nevertheless, by the end of 1943, most of the new factories and annexes were virtually complete, and it could fairly be expected that, with the curve of munitions output continuing to rise steeply, India would contribute materially to the solution of the supply problems of the new South-East Asia Command. But the fulfilment of such hopes was threatened from a new quarter. When India's industrial war effort was planned, the country had been and had expected to continue to be a supply and training ground for distant theatres of war. Since then, it had become an armed camp instantly menaced with attack. The formations which should have moved out westward had remained at home, where they had been joined by a great influx of fresh troops, British, Americans, Chinese and Africans. India was now, in fact, trying to carry out an industrial programme, not, as had been assumed, in a remote tranquillity comparable with that of North America, but under conditions of stress and danger similar in many respects to those under which the British people laboured. And, wholly lacking the resilience which carried Britain through, the Indian economy was buckling under the strain. The railway system, for example, which had not been much improved in the inter-war period and, owing to the diversion of workshop equipment and labour to munitions work, had received altogether inadequate maintenance since 1940, was not far from collapsing utterly under a load heavier than it had ever before been asked to carry. A still more serious danger was the collapse of the currency. The pay and maintenance of the armies now massed within the borders of India had given a final impetus to the upward movement of prices occasioned by the constriction of imports and the diversion of internal resources to war production. All the belligerent countries suffered inflation during the war in varying degrees, but the pressure was naturally most severe upon a people living always near the subsistence margin, whose demand cannot but be inelastic and who do not use banks. India's inflation was certainly the worst within the British Commonwealth and without energetic counteraction might have got completely out of hand.

As an important part of this counteraction the Government of India was constrained to seek relief from the burden of munitions production. In May 1943, in view of the slackening demand for many types of armament, the Ministry of Supply had already recommended certain reductions in the Indian programme. But these did not satisfy the Government of India, which proposed in November that, with a few exceptions, production should be so planned as to meet the needs of the Indian General Staff only, with no imperial surplus. Though the Ministry of Supply reluctantly assented to this in principle, it was none the less dismayed to find early in 1944 that the Indian authorities were curtailing, on their own initiative, the output of stores on which London had been counting. Munitions production in civilian workshops had already been largely 'back-loaded' on to the ordnance factories, in order that the supply of consumer goods might be increased. Now the Government was planning to employ parts even of the ordnance factories on civilian work. Altogether it was hoped to save an annual $10\frac{1}{4}$ crores of rupees, or about £7 million, on the munitions programme.

These moves made it very difficult to preserve harmony between London and Delhi. The situation of 1940-41, when the Government of India had been aiming at the maximum output of munitions and the Ministry of Supply had been counselling caution, was now completely reversed; and it is easy to imagine the latter's feelings when it found itself denied any benefit from capacity which the United Kingdom Government had not only financed but had gone far out of its way to help create. At heavy cost to the British taxpayer and to the British war effort, facilities for munitions production had been established in India, and now that they were on the point of becoming really productive they were to be used for purposes having no direct relation to the war effort. Indian production, it was held in

London, was not a purely domestic concern which the authorities could adjust at will in order to solve their internal economic problems, but an essential element in Commonwealth supply planning – more essential than ever now that large-scale eastern operations were in prospect. On the other hand, it is not hard to appreciate the Indian point of view either. The chronic poverty of the Indian masses (of which the appalling famine in Bengal gave spectacular evidence) was accentuated by the inflationary situation. It was true that in return for their present hardships they were amassing, in the famous sterling balances, a huge store of future wealth, but that did not make the present hardships much easier to bear. London's position was really tenable only if it could be accepted that Indians, like Englishmen or Australians, had freely and deliberately shouldered the burden of the common war and could therefore fairly be expected to do more than provide, in a narrow sense, for their own defence.

The Ministry of Supply's views were represented to the Government of India by Mr Kearns during his visit in February 1944. He made it clear that, while there was no objection to the diversion of some resources from armaments to other work connected with the war effort, such as the repair and maintenance of ships, aircraft, mechanical transport or railway equipment, it would be considered a tragedy if the highly specialised equipment of the ordnance factories were turned over to the kind of jobbing work which the Government of India was believed to envisage, and for which most of it was in no way suited; and he received assurances that there would be no general dispersal of valuable plant in this way. He also vigorously asserted the interdependence of Indian and imperial supply planning, and established the principle that once programmes had been agreed they should not be modified in any way without the concurrence of the Ministry of Supply. Revised targets were now set up for the monthly output of the principal munitions stores throughout 1944, and the Indian authorities agreed that, unless the economic storms blew altogether more fiercely than they expected, these targets should stand unchallenged. But in point of fact few of the programmes now settled were implemented in full; and whilst Indian production in 1944 as a whole was higher than in 1943 it had begun to decline steeply before the end of the year. To take a specific example, it had been planned originally that India should produce anti-tank mines at the rate of 120,000 a month. During 1943 output reached a peak of some 70,000 a month, but towards the end of the year production was stopped on the ground that India herself had no need of this store. At Mr Kearns' instance the full programme was reinstated, but production in 1944 was never more than 40,000 a month.

Thus London had virtually to abandon all hope of an Indian contribution to the general stock of munitions. India's share of the total Ministry of Supply production programme for 1943 had been 2.4 per cent. (£40.6 million). In 1944 it was £23.7 million or 1.7 per cent. of the total programme, and in 1945 £11.5 million or just over one per cent. In the two later years the contribution in munitions was negligible; practically the whole of it was made up of clothing, textile and general stores.

In the final analysis the Ministry could dispense with Indian armaments, but it could not dispense with Indian aid in the supply of goods of civilian type. By 1943 it had become apparent that throughout the United Nations the production of such goods had been cut back a little too far to make room for munitions. The civilian markets had been starved too long not only of luxuries but of necessities as well. Army stocks were running down, many new needs, such as jungle clothing, were waiting to be met, and the blockaded lands of Europe would expect relief to follow on the heels of liberation. Clearly the balance had to be redressed, and it was natural that the British Government should look to India for a large measure of assistance in this regard. One of the gravest world shortages was the shortage of textiles, the supply of which was really a far more appropriate task for India, with its long-established cotton mill industry, than was the manufacture of armaments. Now the production of military clothing and cotton piece-goods along with other consumer goods used by the armed forces, had been very greatly expanded since the outbreak of war, and especially since the summer of 1940; but hopes of further expansion were not to be realised. Here again India's economic difficulties obtruded themselves, and more directly and forcibly here than in the munitions sector. Nothing had contributed more to the growth of inflation than the export of consumer goods, nor was there any simple or more obvious way of mopping up surplus purchasing power than the release of more such supplies to the home market. Thus so far from being willing to make further contributions, the Government of India since the spring of 1943 had been seeking relief from its war supply responsibilities in respect of non-munitions as well as munitions. Unable to secure adequate concessions from the British Government, the Indian authorities resorted to drastic and unilateral action. In March 1944 London was informed that India would accept no further orders from the Central Provision Office, except for articles which were produced only, or could best be produced in India. The qualification exempted jute goods and certain drugs, of which India had been the sole war-time producer; tyres and tubes, the capacity for which had been set up in concert with the British Government; the C.P.O. programme of engineering stores, which was mostly for the benefit of the Engineer-in-Chief, India; and certain types of equipment peculiar to Indian troops. But as far as the great majority of stores was concerned, Britain would be unable to place any supplementary orders for delivery in 1944 and would get nothing at all in 1945.

In view of the critical textile situation it was impossible for London to accept this edict. At the same time it was brought home to the Ministry of Supply that demands on India would have to be reduced to the absolute minimum, for if India was to serve as the base for offensive operations in South East Asia, it was obviously vital that she should not collapse under the mounting pressure of inflation. The whole question of India's role in Stage II was discussed in London at the beginning of 1945 with a Government of India Mission led by Sir Akbar Hydari, Supply Member of the Viceroy's Council, and a compromise was reached. Some concessions were made to the Mission's plea for increased supplies of consumer goods to the home market, but the Mission agreed to maintain large deliveries of army clothing and cotton piece-goods for export throughout 1946. To secure this point the Ministry of Supply willingly granted further concessions in the munitions sector. Thus in the final stages of the war munitions production was relegated to the background of India's war effort, the main feature of which was the supply of textile and general stores and the servicing of the Forces ranged against the Japanese.

(v)

The Record of Achievement

The part played by the eastern hemisphere in the story of overseas supply falls, so far as munitions are concerned, into two distinct phases, with a long interval between them. At the outbreak of war the two largest producers in the area, India and Australia, both had armaments industries in being, from which there flowed during the first two years a substantial quantity of arms and ammunition; and since only a small fraction of their armed forces was as yet committed to action these countries could afford to divert a large part of the flow to beleaguered Britain and to British forces in the Middle and Far East. But after 1941 all this changed. Neither India nor Australia could now spare any appreciable fraction of their munitions output, steadily expanding though it was, for the use of Forces other than their own; and their virtual withdrawal was not adequately compensated by the entry on the scene of South Africa and New Zealand, whose contributions had hitherto been almost

negligible. The year 1942 was thus very nearly a total blank so far
as the supply of munitions from the eastern hemisphere was concerned. In 1943, however, the situation changed again. Whilst
Indian supplies never re-entered the general pool, Australia, having
seen the tide of battle rolled back from her immediate neighbourhood, and having accumulated large stocks of many stores, was able
to resume the export of munitions on a very considerable scale; and
at the same time the South African and New Zealand munitions
factories, having now satisfied most of the demands of their own
Forces, were working almost entirely on United Kingdom account.
Thus in the last two years of war the contribution of the Eastern
Group was larger in volume than it had been in the first two years.
But since in the meantime universal scarcity had given way to fairly
general plenty the real value of the later contribution was much less
than the earlier. The figures in Table 14 show, very approximately,
what proportion of total United Kingdom supply of some of the
main classes of armaments was received at different periods from
the eastern countries.

Proportion of total United Kingdom supply of certain
classes of armaments received from the Eastern Group

Table 14   Per Cent

	1940–1	1942	1943–5
Artillery	1.3	0.1	1.5
Rifles	10.5	—	0.1
Gun and mortar ammunition .	1.4	0.1	5.3
Small arms ammunition .	8.0	1.1	6.7

Besides displaying its distribution in point of time, the figures
show, when allowance is made for the total absence of ships, aircraft,
tanks, mechanical transport, and radio, that the eastern contribution
was at no period a really important element in United Kingdom
munitions supply as a whole. But this is not the whole of the story.
For in the first place munitions were not the only or the most important items supplied by the eastern countries. One other contribution, the provision of a large part of the miscellaneous equipment and
stores used and consumed by the British forces operating east of
Malta, has been touched on in this narrative. Others, still more
important, lie outside its scope, but it must not be forgotten that
the food and the raw materials supplied by the southern Dominions
and India, not to mention South Africa's gold, were at least as vital
to the United Kingdom in war as they are in peace, and that their
production constituted a most valuable part of the war effort of
these countries.

Moreover, even within the munitions sector the computation of the volume of supplies physically transferred to the United Kingdom does not represent the sum total of the aid rendered by the eastern countries. As was suggested at the beginning of this chapter, the division of their munitions output into two parts, one within and one outside the scope of 'overseas supply', is artificial and misleading. So, although it will be appreciated that an adequate study of munitions production in the Eastern Group can neither be written in London nor brought within the limits of this volume, we cannot properly conclude without a brief sketch of the total achievement.

The principal elements in that achievement are set forth in summary form in Table 15, with Canadian production added by way of comparison.

Total munitions production of the Eastern Group and Canada,

September 1939 – August 1945

Table 15

Item	Unit	Australia	India	South Africa	New Zealand	Eastern Group Total	Canada
Destroyers .	Each	3	—	—	—	3	—
Escort vessels and minesweepers .	,,	66	3	—	—	69	295
Combat aircraft .	,,	1,323	—	—	—	1,323	5,178
Other aircraft .	,,	1,758	—	—	—	1,758	10,779
Tanks . .	,,	57	—	—	—	57	5,678
Armoured cars .	,,	270	295	2,116	—	2,681	1,123
Tracked carriers.	,,	5,501	—	—	1,210	6,711	33,987
Field artillery .	,,	1,184	815	274	—	2,273	1,684
Anti-tank guns .	,,	1,802	42	330	—	2,174	4,280
Anti-aircraft guns	,,	768	—	—	—	768	4,588
Mortars . .	,,	5,370	—	11,318	8,707	25,395	20,619
Machine guns .	,,	30,992	6,991	—	—	37,983	251,925
Rifles . .	,,	412,050	580,917	—	—	992,967	901,850
Guns and mortar ammunition .	Thousand rounds	13,398	6,766	6,289	1,198	27,651	72,367
Small arms ammunition .	Million rounds	1,828	969	925	254	3,976	4,350

The general impression conveyed by this table, that Canadian production far exceeded that of the Eastern Group taken together is confirmed by the estimate that in total value it was in fact nearly five times as great ($7,971 million against $1,614 million).[1] In view of their relative populations, incomes and steel outputs this may seem a strange result. It is accounted for by the simple fact that Canada possessed what all the eastern countries, even Australia, lacked – mass-production engineering plants of types readily adaptable to war purposes. Thus, whereas for a while the eastern countries

---

[1] See *North American Supply, op. cit.,* Chapter X.

having made an earlier start, more or less kept pace with Canada, and in some fields kept well ahead, from 1942 onwards, when Canadian industry was fully deployed, they were completely outstripped, in much the same way as Britain was outstripped by the United States.

AUSTRALIA

Australia's supremacy in the Eastern Group emerges fairly clearly from Table 15, and still more clearly from a rough calculation of the relative value of the production of ground munitions only, which yields the following proportions: Australia 51, India 27, South Africa 20, New Zealand 4. Since her lead was certainly much greater in shipbuilding and in aircraft production, it is clear that Australia produced well over half the munitions that were made in the Eastern Group on a whole. Even so, the intensity of her industrial war effort did not compare with that of the United Kingdom or North America. Early in 1942 it was estimated in London that Australians were devoting only about 25 per cent. of their national income to the war effort, as against the United Kingdom's 60 per cent. and Canada's 35 per cent. In part, this merely reflects the fact that Australia was a predominantly agricultural and pastoral country whose primary task, in war as in peace, was the production and export of grain, meat and wool. Nevertheless, it was noted – and this comment could be applied with at least equal validity to the other Dominions – that the production of consumer goods had not been restricted to anything like the same extent as in Britain.

But if munitions production was not particularly intensive, it was extremely comprehensive. In 1943 the Australians were urged by Mr Kearns on behalf of the Ministry of Supply to make themselves as nearly as possible self-supporting, in two senses of the word. In the narrow sense, if they made a particular weapon they should also make all the necessary ammunition, spare barrels, instruments and other ancillaries. In the broader sense, the production of Australian factories should be matched as closely as possible to the needs of Australian troops. This advice was really superfluous. Indeed, if any criticism be advanced against the planning of production it would be that too much was attempted, that the small-scale manufacture of elaborate items was uneconomic and might better have been left to the mass-production industries of the west. To some extent this was a manifestation of the settled Australian policy of establishing, even at heavy cost, the widest possible range of indigenous manufacture. The development of merchant shipbuilding, for example, had been mooted before the war for reasons not primarily strategic, and would probably have been pushed forward even if war had not come. But there were also solid military reasons for a high degree of autarky. So long as Australian troops were intended to fight in Egypt or Malaya as components of larger Commonwealth forces it did not matter that they lacked some of the more elaborate supporting weapons. But the aspect of things was changed when it became apparent that they might be engaged in virtually single-handed defence of their country. In the early months of 1942 the Australians were desperately in need of tanks, Bofors guns and fighter aircraft, and they were far from satisfied with the allocations they were receiving from British and American production. Therefore they pushed ahead with plans to make tanks, Bofors and fighters for themselves. The few score of each of the two former that they produced represented, for them, a great and costly effort, whereas by the latter part of 1943 the United States or Britain could have assigned corresponding quantities almost without noticing the loss. However, there is no doubt that as a result of these enterprises Australian forces did acquire valuable equipment some months earlier than they could have done otherwise. Moreover, from the point of view of economy in shipping it was very obviously desirable that the land and air forces operating in Papua should be supplied from the nearest possible source.

To a remarkable extent Australian production was self-sufficient also in the sense that military equipment was made by locally produced machines out of local raw materials, and made complete with all accessories. Local industry proved itself able to supply the special steel and some of the special-purpose machine tools required for armaments manufacture. Not only were complex instruments such as dial sights and predictors made in Australia, but they were made out of Australian optical glass, the manufacture of which was developed from nothing in the space of two years, after a world shortage had manifested itself in 1940. Australians did not stop short at making airframes but launched out into the manufacture of aero engines as well. Their essay in tank production, though dependent on the supply of power units and some other components from the United States, was a good deal more than the amalgamation of imported sub-assemblies. Moreover they were not always content to follow the lead of others in matters of design. Their tanks and some of their aircraft, though ultimately derived from American models, were peculiarly Australian, and they produced a modified version of the British 25-pounder field gun capable of being transported in bits and pieces through the jungles of New Guinea. Similarly, they evolved new types of special steel, new machines and new manufacturing processes which made a great impression on visiting experts.

Munitions production was developed partly by the extension and multiplication of the peace-time government ordnance factories, partly by the adaptation of civilian engineering industry which not only undertook the manufacture of equipment generally similar to its ordinary products, such as engineering stores, communications equipment and armoured vehicles, but helped the ordnance factories with more specifically armament work. The mobilisation of the resources of private industry took two forms – straightforward 'trade' contracts and the erection at government expense of munitions plants which were operated as 'annexes' by commercial firms. The co-operation of industrialists began to be enlisted in 1938, and was very close during the war years. They made available not only their manufacturing resources but their technical and administrative talents as well, executives of the big private concerns occupying key positions in the Ministry of Munitions, the Department of Aircraft Production and the Shipbuilding Board.

The mixture of government and private war industry is well illustrated in the story of artillery production. At the outbreak of war guns were being made only in the arsenal at Maribyrnong and the only type actually in production was the obsolescent 3-inch anti-aircraft gun. During the war Australia satisfied the bulk of her own needs of most types of gun – 25-pounder field equipments, anti-tank guns (including the heavy 17-pounder model) 3.7-inch and 40-mm. anti-aircraft and 4-inch naval guns – and was able to export several hundreds to British theatres. To achieve this the existing ordnance factory was much enlarged, a second government factory was built at Bendigo, near Melbourne, to take over the naval side, and a private engineering firm, Chas. Ruwolt Proprietary, was brought in to help Maribyrnong with the production of gun carriages and some complete equipments. In addition the manufacture of the smaller anti-tank guns was carried on by means of a wide sub-contracting network.

Small arms on the other hand, except for that small-workshop product the Sten gun, remained a government monopoly. The peace-time factory at Lithgow in New South Wales had capacity adequate for Australia's original objective of 3,000 rifles a week, but when in January 1941, the Government agreed, as part of its Eastern Group commitments, to double this rate of output, fresh plans had to be laid. Further expansion at Lithgow, a smallish town with no room for additional workers and a bad reputation for industrial unrest, was judged unfeasible, especially as the factory was charged with the production of Bren and Vickers machine guns as well as rifles. It was therefore decided to set up a new assembly line at the neighbouring centre of Orange and to build eight small component workshops in the country districts of New South Wales. Lithgow was to carry out forging operations and tool-room work for the whole group. These schemes took time to bring to fruition; the output of rifles did not much exceed two thousand a week in 1942, and the full rate of four thousand a week was never quite attained. As a result of this and of the growing domestic demand, United Kingdom hopes of securing rifles from Australian production remained unfulfilled, only 1,500 being delivered against an order for 100,000. In addition, a few thousand Bren and Vickers machine guns were assigned to British forces in 1944/45. The latter weapon was rather an Australian speciality, the number produced being very nearly as large as in the United Kingdom.

Armoured fighting vehicles, by contrast, were manufactured, in Australia as elsewhere, entirely outside the ordnance factory organisation. The system was that components were made by a number of engineering sub-contractors and assembled in the state-owned railway workshops. The principal product in this group was the Universal carrier, of which 1,500 were shipped to China in addition to those supplied to the Australian Army. But there was also a small output of light armoured cars, scout cars and cruiser tanks, which last were among the most ambitious and controversial items in the Australian programme. They were controversial because they could be made only as the result of a successful incursion into the very tight American components market, and the Australian representatives in Washington had a hard struggle to convince the United States War Department and the British Purchasing Commission that it was worth while to export precious engines and transmissions to Australia. However, they did secure a sufficient allocation for a start to be made with assembly in the summer of 1942. The plans originally laid were very ambitious: several hundred machines were to be produced at a rate of sixty-five a month in 1943. But the actual rate of output did not exceed eleven in any one month, and, since a general surplus of tanks was emerging and the terrain in which the Australian Army was operating was not markedly suitable for tank warfare, production stopped altogether in June 1943, after only fifty-seven machines had been completed.

A striking feature of Australian war production was the contribution of the electrical industry, which included searchlight equipment, field telephones, several kinds of wireless sets and many hundreds of radar sets, including a number of the most advanced centimetric equipments.

More remarkable, however, and of more permanent significance than any aspect of ground munitions production was the Australian achievement in aircraft production and in shipbuilding, both of which involved such large expansion of so small a nucleus as to represent virtually the creation of a new Australian industry. The development of aircraft production in the Commonwealth followed three separate lines. There was the growth of the government-encouraged but privately financed Commonwealth Aircraft Corporation, the transformation of the Australian branch of de Havillands from a sales and servicing organisation into a largely self-sufficient manufacturing unit, and finally the development of direct government enterprise.

The Commonwealth Aircraft Corporation was founded in 1935, as described earlier in this chapter, and was producing trainers well before the outbreak of war. It built and operated a large and well-equipped factory at Fisherman's Bend, near Melbourne, which employed at the peak as many as seven thousand workers and turned out engines and components as well as assembling the finished product. Later, however, engine manufacture was transferred to a new factory at Lidcombe in New South Wales. De Havillands also had established a manufacturing unit at Mascot in New South Wales before the war, but were not then doing much more than assemble imported components. During the war, however, their activities were very much enlarged, and they undertook the complete manufacture (engines being supplied by General Motors-Holden's Limited) of large numbers of elementary and basic trainers, and eventually of combat planes as well. Government enterprise in the field of aircraft production started later, with the formulation of the Beaufort scheme in 1939, but ultimately overshadowed that of private industry. The Beaufort scheme was entrusted originally to an organisation known as the Aircraft Construction Branch, which was responsible to the Minister of Supply Development. In March 1940 it was reconstituted as the Aircraft Production Commission, and in June of that year became a section of the newly-formed Ministry of Munitions. Twelve months later the Commission became a separate Department of Aircraft Production headed by a Minister of the Crown and having general responsibility for the aircraft programme as a whole as well as special responsibility for the production of Beauforts. Under its direct control were two assembly lines, at Fisherman's Bend and Mascot, fed by components made in the workshops of the New South Wales, Victoria and South Australia Government railways. But in addition the Commonwealth Government had to arrange for the construction of a large number of annexes under the control of private firms. These included, besides the Lidcombe engine factory, operated on its behalf by the Commonwealth Aircraft Corporation, plants producing heavy forgings, electrical equipment, hydraulic landing gears, propellers and gun turrets. The magnitude of the whole enterprise can be judged from the fact that it involved the expenditure of over £20 million of government money alone, and was employing over 30,000 workers by 1943.

For a long time the Beaufort was the only combat aircraft contemplated for manufacture in Australia. But the country's growing peril and the inadequacy of allocations from Britain and America inspired the authorities to extend the range of production by including other types. The first and most urgent need was for some kind of interceptor. To avoid the delay of securing fresh jigs and tools the Commonwealth Aircraft Corporation adopted the not altogether satisfactory expedient of evolving a machine constructed out of the same basic components as the Wirraway trainer, but with armament and additional engine power. The first of these quite efficient but essentially makeshift machines, christened Boomerangs, took the air in September 1942. Meanwhile the Corporation had also designed a light torpedo-bomber, but this was not a success and did not go into quantity production. In the last two years of war Australia emerged from her temporary isolation in this as in other respects and rejoined the main highroad of technical progress in aircraft design, adopting certain of the most up-to-date British and American machines. The Beaufort was succeeded by its close relative the twin-engined Beaufighter; the American Mustang fighter took the place of the Boomerang; and de Havillands, having served their apprenticeship on elementary trainers, went on to make their parent firm's most celebrated war-time product, the Mosquito.

The Australian shipbuilding industry, after a brief period of activity during and shortly after the First World War, had practically ceased to exist. Apart from the Cockatoo Docks and Engineering Company, which made an occasional small warship for the Australian Navy in its shipyard on the island of that name in Sydney Harbour, there were only a few small firms engaged in the construction of coastal vessels of less than 500 gross tons. The ocean-going vessels built for the Government between 1917 and 1924 had had to be sold off at a heavy loss to the Australian taxpayer. Despite this experience, however, and despite the continuing disparity in construction costs between Australia and the established shipbuilding countries of the world, the revival of the industry was a project which had strong political and commercial backing throughout the inter-war period. Shortly before the war the movement culminated in government measures providing bounties for construction and remitting duties on imported machinery; and the big steel firm, Broken Hill Proprietary, with the approval of the Commonwealth authorities and the active support of the State Government, planned to lay out a large modern shipyard close to its iron-ore deposits at Whyalla in South Australia. Early in 1940 the Commonwealth Government sounded London about the possibility of British orders for merchant ships, but although London agreed that the development of merchant shipbuilding in Australia would be a useful contribution to the common war effort, no orders were forthcoming. This was a disappointment to the Australians, especially as it was known that cargo steamers were to be built in the Hong Kong ship-yards on United Kingdom account. It was, however, the policy of the Admiralty to reserve shipyard facilities in the Dominions, so far as it was itself concerned, for the construction of warships; and it was in fact on warships that Australian shipbuilding efforts were mainly concentrated during the war. The vessels constructed included three Tribal class destroyers, two of which were completed in 1942 and the third in the spring of 1945, two sloops in 1940, and six frigates, all completed in the last two years of war. The Australian speciality, however, was the fleet minesweeper, of which no less than fifty-eight were built, mostly in the central period of war. Of these four were constructed for the Royal Indian Navy and twenty to Admiralty order, though the latter actually did most of their ser-vice with the Royal Australian Navy. Six other yards, normally engaged on the construction or repair of coastal vessels, co-operated with the Cockatoo Island Dockyard in this achievement. In addi-tion, Australia was a large producer of small craft – tugs, Fairmile launches, assault landing craft and so on – most of which were supplied to the United States forces in the South-West Pacific.

At the same time the Commonwealth Government pressed on with its plans for the creation of a merchant shipbuilding industry. This was an altogether more ambitious project, ocean-going cargo ships being many times larger, though less complex, than the types of warship built in Australia. To direct it an Australian Shipbuilding Board was set up in March 1941, and large sums were spent on the supply of additional equipment to the shipyards and the construction of additional engine-building plants. By the beginning of 1943 most of this work was completed, and the first vessel was actually launched in April of that year. But from that time onward, with the increasing concentration of shipping in the South Pacific, repair work made such large claims on Australian shipyard labour and equipment that the construction programme had to be progressively scaled down; and only ten ships were actually completed during the war. This was a useful increment to the still very inadequate United Nations pool, but on the whole the value of the war-time development of Aus-tralian merchant shipbuilding must be judged by its post-war utility.

NEW ZEALAND

In volume, New Zealand's total munitions production was only a fraction of Australia's, and its character and function were altogether different. The aim was not self-sufficiency in a wide variety of equip-ment, which would have been quite impracticable, but rather a surplus of a few stores selected as particularly suitable for production in a country with very limited industrial experience or equipment. In New Zealand there were no government ordnance factories, and the nearest approach to a specialised munitions firm was the Colonial Ammunition Company, which made .303-inch ball cartridges. Apart from this, munitions production was made possible only by the fact that the General Motors, Ford and Dominion Motor Companies had established automobile plants which could be used to assemble components made in the various small workshops that constituted New Zealand's manufacturing industry. This, incidentally, was a system which called for very skilled direction at the centre. The problem for the Dominion Government, the Eastern Group Supply Council and the United Kingdom Government was to make full use of New Zealand's assets, especially her very intelligent and adaptable labour, without using too much shipping space in the bringing in of raw materials, components and machinery and without setting the country to do what could be done elsewhere more economically. In other words it was necessary to find stores, the manufacture of which was within New Zealand's capabilities and which would yet be of real value to the Commonwealth as a whole.

Unfortunately, during the first eighteen months of war the solution of this problem was left almost entirely to the New Zealand authorities, who made arrangements for the production of small arms ammunition, tracked carriers, mortars, mortar bombs and hand grenades. This was unfortunate, not because the selection was unsuitable or because any opportunity of securing supplies for the United Kingdom was lost – during this period New Zealand was fully occupied in meeting her own requirements – but because this production was not at first fitted into the general scheme of Commonwealth supply. The Ministry of Supply did not take full cognisance of New Zealand capacity until the spring of 1941, when the country was visited by a section of the Roger Mission, and by that time an adequate supply of many of the stores which New Zealand could produce had been arranged elsewhere. Hand grenades were a case in point. At the time of the Mission's visit the initial New Zealand Government order for 200,000 grenades was nearing completion, and in default of external orders the makers would soon have had to be allowed to revert to civil production. But there appeared to be no general scarcity of grenades, and the most London could offer was an order for the negligible quantity of 25,000. As it happened, however, the difficulty was solved by an unforeseen increase in War Office requirements later in the year, which enabled the Ministry of Supply to keep New Zealand grenade makers busy for years to come; and much the same applied to the other stores mentioned above, in each of which New Zealand became one of the leading Eastern Group producers. Dependence on imported components, however, made the manufacture of any but the simplest munitions a precarious business. For instance, once the production of Universal carriers had developed in North America, there was clearly very little to be said for shipping components thence to be assembled on the far side of the Pacific, and New Zealand production accordingly came to an end in 1943. Similarly, a venture into the radio field proved somewhat unfruitful. In December 1943, the Ministry of Supply asked New Zealand authorities to supply 15,000 sets, but owing to delays in the supply of American components only 7,170 were ever produced, and those so late that no outlet could be found for them.

It was no mean achievement on the part of New Zealand to have produced a sizeable export surplus of carriers, 2-inch mortars, mortar bombs, hand grenades and small arms ammunition in addition to meeting her own needs of these and some other stores, including 3-inch mortars and Sten guns. Still more remarkable, however, were her achievements in aircraft production, though limited to propellers, and in shipbuilding, which resulted in the completion of a dozen minesweeping trawlers and a number of smaller craft. Many things were done in New Zealand during the war which had never been done before, such as the production of precision instruments and the operation of the complex automatic machines used in the manufacture of fuses.

SOUTH AFRICA

South African munitions production stands midway between those of Australia and New Zealand, both in total volume and in the variety of its products. The Union did not attempt to make ships (though she made a few small craft and provided servicing and repair facilities for the Royal Navy), aircraft, tanks, small arms, or anti-aircraft guns, but its range of products, including as it did artillery equipments and ammunition, explosives and propellants and a considerable variety of signal and engineer equipment, was very much wider than New Zealand's and the output of individual stores was in nearly every case considerably larger. South Africa had a larger export surplus in proportion to her total output than any other member of the Eastern Group; and even absolutely she was the principal contributor to Central Provision Office munitions stocks. The initial needs of the Union Defence Forces were met at a fairly early stage in the war, and thereafter it was United Kingdom and Eastern Group orders that kept the war factories in production.

The organisation of war production was generally similar to that of Australia, with perhaps a rather greater reliance on government enterprise. Besides setting up a Central Ordnance Factory (C.O.F.A.C.) for the manufacture of artillery, the government made much use of the production organisation of existing bodies under its own control. The Railways and Harbours Administration played a big part in several sectors, and ammunition production was largely entrusted at the outset to the South African Mint, though the Mint factories and annexes later came under the direct control of the War Supply Board. Similarly, the production of instruments was begun by the Trigonometrical Survey at Capetown and carried on by the electrical workshops of the railways. There was also, however, a large contribution from private industry, chiefly from the Rand engineering and explosives firms.

Apart from a few 2-pounder anti-tank guns made by the Mint, artillery equipments were manufactured (that is to say, components were machined, fitted and assembled) in the Central Ordnance Factory. The peak rate of output was high, about thirty-five equipments a month, but the peak was not quickly scaled, nor was it held for long; the number produced throughout the war was only 604. The main trouble was the lack of continuity in demand. The weapon originally chosen for South African production was the 3.7-inch howitzer, but when the Desert war began it was generally agreed that the 6-pounder anti-tank gun would be a more valuable contribution. Production of howitzers was accordingly slowed down and ceased altogether in the summer of 1942, but it was not until the following summer that the adjustment was completed and quantity production of anti-tank guns started. By this time the war had moved away from North Africa, 6-pounders were becoming plentiful and the development of enemy armour was beginning to make them obsolescent. It was therefore decided that the South African factory should gradually revert to howitzers, for which there was a renewed demand in connection with operations in the Far East. But by the time *this* change-over was effected the war was almost over. The moral is clear: in a country of limited resources, where it is only with difficulty that armaments are made at all, changes in the type of product are bound to cause exceptional dislocation and delay. It is therefore desirable that such countries should not attempt to make complex equipment of the type that is outclassed after a short life, but should concentrate on the simple weapons which form a more or less permanent feature of an army's equipment. In marked contrast with the limited usefulness of the Union's artillery production was its output of 3-inch mortars, which represented well over a quarter of total Commonwealth production. There was a steady flow of orders from June 1939 to September 1943, and production, which was undertaken by four Reef engineering firms and two railway workshops, was continuous from early in 1940 until the summer of 1944. Having completed an initial Union Defence Force order for five thousand South Africa went on to make as many again and more for the Eastern Group.

Even more prominent than the 3-inch mortars in the catalogue of South African armaments, were the armoured cars made by Dorman Long (Africa) Ltd. in a government-owned annex near Johannesburg. These, however, cannot properly be classed as a South African product in the full sense of the term, since they were built on chassis imported from North America. Altogether about 6,500 vehicles were completed, nearly half of them on behalf of the Middle East Command. The original model was merely a lightly-armed and ill-protected reconnaissance car, but successive improvements resulted in the evolution of a workmanlike fighting vehicle of considerable value in the Desert war.

In actual value, however, ammunition made up over three-fifths of total production in South Africa, as it did in most of the Eastern Group countries. Large surpluses of 25-pounder and 3.7-inch shell, mortar bombs, grenades, small arms ammunition and above all of aircraft bombs accrued to the Commonwealth forces from an elaborate network of production which included the Mint annexes, a government assembly plant and a number of private contractors and sub-contractors. Other aspects of war production in the Union which may be briefly mentioned were a government small arms factory, which however did not proceed beyond the manufacture of rifle barrels and other components; the production of artillery instruments and of signal equipment, which represented a very great technical achievement but must be regarded as a striking example of the uneconomic autarky imposed on the eastern countries by the drying up of overseas supplies in the earlier part of the war; and the very large output of engineering and general stores, from which India gained substantial relief in the later stages.

There is no doubt that South Africa was the 'discovery' of the Eastern Group. The misgivings about her belligerent intentions and about her industrial resources, which had prevented the United Kingdom authorities from doing more than cautiously encourage the development of a war potential in the thirties, were proved equally groundless in the event. Her total output was not much less than that of India, on which London's hopes were mainly fixed, and her contribution to the Commonwealth pool was vastly greater. Especially notable was the way in which the South Africans overcame their most serious difficulty, the scarcity of factory labour. The solution was found in two expedients of almost equal novelty – the wide use of Africans on operations of which many were at least semi-skilled, and the recruitment of European women workers.

INDIA

The difficulties and disappointments of Indian munitions production have been referred to earlier in this chapter. It should be

appreciated, however, that the disappointment arose from the somewhat extravagant expectations entertained in the latter part of
1940, and that India achieved at least as much as was expected of
her at the outbreak of war. If there was little to spare for Forces
operating outside the country, that was only because India maintained on her own soil far larger Forces than anyone had bargained
for.

War production in India was very much more an affair of
ordnance factories than in any other country. Civilian industry was
active in shipbuilding and in the assembly of vehicles, but the production of weapons and ammunition was concentrated almost
entirely in factories owned and operated by the central Government.
Nor were these factories merely the focal points of an extensive
system of sub-contracting. On the contrary they formed in the
aggregate a self-contained organisation in which the entire process
of manufacture, from the forging of steel to the assembly of the
finished product, was carried on without outside assistance of any
kind. Thus whereas everywhere else the development of war production meant at least in part the progressive conversion of civilian
industry, in India it consisted primarily of the enlargement of the
ordnance factory potential.

In this direction much was done. The seven factories in existence
at the outbreak of war were much extended and improved and nine
other units were brought into service. Three of these had pre-war
nuclei in the Mathematical Instrument Office at Calcutta, the railway workshops at Lucknow and the Public Works Department
shops at Amritsar; the other six were completely new. Some of the
latter were very large, and all were first-class factories well and
indeed lavishly equipped. Their construction, however, and the
collection of machinery from distant parts of the earth, took so long
that, while they undoubtedly represent permanent assets of great
value to the country, the main burden of munitions production in
the Second World War fell upon the pre-war factories, in most of
which the modern machinery acquired during the war served only
to emphasise the antiquated character of the bulk of the plant.

These factories nevertheless did yeoman service, largely because
they were to a great extent allowed a long, steady run on well-
established products. Very little, indeed, was added to the range of
Indian production during the war. Apart from a very few anti-tank
guns, the only artillery equipments produced were the 3.7-inch pack
howitzers designed and brought into production before 1939.
The only automatic weapons made in India were Vickers-Berthier
light machine guns, which had been succeeded everywhere else by
Brens. And the most successful branch of Indian ordnance production was the manufacture of .303-inch rifles, which was carried on

continuously in the same factory throughout the period of rearmament and war. At the end of 1940 the Ministry of Supply Mission reported that without any major addition of plant output could be raised from the current rate of six thousand to ten thousand rifles a month; and this estimate, unlike most of the others made at this time, was fulfilled with remarkable accuracy. The conclusion suggests itself that better results could have been obtained from India at far less cost to the British Exchequer, the Indian economy, and the British pool of machinery and plant if efforts had been concentrated generally on small-scale improvement and reorganisation of existing facilities rather than on the creation of large and costly new capacity.

There were, however, some fresh developments of considerable interest. Aircraft production, indeed, though mooted on more than one occasion, did not materialise. In 1940 an aircraft factory which had been operating in south-west China was bombed by the Japanese, and it was suggested that it might be re-erected in India, whither part of its executive staff had betaken themselves. Nothing came of this, however, nor of a later proposal that gliders might be made by Messrs Tata; and indeed it is difficult to suppose that such projects could possibly have been economic. On the other hand, something was achieved in the matter of shipbuilding. There were a number of firms, mostly in the Calcutta area, which had experience in the construction of tugs, launches and other small vessels, and their resources were used to build small anti-submarine vessels, landing craft and even a few fleet minesweepers for the growing Royal Indian Navy. Merchant shipbuilding, however, was less successful. The desire of India's one important shipping line, the Scindia Steamship Company, to establish indigenous construction appeared to coincide with Britain's desperate need for new tonnage from every possible source. But the coincidence was marred by the fact that engines would have to be supplied from Britain and that up to the end of 1941 shortage of engines was the main impediment to the progress of British shipbuilding. However, in 1942 the Admiralty reluctantly agreed to the delivery of engines from the Clyde, a shipyard was laid out at Vizigapatam and construction began. Then the Japanese bombed Vizigapatam, the labour force dispersed, and although the Indians were eager to start again on the west coast the delay made the whole project unfruitful in the British Government's eyes.

Though there were interests in India which would gladly have taken the opportunity afforded by the war to develop the manufacture of automobiles, the consensus of opinion was that the Indian Army's requirements of mechanical transport could be met adequately by the re-assembly of North American chassis. It was also agreed, however, that India could usefully undertake the production of light armoured vehicles. As in South Africa, 'production' here meant no more than the manufacture of bodies for imported chassis, but nevertheless represented a valuable achievement. Two types of vehicle, a medium armoured car (or light wheeled tank), and a wheeled carrier which was put to a variety of military uses, were produced in considerable numbers.

Strenuous efforts were made during the war to overcome the supreme obstacles to munitions production, or indeed to any advanced form of manufacturing, in India – the scarcity of machine tools and of skilled labour. In view of the obvious difficulties in the procurement of machine tools from overseas, the Government of India worked out in 1941 a scheme for indigenous manufacture. A few machine tool shops were already established, but most of them were very poorly equipped and turned out only the most elementary types of machine. Therefore, they would need both plant and instruction if they were to be of much value to the war effort, and the Ministry of Supply agreed that both should be provided. A travelling team of British machine tool experts reached India at the end of 1942, and helped to educate Indian engineers in the mysteries of their trade. It cannot be said, however, that these measures more than slightly mitigated India's war-time dependence on imported machinery. As for personnel, the United Kingdom provided a fair number of experienced supervisors and technicians. There are always difficulties and dangers in such transplantations; Indian munitions production in the First World War was said to have broken down largely because the staff sent out from England were unable to adapt themselves to working under Indian conditions and with Indian labour. But in the late war, although there were again some failures of adjustment the majority of the imported experts were thought to have done an excellent job. The supply of foremen and chargehands was augmented by a very interesting experiment, associated with the name of Mr Ernest Bevin, whereby young Indians who had displayed technical aptitude were sent to Britain for a course of practical training. There were many opinions about the degree of success obtained by this scheme, but that some good came of it, a long-term good perhaps rather than an immediate benefit to the war effort, there seems no reason at all to doubt.

CONCLUSION

It seems likely that as the historical perspective deepens the activities described in this chapter will take on a significance altogether greater than their very real value at the time would in itself warrant. In the First World War the Dominions had set a seal on their nationhood by sending their young men to join in the defence of the Empire, and the prowess of Indian troops, however little developed their own sense of nationality, had likewise added prestige to the Indian national movement. But the development was incomplete so long as they were dependent on Britain for the bulk of the arms and equipment with which they fought. One of the salient features of the Second World War was that this deficiency was largely made good; all the Dominions (if Australia and New Zealand can be linked as a supply unit) supplied most of their own needs and so emerged as independent nations in a fuller sense. Yet this has only to be stated for doubts to arise. 'Independence' is a term that changes its meaning in an era of the mass production of weapons. Nations with a population of a few millions and a steel output of a few hundred thousand tons a year have less chance of standing alone than ever they had before. Up to about 1944 the industrial development of such countries rather more than kept pace with the technological elaboration of military requirements, but since then the balance has been heavily weighted in favour of the great agglomerations of industrial power. Even in the Second World War the southern Dominions, largely because of their physical isolation and the desperate straits of the United Kingdom, attempted to be self-supporting in munitions production to a higher degree than was then desirable – or likely to be in the future as it seemed to be shaping itself after the war.

The war has left its mark on both the political and the economic life of the countries of the Eastern Group. On the economic side the effects were varied and difficult to assess. It is obvious that the war gave all of them an opportunity to accelerate the process of industrialisation – an opportunity of which they all availed themselves in varying degrees, though Australia and South Africa much more than the others. All of them gained substantially in technical skills and new industrial plant. But the particular skills and machines acquired were not all of much peace-time value; and against the gains had to be set losses through distortion of their normal industrial development. With the exception of South Africa their war-time situation resembled that of the United Kingdom more than that of the North American countries. They were in or near the front line; they lost more markets than they gained; and for the most part their war products bore little relation to the needs of peace – there was for example no production of load-carrying vehicles in the Eastern Group. In basic industrial potential they gained comparatively little, again excepting South Africa. The percentage increase of steel output between 1937 and 1947 was as follows: South Africa 104, Canada 87, the United States 50, India 34, Australia 14 (the United Kingdom minus 4 per cent.).

Nor is it certain that rapid industrialisation is in the interests of the countries concerned. This is a controversial question which hardly lies within the scope of this study. But it may be mentioned that at least one good authority considered that the war left the South African economy not less but more dependent on gold-mining than before, having saddled it with a further burden of essentially unprofitable industry which would have to be indirectly supported from the profits of the Rand. Similarly, at the time of writing it seems to be generally agreed that more agriculture, not more industry, is Australia's greatest need. Her output of most foodstuffs was lower in 1947 than in 1937. Her chief gain from the war was probably the improvement in the terms of trade which she shared with other primary producers; and her particular war-time circumstances prevented her from gaining as much therefrom as did some others. For India, not very much less than for the conquered areas of Asia, the immediate impact of war was economically disastrous, though the sterling balances offered hopes for the future. Thus it seems clear that the war effort of the Eastern Group involved a genuine sacrifice of economic opportunity as well as of men.

Appendices

APPENDIX I

The Combined Munitions Assignments Board: Terms of Reference

The preliminary 'charter' of the Board is contained in the joint statement issued by the Prime Minister and the President on 26th January 1942.[1]

This charter was elaborated in the following directive to the Washington Board, dated 25th March 1942.

1. In accordance with an understanding between the President and the Prime Minister, a Munitions Assignments Board is hereby established, to consist of the following, or of alternates designated by them with authority to act for them: Mr Harry L. Hopkins, Chairman. United States representatives—Admiral W. H. Standley, Major-General R. C. Moore, Major-General M. F. Harmon. British representatives—Admiral Sir Charles Little, Lieut.-General Sir C. Wemyss, Air Marshal D. C. Evill, Major-General J. H. Burns, U.S.A., executive. A corresponding Board is being established in London.

2. Working in close collaboration with the corresponding London organisation, the Board will maintain full information of the entire munitions resources of Great Britain and the United States and translate such resources into combat forces and their material reserves. It will submit such statement to the Combined Chiefs of Staff and keep the estimate up-to-date in the light of war developments and also of variations in production achievements and prospects, as ascertained through effective liaison with the supply authorities. Such periodical revisions will be submitted in order that the Combined Chiefs of Staff may be fully informed and recommend the measures necessary to keep planned requirements programmes in line with—

(a) strategic policy;

(b) changing operational conditions in the effect on war material; and

(c) the realities of production.

3. Under such strategic policies, directives and priorities as have been approved, and in accordance with agreements with the corresponding London organisation, the Board will be responsible for making assignments of the stocks and production of finished war material to the United States and Great Britain and to others of the United Nations.

---

[1] For the text of this statement see Cmd. 6332. The text (which gives also the terms of reference of the Combined Raw Materials Board and the Combined Shipping Adjustment Board) is annexed to *North American Supply*, *op. cit.*, Appendix IV.

APPENDIX II

The Combined Production and Resources Board

The terms of reference of this Board, and of the Combined Food Board, were contained in the following joint statement, issued on 9th June 1942 by the Prime Minister in London and the President in Washington.

In order to complete the organisation needed for the most effective use of the combined resources of the United States and the United Kingdom for the prosecution of the war, there is hereby established a Combined Production and Resources Board and a Combined Food Board.

COMBINED PRODUCTION AND RESOURCES BOARD

The Board shall consist of the Chairman of the War Production Board, representing the United States, and the Minister of Production, representing the United Kingdom.

The Board shall:

(a) Combine the production programmes of the United States and the United Kingdom into a single integrated programme, adjusted to the strategic requirements of the war, as indicated to the Board by the Combined Chiefs of Staff, and to all relevant production factors. In this connection, the Board shall take account of the need for maximum utilisation of the productive resources available to the United States, the British Commonwealth of Nations, and the United Nations, the need to reduce demands on shipping to a minimum, and the essential needs of the civilian populations.

(b) In close collaboration with the Combined Chiefs of Staff, assure the continuous adjustment of the combined production programme to meet changing military requirements.

To this end, the Combined Chiefs of Staff and the Combined Munitions Assignments Board shall keep the Combined Production and Resources Board currently informed concerning military requirements, and the Combined Production and Resources Board shall keep the Combined Chiefs of Staff and the Combined Munitions Assignments Board currently informed concerning the facts and possibilities of production.

To facilitate continuous operation, the members of the Board shall each appoint a Deputy; and the Board shall form a combined staff. The Board shall arrange for such conferences among United States and United Kingdom personnel as it may from time to time deem necessary or appropriate to study particular production needs; and utilise the Joint War Production Staff in London, the Combined Raw Materials Board, the

Joint Aircraft Committee, and other existing combined or national agencies for war production in such manner and to such extent as it shall deem necessary.

COMBINED FOOD BOARD

The purpose of the Board shall be to co-ordinate further the prosecution of the war effort by obtaining a planned and expeditious utilisation of the food resources of the United Nations.

The Board will be composed of the Secretary of Agriculture and of the Head of the British Food Mission who will represent and act under the instruction of the Minister of Food.

The duties of the Board shall be:

To consider, investigate, enquire into, and formulate plans with regard to, any question in respect of which the Governments of the U.S.A. and the United Kingdom have, or may have, a common concern, relating to the supply, production, transportation, disposal, allocation or distribution, in or to any part of the world, of foods, agricultural materials from which foods are derived, and equipment ancillary to the production of such foods and agricultural materials, and to make recommendations to the Governments of the U.S.A. and the United Kingdom in respect of any such question.

To work in collaboration with others of the United Nations towards the best utilisation of their food resources, and, in collaboration with the interested nation or nations, to formulate plans and recommendations for the development, expansion, purchase or other effective use of their food resources.

The Board shall be entitled to receive from any Agency of the Government of the United States and any Department of the Government of the United Kingdom, any information available to such Agency or Department relating to any matter with regard to which the Board is competent to make recommendations to those Governments, and in principle, the entire food resources of Great Britain and the United States will be deemed to be in a common pool, about which the fullest information will be interchanged.

APPENDIX III

Decisions by the Combined Raw Materials Board

The following are given as specimens of decisions by the Combined Raw Materials Board.

A. INTERIM DECISIONS JANUARY 16TH 1942[1]

1. *Hemp Seed 'Insurance' Stockpile.* The Board decided that 33,000 acres in the U.S. should be sown to hemp seed in 1942 for seed propagation purposes in order to make available sufficient seed for planting in 1943 to produce up to 140,000,000 pounds of hemp fibre and 150,000,000 pounds of tow. It was agreed that the question of planting seed for fibre should be reconsidered not later than 1st August 1942, in order to allow time for the necessary preparatory steps.

   Aside from the foregoing the Board decided that 7,000 additional acres should be planted to hemp for hemp fibre in 1942 and that a new scutching mill should be built in order partly to take care of this additional production and partly for experimental purposes in view of the possible large acreage of hemp fibre for 1943 envisaged in the foregoing paragraph.

2. The Board decided that a project to plant 20,000 acres of abaca in Panama and Costa Rica should be approved.

3. The Board decided that an arrangement should be made with the Haitian American Development Company for the planting of 20,000 additional acres of sisal in Haiti.

4. The Board agreed that the New Zealand Government should be contacted with a view to investigating the possibility of their making additional quantity of phormium fibre for 1943 and subsequently. In this connection it was also agreed that the U.S. should lift any quantities available from New Zealand, if through shipping difficulties the United Kingdom were unable to do so.

5. The Board agreed that sisal yarns for rugs should be eliminated both in the U.S. and the U.K.

6. The Board agreed that the use of sisal yarns should be limited in wrapping twines and that jute should be substituted for the finer wrapping twines.

---

[1] This interim decision was confirmed, as Decision No. 4, by the Board on 3rd March 1942. See above Chapter VI.

7. The Board decided that negotiations should be made for procuring additional maximum quantities of Mexican istle.

8. The Board decided that the yardage of pure henequen binder twine should be increased from 500 to 525 feet. It was also agreed that further study should be given to increasing the yardage of binder twine from 525 to 550 feet or more.

9. The Board decided that during 1942 (*a*) the U.S. should make available for shipment to the U.K. 15,000,000 pounds of manila fibre, (*b*) that 135,000,000 pounds of British East African sisal should be made available for shipment to the United Kingdom, (*c*) 235,000,000 pounds of British East African sisal should be made available for shipment to the United States and Canada, (*d*) that sisal from all other sources should go to the United States and Canada.

   In respect of (*a*) above it was agreed that the 15,000,000 pounds of manila fibre would be inclusive of existing Lease-Lend requisitions and not in addition to them.

10. The Board agreed that negotiations should be entered into with the Portuguese Government with a view to purchasing the available supplies of Portuguese East and West African sisal. It was also agreed that the Portuguese colonies, as also British East Africa, should be urged to produce the greatest possible quantity of sisal.

11. The Board agreed that the question of distribution of supplies for the year 1943 and thereafter would be the subject of a revised study as of 1st August 1942.

12. The Board agreed that a revision of manila rope specifications in the U.K., U.S. and Canada, for all purposes including Army, Navy and Merchant marine should be undertaken in order to determine what ropes can be made of sisal and alternatively whether a mixture of sisal and manila might not be advisable in some instances.

13. The Board agreed that the United States and Canadian Departments of Agriculture should enter into a programme for the fullest use of the 'combine' in harvesting.

14. To be undertaken by the
    U.S.   1, 2, 3, 6, 7, 8, 13.
    U.K.   4.
    Jointly   5, 9, 10, 11, 12.

B. EXTRACT FROM C.R.M.B. DECISION ON COPPER

The following decision of the Combined Raw Materials Board in January 1943 illustrates the way in which the complex problem of 'development' was handled for a key material. It takes in copper development in all copper-producing countries, includes conservation even in the matter of steel for brass in cartridges, and touches on economic warfare. It combined both general advice and precise detail.

'5. The appropriate United States and United Kingdom agencies take all necessary steps (especially for making available the requisite material and equipment as needed) to facilitate the execution of the plan for expanding copper production in the Belgian Congo, investigation of which has been completed in accordance with Recommendation No. 3 (d) of Decision No. 44.

6. The appropriate United Kingdom authorities carry out the plan for expanding copper production at the N'Changa mine from 1,250 to 3,000 tons monthly, and the appropriate United States agencies make available as required the materials and equipment necessary for the execution of the plan which need to be supplied from the United States.

7. (a) The appropriate United States authorities take all steps necessary to expedite the completion of projects now under construction and listed in Appendix I of Document No. 118.

(b) The appropriate United States agencies give urgent and sympathetic consideration to copper-producing projects now under investigation by them which would yield significant amounts of copper by the end of 1944.

(c) All copper-producing countries be recommended to give urgent and sympathetic consideration to copper-producing projects which would yield significant amounts of copper by the end of 1944.

8. (a) All necessary steps continue to be taken to obtain the largest possible part of Turkish production of copper, such copper to be shipped to the United States, when and as shipping is available.

(b) The United States make available to the United Kingdom refined copper equivalent to quantities of Turkish copper obtained by the United Kingdom and received by the United States in accordance with (a) above.

9. (a) The appropriate United States and United Kingdom agencies submit to the Board by 1st March 1943, comprehensive reports on the programmes of their respective countries, and also on those of Canada and the other Empire Countries:

    1. (A) To effect the substitution of steel for brass cartridge cases in the range 20 to 105 millimeters; and (B) to substitute steel for brass and other copper bearing alloys in small arms ammunition, both in cartridge cases and in bullet jackets.

    2. To recover and utilise copper bearing battle scrap, including the reforming of used cartridge cases.'

APPENDIX IV

Future of the Combined Boards

The President of the United States and the Prime Ministers of the United Kingdom and Canada issue the following statements:[1]

We announced on 29th August that the Combined Production and Resources Board, the Combined Raw Materials Board and the Combined Food Board would continue to operate on their existing basis for the time being. As then proposed, however, the situation has been further examined with a view to the earliest possible removal of all war-time controls of international trade.

We take this opportunity of paying tribute to the outstanding achievements of the Boards in the full and equitable utilisation of resources for the effective prosecution of the war. This novel experiment in economic collaboration unquestionably hastened the moment of victory.

It is, however, our view that the work of the C.P.R.B. and C.R.M.B. on this existing basis should come to an end. It has accordingly been agreed that these two Boards terminate on 31st December 1945.

There remain, however, a few commodities which call for continued attention inasmuch as they are in global short supply in relation to the needs in consuming countries. For cotton textiles, tin, rubber and hides and leather it is proposed that the committees set up under the Boards which are concerned with these supplies should be continued during such period as the shortage of supply in relation to needs renders necessary. It is also proposed that in all cases representation on the committees should be on an appropriate international basis having regard to their independent status following the dissolution of the Boards. In most cases Committee membership already includes countries having a major interest in the problems involved. In the case of coal there exists an organisation in respect of Europe but special considerations make it desirable that for the time being the coal committees in Washington and London, now under the Boards, continue in their present form. As regards some additional commodities in uncertain supply, the Boards may make suitable distribution arrangements before the end of the year to extend into 1946.

It has been concluded that conditions do not yet permit the dissolution of the Combined Food Board. Because many foodstuffs are still in world short supply and because of their close inter-relationship it is believed desirable to retain the Board as a supervisory and co-ordinating mechanism. The commodity committees of the Board will be abandoned as soon as the foodstuffs with which they deal cease to require international allocation. It is anticipated that the Combined Food Board itself will be dissolved on 30th June 1946, or sooner if conditions permit. However, a

---

[1] Released to the press on 10th December in Washington, London and Ottawa.

few of the commodity committees may have to be retained beyond the termination date to recommend allocations of materials which continue to be in serious short supply. Arrangements were made last summer to associate other major importing and exporting countries with the work of the commodity committees. These committees will continue to operate on this principle.

Index

Index

The suffix letter 'n' denotes a footnote

S.O. Code No. 63-111-3-15*